September–December 1775

Paul H. Smith, Editor

Gerard W. Gawalt, Rosemary Fry Plakas, Eugene R. Sheridan
Assistant Editors

LIBRARY OF CONGRESS WASHINGTON 1977

This volume is printed on permanent/durable paper.

Library of Congress Cataloging in Publication Data

Main entry under title:

Letters of delegates to Congress, 1774–1789.

Includes bibliographical references and indexes.
CONTENTS. v. 1. August 1774–August 1775.—
v. 2. September–December 1775.

1. United States. Continental Congress—History—Sources—Collected works. I. Smith, Paul Hubert, 1931–
JK1033.L47 328.73 76–2592
ISBN 0–8444–0177–3

ISBN for complete set: 0–8444–0177–3
ISBN for this volume: 0–8444–0230–3

For sale by the Superintendent of Documents, U.S. Government Printing Office
Washington, D.C. 20402

Stock No. 030–000–00077–3

Foreword

Well before the signing on July 4, 1966, of Public Law 89–491, establishing a national American Revolution Bicentennial Commission, the Library of Congress began considering how it could contribute to the celebration of the Bicentennial of the American Revolution. In 1968 Congress approved the Library's general plan and subsequently authorized the addition to the Library's staff of several historians, all specialists in early American history. The Library took as the theme for its Bicentennial program "Liberty and Learning" from James Madison, who asked: "What spectacle can be more edifying or more seasonable, than that of Liberty & Learning, each leaning on the other for their mutual and surest support." Reflecting the Library's unparalleled resources for the study of the revolutionary era, its Bicentennial program ranges widely: from the presentation of symposia to the publication of facsimiles and the texts of rare or unique material to the recording of American folk music and the compilation of bibliographies and guides.

In preparing one of those guides, *Manuscript Sources in the Library of Congress for Research on the American Revolution* (Washington: Library of Congress, 1975), the staff of the Bicentennial Office discovered large numbers of letters, written by members of the Continental Congresses, which had not been published in Edmund C. Burnett's magisterial 8-volume edition of *Letters of Members of the Continental Congress,* 1774–89 (Washington: Carnegie Institution, 1921–36). Initially, it appeared that these letters might be published as a supplement to Burnett's work, but as additional unpublished letters of Congressmen turned up and as a cursory survey of other repositories suggested that even more unpublished letters were available, the Library decided that a new, expanded edition would be a valuable and appropriate Bicentennial project.

As the editors of the present work grew to appreciate the magnitude of the task they had undertaken, their admiration for Burnett increased. It is not enough to say that his edition provided the inspiration for their efforts. His research and annotations have stood the test of time and provide the foundation for much of the research which will appear in these volumes. Specialists will sense the editors' dependence on Burnett's pathfinding work, but perhaps few, other than the editors, can fully appreciate the dimensions of his achievement.

The present edition has benefited immensely from the generous cooperation of the editors of several other documentary publications that have a common focus on the era of the American Revolution. From them the Library has borrowed heavily and to them it owes a debt that it can never adequately acknowledge. It is, therefore, a pleasure to give special thanks to the editors of *The Adams Papers, The Papers of Benjamin Franklin, The Papers of Thomas Jefferson, The Papers of Henry Laurens, The Papers of James Madison,* and *The Papers of George Washington* for their assistance and counsel.

Thanks are also due to the Library's Advisory Committee on its American Revolution Bicentennial Program for support and encouragement, especially to the late Adrienne Koch, a member of the original advisory committee, whose enthusiasm for this project was unfailing and who had a central role in seeing that it was properly launched. To the Ford Foundation, which supplied a generous grant to help underwrite the project, we gratefully record our indebtedness. And, finally, we are beholden to the Congress of the United States, which appropriates funds for the publication of these volumes of the papers of its distinguished predecessors and which has unstintingly supported the Library's Bicentennial program.

Elizabeth Hamer Kegan
Assistant Librarian of Congress
for American and Library Studies

Editorial Method and Apparatus

Scheduled to reconvene on September 5 after a five-week summer recess, Congress formally resumed its deliberation on September 13, 1775—the first day a quorum of delegates was present—opening a session that continued without interruption until December 12, 1776, when an approaching British army threatened Philadelphia and forced Congress to flee to Baltimore. The present volume covers the work of the delegates through the last four months of 1775.

In its treatment of documents this edition of delegate letters strives to achieve a middle ground between facsimile reproduction and thorough modernization. The original spelling and grammar are allowed to stand except in cases where editorial changes or insertions are required to make the text intelligible. For example, when a badly misspelled word is misleading, the correct spelling is inserted in roman type in brackets after the word. Moreover, words omitted through oversight have been supplied at appropriate places in italic type in brackets. Obvious slips of the pen and inadvertent repetitions are usually silently corrected. Capitalization and punctuation have been standardized according to certain conventions. Each sentence begins with a capital letter, as do all proper and geographic names as well as days of the week and months of the year. Doubtful cases have been resolved in favor of modern usage; otherwise the usage of the original texts has been followed. Generally, abbreviations, contractions, and monetary signs are preserved as they appear in manuscript except when they are ambiguous or misleading. On the other hand, the thorn and the tilde are consistently expanded. "Ye" always appears as "The," for instance, and "rec̃vd" as "received." Likewise, "pr." and "℘" are always expanded to "per," "pre," or "pro," as the case demands. Finally, superscript letters are always lowered to the line.

Gaps in the text are indicated by ellipses in brackets for missing words and by blank spaces in brackets for missing numbers. Conjectural readings are supplied in roman type in brackets, and editorial insertions in italic type in brackets. Material canceled in manuscript but restored to the printed text is included in italic type in angle brackets ("square parentheses"). Marginalia in letters are treated as postscripts, and postscripts which appear without explicit designation are supplied with a *P.S.* in brackets. Documents are arranged chronologically, with more than one document of the same date being arranged alphabetically according to writer. Documents dated only by the month or by the year are placed at the end of the respective month or year. Place-and-date lines always appear on the same line with the salutation regardless of their position in the manuscript.

A descriptive note at the foot of each entry provides abbreviations indicating the nature and location of the document when it was copied for this project, except for privately owned manuscripts whose ownership is fully explained. The descriptive note also contains information on the document's authorship if explanation is necessary, and endorsements or addresses are quoted when they contain more than routine information. Other editorial practices employed in this work are explained in the sections on editorial apparatus which follow.

TEXTUAL DEVICES

The following devices will be used in this work to clarify the text.

[. . .], [. . . .]	One or two words missing and not conjecturable.
[. . .][1], [. . . .][1]	More than two words missing; subjoined footnote estimates amount of material missing.
[ ]	Number or part of a number missing or illegible.
[ ][1]	Blank space in manuscript; explanation in subjoined footnote.
[roman]	Conjectural reading for missing or illegible matter; question mark inserted if reading is doubtful.
[*italic*]	Editorial insertion in the text.
⟨*italic*⟩	Matter crossed out in manuscript but restored.

DESCRIPTIVE SYMBOLS

The following symbols are used in this work to describe the kinds of documents drawn upon. When more than one symbol is used in the descriptive note, the first to appear is that from which the main text is taken.

RC recipient's copy
FC file copy
LB letterbook copy
MS manuscript
Tr transcript (used to designate not only contemporary and later handwritten copies of manuscripts, but also printed documents)

LOCATION SYMBOLS

The following symbols, denoting institutions holding the manuscripts printed in the present volume, are taken from *Symbols of American Libraries,* 11th ed. (Washington: Library of Congress, 1976).

CSmH Henry E. Huntington Library, San Marino, Calif.

Ct	Connecticut State Library, Hartford
CtHi	Connecticut Historical Society, Hartford
CtNhHi	New Haven Colony Historical Society, New Haven, Conn.
CtNlHi	New London Historical Society, New London, Conn.
CtY	Yale University, New Haven, Conn.
DLC	Library of Congress
DNA	National Archives
DeHi	Historical Society of Delaware, Wilmington
GHi	Georgia Historical Society, Savannah
ICHi	Chicago Historical Society
M-Ar	Massachusetts Archives, Boston
MH	Harvard University, Cambridge, Mass.
MHi	Massachusetts Historical Society, Boston
MWA	American Antiquarian Society, Worcester, Mass.
MdAA	Maryland Hall of Records, Annapolis
MdAn	U.S. Naval Academy, Annapolis
MdBJ-G	John Work Garrett Library, Johns Hopkins University, Baltimore, Md.
MeHi	Maine Historical Society, Portland, Maine
MiD-B	Burton Historical Collection, Detroit Public Library, Detroit, Mich.
N	New York State Library, Albany
NHi	New-York Historical Society, New York
NHpR	Franklin D. Roosevelt Library, Hyde Park, N.Y.
NN	New York Public Library, New York
NNC	Columbia University, New York
NNPM	Pierpont Morgan Library, New York
Nc-Ar	North Carolina State Department of Archives and History, Raleigh
NcU	University of North Carolina, Chapel Hill
Nh-Ar	New Hampshire Division of Archives and Records Management, Concord
NhD	Dartmouth College, Hanover, N.H.
NhHi	New Hampshire Historical Society, Concord
NjHi	New Jersey Historical Society, Newark
NjMoHP	Morristown National Historical Park, Morristown, N.J.
NjP	Princeton University, Princeton, N.J.
OClWHi	Western Reserve Historical Society, Cleveland, Ohio
PHC	Haverford College, Haverford, Pa.
PHi	Historical Society of Pennsylvania, Philadelphia
PPAmP	American Philosophical Society, Philadelphia
PWbH	Wyoming Historical and Geological Society, Wilkes-Barre, Pa.
RBrHi	Bristol Historical and Preservation Society, Bristol, R.I.
RHi	Rhode Island Historical Society, Providence

RPJCB	John Carter Brown Library, Providence
ViHi	Virginia Historical Society, Richmond
ViU	University of Virginia, Charlottesville

ABBREVIATIONS AND SHORT TITLES

Abbreviations and short titles frequently cited in the present volume are identified below.

Adams, *Diary* (Butterfield)
Adams, John. *Diary and Autobiography of John Adams*. Edited by Lyman H. Butterfield et al. 4 vols. Cambridge: Harvard University Press, Belknap Press, 1961.

Adams, *Family Correspondence* (Butterfield)
Butterfield, Lyman H., et al., eds. *Adams Family Correspondence*. Cambridge: Harvard University Press, Belknap Press, 1963–.

Adams, *Works* (Adams)
Adams, John. *The Works of John Adams, Second President of the United States*. . . . Edited by Charles Francis Adams. 10 vols. Boston: Charles C. Little and James Brown, 1850–56.

Am. Archives
Force, Peter, ed. *American Archives: Consisting of a Collection of Authentick Records, State Papers, Debates, and Letters and Other Notices of Publick Affairs*. 4th series. 6 vols. Washington: U.S. Government Printing Office, 1837–53.

Austin, *Life of Gerry*
Austin, James T. *The Life of Elbridge Gerry, with Contemporary Letters to the Close of the American Revolution*. 2 vols. Boston: Wells and Lilly, 1828–29.

Bio. Dir. Cong.
U.S. Congress. *Biographical Directory of the American Congress, 1774–1971*. Washington: U.S. Government Printing Office, 1971.

Burnett, *Letters*
Burnett, Edmund C., ed. *Letters of Members of the Continental Congress*. 8 vols. Washington: Carnegie Institution of Washington, 1921–36.

CHS Bulletin
Connecticut Historical Society Bulletin.

Clark, *Naval Documents*
Clark, William Bell, et al., eds. *Naval Documents of the American Revolution*. Washington: Department of the Navy, 1964–.

DAB
Dictionary of American Biography. Edited by Allen Johnson and Dumas Malone.

DNB
Dictionary of National Biography. . . . Edited by Sir Leslie Stephen and Sir Sidney Lee.

Franklin, *Writings* (Smyth)
Franklin, Benjamin. *The Writings of Benjamin Franklin*. Edited by Albert H. Smyth. 10 vols. New York: Macmillan Co., 1905–7.

JCC
U.S. Continental Congress. *Journals of the Continental Congress, 1774–1789*. Edited by Worthington C. Ford et al. 34 vols. Washington: Library of Congress, 1904–37.

Jefferson, *Papers* (Boyd)
Jefferson, Thomas. *The Papers of Thomas Jefferson*. Edited by Julian P. Boyd et al. Princeton: Princeton University Press, 1950–.

Journals of N.Y. Prov. Cong.
New York. *Journals of the Provincial Congress, Provincial Convention, Committee of Safety and Council of Safety of the State of New York, 1775–1777*. 2 vols. Albany: T. Weed, 1842.

Md. Hist. Magazine
Maryland Historical Magazine.

N.C. Colonial Records
North Carolina. *The Colonial Records of North Carolina*. Edited by William L. Saunders. 10 vols. Raleigh and Goldsboro, N.C.: P.M. Hale et al., 1886–90.

N.H. Provincial Papers
New Hampshire. *Provincial and State Papers*. 40 vols. Concord, 1867–1943.

N.J. Archives
New Jersey Historical Society. *Documents Relating to the Colonial, Revolutionary and Post-Revolutionary History of the State of New Jersey*. Archives of the State of New Jersey. 1st series. 42 vols. Newark and Paterson, N.J., 1880–1949.

NYHS Collections
Collections of the New-York Historical Society.

OED
The Oxford English Dictionary.

Pa. Archives
Pennsylvania Archives. 9 series, 119 vols. in 120. Philadelphia: J. Severns & Co., 1852–56; Harrisburg: state printer, 1874–1935.

PCC
Papers of the Continental Congress. National Archives. Washington, D.C.

PMHB
Pennsylvania Magazine of History and Biography.

Rodney, *Letters* (Ryden)
Rodney, Caesar. *Letters to and from Caesar Rodney, 1756–1784*. Edited by George H. Ryden. Philadelphia: University of Pennsylvania Press, 1933.

Shipton, *Harvard Graduates*

Shipton, Clifford K. *Biographical Sketches of Those Who Attended Harvard College.* Sibley's Harvard Graduates. Boston: Massachusetts Historical Society, 1873–.

Susquehannah Co. Papers

Boyd, Julian P., and Taylor, Robert J., eds. *The Susquehannah Company Papers.* 11 vols. Ithaca, N.Y.: Cornell University Press, 1962–71.

Ward, *Correspondence* (Knollenberg)

Ward, Samuel. *Correspondence of Governor Samuel Ward, May 1775–March 1776, with a Biographical Introduction Based Chiefly on the Ward Papers Covering the Period 1725–1776, and Genealogy of the Ward Family, Thomas Ward, Son of John, of Newport and Some of His Descendants.* Edited by Bernhard Knollenberg and compiled by Clifford P. Monahon. Providence: Rhode Island Historical Society, 1952.

Warren-Adams Letters

Warren-Adams Letters, Being Chiefly a Correspondence among John Adams, Samuel Adams, and James Warren. 2 vols. Massachusetts Historical Society Collections, vols. 72–73. Boston: Massachusetts Historical Society, 1917–25.

Washington, *Writings* (Fitzpatrick)

Washington, George. *The Writings of George Washington.* Edited by John C. Fitzpatrick. 39 vols. Washington: U.S. Government Printing Office, 1931–44.

Webb, *Correspondence* (Ford)

Webb, Samuel B. *Correspondence and Journals of Samuel Blachley Webb.* Edited by Worthington C. Ford. 3 vols. New York: Wickersham Press, 1893–94.

Acknowledgments

To the Library of Congress, the Congress of the United States, and the Ford Foundation this edition owes its existence. It is fitting, therefore, that we take this opportunity to acknowledge the foresight of the Library's administration in planning a timely and comprehensive observation of the American Revolution Bicentennial, of the Congress in funding a Bicentennial Office in the Library, and of the Ford Foundation in granting $500,000 to support this project as a scholarly contribution to the celebration of the Bicentennial. It is with the most profound gratitude that the editors acknowledge their appreciation for this generous support. Our appreciation is also extended to the innumerable persons who have contributed to enriching the holdings of the Library of Congress to make it the premier institution for conducting research on the American Revolution.

The photocopies of the more than 20,000 documents that have been collected for this project have been assembled through the cooperation of several hundred institutions and private persons devoted to preserving the documentary record upon which the history and traditions of the American people rest, and it is to their work that a documentary publication of this nature should ultimately be dedicated. Unfortunately, the many individual contributors to this collecting effort cannot be adequately recognized, but for permission to print documents appearing in the present volume, we are especially grateful to the following institutions: the Algemeen Ryksarchief, The Hague, American Antiquarian Society, American Philosophical Society, Bristol Historical and Preservation Society, John Carter Brown Library, Chicago Historical Society, Columbia University, Connecticut Historical Society, Connecticut State Library, Dartmouth College, Historical Society of Delaware, Detroit Public Library, John Work Garrett Library, Georgia Historical Society, Harvard University, Haverford College, Henry E. Huntington Library, Maine Historical Society, Maryland Hall of Records, Massachusetts Archives Division, Massachusetts Historical Society, Pierpont Morgan Library, Morristown National Historical Park, National Archives, New Hampshire Division of Archives and Records Management, New Hampshire Historical Society, New Haven Colony Historical Society, New Jersey Historical Society, New London County Historical Society, New-York Historical Society, New York Public Library, New York State Library, North Carolina State Department of Archives and History, University of North Carolina, Historical Society of Pennsylvania,

Princeton University, Public Record Office, London, Rhode Island Historical Society, Franklin D. Roosevelt Library, United States Naval Academy, Virginia Historical Society, University of Virginia, Western Reserve Historical Society, Wyoming Historical and Geological Society, Pa., and Yale University. And in addition we express our thanks and appreciation to the following persons: Mr. J. Woodward Redmond, Mr. Kenneth W. Rendell, Mr. Paul C. Richards, Mr. Robert J. Sudderth, Jr., and Mrs. John G. Wood. Finally we owe thanks to the historians who have served on the Library of Congress Advisory Committee on the American Revolution Bicentennial, and especially to Mr. Julian P. Boyd, Mr. Lyman H. Butterfield, and Mr. Merrill Jensen who generously consented to serve as an advisory committee for this project.

Chronology of Congress

September–December 1775

September 13	Achieves quorum and reconvenes; Georgia fully represented for first time.
September 19	Appoints Secret Committee to purchase military supplies abroad.
September 22	Appoints committee to consider "the state of the trade of America."
September 27	Orders publication of corrected journals of Congress.
September 29	Appoints Committee of Conference to confer with General Washington and various New England executives.
October 3	Receives Rhode Island proposal for building an American fleet.
October 5	Recommends to General Washington a plan to intercept British supply ships.
October 6	Recommends that provincial governments arrest persons deemed a danger to "the liberties of America."
October 7	Adopts report on fortification of the Hudson River.
October 13	Resolves to fit out armed vessels; appoints Naval Committee.
October 17	Appoints John Morgan director general of hospitals, replacing Benjamin Church upon his arrest for correspondence with the enemy; appoints committee to estimate damages inflicted by British arms.
October 24	Adjourns to attend funeral of Peyton Randolph.
October 26	Publishes resolution authorizing exports in exchange for arms.
October 30	Increases naval authorization and expands Naval Committee.

November 1	Reaffirms general embargo on exports, extended explicitly to March 1, 1776; commends provincial authorities for ignoring parliamentary trade exemptions designed to undermine American unity.
November 2	Appoints Committee to the Northward to confer with General Schuyler; receives report of Committee of Conference.
November 3	Recommends formation of new provincial government in New Hampshire.
November 4	Adopts resolutions for reconstitution of General Washington's army in Massachusetts, and for defense of South Carolina and Georgia.
November 9	Adopts new oath of secrecy; publishes report of king's refusal to receive Olive Branch Petition.
November 10	Adopts plan for promoting manufacture of saltpetre; orders enlistment of first two battalions of marines.
November 13	Orders publication of new "Rules and Regulations" for Continental Army.
November 15	Receives account of capture of St. Johns.
November 16	Adopts resolves to improve delegates' attendance in Congress.
November 17	Adopts regulations pertaining to prisoners of war.
November 22	Authorizes exemptions to ban on exports to Bermuda.
November 23	Adopts resolves to improve peaceful relations with the Six Nations.
November 25	Adopts regulations pertaining to prize cases.
November 28	Adopts "Rules for the Regulation of the Navy of the United Colonies"; adopts measures for the defense of North Carolina.
November 29	Appoints Committee of Secret Correspondence; resolves to emit $3,000,000 in Continental currency; receives account of capture of Montreal.
December 2	Sends Benjamin Harrison to Maryland to promote defense of the Chesapeake.
December 4	Recommends formation of new provincial government in Virginia; appoints committee to dissuade New Jersey Assembly from separately petitioning king.

December 6 Publishes response to king's August 23 proclamation declaring colonies in state of rebellion.

December 8 Resolves to confine John Connolly for plotting with Lord Dunmore against western Virginia.

December 13 Authorizes construction of 13 ships for Continental Navy.

December 14 Appoints Marine Committee.

December 15 Receives plan for creation of committee to sit during recess of Congress.

December 20 Recommends cessation of hostilities between Connecticut and Pennsylvania settlers in Wyoming Valley.

December 22 Authorizes an attack on Boston; appoints Esek Hopkins commander in chief of Continental Navy.

December 26 Adopts plan for redemption of Continental bills of credit.

December 29 Adopts resolutions for importing and manufacturing salt.

December 30 Recommends Secret Committee negotiations with Pierre Penet and Emanuel de Pliarne for European arms and ammunition.

List of Delegates to Congress

This section lists both the dates on which delegates were elected to terms falling within the period covered by this volume and the inclusive dates of their attendance. The former are generally ascertainable from contemporary state records, but the latter are often elusive bits of information derived from the journals of Congress or extrapolated from references contained in the delegates' correspondence, and in such cases the "facts" are inevitably conjectural. It is not possible to determine interruptions in the attendance of many delegates, and no attempt has been made to record breaks in service caused by illness or brief trips home, especially of delegates from New Jersey, Delaware, Maryland, and Pennsylvania living within easy access of Philadelphia. For occasional references to such periods of intermittent service as survive in the correspondence and notes of various delegates, see the index under individual delegates. Until fuller information is provided in a consolidated summary of delegate attendance in the final volume of this series, the reader is advised to consult Burnett, *Letters,* 1:xli-lxvi, for additional information on conjectural dates of attendance. Brief biographical sketches of all the delegates are available in the *Biographical Directory of the American Congress, 1774–1971,* and fuller sketches of more than half of the delegates can be found in the *Dictionary of American Biography.*

CONNECTICUT

Silas Deane
Elected: November 3, 1774
Attended: September 13 to December 31, 1775 (traveled for the Naval Committee on a mission to New York, November 12?–21)

Eliphalet Dyer
Elected: November 3, 1774
Attended: September 13 to December 31, 1775

Titus Hosmer
Elected: November 3, 1774
Did not attend in 1775

Roger Sherman
Elected: November 3, 1774
Attended: September 13 to November 26; December 23? to 31, 1775

Jonathan Sturges
Elected: November 3, 1774
Did not attend in 1775

DELAWARE

Thomas McKean
Elected: March 16 and October 21, 1775
Attended: September 13 to December 31, 1775
George Read
Elected: March 16 and October 21, 1775
Attended: September 13? to December 25? 1775
Caesar Rodney
Elected: March 16 and October 21, 1775
Attended: September 13? to December 8? 1775

GEORGIA

Archibald Bulloch
Elected: July 7, 1775
Attended: September 13 to November 26? 1775
Lyman Hall
Elected: July 7, 1775
Did not return to Congress in 1775
John Houstoun
Elected: July 7, 1775
Attended: September 13 to November 26? 1775
Noble Wimberly Jones
Elected: July 7, 1775
Did not attend in 1775
John Joachim Zubly
Elected: July 7, 1775
Attended: September 13 to November 9, 1775

MARYLAND

Robert Alexander
Elected: December 9, 1775
Did not attend in 1775
Samuel Chase
Elected: August 14, 1775
Attended: September 13 to November 9? 1775
Robert Goldsborough
Elected: August 14, 1775
Did not return to Congress in 1775
John Hall
Elected: August 14, 1775
Attended: September ? to October 6? 1775
Thomas Johnson
Elected: August 14, 1775
Attended: September 13 to November 30? 1775
William Paca
Elected: August 14, 1775
Attended: September 13 to December 11? 1775

John Rogers
Elected: December 9, 1775
Attended: December 21–31, 1775
Thomas Stone
Elected: August 14, 1775
Attended: September 13 to October 20? 1775
Matthew Tilghman
Elected: August 14, 1775
Did not return to Congress in 1775

MASSACHUSETTS

John Adams
Elected: February 6, 1775
Attended: September 13 to December 8, 1775
Samuel Adams
Elected: February 6, 1775
Attended: September 13 to December 31, 1775
Thomas Cushing
Elected: February 6, 1775
Attended: September 13 to December 31, 1775
John Hancock
Elected: February 6, 1775
Attended: September 13 to December 31, 1775
Robert Treat Paine
Elected: February 6, 1775
Attended: September 15 to December 31, 1775 (traveled with Committee to the Northward, November 12 to December 28)

NEW HAMPSHIRE

Josiah Bartlett
Elected: August 23, 1775
Attended: September 16 to December 31, 1775
John Langdon
Elected: August 23, 1775
Attended: September 16 to December 31, 1775 (traveled with Committee to the Northward, November 12 to December 23)

NEW JERSEY

Stephen Crane
Elected: January 24, 1775
Attended: September 13 to November 9?; December 8–13, 1775
John DeHart
Elected: January 24, 1775
Attended: September 13? to November ? 1775
James Kinsey
Elected: January 24, 1775
Attended: October 9? to November 17? 1775

William Livingston
Elected: January 24, 1775
Attended: September 29? to December 31, 1775
Richard Smith
Elected: January 24, 1775
Attended: September 13–30; December 13–31, 1775

NEW YORK

John Alsop
Elected: April 21, 1775
Attended: September 13 to November 3? 1775
George Clinton
Elected: April 21, 1775
Did not return to Congress in 1775
James Duane
Elected: April 21, 1775
Attended: September 13 to December 31, 1775
William Floyd
Elected: April 21, 1775
Attended: September 13–21?; November 3? to December 31, 1775
John Jay
Elected: April 21, 1775
Attended: September 13–30; October 10 to November 3?; November 22? to December 31, 1775 (traveled with the committee that addressed the New Jersey Assembly on December 5)
Francis Lewis
Elected: April 21, 1775
Attended: September 13 to October 26?; November 2–December 23? 1775
Philip Livingston
Elected: April 21, 1775
Attended: September 13 to October 11; November 30 to December 31, 1775
Robert R. Livingston, Jr.
Elected: April 21, 1775
Attended: September 13 to December ? 1775 (traveled with Committee to the Northward, November 12 to December 10?, when he returned home)
Lewis Morris
Elected: April 21, 1775
Attended: November 9?–ante December 20, 1775 (commissioner negotiating with Indians at Fort Pitt during September and October)
Philip Schuyler
Elected: April 21, 1775
Did not return to Congress in 1775

Henry Wisner
Elected: April 21, 1775
Attended: September 28? to December 31, 1775

NORTH CAROLINA

Richard Caswell
Elected: September 2, 1775
Declined
Joseph Hewes
Elected: September 2, 1775
Attended: October 23 to December 31, 1775
William Hooper
Elected: September 2, 1775
Attended: October 23 to December 31, 1775
John Penn
Elected: September 8, 1775
Attended: October 12 to December 31, 1775

PENNSYLVANIA

Andrew Allen
Elected: November 4, 1775
Attended: November 6 to December 31, 1775
Edward Biddle
Elected: December 15, 1774; November 4, 1775
Did not return to Congress in 1775
John Dickinson
Elected: December 15, 1774; November 4, 1775
Attended: September 13 to December 31, 1775 (traveled with the committee that addressed the New Jersey Assembly on December 5)
Benjamin Franklin
Elected: May 6 and November 4, 1775
Attended: September 13 to December 31, 1775 (traveled with the Committee of Conference, October 6 to November 5? 1775)
Charles Humphreys
Elected: December 15, 1774; November 4, 1775
Attended: September 13 to November 9? 1775
Thomas Mifflin
Elected: December 15, 1774
Did not return to Congress in 1775
Robert Morris
Elected: November 4, 1775
Attended: November 6? to December 31, 1775
John Morton
Elected: December 15, 1774; November 4, 1775
Attended: September 13 to October 13? 1775
George Ross
Elected: December 15, 1774
Attended: September 13 to November 4? 1775

Thomas Willing
Elected: May 6 and November 4, 1775
Attended: September 13 to December 31, 1775

James Wilson
Elected: May 6 and November 4, 1775
Attended: November 9? to December 31, 1775 (commissioner negotiating with Indians at Fort Pitt during September and October)

RHODE ISLAND

Stephen Hopkins
Elected: December 9, 1774
Attended: September 13 to December 31, 1775

Samuel Ward
Elected: December 9, 1774
Attended: September 13 to December 31, 1775

SOUTH CAROLINA

Christopher Gadsden
Elected: February 3 and November 29, 1775
Attended: September 13 to December 31, 1775

Thomas Lynch
Elected: February 3 and November 29, 1775
Attended: September 13 to December 31, 1775 (traveled with the Committee of Conference, October 6 to November 2)

Henry Middleton
Elected: February 3 and November 29, 1775
Attended: September 13 to November 4, 1775

Edward Rutledge
Elected: February 3 and November 29, 1775
Attended: September 13 to December 31, 1775

John Rutledge
Elected: February 3 and November 29, 1775
Attended: September 13 to November 4, 1775

VIRGINIA

Benjamin Harrison
Elected: August 11, 1775
Attended: September 19 to December 31, 1775 (traveled with the Committee of Conference, October 6 to November 2; and for the Naval Committee on a mission to Maryland, December 2–18?)

Thomas Jefferson
Elected: August 11, 1775
Attended: October 2 to December 28, 1775

Francis Lightfoot Lee
Elected: August 15, 1775
Attended: September 13 to December 31, 1775

Richard Henry Lee
Elected: August 11, 1775
Attended: September 24 to December 23, 1775

Thomas Nelson
Elected: August 11, 1775
Attended: September 13 to December 31, 1775
Peyton Randolph
Elected: August 11, 1775
Attended: September 13 to October 21, 1775
George Wythe
Elected: August 11, 1775
Attended: September 13 to December 31, 1775 (traveled with the committee that addressed the New Jersey Assembly on December 5)

Illustrations

"An East Prospect of the City of Philadelphia; taken by George Heap from the Jersey Shore, under the Direction of Nicholas Scull Surveyor General of the Province of Pennsylvania." This detail is from an engraving by Thomas Jefferys based on an etching of the city published in Thomas Jefferys, *A General Topography of North America and the West Indies. Being a Collection of All the Maps, Charts, Plans, and Particular Surveys, That Have Been Published of That Part of the World, Either in Europe or America* (London: R. Sayer, 1768).

"A N.W. View of the State House in Philadelphia taken 1778." On Chestnut Street between Fifth and Sixth streets, the State House was the site of the meeting of the Continental Congress when they reconvened in September 1775. It had served as their meeting place since the convening of the Second Congress in May 1775.

Drawn by Charles Willson Peale. Etching from the *Columbian Magazine*, July 1787.

Published just as Congress was preparing to reconvene in September 1775, this pamphlet was introduced by an 18-page open letter to Lord Dartmouth, secretary of state for the colonies. Zubly's letter contains the fullest expression of his political views dating from his term in Congress, which ended abruptly with his departure from Philadelphia on November 10, 1775. A Georgia delegate and one of the few ordained ministers to sit in the Continental Congress, Zubly was among five delegates—including Robert Alexander, Andrew Allen, Joseph Galloway, and Isaac Low as well—who eventually became avowed loyalists.

The September 26, 1775, entry from the diary of New Jersey delegate Richard Smith, who maintained a record of the proceedings of Congress during the periods he attended between September 1775 and March 1776. In many instances Smith described motions and debates for which no other record has been found in the journals of Congress or in the papers of his fellow delegates. A notable example of this is the warm debate on Edward Rutledge's motion on the use of black soldiers in the Continental Army which Smith noted in this entry.

Harrison, along with Benjamin Franklin and Thomas Lynch, was appointed on September 30, 1775, to a committee "to repair immediately to the camp at Cambridge, to confer with General Washington." A distinguished Virginian and a friend of Washington who sat in both the First and Second Congresses, Harrison was well suited for this important mission. However, because the publication of a scandalous version of his intercepted letter to Washington of July 21, 1775, gave rise to unfavorable rumors about him, some New England delegates felt compelled to explain his appointment to friends.

Miniature by Henry Benbridge. Reproduced through the courtesy of the Virginia Historical Society.

A Wethersfield, Conn., merchant and one of the earliest proponents of strong congressional authority, Deane developed an elaborate plan for a naval establishment in October 1775 when Congress opened debate on proposals for creating a Continental Navy. Although elected to both the First and Second Congresses, he was disappointed when the Connecticut Assembly refused to reelect him in October, and he subsequently decided to linger in Philadelphia after the expiration of his term in January to continue the administrative work in which he had been engaged while on the Naval Committee. When Congress decided in March 1776 to send an agent to France to procure arms, Deane was therefore immediately available for the position, which launched him on a career as agent abroad that led finally to bitter attacks against him and to his ultimate defection to the North ministry near the end of the war.

Engraving by B. L. Prévost, based on a drawing by Pierre Eugène Du Simitière.

In May 1775 Congress appointed a committee to devise means "for the speedy and secure conveyance of Intelligence from one end of the Continent to the other" and at the end of July adopted a report providing for the establishment of a postal system under the direction of Benjamin Franklin as postmaster general, a position Franklin had held under the crown until 1774. By autumn he and his deputies had established a working system, and by December the royal post office in America was discontinued. This table of rates charged for carrying letters between various post offices from New Hampshire to Virginia is evidence that Congress was prepared to assume new executive functions asserting greater central authority whenever required to maintain effective leadership in the struggle against Britain.

From the Papers of the Continental Congress, National Archives and Records Service.

Robert R. Livingston's Notes for a Speech in Congress 265

Page one of notes for a speech Robert R. Livingston delivered on October 27, 1775, while Congress sat as a committee of the whole. In this speech, Livingston, a conservative New York delegate, advanced several arguments opposing the continuation of Congress' nonexportation policy. Despite his arguments, Congress five days later resolved to extend its restrictions on exports until March 1, 1776.

From the Livingston Papers, New-York Historical Society.

Stephen Hopkins 308

Hopkins, former Rhode Island governor, chairman of the Naval Committee, and brother of Commodore Esek Hopkins, was highly regarded by his colleagues. As John Adams, a fellow member of the Naval Committee, recalled: "Upon Business his Experience and Judgment was very Usefull. But when the Business of the Evening was over, he kept Us in Conversation till Eleven and sometimes twelve O Clock. His Custom was to drink nothing all day nor till Eight O Clock in the Evening, and then his Beveridge was Jamaica Spirit and Water. It gave him Wit, Humour, Anecdotes, Science and Learning. He had read Greek, Roman and British History: and was familiar with English Poetry particularly Pope, Tompson [Thomson] and Milton. And the flow of his Soul made all his reading our own, and seemed to bring to recollection in all of Us all We had ever read."

Enlargement of a detail from John Trumbull's painting *The Declaration of Independence, 4 July 1776* in the Capitol rotunda. The gentleman with the hat has traditionally been identified as Stephen Hopkins, according to the key published in John Trumbull, *Description of the Four Pictures, from Subjects of the Revolution, Painted by Order of the Government of the United States, and Now Placed in the Rotunda of the Capitol* (New York: Printed by W. A. Mercein, 1827). Courtesy of the architect of the Capitol.

Posthumous pencil sketch by John Trumbull, 1791. Identified in pencil on the back as Governor Hopkins, the sketch is modeled on his son Rufus Hopkins. The inscription on the front, "Jno. Hopkins," appears to have been added later and is in an unknown hand. Fordham University Library, New York.

For a discussion of the problem of identifying Hopkins, see Irma B. Jaffe, "Fordham University's Trumbull Drawings; Mistaken Identities in *The Declaration of Independence* and Other Discoveries," in *American Art Journal* 3 (Spring 1971): 5-38.

role on several committees appointed to provide gunpowder and arms. However, his appointment to the Committee to the Northward in November 1775 took him on an arduous trip to Albany that brought him greater frustration than satisfaction. Upon his return to Congress he accidentally discovered that John Adams, in corresponding with James Warren during Paine's absence, had disparaged his contributions. Paine confronted Adams with this discovery and widened the breach in the Massachusetts delegation that had already begun to separate the Adamses from Paine, John Hancock, and Thomas Cushing.

Drawn and engraved by James B. Longacre from a sketch by Edward Savage.

John Langdon 516

A Portsmouth, N. H., merchant, Langdon, already a member of the Marine Committee, was appointed on November 2, 1775, to a committee "to repair to the northward, to confer with Gen. Schuyler." He returned briefly to Congress with the committee's report in late December but returned home early in January 1776 to supervise the building of the Continental frigate authorized for construction at Portsmouth. In June 1776 he resigned his position as delegate in order to be appointed the Continental naval agent in New Hampshire, a lucrative post he retained throughout the war.

Etched by Albert Rosenthal, 1888, after a painting by John Trumbull.

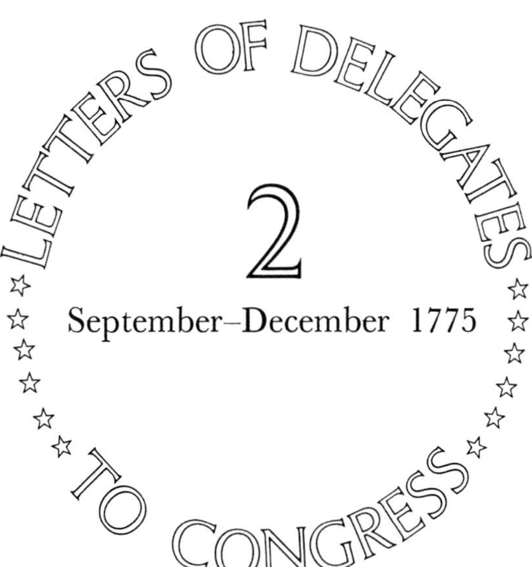
LETTERS OF DELEGATES
2
September–December 1775
TO CONGRESS

John Zubly's Diary

[September 9, 1775]

Saturday, 9. This being the last day for Exportation every body extremely busy. Of the many favorable Reports so much I hope is true that we may expect a favorable Turn of Affairs. Waited on Mr. Hancock who expressed himself very Kindly on the joining of Georgia & has great hopes of a favorable Issue.

MS (GHi).

Silas Deane to Jonathan Trumbull, Jr.

Dear Sir Trenton 10th Sepr. 1775

I was informed by Mr. Vandervoort on the road that You proposed to quit the office of Depy. paymaster General,[1] & had wrote my Brother as he had been Nominated, on the Subject, conclude if this be your Determination that you will write the Congress on the Subject in Season, as Your Successor must have some little Time, to prepare to leave his Business; I wish if You write the Congress You would let me know it by Letter at the same Time.

I am with Esteem Dr Sir Yours Silas Deane

P.S. Tho. my Brother was Nominated his Name is not on the Journal of the Congress so that an Appointment must be made before he can Succeed.

RC (CtHi).

[1] Jonathan Trumbull, Jr., continued to serve as paymaster general in the northern department until July 29, 1778. *JCC*, 11:727.

Samuel Ward's Diary

[September 11, 1775]

11th. Mr. President & Mr. Cushing, S Ward, the Connecti[cu]t Delegs., Mr. Crane of the Jerseys, several Pensylvania, Lower County, Mary[lan]d, Virginia & So. Carolina & Georgia delegates met & adjourned to the next Day.

MS (RHi).

John Zubly's Diary

[September 11–12, 1775]

Monday, 11. Tuesday, 12. Attended Congress but could not make a board.

MS (GHi).

Benjamin Franklin to David Hartley

Dear Sir, Philada. Sept. 12. 1775

I have this Day received your Favours per Capt. Falconer, of which more in my next. With this I send you a number of Newspapers and Pamphlets, by which you will see Things are become serious here. Your Nation must stop short, & change its Measures, or she will lose the Colonies forever. The Burning of Towns, and firing from Men of War on defenceless Cities and Villages filled with Women & Children; The exciting the Indians to fall on our innocent Back Settlers; and our Slaves to murder their Masters; are by no means Acts of a legitimate Government. They are of barbarous Tyranny and dissolve all Allegiance. The Insolence of your Captains of Men of War is intolerable But we suppose they know whom they are to please. I shall endeavour to procure the Petitions so that you may have them against Winter: they cannot be collected suddenly. With the highest Esteem, I am Yours most affectionately.

[*P.S.*] Pray present my Respects to Mr Burke, to whom, & to you I shall write fully by the first safe hand.

RC (DLC). In Franklin's hand, though not signed.

Benjamin Franklin to Jonathan Williams, Jr.

Dear Jonathan, Philada. Sept. 12. 1775

I this Day receiv'd yours per Capt. Falconer, and am vastly oblig'd by your Industry in Packing and Dispatching my Things.[1] Their Arrival makes me very happy, tho' they are not yet come onshore. I have not before written to you, imagining you would hardly be found there; but now I find by Mr Alexr's Letter (to whom my best Respects) that he advises you to stay,[2] for the Chance of something turning up to your Advantage. I have lately heard from your Father. He has made a temporary Exchange of Houses & Furniture with a Mr Putnam of Worcester, who now resides at your House in Boston, and your Family at his House in Worcester, where they were all well about two Weeks since. My Sister is at Warwick with Mrs Greene. She left her House lock'd up with the Furniture in it, but knows not whether she shall ever see it again.

I like your Conduct with Respect to the Jersey Petition. The first Copy had indeed been presented before; by Mr Lee, but that you could not know. If you determine to stay in England, I shall do what I can to throw Business in your Way. But whether America is ever again to have any Connection with Britain either Commercial or Political is at present uncertain. All depends upon that Nation's coming to its Senses. Here we are preparing and determined to run all Risques rather than comply with her mad Demands.

Mr Fergusson, who will deliver this, is a Gentleman of amiable Character in this Country, who visits England on Some Business of his own. If you can do him any Service you will oblige me by it. I recommend him warmly to your Civilities: and likewise Mr Stockton who goes over with him intending to study Law in the Temple.

I desire to be affectionately & respectfully remembred to Mrs Hewson, Miss Dolly Blunt, Mrs Falconer, Mrs. Barwell and all our other Female Friends. I am hurried & can now only add that I am ever Your affectionate Friend & Uncle B Franklin

[*P.S.*] I shall write to you fully, and to Mr Alexander by next Opportunity.

Deliver the inclos'd yourself.[3] I have given you a little Recommendation to the good Bishop.

RC (CtY).

[1] Jonathan Williams, Jr. (1750–1815), Franklin's grandnephew, had been under his uncle's tutelage in London since 1770 and had remained behind when Franklin returned to America. When Franklin became United States commissioner at Paris in December 1776, Williams went to France and became United States commercial agent at Nantes. *DAB*.

[2] Apparently William Alexander (1729–1819), whose daughter, Mariamne, Williams married in 1779.

[3] See Franklin to Jonathan Shipley, September 13, 1775.

Richard Smith's Diary

Tuesday 12 September 1775

I attended at Congress for the first Time since the Adjornment. Mr. Hancock having a Touch of the Gout there was no President in the Chair. The Colonies of New Hampshire and N Carolina absent as also sundry Members from other Colonies. Dr. Franklin read several Letters recieved today by Capt. Falkner from London and informed the Members that he had some Bales of Household Goods on

Board of Falkner, desiring the Congress's Leave to land them. No Objection to it only Willing and John Rutledge thought it irregular to do Business without a President and it was referred.[1] Mr. Gadsden and others moved for an Adjournment to 10 Tomorrow which was complyed with. 3 of the Georgia Delegates were present with Mr. Peyton Randolph and the new Delegates from Virginia, their Credentials not yet delivered and little Business hitherto done this Session.

MS (DLC). This diary, as indicated by certain comments in later entries, is based upon an earlier set of notes, since lost, which Smith made during his service in Congress from September 12, 1775, to March 30, 1776. Smith made this copy no earlier than April 1776, but apart from the presence of some easily identifiable retrospective comments, there is little reason to assume that his diary does not accurately reflect his more contemporary notes. See Smith's Diary, September 15, 30, and December 13, 1775.

[1] Congress approved the unloading and the delivery of Franklin's goods on September 13. *JCC*, 2:247.

Samuel Ward's Diary

[September 12, 1775]

12th. Members from the above Col[onie]s met,[1] were joined by Messrs. Adams. For want of Quorum did no Business, adjourned. Mr. Hopkins came into the City.

MS (RHi).

[1] See Ward's Diary, September 11, 1775.

Benjamin Franklin to Jonathan Shipley

My dear Friend Philada. Sept. 13. 1775.

I write but seldom to you, because at this time the most innocent Correspondence with me may be suspected, and attended with Inconvenience to yourself. Our united Wishes for a Reconciliation of the two Countries, are not I fear soon to be accomplished; for I hear your Ministry are determin'd to persevere in their mad Measures, and here I find the firmest Determination to resist at all Hazards. The Event may be doubtful, but it is clear to me that if the Contest is only to be ended by our Submission, it will not be a short one. We have given up our Commerce; our last Ships, 34 Sail, left this Port the 9th Instant. And in our Minds we give up our Sea Coast (tho' Part may be a little disputed) to the barbarous Ravages of your Ships of War; but the internal Country we shall defend. It is a good one and fruitful. It is with our Liberties, worth defending, and it will itself by its Fertility enable us to defend it. Agriculture is the great Source of Wealth & Plenty. By cutting off our Trade you have thrown us *to the Earth,* whence like *Antæus* we shall rise yearly with fresh Strength and Vigour.

This will be delivered to you by Mr Jonathan Williams, a Nephew of mine, whom I left in my Lodgings. Any thing you think fit to send me, may be safely trusted to his Care and Discretion. He is a valuable young Man, having, with great Industry & excellent Talents for Business, a very honest and good Heart. If he should stay in London, I beg leave to recommend him to a little of your Notice.

I am here immers'd in so much Business that I have scarce time to eat or sleep. The Winter I promise myself will bring with it some Relaxation. This Bustle is unsuitable to Age. How happy I was in the Sweet Retirement of Twyford, where my only Business was a little Scribbling in the Garden Study, and my Pleasure your Conversation, and that of your amiable Family!

With sincere and great Esteem & Respect, I am ever, my dear Friend, Your affectionate & most obedt huml Servant

B Franklin

[*P.S.*] The Perfidy of General Gage in breaking his Capitulation with Boston & detaining their Effects.

The Firing of Broadsides from Men of War into defenceless Towns & Villages filled with Women and Children.

The Burning of Charlestown wantonly without the least Reason or Provocation.

The encouraging our Blacks to rise and murder their Masters. But above all,

The Exciting the Savages to fall upon our innocent Outsettlers, Farmers, (who have no Concern in, and from their Situation can scarce have any Knowledge of this Dispute) especially when it is considered that the Indian Manner of making War, is by surprizing Families in the Night, and killing all, without Distinction of Age or Sex![1] What would be thought of it, if the Congress should hire an Italian Bravo to break into the House of one of your Ministers, and murder him in his Bed? All his Friends would open in full Cry against us as *Assassins, Murderers* & *Villains,* and the Walls of your Parliament House would resound with their Execrations! Of these two damnable Crimes which is the greatest?

These Proceedings of Officers of the Crown, who it is presumed either act by *Instruction,* or know they shall *please* by such Conduct, give People here a horrid Idea of the *Spirit* of your Government.

RC (CtY).

[1] Franklin wrote the remainder of this paragraph at the foot of the page and designated its continuation with an asterisk.

Caesar Rodney to Thomas Rodney

Sir, Philadelphia Sepr. 13th 1775.

I have had no letter from you Since you Returned Home, Expected one by Robert the Post but am dispointted. I am very little if any better than when I wrote you last. Yet able to Attend the Congress[1] and in hopes of getting better before long. Wheat is now Selling tho verry Slowly at 3/6 per buss[he]ll. Much more offerred to Sale than bought as none buy Except a few who want for their own Use. Corn is 1/6 the highest—so soon were the Markets Cut up. Mr. McGarmant will tell you about Loockermans Money—and the Colours will be down by the next Post. Get the ballance of the Bill for the Colours from Loockerman. He paid me ten pounds which you will deduct out of it. I have had private Conversation with Nat. Fortner who is just from London. He tells me he is Convinced that our differences will be Soon Settled, on our own Terms, And Says it is more than two to one that there is before this day an intire Change in the Ministry.

I am Yrs. &c. Caesar Rodney

RC (PHC).

[1] Caesar Rodney had apparently gone directly from Newcastle to Philadelphia on September 4. "I Intended when I left Dover to have Returned before I went to the Congress. But the Assembly's Continuing to Set so much longer than I Expected has put it out of my power—Monday being the day to which the Congress is adjourned. . . . I shall (tomorrow) proceed to Philadelphia." Rodney to Elizabeth Rodney, September 3, 1775, PHC.

Richard Smith's Diary

[September 13, 1775]

Wednesday 13th. Mr. President (Hancock) in the Chair. The Credentials of the Georgia, Virginia and Maryland Delegates were read and accepted without any Objection. The Marylanders were the same as at the last Session. An Order was made that the Pennsa. Delegates shall send off to Gen. Washington under a proper Guard, the remainder of his Money amounting in the whole to 700,000 Dollars, and they were at the same Time to send the Cloathing for Two Regiments lately seized at Philada.[1] Duane & Rob. R. Livingston came today from the Indian Treaty at Albany. Another Treaty is about to be held at Pittsburg.[2] Dr. Franklins Goods allowed to be landed. A great Number of Letters and Papers were read, some from Gen. Washington[3] giving a particular State of his Army, they want Powder and Money—some from Gen. Schuyler[4] stating his Situation

Pennsylvania State House

—others from Col. Lewis Morris & Jas. Wilson[5] Dated at Fort Pitt recommending an Expedition agt. Detroit to be conducted by Col. Arthur St. Clair—others from Gov. Trumbull and sundry more.

MS (DLC).

[1] Although Congress this day ordered the Pennsylvania delegates to send Washington $527,480, not until the following day did it instruct them to forward clothing to him. *JCC,* 2:245, 248.

[2] Commissioners from Congress and from Virginia concluded a treaty of friendship with various Western Indian tribes at Pittsburgh in October 1775. See Richard Henry Lee to Washington, November 13, 1775; and Reuben Gold Thwaites and Louise Phelps Kellogg, eds., *The Revolution on the Upper Ohio, 1775–1777* (Madison: Wisconsin Historical Society, 1908), pp. 25–127.

[3] Washington's letters to the president of Congress of August 4 and 31, together with accompanying enclosures, are in PCC, item 152, 1:51–106; and *Am. Archives,* 4th ser. 3:26–36, 243–55, where, however, the latter letter is incorrectly dated August 23.

[4] Schuyler's letter to Hancock of July 16 is in PCC, item 153, 1:47; those to Hancock of July 21 and August 2 are printed in *Am. Archives,* 4th ser. 2:1702–4 and 3:11–12; and that to the Indian commissioners for the northern department of August 31 is in ibid., 3:493–94.

[5] Not found.

Samuel Ward's Diary

[September 13, 1775]

13th. Met. The President took the Chair the first Time. Letters from Genls Washington (two from G. Washn. to Genl Gage & one from Gage), Schuyler, &c, read.[1] Leave granted to Dr. Franklin to receive his Books Papers &c, just arrived. Leave granted to two Virginia Men to reload & export a Cargo which was shiped timely on Board a Vessel cast away.[2] Mr. Hopkins was with us untill One.

MS (RHi).

[1] Ward inserted the parenthetical comment between the lines of his diary, marking the point of insertion following Schuyler's name, but obviously intended to add it after Washington's.

[2] On this point, see *JCC,* 2:246–47.

John Zubly's Diary

[September 13, 1775]

Wednesday, 13. Took Seat at the Congress. Preachd for Mr. Weinbery. Act 16:31.4, & agreed D[eo] V[olante] to preach every Wednesday.

MS (GHi).

Richard Smith's Diary

Thursday 14 Septr. [1775]

Letters read from Gen. Schuyler and others.[1] Col. Francis sent the Journal of the late Indian Treaty at Albany to the Congress which was read.[2] Several Members from Virginia, Maryland, Jersey, N York & Connecticut added to the Pennsa. Delegates appointed last Session to settle Accounts. The Georgia Delegates laid the Proceedings of their Provincial Convention before Us Cont'g a Petition to the King, another to certain Resolves and other Matters,[3] and motioned for Leave to sell the Cargoes of Two Ships which were shipped without Knowledge of their Agreement of Non Importn. and motioned also for Exportation of certain Articles under certain Limitations. These Motions were opposed by Chase and J. Adams and supported by Nelson, Houstoun & Dr. Zubley, the latter out of Humor with Chase. The Consideration of it was put off till Tomorrow. The proposed Expedition to Detroit canvassed and disagreed to & various other Matters.

MS (DLC).

[1] Schuyler's letters to Hancock of July 26, 27, 28 and August 6, together with accompanying enclosures, are in PCC, item 153, 1:63-86, 102-7; and *Am. Archives,* 4th ser. 2:1729-31, 1734-35, 1745-47, and 3:48-49.

[2] On this point, see ibid. 3:473-95.

[3] On the proceedings of the Georgia Provincial Congress, held in Savannah July 4-17, 1775, see ibid. 2:1543-68.

Samuel Ward's Diary

[September 14, 1775]

14th. Met, a Number of Letters from Genl. Schuyler &c, read. Dr. Stringer appoin[te]d chief Physician & Surgeon to Genl. Schuylers Army to be pd. for his Medicines & supplies the same Pay as the other chief Phy[sician].[1] The Motion from Georgia consid[ere]d & referred. (Mr. Hopkins until one.) The Address of that Provincial Con[vention] to the King read & their resolves. Treaty with the Six Nations read, a Plan for taking Fort Detroit proposed by Mr. Willson & Colo. Morris rejected. Colo. Morris appointed a Commissr. at the Indian Treaty for the middle Department.

MS (RHi).

[1] Samuel Stringer (1734-1817), Albany doctor and sometime chairman of the Albany Committee of Correspondence in 1775, was Gen. Philip Schuyler's personal physician before being appointed this day as director of the hospital and chief physician and surgeon for the army in the northern department. Joel Munsell, *The Annals of Albany,* 10 vols. (Albany: J. Munsell, 1850-59), 6:124; Don R. Gerlach,

Philip Schuyler and the American Revolution in New York, 1733–1777 (Lincoln: University of Nebraska Press, 1964), p. 285; and *JCC,* 2:249–50.

John Adams' Diary

1775. Septr. 15. Fryday.

Archibald Bullock and John Houstoun Esquires, and the Revd. Dr. Zubly, appear as Delegates from Georgia.[1]

Dr. Zubly is a Native of Switzerland, and a Clergyman of the Independent Perswasion, settled in a Parish in Georgia. He speaks, as it is reported, Several Languages, English, Dutch, French, Latin &c. —is reported to be a learned Man. He is a Man of a warm and zealous Spirit. It is said that he possesses considerable Property.

Houstoun is a young Gentleman, by Profession a Lawyer, educated under a Gentleman of Eminence in South Carolina. He seems to be sensible and spirited, but rather inexperienced.

Bullock is cloathed in American Manufacture.

Thomas Nelson Esquire, George Wythe Esqr., and Francis Lightfoot Lee Esq. appeared as Delegates from Virginia.

Nelson is a fat Man, like the late Coll. Lee of Marblehead. He is a Speaker, and alert and lively, for his Weight.

Wythe is a Lawyer, it is said of the first Eminence.

Lee is a Brother of Dr. Arthur, the late Sheriff of London,[2] and our old Friend Richard Henry, sensible, and patriotic, as the rest of the Family.

Deane says, that two Persons, of the Name of De Witt of Dutch Extraction, one in Norwich the other in Windham, have made Salt Petre with Success—and propose to make a great deal. That there is a Mine of Lead at Middletown, which will afford a great Quantity. That Works are preparing to smelt and refine it, which will go in a fortnight. There is a Mine at Northampton, which Mr. W. Bowdoin spent much Money in working, with much Effect, tho little Profit.

Langdon and Bartlett came in this Evening, from Portsmouth.[3] 400 Men are building a Fort on Pierce's Island to defend the Town vs. Ships of War.

Upon recollecting the Debates of this Day in Congress, there appears to me a remarkable Want of Judgment in some of our Members. Chace is violent and boisterous, asking his Pardon. He is tedious upon frivolous Points. So is E. Rutledge. Much precious Time is indiscreetly expended. Points of little Consequence are started, and debated [*with*] warmth. Rutledge is a very uncouth, and ungracefull Speaker. He shruggs his Shoulders, distorts his Body, nods and wriggles with his Head, and looks about with his Eyes, from side to side, and Speaks thro his Nose, as the Yankees Sing. His Brother John dodges his Head too, rather disagreably, and both of them Spout out their Language in a rough and rapid Torrent, but without much Force or Effect.

Dyer is long winded and roundabout—obscure and cloudy. Very talkative and very tedious, yet an honest, worthy Man, means and judges well.

Sherman's Air is the Reverse of Grace. There cannot be a more striking Contrast to beautifull Action, than the Motions of his Hands. Generally, he stands upright with his Hands before him. The fingers of his left Hand clenched into a Fist, and the Wrist of it, grasped with his right. But he has a clear Head and sound Judgment. But when he moves a Hand, in any thing like Action, Hogarths Genuis could not have invented a Motion more opposite to grace. It is Stiffness, and Aukwardness itself. Rigid as Starched Linen or Buckram. Aukward as a junior Batchelor, or a Sophomore.

Mr. Dickinsons Air, Gate, and Action are not much more elegant.

MS (MHi). Adams, *Diary* (Butterfield), 2:172–73.

[1] This entry is apparently retrospective, since the credentials of the Georgia delegates were entered into the journals on September 13. *JCC*, 2:240–42.

[2] That is, William Lee.

[3] For the arrival of the New Hampshire delegates, see Josiah Bartlett to Mary Bartlett, September 16, 1775.

Silas Deane to Elizabeth Deane

My Dear Philadelphia Septr 15th 1775

I wrote you from Trenton, last Sunday,[1] but miss'd a Conveyance untill on Tuesday, by the Stage, to Care of Mr. Hazard. Hope You received it. I think I promised you a long Letter in it as soon as I arrived here, which shall disappoint you of, tho' this by Brown is sure of coming safe to hand for which want of Spirits occasioned by a sever cold must be my excuse.

I have been casting in my Mind how to procure you a passage to this place. Suppose Mr. Webb who wants to come, at least as farr as N. York could contrive to put his *light Horse,* with Two others, into Browns Stage and so come on, to New York, where I would meet you, with my Carriage. Think of this and write me by the first post after the Receipt of this. Tell my Brother Simeon, that Monsieur *Tetard* is gone Chaplain to the New York Forces, so that his views of studying with him are over, for the present.

The Congress have hardly begun Business, New Hampshire, & N. Carolina being absent.[2] This City is still busy in military parade, & preparation. It is well they are for something is Necessary to keep them employed, and to divert their Attention from the Melancholy appearance of their River destitute of Navigation. No less than Sixty Sail left this place, on the day the Nonexportation took place, & None have arrived since except one Shipp from London. There is Nothing New worth sending you thus farr. Pray forward me a Lettr. from your Father, as soon as received. I am my Dear yours

S Deane

RC (CtHi).

[1] Deane's letter to his wife of September 10 briefly described his journey southward and reported that: "*Govr. Ward* joined Us at New Haven, & *Mr. Cushing*, so that We have had just Company eno. to be agreeable. Col. Dyer has been unwell, but not so as to delay Us." CtHi.

[2] Although the New Hampshire delegates arrived this day, the first mention of the arrival of any of the North Carolina delegates is contained in Secretary Thomson's October 12 entry in the journals recording John Penn's appearance. *JCC*, 2:252, 3:290. Robert Treat Paine, the last of the Massachusetts delegates to take his seat at this session of Congress, attended for the first time this day, having arrived in Philadelphia the preceding evening. Robert Treat Paine's Diary, September 14 and 15, 1775. MHi.

Eliphalet Dyer to Joseph Trumbull

Dear Sir Philadelphia Septr 15th 1775

I recievd yours with a Continuando to the 5th Instant in which you mention the Article of flower you proposed to get from this place &c. The Generalls letter is laid before the Congress[1] & they have taken the matter up but not yet determined Upon but they at present seem rather Averse to Water carriage for 2 reasons. The one the fear of loss the other the fear of Gain to the Enemy. There is now flower enough att York. It has fallen there 3 or 4/ per hund the last Week as I am Informed by their delegates. It has fallen much here I believe to about 12/6 (ie) the midling sort. I can only say at this time you must depend upon Connecticutt for the present but a few days will determine what the Congress will do & shall give you the earliest Intelligence. As to Cash there will be a Supply for the Military Chest immediately sent forword but if they conclude to send Flower from here or York no doubt orders may be given on the Treasurer to the amount. As to the article of pork I have no doubt but the Method you propose of having the hogs drove down on the foot & salted there will be agreable as it must Save a great expence but what Army or how many will be kept up thro the Winter is Impossible to determine. The Congress will soon take that matter under Consideration. I hope there may be some way found out whereby the best officers & those most Worthy may be appointed.

By the last accounts from England it appears the K——g is Obstinately bent to prosecute the Warr against the Americans as appears by the K——s answer to the London Petition.[2] But it rather seems there will be no reinforcement to Genll Gage this fall. I hope a good account may be given of those here in due time. Let me hear wether my son is with you & how he does. Due regards to all Friends & am yours Elipht Dyer

[*P.S.*] Since my last we have recievd from Doctr Church an Invoice for a large quantity of Druggs.[3] As I had sent my son a large quantity of Rhubarb and it is now Scarce here I have engaged to Supply him with that Article I believe Cheaper than can be got here. I have shewd a Sample to the best appothecary here who say it is Cheap at 3 doll[ar]s per lb by 50 wt togeather. I have ordered my son Benjn to send forword to you about 56 lb the quantity Doctr Church sent for, at that price tho it is low, which you will be so kind as to deliver to him as soon as it comes to hand. The other articles we shall procure as soon as may be & forword. Your E D

RC (CtHi).

[1] Probably Washington's September 7 letter to Congress, endorsed "No. 6," and enclosing Commissary Trumbull's proposals for purchasing flour and pork economically. PCC, item 152, 1:109–14; and *Am. Archives,* 4th ser. 3:662–63. Congress continued consideration of this letter on September 16 and on the 21st appointed a committee to consider means of provisioning the army. *JCC,* 2:253, 3:257–58.

[2] On July 14, 1775, the lord mayor, aldermen, and Commons of the City of London petitioned the king, urging him to desist from the use of force against America. The king replied that he must continue to use force as long as there was any resistance. *Am. Archives,* 4th ser. 2:1602–3.

[3] On the previous day Congress had appointed Dyer to a committee "to devise ways and means for supplying the continental army with Medicines." *JCC,* 2:250.

John Hancock to Lewis Morris and James Wilson

Gentlemen, Congress Chamber Septr. 15th. 1775.

Your Letter of the 6th Inst.[1] was duely recd. and communicated to the Congress, who immediately took into Consideration the proposed Expedition against Detroit: and as the Season is so far advanced, and the Congress have not sufficient Light to direct their Judgment, they can not undertake to give their Countenance to the proposed Enterprize; more especially as an Enterprize is now on Foot, which, if successful, will necessarily draw that Place after it.

Inclosed you have two Resolves passed in Congress, relative to the Appointment of Col. Morris and Doctr. Walker,[2] as Commissioners for Indian Affairs. If Doctr. Walker should not be present when this reaches you, it may be proper to dispatch an Express to him, and notify him of his Appointment.

LB (DNA: PCC, item 12A).

[1] On this letter, now lost, see also Richard Smith's Diary, September 13, 1775.

[2] Thomas Walker (1715–94), a Virginia physician and explorer deeply involved in western land speculation, and Lewis Morris, a delegate from New York, were appointed commissioners for Indian affairs in the middle department on September 14–15, for the express purpose of concluding a treaty of friendship with the Ohio Indians at Pittsburgh. *JCC*, 2:251; and *DAB*.

John Jay to Stephen Rapalje

Sir Philad. 15 Septr. 1775

We are informd that a considerable Quantity of Drugs & Medicines are in yr. Possession belonging to a Gent. in England or Ireland. The Congress are desirous of purchasing such of them as may be of use to the army, & I am desired to apply to you for that Purpose. Be so kind therefore as to inform me by the first opportunity whether you will dispose of them. Be assured that yr. Compliance will be very agreable to the Congress.[1] I am Sir yr. very hble Servt.

J. Jay

FC (NNC).

[1] On September 23 Congress ordered the committee on supplying the army to "buy a parcel of Drugs in the hands of Mr. Rapalje, which he offers at the prime cost." *JCC*, 3:261.

George Ross to James Wilson

Dear Sir Phida. 15th Septr. 1775

The Affair of Detroit has been considered in Congress and the result you will have in a Letter from the President.[1] It was thought too late in the Season. The Intelligence was not clear enough. That Cannon might me [*be*] Necessary. That as the Treaty at Albany has been very happily Concluded The Indians might take Offence. That perhaps the Indians in your department might take it amiss and Lastly that Should Genl. Shuyler Suceed as has Embarged 15 days Detroit would Fall of Course. I say those Reasons determined the Congress unanimously to delay the Expedition at this time. We have little to do. All waiting with Anxiety to hear from Schuyler.

All is Quiet at Boston. The Best Intelligence from England shews we must depend on our own Steady measures. I have heard From Jammy, he is well. I have not lately heard from Mr. Biddle, by the last accounts he was better. My Complymts. to Col. Morris Mr. Lawrence & all Friends. Coll. Thompson is well & greatly Esteemed.

There is another Brigadier Wanting For the Army. I hope to have

Col. Armstrong appointed. I am with great affection Your Sincere Friend & Hble Servt. Geo. Ross

RC (MeHi).

[1] For Congress' negative response to a proposed expedition against Detroit, recommended in Morris and Wilson's letter of September 6, see John Hancock to Lewis Morris and James Wilson, September 15, 1775, and *JCC*, 2:251.

Richard Smith's Diary

Friday 15 Septr. [1775]

Debates upon Indian Commissioners for the Middle Department. Henry and Franklin being unable to attend at Pittsburg, Col. Lewis Morris & Dr. Thomas Walker appointed to attend there Hac Vice.[1] Then the Affair of the Two Cargoes at Georgia referred from Yesterday, was largely agitated & in the End a Resolution drawn by Jay took place importing that the cargoes should be sold and the Proffits if any put into the Hands of the Georgia Convention or Comee. of Safety to be applied in Defence of the Province. An incidental Matter took up some Time viz, Whether Mr. Nelson should vote for Virginia he being the only Delegate present[2] & whether any lesser Number than the Quorum shall represent any Colony. Mr. Nelson waved his Question & the other went off without a Determination. (Since that Time no Colony votes without the Quorum present as limited by their Colony. Some authorize 3, some 2, some one Delegate to give a Vote.) Two of the Georgia Delegates are possessed of Homespun Suits of Cloaths, an Adornment few other Members can boast of, besides my Bror. Crane and myself.

MS (DLC).

[1] Although Dr. Walker was appointed commissioner of Indian affairs this day, Morris' appointment had been made on September 14. *JCC*, 2:251.

[2] Francis Lightfoot Lee and George Wythe were in Philadelphia but had been inoculated for small pox and were in seclusion, and Peyton Randolph was ill. See Samuel Ward to George Washington, September 17, 1775. According to his later account with Virginia, Thomas Nelson had been in attendance for a few days. His claim for expenses as a delegate included the following entries: "To Travelling to Phila. 300 Miles @ 1/–Mile £15. To Attendance in Congress from Sepr 10th till Feby 22d is 165 days @ 45/–£371–5." NN.

Samuel Ward's Diary

[September 15, 1775]

15th. Met, Dr. Walker of Virginia appointed a Commissioner in the Room of Mr. Henry. Goods arrived in Georgia before 6th Augst.

last to be sold or reshiped at the option of the Proprietors; if sold, first Cost & Charges to be reimbursed the Owners, the Profits to be applied by the provincial Congress for the Defence of the Colony. (Mr. Hopkins until 1/2 past one.)

MS (RHi).

John Adams' Diary

1775 Sept. 16. Saturday.

Walking to the Statehouse this Morning, I met Mr. Dickinson, on Foot in Chesnut Street. We met, and passed near enough to touch Elbows. He passed without moving his Hat, or Head or Hand. I bowed and pulled off my Hat. He passed hautily by. The Cause of his Offence, is the Letter no doubt which Gage has printed in Drapers Paper.[1]

I shall for the future pass him, in the same manner. But I was determined to make my Bow, that I might know his Temper.

We are not to be upon speaking Terms, nor bowing Terms, for the time to come.

This Evening had Conversation with Mr. Bullock of Georgia. I asked him, whether Georgia had a Charter? What was the Extent of the Province? What was their Constitution? How Justice was administered? Who was Chancellor, who Ordinary? and who Judges?

He says they have County Courts for the Tryal of civil Causes under £8—and a C[hief] Justice, appointed from Home and 3 other Judges appointed by the Governor, for the decision of all other Causes civil and criminal, at Savanna. That the Governor alone is both Chancellor and Ordinary.

Parson Gordon of Roxbury, spent the Evening here.[2] I fear his indiscreet Prate will do harm in this City. He is an eternal Talker, and somewhat vain, and not accurate nor judicious. Very zealous in the Cause, and a well meaning Man, but incautious, and not sufficiently tender of the Character of our Province, upon which at this Time much depends. Fond of being thought a Man of Influence, at Head Quarters, and with our Council and House, and with the general Officers of the Army, and also with Gentlemen in this City, and other Colonies. He is a good Man, but wants a Guide.

MS (MHi). Adams, *Diary* (Butterfield), 2:173–75.

[1] That is, Adams' letter to James Warren, July 24, 1775. For another personal evaluation of the letter's impact, see Adams to Abigail Adams, October 2, 1775.

[2] William Gordon (1728/29–1807), a dissenting clergyman from England, became pastor of a Roxbury, Mass., parish in 1772. Gordon, a correspondent of Lord Dartmouth and an outspoken Whig by 1775, was made chaplain of the Massachu-

setts Provincial Congress in May of that year. He also wrote widely for the newspapers and spent much of his time during the war collecting material for a history of the conflict, *The History of the Rise, Progress, and Establishment, of the Independence of the United States,* 4 vols. (London: Printed for the author, 1788). Shipton, *Harvard Graduates,* 13:60–85.

Josiah Bartlett to Mary Bartlett

My Dear Philadelphia Saturday Septembr 16th [1775]

I arrived yesterday at this place about noon, after a pretty agreable Jorney having had no rain Since the Day I Set out till a Small Shower last thursday. After we Got in yesterday it rained most of the afternoon. I hope & trust that you & my family are well as nothing will Give me So much Uneasiness as to hear any of you are Dangerously Sick in my absence But I hope & trust kind Providence will bring us all togather again in Safety. I am well Except Something of a Cough as is usual after a Great Cold that I took on my Jorney. The Small Pox is in the City. Some of the members of the Congress are now under Innoculation & Some have taken [. . .] as hitherto to Escape it. Which I Shall Do I am not fully Determined, altho all agree there is no Danger in Innoculation, yet it will hinder me at least a fortnight from my Duty at Congress. I have nothing new to inform you of Except that the Storm [that] we had the Sabbath before I Set out from home [was] very Severe in New York, New Jersey & Pensylvania [doin]g Great Damage tearing Down trees &c &c [the] accont of which you will probably See in the Publick Prints. [I] wrote you from Woborn [and] from Windsor in Connecticut both of which I hope you have Received. Remember my Love to my Children and to all Enquiring Friends, Particularly to Lieut. Pearson & Capt. Calef and their families. I Shall frequently write to you and want to hear from you & my family, hope you will not neglect to write now I am here and you know where they will find me. I am yours &c

Josiah Bartlett

RC (NhHi).

John Hancock to the New York Provincial Congress

Sir Philadelphia, Septem. 16th, 1775.

Herewith I transmit you a Commission for Mr. Flemming, Deputy Adjutant General with the rank of Colonell agreeable to the recommendation of your Congress, which I have dated the Day of his Appointment.[1]

I also forward you four Hundred Commissions for the officers of your Forces under the Command of General Schuyler, which you will please to have regularly fill'd up with the Names of those Gentlemen who were Appointed by your Congress, & Transmit them to General Schuyler to be Deliver'd them. You will observe they are not Dated. You will please to Supply the Dates according to the Time of the Appointment of each, as their pay should Commence from that time, and as I was not furnish'd with a List of the names nor the Time, was Oblig'd to give you the trouble of completing the commissions. You will please to acknowledge the Receipt of them.

I have nothing in Charge from Congress to Communicate. When I have, you shall be early Acquainted therewith.

I have the honour to be with much esteem, Sir, Your most Obedt hum Servt. John Hancock Presidt.

RC (N). *Journals of the N. Y. Prov. Cong.*, 2:4. Addressed: "Honl. P.V.B. Livingston Esqr. &c." RC damaged; missing words supplied from Tr.

[1] On September 14 Congress had confirmed the New York Provincial Congress' appointment of Edward Flemming as deputy adjutant-general with the rank of colonel in the army of the northern department. *JCC*, 2:249; and *Am Archives*, 4th ser. 3:564. The Provincial Congress' letter of September 9 to the New York delegates recommending Flemming is in PCC, item 67, 1:37.

Richard Smith's Diary

Saturday 16 Sepr. [1775]

The greater Part of the Time lost in considering Whether One Officer in our Army may be allowed to hold Two Commissions. It was postponed, this was on read'g. Gen Washingtons Letters,[1] other Parts of his Letters gone into & some small Matters settled.

MS (DLC).

[1] See Samuel Ward to Washington, September 17, and Washington's letters to Hancock of August 4 and 31, 1775, Washington, *Writings* (Fitzpatrick), 3:390–99, 461–63.

Samuel Ward's Diary

[September 16, 1775]

16th. Entered upon Genl. Washingtons Letters referred to Monday. Next Tuesday assigned for Consideration of the Trade of the

Colonies.[1] A Motion that no Provisions Hides or Leather Sheepskins Flaxseed be exported postponed.[2] (Mr. Hopkins until one.)

MS (RHi).

[1] Congress chose Wednesday, September 20, not Tuesday, September 19, to consider the state of American commerce. *JCC*, 2:253.

[2] See *JCC*, 3:268–69.

John Zubly's Diary

[September 16, 1775]

Saturday. I made a point of it in every Company to contradict & oppose every hint of a desire of Independency or of breaking our Conexion with Great Britain.[1] [. . .] Went home with Mr. Schlatter.

MS (GHi).

[1] Zubly had more fully stated his views on America's connection with Britain in his long letter to Lord Dartmouth, September 3, 1775: "The question, my Lord, which now agitates *Great Britain* and *America*, and in which your Lordship has taken such an active part, is, whether the Parliament of *Great Britain* has a right to lay taxes on the *Americans*, who are not and and cannot there be represented; and whether the Parliament has a right to bind the *Americans* in all cases whatsoever? . . . Let a declaratory bill be passed that, any law and usage to the contrary notwithstanding. *America* is entitled to all the common rights of mankind, and all the blessings of the *British* Constitution, that the sword shall never be drawn to abridge, but to confirm her birthright, and the storm instantly becomes a calm, and every *American* thinks himself happy to contribute to the necessities, defence, and glory of *Great Britain*, to the utmost of his strength and power. . . . The people in *England* are made to believe that the *Americans* want to separate from them, or are unwilling to bear their part of the common burden. No representation can be more false; but, my Lord, a Nation cannot be misled always, and when once the good people of *Great Britain* get truer notions of the matter, they will naturally wreak their resentment on those by whom they have been grossly misinformed or wretchedly deceived. . . . The *Americans* have always shown an affectionate regard to the King, and they are truly sensible of the necessity and advantage of a perpetual union with the Parent State; but undeserved severities cannot be productive of any pleasing returns. . . . To restore peace and harmony, nothing is necessary than to secure to *America* the known blessings of the *British* Constitution. This may be done in a moment, and without any disgrace or risk. Let the *Americans* enjoy, as hitherto, the privilege to *give* and *grant* by their own representatives, and they will give and grant liberally; but their liberty they will never part with but with their lives." *Am. Archives*, 4th ser. 3:634–39. (From Zubly's pamphlet *The Law of Liberty*; see illustration.)

John Adams' Diary

1775 Septr. 17th. Sunday.

Mr. Smith, Mr. Imlay and Mr. Hanson, breakfasted with us. Smith is an Englishman, Imlay and Hanson N. Yorkers.

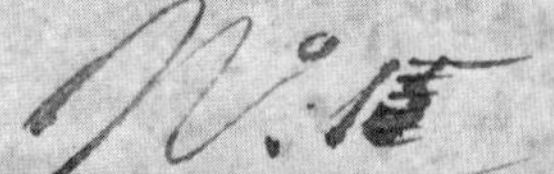

THE LAW OF *LIBERTY.*

A SERMON

ON

AMERICAN AFFAIRS,

PREACHED

AT THE OPENING OF THE PROVINCIAL CONGRESS OF *GEORGIA.*

ADDRESSED

TO THE RIGHT HONOURABLE THE EARL OF *DARTMOUTH.*

WITH AN APPENDIX,

GIVING A CONCISE ACCOUNT OF THE STRUGGLES OF SWISSERLAND TO RECOVER THEIR LIBERTY.

BY JOHN J. ZUBLY, *D. D.*

IS. XI: 13. EPHRAIM SHALL NOT ENVY JUDAH, AND JUDAH SHALL NOT VEX EPHRAIM.

PHILADELPHIA:
PRINTED BY HENRY MILLER. MDCCLXXV.

The Law of Liberty by John Joachim Zubly

Heard Sprout [Sproat], on 3 Tit. 5. Not by Works of Righteousness, which We have done, but according to his Mercy he saved us, through the Washing of Regeneration and the Renewing of the holy Ghost.

There is a great deal of Simplicity and Innocence in this worthy Man, but very little Elegance or Ingenuity. In Prayer, he hangs his Head in an Angle of 45° over his right Shoulder. In Sermon, which is delivered without Notes, he throws himself into a Variety of indecent Postures. Bends his Body, Points his Fingers, and throws about his Arms, without any Rule or Meaning at all. He is totally destitute of the Genius and Eloquence of Duffil [Duffield], has no Imagination, No Passions, no Wit, no Taste and very little Learning, but a great deal of Goodness of Heart.

MS (MHi). Adams, *Diary* (Butterfield), 2:175–76.

John Adams to Abigail Adams

My Dear Philadelphia Septr. 17. 1775

This is the first Time, that I have attempted to write, since I left you. I arrived here in good Health, after an agreable Journey, last Wednesday; There had not been Members enough to make a House, several Colonies being absent, so that I was just in Time. The next day, an adequate No. appeared, and Congress has sat ever since.

Georgia is now fully represented, and united to the other Twelve.

Their Delegates are Dr. Zubly, a Clergyman of the independant Perswasion who has a Parish in that Colony and a good deal of Property. He is a Native of Switzerland, is a Man of Learning and Ingenuity. It is said he is Master of several Languages, Greek, Latin, French, Dutch and English. In the latter it is said, he writes tolerably. He is a Man of Zeal and Spirit, as We have already seen upon several occasions.

However, as he is the first Gentleman of the Cloth who has appeared in Congress, I can not but wish he may be the last. Mixing the sacred Character, with that of the Statesman, as it is quite unnecessary at this Time of day, in these Colonies, is not attended with any good Effects. The Clergy are universally too little acquainted with the World, and the Modes of Business, to engage in civil affairs with any Advantage. Besides those of them, who are really Men of Learning, have conversed with Books so much more than Men, as to be too much loaded with Vanity, to be good Politicians.

Mr. Bullock is another of the Georgian Delegates, a sensible Man, a Planter I suppose. Mr. Houstoun is the third, a young Lawyer of Modesty as well as sense and Spirit which you will say is uncommon.

Mr. Jones and Dr. Hall are not yet arrived.

Mr. Henry is made a General in Virginia, and therefore could not come. Mr. Pendleton and Coll. Bland excused them selves on Account of Age and ill Health. Messrs. Nelson, Wythe, and Lee, are chosen and are here in the Stead of the other three. Wythe and Lee are inoculated. You shall hear more about them. Altho they come in the Room of very good Men, We have lost nothing by the Change I believe. Remember me in the tenderest Language, to all our little Folks. I am yours.

RC (MHi) . Adams, *Family Correspondence* (Butterfield) , 1:280–81.

John Adams to James Warren

Dr Sir Philadelphia Septr. 17. 1775

I have nothing in particular to write. Our most gracious K—— has given a fresh Proof of his Clemency, in his answer to the City. But no more of Politicks, at present. If this Scratch of a Pen should fall into the Hands of the wiseacre Gage, as long as I confine myself, to Matrimony, and Horsemanship, there will be no Danger.

Be it known to you then that two of the most unlikely Things, within the whole Congress of Possibility, have really, and actually happened. The first is the Suden Marriage of our President, whose agreable Lady honours us with her Presence and contributes much to our good Humour, as well as to the Happiness of the President. So much for that.

The next Thing is more wonderfull Still.

You know the aversion, which your Secretary[1] has ever entertained to riding, on Horseback. He never would be perswaded to mount a Horse. The last time we were here, I often laboured to perswade him, for the Sake of his Health, but in vain. Soon after We Sat out, on the last Journey, I reflected that Some Degree of Skill and Dexterity in Horsemanship, was necessary to the Character of a Statesman. It would take more Time and Paper than I have to Spare, to shew the Utility of Horsemanship to a Politician; So I shall take this for granted. But I pointed out the particulars to him, and likewise shewed him that Sociability would be greatly promoted, by his mounting one of my Horses.

On Saturday the second day of September 1775, in the Town of Grafton He was prevailed on to put my Servant with his, into Harrisons Chaise and to mount upon my Horse, a very genteel, and easy little Creature. We were all disappointed and Surprised. Instead of the Taylor riding to Brentford We beheld, an easy, genteel Figure, upon the Horse, and a good deal of Spirit and facility, in the Management of the Horse, insomuch that We soon found our Servants were making Some disagreable Comparisons, and Since our arrival here I am told that Fessenden (impudent Scoundrel!) reports that the Secretary rides fifty per Cent better than your Correspondent.

In this manner, We rode to Woodstock, where we put up for the Sabbath. It was Soon observed that the Secretary, could not Sit So erect in his Chair as he had Sat upon his Horse, but Seemed to be neither sensible of the Disease or the Remedy. I Soon perceived and apprised him of both. On Sunday Evening, at Mr Dexters, where we drank Coffee & Spent an agreable Evening I perswaded him to purchase two yards of flannell which we carried to our Landlady, who with the assistance of a Tayler Woman in the House, made up a Pair of Drawers, which the next Morning were put on, and not only defended the Secretary from any further Injury, but entirely healed the little Breach which had been begun.

Still an Imperfection remained. Our Secretary had not yet learned to mount and dismount. Two Servants were necessary to attend upon these Occasions, one to hold the Bridle and Stirrup, the other to boost the Secretary. This was rather a ridiculous Circumstance Still. At last, I undertook to instruct him the necessary Art of mounting. I had my Education to this Art, under Bates, the celebrated Equerry, and therefore might be Supposed to be a Master of it. I taught him to grasp the Bridle, with his Right Hand over the Pummell of his Saddle, to place his left Foot firm in the Stirrup; to twist his left Hand into the Horses Main, about half Way between his Ears and his Shoulders, and then a vigorous Exertion of his Strength would carry him very gracefully into the Seat, without the least Danger of falling over on [the] other Side. The Experiment was tryed and Succeeded to Admiration.

Thus equipped and instructed, our Horseman rode all the Way from Woodstock to Philadelphia, Sometimes upon one of my Horses, Sometimes on the other—and acquired fresh Strength, Courage, Activity and Spirit every day. His Health is much improved by it, and I value myself, very much upon the Merit of having probably added Several Years, to a Life So important to his Country, by the little Pains I took to perswade him to mount and teach him to ride.

Sully and Cecil were both Horsemen, and you know I would not have our Americans inferiour to them in the Smallest Accomplishment.

Pray Mrs Warren to write to me. I would to her, if I had half so much Time.

RC (MHi). In Adams' hand, though not signed.

[1] Samuel Adams.

Silas Deane to Joseph Trumbull

Dear Sir Philadelphia Sepr. 17th. 1775

I write, because I owe You a Lettr. & wish for another, not That I have anything to send you private or public deserving Notice since Our Arrival. The Congress is well nigh full, little Business has as yet been done, but This Week it will be seriously entered upon, and I wish in Vain, that Mr. Mifflin was here. Mr. Biddle continues dangerously ill, Mr. Willson at Fort Pitt on an Indian Treaty, & Mr Willing a Constant attendant on Congress, will give Mr. Mifflin a proper Idea of the representation of this Colony, to whom present my sincerest respects. Hope Mrs. Mifflin arrived in safety, had the pleasure, of seeing her on the Road. Whenever you have Leisure you will oblige Me by a Lettr. Let it be ever so short, but the longer the better. I am Dear Sir Your much obliged & Very hum. Sevt

Silas Deane

RC (CtHi).

Samuel Ward to George Washington

Dear Sir Philadelphia 17th Sepr. 1775

Having nothing of immediate Consequence to communicate & determining to sett out for this City in a few Days after the Receipt of yr. favor, I deferred acknowledging it until my arrival here.

I am greatly obliged to you for the very kind notice which you was pleased to take of my Son & the favorable Light in which you view him. The Advantages of travelling he wants but those of a liberal Education he enjoys; he has seen some of the best Company in our Colony and from his moral & political Principles I flatter myself his Conduct will make him not unworthy of your future Regard every Instance of which I shall most gratefully acknowledge.

With Pleasure I observe that you have lately received some Powder & expect some Lead & Arms from our Colony. I hope the Measures taken by Congress and by the Colonies will furnish you with such Quantities as will allow the freest Scope to your military Plans & Operations.

That Part of your Letter relative to removing the Stock from the Islands & Sea Coasts I laid before our Genl. Assembly. I shewed the necessity of immediately doing it in the most forcible Terms & such Measures were immediately adopted as have I imagine secured all our Cattle from the Enemy by this Time.

The innumerable Difficulties which you must have encountered in the Command of an Army under different Establishments in Want of Arms Ammunition, regular Supplies of Provisions, a military Chest, experienced officers a due Organization & a hundred other Things I have some tho' not an adequate Conception of but from the Accts. which I have the Pleasure to receive from my Friends in Camp I doubt not but your wise & steady Attention to the Service will surmount all obstacles & that by the opening of next Campaign you will have the finest Army under Your Commd. which ever was formed in America. I am too sensible of the Multiplicity of Business in which you are engaged to flatter Myself with a regular Correspondence but whenever you shall communicate any thing necessary for the public Good to Me you may rely upon my best & constant Endeavours both in our own Colony & in Congress to promote the Service. I most chearfully entered into a solemn Engagement upon your Appointment to support you with my Life & Fortune and shall most religiously & with the highest Pleasure endeavour to discharge that duty.

The Congress began to do Business Last Wednesday but many Members are still absent; Colo. Lee, Colo. Harrison & Mr. Jefferson & the No. Carolina Delegates & some others are not arrived. Mr. Randolph has been confined with a fever two or three Days. Messrs. Wythe & Lee are under Enoculation so that Colo. Nelson alone attends from your Colony.

We entered into the Consideration of your Letters *yesterday,* for Want of a thorough Knowledge of military affairs it was not so well understood how an officers having several Appointments could make any Difference in Rank for instance how a Genl. officers having a Regiment or Company or a Feild officers having a Compy. could alter his Rank. It seemed to be the general Opinion that all officers should receive Pay only for one Commission & that for their highest & that when the Army was reformed no Person should sustain more than one office but some seemed to apprehend that if a Genl. officer appointed by his Colony as Colonel of a particular Regiment or a Field officer as Captain of a Company were refused by the Congress Commissions as such that the Colonies would appoint other Colonels & Captains in their Places that this increase of officers would augment the Difficulties attending the Reduction of the Troops if such a Measure should be adopted. Upon the whole the matter was referred & as soon as your several Letters are considered you will be acquainted with the Sentiments of the Congress.

⟨*We have no News here from England later than 18th July. By the Kings Answer to the Petition of the Lord Mayor Aldermen & Commons of the City of London it appears He is determined to pursue & enforce his Measures.*[1] *God be thanked that however severe the Contest may prove We are now in such a happy Way that the End must be the Establishment of American Liberty.*⟩

FC (RHi).

[1] See Eliphalet Dyer to Joseph Trumbull, September 15, 1775, note 2.

John Adams' Diary

1775 Septr. 18. Monday.

This Morning John McPherson Esq. came to my Lodging, and requested to speak with me in Private. He is the Owner of a very handsome Country Seat, about five Miles out of this City: is the Father of Mr. McPherson, an Aid de Camp to General Schuyler. He has been a Captain of a Privateer, and made a Fortune in that Way the last War. Is reputed to be well skilled in naval Affairs. He proposes great Things. Is sanguine, confident, positive, that he can take or burn every Man of War, in America. It is a Secret he says. But he will communicate it to any one Member of Congress upon Condition, that it be not divulged during his Life at all, nor after his Death but for the Service of this Country. He says it is as certain as that he shall die, that he can burn any Ship.[1]

In the afternoon Mr. S.A. and I made visit at Mrs. Bedfords to the Maryland Gentlemen. We found Paca and Chase and a polite Reception from them. Chase is ever social and talkative. He seems in better Humour, than he was before the Adjournment. His Colony have acted with Spirit in Support of the Cause. They have formed themselves into a System and enjoyned an Association, if that is not an Absurdity.

MS (MHi). Adams, *Diary* (Butterfield), 2:176.

[1] John Macpherson (1726–92), Philadelphia privateer-merchant, was one of several persons to propose plans for using an explosive torpedo to destroy ships at anchor. Congress endorsed Macpherson's scheme on October 19, 1775, and he subsequently went to Boston to implement it. *JCC,* 3:296, 300, 301; James Warren to John Adams, November 5, 1775, *Warren-Adams Letters,* 1:177; "Mount Pleasant and the Macphersons," in Thomas A. Glenn, *Some Colonial Mansions and Those Who Live in Them,* 2d ser. (Philadelphia: Henry T. Coates & Co., 1900), pp. 445–72.

George Ross to the Lancaster County Committee of Correspondence

Gent Philada. 18th Septr. 1775

I embrace with pleasure the Earliest opportunity to express the Deep sense of Gratitude I entertain of the Honourable Testimony the County of Lancaster have given of my Publick Conduct in the Arduous task I have been entrusted with.

Being Heartily & Conscientiously engaged in this best of Causes —The support of the just rights & Libertys of my Country, I shall ever Esteem it the most Honourable & happy period of my Life that the small mite I have cast in for the Service of the Common Cause meets with the Approbation of my Worthy Constituents.

Rest Assured I shall persevere in the line of Conduct you have been pleased to approve untill Peace & Happiness shall be restored to this much Injured & distressed Country. I am with the Greatest respect Your much Obliged & Obedt. Hble Servt. Geo. Ross

[*P.S.*] A Map of the Seat of Warr in Massachusetts Bay Accompanys this which I beg the Committee will be pleased to accept from their obliged Servt. G.R.

RC (DLC).

Richard Smith's Diary

[September 18, 1775]

Monday 18. Motion to appoint a Comee. to procure 500 Ton of Gunpowder, from abroad, together with 10,000 Stand of Arms 20,000 Gun Locks &c with power to draw on the Continental Treasury for the Amount, was carried by Vote,[1] the Payment in Produce was opposed & the further Consideration postponed. Comee. on the Accounts asked Direction how to settle them & the Matter left unsettled.[2] Motion by E. Rutledge to enlarge Col. Fenton a Prisoner in Connectt. from New Hampshire, opposed by Langdon and deferred. Letter from Gen. Schuyler giving an Account of his being at Isle aux Noix & postponing the Attack on Carlton at St. Johns till he sounds the Canadians, after having a small Skirmish.[3]

MS (DLC).

[1] On this point, see *JCC*, 2:253–54.

[2] According to the journals, this day Congress agreed that the committee of accounts should pay $5,303, continental currency, for the expenses incurred by Pennsylvania in raising eight companies of riflemen under congressional resolves of June 14 and 22, although the method of payment was not specified. *JCC*, 2:89, 104, 237, 248n, 250, 254.

[3] Schuyler's letter to Hancock of September 8, together with accompanying enclosures, including a September 5 Address to the Inhabitants of Canada, are in PCC, item 153, 1:125–37; and *Am. Archives*, 4th ser. 3:669–72.

Samuel Ward's Diary

[September 18, 1775]

18th. Agreed that proper Persons be appointed to a Commee. to procure 500 Tons Powder & if not so much to be had Salt petre to make up that quantity. 40 brass field Pieces, 20000 double bridled

Gunlocks, 10000 stands of Arms flints. Recd. an Express from Genl. Schuyler, he made his landing good, repulsed the Party that attacked him & returned to Isle of Noix. (Mr. Hopkins till 1/2 past one.)

MS (RHi).

John Adams to James Warren

Dear Sir Philadelphia Septr. 19. 1775

I have but a Moments Time to write and nothing of Importance to Say.

Mr Randolph, our former President is here, and Sits very humbly in his Seat, while our new one continues in the Chair, without Seeming to feel the Impropriety.[1] Coll Nelson, a Planter, Mr Wythe, a Lawyer, and Mr Francis Lightfoot Lee, a Planter, are here from Virginia, instead of Henry, Pendleton and Bland. Henry is General of Virginia—the other two are old and infirm. I am well pleased that Virginia has Set the Example of changing Members, and I hope that Massachusetts will follow it, and all the other Colonies. I Should be glad upon a new Election to be relieved from this Service. This Climate does not agree with my Constitution, So well as our own: and I am not very well fortified you know against the Inclemencies of any.

This Congress, I assure you, feels the Spirit of War, more intimately than they did before the Adjournment. They set about Preparations for it, with Seriousness and in Earnest.

RC (MHi). In Adams' hand, though not signed.

[1] A reference to John Hancock's continuation in the presidency, which many delegates apparently assumed would be resumed by Randolph upon his return to Congress.

Silas Deane's Diary

[September 19, 1775]

Monday [*i.e.* Tuesday] 19th. At Congress. On Committee for Settling Accts.[1] On do. for answering Genl. Schuyler.[2] On do. for contracting for Powder &c.[3]

MS (CtHi). *CHS Bulletin* 29 (July 1964): 96.

[1] Deane was one of five delegates added September 14 to the committee of accounts, which Congress reorganized September 25 to include one delegate from each colony. *JCC,* 2:250, 3:262.

[2] A committee of four, appointed September 19 to draft a reply to General Schuyler's September 8 letter, reported a letter the following day, which was then approved for the president's signature. *JCC,* 2:255–56. See John Hancock to Philip Schuyler, September 20, 1775.

[3] This day Congress also appointed Deane to a nine-member secret committee initially charged with contracting for importation of gunpowder and arms. *JCC,* 2:253–55.

John Hancock to George Washington

Sir, Congress Chamber 19 Septr 1775

The Congress have sent to you by Major William Coates, & Captain Joseph Copperthwait five hundred twenty seven thousand four hundred and eighty dollars continental Money to be delivered to the paymaster & subject to your Order for the use of the Army under your Command.[1]

I have the honour to be, Sir, Your most Obedt & huml servt.

John Hancock President

[*P.S.*] The Cloathing is on the way.[2] Your Letters are now under the Consideration of Congress, & you will soon hear from us. Pray forward your plans for Winter &c as soon as possible.

RC (DLC).

[1] See *JCC,* 2:245.

[2] See *JCC,* 2:248.

Richard Smith's Diary

Tuesday 19 Septr. [1775]

Arguments on Gen Schuylers Letter Whether he shall make a Post at Isle aux Noix and what is best to be done in his Situation, a Comee of Three named By Ballot to report their Opinion.[1] A Committee of 9 chosen by Ballot for procuring Arms & Ammunition. Agreed to banish John Fenton to England at his own Request after considerable Debate. Dr Franklin the PostMaster General desired the Delegates of New Jersey to nominate Deputy PostMasters throughout that Colony which we did accordingly.

MS (DLC).

[1] See Silas Deane's Diary this date, note 2.

Samuel Ward's Diary

[September 19, 1775]

19th. Took into consideration Gen Schuyler's Letters; appointed a Comee. to answer them. Gave Colo. Fenton leave to go to Engd. or Irland, he not to take up arms against us. Appointed Mr. Willing, Dr. Franklin, Mr. P. Livingston, Mr. Alsop, Mr. Dean, Mr. Dickinson, Mr. Langdon, Mr. McKean & Mr. Ward a Comee. for purchas[ing] Powder &c. Mr. Hopk[in]s as usual.

MS (RHi).

John Adams' Diary

1775. Septr. 20. Wednesday.

Took a Walk in Company with Govr. Ward, Mr. Gadsden and his Son, and Mr. S. Adams, to a little Box in the Country, belonging to old Mr. Marshall, the father of three Sons who live in the City.[1] A fine facetious old Gentleman, an excellent Whigg. There We drank Coffee. A fine Garden. A little Box of one Room. Very chearfull and good humoured.

MS (MHi). Adams, *Diary* (Butterfield), 2:176–77.

[1] Christopher Marshall (1709–97), retired Philadelphia pharmacist and Quaker patriot, who kept an informative diary during the war. *DAB;* and Christopher Marshall, *Extracts from the Diary of Christopher Marshall, Kept in Philadelphia and Lancaster during the American Revolution, 1774–1781,* ed. William Duane (Albany: Joel Munsell, 1877), p. 43.

John Hancock to the New York Provincial Congress

Gentlemen Philadelphia, Sept. 20th, 1775.

As General Schuyler is engaged in an Expedition of immense consequence to the United Colonies, and it being of the last importance that he be properly supported, in order to insure success, or at least prevent a Repulse, I am directed by the Congress to write to you and direct you immediately to send forward the whole of the Troops, order'd to be Raised in your Colony, properly equipped, in order to Join General Schuyler as soon as possible.

I am Gentlemen Your most Obedt hum Servt

John Hancock President

RC (N). LB (DNA: PCC, item 12A). RC damaged; missing words supplied from LB.

John Hancock to Philip Schuyler

Sir, Septr. 20th. 1775.

Your Letter of the 8th. Inst was recd. yesterday, and laid before the Congress. I am directed to express their Approbation of your

Conduct, as stated in your Letter. Your taking Possession of the Isle au Noix, and the proposed Measures for preventing the Enemies Vessels from entering the Lake, appear to them highly expedient and necessary.[1]

The Congress have such a Sense of the Importance of that Post, as to wish it may not be abandoned without the most mature Consideration, or the most pressing Necessity.

They view the Expedition entrusted to your Care as of the greatest Consequence to the general Cause; and as they clearly foresee, that its Influence whether successful, or otherwise, will be great and extensive, They are desirous that Nothing necessary to give it a fortunate Issue, may be omitted.

They have ordered all the Forces raised in New York, immediately to join you; and those under Genl. Worster to march immediately to Albany, from whence if you should think such Reinforcement necessary, you will be pleased to order them.

Should you stand in Need of farther Reinforcement, the Congress desire you will apply to Genl. Washington.

The Congress repose the highest Confidence in the Abilities, the Zeal, and the Alacrity of the Officers, and Forces employed on this Expedition. They are determined to spare neither Men, nor Money; and should the Canadians remain neuter, flatter themselves, that the Enterprize will be crowned with Success, notwithstanding the great and various Difficulties, to which it has been, and still is exposed.

It is with great Concern that the Congress hear of your Indisposition. They desire me to assure you of their warmest Wishes for your Recovery; and to request, that in discharging the Duties of your Station, you will not omit the Attention due to the Re-establishment of your Health.

By Order of the Congress, I am &c John Hancock, Prest.

LB (DNA: PCC, item 12A). On the authorship of this letter, see Silas Deane's Diary, September 19, 1775, note 2.

[1] See Richard Smith's Diary of this date for an indication that Congress was far from unanimous in its approval of Schuyler's withdrawal from St. Johns to the Isle aux Noix.

John Hancock to David Wooster

Sir, Philada. Sept. 20th. 1775.

The Necessity of supporting Genl. Schuyler in the important Enterprize he is now engaged in, has induced the Congress to direct you, immediately on Receipt of this, to march with the Troops under your Command to Albany, there to wait the Orders of Genl. Schuyler in Case he should want your Assistance; and you will please without Loss of Time to proceed.

By Order of the Congress. John Hancock President

LB (DNA: PCC, item 12A). Addressed: "To David Worster Esqr. Brigadr. Genl. in the Army of the united Colonies, and Commander of the Connecticut Forces, at Harlem."

Benjamin Harrison to William Palfrey

Dear Sir Phida Sepr. 20th. 1775

I Recd. your acceptable Favour last Night, and Mr Byrds going for Camp gives me an opportunity of answering it, tho' not so fully as I could wish, having been but one Day here and much Business of this sort to do, you may assure yourself on this and every other Occasion my best Endeavours shall be used to Serve you. I think what you propose is just and I make no doubt but the Congress will think as I do when the matter comes before them.[1]

I am truily affected with your Situation, and that of many other worthy Familys now suffering under the Hand of Tyrany, but I hope we shall soon see better Days.

Gage and his associates may Rejoice as much as they please at the possession of my Letter but the Publication of it reflects more Dishonour on him than the writing it dos on me.[2] I knew him a Slave, lost to all Sense of Honour, but suppos'd he would endeavour to keep up the appearance of the Gentleman. I am mistaken, and he is a R—— Compleat. I hope it will be no prejudice to your worthy General, if not I am content, as there is no mortal that such a thing will set easier on than myself.

I shall be glad to hear from you now & then if you can spare the time. I fear the Foxes will keep themselves close and not give you an oppy. to hunt them down, which I make no Doubt you are able & willing to do, if they should take it in their Heads to come out.

Pray present my Compliments to Genl Lee I shall be glad to hear from him if he has Leasure. I am Dr Sir Your affect Servt

Benja Harrison

RC (MH).

[1] See John Hancock to Palfrey, September 25, 1775. Although Palfrey was apparently interested in obtaining a different position in the army, he remained aide-de-camp to General Lee until March 6, 1776, when he briefly served as aide-de-camp to Washington before being appointed paymaster-general on April 27, 1776. Washington, *Writings* (Fitzpatrick), 4:369; and *JCC*, 4:315.

[2] Undoubtedly a reference to Harrison's letter to Washington of July 21, 1775.

Robert R. Livingston, Jr., to John Stevens

Dr. Sir 20th Sepr 1775 Philadelphia

I enclose you £90.1.0 of the £150 received agreeable to your order from Willing & Morris the remainder I retain in my hands. I could not receive it time enough to remit it by the last post or you should have had it sooner.

I do not know of any thing here worth relating but what is contained in the paper to wit the King's answer to the City of London & the little Skirmish of Schuylers. Their does not seem to be any great appearance of relaxation in the answer, I am much afraid that his majesty plays too carelessly, considering the greatness of the stake. Mr. Watts has been listned to with some attention by the ministry,[1] & has advised that they can not expect a reconciliation, but through the medium of the Congress. God knows what they may determine but prudence bids us prepare for the worst.

I suppose you have heard that Mrs. Browne is gone & taken Sally with her? If you havnt, it will be a peace of news for her sisters. I beg leave to present my respects to our friends at the Valley & remain Your Most Aff. Hum. Servt. Robt R Livingston Junr

RC (NjHi).

[1] John Watts (1715–89), New York merchant and provincial councillor, had fled to England in May 1775 following accusations that he had requested the dispatch of British troops to New York to curb local revolutionary leaders. *NYHS Collections* 61 (1928): ix-xiv; and Roger J. Champagne, "New York's Radicals and the Coming of Independence," *Journal of American History* 51 (June 1964): 23.

Thomas Lynch to Philip Schuyler

Dear Sir Phila Sepr. 20 1775

I[t] gives me great Concern to find your Health so much injured. Don't you know that it is the Duty of a General to take the utmost Care to bring his Army into the Field in good Health. If so, how much care is to be taken of the Head. You must spare your Body, & not expect it can possibly keep pace with such a Spirit if you push it too far, or it will leave you & us, in the Lurch, in short you will kill our General.

I see the Difficulties with which you are Surrounded. These can only add glory to the Success of your Enterprize. The Congress are awake at last & feel the importance of your Expedition, that every thing depends on its Success, and I think you may depend on every Support that is consistent with the Delay that attends popular Assemblies.

There will arise a Difficulty (and God knows you need no additional ones) about the old Genl. of Connecticut,[1] perhaps it may be of Use to have a General to Command at Fort George & receive the Supplies, or is Ticonderoga a better Station for that purpose.

We who know the officers commanding our Northern Army, have no doubt that every thing [*is*] done that Man can do. Cant you get Winter Quarters in Canada even shoud you not get Montreal, we hear the 2500 Highlanders are raising (tis thought) for Canada, and the Papers mention Cloathing being intended for 3000 Men to be raised in Canada is ordered from London. You being there can prevent all this even if St. Johns stands as it does, & is it not possible to interpose your Forces between that Post & Supplies so as to starve them. (A pretty Fellow to be taking Canada in the Comee Room at Philad. say you.) I knock under.

Colo. Arnold is on his Way to Canada by way the Genl mentioned to y[ou] and will I hope make a powerful diversion in Your Favour.

I beg my best Comp[lime]nts to Genl Montgomery, Colo. Campbell &c. I am Sir your most Obedt. Th Lynch

RC (NN).

[1] David Wooster, who apparently resented the fact that he was outranked by Schuyler. The two men subsequently quarreled once they joined forces in northern New York. Benson J. Lossing, *The Life and Times of Philip Schuyler,* 2 vols. (New York: Sheldon & Co. 1860–73), 1:433–42; and *DAB.*

[2] To facilitate Schuyler's advance on Montreal, Washington had ordered a detachment under the command of Benedict Arnold to strike at Quebec by way of the Kennebec River. Washington, *Writings* (Fitzpatrick), 3:436–39, 491–96.

Maryland Delegates to the New York Committee of Safety

Philadelphia, September 20, 1775. In response to a letter from the New York committee, Thomas Johnson, Samuel Chase, and William Paca return a noncommittal reply pertaining to the character of Dr. George Nicholson, who "came a stranger into Annapolis, in Maryland, about two years ago . . . and has uniformly as far as we have ever understood, expressed himself friendly to the cause of American liberty."[1]

MS not found; abstracted from *Journals of N. Y. Prov. Cong.*, 1:155.

[1] *Am. Archives,* 4th ser. 3:907. The New York Committee of Safety's letter of September 15, inquiring about Nicholson's character in order to evaluate intelligence he had recently provided them, is in ibid., p. 897.

New Hampshire Delegates to Matthew Thornton

Dear Sir Philadelphia Septembr 20th 1775

Yesterday it was moved in Congress to Discharge Col Fenton from his confinement.[1] It Seems that he living at Hartford had opportunity to See Several of the members as they passed to & from the army & by his politeness & address and by telling how much he had suffered had prejudiced some of them that he had been hardly Dealt with by us. The Copy of a letter from General Putnam was also Produced wherein he Says "that the Populace had Siezed him and Carried him before the Congress of N Hampshire and that after a full hearing they could not find that he had Done any thing against the Liberties of America in *Word* or *Deed*" but for fear that he might, had "ordered him to be Confined." But as we knew the whole of that affair we Convinced the Congress that our Convention had Done right.[2] The Congress then Passed a Resolve to this Effect "that whereas the Convention of the Colony of New Hampshire had *prudently* & *justly* ordered Col John Fenton to be Confined and that he being now Desirous to Remove to Great Brittain or Ireland therefore Resolved that General Washington be Directed to allow Col Fenton to Repair forthwith to New York and from thence to Great Brittain or Ireland on his Giving his Parole not to take up arms against America" which order your Delegates Consented to thinking it better than Keeping him Confined at the publick Expence.

As to Publick news you will See it in the Publick prints and we have no other that we can at present Communicate. We should be glad to Receive from you all possible Intelligence of our affairs and shall think it our Duty to write you often Even tho it were only to tell you we have nothing new to inform you of. We are your Most Obedient Humble Servants

Josiah Bartlett

John Langdon

RC (Nh-Ar). Written by Bartlett and signed by Bartlett and Langdon. Addressed: "Mathew Thornton Esqr. Chairman of the Committee of Safety, N. Hampshire, to be Communicated."

[1] See Richard Smith's Diary, September 19, 1775; and *JCC*, 2:255.

[2] The New Hampshire Provincial Congress on June 29 voted that "Colo. John Fenton is not a friend to this country." The next day his papers were seized, and he was ordered confined "till further orders from this Congress." He was subsequently sent to army headquarters in Cambridge. *N. H. Provincial Papers*, 7:543–45. For New Hampshire's official explanation of this event, see New Hampshire Committee of Safety to their Delegates in the Continental Congress, July 8, 1775, ibid., pp. 559–60.

New York Delegates to the New York Committee of Safety

Gentlemen Philad. 20th Septem. 1775

We have the Honour of your favour of the 9th Instant which we instantly communicated to the Congress.[1] Deputy Adjutant Flemming's Commission, with the Rank of Colonel, and a number of blanks, which you request have already been forwarded; and you may be assured that we shall be attentive to your want of powder, and embrace every Opportunity to supply it.

The Article of Tea gives us real Anxiety. We sincerely wish to relieve our suffering Fellow Citizens by Enabling them to dispose of what, so much to their Misfortune lies useless and perishing upon their Hands. You can not be insensible of the Delicacy of this Subject, and how many difficulties we have to struggle with to accomplish your humane Request. Whether we shall succeed or not it is out of our Power to determine. We are not without Hopes: but whatever may be the Event, you may rely upon our utmost Exertions to obtain the Permission which you solicit.

We have the Honour to be Gentn. Your most Obedt. humble Servants

Jas. Duane
John Jay
John Alsop
Robt. R. Livingston, Junr.
Frans. Lewis

RC (N). Written by Duane and signed by Alsop, Duane, Jay, Lewis, and Livingston. *Journals of N. Y. Prov. Cong.*, 2:17–18. RC damaged; missing words supplied from Tr.

[1] For the Committee of Safety's letter to the New York delegates of September 9, see *Am. Archives*, 4th ser. 3:680–81.

Richard Smith's Diary

[September 20, 1775]

Wednesday 20. An Expedition is on Foot against the Kings Forces in Canada via Kennebec under Col. Arnold from Washingtons Camp at Cambridge. Comee. brought in the Draught of a Letter from our President to Gen Schuyler. Large Controversy on some Parts of it & particularly how far we shall express Approbation of his late Proceedings in retreating to Nut Island[1] &c. Gen. Wooster with a considerable Detachment ordered to join Schuyler. This Morning a Letter in French was delivered to the President directed for Gen. Washington said to be from the Governor of Hispaniola.[2] Whether the Letter shall be opened and whether by a select Comee. or by the

President, were made Questions. The general Opinion seemed to be that the President should open it & the Secretary (Charles Thomson) translate it and if of a public Nature that it should be laid before Congress but it was dropt. Major Robert Rogers was at the State House today; he is just come from England & is upon the Kings Halfpay.[3]

MS (DLC).

[1] That is, Isle aux Noix.

[2] Not found.

[3] Robert Rogers (1731–95), commander during the French and Indian War of the celebrated "Rogers' Rangers," had recently returned to America from England as a major on half-pay, after an extended term in debtors prison. Ill-informed about the dispute between Britain and the colonies, he was ostensibly neutral but was regarded with suspicion by both sides. Arrested but soon released by the Americans in September 1775, he continued to be suspected and was again arrested in July 1776, shortly after which he escaped and fled to the British lines, where he returned to active duty as commander of the Queen's Rangers in the British provincial service. John R. Cuneo, *Robert Rogers of the Rangers* (New York: Oxford University Press, 1959), chap. 23; and *JCC*, 3:259.

Samuel Ward's Diary

[September 20, 1775]

20th. Finished Letter to Genl. Schuyler, Copy to be sent Genl. Washington. Genl. Washingtons Letter resumed.[1] Mr. Gridly to have a Com[missio]n as Colo. State of Trade referred. Mr Hopk[ins] as usual.[2]

MS (RHi).

[1] See Washington's letter to Hancock of August 4. Washington, *Writings* (Fitzpatrick), 3:390–99.

[2] John Zubly wrote in his diary for this date: "Thro Mercy recovering, attended Congress & preach[ed] for Mr. Weyberg. Act 16:31.6." GHi.

John Adams' Diary

1775. Septr. 21. Thursday.

The famous Partisan Major Rogers came to our Lodgings to make Us a Visit.[1] He has been in Prison—discharged by some insolvent or bankrupt Act. He thinks We shall have hot Work, next Spring. He told me an old half Pay Officer, such as himself, would sell well next Spring. And when he went away, he said to S.A. and me, if you want me, next Spring for any Service, you know where I am, send for me. I am to be sold. He says the Scotch Men at home, say d—n that Adams and Cushing. We must have their Heads, &c. Bernard used to d—n that Adams—every dip of his Pen stung like an horned Snake, &c. Paxton made his Will in favour of Ld. Townsend, and by that Maneuvre got himself made a Commissioner. There was a great deal of Beauty in that Stroke of Policy. We must laugh at such sublime Strokes of Politicks, &c. &c. &c.

In the Evening Mr. Jona. Dickinson Sergeant of Prince Town, made a Visit to the Sec.[2] and me. He says he is no Idolater of his Name Sake. That he was disappointed when he first saw him. Fame had given him an exalted Idea: but he came to N. Jersey upon a particular Cause, and made such a flimsy, effeminate, Piece of Work of it, that he sunk at once in his Opinion.

Serjeant is sorry to find a falling off in this City—not a third of the Battalion Men muster, who mustered at first.

D[ickinson] he says sinks here in the public opinion. That many Gentlemen chime in with a spirited Publication in the Paper of Wednesday, which blames the conduct of several Gentlemen of Fortune, D., Cad[walader], R[hoads], and J. Allen &c.[3]

MS (MHi). Adams, *Diary* (Butterfield), 2:177.

[1] See Richard Smith's Diary, September 20, 1775, note 3. In a letter of October 10, 1775, to Lord Dartmouth, Governor Tryon of New York enclosed a manuscript captioned "Private Intelligence, Sep 1775," and endorsed "The above are the sentiments on an Eastern Delegate of the Continental Congress. ⟨*Received*⟩ Communicated by Mjr ——— R ——." It is quite possible that the "Eastern Delegate" referred to was John, or more likely, Samuel Adams, whose "sentiments" were communicated to Rogers during the meeting described in this entry of Adams' diary. The complete text of the document reads: "They dont wish for independency but will not be Taxed at the Requisition of Parliament, but on Representation of the Minister they will Contribute, but at theyr own discretion and their own mode of Raising the Money. They have sent Home their last Proposal and are waiting for an answer, and if not settled this winter, they will open the Ports to all Europe.

"Other Powers will espouse their Cause when apply'd to with their Ships.

"That they are Confident they will be in possession of Montreal and Quebec this Year.

"If no settlement this winter, all the Ports in the interior Country will be seized and Privateers fitted out at such Ports that men of War cannot enter, and will seize the Homeward bound, West India Men or any others they can Master.

"They have laid Plans for plenty of ammunition this Winter.

"If Russians or [foreign] auxiliary's are sent over they will set up an Independency.

"If the Ice freezes over Boston Harbour this Winter they will burn the Ships of War and the Town. If affairs are settled an Act of Indemnity and free Pardon will be required for all the officers and all concern'd.

"No Regular Troops to be allowed to Remain in America as they have People enough to defend themselves, and assist his Majesty with Men against other Powers. Requisition in Money will be required for the burning of Charlestown and other Damages of the like Nature &c &c." PRO: C.O. 5, 1106:565–70.

[2] That is, Samuel Adams.

[3] An article defending an attack on two Philadelphia loyalists September 6 and

criticizing the protection of them by several "men of fortune" appeared in the *Pennsylvania Journal; and the Weekly Advertiser,* September 20, 1775. A description of the attack is in Christopher Marshall, *Extracts from the Diary of Christopher Marshall, Kept in Philadelphia and Lancaster, during the American Revolution, 1774–1781,* ed. William Duane (Albany: Joel Munsell, 1877), pp. 41–42.

Silas Deane's Diary

[September 21, 1775]

Thursday 21st. At Congress. Appd. on Comme. for purchasing Goods &c.[1]

MS (CtHi). *CHS Bulletin* 29 (July 1964): 96.

[1] The committee to consider the proposals of Commissary General Joseph Trumbull for provisioning the army, which submitted a report on October 19. *JCC,* 3:257–58, 299.

New York Delegates to the New York Committee of Safety

Gentlemen Philad. 21st Septemr. 1775

Be pleased by the first Opportunity to favour us with a particular Account of the Number of Men raised in our Colony in pursuance of the Orders of the Congress when the several Detachments marched; where they are at present; whether they are armed, and what Steps were taken for that purpose! We also wish to know the progress made in erecting the works in the highlands, whether the materials are purchased or what proportion, and when they may probably be compleated? Inform us also of the exact Quantity of powder our Colony has, at their own Expence, forwarded to either Army, that it may be replaced out of the continental Stock as soon as it can be afforded.

We are Gentlemen Your most Obedient humble Servants

Phil. Livingston John Jay
Jas. Duane Robt. R. Livingston, Junr.
John Alsop Wm. Floyd
Frans. Lewis

P.S. Acquaint us likewise of the prices you gave for the different sort of Cloath for Tents, & the making.[1]

RC (N). Written by Duane and signed by Alsop, Duane, Floyd, Jay, Lewis, Philip Livingston, and Robert R. Livingston. *Journals of N. Y. Prov. Cong.,* 2:83–84. RC damaged; missing words supplied from Tr.

[1] For the New York Provincial Congress' response to these queries, see *Am. Archives,* 4th ser. 3:1268–69.

Richard Smith's Diary

Thursday 21 Septr. [1775]

On a Question Whether Col. Armstrong or Col. Fry shall be Brig. Gen. in the Room of Pomeroy retired, the Colonies were divided 6 against 6, North Cara. being absent, consequently there was no Appointment. A Comee. of 5 was raised to consider of the best Method to convey 10 or 15000 Barrels of Flour and other Provisions to Gen. Washn. Much said about the Accounts of Col. Thompsons Riflemen, this Gent. had 5000 Dollars advanced to Him but his Accots. are yet unpaid & one demands Interest. The Judge Advocate (Tudor's) wages were raised at his Request from 20 Dollars to 50 Dollars per Month.[1]

MS (DLC).

[1] In response to William Tudor's letter to General Washington of August 23, which is in PCC, item 152, 1:99–101; and *Am. Archives,* 4th ser. 3:245.

Samuel Ward's Diary

[September 21, 1775]

21st. Sund[r]y Accts preferred & postpd. Appointment of a brigd. Genl. deferred until the Army is new modelled. Gen. Washington to commission as Brigade Majors Box, Sam. Brewer & Scammal [Scamell]. Gen. Schuyler to appoint a Brigade Major. Judge Advocates Pay for him[sel]f & clerk 50 Doll[ar]s per Month. A Comee. appointed to consider of the best Means of supplying our Army, their Names Mr. Dean Mr. Ward Mr. Cushing Mr. P. Livingston Mr. Willing. An Acct. for Duck &c of James Millikin [Milligan] Jr. allowd. Comee. of Berks county's Accts £2038.7.1 for rifle Men under Colo. Thompson referred to the Comee. Colo. Thomp[son] to send an Acct. how he disposed of the M[one]y 5000 Dollars. Mr. Hopkins as usual.

MS (RHi).

Samuel Ward to Henry Ward

Dear Brother Philadelphia 21st. Sepr. 1775

The merchant who has a good Customer who he knows will pay

all Accts. well does not stop shiping him Goods although a remitance may not be made so soon as he wishes, upon this principle exclusive of the Pleasure which I take in communicating any thing which I think will be acceptable to You I might write by this Post 'though I have not the Pleasure of a Letter from you.

The Check which Genl. Schuyler has recieved near St. Johns youl have an Acct. of in the Papers. The Loss is very trifling & such Measures are taken as I believe will inable him to proceed and crown the Expedition with Success; I feel much for him. He was so ill when he wrote Us that he was not able to hold a Pen. The Colonies of Connecticut & New York were to supply him with Men & Money &c; the first readily obeyed every Order of Congress, the last (their Delegates plead want of money &c) have never supplied him properly & I believe mere fatigue & Chagrine at the Disappointments he has recd. have made him sick.

We have the Honor of the Deputy Governors Letter & should jointly have acknowledged it but I was so engaged yesterday & last Evening that I could not draught an Answer & should I wait to find Mr. Hopkins this Morning the Post would be out. We made Mr. Redwood so much Trouble that We had agreed before I left the City last to remove upon our Return. I dont know the House in which he lodges but he tells Me the Family is very clever; be kind enough to let his Family know that they are both very well.

Present my most respectful Regards to Govr. Cooke. We had his Letter[1] read in Congress and it was very acceptable; the Intelligence of the Marching of Arnold with his Detachment was the first Acct. recd. here of it, happily the important Object recommended by him hath been taken into Consideration. Supplies full as large as he would wish are agreed upon & I doubt not will be most seasonably procured. And it is with the greatest Pleasure that I can assure You that the Congress is not only very unanimous but very spirited. Every Measure for the Defence of the Country & pushing our Enemies to a Submission is chearfully come into and at the same Time that Attention is paid to the Principles of Oeconomy We are determined to spare neither Men nor Money in securing our just Rights & Liberties.

I have inclosed you a Copy of the Petition of the Province of Georgia to the King.[2] That Spirit of Freedom that Vein of Piety that good sense that manly Firmness & Decency void of all that low submissive creeping Address usually contained in Performances of that Sort do great Honor to the Province & particularly to the Gentleman who drew it (Dr. Zubly). You will communicate it to the Depy. Govr. & other Gentlemen but by no Means suffer it to go out of your Hands (unless to his Honor) or a Copy to be taken for I would not have it get abroad through Me upon any Acct.

I have no other Accts. from our Colony than what my Daughter gives Me & the Papers contain. I must desire you to write Me very particularly what the State of the Town of Newport is, what the Men of War (if such Wretches as attack & plunder the innocent & defenceless deserve that Character) are about & in Short every thing of consequence as well from home as the Army &c. I must conclude or my Letter will be left. I am Yours most affectionately

Sam Ward

RC (RHi).

[1] Not found and not mentioned in the journals.

[2] See *Am. Archives,* 4th ser. 2:1556–57.

Silas Deane to Elizabeth Deane

My Dear Phila. 22d Sepr. 1775.

This by Mr. Bird, of Virginia, is my fourth Lettr. since I left home, but have not had the pleasure of receiving one Line save from my Brother Bars [Barnabas][1]. I wish to know, whither You propose to keep Your Word, & see Philadelphia. If so, in what readiness are you, and how do you propose to set out? I sent a peice of Linnen by Capt Champlin, which cost Six Shillings this Currancy per Yd—which hope You have received.

The Congress begin to Talk out Doors of adjourning Eastward as farr as Albany or Hartford, therefore judge it best, for You, to set out as early, as the first of October for this place. Have Nothing New worth sending You. Compts. To all Freinds. Love to the Family. Am in my old usual Way Committeeing it away, & busy. As Usual, am Your Affectionate Husband[2] Silas Deane

RC (CtHi).

[1] Deane also wrote a letter to his stepson Samuel Webb on September 16 complaining that Webb owed him a letter. Webb, *Correspondence* (Ford), 1:106.

[2] For the continuation of this letter, see Deane to Elizabeth Deane, September 24, 1775.

Richard Smith's Diary

[September 22, 1775]

Friday 22. Andrew MacNair Doorkeeper's Accot. ordered to be paid. A Letter from John Haring Chairman of the Comee. of Safety in New York and a Letter from Lewis Morris & James Wilson at Fort Pitt read.[1] Major Rogers ordered to be discharged if Nothing appears agt. Him but being a Half Pay Officer, he was arrested by the Comee.

of Safety of Pennsylvania. A Committee of 7 appointed by Ballot to consider the State of Trade in America. Wm. Shads Accot. as Messenger ordered to be paid.

MS (DLC).

[1] Haring's two letters to Congress of September 19, together with accompanying enclosures, are in PCC, item 67, 1:41–62, 71; and *Am. Archives*, 4th ser. 3:732–37. Morris and Wilson's letter of September 14 has not been found, but for an indication of its contents see Smith's Diary, September 25, note.

Samuel Ward's Diary

[September 22, 1775]

22nd. Letters from provincial Congress of New York estimate & Plan of fortifications on the highlands referred to tomorrow.

Letters from Mr. Morris & Mr. Wilson relative to disturbances between Virginians & Pennsylvanians near Pittburgh referred to the morrow.[1] Doorkeepers Accts. allowed. Upon Majr. Rogers being taken into Custody ordered that if nothing but his being on half pay be found against him that he be discharged on Parole. Dr. Franklin, Mr. J. Rutledge, Mr. Jay, Mr. Randolp, Mr. Johnston, Mr. Dean & Mr. Willing appoind. a Comee. to take into Consideration State of the Trade of the Colonies. A Missengers Accts. allowed. Mr. Hopkins as usual.

MS (RHi).

[1] On this point, see *JCC*, 3:262, 283.

John Adams' Diary

1775. Saturday. Septr. 23.

Mr. Gordon came and told us News, opened his Budget. Ethan Allen with 500 green mountain Boys, were entrenched half Way between St. Johns and Montreal, and had cutt off all Communication with Carlton, and was kindly treated by the French. A Council of War had been held, and it was their opinion that it was practicable to take Boston and Charlestown: but as it would cost many Lives, and expose the Inhabitants of Boston to destruction it was thought best to postpone it for the present.

Major Rogers came here too this Morning. Said he had a Hand and an Heart: tho he did not choose by offering himself to expose himself to Destruction.

I walked, a long Time this Morning, backward and forward, in the Statehouse Yard with Paca, McKean and Johnson. McKean has no

Idea of any Right or Authority in Parliament. Paca contends for an Authority and Right to regulate Trade, &c.

Dyer and Serjeant of Princetown, spent the Evening here. S. says that the Irish Interest in this City has been the Support of Liberty. Maes [Mease] &c. are leaders in it. The Irish and the Presbyterian Interest coalesce.

MS (MHi). Adams, *Diary* (Butterfield), 2:178.

John Adams' Notes of Debates

1775. Saturday. Sept. 22d [*i.e.* 23d].[1]

S[amuel] A[dams] moved, upon Mifflins Letter, that a Sum be advanced from the Treasury for Mifflin and Barrell.[2]

Mr. E. Rutledge wished the Money might be advanced upon the Credit of the Qr. Mr. General. Wished that an Enquiry might be made whether Goods had been advanced. If so, it was against the association.

Lynch wish'd the Letter read. S. Adams read it.

Jay. Seconded the Motion of E. Rutledge that a Committee be appointed to enquire if Goods are raised vs. the association.

Gadsden wished the Mo[tion] put off. We had other Matters of more importance.

Willing. Thought that Goods might be purchased upon four Months Credit. We should not intermix our Accounts.

Paine. We have not agreed to cloath the Soldiers, and the Qr. Mr. Genl. has no Right to keep a Slop Shop any more than any Body else. It is a private Matter. Very indigested Applications are made here for Money.

Deane. The Army must be cloathed, or perish. No preaching vs. a Snow Storm. We ought to look out, that they be kept warm and that the Means of doing it be secured.

Lynch. We must see that the Army be provided with Cloathing. I intended to have moved this very day that a Committee be appointed to purchase woolen Goods in this City and N. York, for the use of the Army.

E. Rutledge. I have no objection to the Committee. I meant only that the poor Soldiers should be supplied with Goods and Cloathing as cheap as possible.

Lewis. Brown of Boston bought Goods at N. York and sent em up the North River, to be conveyed by Land to Cambridge.

Dyer. Wanted to know whether the Soldiers would be obliged to take these Goods. Goods cheaper in York than here.

Sherman. The Sutlers, last War, sold to the Soldiers who were not obliged to take any Thing. Many will be supplied by Families with their own Manufacture. The Qr. Mr. General did not apply to Congress, but to his own private Correspondents.

Deane. The Soldiers were imposed on by Sutlers last War. The Soldiers had no Pay to receive.

Lynch. A Soldier without Cloathing is not fit for Service, but he ought to be cloathed, as well as armed, and we ought to provide as well as it can be done, that he may be cloathed.

Nelson. Moved that 5000£ st. be advanced to the Qr. Mr. Genl. to be laid out in Cloathing for the Army.

Langdon. Hoped a Committee would be appointed.

Sherman liked Nelsons motion with an Addition that every Soldier should be at Liberty to supply himself in any other Way.

Reed. Understood that Mass. Committee of Supplies had a large Store that was very full.

Sherman. For a Committee to enquire what Goods would be wanted for the Army, and at what Prices they may be had and report.

Gadsden. Liked that best.

Johnson. Moved that the Sum might be limit[ed] to 5000£ st. We dont know what has been supplied by Mass., what from Rhode Island, what from N. York, and what from Connecticutt.

S. Adams. Liked Nelson's Motion.

Ward. Objected to it, and preferred the Motion for a Committee.

Nelson. The Qr. Mr. is ordered by the General to supply the Soldiers, &c.

Paine. It is the Duty of this Congress to see that the Army be supplied with Cloathing at a reasonable Rate. I am for a Committee. Qr. Mr. has his Hands full.

Zubly. Would it not be best to publish Proposals in the Papers for any Man who was willing to supply the Army with Cloathing, to make his offers.

Harrison. The Money ought to be advanced, in all events. Content with a Committee.

R. R. Livingston.

Willing. Proposed that We should desire the Committee of this City, to enquire after these Goods and this will lead them to an Enquiry, that will be beneficial to America.

Chase. The City of Philadelphia has broke the association by raising the Price of Goods 50 per Cent. It would not be proper to purchase Goods here. The Breach of the association here is general, in the Price of Goods, as it is in N. York with Respect to Tea. If We lay out 5000£ here we shall give a Sanction to the Breaches of the association. The Breach is too general to be punished.

Willing. If the Association is broke in this City, dont let us put the Burden of Examining into it upon a few, but the whole Committee.

N. York have broke it, entirely. 99 in 100 drink Tea. I am not for screening the People of Philadelphia.

Sherman. I am not an Importer, but have bought of N. York Merchants for 20 years, at a certain Advance on the sterling Cost.

R. R. Livingston. Thought We ought to buy the Goods where they were dearest, because if We bought em at N. York where they were cheapest, N. York would soon be obliged to purchase in Phil. where they are dearest and then the loss would fall upon N. York. Whereas in the other Way the Loss would be general.

Jay. We had best desire the Committee of this City to purchase the Quantity of Goods at the Price stated by the Association and see if they were to be had here at that Price.

This Debate terminated in a Manner that I did not foresee. A Committee was appointed to purchase 5000£ st.s worth of Goods, to be sent to the Qr. Mr. and by him be sold to the Soldiers at first Cost and Charges. Qr. Mr. to be allowed 5 Pr. Cent for his Trouble.

Mr. Lynch, and Coll. Nelson and Coll. Harrison indulged their Complaisance and private Friendship for Mifflin and Washington so far as to carry this.

It is almost impossile to move any Thing but you instantly see private Friendships and Enmities, and provincial Views and Prejudices, intermingle in the Consulation. These are degrees of Corruption. They are Deviations from the public Interest, and from Rectitude By this Vote however, perhaps the poor Soldiers may be benefited, which was all I wished, the Interest of Mr. Mifflin being nothing to me.

MS (MHi). Adams, *Diary* (Butterfield), 2:178–81.

[1] The diary entries of Richard Smith and Samuel Ward make it clear that this debate occurred on September 23. For the official action on the appointment of a committee "to purchase a quantity of woolen goods for the use of the army," see *JCC*, 3:260.

[2] Although this letter has not been found, it was probably that of Thomas Mifflin to William Barrell, September 11, 1775. In his letter of September 21, Barrell acknowledges the receipt of Mifflin's letters of September 6 and 11 but says he is unable to obtain credit to fill the quartermaster general's request for coarse woolens. "I have concluded to make an application to some of the Delegates," Barrell wrote, "and if they approve lay your last Letter before the Congress to Induce them to advance a part of the Money." William Barrell to Thomas Mifflin, September 21, 1775, DLC. The following debate is the result of Barrell's actions.

Richard Smith's Diary

Saturday 23 Septr. [1775]

A Letter from Thos. Mifflin Quarter Master to the Army directed to Wm. Barrell Mercht. was read, desiring Him to forward Cloathing for the Army, the Congress took that Subject into Consideration & appointed by Ballot a Comee. of 5 to supply the Two Armies with Cloathing to the Amount of £5000 sterl[in]g, and allowed each Quarter Master 5 per Cent for selling out to the Soldiers.

MS (DLC).

Samuel Ward's Diary

[September 23, 1775]

23rd. Upon reading a Letter from the Qr. master Genl. relative coarse Goods for cloathing the Soldiers ordered that Mr. Lewis, Mr. Willing, Mr. Deane, Mr. Alsop, Mr. Langdon be a Comee. to purchase £5000 worth coarse woolen Goods for the use of the conti[nental] Army to be placed in the hands of the quarter master Genl. for the soldiers at prime cost & charges, the qr. master to have 5 per Cent for his trouble. Some Accts allowed.[1] The Letters from Morris & Willson referred to Monday. (Mr. Hopkins as usual.) A parcel [*of*] medicines for the hospital ordered to be bought.

MS (RHi).

[1] See *JCC*, 3:260.

John Adams' Diary

1775. Septr. 24. Sunday.

Dyer is very sanguine that the 2 De Witts, one of Windham, the other of Norwich, will make Salt Petre in large Quantities. He produces a Sample, which is very good.

Harrison is confident that Virginia alone will do great Things from Tobacco Houses. But my faith is not strong, as yet.

Ld. North is at his old Work again. Sending over his Anodynes to America—deceiving one credulous American after another, into a Belief that he means Conciliation, when in Truth he means nothing but Revenge. He rocks the cradle, and sings Lullaby, and the innocent Children go to Sleep, while he prepares the Birch to whip the poor Babes. One Letter after another comes that the People are uneasy and the Ministry are sick of their Systems. But nothing can be more fallacious. Next Spring We shall be jockied by Negociation, or have hot Work in War. Besides I expect a Reinforcement to Gage and to Carlton, this fall or Winter.

Heard Mr. Smith of Pequay [Pequea], at about 40 Miles towards Lancaster, a Scotch Clergyman, of great Piety as Coll. Roberdeau says: The Text was Luke 14:18. And they all with one Consent began to make excuse. This was at Duffills Meeting. In the afternoon, heard our Mr. Gordon, in Arch Street. The Lord is nigh unto all that call upon him.

Call'd upon Stephen Collins who has just returned.[1]

Stephen has a Thousand Things to say to Us, he says. A Thousand observations to make.

One Thing he told me, for my Wife, who will be peeping here, sometime or other, and come across it. He says when he call'd at my House, an English Gentleman was with him, a Man of Penetration, tho of few Words. And this silent, penetrating Gentleman was pleased with Mrs. Adams, and thought her, the most accomplished Lady he had seen since he came out of England. Down Vanity, for you dont know who this Englishman is.

Dr. Rush came in. He is an elegant, ingenious Body. Sprightly, pretty fellow. He is a Republican. He has been much in London. Acquainted with Sawbridge, McCaulay, Burgh, and others of that Stamp. Dilly sends him Books and Pamphletts, and Sawbridge and McCaulay correspond with him. He complains of D[ickinson]. Says the Committee of Safety are not the Representatives of the People, and therefore not their Legislators; yet they have been making Laws, a whole Code for a Navy. This Committee was chosen by the House, but half of them are not Members and therefore not the Choice of the People. All this is just. He mentions many Particular Instances, in which Dickenson has blundered. He thinks him warped by the Quaker Interest and the Church Interest too. Thinks his Reputation past the Meridian, and that Avarice is growing upon him. Says that Henry and Mifflin both complained to him very much about him. But Rush I think, is too much of a Talker to be a deep Thinker. Elegant not great.

In the Evening Mr. Bullock and Mr. Houstoun, two Gentlemen from Georgia, came into our Room and smoked and chatted, the whole Evening. Houstoun and Adams disputed the whole Time in good Humour. They are both Dabbs at Disputation I think. H. a Lawyer by Trade is one of Course, and Adams is not a Whit less addicted to it than the Lawyers. The Q. was whether all America was not in a State of War, and whether We ought to confine ourselves to act upon the defensive only. He was for acting offensively next Spring or this fall if the Petition was rejected or neglected. If it was not answered, and favourably answered, he would be for acting vs. Britain and Britains as in open War vs. French and frenchmen. Fit Privateers and take their Ships, any where.

These Gentlemen give a melancholly Account of the State of Georgia and S. Carolina. They say that if 1000 regular Troops should land in Georgia and their commander be provided with Arms and Cloaths enough, and proclaim Freedom to all the Negroes who would join his Camp, 20,000 Negroes would join it from the two Provinces in a fortnight. The Negroes have a wonderfull Art of communicating Intelligence among themselves. It will run severall hundreds of Miles in a Week or Fortnight.

They say, their only Security is this, that all the Kings Friends and Tools of Government have large Plantations and Property in Negroes. So that the Slaves of the Tories would be lost as well as those of the Whiggs.

I had nearly forgot a Conversation with Dr. Coombe concerning assassination, Henry 4., Sully, Buckingham &c. &c. Coombe has read Sullys Memoirs with great Attention.

MS (MHi). Adams, *Diary* (Butterfield), 2:181–83.

[1] Collins had been to Massachusetts. See John Adams to Abigail Adams, July 4, 1775, note.

Silas Deane to Elizabeth Deane

Sunday Sepr. [24, 1775]

This was to have gone by Mr Bird of Virginia but he set out without my knowledge of the Time. The Weather is very cool here for this Season, therefore if you determine on coming down the Time fixed above will be a good one though by the Way I see no End to Our Business, & it is as extensive as endless.

How ran Elections? Though personally I do not feel myself Interested however agreeable to one of my Sensibility the suffrages of ones Countrymen are, yet one great Object swallows up like Aarons Rod all the Lesser. *Liberty,* or *Death* is before Us, & I can conceive of No Alternative, if the former it will take a long Time to obtain, & afterwards settle it, on a permanent Basis. If the Latter (as I trust no American patriot will so desert himself as to prefer a short existence in Slavery to it) why then, it will but Shorten a Life of Care and Anxiety.

We expect intelligence from G Brittain every hour. I am impatient for it, not that I think it will alter our Measures, for I am very confident as to the Complexion of it before it arrives but that the least & every Shadow of an excuse, for not pursuing the most vigorous Measures may be removed from the really Timid, & those pretendedly so. You must not expect Long Letters from Me, as I am more taken up, than when here last Summer and among other Things, the Settlement of Our Continental Expences & Charges of the Warr has fell to the Lot of a Comme. of which I am one. I have therefore No Time of my own. If I had it Should be yours & my Freinds, so excuse Me to Mr. Hosmer &c. Adieu.

[*P.S.*] Have You heard anything of Your missing Lettr?

I dined Yesterday with Mr. Rutledge & Lady. She inquired after You, and says You promised her to come down with Me.

RC (CtHi) . A continuation of Deane to Elizabeth Deane, September 22, 1775.

John Adams' Diary

1775. Septr. 25. Monday

Rode out of Town and dined with Mr. Macpherson. He has the most elegant Seat in Pensilvania, a clever Scotch Wife and two pretty daughters. His Seat is on the Banks of Schuylkill.

He has been Nine Times wounded in Battle. An old Sea Commander, made a Fortune by Privateering. An Arm twice shot off, shot thro the Leg. &c. He renews his Proposals of taking or burning Ships.

Spent the Evening with Lynch at the City Tavern. He thinks the Row Gallies and Vesseau de Frize inadequate to the Expence.[1]

MS (MHi) . Adams, *Diary* (Butterfield) , 2:183.

[1] Members of Congress later went for a ride on the row galleys, built by the Pennsylvania Committee of Safety for the defense of Philadelphia on the Deleware River. See the diaries of John Adams, Richard Smith, and John Zubly, September 28, 1775.

John Adams' Notes of Debates

1775 Monday. Sept. 24 [*i.e.* 25]

An Uneasiness, among some of the Members concerning a Contract with Willing & Morris, for Powder, by which the House, without any Risque at all will make a clear Profit of 12,000£ at least.[1]

Dyer and Deane spoke in public, Lewis to me in private about it. All think it exorbitant.

S. Adams desired that the Resolve of Congress, upon which the Contract was founded might be read: he did not recollect it.

De Hart. One of the Contractors, Willing, declared to this Congress that he looked upon the Contract to be that the first Cost should be insured to them, not the 14£ a Barrell for the Powder.

R. R. Livingston. I never will vote to ratify the Contract in the sense that Morris understands it.

Willing. I am as a Member of the House, a Party to that Contract, but was not privy to the Bargain. I never saw the Contract, untill I saw it in Dr. Franklins Hand. I think it ensures only the first Cost.

My Partner thinks it ensures the whole. He says that Mr. Rutledge said at the Time, that Congress should have nothing to do with Sea risque. The Committee of this City offered 19£. I would wish to have nothing to do with the Contract: but to leave it to my Partner, who is a Man of Reason and Generosity, to explain the Contract with the Gentlemen who made it with him.

J. Rutledge. Congress was to run no Risque only vs. Men of War and Customhouse officers. I was surprized this Morning to hear that Mr. Morris understood it otherwise. If he wont execute a Bond, such as We shall draw, I shall not be at a loss what to do.

Johnson. An hundred Ton of Powder was wanted.

Ross. In Case of its Arrival Congress was to pay £14. If Men of War, or Custom house officers, should get it, Congress was to pay first Cost only as I understood it.

Zubly. We are highly favoured. 14£ We are to give if We get the Powder: and 14£ if We dont get it. I understand Persons enough will contract to supply Powder at 15£ and run all risques.

Willing. Sorry any Gentleman should be severe. Mr. Morris's Character is such that he cannot deserve it.

Lynch. If Morris will execute the Bond, well, if not the Committee will report.

Deane. It is very well that this matter has been moved and that so much has been said upon it.

Dyer. There are not Ten Men in the Colony I come from, who are worth so much Money as will be made clear by this Contract.

Ross. What has this Matter to the present debate, whether Connecticutt Men are worth much or no. It proves there are no Men there whose Capital or Credit are equal to such Contracts. That is all.

Harrison. The Contract is made and the Money paid. How can We get it back?

Johnson. Let us consider the Prudence of this Contract. If it had not been made Morris would have got 19£, and not have set forward a second Adventure.

Gadsden. Understands the Contract as Morris does, and yet thinks it a prudent one, because Morris would have got 19£.

J. Adams. — — — — &c. &c. &c.

Cushing. I move that We take into Consideration a Method of keeping up an Army in the Winter.

Gadsden. Seconds the Motion and desires that a Motion made in Writing some days ago, and postponed may be read as it was. As also Passages of G. Washingtons Letter.

S. Adams. The General has promised another Letter in which We shall have his Sentiments. We shall have it tomorrow perhaps.

Lynch. If We have, We shall only loose the Writing of a Letter.

J. Adams moved that the Generals Advice should be asked concerning Barracks &c. and that a Committee be appointed to draught a Letter. Lynch seconded the Motion.

A Committee was appointed. Lynch, J. Adams, and Coll. Lee the Men.[2]

Sherman moved that a Committee be appointed of one Member from each Colony, to receive, and examine all Accounts.

S. Adams seconded the Motion.

Harrison asked is this the Way of giving Thanks?

S. Adams. Was decent to the Committee for Rifle Mens Accounts, meant no Reflections upon them, was sorry that the worthy Gentleman from Virginia, conceived that any was intended. He was sure there was no foundation for it.

Paine. Thought that Justice and Honour required that We should carefully examine all Accounts, and see to the Expenditure of all public Monies.

That the Minister would find out our Weakness, and would foment divisions among our People.

He was sorry that Gentlemen could not hear Methods proposed, to settle and pay Accounts in a manner that would give Satisfaction to the People, without seeming to resent them.

Harrison. Now the Gentlemen have explained themselves he had no Objection, but when it was proposed to appoint a new Committee in the Place of the former one, it implied a Reflection.

Deane. ———.

Willing. These Accounts are for Tents, Arms, Cloathing, &c. as well as Expences of the Riflemen, &c.

Nelson moved that 20,000 dollars be voted into the Hands of the other Committee to settle the Accounts.

S. Adams. Seconded the Motion, but still hoped that some time or other, a Committee would be appointed of one Member from each Colony, to examine all Accounts because he thought it reasonable.[3]

MS (MHi). Adams, *Diary* (Butterfield), 2:183–86.

[1] This contract was entered into by the secret committee appointed on September 18 by Congress "to contract and agree for the importation and delivery of any quantities of gunpowder, not exceeding, in the whole five hundred tons." *JCC*, 2:253. There is no mention of this debate in the journals, *JCC*, 3:261–62, but see Secret Committee Minutes of Proceedings, September 27, 1775.

[2] This committee, which was appointed to answer Washington's letters to Hancock of August 4 and 31, brought in a draft letter the following day, which Congress then approved and sent to Washington over Hancock's signature. See *JCC*, 3:261–63; and John Hancock to George Washington, September 26, 1775.

[3] This day Congreess appointed a committee of claims, consisting of one delegate from each colony. *JCC*, 3:262. John Zubly's diary entry for September 25 reads: "Attended Congress. Put on the Committee to examine accounts." GHi.

Eliphalet Dyer to Joseph Trumbull

Sr Philadelphia Septr 25th 1775

I recievd yours of the 14th Instant and am Very glad that Scoundrel of an Avery is disappointed in his Vain expectations & wish every other rascall may share the same fate.

Am glad to hear of my sons Arrival at the Camp and if he may be on good Terms with the officers & Company over which he is Appointed am not so much Concerned about the Others especially if he can have the good Will of Genll Putnam & some Other principal officers to Support him. As to Wales & Bingham there was but Very few thot them fitt for the least Command when they Obtained it. As to Wales he is a Sour disaffected fellow wherever he is, and has been specially Piqued against me for some years. Bingham I know not so much about. He has rather appeared to be a still quiet fellow & of but little Influence, but hope Capt Thos with the Assistance of his friends will be Able to make his way good.

The Money Ordered by Congress was forworded soon after our Arrival and were Surprised to find that Nothing had been done by the delegates of this Province, Who were especially entrusted to Send forward the Money as also a Number of Tents & other Necessaries for the Army but when we came here found Nothing had been done in our recess. For ought I can See at present you must depend principally upon Connecticutt for the Provision Supplys for the Army the bread kind as well as Others. I wish our Soldiery would be Content with Rye & Indian [*corn*] two or 3 times a week. Believe then our Colony could easily furnish the whole. You must set the farmers in Connecticutt Immediately to thresh out their Wheet &c. Perhaps You may get some flower from York & from the Western part of our Colony as far as Norwich by Water till that river is froze up. The Congress in generall seem Averse to Venture it by Water from this place at present tho a Comtee is appointed to Consult that Affair as well as some Others Who Still have the matter under Consideration.[1] It may be decided in two or 3 days but I cannot Advise you to slack your hand as to any other way or Method of Providing you think prudent. For the present it is as yet quite undetermined What force will be Necessary to be kept up thro the Winter. I know your Trouble & expences is great and your present allowance but small but believe the Congress will be disposed to make you a proper allowance. It will be best for you to keep a good account of your expenses, Clerks, Store keepers &c as it is not expected their pay will come out of your small pittance and it would be well for you to be prepared to make a proper representation to the Congress of the State of your business Contracts Number of persons you are oblidgd to employe & to Transact with, the quantitys you Supply, the Vast sums that goe thro your hands & the Numbers you have to pay out to, to which it will be Well to have the Generalls (at least) & the other Generall officers recommendation for further Allowance. I should think a small Commission might be best as the Amount would not be so Obvious to every Vulgar eye to make their Invidious reflections upon, but as all is uncertain, you must take good and prudent care to guard your self against loss. Tell my son I wrote to him a few days agoe & put him in mind to write to me for he is Very Slack about letter writing, but hope you will favor me with your observations from time to time, how he makes out &c. The time of his joining the Army I know may occasion the uneasiness if any. Remember me to all Friends & am Sincerely yours.

Elipht Dyer

RC (CtHi).

[1] The committee appointed on September 21 to recommend means of provisioning the army reported to Congress on October 19. *JCC*, 3:257, 299.

Benjamin Franklin to Ebenezer Hazard

Sir

Philad. Sept. 25. 1775

It seems the more necessary to establish Speedily a Post to Albany, as we have an Army on your Frontiers. I hope you have found a Rider willing to go on more reasonable Terms than those mention'd in yours of the 6th appear to be, compar'd with what is given to the New London Riders. But if there are Reasons why he should have more, of which you can best judge, agree with him & let him proceed as soon as possible.

Mr Goddard is expected in a few Days from the Southward, where he went to settle those Offices. As soon as he returns we shall open the Office here, and proceed regularly Northward. By him I shall send your Commission & Instructions. I am Sir, Your most huml Servt

B Franklin

[*P.S.*] I request your Care of the Enclos'd, & a Packet with the same Direction.

RC (PPAmP).

John Hancock to William Palfrey

Dear Palfrey,

Philadelphia 25th Septr. 1775

Your Letter from Marblo. [Marlborough] of 3d Inst. is now before me, the first part of it has been very sufficiently Answer'd in the

Publick Papers. I am much obliged to you for your good wishes on that Event, and I shall be exceedingly happy when I find myself quietly Settled in Boston.

I Note what you Say respecting your present Scituation in the Army, & your Desire of acting in a different Department. I could wish you had pointed out particularly what Vacancies there were distinct from the Army, or whether there was a prospect of any New Alterations, or Additions of offices propos'd to be Recommended by the General to Congress. Of this give me the earliest Notice, or as it is, write me as soon as possible your inclination. I am the rather urgent that you be speedy in this, as in a few days we shall likely Take up a total Reform of the Army, & make effectual provision in all Departments for the Winter, of course in all the Supplies new offices must be Establish'd &c. Say nothing, but to particular friends. Give me your mind freely. I shall then talk with Coll Harrison who is a good Man. I must get a place for my Brother, if you See him Talk with him, if not, do write him & get his mind & write me in your next, don't fail, if you Send to him on purpose. I want to assist Docr Perkins. I must Close, as I am Call'd on in my Departmt. Remem[ber] me to all Friends. I am Your Real Friend John Hancock

[*P.S.*] Colo. Harrison has wrote you.[1]

I have been sadly Afflicted with the gout, but am abroad. Mrs. Hancock's Complimts. She is not very well.

Pray make a point of Seeing Coll. Orne, & by all means beg him to Send my Salt Fish by one of the Return Waggons to Philada. I have wrote him.

RC (MH). Addressed: "To William Palfrey Esqr. Aid de Camp to General Lee at Cambridge."

[1] See Benjamin Harrison to William Palfrey, September 20, 1775.

Richard Smith's Diary

[September 25, 1775]

Monday 25. A Comee. of 3 named to draw an Answer to Gen Washingtons Letters. An Order passed for Payment of Accots. amounting to near 2000 Dollars. A Committee of 13, one from each Colony (myself for N Jersey) was named for Settling what Accounts may come this Session. De Hart moved to restrict all Conventions & Assemblies from issuing any more Paper Money and to recall what they have done without Permission from hence, he was not seconded. On reading Wilson & Morris's Letters and other Papers Willing moved that the Congress would interfere in settling a temporary Line between Virginia & Pennsylvania. A Letter was read from the Delegates of those Two Colonies to the Inhabitants recomm'g. Peace &c.[1] Several Orders of the King in Council Dated in June last relative to this Line were read.

MS (DLC).

[1] See Virginia and Pennsylvania Delegates to the Inhabitants West of Laurel Hill, July 25, 1775. At the same time Wilson and Morris wrote to Congress, Wilson also dispatched a letter to John Montgomery from Pittsburgh discussing the topic of the Pennsylvania-Virginia dispute. "It is surely a very extraordinary Step in the Virginians to take Possession of Fort Pitt with an hundred Men after the Recommendation addressed to the Inhabitants to the Westward of the Laurel Hill by the Delegates of both Provinces. Our Part of it was, 'That all Bodies of armed Men kept up under either Province be dismissed.' We could not be deemed so stupid and inconsistent as to think it would not be equally hurtful to send new Bodies, as to retain the old ones.

"This Manoevre of the Virginians has occasioned the Application which Col. Morris and I have sent, in Behalf of the People, to the Congress, by the Express who delivers you this Letter. Certainly something ought to be done for the distressed and impoverished People who settled here while the Jurisdiction of Pennsylvania was peaceably acquiesced under. Your Heart would bleed for them if you knew all they have suffered, and all they are likely to suffer.

"As the Indians have not yet come in to the Treaty, it is impossible for me now to give you any satisfactory Answer, whether their Humour may render it proper that Troops should be ordered to the Frontiers of this Province, but I will not fail to give you one, so soon as it shall be in my Power." James Wilson to John Montgomery, "at the Indian Queen, Philadelphia," September 14, 1775. PHi.

Samuel Ward's Diary

[September 25, 1775]

25th. The Comee. appoind. to audit the Rifle Accts. &c authorized to draw for a Sum not exceeding 2000 Doll[ar]s. Colo. Lee, Mr. J Adams & Mr. Lynch a Comee. to take Genl. Washingtons Letter into Consideration & report. A Comee. for auditing all Accts. appointed, Mr. Langdon, Mr. Cushing, Mr. Ward, Mr. Dean, Mr. Lewis, Mr. Smith, Mr. Willing, Mr. Rodney, Mr. Johnson, Mr. Nelson, Mr. Gadsden, Dr. Zubly. Letters from Coll. Morris & Mr. Willson taken into Cons[ideratio]n & referred. (Mr. Hopkins as usual; shall not ment[ion] it again unless he sitts all Day.)

MS (RHi).

John Adams to Abigail Adams

My Dear Philadelphia Septr. 26. 1775

I have not written the usual Compliment of Letters since I left Braintree; nor have I received one Scratch of a Pen from any Body, till the last Evening, when the Post brought me a Line from Mrs. Warren, in which she informs me that you had been ill, but was better. I shall be unhappy till I hear farther from you, tho I hope for the best.

I have enjoyed better Health, this session than the last, and have suffered less from certain Fidgets, Pidlings, and Irritabilities which have become so famous. A more serious Spirit prevails than heretofore. We shall soon be in Earnest. I begin to think We are so. Our Injunctions of Secrecy are so much insisted on, that I must be excused from disclosing one Iota of any Thing that comes to my Knowledge as a Member of the Congress. Our Journal of the last session however, I conjecture will be speedily printed and then I will inclose it to you.

I want to be informed from Hour to Hour, of any Thing which passes in Boston—whether our Friends come out—what Property they bring?—how they fare in Town? How the Tories subsist &c. &c. &c. Whether the Troops are healthy or sickly?

I also want to know every Thing which passes in our Army. The Feats and Exploits of our little Naval Armaments would be very agreable.

Tudor is made easy. He must keep a Clerk, or there will be Jealousies. Indeed it is his Duty for it is impossible he can do the Business himself, and if that is not done, Injustice to the public will be done.[1]

I have seen the Utility of Geometry, Geography, and the Art of drawing so much of late, that I must intreat you, my dear, to teach the Elements of those Sciences to my little Girl and Boys. It is as pretty an Amusement, as Dancing or Skaiting, or Fencing, after they have once acquired a Taste for them. No doubt you are well qualified for a school Mistress in these Studies, for Stephen Collins tells me the English Gentleman, in Company with him, when he visited Braintree, pronounced you the most accomplished Lady, he had seen since he left England. You see a Quaker can flatter, but dont you be proud.

My best Wishes and most fervent Prayers attend our little Family. I have been banished from them, the greatest Part of the last Eighteen Months but I hope to be with them more, in Time to come. I hope to be excused from attending at Philadelphia, after the Expiration of the Year. I hope that Dr. Winthrop, Mr. Sever, Mr. Greenleaf, Coll. Warren, Mr. Hawley, Mr. Gerry, some or all of them will take their Turns, in the States[2]—and suffer me, at least to share with my Family, a little more than I have done, the Pleasures and Pains of this Life, and that I may attend a little more to my private Affairs that I may not be involved in total Ruin, unless my Country should be so and then I should choose to share its Fate.

RC (MHi). Adams, *Family Correspondence* (Butterfield), 1:285–86.

[1] On September 21, Congress had voted to pay William Tudor, as judge advocate general, "for himself and clerk, fifty dollars per month." *JCC,* 3:257.

[2] That is, Congress.

John Adams to James Warren

Dr Sir Philadelphia Septr. 26. 1775

This Afternoon, and not before I received a Line from the excellent Marcia, which [*is*] the first and only Letter I have received from the Family to which She belongs Since I left Watertown. Be pleased to thank her for this Favour, and to let her know that She must certainly have misinterpretted Some Passage in my Letter Since I never thought either Politicks or War, or any other Art or Science beyond the Line of her Sex:[1] on the contrary I have ever been convinced that Politicks and War have in every Age, been influenced, and in many, guided and controuled by her Sex. Sometimes it is to be feared by the unworthy Part of it: but at others, it must be confessed by the amiable and the good.

But, if I were of opinion that it was best for a general Rule that the fair should be excused from the arduous Cares of War and State; I should certainly think that Marcia and Portia ought to be Exceptions,[2] because I have ever ascribed to those Ladies, a Share and no small one neither, in the Conduct of our American Affairs.

I have nothing new to communicate. Every Thing has been done, and is now doing, to procure the *Unum Necessarium.* I wish I could give you a more agreable account of the Salt Petre Works in this City. I fear they have chosen injudiciously a Place for their Vatts, Vaults and Buildings, a low marshy Place which was lately overflowed by the Storm. Still We have Sanguine Accounts of the Skill and Success of some operators.

Coll Dyer produces a Sample of excellent Salt Petre, made by two De Witts, one of Norwich the other of Windham, and he is confident that they can and will make large Quantities. Coll Harrison of Virginia, whose Taste in Maderia, I know, and in Girls I believe, and in Salt Petre I hope to be much Superiour to his Judgment in Men, is very confident that they are making large Quantities from Tobacco House Earth, in his Colony.

We are hourly expecting Intelligence from Canada, as well as Massachusetts, and from London.

My dear Sir, Let me intreat you to do every Thing in your Power to get ready the Accounts of all that our Province has done and expended in the Common Cause, for which they expect or hope to be reimbursed by the United Colonies.[3] It has ever appeared to me a Thing of much Importance, that We should be furnished with these Accounts as soon as possible. From present appearances, our session will not be long, and if We should not be furnished with the Necessary Papers, very soon, We shall not be able to obtain any Reimbursement this Fall; and the next Spring We may be involved in so many Dangers, as well as new Expences as to render our Chance for obtaining Justice, more precarious. You know that your Delegates have been here, almost the whole Time since the Commencement of Hostilities, and therefore can say nothing of their own knowledge concerning your Exertions or Expences, but must depend altogether upon Information from the General Court.

This is really a Strong Reason for a Change in the Delegation. We have been absent so long from our native Country as to be a Kind of Aliens and Strangers there. If it is good Policy to reelect one of the old Delegates, because he is personally knowing to what has passed here, it is equally good Policy to elect some new ones, because they are Witnesses of what has passed with you. For my own Part, as my political Existence terminates with the Year, I Sincerely wish to be exempt in the next Election. I long to be a little with you in the General Court, that I may see and hear, and feel with my Countrymen, and I ardently wish to be a little with my Family, and to attend a little to my private Affairs. To be frank and candid to a Friend, I begin to feel for my Family. To leave all the Burthen of my private Cares, at a Time when my affairs are in so much Perplexity, to an excellent Partner, gives me Pain for her. To leave the Education of a young Family, entirely to her, altho I know not where it could be better lodged, gives me much Concern for her and them.

I have very little Property, you very well know, which I have not earned myself, by an obstinate Industry, in opposition to the Malice of a very infirm Constitution, in Conjunction with the more pernicious Malice of Ministerial and gubernatorial Enemies. Of the little Acquisitions I have made, five hundred Pounds Sterling is sunk in Boston in a Real Estate, four hundred sterling more is compleatly annihilated in a Library that is now wholly useless to me and mine, and at least four hundred sterling more, is wholly lost to me, in Notes & Bonds not one farthing of the Principal or Interest of which, can I obtain, and the Signers are dying, breaking, flying every day.

It is not compleatly two years since my Business has been totally ruined by the public Confusions. I might modestly estimate the Profits of my Business before this Period at three hundred sterling a Year, perhaps more. I think therefore I may fairly estimate myself a sufferer immediately, to the amount of two Thousand Pounds sterling. I have purchased Lands, which these Causes have prevented me from paying for, and the Interest is running on without a Possibility of my paying it, and I am obliged to hire Labour yearly upon my Farm to no Small amount.

In the mean Time, all that has been granted me by the general Court for the sessions of this Congress last Fall and this Spring has not defrayed my necessary Expences, however Strange it may appear.

The Conclusion from all this is, that I am rushing rapidly into Perplexities and Distresses in my private affairs from which I can never extricate myself. By retreating from public Life, in some Measure I might preserve myself and Family from a Ruin, which without it will be inevitable. I am willing to sink with my Country, but it ought not to be insisted on that I Should Sink myself without any Prospect of contributing by that Means to make it Swim. I have taken my Trick at Helm, when it was not easy to get Navigators who would run the Risque of the Storm. At present the Course is plain whatever the Weather may be, and the prospect of that is much better than it was when I was called to assist in steering the ship.

RC (MHi). In Adams' hand, though not signed.

[1] In a letter of September 4, 1775, Mercy Otis Warren had chided Adams for insinuating in his letter of August 26 that war and politics were "beyond the line of my sex." *Warren-Adams Letters,* 1:104–5, 106–7.

[2] Portia was a pseudonym for Abigail Adams, as Marcia was for Mercy Otis Warren.

[3] On December 4, 1775, Congress resolved that "the sum of 443,333 1/3 Dollars be paid to the Colony of Massachusetts" in partial payment of that province's account. *JCC,* 3:403.

John Adams to Mercy Warren

Madam Philadelphia Septr. 26. 1775

Your Favour, by my Friend Collins, never reached me till this Evening. At Newport, concluding to go by Water, he put it into the Post Office, least it Should meet with a Fate as unfortunate as Some others. I call them unfortunate after the manner of Men for, altho they went into Hands which were never thought of by the Writer, and notwithstanding all the unmeaning Noise that has been made about them, they have done a great deal of good. Providence intended them for Instruments to promote valuable Purposes, altho the Writer of them, thought so little of them that he never could have recollected one Word in them, if they had been lost. The most that I care about them, is the indecent Exposure of the Name of a Lady, who cannot be put to Pain, without giving me Uneasiness by Sympathy.

I boasted, Madam, of my Happiness, in my last to you, because I know you could excuse the appearance of Vanity, and because I knew very well that the Person who So deservedly holds the first

Place in your Heart, could Say by Experience, that an Happiness so perfect was not merely ideal.

I am much obliged to you, for your kind Information concerning the Health of a Lady whom I esteem so highly. I presume her Indisposition has been the Cause why I have not heard from her before. I rejoice to hear she is better. I Hope my invariable Friend is better and that I shall receive a long Letter from him, Soon. My best Wishes attend him, as well as all His.

RC (MHi). In Adams' hand, though not signed.

Samuel Adams to Elbridge Gerry

My dear Sir Philada Sept 26 1775

I arrived in this City on the 12 Instant having rode full three hundred Miles on horseback, an Exercise which I have not used for many years past. I think it has contributed to the Establishment of my Health, for which I am obligd to my Friend Mr John Adams who kindly offered me one of his Horses the day after we set off from Watertown.

I write you this Letter, principally to put you in Mind of the promise you made me to give me Intelligence of what is doing in our Assembly and the Camp. Believe me sir it is of great Importance that we should be informd of every Circumstance of our Affairs. The Eyes of Friends and Foes are attentively fixed on our Province, and if Jealousy or Envy can sully its Reputation, you may depend upon it they will not miss the opportunity. It behoves our Friends therefore to be very circumspect, and in all their publick Conduct to convince the World, that they are influenced not by partial or private Motives but altogether with a View of promoting the publick Welfare.

Some of our Military Gentlemen have, I fear, disgracd us; It is then important that every Anecdote that concerns a Man of real Merit among them (and Such I know there are) be improvd, as far as decency will admit of it, to their Advantage and the Honor of a Colony which for its Zeal in the great Cause as well as its Sufferings, deserve so much of America.

Until I visited head Quarters at Cambridge, I had never heard of the Valor of Prescot on Bunkers Hill, nor the Ingenuity of Knox and Waters in planing the celebrated Works at Roxbury. We were told here that there were none in our Camp who understood this Business of an Engineer, or any thing more than the manual Exercise of the Gun. This we had from great Authority, and for want of more certain Intelligence were obligd at least to be silent. There are many military Geniuses at present unemployd and overlookd, who I hope, when the

Army is new modelld, will be sought after and invited into the Service of their Country. They must be sought after, for modest Merit declines pushing it self into publick View. I know your disinterested Zeal and therefore need add no more than to assure you that I am with cordial Esteem Your Friend Saml Adams

RC (NjHi).

Silas Deane's Diary

[September 26, 1775]

Tuesday 26th. At Congress.[1] Col. Williams, & Mr. Wales arrived. Spent for Physic for Horses—2/.

Wrote to Govr. Trumbull, a Lettr. of Notice of sending forward the Money by Landman & Coit.

MS (CtHi). *CHS Bulletin* 29 (July 1964): 96A.

[1] John Zubly briefly recorded in his diary this date: "Attended Committee & Congress." GHi.

John Hancock to George Washington

Sir, Philadelphia Septemr. 26th. 1775

Upon considering your Letter of 4th August the following Points appear'd so exceedingly important, that I am Directed to Desire you will Consult such of your Officers as you think proper, upon the most prudent & effectual Methods of Accomplishing them.

These are the Continuation of the Army, now under your Command, in the Service of the Continent after the terms of Enlistments shall have been Compleated. The Reducing the severall Corps of Provincials, which at present compose your Army, into one Body of Continental Forces, what Number will be necessary for the Winter Campaign, & what Rations should be Allow'd the Men, and what farther Regulations may be necessary for the Government of those Forces.

Upon these Heads the Congress wish to be favour'd with the Result of your Deliberations as soon as possible, as the Time of Enlistment in Connecticutt draws to a Conclusion.[1]

The Congress Desire you will Take the proper Steps to provide your Troops with necessary Cover and Fuel for the Winter, as it is highly probable, that the Service of the Army will be wanted during that whole Season at least; and that you lay before Congress an Estimate of the Expence, which may be necessary for these Services.

As making any Alterations in the present Appointments of the Officers of different Colonies, and the Reduction of those Regiments which cannot be Compleated to their full Establishments may Create great Jealousies and Uneasiness, the Congress are of Opinion that at present no Step should be taken therein, as the New Modelling the whole is so soon Expected, when those inconveniencies may be Remedied without Danger.

The Congress desire you will give them your Opinion, whether the Pay of the Private Men, which is consider'd as very high, may not be Reduc'd, and how much.

Agreeable to the order of Congress I inclose you Copy of a Letter from General Schuyler, with sundry papers Inclos'd.[2]

Application having been made to Congress for the Discharge of Coll John Fenton, at present Confin'd at Hartford they pass'd a Resolution that he be allow'd to proceed to New York, and from thence to London upon his giving his Parole not to Take up Arms against the Continent during the present Contest.[3]

It is Determin'd by Congress that you Issue a Commission to Mr Gridley as Colonell only, and to Suspend the appointment of a Brigadier General for the present. They Recommend to you to Grant Commissions to Messrs. Box, Scammell & Samuel Brewer as Brigade Majors.[4]

The Memorial from Mr. Tudor the Judge Advocate was laid before Congress, and upon Consideration it was Resolved that he be allow'd & paid Fifty Dollars per Month for himself & Clerk from the Time of his Appointment, & I Transmitt him by this Express his Commission and the Resolution of Congress.

Some Difficulty having arisen in the Settlement of the Accotts. of the severall Rifle Companies as to Supplies of Money &c particularly with Respect to Coll. Thompson, and the Congress having on the 29th July last Advanc'd to Colonell Thompson Five Thousand Dollars for the Service of his Battalion, I am directed to Desire you will order Coll Thompson to Exhibit to you an Accott. of the Expenditure of the said Five Thousand Dollars, which you will please to Transmitt to me to be laid before Congress, by which the severall Accotts. may easily be Accomodated.

I have nothing further in Charge to Communicate. You will please to Return Fessenden as soon as you conveniently can.

I have the honour to be with great Respect & Esteem, Sir Your most Obedt huml Servt. John Hancock President

[*P.S.*] I have Sent you Eleven Bundles contg 550 Commissions.

RC (DLC). On the authorship of this letter, see John Adams' Notes of Debates, September 25, 1775, note 2.

[1] Washington's responses to these inquiries are in his letters and enclosures to Hancock of October 5 and 12. PCC, item 152, 1:181–240; and *Am. Archives,* 4th ser. 3:956–64, 1037–49.

[2] Hancock is referring here to Schuyler's letter to him of September 8 and accompanying enclosures. Ibid., pp. 669–72.
[3] See *JCC,* 2:255.
[4] See *JCC,* 2:256; and 3:257.

Richard Henry Lee to George Washington

Dear Sir Philadelphia 26th Septr. 1775

Two days ago I arrived here from Virginia, which the late short adjournment just allowed me time to visit and return from. I brought two letters from thence for you which come with this. Having some business with Colo. Mason, I travelled that road and having sent to your Lady to know if she had any commands this way, had the pleasure to learn that all were well at Mount Vernon. As I suppose it will be agreable to you to know what is passing in Virginia, I have inclosed you the proceedings of our last Convention, with two of Purdies Gazettes. I am greatly obliged to you for your favor of August the 29th,[1] and you may be assured I shall pay great attention to it. When I mentioned securing the entrance of the harbour of Boston, it was more in the way of wishing it could be done, than as conceiving it very practicable. However the reasons you assign are most conclusive against the attempt. I assure you, that so far as I can judge from the conversation of Men, instead of their being any who think you have not done enough, the wonder seems to be that you have done so much. I believe there is not a Man of common sense and who is void of prejudice, in the world, but greatly approves the discipline you have introduced into the Camp; since reason and experience join in proving, that without discipline Armies are fit only for the contempt and slaughter of their Enemies. Your labors are no doubt great both of mind and body, but if the praise of the present and future times can be any compensation you will have a plentiful portion of that. Of one thing you may certainly rest assured that the Congress will do every thing in their power to make your most weighty business easy to you. I think you could not possibly have appointed a better Man to his present Office than Mr. Mifflin. He is a singular Man, and you certainly will meet with the applause and support of all good men by promoting and countenancing real Merit and public virtue, in opposition to all private interests, and partial affection. You will see in the proceedings of our Convention, that they have agreed to raise the pay of our Rifle Officers & Men to the Virginia standard. It may perhaps encourage them to be told this.

We have no late accounts from England, but from what we have had that can be relied on, it seems almost certain, that our Enemies there must shortly meet with a total over throw. The entire failure of all their schemes, and the rising spirit of the people strongly expressed by the remonstrance of the Livery of London to the King, clearly denote this. The Ministry had their sole reliance on the impossibility of the Americans finding money to support an army, on the great aid *their* cause would receive from Canada, and consequent triumph of their forces over the liberties and rights of America. The reverse of all this has happened, and very soon now, our Commercial resistance will begin sorely to distress the people at large. The Ministerial recruiting business in England has entirely failed them, the Ship builders in the royal yards have mutinied, and now they are driven as to their last resort to seek for Soldiers in the Highlands of Scotland. But it seems the greatest willingness of the people there cannot supply more than one or two Thousand men, A number rather calculated to increase their disgrace, than to give success to their cause.

I beg your pardon for engaging your attention so long, and assure you that I am with unfeigned esteem dear Sir Your affectionate friend and Countryman Richard Henry Lee

RC (DLC).

[1] See Washington, *Writings* (Fitzpatrick), 3:450–54.

Richard Smith's Diary

[September 26, 1775]

Tuesday 26 Septr. Comee brought in a Letter to Gen Washington,[1] in the Course of it E Rutledge moved that the Gen. shall discharge all the Negroes as well Slaves as Freemen in his Army. He (Rutledge) was strongly supported by many of the Southern Delegates but so powerfully opposed that he lost the Point.[2] The Question of the Lines between Penna. & Virginia agitated but Nothing determined.[3] The Letters between Washington & Gage ordered to be published,[4] then the Journal was read in Order for Publication and some Parts of it ordered not to be printed as improper for Public Inspection particularly all that was there about fortifying the Passes on Hudsons River & the Directions to the New Yorkers to arm themselves &c.

MS (DLC).

[1] See John Hancock's letter to Washington, this date.

[2] Although small numbers of blacks had served in the provincial forces of all the New England colonies before the establishment of the Continental Army in June 1775, and although Congress had placed no racial restrictions on military service, as early as July 10, 1775, Adjutant-General Horatio Gates ordered continental officers not to enlist blacks. In spite of Congress' rejection of Rutledge's motion on

that the Congress would interfere in settling a temporary Line between Virginia & Pennsylvania, a Letter was read from the Delegates of those Two Colonies to the Inhabitants recommg. Peace & several Orders of the King in Council Dated in June last rela=tive to this Line were read.

Tuesday 26 Septr. Comee brought in a Letter to Gen Washington, in the Course of it E Rutledge moved that the Gen. shall discharge all the Negroes as well Slaves as Freemen in his Army, he (Rutledge) was strongly supported by many of the Southern Delegates but so powerfully opposed that he lost the Point — the Question of the Lines between Penna. & Virginia agitated but Nothing determined — the Letters

Diary of Richard Smith

between Washington & Gage ordered to be published, then the Journal was read in Order for Publication and some Parts of it ordered not to be printed as improper for Public Inspection particularly all that was there about fortifying the Passes on Hudsons River & the Directions to the New Yorkers to arm themselves &c.

Wednesday 27. 160,000 Dollars ordered to be advanced to Connectt. in part of their Claim on the Congress. Willing from the Comee. on Accounts asked Whether a Charge should be allowed made by the Comee. of Northampton County in Pennsa. for their Time & Trouble in settling

September 26, Gates' exclusionary recruitment policy was endorsed by a council of war, consisting of Washington and eight of his subordinates, on October 8, when the questions of accepting Negroes into the continental service and distinguishing between free blacks and slaves were decided in the negative. Later in the same month Washington reported to the "Committee of Conference" the council's opinion on these points, and the committee concurred in its recommendations. Washington thereupon issued general orders of October 31 and November 12, forbidding the enlistment of Negroes into the Continental Army, although on December 30 he modified these orders to permit the recruitment of free blacks, fearful that disgruntled protestors might otherwise join British units. When Washington informed Hancock of his decision and asked Congress to signify its opinion, Congress responded with a resolution of January 16, 1776, approving the enlistment of free blacks already in Washington's army but forbidding the acceptance of others. On this point, as well as on the more general subject of the employment of black soldiers in the War for Independence, see Benjamin Quarles, *The Negro in the American Revolution* (Chapel Hill: University of North Carolina Press, 1961), pp. 9–18, and chaps. 4 and 5 passim. See also *JCC,* 4:60; Washington, *Writings* (Fitzpatrick), 4:7n.16, 57, 86, 194–95; Committee of Conference Minutes of Proceedings, October 23–24, 1775; and Richard Smith's Diary, January 16, 1776.

[3] According to the journals, the Virginia and Pennsylvania delegates were absent this day, requiring Congress to postpone consideration of a letter from Lewis Morris and James Wilson about the boundary dispute between these two provinces. *JCC,* 3:262. On this point, Samuel Ward laconically noted in his diary this day: "Letters from Colo. Morris &c refd. Letter to G. Washington." RHi.

[4] Between August 11 and 19 Washington and Gen. Thomas Gage exchanged letters accusing each other of mistreatment of prisoners of war. Washington's letter to Gage of the 11th, Gage's reply of the 13th, and Washington's rebuttal of the 19th were widely printed in American newspapers. *Am. Archives,* 4th ser. 3:245–47.

John Adams' Diary

1775. Septr. 27. Wednesday.

Mr. Bullock and Mr. Houstoun, the Gentlemen from Georgia, invited S.A. and me to spend the Evening with them in their Chamber, which We did very agreably and socially. Mr. Langdon of N. Hampshire was with us.

Mr. Bullock after Dinner invited me to take a ride with him in his Phaeton which I did. He is a solid, clever Man. He was President of their Convention.

MS (MHi). Adams, *Diary* (Butterfield), 2:186.

John Adams' Notes of Debates

1775. Septr. 27.

Willing in favour of Mr. Purveyances Petition.[1] Harrison vs. it. Willing thinks the Non Exportation sufficiently hard upon the

Farmer, the Merchant and the Tradesman, but will not arraign the Propriety of the Measure.

Nelson. If We give these Indulgences, I know not where they will end. Sees not why the Merchant should be indulged more than the Farmer.

Harrison. It is the Merchant in England that is to suffer.

Lynch. They meant gain and they ought to bear the Loss.

Sherman. Another Reason. The Cargo is Provisions and will probably fall into the Hands of the Enemy.

R. R. Livingston. There is no Resolve of Congress vs. exporting to foreign Ports. We shall not give Licence to deceit, by clearing out for England.

Lynch. Moves that the Committee of this City, be desired to enquire whether Deans Vessel taken at Block Island and another at Cape Codd, were not sent on Purpose to supply the Enemy.

Reed. The Committee of this City have enquired of the owners of one Vessell. The owners produc'd their Letter Books, and were ready to swear. The Conduct of the Captain is yet suspicious. Thinks the other Enquiry very proper.

Lee. Thinks Lynches Motion proper. Thinks the conduct detestible Parricide—to supply those who have Arms in their Hands to deprive us of the best Rights of human Nature. The honest Seamen ought to be examined, and they may give Evidence vs. the guilty.

Hancock. Deane belongs to Boston. He came from W. Ind[ies] and was seized here, and released. Loaded with flour and went out.

MS (MHi). Adams, *Diary* (Butterfield), 2:186–87.

[1] Congress tabled Samuel and Robert Purviance's petition, which requested permission to export a cargo of wheat after the nonexportation deadline of September 10. See *JCC*, 3:264.

Silas Deane's Diary

[September 27, 1775]

Wednesday 27th. At Congress & on Com[mitte]es all Day.[1] Col. W[illia]ms & Mr. Wales Order for Money, had it Voted them.

MS (CtHi). *CHS Bulletin* 29 (July 1964): 96A

[1] Deane apparently often added several diary entries together retrospectively and in the process sometimes confused the chronology of events. The following sentence actually appears on the next line of his manuscript diary after the words "Thursday 28th. at ditto," but it is clear from the journal of Congress and the diary of Richard Smith that the business of William Williams and Nathaniel Wales was considered by Congress the 27th. Williams and Wales applied to Congress on behalf of the Connecticut Council of Safety for reimbursement of

£65,000 already advanced by Connecticut for the supply of the army. *JCC,* 3:263; and *Am. Archives,* 4th ser. 3:674.

Caesar Rodney to Thomas Rodney

Philadelphia Sepr. 27th 1775. Discusses the impending elections in Delaware and expresses particular apprehension over the divisions that may arise. "This gives me much Concern, more Especially when our public affairs require the greatest unanimity, for our union is our Strength." Is even more concerned, he cautions his brother, "that you intend to leave Mr. Barrett out of your ticket as Sheriff."

RC (NN) . Rodney, *Letters* (Ryden) , pp. 64–65.

Secret Committee Account

[September 27, 1775–August 26, 1776]

Abstract of Monies Advanced to Sundry persons by the Secret Committee on Special Contracts.[1]

Persons	Dates	Sums D[o]ll[ar]s
Willing, Morris, & Co.	27th Sepr. 1775	45,000
Ph. Livingston, Jo. Alsop & Frs. Lewis	9th Octr.	36,000
Alexander Gillon	27th Ocr.	45,000
Nathl. Shaw	8th Novr.	21,000
John Langdon	8th Novr.	15,000
Ths. Mumford	28th Novr.	28,500
Saml. Mifflin & George Clymer	30th Novr.	7,500
J. & Peter Chevalier	5th Decembr.	11,500
Esek Hopkins	11th Decembr.	6,000
Willing Morris & Co.	14th Decembr.	14,000
Ths. Yorke	19 Decembr.	5,350
Blair Meclenachan	22d Decembr.	4,550
John Brown	25 Decembr.	20,000
Ths. Greene	26 Decembr.	10,000
Bayard, Jackson & Co.	26 Decembr.	15,000
Philip Livingston	8th Jany. 1776	20,000
John Langdon	8th Jany.	10,000
Deane, Silas & Barnabas	11th Jany.	30,000
Willing, Morris & Co.	5th Feby.	80,000
Nathl. Greene & Co.	6 Feby.	10,000
Nichls. & John Browne	6th Feby.	24,000

Hodges Bayard & Co.	13th Feby.	23,333.30
J. Alson,[2] F. Lewis, P. Livingston, S. Deane & Robert Morris	19th Feby.	200,000
Robert Morris & John Ross	1st March	90,000
Ths. Yorke	17th June	5,400
	18th June	5,000
Josa. & Adam Babcock	7th March	20,000
Guinet Button	12 July	20,000
Hewes & Smith	26 Augt.	20,000
Total	D[o]ll[ar]s	841,633.

MS (MH). In the hand of Richard Henry Lee. Lee was appointed to the committee in March 1776. *JCC,* 4:215.

[1] More information regarding the contracts listed in this account is available in the various entries of the Secret Committee Minutes of Proceedings, the majority of which are printed under the dates indicated in the middle column of this list. In seven instances the date on which advances were recorded varies slightly from that on which the corresponding contract was recorded in the Secret Committee Minutes of Proceedings, and the advance made to John Langdon on January 8, 1776, apparently does not pertain to any of the transactions discussed in the committee's proceedings.

[2] That is, John Alsop. See Secret Committee Minutes of Proceedings, February 20, 1776.

Secret Committee Minutes of Proceedings

Committee Chamber Sepr. 27th. 1775, Philadelphia.

At the Meeting of the Committee of Secrecy appointed by the Honble continental Congress of the 13 U[nited] C[olonies] in N. A. present—Saml. Ward, John Langdon, Silas Deane, John Alsop, Philip Livingston, Benjamin Franklin, John Dickenson & Thos. McKean Esqrs—Members of the said Committee of Secrecy.[1]

A Contract was enterd into by Thos. Willing & Robert Morris & Co.[2] of the City of Philadelphia in the Province of Pensylva., Merchts. of the one part, with Samuel Ward, John Langdon, Silas Deane, John Alsop, Philip Livingston, Benjamin Franklin, John Dickenson & Thos. McKean the aforesaid Members of the other part as follows vizt.—That the sd. Thos. Willing, Robert Morris* & Co. shall & will, with the utmost speed & secrecy send a ship or vessel to some part of Europe & there purchase at the cheapest rate they can a thousand barrels of good powder, twelve good brass guns (six pounders), two thousand stand of good arms vizt. Soldiers muskets & bayonets & five thousand gunlocks double bridled, of a good quality, & in case the aforesaid quantity of powder cannot be procurd, that they shall & will purchase as much Saltpetre & sulphur if to be had as will make as much powder as shall be deficient.

As by the sd. Contract copied into the Register of the Contracts of the sd. Committee of Secrecy p. 2 &c bearing date the day & year aforesaid, reference being thereunto had, more fully & at large appears.

* N.B. Mr. Patterson Coll[ecto]r in the port of Philadelphia in the years 1773, 1774, says that in those years protested Bills returnd against Mr. R. Morris for about 50,000 ster. A. Lee had it from Mr. W. Livingston.

MS (MH). Extracted from a 138-page document in the Lee Family Papers consisting of the Secret Committee's minutes of meetings and extracts from the journals of Congress pertinent to the committee's work for the period September 18, 1775–September 10, 1777. Endorsed: "Copy, Journal of the Secret Committee, N. 2d"; and captioned: "The proceedings of the Committee of Secrecy appointed by the Honble Congress of the thirteen United Colonies, 1775." The copyist's final entry indicates that this document was made sometime after October 5, 1778, the day the committee met pursuant to a congressional resolve of September 4, 1778, and agreed to hire "a capable Clerk" to assist in settling the committee's accounts and preparing them for delivery to the Committee of Commerce. See *JCC*, 12:878–79.

[1] Thomas Willing was also a member of this committee, which Congress appointed September 18 "to contract and agree for the importation and delivery of . . . gunpowder." Subsequently known as the Secret Committee, it was granted significant decision-making powers and ultimately became the manager of extensive exportation and importation operations crucial to the war effort. *JCC*, 2:253–55, 3:280, 336.

[2] Although there was a heated discussion of the Willing, Morris & Co. contract in Congress on September 25, the contract was apparently not completed until the 27th, when the company was also advanced $45,000. See Secret Committee Account, September 27, 1775–August 26, 1776; and John Adams' Notes of Debates, September 25, 1775. See also Secret Committee Minutes of Proceedings, February 5, 1776.

Richard Smith's Diary

[September 27, 1775]

Wednesday 27. 160,000 Dollars ordered to be advanced to Connectt. in part of their Claim on the Congress. Willing from the Comee. on Accounts asked Whether a Charge should be allowed made by the Comee. of Northampton County in Pennsa. for their Time & Trouble in settling certain Accounts, Mr. Willing was directed not to allow it.[1] The Journal continued to be read & various Parts ordered not to be published, as the Instructions to Gen Washn., the Directions to the German Ministers &c. A Petition was read from Messrs. Purviance of Baltimore praying Leave to ship off a Cargo of Wheat which the late Storm prevented, refused & ordered to lie on the Table.[2]

MS (DLC).

[1] This day Congress did, however, approve the payment of more than $3,000 to the Northampton County committee for expenses incurred in raising rifle companies for the Continental Army. *JCC*, 3:264.

[2] John Zubly briefly noted in his diary this day: "Attended Committee & Congress. Preached for Mr. Stillman. Math. 8:25." GHi.

Samuel Ward's Diary

[September 27, 1775]

27th. Copy of Journal presented & partly read. Kettles, Kanteans &c allowed the soldiers. 160,000 Doll[ar]s ordered to Com[mitte] on Acct. Several Accts., Rob Erwin &s allowd.[1] Journal read & ordered to be printed.[2]

MS (RHi).

[1] For the accounts approved by Congress this day, see *JCC*, 3:263–64.

[2] Despite congressional authorization this day to print selections of its proceedings "of the last session," not until December 1775 was such a volume published. *JCC*, 3:514.

Willing, Morris & Co. to Messrs. Wm. Baynes & Co.

Philada. Sepr. 27. 1775. "We[1] wrote you last on the 11th Instant, & since that Period all Exportation of this Country Produce has ceased, indeed there has not been any brought to Market for Sale, consequently no Prices can be quoted. The Act of Parliament leaves New York, the three lower Counties on Delaware, North Carolina & Georgia at Liberty to export to Foreign Countries & we expect they will avail of this exemption by & by, as they are not restrained by the Congress, but at present no Body dare move in the Export from those Places, as the People at large seem disposed to prevent Exportation totally, but their Folly will be their Punishment, & we shall not be surprised to see a different Disposition prevail in this Point in a short time. . . . We have not heard yet the Arrival of the Union, Capt. Steel, in the Mediterranean, but expect she will arrive to a good Market, indeed its very probable that all the Foreign Markets will be good, soon as they know of a certainty that the Exports from this Country will be stopped. Should the Exports from New York & the lower Counties take place by & by, we shall come in for a Share of them & by that means send some farther Supplies to Mr. Gorge, Messrs. Gregory & Guille, Messrs. Martins &c., as we judge that

Business must be very valuable, so long as the other Colonies are shut up."

Tr (PRO: C.O. 5, 134).

[1] Thomas Willing and Robert Morris, partners since 1754, utilized their positions as Philadelphia merchants and prominent political leaders to engage in many of the most lucrative commercial enterprises available to American merchants during the War for Independence. Successively members of Congress from May 1775 to October 1778, and throughout the war privy to nearly all the significant economic intelligence available to Congress, Willing and Morris maintained a commercial correspondence suggestive of the wide range of commercial opportunities open to advantageously placed merchants.

John Adams' Diary

1775. Sept. 28. Thursday.

The Congress, and the Assembly of this Province were invited to make an Excursion upon Delaware River in the new Row Gallies built by the Committee of Safety of this Colony. About Ten in the Morning We all embarked.[1] The Names of the Gallies are the Washington, the Effingham, the Franklin, the Dickenson, the Otter, the Bull Dog, and one more, whose Name I have forgot. We passed down the River by Glocester where the Vesseau de Frize are. These a[re] Frames of Timber to be fill'd with Stones and sunk, in three Rowes, in the Channell.

I went in the Bull Dog Captn. Alexander Commander. Mr. Hillegas, Mr. Owen Biddle, and Mr. Rittenhouse, and Capt. Faulkner [Falconer] were with me. Hillegas is one of our Continental Treasurers, is a great Musician—talks perpetually of the Forte and Piano, of Handell &c. and Songs and Tunes. He plays upon the Fiddle.

Rittenhouse is a Mechannic, a Mathematician, a Philsosopher and an Astronomer.

Biddle is said to be a great Mathematician. Both are Members of the American Philosophical Society. I mentioned Mr. Cranch to them for a Member.

Our Intention was to have gone down to the Fort but the Winds and Tide being unfavourable We returned by the City and went up the River to Point no Point, a pretty Place. On our Return Dr. Rush, Dr. Zubly and Counciller Ross, Brother of George Ross, joined us.

Ross is a Lawyer, of great Eloquence, and heretofore of extensive Practice. A great Tory, they say, but now begins to be converted. He said the Americans were making the noblest and firmest Resistance to Tyranny that ever was made by any People. The Acts were founded in Wrong, Injustice and Oppression. The great Town of Boston had been remarkably punished without being heard.

Rittenhouse is a tall, slender Man, plain, soft, modest, no remarkable Depth, or thoughtfullness in his Face—yet cool, attentive, and clear.

MS (MHi). Adams, *Diary* (Butterfield), 2:187–88.

[1] On the subject of this trip, see the diary entries of Robert Treat Paine, Richard Smith, and John Zubly, this date, and John Jay to Sarah Jay, September 29, 1775. Silas Deane, who was also present on the cruise, erroneously dated his brief diary entry this day: "Friday 29th. In Committee in the Morning, thence went to take a Sail in the Gondola's—Col. Wms. with Us." CtHi.

John Adams to James Warren

Dr sir Philadelphia Septr. 28. 1775

I write at this Time, only to remind you that I have recd no Letters.

Let me intreat the earliest Attention of our Houses, to the Accounts and Vouchers of our Province. Accounts must be exact and Vouchers genuine, or We shall suffer. The whole attention of every Member of both Houses, would be not improfitably employed upon this subject untill it is finished.[1]

The Accounts, I mean, are of Ammunition, such as Powder, Ball, Cartridges—Artillery, Cannon, Field Pieces, Carriages—Camp Equipage, Cantins, Kettles, Spoons &c Tents, Canvas &c &c &c. Provisions, Bread, Meat, Meal, Peas, every Thing in short. In fine it is idle for me to enter [in] to detail—The Pay and Cloathing of the Troops &c &c.

But I must entreat, to have these Accounts and Vouchers. I do beseech that it may be remembered that I was importunate, on this Head with Several Gentlemen, when I was with you.

RC (MHi). In Adams' hand, though not signed.

[1] Adams was probably stimulated to raise this subject by Congress' appointment of a committee of claims on September 25. *JCC*, 3:262–64.

Robert Treat Paine's Diary

[September 28, 1775]

Fair. Fine day. The Congress Comttee of the City & Some of Assembly went down the River in the Row Gallies designing to dine at the Fort, but Wind & Tide being a head we went up to Point no Point, returned.

MS (MHi).

Richard Smith's Diary

Thursday 28 Septr. [1775]

No Congress. The Members dined by Invitation on Board of the Row Gallies which sailed down to the Chevaux de Frize near Mud Island & up to Point no Point.[1] I amused myself all the Morning in M. du Simitiere's curious Museum.

MS (DLC).

[1] Samuel Ward noted in his diary this day: "Attended the Invitation of the City on board the Gallies." RHi.

Henry Wisner to John Haring and John McKesson

Gentlemen. Philadelphia Sept. 28. 1775

By the first safe opportunity I send you[1] the 32 articles of agreement for the due regulation and government of the associations in the colony of Pennsylvania.[2]

I beg the favor of you to let me know as quick as possable whether the Saltpeter has arrived from Connecticut that your committee of safety informed me a few days ago when last in town. Also if any accounts from that which was expected another way. I want to send to the workman as quick as possible but dare not send him until I can get some Saltpeter at least a few hundred weight.

I am gentlemen your ashured friend and Very Humble Servant,

Henry Wisner

RC (N). *Journals of N. Y. Prov. Cong.*, 2:85. RC damaged; missing words supplied from Tr.

[1] John Haring and John McKesson were, respectively, chairman of the New York Committee of Safety and secretary to the New York Provincial Congress.

[2] For Pennsylvania's articles of association, adopted by that province's Committee of Safety on August 19, see *Am. Archives,* 4th ser. 3:502–4.

John Zubly's Diary

[September 28, 1775]

Thursday, 28. At the Invitation of the Committee of this City the Congress sailed in the Row Gallies to see the Preparations to Stop up the River, but Wind & tide being Contrary could not effect it. Sailed to Point no Point. The Galley on board which I was carried away her fore mast. It was observed that the Thermometer this summer had risen at Philada to 96.

MS (GHi).

John Jay to Sarah Jay

My dear Sally Ph. 29 Septr. 1775

My last to you was by Mr. Graham which I hope you have recd. It would give me Pleasure to have an opportunity of acknowledging the Receipt of one from you. I sometimes fear you are indisposed and that your Silence proceeds from a Desire of concealing it.

Your Papa is hearty & well.[1] The Congress spent Yesterday in Festivity. The Com[mitte]e of Safety were so polite as to invite them to make a little voyage in their Gondolas as far as the Fort which is about 12 Miles from the City. Each Galley had its Company & each Company entertained with Variety of musick &c! &c! We proceeded six or Eight Miles down the River when the Tide being spent & the wind unfavorable We tacked about & with a fine Breese returned, passed the City & landed six miles above the Town at a pretty little Place called Paris Villa. It appears to have been the Property of a Gentleman of some Taste—a Garden, a close walk, a Summer House &c. much out of order & partly in Ruins. I wished you & a few select friends had been with me. This Idea tho amidst much noise and mirth, made me much alone. Adieu my beloved. I am most sincerely yours John Jay

RC (NNC).

[1] William Livingston.

Richard Smith's Diary

[September 29, 1775]

Friday 29. Letters from Gen. Washington with a Return of his Army, about 19,000 effective Men who are to be disbanded in Decr. by the Terms of Inlistment, he prays Directions how to keep or raise an Army. Expenses run very high, great Want of Powder & Money.[1] Chief Part of the Morn'g. was spent on a Motion to send a Comee. of the Congress to the Army to take proper Measures for the Winter Campaign, it passed in the Affirmative. Some Powder said to be just arrived in Delaware, our Comee. were desired to purchase it. Above 80 of our Men have deserted to Gen. Gage in the Course of this Campaign accordg to Gen Washns. Dispatches.

MS (DLC).

[1] Washington's letter to Hancock of September 21, together with enclosures, is in PCC, item 152, 1:119–44; and *Am. Archives,* 4th ser. 3:760–71.

Samuel Ward's Diary

[September 29, 1775]

29th. A letter from Gen Washington. Several Accts. all[owe]d. The powder Comee. to purch[ase] [. . .] said to be arrived. President to sign all Orders on the Treasury. Three Members appointed to go to the Camp to consult Genl. Washington, the Govs. Conn[ecticu]t & Rhode [Island], the president of the congress of New Hampshire, & the Council of the Massachusts upon the most effective Method of continuing supporting & regulating a continental Army.[1]

MS (RHi).

[1] Although this day Congress approved the formation of a committee to consult with Washington and New England officials on military matters, members of the committee were not actually appointed until the following day. *JCC,* 3:266. For a discussion of sentiment in Congress against appointing such a committee, see Ward to Henry Ward, September 30, 1775.

John Adams to James Warren

Dr sir Philadelphia Septr. 30. 1775

Mr Lynch, Coll Harrison, and Dr Franklyn are preparing for a Journey to Watertown and Cambridge, one of whom will do me the Favour of taking this Letter.

Mr Lynch, you have seen before. He is an oppulent Planter of great Understanding and Integrity and the best affections to our Country and Cause.

Coll Harrison is of Virginia, and the Friend and Correspondent of the General, but it seems by a certain Letter, under some degree of Prejudice against our dear New Englandmen. These Prejudices however, have arisen from Misrepresentation and may be easily removed.

Dr Franklyn needs nothing to be said. There is no abler or better American, that I know of.

I could wish a particular Attention and Respect to all Three.

I know you will be pleased to be introduced to these Gentlemen, because it will give you an opportunity of serving your Country.[1] I am your Friend John Adams

RC (MHi).

[1] Adams wrote a second letter this day to Warren containing substantially the same information about the delegates appointed to confer with General Washington and several New England leaders, who were to discuss "various Matters of importance—such as a Plan for continuing the Army this Winter, and another for raising one next Spring." He also added the query: "Will it not be excellent

Politicks to make Dr. Franklin welcome by making him a grant of what is due him from the Province?" John Adams to James Warren, September 30, 1775, extract in *Parke-Bernet Galleries Catalog,* no. 251 (January 22, 1941), part 2, p. 1. On October 23, the Massachusetts General Court ordered the payment of £1854 to Benjamin Franklin for his services as agent of the province. Proceedings of the Massachusetts House of Representatives, *Am. Archives,* 4th ser. 3:1472.

Silas Deane's Diary

[September 30, 1775]

Saturday—Unwell—Mr. Jay went home.[1] Expences for paper and Sealing Wax—0.5.0, For Trimming horses—2.6, For Shoeing ditto—10.0.

MS (CtHi). *CHS Bulletin* 29 (July 1964): 96A.

[1] Jay returned to Congress by October 10, as indicated by the record of his remarks in John Adams' Notes of Debates for that date. Burnett, who did not have access to Deane's diary, was unable to include this absence in his otherwise comprehensive account of Jay's attendance in Congress from September 1774 to April 1776. Burnett, *Letters,* 1:liv.

John Hancock to Jonathan Trumbull, Sr.

Sir, Philada. Sepr. 30th. 1775.[1]

The Congress have recd. sundry Letters from General Washington Containing Matters of great Importance, touching the supporting and regulating the Continental Army.

As the Congress are desirous of the fullest Light on these Subjects before they come to a final Determination, they have appointed three of their Members—viz Mr. Lynch, Doctor Franklyn, and Mr. Harrison to wait on the Genl. and confer with him, and with the Governors of Connecticut & Rhode Island, and with the Council of Massachusetts Bay, and the President of the Convention of New Hampshire.[2]

The Committee will set out as soon as possible, and expect to be at the Camp by the 12th. of next Month.

Of this I am desired to inform you, and to request you will meet the Committee on that Day. In Case the Business of your Colony will not admit of your personal Attendance, it is the Desire of the Congress that you appoint a proper Person or Persons to represent your Colony at the Conference with their Committee. I have the Honor to be Hond. Sir yr. &c J. Hancock Prest.

LB (DNA: PCC, item 12A).

[1] *JCC,* 3:265–66. Hancock sent similar letters this day to Rhode Island Deputy

Governor Nicholas Cooke, the Massachusetts Council, and the New Hampshire Convention. PCC, item 12A, 1:6–7.

[2] For the proceedings of the conference among Washington, the delegates from Congress, and representatives from the aforementioned New England provinces, which was held at Cambridge October 18–22, see *Am. Archives,* 4th ser. 3:1156–61. For the proceedings of the conference between Washington and the three delegates held the following two days, see Committee of Conference Minutes of Proceedings, October 23–24, 1775.

John Hancock to George Washington

Sir Philadelphia Septemr. 30th. 1775

Your Letters No 4, 5 and two other Letters not Numberd, with the Inclosures have been duly Receiv'd and laid before Congress.[1]

As there are Sundry matters contain'd in your Letters which are of great importance, and on which the Congress, before they come to a final Determination, are Desirous to have the Advantage of your Experience and Knowledge, They have Appointed three of their Members, Vizt. Mr. Lynch, Doctor Franklin & Mr Harrison to wait on you, Confer with you and the Governors of Connecticutt & Rhode Island, the Council of Massachussets Bay, and the President of the Convention of New Hampshire, (to whom I have wrote on the Subject by order of Congress,) and such other Persons as to the said Committee shall seem proper, touching the most effectual Method of Continuing, Supporting and Regulating a Continental Army.

The Committee will set out as soon as possible, and Expect to be with you by the 12th of next Month.

I have the Honour to be with the greatest Esteem, Sir, Your most Obedt. huml Servt John Hancock President

[*P.S.*] The Inclos'd Letter to the Council of Massachusetts you will please to order to be Deliver'd. And the Letter to the President of the Convention of New Hampshire you will please to forward by Express as soon as possible.

RC (DLC).

[1] For the response of Congress to these letters, the minutes of the conference at headquarters to discuss Washington's inquiries, and the recommendations resulting from those discussions, see Committee of Conference Minutes of Proceedings, October 23–24, 1775, note 1.

Richard Smith's Diary

Saturday 30 Septr. [1775]

A Comee. of 3, viz Harrison, Franklin & Lynch was appointed by

Ballot to proceed to the Camp at Cambridge. Harrison & Dyer had an equal Number of Votes, the Question was taken Whether the Comee. shall consist of 3 or 4. It was carried for 3. Then the Vote was passed for a 3d Committee Man when Harrison was chosen. A Comee. of 5 was chosen to draw up Instructions for those Gentlemen.[1] On Motion of Dr. Franklin the resolution that the Postage should be 20 per Cent less than the Kings Postage was suspended till further Order, he being fearful that the reduced Postage at this Time may not be sufficient to pay all Charges.[2] An Application was made from the Philada. Comee. to give a Regulation Whether or not the Trade Coastwise shall be continued, and a particular Vessel bound to Gloucester in Mass. Bay shall be permitted to proceed. After Debate the Matter was postponed. An Application was made to the Congress by Capt John MacPherson offering to destroy all the British Fleet at Boston if permitted—postponed. (I believe he was afterwards permitted to go & that he came back without effectg. any Thing.)[3] McKean & Willing moved for Us to interfere in the Dispute between Connecticut & Pennsa. for that there is immediate Danger of Hostilities between them on the Susquehannah—deferred till Monday. The Congress adjorned till Monday to meet at the Lodge in Lodge Alley because the Election is to be then held at the State House.[4]

MS (DLC).

[1] This committee reported to Congress October 2 a set of instructions for the delegates appointed to consult with Washington at Cambridge, which Congress approved the same day. *JCC*, 3:270–71.

[2] Congress had originally approved on July 26, 1775, the resolution on postal rates it now suspended. *JCC*, 2:208.

[3] For a discussion of Captain Macpherson and his proposal for destroying the British fleet, see John Adams' Diary, September 18, 1775, and the accompanying note. On October 20 Congress approved the payment of $300 to help Macpherson put his plan into effect, but Washington thought the whole scheme chimerical and nothing came of it. *JCC*, 3:301; and Washington, *Writings* (Fitzpatrick), 4:71–72.

[4] Smith went to Burlington October 1 to supervise the printing of a new emission of New Jersey paper money and to serve as clerk of the provincial assembly and did not return to Congress until December 13. See Smith's diary, October 1, December 12, 1775. DLC.

Samuel Ward's Diary

[September 30, 1775]

30th. Dr. Franklin, Mr. Lynch & Colo. Harrison the Comee; John Rutledge, Colo. Lee, R R Livingston, S. Adams & Mr. Johnston a Comee to draw Instructions for the above Comee. President to write to Genl. Washington to acquaint him with the Appoint. & the Govrs. Council & President desiring them to attend the Comee 12th Octr.

next. Postage of Letters to be same as usual. Some Accts. allowed, a Complaint made by Delegates against the Conn[ecticu]t People at Susquehannah, a Reprt from the Comee. for considering of the Trade &c read.

MS (RHi).

Samuel Ward to Henry Ward

Dear Brother Philadelphia 30th Sepr. 1775

I determined to have wrote You every Post but I am upon several Committees for very important Purposes which takes up My Time so that I was forced to omit writing to you by last Post; what can be the Reason that I have never recd. one Line from You I cannot conceive. I am willing to suppose a hundred Causes rather than Want of affection and so continue to write.

In our Letter to the Depy. Govr.[1] the principal Things which you had at Heart are taken some Notice of. The Comee. to whom I designed to present his Honors Letter relative to Capt. Hopkins hath not yet met. I am one of them & design to get a Meeting on Monday next if possible. Business cannot be done here with the same Dispatch as in New England but I have this Satisfaction that I am never absent either from Comees. or Congress.

A Letter from Genl. Washington relative to the forming a new Army, and that Paragraph of Govr. Cooke's Letter that only Capt. Ward amongst all the Rhode Island officers had received a continental Commission alarmed the Congress, or rather some Members of it. A Motion was made that a Comee. should be appointed to consult Genl. Washington, the Depy. Govr. of Rhode Island, the Govr. of Connecticut, the Council of the Massachusetts Bay & the President of the Congress of New Hampshire upon the best Method of continuing supporting & regulating a continental Army. Mr. Adams the Con[necticu]t Gentlemen & myself were against it & many others but least We should be supposed to think our Army would not bear Inspection We did not exert ourselves and suffered the Motion to be carried without calling the Colonies when a Major[it]y of them were against it. Letters to the Governors &c go by this Express that they may meet the Comee. 12th next Month at Cambridge. The Gentn. fond of the Motion wished a very different Comee. from that actually appointed. I saw their Aim and proposed to the New England Cols. a Plan for defeating them & succeeded saving that We failed in getting Colo. Dyer appointed with the other Gentn. The Comee. as it now stands is Dr. Franklin Mr. Lynch & Colo. Harrison, the two first You are well acquainted with the last is a Virginian a Friend of Liberty a Man of

Sense & Spirit but not at all Times so wise & judicious as some from that glorious Colony.[2] A Comee. is appointed to draw Instructions for them I imagine they will sett out on Tuesday next. I wish You could accompany Govr. Cooke to Cambridge. Your Advice & Pen I think would do your Country most essential Service. It is agreed that an Army for the Winter must be formed out of that now in Service, the Southern Gentlemen wish to reduce the Wages of the privates and raise those of the Officers. With Regard to the last they are right for in the present Camp officers can't support themselves upon their present Pay, as to the first they are certainly wrong for no Man can live tolerably for less. They could hire they say good Men in the Southern Colonies for ten shillings per Month less but I believe they would not be so good by twenty. A Letter to General Washington would have superceded the necessity of any Comee. but as we have suffered one I would have the best made of it. Upon this Principle I ardently wish You to attend the Depy. Govr. & at the same time that you nobly sacrifice every other Consideration to the Good of America, I would have you take Care of the New England Colonies in general (the great Support of Liberty) & of our own little Colony in particular. Neither of the Gentn. save Dr. Franklin is equal to you in natural or acquired abilities. Some of the southern Gentn. seem to consider this matter as an affair between New England & the other Colonies & upon that Plan balloted for Gentn. only of the other Colonies. (Colo. Dyer & Colo. Harrison had equal Votes at first, upon a second Tryal another Southern Member came in & turned the Vote for Colo. Harrison). I believe he will do well. I wish our Troops to reinlist but wish the Terms may be good.

An unhappy Dispute subsists between the Virginians & the Pennsylvanians & another between the latter & Connecticut both which are before the Congress & I hope such Measures will be adopted as may prevent the sad Mischiefs which they threaten us with.

Mr. Goddard hath been to the southward and established Post offices & Riders quite to Georgia & Dr. Franklin as he comes to the north will establish proper offices that Way.

No News from England since my last. The Gen[tleme]n of Georgia deserve the Character I gave you of them. They are some of the highest Sons of Liberty I have seen & are very sensible & clever. Mr. Wythe & Mr. Lee of Virginia have been under Enoculation ever since my last that I can say no more of them than I did then; saving that unhappy Jealousy of New England which some weak Minds are possessed with great Unanimity prevails in Congress. Our Measures are more Spirited and I believe We are now ready to go every Length to secure our Liberties. John Adams Letter[3] has silenced those who opposed every decisive Measure, but the moderate or as I consider them the Enemies of our Cause have caused Copies of it to be sent throughout the Province in Hopes by raising the Cry of Independence to throw the Friends of Liberty out of the new Assembly the Choice of which commences next Monday but I believe they will fail & that the House will be more decisive than ever. One Comfort We have that divine Wisdom & Goodness often bring Good out of ill; that the Issue of this severe Contest will be the Establishment of our Liberties I as firmly believe as I do my Existence for I never can think God brought us into the Wilderness to perish or what is worse to become Slaves but to make us a great & free People.

If you have any kind of Intelligence from Quebec let Me have that & any thing else in your next. I am concerned for my Son least the severe Fatigues of the Expedition should overcome him. God bless you & yours my dear Bror. I am most affectionately your

Sam Ward

P.S. The Express being just going I have wrote as fast as I could & scarcely know what.

Mr. Hopkins & Lady are very well. Make my most respectful Compliments to the Depy. Govr. & his Family. I thought the rude Sketch now given of the Sentiments of Congress &c would not be unacceptable & might let you into the Principles of the chief People.

You'l observe I have wrote principally to You & communicate no Parts but such as are proper.

RC (RHi).

[1] Not found.

[2] For an indication of why Harrison's reputation was temporarily under a cloud, see the intercepted letter of Harrison to George Washington, July 21, 1775, note 3.

[3] A reference to John Adams' letter to James Warren of July 24, 1775, which was intercepted by the British and widely printed in English and American newspapers.

Henry Wisner to John Haring and John McKesson

Gentlemen Philadelphia September 30th 1775

Enclosed I Send you the Military articles Delivered out by the Commitee of Safety, for the Coloney of Pennsylvania. After I had Wrote the inclosed Letter[1] I found that the associators generally Refused signing and that they had printed their Reasons for So Doing.[2] I then thought Best to wait till I could Send Both together Which I hope May Apologise for my not Sending Sooner. It is Some Matter of Doubt with me whether our people will Be prevaild on to Signe them—I rather think they will not. However you will Be Best Judges of that, and the propriaty of So Doing if it May Be Done. I Beg you to Send Me an answer to that part of the enclosed Letter that Relates to Saltpeter as quick as posable. Direct My Letters to the Care of William Will in the Corner of Second and Arch Streets.

If You Deliver it to Henry Will, puteror [pewterer] in N York, he will Send it As he Very frequently Coresponds with his Brother.

I am gentlemen your Humble Servant Henry Wisner

RC (N). *Journals of N. Y. Prov. Cong.*, 2:85. RC damaged; missing words supplied from Tr.

[1] See Henry Wisner to John Haring and John McKesson, September 28, 1775.

[2] On September 27 the Pennsylvania Assembly received an address signed by privates from 30 provincial militia companies, which explained their refusal to accept the articles of association adopted by the Pennsylvania Committee of Safety. *Am. Archives*, 4th ser. 3:821–22.

John Zubly's Diary

[September 30, 1775]

Saturday, 30. Frost & very cold. Dispatched Packet to Mr. Tennent with Letters[1] to Committee at Savannah.

MS (GHi).

[1] Not found.

Virginia Delegate to Unknown

[September ? 1775][1]

We have hopes here of an accommodation with Great Britain, notwithstanding the unfavourable answer his majesty has given the city of London, and the order to governour Tryon for the men of war to beat down the towns if we are not quiet. The ministry themselves agree that it must be made up, and will, in all probability take hold of the offer made them by the congress in their petition. Orders are sent, it seems, to Boston, to treat the people with lenity, and to suffer them to remove with their effects.

MS not found; reprinted from the *Virginia Gazette* (Pinkney), October 12, 1775. Printed under the heading: *"Extract of a letter, to a gentleman in this city, from one of the delegates from this colony to the congress."*

[1] This letter was probably written after the delegates had learned in mid-September of the king's response to the petition of the city of London but before the beginning of October when they became more pessimistic over prospects for a peaceful accommodation with Britain as a result of accounts recently received from correspondents in London. See, for example, Eliphalet Dyer to Joseph Trumbull, September 15, and Samuel Adams to James Warren, October 3, 1775.

John Adams to Abigail Adams

My Dear Philadelphia Octr. 1. 1775

This Morning, I received your two Letters of September 8th. and September 16th. What shall I say? The Intelligence they contain, came upon me by Surprize, as I never had the least Intimation before, that any of my Family was ill, excepting in a Card from Mrs. Warren received a few days ago, in which she informed me that Mrs. Adams had been unwell but was better.[1]

You may easily conceive the State of Mind, in which I am at present. Uncertain and apprehensive, at first I suddenly thought of setting off, immediately, for Braintree, and I have not yet determined otherwise. Yet the State of public Affairs is so critical, that I am half afraid to leave my Station, Altho my Presence here is of no great Consequence.

I feel—I tremble for You. Poor Tommy! I hope by this Time, however, he has recovered his plump Cheeks and his fine Bloom. By your Account of Patty I fear—but still I will hope she has been supported, and is upon the Recovery.

I rejoice to learn that Nabby and her Brothers have hitherto escaped and pray God that his Goodness may be still continued to them. Your Description of the distressed State of the Neighbourhood is affecting indeed.

It is not uncommon for a Train of Calamities to come together. Fire, Sword, Pestilence, Famine, often keep Company, and visit a Country in a Flock.

At this Distance I can do no good to you nor yours. I pray God to support you—I hope our Friends and Neighbours are kind as usual. I feel for them, in the general Calamity.

I am so far from thinking you melancholly, that I am charmed with that Admirable Fortitude, and that divine Spirit of Resignation which appears in your Letters. I cannot express the Satisfaction it gives me, nor how much it contributes to support me.

You have alarmed me however, by mentioning Anxieties which you do not think it prudent to mention to any one. I am wholly at a Loss to conjecture what they can be. If they arise from the Letters,[2] be assured that you may banish them forever. These Letters have reached Philadelphia, but have produced Effects very different from those which were expected from the Publication of them. These Effects I will explain to you sometime or other. As to the Versification of them, if there is Wit or Humour in it laugh—if ill Nature, sneer—if mere Dullness, why you may even yawn or nod. I have no Anger, at it, nay even scarcly contempt. It is impotent.

As to Politicks, We have nothing to expect but the whole Wrath and Force of G. Britain. But your Words are as true as an oracle

"God helps them, who help them selves, and if We obtain the divine Aid by our own Virtue, Fortitude and Perseverance, We may be sure of Relief."

It may amuse you to hear a Story. A few days ago, in Company with Dr. Zubly, somebody said, there was nobody on our side but the Almighty. The Dr. who is a Native of Switzerland, and speaks but broken English, quickly replied "Dat is enough. Dat is enough," and turning to me, says he, it puts me in mind of a fellow who once said, The Catholicks have on their side the Pope, and the K. of France and the K. of Spain, and the K. of Sardinia, and the K. of Poland and the Emperor of Germany &c. &c. &c. But as to them poor Devils the Protestants, they have nothing on their side but God Almighty.

RC (MHi). Adams, *Family Correspondence* (Butterfield), 1:289–91.

[1] In her two letters Abigail had described the ravages of a "Distemper" that was sweeping through the Adams family and the neighborhood of Braintree. Adams, *Family Correspondence* (Butterfield), 1:276–80.

[2] A reference to the capture and publication of Adams' letters of July 24, 1775, to Abigail and James Warren. For other optimistic assessments of the effect of their publication, see Adams' letters to Abigail and to James Warren, October 2, 1775.

John Adams to William Tudor

Dr Sir Philadelphia Octr. 1. 1775

I have at last the Pleasure to mention to you what I Suppose Mr H[ancock] has informed you of before, vizt that the Pay of the Judge Advocate is raised to fifty dollars per Month for himself and his Clerk, and this is to be allowed from the day he entered upon the service.[1]

There was an Expresion in your Representation to the General which alarmed me much, and put me to some Pain lest it should excite a Disgust.[2] It was this "The Congress as I have been informed were wholly unacquainted with the Duties of a Judge Advocate, especially in the continental Army." If this had been true, yet it was indecent to tell them of it, because they ought to be presumed to know all the Duties of this officer, but most especially in their own Army. The Construction that I put upon it, was that the Congress had never been made Acquainted with the orders of the General to the Judge to attend every general Court Martial, which made the Duty in the American Army, essentially greater than in any other. By this Interpretation, satisfaction seemed to be given and by the favourable Representation of the General, together with the friendly Notice of General Gates to Some Members who had been at the Camp, this Matter was at last well understood, and Justice was done.

I am very Sorry to learn, that you have been Sick, but rejoice to hear you are better. I have this Morning received from my dear Mrs Adams, two Letters which have put all my Philosophy to the Proof. Never Since I had a Family was it in such Distress, altho it has often seen melancholly Scenes. I tremble for fear my Wifes Health should receive an irreparable Injury from the Anxieties, and Fatigues, which I know she will expose herself to, for the relief of her Family in their present Sick Condition. I fear too the Contagion of such an Hospital of an House. Whether to return I know not. We expect every Hour, momentous Intelligence from England, and from Schuyler and from Washington. And altho, my Presence here is not of any great Consequence, yet some of my Constituents may possibly think it of more than it is, and be uneasy, if I should be absent. At least, if I am here, and any thing goes differently from my Wishes, I shall have the Satisfaction to reflect that I have done all I could however little it might be. Yet if I Stay here, I shall not be happy, till I know more from Braintree. Perhaps I may receive another Letter in a day or two. My Respects to your Father and Mother, and all Friends. Pray write me if you are well enough. I am, sir, your Friend. John Adams

RC (MHi).

[1] Congress had taken this action on September 21. *JCC,* 3:257.

[2] Tudor's letter to Washington, dated August 23, 1775, which Washington enclosed in his August 31 letter to John Hancock, is in PCC, item 152, 1:99–101; and *Am. Archives,* 4th ser. 3:245.

John Adams to James Warren

Dear sir Philadelphia Octr. 1. 1775

This Morning I received your kind Favours of the 11th and 19th Ult.—with the Inclosures. Drapers Paper is a great Curiosity and you will oblige me by sending it as often as possible.

The foreign News you mention, is all a Delusion my Friend.[1] You may depend upon it, every Measure is preparing by the Ministry to destroy us if they can, and that a Sottish Nation is Supporting them.

Heaven helps those who help themselves, and I am happy to find a Disposition so rapidly growing in America to exert itself.

The Letters, by your Packett from my Family, have given me Serious Concern indeed. I am much at a Loss what Course to take. I have thoughts on returning home—I fear my dear Mrs Adams's Health will sink under the Burthen of Care that is upon her. I might well enough be Spared from this Place, where my Presence is of no Consequence, and my Family might derive some Advantage from my being there, and I might have an opportunity of attending a Conference between a Comtee. of this Congress and the Council of Mass. where perhaps I might be of more Service than I can here. However

I am not determined—My Friend, your secretary[2] is very much averse to my going. I dont know what to do.

The Comtee, who are going to the Camp, are Dr Franklin Mr Lynch and Coll Harrison, who I hope will be received with Friendship and Politeness—by all our Friends.

I assure you, Sir, there is a serious Spirit here—Such a Spirit as I have not known before.

The Committee by whom this Letter will go are determined Americans. I fear that two of them, I mean Mr L. & H. may have received some unfavourable Impressions from Misrepresentations, concerning our Province, but these will be easily removed, by what they will see and hear, I hope. I wish that every Civility may be shewn them, which their Fortunes, Characters and Stations demand.

Our News from England, is, Troops from England, Scotland, Ireland, and Hanover—Poor old Britania! I am, your Friend

John Adams

RC (MHi).

[1] See *Warren-Adams Letters,* 1:108.

[2] That is Samuel Adams.

Silas Deane to Elizabeth Deane

My Dear [October 1, 1775][1]

Yours of the 24th Ulto. received yesterday. I thank you for welcoming Me to the *Lovely City of Philadelphia,* but I hardly know a place, but I should be happier in, save among my distressed sick Neighbors at Wethersfeild. The sight of the Eye affects even the hardest heart, mine is too easily affected, & public miseries are surely enough for one thinking feeling mind at a Time. Of these the prospect, the Apprehension is ever before Me, not only on my heart, but as I may say in my hand continually. My sincerest condolance awaits however, all the unfortunate, those in Wethersfeild in particular, whose remembrance of Me, so repeatedly in my absence, will ever render them dear to Me, while I have sense, or recollection left. Mr. May's loss must be a cutting one, as he is fond of his Children, & I think had great reason to be fond of this. But I often say to myself, *Blessed are the Dead,* if as Hamlet says, in that same Sleep of theirs, there were no Dream. You will think Me Melancholy, and you are not much out of the way. The Soul distressing Uncertainty in which We are, respecting Our Northern Friends, with the weight, and fatigue of Business, is almost Too much. I will shake it off for a more agreeable Subject your proposed Journey. The Col. proposed, for Brown, to bring you as farr as New York, where one of Us would meet You, on previous Notice. I do not like Browns Coa[ch and] made no bargain but directed him to shew it to Mr. Webb, & you, [for] your Opinion of that plan. The Season is advancing, and I am sure the Business of the Congress will not soon be compleated. By all the accts. from London the inveteracy of the Ministry is increasing, and nothing in their power, will be left unattempted to reduce Us to their humiliating Terms. The reduction of Montreal, & Quebeck would put a very good Face on Our Affairs, & give the Ministry a blow indeed. The most cool & moderate Men among Us, now sing the same song, which I rung in their Ears, last May & June, untill they almost call'd Me mad, and tell me plainly every day, We now wish we had followed Your advice in Season.

This is some satisfaction, but the poorest in the World, to have Your Opponents own you were right, when too late to take advantage of it either for them or Ourselves. I will however hope the best. I was urged Week before last, on hearing of Genl. Schuylers illness to go in person to that Army, not so much to command as to advise, & assist. This was in a private Clubb, but I discouraged the proposal, and it went no farther. I have vanity enough to think myself a tolerable good contriver, & manager in such an assembly as this, but am not Vain eno. to think myself fit for a General officer. I have indeed tho't it my duty to stay here, otherwise should have gone Northward [on] a former Occasion. I am inlisted in the general Service & must take my post if possible where I have a Chance of doing most service.

I think that the 10th of this Mo. will be late eno. for you to set out, if you can be ready by that Time. This comes by Col. Williams, & Mr. Wales, who have paid Us a Visit,[2] the former cool & stiff as you please, but I trust I have not been deficient in complaisance to him. I suppose Connecticut politicians have been busy, & that the Nomination will be varied, but I hope not very greatly, as I wish for the old steady plan of the Colony in preferance to every private View, either for myself, or Freinds. Am a little surprized that Col. Seymour miss'd his Election for Hartford, but duplicity and haughtiness are two the worst ingredients, in Nature, for a Connecticut Statesman. Adieu to this Subject. I suppose all Freinds are well, my Love to them. When is Sally to be married? I am my Dear your Affectionate Husband S. Deane

RC (CtHi).

[1] This letter to his wife is undoubtedly the one Deane mentioned in his diary entry for October 1 and which he forwarded by William Williams and Nathaniel Wales when they left Philadelphia on the second. *CHS Bulletin* 29 (July 1964): 96A.

[2] For details on the purpose of their visit to Philadelphia, see Deane's Diary, September 27, 1775, note.

Eliphalet Dyer to Zebulon Butler

Sr Philadelphia Octobr 1st 1775

We are Again Alarmed with a report here that you have ordered three hundred Men over on the West branch all Armed & with tools of every kind to erect a fort there & to Molest the Inhabitants on the West branch. We should be glad of a True & just Information from you & some other principal Gentn of ours with respect to the Matters Alledged & the true state of the Affair.[1] The times you Know Now are Very Critical therefore require the Utmost prudence & tho many things may be lawfull yet not expedient it is better to make friends by every Concilliatory method than drive or Use force. Let the people on the West branch see & feel the benefit of being under Connecticutt. We ought to be Carefull not to make our selves enemies in this Colony. Principally on that Account I have before recommended the Confirmation of Esqr Paulings [Henry Pawling's] purchase from Chilliway not so much from the justice as the Policy & as he has purchased a right. I hope his son may be allowed to have it fixd in part or the whole on this purchase he made of Chilliway as Esqr Pauling is one of the Assembly and Considerable Influence in this County. Our Enemies are Indeavouring to make their Interest in the Pensylvania Assembly & if they should take up the matter it would give us much more Trouble than from any other quarter. I am therefore Indeavoring to make as many Friends here as possible. You will therefore from these reasons Indeavor to make our people easy with Esqr Paulings son setting on that right as it may make many friends here. I hope affairs may be Conducted with Temperance Prudence & moderation for the present and with sincere Regards to our Friends at Westmoreland am Yr Hle Servt Elipht Dyer

P.S. Let me hear from you as soon as may be. Yours E D

RC (PWbH).

[1] William Judd's expedition, which was authorized by Butler and the Susquehannah Company to establish a Connecticut settlement at Warrior's Run on the west branch of the Susquehannah, was attacked on September 25 by the Pennsylvanians settled at Sunbury. Judd and other Connecticut men were sent to jail in Philadelphia, and the jurisdictional dispute between Pennsylvania and Connecticut was referred to Congress for solution. For other references to this dispute, see Dyer to William Judd, July 23, 1775, note.

John Adams to Abigail Adams

My Dear Philadelphia Octr. 2. 1775

Every Thing here is in as good a Way as I could wish, considering the Temper and Designs of Administration. I assure you, the Letters have had no such bad Effects, as the Tories intended, and as some of our shortsighted Whiggs apprehended: so far otherwise that I see and hear every day, fresh Proofs that every Body is coming fast into every political Sentiment contained in them. I assure you I could mention compliments passed upon them: and if a serious Decision could be had upon them, the public Voice would be found in their Favour.

But I am distressed with Cares of another Kind. Your two Letters are never out of my Thoughts. I should have mounted my Horse this day for Braintree, if I had not hopes of hearing further from you in a Day or two.

However, I will hope that your Prospects are more agreable than they were, and that the Children are all better as well as the rest of the Family and the Neighbours. If I should hear more disagreable Advices from you I shall certainly come home, for I cannot leave you, in such Affliction, without endeavouring to lessen it, unless there was an absolute Necessity of my staying here, to do a Duty to the Public, which I think there is not.

I must beg to be excused my dear from hint[ing] any Thing for the future of public Persons or Things. Secrecy is so much exacted: But thus much I can say, that I never saw so serious and determined a Spirit.

I must also beseech you to be cautious what you write to me and by whom you send. Letters sent to the Care of Coll. Warren will come Safe.

My Regards with all proper Distinctions to my Relations and yours, my Friends and yours, my Acquaintances and yours.

This will go by Major Bayard, a Gentleman of the Presbyterian Perswasion in this City, of excellent Character to whom I am indebted for a great many Civilities.

RC (MHi). Adams, *Family Correspondence* (Butterfield), 1:291–92.

John Adams to William Sever

Dr sir Philadelphia Octr. 2. 1775

I do my self the Honour of writing to you[1] for the Sake of introducing to you Three Gentlemen, whose Characters and Embessy will render any private Introductions unnecessary. Dr Franklyn, Mr Lynch and Coll Harrison are a Committee from this Congress to consult the General and the Council of the Massachusetts, the Governors of Connecticutt and Rhode Island, and the President of the Congress of New Hampshire, upon Points of great Consequence, concerning the Army, which they will open to you.

We are in Hopes of News, every Day, from Genl. Schuyler and from Cambridge. The last Advices from England are rather alarming. But We expected no better. If Powder can be imported or Petre made, We need not dread their Malice. I am sir, with great Respect and Esteem your very huml sert John Adams

RC (MHi photostat).
[1] William Sever (1729–1809), Kingston, Mass., merchant, served briefly as president of the Massachusetts Council in July 1775. Shipton, *Harvard Graduates,* 11:575–78.

John Adams to James Warren

Dr sir Philadelphia Octr. 2. 1775

I believe you will have a surfeit of Letters from me, for they will be as inane, as they are numerous.

The Bearer of this is Major Bayard a Gentleman of this City of the Presbyterian Persuasion of the best Character and the clearest affections for his Country. I have received so many Civilities from him, that I could not refuse myself the Pleasure of introducing him to you.

Our obligations of Secrecy, are so braced up, that I must deny myself the Pleasure of Writing Particulars.[1] Not because some Letters have been intercepted, for notwithstanding the Versification of them, they have done good, tho they have made some People grin.

This I can Say with Confidence, that the Propriety and Necessity of the Plan of Politicks so hastily delineated in them is every day, more and more confessed, even by those Gentlemen who disapproved it at the Time when they were written.

Be assured, I never Saw, So Serious and determined a Spirit as I see now every day.

The high Spirited Measures you call for will assuredly come. Languid and disas[trous] Campaigns are agreable to Nobody.

Young Mr Lux desires his Compts to you and your Lady. He is vastly pleased with his Treatment both from you and her.

Remember me to her. I have Shocking Letters from her Friend at Braintree,[2] Such as have put my Phylosophy to the Tryal. I wait only for another Letter to determine, whether I shall come home.

RC (MHi). In Adams' hand, though not signed.
[1] It is not clear to what action Adams is referring. The journals record resolutions of secrecy adopted on May 11 and November 9, 1775. *JCC,* 2:22, 3:342–43.
[2] That is, Abigail Adams.

John Adams to John Winthrop

Dr sir Philadelphia Octr. 2. 1775

I do myself the Honour of writing you a very few Lines, just for the Sake of introducing to you, the Gentlemen who compose a Committee of this Congress, who are to consult with your Hon. Board,[1] about a Plan for continuing the Army.

I conjecture that the Reduction of the Pay of the private Soldiers, and the Introduction of Some Gentlemen from other Colonies, into the Service as officers will be principal objects.

The Pay of the Privates is generally, if not universally thought to be too high,[2] especially in Winter: but whether a Reduction of it would not give Such a Disgust as to endanger the Service, I dont know. If the War should continue, and the Pay is not reduced this Fall this Congress will certainly reduce it next Spring, and in a Way that will perhaps be dangerous, at least attended with many Inconveniences. This Way will be by each Colony furnishing its Quota of Men as well as Money.

The other Thing that is wished by many is not so reasonable. It is altogether absurd to Suppose, that the Council of Massachusetts should appoint Gentn. from the southern Colonies, when Connecticutt, Rhode Island and N. Hampshire do not. But it is idle to expect it of either.

The Council, if they are Men of Honour cannot appoint Gentlemen whom they dont know, to command Regiments or Companies in their service. Nor can they pay a Regard to any Recommendation of Strangers, to the Exclusion of Persons whom they know. Besides it is certain that the Massachusetts has Numbers of Gentlemen, who have no Command in the Army at all, and who would now be glad to get in, who. are better qualified, with knowledge both of Theory and Practice than any who can be had upon the Continent. They have been more in War, and longer in the study of it. Besides can it be Supposed that the private Men will be easy to be commanded by Strangers to the Exclusion of Gentlemen, whom they know being their Neighbours. It is moreover a Reflection, and would be a Disgrace upon that Province to send abroad for Commanders of their own Men, it would suppose that it had not Men fit for officers than which nothing can be further from the Truth.

But I must desist. We have heard nothing from the Comtee appointed to write to Us, as yet. Nor from that about Lead and Salt.

I pray you Sir that We may have the accounts and Vouchers sent Us, that our poor suffering Province may obtain a Reimbursement. I am, with great Respect &c

RC (MHi). In Adams' hand, though not signed.

[1] That is, the Massachusetts Council.
[2] On July 29, 1775, Congress had approved a monthly salary for privates of 6 2/3 dollars. *JCC*, 2:220.

Josiah Bartlett to Mary Bartlett

My Dear wife & family Philadelphia October 2nd 1775

I Can now with pleasure inform you that I have been Inoculated for the Small Pox and am almost Got well of it. I had it very favorable not above 20 Pock or thereabout Tho I was Confined by the fever to the House 5 or 6 Days. It is 4 weeks this Day Since I left Kingstown and have not heard from you Since I Saw you. I want very much to hear from you. Tho I know you have the Same almighty preserver in my absence as when I was with you So I Endeavor to rest Satisfied knowing that my uneasiness will Do you no Good. This is the fourth Letter I have Sent you Since I Left home and hope within a few Days I Shall Receive one from you. When I Shall Return I Can Give no better account than when I left you but as Soon as I Can you may be Sure I Shall Return with great pleasure. The Living in so Grand a City without the pleasure of a free Country air is not very agreable to me. I have nothing of Publick news more than you will See Duyly in the Publick papers and private affairs I may not Communicate. Gideon George is well.

Remember me to all my acquaintance.

You need be under no fear of the Small Pox by this Letter tho it would be very safe to hold all my Letters over the Smoke a Little before you handle them much as the Small Pox is very frequent in the City. I am &c Josiah Bartlett

RC (NhHi).

Eliphalet Dyer to Joseph Trumbull

Sr Philadelphia Octobr 2nd 1775

I receivd yours of the 21st of Septembr & Immediately returned an Answer by Fessenden an express. I have sent you several letters before by the Common posts but it seems you had not receivd them when you wrote yours of the 21st Ultmo but most probable they came to hand soon after. I do not at present see any prospect of your getting flower from this place. What they have sent has been taken by the Enemys Ships of Warr which discourages the Congress' permitting any more being Shipd, from hence that believe you must depend on Connecticutt & New York. But of this you will be more particularly advised by the Gentn. Viz Doctr Franklin Mr Lynch & Coll Harrison who are appointed a Comtee to attend the Genll at Cambridge and other G[eneral] Officers he shall think proper on many Important Matters. Govr Trumbull & Depty Govr Cook & the president of New Hampshire Convention are desired to be with them in Consultation. The Matter of providing the Army no doubt will be part of their deliberations. By the last accounts from England there appears no prospect of Concilliatory measures—but every thing looks rather hostile. We ought therefore to do the best & prepare for the worst. I want to hear how matters are like to goe with respect to my son, you wrote me there was some grumbling.[1] Indeed in this day I am Sensible I can take no one Step but I must meet with some plague & Trouble. Sometimes I think I have rather more than my share but I'll Indeavor to put on patience and Solace my self with a Consciousness that I am steadily Indeavouring to serve my Country to the best of my power. I had a hint in a letter that he was about returning home. You will Advise him I dare say to what you think best, consulting other Friends. Respects to Genll Putnam &c &c & am yours

Elipht Dyer

[*P.S.*] Majr Bayard from this City a Gentn of an Amiable Carracter is on a Visit to the Army. Your Notice & Civilitys to him will be most agreable. He may know I mentiond him in my letter as I Informd him I had.

RC (Ct).

[1] By general order of October 7, General Washington recognized Thomas Dyer's Connecticut commission as captain in the Thirty-fourth Regiment of Foot. Washington, *Writings* (Fitzpatrick), 4:20.

New Hampshire Delegates to Matthew Thornton

Sr. Philad 2d Octobr. 1775

Agreable to your desire, that we should write, as often as may be, have taken this early opportunity, tho' little or nothing to Communicate.

Before this Comes to hand, doubtless, you'll Receive [*a*] letter from our President desire'g your Attendance at head Quarters, to Consult with a Committee from this Congress, Relative to the Army.[1] Doctr. Franklin, Mr. Lynch and Colonal Harrison are the Committee.

We humbly beg leave here to Suggest whether it would not be [*a*] good oppertunity to mention the Convu[lse]d state of our Colony and the absolute Necessaty of Govermt. and also to forward by them a Petition from our Convention, to take government. We have Consulted many of the members on the Matter and as Soon as Colonal Bartlet is able to Attend the house (which will be in a few days, as he's almost well of the Small pox) shall Motion for leave to take the same government as Massachusetts Bay.[2]

You'll also give us leave to urge the forwarding of our Acct. Against the Continent, immediately, otherwise, there may not be money in the Continential Treasury as great Sums are dayly Drawing from thence; the Consequence of which will be, shall be obliged to wait for another emition.

There has nothing been Transacted in Congress as yet that we are at Liberty to Communicate. The Journals are not yet Printed, tho' ready for the press, but will be soon.[3]

You'll give us leave to Repeat our Desire that our Convention, or Committee of Safety will forward a Petition for government, seting forth the absolute Necessaty of it, the impossability of Taxg. without which is a thing that must be done, as it would Ruine us to be emitting paper on every Occasion. You'll pardon us throwg out these hints.

We are sr. your most [. . . .] Josiah Bartlett

John Langdon

RC (Nh-Ar). Written by Langdon and signed by Bartlett and Langdon.

[1] John Hancock to the New Hampshire Convention, September 30, 1775.

[2] Bartlett and Langdon put this question before Congress on October 18, and Congress appointed a committee to consider the issue on October 26, leading to the adoption on November 3 of a resolve "that it be recommended to the provincial Convention of New Hampshire, to call a full and free representation of the people, and that the representatives, if they think it necessary, establish such a form of government, as, in their judgment, will best produce the happiness of the people, and most effectually secure peace and good order in the province, during the continuance of the present dispute between G[reat] Britain and the colonies." *JCC,* 3:298, 307, 317, 319. New Hampshire's subsequent action in establishing a government is discussed in Jere R. Daniell, *Experiment in Republicanism, New Hampshire Politics and the American Revolution, 1741–1794* (Cambridge: Harvard University Press, 1970), pp. 108–12.

[3] Congress had directed that the journals be printed by order of September 27, although they did not actually appear until December. *JCC,* 3:264, 514.

Robert Treat Paine's Diary

[October 2, 1775]

Fair. Warm. Congress Sett at Lodge Hall, the State House being taken up by the Elections.[1]

MS (MHi).

Benjamin Harrison

[1] Provincial elections for county officials and representatives to the Pennsylvania Assembly were held this day. *Pennsylvania Journal; and the Weekly Advertiser*, October 4, 1775. Silas Deane also noted in his diary this day that Congress "met at the Lodge," as did John Zubly, who wrote, "Attended Congress at the Masons Lodge." *CHS Bulletin* 29 (July 1964) : 96A; and John Zubly's Diary, GHi.

Samuel Ward's Diary

Octr. 2d. [1775]

The above report[1] read again & referred to a Comee. of the whole congress to Morrow Morning. Instructions to Genl. Washington. Soldiers to be pd. by callender Months.

MS (RHi).

[1] That is, the report of the committee on trade. See *JCC*, 3:268–69.

Samuel Adams to Elbridge Gerry

Philada Octob 3 1775. Introduces the bearers, Maj. John Bayard and Lt. John Henry of Philadelphia, who are going to the American camp at Cambridge.[1] Also urges Gerry to "hasten with all convenient Speed our Colonys Account of Expenses."

RC (ViU).

[1] This day John Hancock also wrote a letter of introduction for Bayard and Henry addressed to Moses Gill, John Pitts, Elbridge Gerry, and Azor Orne. Facsimile RC, *Paul C. Richards Catalog*, no. 54 (1970), item 138.

Samuel Adams to James Warren

My dear Sir Philada. Octob 3 1775

I take the Liberty of recommending to your Notice Mr Bayard a worthy Inhabitant of this City who with his Friend Mr Henry intends to make a Visit to the American Camp. They are both honest Whigs, and as such I am sure they will be duly regarded by you.

This day Dr Franklin setts off for Cambridge, being deputed by the Congress in Conjunction with Mr Lynch of South Carolina and Coll Harrison of Virginia to consult with the General and some Gentlemen of the four New England Colonies concerning the most effectual Methods of continuing supporting and regulating the Continental Army. This Embassy I conjecture will be attended with great and good Consequences.

The Intelligence receivd by the July Packett which arrivd at New

York a few days ago, has convincd some, who could not be prevaild upon to believe it before, that it is folly to supplicate a Tyrant, and that under God, our own virtuous Efforts must save us. I hope, that our Troops will before long force their Way into Boston. If such a Design should be in Contemplation, I dare say you will encourage it to the utmost of your Power.

Mr Lynch is a Man of Sense and Virtue. Coll Harrisons Character may be drawn from his Confidential Letter publishd not long ago in Madam Drapers Gazette.[1] I hope these Gentlemen will be treated with all the Respect which is due to the publick Character they sustain. I mentiond to my valueable friend Coll Lee (Brother of my trusty Correspondent Dr Lee of London) his going upon this Embassy. Indeed he could not have been well spared from the Congress, and therefore I was the more easily satisfied with his Objection, which was the Want of Health. You would have been exceedingly pleasd with him.

In your Letter to Mr J A you promise to write to me. I shall be happy in receiving your Letters by every opportunity. If I am not much mistaken, a short time will afford you a delightful Subject to write upon. Our Army must not long remain inactive. They must improve the golden Season, before the Rebels can be reinforcd, which probably will be this fall.

We are expecting every Moment important News from General Schuyler. May God prosper our Designs in that Quarter.

I wish you would inform me, how Affairs are carried on in General Assembly. Adieu S A

RC (MHi).

[1] Harrison's intercepted letter to Washington of July 21, 1775, containing a spurious passage pertaining to a suggestive sexual incident, was printed in the *Massachusetts Gazette; and the Boston Weekly News-Letter,* August 17, 1775.

Silas Deane to Elizabeth Deane

My Dear Philadelphia Octo. 3d 1775

I wrote You Yesterday, per Col. Williams, but Col Harrison sitting out This Day, with Doct. Franklin, and Mr Lynch, for the Camp, he promised just to call, & tell You I was well.[1] I wish Your Father could see the Doctr., on his road or return, on Acct of the post Office, & other Matters which I think he well may, as these Gentlemen go to Lebanon. Suppose on the receipt of this, You sent a Lad to Your Father to meet them at that place, knowing first of them, when they will be There, which you may easily do. Pray let me know, when you propose to set out for This City, that I may be in readiness to meet You. I am my Dear your's Affectionately Silas Deane

[*P.S.* The] inclosed you will peruse & forward or Not [. . .] the Gentlemen shall direct.

RC (CtHi).
[1] According to his diary, Deane spent October 3d "at the Lodge AfterNoon at Committee." *CHS Bulletin* 29 (July 1964): 96A.

Benjamin Franklin to David Hartley?

Dear Sir, Philadelphia 3 October, 1775.

I wish as ardently as you can do for peace, and should rejoice exceedingly in coöperating with you[1] to that end. But every ship from Britain brings some intelligence of new measures that tend more and more to exasperate; and it seems to me, that until you have found by dear experience the reducing us by force impracticable, you will think of nothing fair and reasonable.

We have as yet resolved only on defensive measures. If you would recall your forces and stay at home, we should meditate nothing to injure you. A little time so given for cooling on both sides would have excellent effects. But you will goad and provoke us. You despise us too much; and you are insensible of the Italian adage, that there is no *little enemy*. I am persuaded that the body of the British people are our friends; but they are changeable, and by your lying gazettes may soon be made our enemies. Our respect for them will proportionably diminish, and I see clearly we are on the high road to mutual family hatred and detestation. A separation of course will be inevitable. It is a million of pities so fair a plan as we have hitherto been engaged in, for increasing strength and empire with public felicity, should be destroyed by the mangling hands of a few blundering ministers. It will not be destroyed; God will protect and prosper it, you will only exclude yourselves from any share in it. We hear, that more ships and troops are coming out. We know, that you may do us a great deal of mischief, and are determined to bear it patiently as long as we can. But, if you flatter yourselves with beating us into submission, you know neither the people nor the country. The Congress are still sitting, and will wait the result of their *last* petition. Yours, &c.

B. Franklin

MS not found; reprinted from Benjamin Franklin, *The Works of Benjamin Franklin . . .*, ed. Jared Sparks, 10 vols. (Boston: Hilliard, Gray, and Co., 1836–40), 8:161–62.
[1] Sparks printed this letter under the caption "To a Friend in England," noting that it was probably to Hartley. Although William Temple Franklin conjectured that it was written to Richard Price, Franklin's mention of Dr. Price in his letter to Joseph Priestley of this date strongly suggests that he was not the recipient.

Benjamin Franklin to Joseph Priestley

Dear Sir, Philadelphia, 3 October, 1775

I am to set out to-morrow for the camp,[1] and, having but just heard of this opportunity, can only write a line to say that I am well and hearty. Tell our dear good friend, Dr. Price, who sometimes has his doubts and despondencies about our firmness, that America is determined and unanimous; a very few Tories and placemen excepted, who will probably soon export themselves. Britain, at the expense of three millions, has killed one hundred and fifty Yankees this campaign, which is twenty thousand pounds a head; and at Bunker's Hill she gained a mile of ground, half of which she lost again by our taking post on Ploughed Hill. During the same time sixty thousand children have been born in America. From these *data* his mathematical head will easily calculate the time and expense necessary to kill us all, and conquer our whole territory. My sincere respects to ——, and to the club of honest whigs at ——. Adieu. I am ever yours most affectionately, B. Franklin

MS not found; reprinted from Benjamin Franklin, *The Works of Benjamin Franklin. . .*, ed. Jared Sparks, 10 vols. (Boston: Hilliard, Gray, and Co., 1836–40), 8:160–61.

[1] On September 30, Franklin had been appointed to the committee to go to camp at Cambridge to confer with General Washington. *JCC*, 3:266.

Benjamin Franklin to William Strahan

Philadelphia, October 3. 1775.

Since my Arrival here I have received Four Letters from you, the last dated August 2, all filled with your Reasonings and Persuasions, and Arguments and Intimidations on the Dispute between Britain & America, which are very well written, and if you have shewn them to your Friends the Ministers, I dare say, they have done you Credit. In Answer I can only say that I am too fully engaged in actual Business to write much; and I know your Opinions are not easily changed. You wish me to come over with Proposals of Accommodation. Your Ministers have made that impracticable for me, by prosecuting me with a frivolous Chancery Suit in the Name of Whately, by which, as my Sollicitor writes me, I shall certainly be imprisoned if I appear again in England. Nevertheless, send us over hither fair Proposals of Peace, if you choose it, and no body shall be more ready than myself to promote their Acceptation: For I make it a Rule not to mix personal Resentments with Public Business. They have voted me here 1000 Dollars per annum as Postmaster General, and I have devoted the whole Sum to the Assistance of such as have been disabled in the Defence of their Country, that I might not have, or be suspected to have the least interested Motive for keeping the Breach open. My Love to Mrs. Strahan and Peggy. I am ever Dear Sir, your affectionate humble Servant B. Franklin.

[*P.S.*] Present my respectful Compliments to my dear Friend Sir John Pringle; and to Mr. Cooper when you see him. I am to set out for the Camp tomorrow.

Tr (PRO: C.O. 5, 134).

John Hancock to George Washington

Sir Philadelphia Octor. 3d. 1775

The Congress have this Day order'd Three Hundred Thousand Dollars in Addition to the Seven Hundred Thousand to be Sent to the Paymaster for the use of the Army under your Command, which the Committee appointed to Confer with you have taken Charge of,[1] and of which I have inform'd the Pay Master General.

By order of Congress I inclose you several Resolutions enter'd into by them;[2] with respect to the severall matters mention'd in your Letter I must Refer you to the Committee of Congress who are instructed to Confer with you on the particular Subjects.

Should the Commissions Transmitted you by Fessenden not be sufficient, upon the first Notice I will forward the Number you Require.

I have the honour to be, Sir Your most obedt servt.

John Hancock Presidt.

RC (DLC).

[1] See *JCC,* 3:273.

[2] The resolutions in question were adopted by Congress October 2 and 3 and concerned the pay of Continental soldiers, the salting of provisions for the Continental Army, and the additional remuneration for Washington's forces in the event of an assault on Boston. *JCC,* 3:272–74.

Samuel Ward's Diary

Octr. 3rd. [1775]

Several Accts. allowed. Carbines & pistols sold to Comee of Safety.[1]

The Genl. may give to the Army 1 M[onth]s pay upon taking

[Boston?]. Commissy. Genl. to contract for such Quant. Beef & Pork as the Genl. thinks necessary & Salt it up at the Camp. 300000 Dollars to go by the Comee. to Paymaster Genl. Expences of the Comee. to be paid by Conti[nen]t. The Comee. to confer with Mr. Rittenhouse. Presented our Instructions for carrying on the War effectually & building an American fleet.[2]

MS (RHi).

[1] This day Congress authorized the sale to the Pennsylvania Committee of Safety of a number of arms which had been originally procured for the Hussar company whose formation Congress had approved in July and discountenanced in August 1775. *JCC*, 2:173, 238, 3:272–73.

[2] Ward presented Congress with instructions from the Rhode Island Assembly calling upon Ward and Hopkins to persuade their fellow delegates to undertake the construction of a Continental navy. *JCC*, 3:274–75.

John Adams' Notes of Debates

Oct. 3 [*i.e.* 4, 1775].[1]

Johnson. I should be for the Resolutions about Imports and Exports, standing, till further order.

I should be vs. giving up the Carriage. The Grower, the Farmer gets the same, let who will be the Exporter. But the Community does not. The Shipwright, Ropemaker, Hempgrower, all Shipbuilders, the Profits of the Merchant are all lost, if Foreigners are our sole Carriers, as well as Seamen, &c. I am for the Report standing, the Association standing.

J. Rutledge. The Question is whether We shall shut our Ports entirely, or adhere to the Association. The Res[olutions] we come to, ought to be final.

Lee. N. Carolina is absent. They are expected every Hour. We had better suspend a final Determination. I fear our determination to stop Trade, will not be effectual.

Willing. N.C. promised to put themselves in the same situation with other Colonies.[2] N. York have done the same. Our Gold is lok'd up, at present. We ought to be decisive. Interest is near and dear to Men. The Committee of Secrecy[3] find Difficulties. Merchants dare not trade.

Deane. Sumptuary Laws, or a Non Imp[ortation] were necessary, if We had not been oppressed. A N[on] Export was attended with Difficulty. My Colony could do as well as others. We should have acquiesced in an immediate Non Export. or a partial one. Many voted for it as an Object in Terrorem. Merchants, Mechanicks, Farmers, all call for an Establishment.

Whether We are to Trade with all Nations except B[ritain], Ireland and West Indies, or with one or two particular Nations, We cannot get ammunition without allowing some Exports, for The Merchant has neither Money nor Bills, and our Bills will not pass abroad.

R. R. Livingston. We should go into a full Discussion of the Subject. Every Gentleman ought to express his Sentiments. The 1st Q. is how far we shall adhere to our Association—What advantages we gain, What Disadvantages we suffer by it. An immediate Stoppage last year would have had a great Effect: But at that time the Country could not bear it. We are now out of Debt, nearly.

The high Price of Grain in B. will be an advantage to the Farmer. The Price of Labour is nearly equal in Europe. The Trade will be continued and G.B. will learn to look upon America as insignificant. If We export to B. and dont import, they must pay Us in Money. Of great Importance that We should import. We employ our Ships and Seamen. We have nothing to fear but Disunion among ourselves. What will disunite us, more than the Decay of all Business. The People will feel, and will say that Congress tax them and oppress them worse than Parliament.

Ammunition cannot be had unless We open our Ports. I am for doing away our Non Exportation Agreement entirely. I see many Advantages in leaving open the Ports, none in shutting them up. I should think the best way would be to open all our Ports. Let us declare all those Bonds illegal and void. What is to become of our Merchants, Farmers, Seamen, Tradesmen? What an Accession of Strength should We throw into the Hands of our Enemies, if We drive all our Seamen to them.

Lee. Is it proper that Non Export. Ag[reemen]t should continue. For the Interest of Americans to open our Ports to foreign Nations, that they should become our Carriers, and protect their own Vessells.

Johnson. Never had an Idea that We should shut out Export. Agreement closer than it is at present. If We leave it as it is, We shall get Powder by Way of N. York, the lower Counties and N. Carolina. In Winter our Merchants will venture out to foreign Nations. If Parliament should order our Ships to be seized, We may begin a Force in Part to protect our own Vessells, and invite Foreigners to come here and protect their own Trade.

J. Rutledge. We ought to postpone it, rather than not come to a decisive Resolution.

Lee. We shall be prevented from exporting if B[ritish] Power can do it. We ought to stop our own Exports, and invite foreign Nations to come and export our Goods for Us.

I am for opening our Exportations to foreigners farther than We have.

Willing. The Gents. favorite Plan is to induce foreigners to come here. Shall We act like the Dog in the Manger, not suffer N.Y. and the lower Counties and N. Carolina to export because We cant. We may get Salt and Ammunition by those Ports. Cant be for inviting foreigners to become our Carriers. Carriage is an amazing Revenue. Holland and England have derived their maritime Power from their Carriage. The Circulation of our Paper will stop, and [lose?] its Credit without Trade. 7 Millions of Dollars have been struck by the Continent and by the separate Colonies.

Lee. The End of Administration will be answered by the Gentns. Plan. Jealousies and Dissensions will arise and Disunion and Division. We shall become a Rope of Sand.

Zubly. The Q. should be whether the Export should be kept or not.

Chace. I am for adhering to the Association and think that We ought not to determine these Questions this day. Differ from R. Livingston, [*who holds that*] our Exports are to be relaxed except as to Tobacco and Lumber. This will produce a Disunion of the Colonies. The Advantage of cultivating Tobacco is very great. The Planters would complain. Their Negro females would be useless without raising tobacco.

That Country must grow rich that Exports more than they import. There ought not to be a partial Export to Great Britain. We affect the Revenue and the Remittance, by stopping our Exports. We have given a deadly Blow to B. and Ireland, by our Non Export. Their People must murmur, must starve. The Nation must have become Bankrupt before this day if We had ceased Exports at first. I look upon B., I. and W.I. as our Enemies, and would not trade with them, while at War.

We cant support the War and our Taxes, without Trade. Emissions of Paper cannot continue. I dread an Emission for another Campaign. We cant stand it without Trade.

I cant agree that N.Y., the lower Counties and N. Carolina, should carry on Trade. Upon giving a Bond, and making Oath, they may export. I am vs. these Colonies trading according to the restraining Act. It will produce Division. A few Weeks will put us all on a footing. N. York &c. are now all in Rebellion as the Ministry call it, as much as Mass. Bay.

We must trade with foreign Nations, at the Risque indeed. But We may export our Tobacco to France, Spain or any other foreign Nation. If We treat with foreign Nations, We should send to them as well as they to Us.

What Nation or Countries shall We trade with. Shall We go to there Ports and pay duties, and let them come here and pay none.

To say you will trade with all the World, deserves Consideration.

I have not absolutely discarded every Glimpse of a Hope of Reconciliation. Our Prospect is gloomy. I cant agree, that We shall not export our own Produce. We must treat with foreign Nations upon Trade. They must protect and support Us with their Fleets.

When you once offer your Trade to foreign Nations, away with all Hopes of Reconciliation.

E. Rutledge. Differs with all who think the Non Exportation should be broke, or that any Trade at all should be carried on.

When a Commodity is out of Port, the Master may carry it where he pleases.

My Colony will receive your Determination upon a general Non Export. The People will not be restless. Proposes a general Non Export, untill next Congress.

Our People will go into Manufactures, which is a Source of Riches to a Country. We can take our Men from Agriculture, and employ them in Manufactures.

Agriculture and Manufactures cannot be lost. Trade is precarious.

R. R. Livingston. Not convinced by any Argument. Thinks the exception of Tobacco and Lumber, would not produce Disunion. The Colonies affected can see the Principles, and their Virtue is such that they would not be disunited.

The Americans are their own Carriers now, chiefly. A few British Ships will be out of Employ.

I am vs. exporting Lumber. I grant that if We trade with other Nations, some of our Vessells will be seized and some taken. Carolina is cultivated by rich Planters—not so in the northern Colonies. The Planters can bear a Loss and see the Reason of it. The northern Colonies cant bear it.

Not in our Power to draw People from the Plough to Manufacturers.

We cant make Contracts for Powder, without opening our Ports. I am for exporting where B. will allow Us, to Britain itself. If We shut up our Ports, We drive our Sailors to Britain. The Army will be supplied, in all Events.

Lee makes a Motion for 2 Resolutions. The Trade of Virginia and Maryland may be stopped by a very small naval Force. N. Carolina is badly off. The Northern Colonies are more fortunate.

The Force of G.B. on the Water being exceedingly great, that of America, almost nothing—they may prevent allmost all our Trade, in our own Bottoms.

G.B. may exert every Nerve next Year, to send 15, 20, or even 30,000 Men to come here.

The Provisions of America are become necessary to several Nations. France is in Distress for them. Tumults and Attempts to destroy the Grain in the Year [*Ear*]. England has turned Arable into

Grass—France into Vines. Grain cant be got from Poland, nor across the Mediterranean. The Dissentions in Poland continue. Spain is at War with the Algerians, and must have Provisions. It would be much safer for them to carry our Provisions than for Us. We shall get necessary Manufacturers and Money and Powder.

This is only a temporary Expedient, at the present Time, and for a short Duration—to End when the War ends. I agree We must sell our Produce. Foreigners must come in 3 or 4 Months. The Risque We must pay, in the Price of our Produce. The Insurance must be deducted. Insurance would not be high to foreigners on account of the Novelty. It is no new Thing. The B. Cruizers will be the Danger.

MS (MHi). Adams, *Diary* (Butterfield), 2:188–92.

[1] Adams apparently misdated this entry, which pertains to debates when Congress was convened as a committee of the whole "to take into consideration the state of trade of these Colonies." Congress first sat as a committee of the whole for that purpose on October 4 and continued to do so intermittently until at least November 21. *JCC*, 3:268, 275–76, 291–93, 301, 307–8, 312, 361. But see also *JCC*, 3:314–15, 362–64, 455.

[2] Much of this debate concerned action to be taken with regard to allowing exports from the ports of New York, North Carolina, Georgia, and the Lower Counties (Delaware), which Parliament had not yet "closed" by the Restraining Acts of March-April, 1775. Merrill Jensen, *The Founding of a Nation, a History of the American Revolution, 1763–1776* (New York: Oxford University Press, 1968), pp. 649–50.

[3] The committee appointed September 18 "to contract and agree for the importation and delivery of . . . gunpowder." *JCC*, 2:253.

Samuel Ward's Diary

[October 4, 1775]

4th. Allowed a Vessel going to So. Carolina to carry certain Stores enumerated. Resolved into a Comee. upon the Trade of the Colonies. (Additional Instru[ctio]n to the Comee first Given.)[1]

Only 189467 Doll[ar]s ready of the 300000 yest[erda]y ordered.[2] Some Accts allowed, then went into a Comee. of the whole &c. Mr. Ward reported that the Comee. had taken into their Consideration &c and desired Leave to sett again to Morrow to take into their further Consid[eratio]n &c which was accordingly resolved.

MS (RHi).

[1] The additional instructions in question became the seventh article of the instructions given to the committee to confer with Washington and is so designated in the text of these instructions copied into the Hancock letterbook in PCC, item 12A, 1:9. See also *JCC*, 3:271, 276.

[2] See *JCC*, 3:275.

John Adams' Notes of Debates

Octr. 5. [1775]

Gadsden. I wish we may confine ourselves to one Point.[1] Let the Point be whether We shall shut up all our Ports, and be all on a footing. The Ministry will answer their End, if We let the Custom houses be open, in N.Y., N.C., the lower Counties and Georgia. They will divide us. One Colony will envy another, and be jealous. Mankind act by their feelings. Rice sold for £3—it wont sell now for 30s. We have rich and poor there as in other Colonies. We know that the excepted Colonies dont want to take Advantage of the others.

Zubly. Q. whether the Custom houses be stopped, and the Trade opened to all the World. The object is so great that I would not discuss it, on Horse back, riding Post haste. It requires the debate of a Week. We are lifting up a Rod—if you dont repeal the Acts, We will open our Ports.

Nations as well as Individuals are sometimes intoxicated. It is fair to give them Notice. If We give them Warning, they will take Warning. They will send Ships out. Whether they can stop our Trade, is the Question. N. England I leave out of the Question. N.Y. is stopped by one Ship. Philadelphia says her Trade is in the Power of the fleet. V[irginia] and Maryland, is within the Capes of Virginia. N. Carolina is accessible. Only one good Harbour, Cape Fear. In G[eorgia] We have several Harbours, but a small naval Force may oppose or destroy all the naval Force of Georgia.

The Navy can stop our Harbours and distress our Trade. Therefore it is impracticable, to open our Ports.

The Q. is whether we must have Trade or not. We cant do without Trade. We must have Trade. It is prudent not to put Virtue to too serious a Test. I would use American Virtue, as sparingly as possible lest We wear it out.

Are We sure one Cano will come to trade? Has any Merchant received a Letter from Abroad, that they will come. Very doubtfull and precarious whether any French or Spanish Vessell would be cleared out to America. It is a Breach of the Treaty of Peace. The Spaniards may be too lazy to come to America. They may be supplied from Sicily. It is precarious, and dilatory—extreamly dangerous —and pernicious.

I am clearly vs. any Proposition to open our Ports to all the World. It is not prudent to threaten.

The People of England will take it we design to break off, to separate. We have Friends in Eng. who have taken this up, upon virtuous Principles.

Lee. I will follow Mr. Gadsden and simplify the Proposition, and confine it to the Q. whether the Custom houses shall be shut? If they are open, the excepted Colonies may trade, others not, which will be unequal. The Consequence Jealousy, Division and Ruin. I would have all suffer equally. But We should have some Offices, set up, where Bond should be given that Supplies shall not go to our Enemies.

MS (MHi). Adams, *Diary* (Butterfield), 2:192–94.

[1] A continuation of the debate in the committee of the whole on "the state of the trade" of the colonies. *JCC*, 3:276.

John Adams to William Heath

Sir Philadelphia Octr. 5th. 1775

I never had the Pleasure of a Correspondence or any particular Acquaintance with you,[1] which can justify the Freedom I have taken of giving you this Trouble. But as the good of our Country, which I know is your first Consideration, is my Motive, I presume you will think it a Sufficient Apology.

In the present State of America, which is so novel and unexpected, and indeed unthought of by Numbers of Persons in every Colony, it is natural to expect Misapprehensions, Jealousies and Misrepresentations in Abundance: and it must be our Care to attend them, and if possible explain what is misunderstood and state truly what is misrepresented.

It is represented in this City, by Some Persons, and it makes an unfriendly Impression upon Some Minds, that in the Massachusetts Regiments, there are great Numbers of Boys, Old Men, and Negroes, Such as are unsuitable for the service, and therefore that the Continent is paying for a much greater Number of Men, than are fit for Action or any Service. I have endeavoured to the Utmost of my Power to rectify these Mistakes as I take them to be, and I hope with Some success, but still the Impression is not quite removed.

I would beg the favour of you therefore sir, to inform me whether there is any Truth at all in this Report, or not. It is natural to suppose there are some young Men and some old ones and some Negroes in the Service, but I should be glad to know if there are more of these in Proportion to the Massachusetts Regiments, than in those of Connecticutt, Rhode Island and New Hampshire, or even among the Rifle Men.

You may depend, Sir upon my Using the most prudent Caution in the Use of your Letter, and especially of your Name but I could certainly make a good Use of a Letter from you upon the Subject. Great Fault is likewise found in Several Parts of the Continent of the Massachusetts officers, whom I believe, taken on an average, and in Proportion to Numbers to be equal at least if not Superiour to any other Colony.

I must confess I had another View in giving you this Trouble which was to introduce to your Attention, Dr Franklin Mr Lynch and Coll Harrison, a Committee from this Congress to consult with the General and with the New England Colonies, concerning a Plan for future Armies. Mr Lynch is from S. Carolina, Coll Harrison from Virginia, both Gentn. of great Fortune, and respectable Characters, Men of Abilities and very Staunch Americans. Dr Franklyn needs no words of mine.[2] I am, sir, with great Respect, Your very humb servant

John Adams

RC (MHi).

[1] William Heath (1737–1814), Roxbury, Mass., farmer, representative to the Massachusetts General Court and provincial congress, and a major general in the state militia, had been appointed a brigadier general of the Continental Army in June 1775. *Appleton's Cyclopaedia of American Biography*.

[2] John Adams wrote a similar letter this day to Gen. John Thomas. "I presume to give you the trouble of this letter, for the sake of asking your attention to three gentlemen, a Committee of this Congress, who will have a desire to visit you as well as an inclination to see your lines at Roxbury. These gentlemen are Dr. Franklyn, Mr. Lynch of S. Carolina and Coll. Harrison of Virginia. . . . From England we hear of nothing but ministerial ill-will, desperation, and preparations for revenge. With the blessing of heaven, however, upon our endeavours I humbly hope and trust we shall, resist them with success. . . . Certain prejudices are propagated here by a few ill-affected persons in the City, that the Massachusetts forces contain a great number of old men, boys and negroes, more in proportion than the troops of the other Colonies." Extract in *Parke-Bernet Galleries Catalog*, no. 863 (April 21, 1947), pp. 1–2.

James Duane's Notes of Debates

[October 5? 1775][1]

Zubel's [Zubly's] argument.

Custom Houses ought to be shut.

Because it will put all the Colonies on a footing.

Inconveniences.

1st. If shut up Man of War will be our Custom house officer.

2d. No ship can be entered.

3d. All must be subject to seizure and confiscation.

4th. What will be the state of trade between the present time and the period fixed by the Resolutions?

5th. Between the period fixed and time of foreigner's arrival will take further time.

6th. When they arrive they are subject to seizure.

7th. They will then sell dear and buy cheap.

8. If we must trade with foreigners, it will be certain—nor quit costs—precarious pernicious.

9. It is in nature of a threat by which we have gained nothing hitherto.

Lee for preparation.

1. If exempted Colonies Trade as usual—others will be discontented, jealous— Ruin—must all be in the same situation.

1st. Decisive offense by opening ports.

2d. If treaty fails no consequence.

3th. Agent could not have answered—not knows sense of Cong.

4th. Might obtain assistance by sea.

5th. Necessity of winter supply in Virginia.

Tr (NN).

[1] John Adams' Notes of Debates for October 5 indicate that the remarks recorded here by Duane were probably made by Zubly and Lee on this date.

John Hancock to Nicholas Cooke

Sir Philada. Octr. 5. 1775.

The Congress having received certain intelligence of the sailing of two north Country built Brigs of no force from England on the 11 of August last loaded with 6000 stand of Arms and a large quantity of powder & other stores for Quebec without a convoy: and it being of importance if possible to intercept them, I am directed by Congress to desire you[1] with all possible expedition to dispatch the armed vessels of the Colony of Rhode Island on this service that the vessels you dispatch be supplied with a sufficient number of men, stores &c and particularly with oars: That you give the commander or commanders such instructions as are necessary as also proper encouragement to the marines & seamen that shall be sent on this enterprize, which instructions &c are to be delivered to the commander or commanders sealed up with orders not to open the same until out of sight of land on account of secresy.[2]

As there is also advice that a large quantity of Brass ordinance military stores & provisions are sending out to Boston, you are to give orders to seize all transports laden with ammunition cloathing or other stores for the use of the Ministerial Army or Navy in America; and that the said vessels with their cargoes when taken be secured in the most convenient places for the use of the Continent.

For the encouragement of the men employed in this service I am ordered to inform you that the Congress have resolved that the Master, Officers and Seamen shall be entitled to one half of the value of the prizes by them taken, the wages they receive from the Colony notwithstanding.[3]

The ships or vessels of war are to be on the Continental risque & pay during their being thus employed.

On this subject I have wrote to General Washington & desired him to dispatch one or more vessels from the Massachusetts Bay on this Service.

I have the honour to be, Sir Your most Obedt Servt.

John Hancock Presidt.

RC (MH). Written by Charles Thomson and signed by Hancock.

[1] Nicholas Cooke (d. 1782), Providence merchant, was at this time deputy governor of Rhode Island. Upon the ouster from office of loyalist Governor Joseph Wanton by the Rhode Island Assembly in October 1775, Cooke was elected to succeed him and continued to serve in this capacity through 1777. Matt B. Jones, ed., "Revolutionary Correspondence of Governor Nicholas Cooke, 1775–1781," *Proceedings of the American Antiquarian Society*, new ser. 36 (1926): 231–32.

[2] Cooke was unable to comply with Congress' request for assistance because one of the two armed vessels Rhode Island then had was on a return voyage to the province from Bermuda, while the other was unfit for sea duty. See Cooke's letters of October 10 to Washington and to the Rhode Island delegates. *Am. Archives*, 4th ser. 3:1007; and Ward, *Correspondence* (Knollenberg), pp. 98–99. Both British ships subsequently eluded American efforts to intercept them, and made their way safely to Quebec. Washington, *Writings* (Fitzpatrick), 4:23, 33–34, 152.

[3] See *JCC*, 3:279.

John Hancock to the Massachusetts Council

Gentlemen Philadelphia Octor. 5. 1775

It having been Represented to the Congress that you have in the Employ of the Colony of Massachusetts Bay Two Arm'd Vessells, and a particular Service being Recommended to General Washington, the Prosecution of which will require those Vessells, I am directed by the Congress to inform you that General Washington is Instructed to make application to you for those Vessells; and I am particularly Authorized to desire you will put said Vessells for this Service under the General's Command & Direction, and that you furnish him instantly with every Necessary in your power at the Expence of the Continent.[1]

And in case those arm'd Vessells cannot be Employ'd in this Service, you are earnestly requested to afford your utmost assistance in every matter that the General may have Occasion to apply to you upon in the prosecution of the publick service.

I have the Honour to be with Esteem Gentlemen Your most Obt. Hble Servt. John Hancock Prest.

N.B. The Vessell's to be on the Continental Risque and pay, during their being Employed in this Service.[2]

Tr (M-Ar).

[1] Massachusetts, contrary to Hancock's understanding of the situation, had no armed vessels at its disposal at this time. Washington therefore was obliged to make use of two armed schooners, under the commands of Captains Nicholson Broughton and John Selsam, which he had already had outfitted to intercept British supply ships bound for Boston. Washington, *Writings* (Fitzpatrick), 4:23–24, 33–34. For additional information about naval operations carried out under Washington's auspices, see William Bell Clark, *George Washington's Navy* (Baton Rouge: Louisiana State University Press, 1960), passim.

[2] This day Hancock sent a similar letter to Gov. Jonathan Trumbull of Connecticut. Ct. Trumbull ordered a ship to go to the assistance of Washington, but before setting sail it was judged to be unseaworthy and thus was kept from embarking on this mission. See Trumbull to John Hancock, October 17, 1775. *Am. Archives*, 4th ser. 3:1082.

John Hancock to William Palfrey

Dear Palfrey Philadelphia Octor. 5. 1775

This will be handed you by my Friend Coll Harrison of Virginia one of our Delegates, who with Docr Franklin & Mr Lynch are appointed a Committee by Congress to hold a Conference with General Washington, Govr Trumbull &c on Matters of importance. I Beg you would endeavour that they be Treated with the utmost Civility by our Provincial General officers, it will have a very good Effect, do promote this. I need not desire your particular Attention to Coll Harrison, many motives you have to induce you to that, now is your Oppory. to mention to him your Scituation,[1] I have Confer'd with him on the Subject, his Disposition is good, & if any opening he will Exert himself for you. I wrote you by Fessenden. I have this moment Rec'd your Letter by Mr. Tracey &c. I shall do every thing to gratify him & his Compa[ny].

Do write me often. I must Close, Refer you to Coll Harrison.

I am Your Friend John Hancock

[*P.S.*] Don't forget my Brother, mention him to Coll Harrison. I did not do it myself, but desire Harrison to mention him to the General. Don't forget.

RC (MH). Addressed: "To William Palfrey Esqr. Aid De Camp to General Lee at Cambridge."

[1] On Palfrey's "Scituation," see Hancock to Palfrey, September 25, 1775. See also Benjamin Harrison to Palfrey, September 20, 1775, note 1.

John Hancock to George Washington

Sir Philadelphia Octobr. 5th. 1775

The Congress having this day Rec'd certain Intelligence of the Sailing of Two North Country built Brigantines, of no Force, from England on the 11th. of August last, loaded with Six Thousand Stand of Arms, a large Quantity of Powder, & other Stores for Quebec, without Convoy, and as it is of great importance if possible to intercept them, I am order'd by the Congress to Give you this information, and to Desire you immediately to Apply to the Council of the Massachusetts Bay for the Two Arm'd Vessells in their Service, and Dispatch the same, with a sufficient Number of people, Stores &c particularly a Number of Oars in order if possible to intercept said Brigantines and their Cargoes, and secure the same for the Use of the Continent. It is also their Desire that you Give orders to the Commanders of the Vessells you Send on this Service to Seize and take any other Transports laden with Ammunition, Cloathing or other Stores for the Use of the Ministerial Army or Navy in America which they may meet with, & Secure them in the most convenient places for the use of the Continent.

That you Give the Commander or Commanders such instructions as are necessary, and also proper incouragements to the Marines and Seamen that shall be Sent on this Enterprize. That the instructions you shall Give be Deliver'd to the Commander or Commanders Sealed up, with Orders not to Open the same untill out of Sight of Land on Accott. of Secrecy. If the Vessells in the Service of Massachusetts Bay can be Readily obtain'd you are to Employ them, and others if you shall think necessary to Effect the purposes aforesaid; if they cannot, then you will Employ such as can be soonest fitted out. At the same time I am directed to inform you that the Rhode Island and Connecticutt Vessells of Force, if possible, will be directly sent after to the Assistance of those you Send out, for which purpose I write by order of Congress to those Governmts. by this Conveyance.

For the Encouragement of the Men employ'd in this Service, I am to inform you that the Congress have Determin'd that on this Occasion, the Master, Officers and Seamen shall be entitled to one half of the Value of the Prizes by them taken, the Wages they Receive from their respective Colonies notwithstanding.

It is further Resolved that the Ships or Vessells of War employ'd in this Service are to be on the Continental Risque and pay during their being thus Employ'd.

For further Intelligence I Refer you to the Inclos'd, which have not Time to Copy, as I am order'd to Dispatch the Express immediately.

I have the honour to be, Sir Your most Obedt hum Sevt.

John Hancock Presidt.

[*P.S.*] The Inclos'd please to order to be Del[ivere]d to the Council of Massa[chuset]ts Bay.

RC (DLC).

John Hancock to George Washington

Sir, 5 Octr. [17]75

By a very intelligent person just arrived from London[1] we have certain intelligence that a large number of Brass cannon from 24 to 4 pounders are preparing at the tower and were to be sent to Boston immediately, that 400 of the train of artilery were to be sent with them; that transports were taken up by Government to carry several regiments from Ireland to New York, that 17 of the transports lay at Deptford when he left England; that he expected they would sail from Ireland by the last of Septr.

The following is an extract from a person of credit in London[2] dated 31 July which came by the above gentleman.

"The plan of operation they have at present in ajitation or which I might properly say, actually determined on and transmitted to Boston is as follows.

"With the assistance of Govr. Tryon (who is much relied on for the purpose) to get immediate possession of New York & Albany—to fill both of these cities with very strong garrisons—to declare all Rebels who do not join the Kings forces—to command the Hudsons and East Rivers with a number of small men of war & cutters stationed in different parts of it, so as wholly to cut off all communication by water between New York and the provinces to the Northward of it & between New York & Albany except for the Kings Service and to prevent also all communication between the city of New York & the provinces of New Jersey, Pensylvania and those to the southward of them. By these means Administration & their friends fancy that they shall soon either starve out or retake the garrisons of Ticonderoga & Crown Point & open & maintain a safe intercourse & correspondence between Quebec Albany & New York & thereby afford the fairest opportunity to their Soldiery & the Canadians (In conjunction with the Indians to be procured by G.J.) [3]—to make continual irruptions into New Hampshire, Massachusetts Bay & Connecticut and so distract & divide the provincial forces as to render it easy for the British army at Boston to defeat them: but the spirits of the Massachusetts people depopulate their country & compel an absolute subjection to Great Britain. Another good effect to be deduced from this extensive plan, as government apprehend, is that as New York will by this method be prevented from supplying the Massachusetts army near Boston with flour &c. as they heretofore have done through the medium of Connecticut, And the New Jersey and Pensylvania people will not be able to transport provisions across the country, & the colony of Connecticut does not raise corn sufficient for the supply of herself and the Massachusetts bay, The inhabitants & troops of this province must inevitably of course be in a short time destroyed by diseases and famine and to this train of facts let me add; that in consequence of General Gage's desire brought by Captn. Chadds one hundred flat bottomed boats are at present building at Deptford in order to be sent immediately to America—but for what particular purpose I have not yet been able to learn. Many American gentlemen have however been lately asked by a Lord high in the American department, what sized vessels can go loaded from hence to Albany—what is the depth of water at the Overslaw (I think that is the name of the shallowest place in the North River)—whether the ship belonging to Albany in the London trade is alway obliged to unload part of her cargo before she can get to Albany and what proportion of it. Whether if batteries were erected at the highlands, they would not prevent vessels from going up & down the North River. And where would be the best places on that river to hinder the New Jersey people &c from sending flour &c in the winter through Connecticut to the Massachusetts bay. These are the proper operations to the northward. As to the southward—Commodore Shuldam is preparing with all expedition to go to Virginia at the earnest request of Lord Dunmore with a number of Frigates, Cutters &c which are to be employed in obstructing all communication by water inland between the Carolinas, Virginia, Maryland, Pensylvania & the northern Colonies and in order to keep the Virginians & Marylanders engaged at home and prevent their affording any assistance to New York or the Massachusetts Bay. Those frigates & cutters are to destroy the towns of Virginia & Maryland and spread devastation over the plantations bordering on the navigible rivers. Shuldam is also to detach some of his fleet to lie before Philada & Charles town S. C. and fire on these cities, if they afford the least assistance to the Massachusetts Bay."

There are several other letters which confirm the above and farther intimate the resolutions of Administration to take into pay 20,000 Hessians & Hanoverians. But as this must have the sanction of parliament it is apprehended they will not be sent out this fall.

The Gentlemen appointed to wait on you are to set out tomorrow Morning.

I am Your most obedt sert John Hancock Prest.

RC (DLC). Written by Charles Thomson and signed by Hancock.

[1] Capt. Thomas Read. See Samuel Ward's Diary this date, note 2.

[2] This day Congress received intelligence of intended British military and naval operations in the form of three letters from a London correspondent, two of them dated July 31 and the third August 7. The author and recipient of these letters remain unknown, although Samuel Ward's letter this day to his brother Henry clearly states that they were written to Benjamin Franklin. It seems equally clear, however, that the recipient was not a delegate, for Ward stated in his diary that the recipient asked to attend Congress. An ambiguous reference to the "inclosures in Dr. Shippens letter," which Richard Henry Lee mentioned in a letter to Washington three days later, suggests that William Shippen, Jr., may also have had a hand in transmitting copies of these or similar documents to the general. The letters are in *Am. Archives,* 4th ser. 3:1280–82. See Samuel Ward's Diary and Ward to Henry Ward, October 5; and Richard Henry Lee to George Washington, October 8, 1775.

[3] Guy Johnson, superintendent of Indian affairs for the northern department.

Virginia Delegates to the Williamsburg Committee of Safety

Gentlemen Philadelphia 5th Octr. 1775

The inclosed extracts from London letters yesterday laid before the Congress will sufficiently explain to you without a comment what extensive and destructive mischief is projected against our Colony with some others.[1] We have deemed it an incumbent duty to give you the earliest intelligence of our danger, that every possible precaution may be used to render the pernicious design abortive. The most effectual method of doing this, your wisdom will best determine, but it would seem a very important concern to leave undone nothing that can render us more secure from the further machinations of our inveterate, unprincipled, and (with respect to the situation & circumstances of Virginia) our well informed enemy Lord Dunmore. His influence with a most abandoned Ministry, his ardent zeal for the ruin of our Country, and his extensive acquaintance with the Colony certainly renders him an Object deserving particular care. We apprehend that Batteries placed on particular hights on James, York, & Rap. Rivers might greatly circumscribe this ruinous rogue, and it may be worthy of enquiry, whether the Cannon at Hampton, York & Williamsburg may not be removed for this purpose. It is said that near the mouth of Currotoman some good Cannon lay [buried?] in the Sand, which may be raised and placed to advantage on that river. We hope, from an insertion in Purdies Gazette, that our Colony powder is arrived, which, if true, will serve to furnish these Batteries, and we suppose Ball may be obtained from the Furnaces. There is no powder here that can possibly be spared, and the wicked activity, and power on the Sea of our enemies, renders it so essential and indispensable a duty on our Colony in particular to push the making of Salt Petre with unremitting diligence, that we earnestly entreat you will move the whole Colony most strongly on this point. All N. Am. expects it, and the safety of the whole does absolutely demand it; without this internal and essential security, the liberty & rights of America rest on doubtful ground. Perhaps, if a proper System of Look outs was formed by Colonies along the Bay, & from the mouths of the Rivers upwards, such quick notice of the appearance of warlike Vessels might be given as to enable the Inhabitants to guard against the evil, and in many instances to repel it with proper chastisement. It must certainly tend much to the public security if the Country could be prevailed on to execute the Patrol Law with diligence and attention, yet in such a manner as not to alarm the Slaves by too sudden a change from the late general intermission of this salutary regulation. We hope to be pardoned for these hints, and that they will be attributed to zeal for our Countrys good, and anxiety for its impending evils.

We have the honor to be with much esteem & regard Gentlemen:

FC (MH). Unsigned draft in the hand of Richard Henry Lee.

[1] These reports of intended British military operations included plans for sending naval forces to destroy towns and plantations along the Virginia coast. See preceding letter of John Hancock to George Washington, this date.

Samuel Ward's Diary

[October 5, 1775]

5th. Congress accord. to the Order of the Day went into a Comee. of the whole &c, after some Debate a Member produced a Number of Letters from England[1] which were read & Capt. Read[2] just arrived & the Gentn. to whom the letters were wrote desired to attend the Congress.[3] Expresses sent to Genl. Washington, Govr. Cooke & Govr. Trumbull to send out several Vessels to intercept two Transports with Powder &c. Encouragement given to the Men &c, the Vessels to go on the Service to be at the Risque of the Continent.

MS (RHi).

[1] Benjamin Franklin. See Ward to Henry Ward, this date.

[2] Thomas Read, captain of the *Aurora*, recently arrived from London, and brother of Delaware delegate George Read. Clark, *Naval Documents*, 2:314n.

[3] See John Hancock to George Washington, October 5, 1775, 2d letter, note 2.

Samuel Ward to Nicholas Cooke

Sir Philadelphia 5th. Octr. 1775

I laid that Part of your Honors Letter relative to the proposed Voyage and your first Letter upon the Same Subject before the Comee. of Secresy[1] & I am instructed to acquaint You That they approve of the Plan and in Behalf of the united Colonies agree to advance a sufficient Sum of continental Money to purchase sixty or eighty Tons of good Gun Powder as suits You best, to run the Risque of the Money & Powder the Persons intrusted behaving with Fidelity And to give the same Commissions & Freight which they give to other Persons for the like Service which you may rely upon to be a handsome Compensation for the Service. The Money shall be paid to your Order on Sight. The Committee make it a Rule when they advance Money[2] to take good Bonds for the faithful Performance of the Contract on the Part of those who receive it. Your Honor will be pleased to take such Bonds if you should advance the Money for the Voyage until we can replace it with continental Money; the Bonds must be made payable to Thomas Willing Benjamin Franklin Philip Livingston John Alsop Silas Dean John Dickinson John Langdon Thomas McKean & Samuel Ward Esqrs. in Trust for & to the Use of the thirteen united Colonies in North America. The Condition that the money shall be faithfully laid out in France for good Gunpowder upon the best Terms & delivered to the above Comee. for the use of the sd. united Colonies in some Part of the Colonies of Rhode Island or Connecticut the Danger of the Seas & Enemies excepted. If the whole Quantity of Gun Powder cannot be got the Comee. would have as much Salt Petre with a proportionate Quantity of Sulphur to manufacture with it purchased as will make up the proposed Quantity of Powder. The Bonds may specify that & also that if the Powder Salt Petre & Sulphur cannot be had as above directed that the Money shall be returned to the Comee. above sd.

The Comee. would have waited for your particular Terms upon which the Voyage should have been undertaken but thought it would occasion a Delay of several Weeks & possibly frustrate the Voyage, they therefore directed Me to propose to your Honor if hard Money or good Bills of Exchange can be got, immediately to procure the same & dispatch the Vessel as soon as possible.

It is expected that Provisions will be allowed to be exported to foreign Countries agreable to the non exportation Agreement, if so the Money may be laid out here in flour at a low Rate.

If the Voyage cannot be undertaken without the Moneys being first sent from hence or if any other unforseen Event retards it let Capt. Hopkins come here immediately or acquaint us with it in any other Way & every thing reasonable on our Parts shall be done to expedite the Voyage. I have the Honor to be in Behalf of the Committe of Secresy Sir Your most obedient humble Servant

Sam Ward

P.S. The Commee will if good firearms & Gunlocks are to be had at the Place proposed to go to advance the Money for two thousand stands of good Arms & five thousand good double bridled Gunlocks. Nothing of this matter ought to transpire save to the concerned if these last Articles are engaged for the Bonds must contain the Matter.

RC (MH).

[1] Neither of these letters from Cooke has been found, but they almost certainly relate to a plan for procuring gunpowder from Bayonne which he had proposed to Washington early in September, on which see *Am. Archives*, 4th ser. 3:682–83, 709–10. Whether the projected voyage to Bayonne was ever undertaken is uncertain.

[2] To judge from one surviving record of the committee's transactions, there is no indication that an advance was ever paid to Cooke for this proposed undertaking. See Secret Committee Account, September 27, 1775–August 26, 1776.

Samuel Ward to Henry Ward

Dear Brother Philadelphia 5th Octr. 1775

I wrote you this Morning by Post. Since that Time I have seen a Number of Letters from Gentlemen of Character in England to Doctor Franklin. The Master of the Ship a sensible Man (Bro[the]r to one of the Delegates of the lower Counties) I have also seen,[1] and the general Tenor of all the Letters and the Captain's Information is that the Ministry is determined at all Events to conquer America. The Dr. being asked whether his Intelligince was from Gentn. who had frequently corresponded with him & whether their Advices generally were found true, he answered that it was generally good: being asked whether he thought they were a sufficient Foundation for America to proceed upon he answered He thought they were & that We ought to take all possible Care of ourselves. He observed that it was not certain; for that upon the Arrival of the Petition the Ministry might think best to relax a little but it was by no means to be trusted to. We ought to be prepared for the worst: I hope every measure will be taken to put the Town of Providence into a further State of Defence & every Part of the Colony which can be made tenable. Poor Newport You know I have long been concerned for I wish they would secure all their most valuable Effects in the Country indeed I wish the Friends of their Country would move out of Town but if not let all their most valuable Effects be secured. A Number of Men of War are coming over, Troops are to be sent to New York & Virginia to be under the Command of Govrs. Tryon & Dunmore, they propose to take Possession of Albany & keep up a Communication with Canada by the North River & to keep Frigates and Cutters in the East River and all along the Coast. I may write again possibly but must conclude for I am greatly fatigued having been writing ever since Light save while at Breakfast or in Congress. Once more my dear Bror. adieu. Yours most affecy. Sam Ward

P.S. This News will have a more happy Effect for they will induce the most spirited Measures. I wish this Letter may be communicated saving Dr. Franklins Name and the Captains being Bror. &c which I would have communicated to no Person whatever. I wish the People of Newport may know my Sentiments but have not Time to write.

RC (RHi). Endorsed: "Nothing of this to be printed."

[1] See Ward's Diary this date, note 2.

John Adams' Notes of Debates

Octr. 6. [1775]

Chase. I dont think the Resolution goes far enough.[1] Ld. Dunmore has been many Months committing Hostilities vs. Virginia, and has extended his Piracies to Maryland. I wish he had been seized, by the Colony, Months ago. They would have received the Thanks of all North America.

Is it practicable now? Have the Committee any naval Force? This order will be a mere Piece of Paper. Is there a Power in the Committee to raise and pay a naval Force? Is it to be done at the Expence of the Continent. Have they Ships or Men.

Lee. I wish Congress would advise Virginia and Maryland to raise a Force by Sea to destroy Ld. Dunmores Power. He is fond of his Bottle and may be taken by Land, but ought to be taken at all Events.

Zubly. I am sorry to see the very threatening Condition that Virginia is likely to be in. I look on the Plan We heard of yesterday to be vile, abominable and infernal—but I am afraid it is practicable. Will these Mischiefs be prevented by seizing Dunmore. Seizing the K's Representatives will make a great Impression in England, and probably Things will be carried on afterwards with greater Rage.

I came here with 2 Views. One to secure the Rights of America. 2. A Reconciliation with G. Britain.

Dyer. They cant be more irritated at home than they are. They are bent upon our Destruction. Therefore that is no Argument vs. seizing them. Dunmore can do no [*more?*] Mischief in Virginia—his Connections in England are such that he may be exchanged to Advantage. Wentworth is gone to Boston. Franklyn is not dangerous. Pen is not. Eden is not.

Johnson. Dunmore a very bad Man. A defensive Conduct was determined on, in the Convention of Virginia. I am for leaving it to Virginia.

We ought not to lay down a rule in a Passion. I see less and less Prospect of a Reconciliation every day. But I would not render it impossible. If We should render it impossible, our Colony would take it into their own Hands and make Concessions inconsistent with the Rights of America. N.C., V., P., N. York, at least have strong Parties, each of them of that Mind. This would make a Disunion. Five or six Weeks will give Us the final Determination of the People of G. Britain. Not a Governor in the Continent has the real Power, but some have the Shadow of it. A Renunciation of all Connection with G.B. will be understood by a step of this Kind. 13 Colonies connected with G.B. in 16 Months have been brought to an Armed Opposition to the Claims of G.B. The line We have pursued has been the Line We ought to have pursued. If what we have done had been proposed two Years ago, 4 Colonies would not have been for it.

Suppose we had a dozen Crown Officers in our Possession. Have We determined what to do with them? Shall we hang them.

Lee. Those who apply general Reasons to this particular Case will draw improper Conclusions. Those Crown Officers who have advised his Lordship vs. his violent Measures, have been quarrell'd with by him.

Virginia is pierced in all Parts with navigable Waters. His Lordship knows all these Waters and the Plantations on them. Shuldam is coming to assist him in destroying these Plantations. We see his Influence with an abandoned Administration, is sufficient to obtain what he pleases.

If 6 Weeks may furnish decisive Information, the same Time may produce decisive destruction to Maryland and Virginia. Did We go fast enough when We suffered the Troops at Boston to fortify.

Zubly. This is a sudden Motion. The Motion was yesterday to apprehend Govr. Tryon. We have not yet conquered the Army or Navy of G.B. A Navy, consisting of a Cutter, rides triumphant in Virginia. There are Persons in America who wish to break off with G.B. A Proposal has been made to apply to France and Spain—before I agree to it, I will inform my Constituents. I apprehend the Man who should propose it would be torn to pieces like De Wit.

Wythe. It was from a Reverence for this Congress that the Convention of Virginia, neglected to arrest Lord Dunmore. It was not intended suddenly, to form a Precedent for Govr. Tryon. If Maryland have a Desire to have a Share in the Glory of seizing this Nobleman, let them have it.

The 1st. objection is the Impracticability of it. I dont say that it is practicable, but the attempt can do no harm.

From seizing Cloathing in Delaware, seizing the Transports &c., the Battles of Lexington, Charlestown, &c., every Man in Great Britain will be convinced by Ministry and Parliament that We are aiming at an Independency on G.B. Therefore We need not fear from this Step disaffecting our Friends in England. As to a Defection in the Colonies, I cant answer for Maryland, Pensylvania, &c. but I can for Virginia.

Johnson. I am not vs. allowing Liberty to arrest Ld. Dunmore—there is Evidence that the Scheme he is executing was recommended by himself. Maryland does not regard the Connection with G.B. as the first good.

Stone. If We signify to Virginia, that it will not be disagreable to us, if they secure Ld. Dunmore, that will be sufficient.

Lewis moves an Amendment, that it be recommended to the Council of Virginia, that they take such Measures to secure themselves, from the Practices of Lord Dunmore, either by seizing his Person, or otherwise as they think proper.

Hall. A Material Distinction between a peremptory order to the Council of Virginia, to seize his Lordship, and a Recommendation to take such Measures as they shall judge necessary, to defend themselves against his Measures.

Motion to export Produce for Powder.[2]

Sherman. I think We must have Powder, and We may send out Produce for Powder. But upon some Gentlemens Principles We must have a general Exportation.

Paine. From the observations some Gentlemen have made I think this Proposition of more Importance than it appeared at first. In Theory I could carry it further, even to Exportation and Importation to G.B. A large Continent cant Act upon Speculative Principles, but must be govern'd by Rules. Medicines, We must have—some Cloathing, &c. I wish We could enter upon the Question at large, and agree upon some System.

Chase. By the Resolution We may send to G.B., Ireland and W. Indies.

Lee. Suppose Provisions should be sold in Spain for Money, and Cash sent to England for Powder.

Duane. We must have Powder. I would send for Powder to London, or any where. We are undone if We hant Powder.

Dean. I hope the Words "Agreable to the Association" will be inserted. But I would import from G.B. Powder.

R. R. Livingston. We are between Hawk and Buzzard. We puzzle ourselves between the commercial and warlike opposition.

Rutledge. If Ammunition was to be had from England only, there would be W[eigh]t in the Gentlemans Arg[ument]. The Captn. Reed told us Yesterday that he might have bro't 1000 Blls. of Powder. Why? Because he was not searched. But if he had attempted to bring Powder, he would have been search'd. I would let the As-s[ociation] stand as it is, and order the Committee to export our Provisions consistent with it.

Lee. When a Vessell comes to England vs. our Association, she must be observed and watched. They would keep the Provisions, but not let us have the Powder.

Deane. I have not the most distant Idea of infringing the Association.

Duane. The Resolution with the Amendment amounts to nothing. The Committee may import now consistent with the Association. I apprehend that by breaking the Association We may import Powder, without it not. We must have Powder. We must fight our Battles in two or three Months, in every Colony.

J. Rutledge. They may export to any other Place and thence send Money to England.

New York Letter, concerning a Fortification on the high Lands, considered.[3]

Dyer. Cant say how far it would have been proper to have gone upon Romains Plan in the Spring, but thinks it too late now. There are Places upon that River, that might be thrown up in a few days, that would do. We must go upon some Plan that will be expeditious.

Lee. Romain says a less or more imperfect Plan would only be beginning a Strong hold for an Enemy.

Deane. An order went to N. York. They have employed an Engineer. The People and he agree in the Spot and the Plan. Unless We rescind the whole, We should go on. It ought to be done.

MS (MHi). Adams, *Diary* (Butterfield), 2:194–98.

[1] That is, the resolution of October 6 to recommend "to the several provincial Assemblies or Conventions, and councils or committees of safety, to arrest and secure every person in their respective colonies, whose going at large may, in their opinion, endanger the safety of the colony, or the liberties of America." *JCC*, 3:280.

[2] See *JCC*, 3:280.

[3] New York Committee of Safety to the Continental Congress, September 19, 1775. Bernard Romans, engineer and cartographer, had been engaged by the New York Provincial Congress to draw plans for fortifications on the Hudson River. His plans and specifications for the Highland defenses were enclosed in this letter to Congress. *Am. Archives*, 4th ser. 3:732–36, with the drawings following p. 736.

John Adams to Josiah Quincy

Dear Sir Octr. 6. 1775

Two days ago I had the Pleasure of yours of Septr. 22. I am very Sorry to learn from your Letter that you have occasion for any Advice of mine, and have not had an opportunity of take it. I fully intended to have made you a visit,[1] but my stay was so short and I had so many Engagements that it was out of my Power.

That a great Revolution, in the affairs of the World, is in the Womb of Providence, Seems to be intimated very Strongly, by many Circumstances: But it is no Pleasure to me to be employed in giving Birth to it. The Fatigue, and Anxiety, which attends it are too great. Happy the Man, who with a plentifull Fortune, an elegant Mind and an amiable Family, retires from the Noises, Dangers and confusions of it. However, by a Train of Circumstances, which I could neither foresee nor prevent, I have been called by Providence to take a larger share in active Life, during the Course of these Struggles, than is agreable either to my Health, my Fortune or my Inclination, and I go through it with more Alacrity and Chearfullness than I could have expected. I often envy the Silent Retreat of some of my Friends. But if We should so far succeed as to secure to Posterity the Blessings of a free Constitution, that alone will forever be considered by me as an ample Compensation for all the Care, Fatigue, and Loss that I may sustain in the Conflict.

I am much obliged by your kind Explanation of your opinion that the Harbour might be locked up. I must confess, altho I was born so near it, I never before understood the Course of the Channell, and the Situation of the Harbour so well. I have carefully compared your Descriptions of Squantum, the Moon, Long Island, Gallops Island, Lovells Island, and Georges, the Narrows and Nantaskett Road, with "A Plan of the Town and Chart of the Harbour of Boston, exhibiting a View of the Islands, Castle, Fort, and Entrances into the Said Harbour, which was published in London, last February." This Plan I know to be inaccurate in some Particulars, and the Chart may be so in others: but by the best Judgment I can make, upon comparing your Facts with the Chart, and considering the Depths of Water marked on this Chart, I think it extreamly probable, with you that nothing but Powder and Cannon are wanting, to effect the important Purposes you mention, that of making Soldiers and Sailors Prisoners at Discretion.

Dr Franklyns Row Gallies are in great Forwardness. Seven of them are compleated, manned, armed &c. I went down the River the other Day with all of them.[2] I have as much Confidence in them as you have. But the People here have made what some call Chevaux De Frise & others Vesseaux de Frise, Machines to be sunk in the

Channell of Delaware River. Three Rows of them, are phased in the River, with large Timbers barbed with Iron. They are frames of Timber Sunk with stone Machines very proper, for our Channell in the Narrows[. . . .][3]

RC (MHi). In Adams' hand, though not signed. Recipient identified through Quincy's September 22 letter to Adams discussing the defense of Boston harbor, the chief topic of Adams' response. Josiah Quincy to John Adams, September 22, 1775, MHi.

[1] Josiah Quincy (1710–84), merchant, gentleman farmer, and local political leader in Braintree, Mass. Shipton, *Harvard Graduates*, 8:463–75.

[2] See John Adams' Diary, September 28, 1775.

[3] Although the remainder of the MS is missing, an extract from the two missing pages was printed in an 1894 dealer's catalog. "We have favourable accounts from Schuyler. He will have the Province of Canada.

"Our accounts from England breath nothing but war and revenge. What pains and expense, and misery that stupid people will endure for the sake of driving the Colonies to the necessity of a separation, and of alienating their best friends." *William E. Benjamin Catalog*, no. 60 (April 1894), p. 18.

Robert Treat Paine's Diary

Fair. Comittee set off for the Camp.[1] [October 6, 1775]

MS (MHi).

[1] That is, the committee of Congress appointed on September 29 "to repair immediately to the camp at Cambridge" to consult with General Washington and New England leaders. *JCC*, 3:265. Although Franklin reported to Joseph Priestley on October 3 that he was "to set out to-morrow," and Christopher Marshall noted in his diary entry of October 4 that "this afternoon . . . three of the delegates, set out for Boston," Hancock wrote to Washington on October 5 that the committee was "to set out tomorrow Morning." Benjamin Franklin to Joseph Priestley, October 3, 1775; Christopher Marshall, *Extracts from the Diary of Christopher Marshall, Kept in Philadelphia and Lancaster during the American Revolution, 1774–17781*, ed. William Duane (Albany: Joel Munsell, 1877), p. 44: and John Hancock to George Washington, October 5, 1775, 2d letter. Apparently Paine's testimony can be relied upon, although Silas Deane, adding to the confusion, wrote in his misdated diary entry for Saturday, October 7: "Saturday Octo. 6th. at Congress. Messrs Franklin &c sat out on Journey." *CHS Bulletin* 29 (July 1964): 96A.

Samuel Ward's Diary

[October 6, 1775]

6th. Letters from Gens. Schuyler & Montgomery. £20000 Pena. Currency in silver or Gold to be got for contin[enta]l Money for the Canada Expedn. Recomd. to provincial Assemblies & Conventions [*and*] Comees. of Safety to arrest & secure such Persons whose going at large may endanger such Colonies or the Liber[t]y of America. (This to be transmitted.) Comee. for Importation of Pow[de]r to export agreable to the continental Association as much Provisions or other Produce of these Colonies as they shall judge expedient for the Purchase of Arms & Ammunition. A Comee. appointed to consider of the Fortifications ordered to be erected on Hudsons River. Farther Report of the Comee. for concerting a Plan for intercepting certain [*vessels*] read. Ordered that the Congress[1] resolved into a Comee. of the whole to take into their Consideration the State of the Trade. Consideration of the Instructions to the Delegates of Rhod Isd. put off to tomorrow.

MS (RHi).

[1] Ward inserted the preceding four words above the line after he had originally completed the sentence but subsequently neglected to change "resolved" from the past tense.

John Adams' Notes of Debates

Octr. 7. [1775]

Chase. It is the maddest Idea in the World, to think of building an American Fleet.[1] Its Latitude is wonderfull. We should mortgage the whole Continent. Recollect the Intelligence on your Table—defend N. York—fortify upon Hudsons River.

We should provide for gaining Intelligence—two swift sailing Vessells.

Dyer. The Affair of Powder from N. York should be referr'd to the Committee.

Hopkins. No Objection to putting off the Instruction from Rhode Island, provided it is to a future day.[2]

Paine. Seconds Chace's Motion, that it be put off to a future day Sine die.

Chace. The Gentleman from Maryland never made such a Motion. I never used the Copulative. The Gentleman is very sarcastic, and thinks himself very sensible.

Zubly. If the Plans of some Gentlemen are to take Place, an American Fleet must be a Part of it—extravagant as it is.

Randolph moves that all the orders of the day should be read every Morning.

Deane. I wish it may be seriously debated. I dont think it romantic, at all.

J. Rutledge. Move that some Gentn. be appointed to prepare a Plan and Estimate of an American Fleet.

Zubly seconds the Motion.

Gadsden. I am against the Extensiveness of the Rhode Island Plan, but it is absolutely necessary that some Plan of Defence by Sea should be adopted.

J. Rutledge. I shall not form a conclusive opinion till I hear the Arguments. I want to know how many Ships are to be built and what they will cost.

S. Adams. The Committee cant make an Estimate untill they know how many Ships are to be built.

Zubly. Rhode Island has taken the lead. I move that the Delegates of R.I. prepare a Plan, give us their opinion.

J. Adams. The Motion is entirely out of order. The Subject is put off for a Week, and now a Motion is to appoint a Committee to consider the whole subject.

Zubly, Rutledge, Paine, Gadsden, lightly skirmishing.

Deane. It is like the Man that was appointed to tell the Dream and the Interpretation of it. The Expence is to be estimated, without knowing what Fleet there shall be, or whether any att all.

Gadsden. The design is to throw it into Ridicule. It should be considered out of Respect to the Colony of R. Island who desired it.

Determined against the appointment of a Committee.[3]

Report of the Committee for fortifying upon Hudsons River considered.[4]

J. Rutledge. I think We should add to the Report, that they take the most effectual Measures to obstruct the Navigation of Hudsons River by Booms or otherwise.

Gadsden seconds the Motion.

Deane doubts the Practicability of obstructing it with Booms, it is so wide.

The Committee said 4 or 5 Booms chained together, and ready to be drawn across, would stop the Passage.

The Congress of N.Y. is to consult the Assembly of Connecticutt and the Congress of N. Jersey, the best Method of taking Posts and making Signals, and assembling Forces for Defence of the River.

Gadsden. Moves that all the Letters, laid before us from England, should be sent to the Convention of N. York. Tryon is a dangerous Man, and the Convention of that Colony should be upon their guard.

Lee. I think the Letters should by all means be sent.

Rutledge. Dr. F. desired they might not be printed. Moves that Gen. Wooster with his Troops may be ordered down to N. York.[5]

Duane. Moves that Woosters Men may be employed in building the Fortifications.

Dyer 2ds the Motion allowing the Men what is usual.

Sherman. Would have the order conditional, if Schuyler dont want them. Understands that N.Y. has the best Militia upon the Continent.

R. Livingston. They will be necessary at the Highlands.

Dyer thinks they ought to have the usual allowance for Work.

S. Adams. Understands that the Works at Cambridge was done without any Allowance, but that G[eneral] W[ashington] has ordered that for future works they be allowed half a Pistareen a day.

Langdon would not have the order to Wooster, but to Schuyler for he would not run any risque of the northern Expedition.

Rutledge thinks Schuyler cant want them. He waited only for Boats to send 500 Men more.

Sherman. Would it not be well to inform Schuyler of our endeavours to take the Transports and desire him to acquaint Coll. Arnold of it.

Rutledge. He may cooperate with Arnold in taking the Transports. I hope he is in Possession of Montreal before now.

Deane. I wish that whatever Money is collected, may be sent along to Schuyler.

E. Rutledge. We have been represented as beggarly fellows, and the first Impressions are the strongest. If We eat their Provisions and dont pay, it will make a bad Impression.

Ross. Produces a Resolve of the Assembly of Pensylvania that their Delegates lay the Connecticutt Intrusion before Congress, that something may be done to quiet the Minds.[6]

J. Rutledge moves that the Papers be referr'd to the Delegates of the two Colonies.

Willing. Thinks them Parties and that they must have an Umpire.

Sherman. Thinks they may agree on a temporary Line.

Lee. Moves that Parliamentary or ministerial Post may be stopp'd, as a constitutional Post is now established from N.H. to G.[7]

Langdon 2d[s] the Motion.

Willing. Thinks it is interfering with that Line of Conduct which we have hitherto prescribed to ourselves—it is going back beyond the Year 1763.

Lee. When the Ministry are mutilating our Correspondence in England, and our Enemies here are corresponding for our ruin, shall We not stop the ministerial Post.

Willing. Looks upon this to be one of the offensive Measures which are improper at this Time—it will be time enough to throw this aside when the Time comes that we shall throw every Thing aside—at present We dont know but there may be a Negociation.

Dyer. We have already superceeded the Act of Parliament effectually.

Deane is for a Recommendation to the People to write by the constitutional Post, not forbid a Man to ride.

S. Adams thinks it a defensive Measure, and advising People not to write by it, looks too cunning for me. I am for stopping the Correspondence of our Enemies.

Langdon. Administration are taking every Method to come at our Intentions, why should not we prevent it.

Duane. I shall vote vs. it. It may be true that We are come to the Time when We are to lay aside all. I think there should be a full Representation of the Colonies. N.C. should be here.

Deane 2d[s] the Motion for postponing it.

Zubly. The Necessity of this Measure does not appear to me. If We have gone beyond the Line of 1763 and of defence without apparent Necessity it was wrong, if with Necessity right. I look upon the Invasion of Canada a very different Thing. I have a Right to defend myself vs. Persons who come vs. me, let em come from whence they will. We in G. have gain[ed] Intelligence by the K's Post that We could not have got any other Way. Some Gentlemen think all Merit lies in violent and unnecessary Measures.

S. Adams. The Gentlemans Argument would prove that We should let the Post go into Boston.

Moreton. Would not this stop the Packett. Would it not be ordered to Boston. Does the Packett bring any Intelligence to Us that is of Use?

Lee. No Intelligence comes to Us, but constant Intelligence to our Enemies.

Stone. Thinks it an innocent Motion, but is for postponing it, because he is not at present clear. He thinks that the setting up a new Post has already put down the old one.

Paine. My opinion was that the Ministerial Post will die a natural death. It has been under a Languishment a great while. It would be Cowardice to issue a Decree to kill that which is dying. It brought but one Letter last time, and was obliged to retail Newspapers, to bear its Expences. I am very loath to say that this Post shall not pass.

Lee. Is there not a Doctor Ld. North who can keep this Creature alive.

R. R. Livingstone. I don't think that Tory Letters are sent by the Royal Post. I consider it rather as a Convenience than otherwise. We hear 5 times a Week from N.Y.

The Letters upon our Table advise us to adopt every conciliatory Measure, that we may secure the Affections of the People of England.

MS (MHi). Adams, *Diary* (Butterfield), 2:198–202.

[1] Although these debates of October 7 represent the earliest formal discussion of the proposal to create an American navy, an issue in which he was greatly interested, Adams did not record his own views in these notes of debates. But in a letter to James Warren this day he outlined his plans to open the ports of America and establish a naval defense, and years later, when writing his auto-

biography, he reviewed in detail the growth of Congress' interest in naval affairs during October and November 1775. See John Adams to James Warren, October 7, 1775; and Adams, *Diary* (Butterfield), 3:342–50.

[2] For the text of the Rhode Island proposal for an American fleet, see *JCC*, 3:274.

[3] Congress this day "deferred" consideration of the subject until October 16 and subsequently postponed further debate until December 11. *JCC*, 3:281, 420.

[4] The committee's report, as adopted, is in *JCC*, 3:281–82.

[5] See *JCC*, 3:282–83.

[6] See *JCC*, 3:283. For further explication of the Wyoming Valley controversy, see Silas Deane to Thomas Mumford, October 15, 1775.

[7] The journals do not record a separate discussion on this subject this day. *JCC*, 3:281–83.

John Adams to Abigail Adams

My dear Philadelphia Octr. 7th. 1775

Yesterday, by the Post, I received yours of Septr. 25th., and it renewed a Grief and Anxiety, that was before almost removed from my Mind. Two days before I had the Pleasure of a very valuable Letter from Coll. Quincy, in which he kindly informed me that you and Our Family were so much better that you and my dear Nabby, had made a Visit at his House: and Mr. Williams, who brought the Letter acquainted me that he had been to Braintree after the Date of it, that you was in good Spirits, that Tommy was so much better as to be playing abroad, and that he hoped Patty was not dangerous: you will easily believe that this Information gave me great Pleasure and fine Spirits: It really relieved me from a heavy Load: But your last Letter has revived my Concern. I will still hope however that your excellent Mother will yet be spared for a Blessing to her Family and an Example to the World.[1] I build my Hopes of her Recovery, upon the Advantage of a Constitution which has hitherto sustained so many Attacks and upon a long Course of exact Temperance which I hope has deprived the Distemper of its most dangerous food and Fuel. However, our Lives are not in our own Power. It is our Duty to submit. "The Ways of Heaven are dark and intricate." Its designs are often inscrutable, But are always wise and just and good.

It was long before I had the least Intimation of the Distress of the Family, and I fear, that your not receiving so many Letters from me as usual may have been one Cause of Infelicity to you. Really, my dear, I have been more cautious than I used to be. It is not easy to know whom to trust, in these times, and if a Letter from any Person in the situation I am in, can be laid hold of, there are so many Lies made and told about it, so many false Copies taken and dispersed, and so many false Constructions put, that one ought to be cautious.

The Situation of Things, is so alarming, that it is our Duty to prepare our Minds and Hearts for every Event, even the Worst. From my earliest Entrance into Life, I have been engaged in the public Cause of America: and from first to last I have had upon my Mind, a strong Impression, that Things would be wrought up to their present Crisis. I saw from the Beginning that the Controversy was of such a Nature that it never would be settled, and every day convinces me more and more. This has been the source of all the Disquietude of my Life. It has lain down and rose up with me these twelve Years. The Thought that we might be driven to the sad Necessity of breaking our Connection with G.B. exclusive of the Carnage and Destruction which it was easy to see must attend the separation, always gave me a great deal of Grief. And even now, I would chearfully retire from public life forever, renounce all Chance for Profits or Honours from the public, nay I would chearfully contribute my little Property to obtain Peace and Liberty. But all these must go and my Life too before I can surrender the Right of my Country to a free Constitution. I dare not consent to it. I should be the most miserable of Mortals ever after, whatever Honours or Emoluments might surround me.

RC (MHi). Adams, *Family Correspondence* (Butterfield), 1:294–96.
[1] Elizabeth Quincy Smith died on October 1. Ibid, pp. 293–94.

John Adams to James Warren

Dr sir Philadelphia Octr. 7th. 1775

The Debates, and Deliberations in Congress are impenetrable Secrets: but the Conversations in the City, and the Chatt of the Coffee house, are free, and open. Indeed I wish We were at Liberty to write freely and Speak openly upon every Subject, for their is frequently as much Knowledge derived from Conversations and Correspondence, as from Solemn public Debates.

A more intricate and complicated Subject never came into any Mans thoughts, than the Trade of America.[1] The Questions that arise, when one thinks of it, are very numerous.

If The Thirteen united Colonies Should immediately Surcease all Trade with every Part of the World, what would be the Consequence? In what manner, and to what degree, and how Soon, would it affect, the other Parts of the World? How would it affect G. B., Ireland, the English West India Islands, the French, the Dutch, the Danish, the Spanish West India Islands? How would it affect the Spanish Empire on the Continent? How would it affect the Brazills and Portuguese Settlements in America? If it is certain that it would distress Multitudes in these Countries, does it therefore follow that it would induce any foreign Court to offer Us Assistance, and to ask us for our Trade or any Part of it? If it is questionable whether foreign States would venture upon Such Steps, which would perhaps be Violations of Treaties of Peace, and certainly would light up a War in Europe, is it certain that Smugglers, by whom I mean private Adventurers belonging to foreign Nations, would come here, through all the Hazards they must run. Could they be suffered to clear out for America in their own Custom houses? Would they not run the risque of Seizure from their own Custom house officers, or of Capture from their own Men of War? Would they not be liable to be visited by British Men of War, in any Part of the ocean, and if found to have no Clearances be seized? When they arrive on any Part of the Coast of N. America, would they not be seized by Brittish Cutters, Cruizers, Tenders, Frigates without Number: [But] if their good Fortune should escape all these Risques, have We harbours or Rivers, sufficiently fortified, to insure them Security while here? In their Return to their own Country would they not have the Same Gauntlett to run.

In Short, if We stop our own ships, have We even a Probability that the ships of foreign Nations, will run the Venture to come here, either with or without the Countenance and Encouragement of their Severall Courts or States public or private open or secret? It is not easy for any Man precisely and certainly to answer this Question. We must then say all this is uncertain.

Suppose then We assume an intrepid Countenance, and Send Ambassadors at once to foreign Courts. What Nation shall We court? Shall We go to the Court of France, or the Court of Spain, to the States General of the United Provinces? to the Court of Lisbon, to the Court of Prussia, or Russia, or Turkey, or Denmark, or where, to any, one, more, or all of these? If We Should is there a Probability, that Our Ambassadors would be received, or so much as heard or seen by any Man or Woman in Power at any of these Courts. He might possibly, if well skill'd in intrigue, his Pocketts well filled with Money and his Person Robust and elegant enough, get introduced to some of the Misses, and Courtezans in keeping of the Statesmen in France, but wd not that be all.

An offer of the Sovereignty of this Country to France or Spain would be listened to no doubt by Either of those Courts, but We should Suffer any Thing before We shd offer this. What then can We offer? An Alliance, a Treaty of Commerce? What Security could they have that We should keep it. Would they not reason thus. These People intend to make Use of Us to establish an Independency but the Moment they have done it: Britain will make Peace with them, and leave Us in the Lurch and We have more to dread from an alliance Between Britain and the United Colonies as an independent state, than We have now they are under one corrupted Administration. Would not Spain reason in the Same manner, and say further, our Dominions in South America will be soon a Prey to these Enterprizing and warlike Americans, the Moment they are an independent State. Would not our Proposals and Agents be treated with Contempt! And if our Proposals were made and rejected, would not this sink the Spirits of our own People, Elevate our Enemies and disgrace Us in Europe.

If then, it will not be Safe to Stop our own Ships entirely, and trust to foreign Vessells coming here either with or without Convoy of Men of War, belonging to foreign States, what is to be done? Can our own People bear a total Cessation of Commerce? Will not Such Numbers be thrown out of Employment, and deprived of their Bread, as to make a large discontented Party? Will not the Burthen of supporting these Numbers, be too heavy upon the other Part of the Community? Shall We be able to maintain the War, wholly without Trade? Can We support the Credit of our Currency, without it?

If We must have Trade how Shall We obtain it?

There is one Plan, which alone, as it has ever appeared to me, will answer the End in some Degree, at first. But this is attended with So many Dangers to all Vessells, certain Loss to many, and So much Uncertainty upon the whole, that it is enough to make any Man, thoughtfull. Indeed it is looked upon So wild, extravagant and romantic, that a Man must have a great deal of Courage, and much Indifference to common Censure, who should dare to propose it.

"God helps those who help themselves," and it has ever appeared to me since this unhappy Dispute began, that We had no Friend upon Earth to depend on but the Resources of our own Country, and the good sense and great Virtues of our People. We shall finally be obligd to depend upon ourselves.

Our Country furnished a vast abundance of materials for Commerce. Foreign Nations have great Demands for them. If We should publish an Invitation to any one Nation or more, or to all Nations, to send their ships here, and let our Merchants inform theirs that We have Harbours where the Vessells can lie in Safety, I conjecture that many private foreign Adventurers would find Ways to send Cargoes here thro all the Risques without Convoys. At the Same Time our own Merchants would venture out with their Vessells and Cargoes, especially in Winter, and would run thro many Dangers, and in both these Ways together, I should hope We might be supplied with Necessaries.

All this however Supposes that We fortify and defend our own Harbours and Rivers. We may begin to do this. We may build Row Gallies, flatt bottomed Boats, floating Batteries, Whale Boats, Vesseaux de Frize, nay Ships of War, how many, and how large I cant Say. To talk of coping Suddenly with G. B. at Sea would be Quixotism indeed. But the only Question with me is can We defend our Harbours and Rivers? If We can We can trade.[2]

RC (MHi). In Adams' hand, though not signed.

[1] Adams' later recollections of the debates on this subject are in his autobiography. Adams, *Diary* (Butterfield), 3:327–29.

[2] It is unclear whether the letter ended here or part of the MS is missing.

Samuel Adams to James Warren

Dear sir, Philade Octob 7 1775

Yesterday Capt Read arrivd here from London which place he left the 5th of August and Falmouth the 11th. He brings Advice that there is not the least Appearance of a Relaxation of ministerial Measures—That the ——— speaks of them with the utmost Satisfaction—that 2000 Troops are raising to be sent to America immediately, either to Boston or New York. The Parliament is to meet in November when a Bill will be brought in to enable our most gracious Sovereign to send for & employ 16000 Hessians, to subdue his Subjects in America. The Necessity of the times requires the utmost Activity and Vigor on this side of the Atlantick. Pray get ready our Colony Accounts with all convenient Speed. I am now in Congress and can add no more than that I am with the warmest Affection your Friend Saml Ad[ams]

RC (MHi).

Silas Deane to Elizabeth Deane

My Dear Philada Octo 7th 1775

J Webb tells Me you talk of not coming to See me. I don't know but you are in the right of it, for my Business here will give Me no Time to wait on You except between the hours of Ten at Night, and seven in the Morning, out of which if we borrow from Sleep it will not be much. I rise at Six, write untill Seven dress & breakfast by Eight go to the Committee of Claims untill Ten, then in Congress untill half past Three or perhaps four—Dine by five, & then go either to the Committee of Secrecy, or of Trade untill Nine, then Sup & go to Bed by Eleven. This leaves little Room for diversion, or any thing else, and to Tell You the Truth I expect this kind of Life must be my Lot for some time. I shall however Steal Away & meet You at New York unless my Brother to whom I have wrote, or J. Webb will wait on You quite down. I think it will be for the Interest of one or both to be here just at this Time. You have Wrote Me but Two Letters since I left home. Love to all. I am yours S D

RC (CtHi).

John Hancock to Philip Schuyler

Sir Philadelphia Octr. 7th 1775

By Intelligence received from England and laid before the Congress on the 5th Instant,[1] we are well assured that two North Country Briggs were dispatched from England to Quebec on the 11th of August with a very large Quantity of Arms, Ammunition and Cloathing. If you should be happy enough to possess yourself of Montreal, it is the earnest Desire of the Congress, that you take Measures if those Vessels should arrive, to seize them and secure their Cargoes for the Use of the Continent. It is also the Desire of the Congress that you secure for the same purpose all Military Stores belonging to the King.

I am also to inform you that we have Intelligence that Administration are obstinately determined to pursue every Measure in their power to subjugate the Colonies, and in Order to execute their purpose, they have determined to send over five more Regiments viz: 17th, 27th, 28th, 46th & 55th to New York.

Their plan is that these Troops "with the assistance of Governor Tryon, who is much relied [*on*] for the purpose to get immediate possession of New York and Albany—to fill both these Cities with very strong Garrisons—to declare all Rebels, who do not join the King's Forces—to command the Hudson and East Rivers, with a Number of small Men of War and Cutters stationed in different parts of it so as wholly to cut off all Communication by Water between New York & the provinces to the Northward of it, and between New York and Albany except for the King's Service & to prevent also all Communication between the City of New York and the provinces of Jersey Pennsylvania and those to the Southward of them. By these Means Adm——n and their Friends fancy that they shall soon either starve out or retake the Garrisons of Ticonderoga & Crown Point and open and maintain a safe Intercourse and Correspondence between Quebec Albany and New York & thereby afford the fairest Opportunity to their Soldiery and Canadians in Conjunction with the Indians to be procured by G[uy] J[ohnson] to make continual Irruptions into New Hampshire, Massachusetts and Connecticut and so distract and divide the provincial Forces as to render it easy for the British Army at Boston to defeat them, break the Spirit of the Massachusetts people, depopulate their Country and compel an absolute Subjection to Great Britain. Another good Effect to be deduced from this extensive plan as Government apprehend is that as New York will by this Method be prevented from supplying the Massachusetts army near Boston with Flour &c as they have heretofore done through the Medium of Connecticut: and the New Jersey and Pennsylvania people will not be able to transport provisions across the Country: and as the Colony of Connecticut does not raise Corn sufficient for the Supply of herself & the Massachusetts Bay, the Inhabitants and Troops of this province must inevitably of Course by [*be*] in a short Time destroyed by Diseases & Famine, and to this Train of Facts let me add, That in Consequence of Genl. Gage's desire brought by Capt. Chadd one hundred flat Bottomed Boats are at present building at Deptford &c in Order to be sent immediately to America. But for what particular purpose I have not yet been able to learn. Many American Gentlemen have however been lately asked by a Lord high in the American Department, what sized vessels can go loaded from hence to Albany? What is the Depth of Water at the Overslaw. I think that is the Name of the shallowest place in the North River? Whether the ship belonging to Albany in the London Trade is always obliged to unload part of her Cargo before she can get to Albany and what proportion of it? Whether if Batteries were erected at the Highlands, they would not prevent Vessels from going up and down the North River? and where it would be the best place on that River to hinder the New Jersey people &c. from sending Flour &c. in the Winter through Connecticut to the Massachusetts Army. These are the proposed Operations to the Northward."

I hope the Success of the Enterprize you are engaged [*in*] and the happy Change in the Disposition of the Canadians & Indians will disappoint and defeat the infernal purposes of administration.

Your Letters of the 25th & 28th Ult. have been laid before the Congress.[2] Measures are taking to collect a Quantity of Gold and Silver, which when collected will be sent to you by the safest & speediest Conveyance, when I shall again address you. I am with great Esteem Sir Your very humble Servant

John Hancock President

Tr (NN).

[1] On the nature of this "Intelligence," and for the provenance of that section of this letter enclosed in quotation marks, see Hancock to George Washington, October 5, 1775, 2d letter, note 1.

[2] Schuyler's letters to Hancock of September 25 and 28, together with accompanying enclosures, are in PCC, item 153, 1:166–79; and *Am. Archives*, 4th ser. 3:796–98, 826–27.

New Hampshire Delegates to Matthew Thornton

Sr. Philade. 7th Octob. 1775

We wrote you a few days since fully Desiring the Acct. of our Supplies, to be forwarded immediately as also the Number of inhabitants, as soon as may be. This Serves Chiefly, to inclose a Resolve of the Congress, which we were order'd to forward to the Several Conventions immediately that they might take Such Spirited measures as to them, Might Seem Meet.[1]

By the last Advices from London the Ministry Seem wickedly inclined to burn more towns, therefore we would humbly Suggest the propriety of Secureg our Sea port, as thereby we should not only Secure the Capital, but prevent the Sons of Depredation, from Ravageg the country, and thereby compleatg their Diabolical Designs. By Express Just Arrived from Gen. Schuyler We are likely *soon* to be in possession of St. John's and Canada, as the former is held Besiged by our Troops, and the Canadians join us, the Indians are also Friendly.

We are Sr. with Respect Yor most H.O. Servts

Josiah Bartlett

John Langdon

RC (Nh-Ar). Written by Langdon and signed by Bartlett and Langdon.

[1] Probably the resolve of October 6 recommending the arrest of every person "whose going at large may . . . endanger the safety of the colony, or the liberties of America." *JCC*, 3:280.

Samuel Ward's Diary

[October 7, 1775]

7th. Letters from N. York read. Consideration of Rhode [Islan]d Ins[t]r[uctions] to be heard next Monday week. The Money order'd for the Goods.[1] Reprt of the Comee. who took into Consideration the Letter relative to Fortification on Hudsons river accepted & recommendn. to the provinc[ial] Congress accordingly.[2] Genl. Wooster order'd (unless counter order'd by Genl. Schuyler) to come down to the Highlands leave as many Troops as the Managers of the Works think necessary & repair with the remainder to New York. Dispute between Pennsylvanians & Connect[icut] People referred to [their?] Delegates to reprt on Monday next. Agreed to resolve into a Comee. on Monday to consider the state of Trade. Letters from Colo. Morris & Mr. Willson referred to next Monday.

MS (RHi).

[1] Congress appointed a committee on September 23 to purchase £5,000 sterling

worth of woolens for the Continental Army and this day resolved to order the Continental treasurers to provide the money to pay for these goods. *JCC*, 3:260, 281.

[2] See *JCC*, 3:281–82.

John Adams to James Warren

Dear Sir October the 8. 1775

You will not think your Time misspent in Perusing any Plans for the service of your Country, even altho they may prove, upon Examination chimerical. There are two Channells only, through which Vessells of large Burthen, can pass, to and from Boston: one is between the West Head of Long Island and the Moon: It is a mile wide, but incumbered with Rocks and too shallow for a Man of War of more than twenty Guns. The other is between Long Island and Deer Island, a mile and a half from Point to Point, the only Channell, thro which capital Ships can pass, leads through the Narrows, between Gallops Island and Lovells Island where it is not wider, than the length of a fifty Gun Ship. In the Interval between Gallops and George's, is Nantaskett Road where, five Men of War are now Stationed: for what other End, do you Suppose, than to guard the Narrows from being obstructed?

The Moon communicates with Squantum, at low Water, even without a Canoe. A Fort, therefore, upon Squantum, may be so placed as to secure a Retreat from the Moon to Squantum and from that to the Main: one upon the East Head of the Moon, and another on the West Head of Long Island, secures the Communication, and covers a Retreat from the latter to the former: Another, on the Summit of Long Island, covers the shore on each Side. A strong Battery at the East Head of Long Island, commands the Ship Channell, the Narrows, and Nantaskett Road. Consequently by Sinking Hulks or Vesseaux de Frise, in the Narrows, We might prevent any Vessell of great Force from going out, or coming in.

In the Month of February last, "a Plan of the Town and Chart of the Harbour of Boston," was published in London—I think in a Magazine. I wish you would examine this Project by that Plan, and give me your opinion.

I dont trouble Washington with any of these Schemes, because I dont wish to trouble him with any Thing to no Purpose. But if I could command a Thousand Tons of Powder, and an hundred Pieces of heavy Cannon I would Scribble to him till he would be weary of me. Mean Time It may not be amiss for me to amuse myself with some of my Friends, in Speculations of this kind, because some good may Some time or other Result from them.

Can no use be made of Rowe Gallies, with you? Eight or Ten are compleated here. Can they be used in the Vineyard Sound? Would not their heavy Metal demolish a Cruizer now and then? There is a Shipwright escaped from Boston, who [*has*] been several Years a Prisoner in a Turkish Galley, and has a Model of one. Coll. Quincy knows him. Or I could procure you Directions from this Place, how to construct them.

We have just received by an express from Schuyler, very promising Intelligence concerning the operations of the Northern Army. Ethan Allen are in the Heart of the Country joined by 200 Canadians. Montgomery was beginning to bombard St Johns.

If We should be successful in that Province, a momentous, political Question arises. What is to be done with it? A Government will be necessary for the Inhabitants of Canada, as for those of the Massachusetts Bay? and what Form of Government, shall it be? Shall the Canadians choose an House of Representatives, a Council and a Governor? It will not do to govern them by Martial Law, and make our General Governor. This will be disrelished by them as much as their new Parliamentary Constitution or their old French Government.

Is there Knowledge and Understanding enough among them, to elect an assembly, which will be capable of ruling them and then to be governed by it—who shall constitute their Judges and civil Officers?

This appears to me as serious a Problem as any We shall have to solve.[1]

When I was at Watertown, a Comtee. of both Houses was appointed to Correspond with Us. We have not recd any Letter from it.

Another was appointed to enquire after Virgin Lead and leaden ore and the Methods of making Salt and acquaint Us with their Discoveries. We have not heard from this Comtee.

Please to send the enclosed News Paper to my Wife, when you have read it.

RC (MHi). In Adams' hand, though not signed.

[1] The remainder of this paragraph, six lines of text, has been inked out.

Richard Henry Lee to George Washington

Dear Sir, Philadelphia 8th Octr. 1775

A Ship in 7 weeks from London brings us pretty perfect intelligence of the infernal designs of our Ministerial enemies,[1] as you will see by the inclosures in Dr. Shippens letter. I believe they are the most perfect that could be obtained, and so may be much relied on.

God grant our successes at Boston and in Canada may disappoint, and thereby ruin these fatal foes to the liberty and happiness of the British empire.

My love, if you please, to Gen. Lee, Mifflin, Griffen and my other friends with you.

May heaven preserve you, and give your Army success in the most glorious cause that was ever contended for by human nature.

I am dear Sir your affectionate friend and obedient Servant

Richard Henry Lee

RC (DLC).

[1] See John Hancock to Washington, October 5, 1775, 2d letter.

Silas Deane's Diary

Monday Octo. 8th [*i.e.* 9th, 1775].

At Congress. At Committee buying goods.[1] Exp[ence]s 2/.

MS (CtHi). *CHS Bulletin* 29 (July 1964): 96A.

[1] Probably the committee appointed on September 23 to purchase woolens for clothing the army. On October 7 Congress ordered the continental treasurers to pay this committee £5,000 sterling for that purpose. *JCC*, 3:260, 281.

John Hancock to the New York Provincial Convention

Gentlemen Philadelphia, Octor. 9th, 1775.

Your Letters of the 6th inst. have been laid before Congress. They have issued an order for One Ton of Powder to be Sent to New-York, but I am directed to inform you, if you can with safety spare it or any part, it is the wish of Congress you would immediately forward it to General Schuyler.[1]

In Answer to your Letter Respecting the Brig[antin]e Mary, Capt Wallace, which put into your port to Repair, I am order'd to Acquaint you, that the Congress Recommend that she proceed on her Voyage with the Cargo after being Refitted.[2]

In Consequence of your Letter to Congress Inclosing a plan & Estimate of the Fort Erecting on the Highlands of North River, I now Inclose you the Resolution of Congress thereon to which Refer you. I also Inclose you a Resolve of Congress respecting those who are in your Opinion dangerous by being at large, to which also Refer you.[3]

Your proposall inclos'd respecting the Importation of Gunpowder is submitted to a committee—the resolution of Congress thereon shall be transmitted you.[4]

I have wrote Genl Wooster, at Albany, by order of Congress, to proceed to the Fort now building at North River, & there leave as many of his Troops as the Conductor of the Works shall think necessary to Expedite the Works, & with the Remainder to proceed to New York & there Remain.

By Desire of your Delegates I inclose you some Extracts of Letters from London, laid before Congress.

I am Gentlemen Your most Obedt sevt.

John Hancock Presidt.

RC (N). *Journals of N. Y. Prov. Cong.*, 2:5. RC damaged; missing words supplied from Tr.

[1] See *JCC*, 3:284. The New York Provincial Congress' letters of October 6 are in PCC, item 67, 1:91–95; and *Am. Archives*, 4th ser. 3:971–72, 1272–74.

[2] On the case of Capt. Robert Wallace, see the New York Provincial Congress' second letter to Congress of October 6 in *Am. Archives*, 4th ser. 3:972, 1273–74. There is no mention in the journals of any action on this matter.

[3] For these resolves see *JCC*, 3:280, 281–82.

[4] The New York Provincial Congress' proposal for procuring gunpowder is in a letter to Congress of October 4, with accompanying enclosure, on which see PCC, item 67, 1:79–83; and *Am. Archives*, 4th ser. 3:944. Congress referred the matter to the Secret Committee this day. *JCC*, 3:286.

John Hancock to Philip Schuyler

Sir, Philada. Octr 9th. 1775.

The enclosed Intelligence[1] was designed to be forwarded on the Day of its Date, but the Arrival of fresh Advices from you prevented it.

I now by order of Congress enclose you sundry Resolutions, entered into by them the 14th. of Sepr. last respecting the Appointment of Mr. Stringer as Director of the Hospital and Chief Physician, and several other Orders respecting the Hospital, and a Direction to the Commissary to pay Doctr. Stringer the Amount of Costs of Medicines purchased by him for the Use of the Army and Orders that the Commissary furnish such other Medicines as you shall direct.[2]

I am directed by the Congress to inform you that if you judge it necessary, they approve of your appointing a suitable Person for a Brigade Major in your Department.

Your several Letters have been duely laid before Congress, and are now under the Consideration of a Committee;[3] as soon as they report, and the Congress have come to Resolutions thereupon, the Result shall be immediately transmitted to you. But they have directed me to forward to you by this Express under the Escort of two of the light Horse of this City what Silver and Gold can be collected in the Time, least you should be in Want; and I have accordingly sent you six Thousand three Hundred and sixty four Pounds Philada. Currency.

A further Sum will be forwarded you by the Express that carries you the Resolutions of Congress on the various Parts of your Letters, which will be dispatched in a few Days.

I have Nothing further in Charge from Congress to communicate. I hope your next will give us the pleasing Account of the Restoration of your Health.[4] That you may have the full Enjoyment of that Blessing, and that Success may crown your Expedition is the Wish of, Sir, your most obedt. hble Servt. J.H. Prest.

[*P.S.*] You will please to acknowledge the Receipt of the Money. Enclosed is the Invo. of the Money.

LB (DNA: PCC, item 12A).

[1] Not found but perhaps the same intelligence from England discussed in Hancock to George Washington, October 5, 1775, 2d letter, note 2.

[2] See *JCC*, 2:249–50.

[3] See *JCC*, 3:284–85.

[4] Richard Henry Lee also wrote to Schuyler this day, expressing his concern for the general's health, stressing the importance of securing Canada, and informing him of large stores of ammunition and clothing coming to Quebec from London. Typescript summary of Richard Henry Lee to Schuyler, October 9, 1775, Schuyler Papers, NN.

John Hancock to David Wooster

Sir, Philada. Octr. 19th [*i.e.* 9th] 1775[1]

General Schuyler having by Letter informed the Congress that he believed he should have no Occasion to employ the Troops under your Command, I am desired by the Congress to direct that you immediately proceed with the Troops under your Command to the Batteries erecting on the Highlands in North River, and there leave as many of your Troops, as in the opinion of the Conductor will be necessary for expediting the Completion of the Works there, and that you repair with the Remainder of the Troops to New York, and there continue until further Orders from the Congress.[2] But in Case you should have any Orders from Genl. Schuyler, previous to the Receipt of this, to join the Army under his Command, or in any Way to be aiding to his Expedition, you are wholly to conform yourself to his Directions, the above Orders of Congress notwithstanding.

I am &c J.H. Prest.

LB (DNA: PCC, item 12A).

[1] The location of this letter in Hancock's letterbook and the date of the resolution of Congress alluded to by Hancock indicate that the president composed this letter on October 9, not October 19. PCC, item 12A, 1:12.

[2] The letter in question from Schuyler was written September 28, but the decision to reassign Wooster was made by Congress October 7. *Am. Archives*, 4th ser. 3:826–27; and *JCC*, 3:282–83.

New Jersey Delegates to the President of the New Jersey Provincial Congress

Sir [October 9, 1775]

The Continental Congress have this Day Agreed to Recommend to the Jersey Congress to Raise two Battallions for *one year* to Consist of 8 Companys of 68 Men to be sent to New York as soon as raised where it is expected their Assistance may be Wanted this Winter or early in the Spring. In Case the present Unhappy differences should be soon Settled & they discharged sooner the Men to receive one Months pay extra ordinary.

The Troops hitherto raised in any of the Colonys have had the Appointment of the Colonells and All the Inferier Officers and the Men 50 Shillings per Month.

It is Voted by the Congress that 5 Dollars per Month should be paid to the Jersey Troops and we have had a Considerable Debate whether the provincial Congresses Should have the Appointment of the field Officers of the Regiment or only the Captains & the Officers downward.

The Reason of Lessening the pay is The Expences of the Continent are so enormous and so beyond the Abilitees to pay that the Congress propose to Lessen All the pay after December.

Whether the Last proposition will take place or not is Undetermined that is Whether the Continental Congress or the Several provincial Congresses shall Appoint the Regimental field officers. ⟨*From what has Already past in Congress We believe the Majority of the Congress will incline to take the Appointment of the field officers of the Regiments into their Own hands. Whether the New England Colonies will submitt to that Inclination We doubt.*⟩

We beg the favor of You to lay this before the New Jersey Congress and Request of them to Return an Answer to the Continental Congress Whether on *these Terms* the Troops Can be had in Jersey and Whether the Congress will putt the Recommendation in practice.[1]

As Delegates of New Jersey We think it our Duty to state these Facts for Your Consideration without any Observation of Our Own Not doubting but that You will bestow the proper Consideration on the subject and Come to that Determination which Your Duty and the Common Interest Dictate.

You will receive We Expect a Letter from the president inclosing the Minutes of the Continental Congress relating to this Matter which will More particularly Mention the Terms.

We are with great Respect Your Frds and Serts

Js Kinsey

Wil: Livingston

MS not found; reprinted from Burnett, *Letters*, 1:223–24.

[1] At first the New Jersey Provincial Congress was reluctant to grant Congress the appointment of field officers for the colony's battalions, but in time a compromise was reached whereby the provincial congress submitted nominees which Congress then approved. See *JCC*, 3:289, 335; *Am. Archives*, 4th ser. 3:1050–51, 1240; and William Livingston to William Alexander, November 8, 1775.

New York Delegates to the New York Provincial Convention

Gent. Philadelphia 9th Octor. 1775.

We recd. your favour of the 4th. inst[an]t[1] containing an account of the troops raised in our Colony; of which we shall make the proper use. The Congress approve highly of your diligence in the erection of fortifications on Hudsons River, you will I believe receive by this conveyance their sentiments on this subject, as well as extracts of some letters that shew its propriety, & the designs of administration against us.

We sincerely lament the necessity to which the want of gun powder may reduce us, & have endeavoured as far as lies in our power to remove it by procuring you at the continental expence one ton, which was all that could be obtained. You will take care not to forward this, unless you know how to supply yourselves, for it is not the design of the Congress that you should at any time be intirely at the mercy of your enemy.[2]

We shall take care to get your artillery company put upon a proper footing, in which we apprehend no difficulty. As to the want of Cloathing for our troops, we are not without hopes that may be provided for in Canada, of which we cannot but flatter ourselves they will shortly be in possession.

We remain Gent with the greatest respect Your Most Obt. Hum. Servt.

Phil. Livingston Jas. Duane

John Alsop Robt R. Livingston Junr.

RC (N). Written by Robert R. Livingston, Jr., and signed by Livingston, Alsop, Duane, and Philip Livingston. *Journals of N. Y. Prov. Cong.*, 2:18. RC damaged; missing words supplied from Tr.

[1] For this letter, see *Am. Archives*, 4th ser. 3:1268–69.

[2] This day Congress resolved that James Duane procure a ton of gunpowder for the New York Provincial Convention from the Pennsylvania Committee of Safety and that the New York body forward as much of it as could be spared to General Schuyler. *JCC*, 3:284.

Robert Treat Paine's Diary

[October 9, 1775]

Fair. Congress sat again in State House.

MS (MHi).

Rhode Island Delegates to Nicholas Cooke

Sir Philadelphia 9th Octr. 1775

By a Number of Letters from England & the public Papers it clearly appears that Administration is determined upon the most sanguinary & violent Measures. We ought to be prepared for the worst, The Town of Providence We hope is secure if not We would advise to such additional works as the Fall will admit & necessity requires. The People in Newport We hope have secured their best Effects in Places of Safety. We think indeed that it would be for theirs & their Countrys Interest that they should abandon the Town. We are afraid (like the unhappy People of Boston) that they will stay too long. We doubt not but your best Endeavours will be used to secure as much as possible every Part of the Colony.

The ministry depends much upon Canada. Their Plan by the best Intelligence is to take Possession of New York, Hudsons River & Albany keep open a Communication with Canada, cut off all Intercourse between New England & the other Colonies sett the Canadians & Indians upon our Frontiers, and arm all our domestic Enemies against Us. Govr. Martin & Lord Dunmore have been indefatigable this last Way & Lord Wm. Campbell Govr. of So. Carolina being suspected of such Intentions pledged his Word & Honor that there was not a Word of Truth in the Charge, since which they have the fullest Proof of his Guilt, He hath taken Shelter on board a Man of War with one of his Agents, the People are in Pursuit of the others. Things grow daily more serious, Our Enemies are making their greatest Efforts, let not this discourage but animate Us to double our

Vigilence & exert every Nerve in the Service of our Country.

Upon Motion that it should be recommended to the Convention of Virginia to arrest & secure Lord Dunmore a general Resolution was come into a Copy of which is inclosed.[1] This as to our Colony is a matter of great Delicacy especially in New port. Some Letters advise to the seizing all Govrs. & crown officers on the Continent as the surest Way to preserve our maritime Towns. Whether such a measure would have that happy Effect or precipitate an Attack upon them You who are upon the Spot & well acquainted with the State of the Colony in all Respects can best determine. New Hampshire some time since seized the Money in the public Treasury. She has lately disarmed all the Torries & crown officers. Connecticut disarmed two whole Towns, other Colonies have seized public Money's & Supplied them to provincial Uses. We are clear that such measures when necessary for the public Safety are perfectly justifiable. As to this particular Matter We submit it wholly to your Honor only suggesting whether it will not be best to keep the inclosed matter Secret save from a few trusty Friends until the next assembly, & then communicate it under the strongest Injunctions of Secresy that our Enemies may get no Knowledge of it & that such Measures may be taken as the public Safety shall require. May infinte Wisdom direct & prosper all your Councils.

By Letters from Genl. Schuyler of 19th Sepr. We are informed that the American Troops had surrounded St. Johns & cut off the Enemies Communication with Montreal; before this Time We hope they are in Possession of both for as our People are joined by the Canadians they will have nobody to contend with but the few Regulars in that Country; by these happy Acquisitions to which We hope Quebec will be soon added We shall altogether disappoint the most favourite Plan of the Ministry. We are, with great Regard Sir your most obedient hble Servants Step Hopkins

Sam. Ward

[*P.S.*] By other Letters by express from St. John's of the 24 Sept. we are informed our Troops were Masters of Chamblee began to play on St. John's and in two Days expected to be in possession of it. Many Canadians having then joined them and our Success seemed to be certain in that Quarter.[2] S Hopkins

RC (RHi). Body of letter written by Ward and signed by Ward and Hopkins. Postscript written and signed by Hopkins.

[1] See *JCC*, 3:280.

[2] In reality Fort Chambly did not surrender to American forces under General Montgomery until October 17, nor St. Johns until November 2. Gustave Lanctot, *Canada & the American Revolution, 1774–1783,* trans. Margaret M. Cameron (Toronto and Vancouver: Clarke, Irwin & Co., 1967), pp. 90–91.

Caesar Rodney to Thomas Rodney

Sir Philadelphia Monday Octr. 9th 1775

I Received your letter by Mr. Barrett dated the 2d of Octr., but rather Suppose it was dated the 3d, wherein you inclosed me a list of the Poles, which gives me an Oppertunity to Congratulate You on Your Safe arrival uppon the Stage of Honor, Trouble, Expense and Abuse.[1] Therefore Would advise you to be Carefull to deserve as much of the first Article as your Station affords, and to be Equally Carefull not to Seek or deserve either of the latter; for they will come, when they will come, and Let me tell You that it is Honorable for a man to be puncktual in the discharge of Every public Trust, Therefore Expect to See all the Representatives for Kent, at Newcastle on the 20th of this Instant, and not be dropping in, for a week following the day they ought to have met.

As it is a verry great disadvantage to me to be so much from my private Concerns, I hope therefore you will between this and your Coming to Newcastle, put All my business as well as your own upon the best footing you possibly Can, or Else when both are away We Shall doubly Suffer.

I am Sorry Circumstances turned out so Contrary to your Good intentions toward John Bullen. But Your Carrying Sipple so near him as to put it in the power of the others to Shoot him ahead Certainly Broke your Scheme with Respect to him—for tho it was Just and Right that Bullen (according to your party Agrement) Should have the Commission, Yet as those Manuveries of party are, and ought to be unknown to a Governor, and as it is a Just Rule of Conduct in him to give the Commission to the highest in Vote[s], I Could not Serve Bullen unless I had asked as a favour, which (I dare say you will be of opinion with me) would have been paying too dear for a Commission of no more importance than that of a Coroner. You may perhaps have it in Your power to take better Care of him another time. But we Shall talk More of this another time.

On Fryday about Eleven OClock at night Doctr. Kearsly of this City was Seized by Order of the Committee of Observation,[2] for having wrote Letters to England injurious & distructive to us in the American Contest, and wicked with Respect to this City, and is now Confined in Goal Together with one Brooks who Came here with Governor Skeen, Mr. Carter an apothecary who was in partnership with Speakman, and one Mr. Snowden, all of whom were Aiding the Doctr. in his plan. You must know Kearsly has been a Considerable time Since Marked out as a thorough-paced Tory, for Which, together with his having Insulted the people he was (Since I Came to Town last) Carted through the Streets. But the offence for Which he is now Confined is thus Circumstanced. On Wednesday last A Ship

Sailed out of this port for London, in Which Mr. Carter was going passenger. A few days before she Sailed, Young Dewees, son of the Sheriff went to pay Doctr. Kearsly Some Money and Comeing Suddenly in to his Room found him and Carter together, with a bundle of Papers before them, which they Hussel'd up in Seeming Confusion. This, with Kearsly's Tory Carrictor gave Dewees Suspition, and he Accordingly informed a few of the Committee Who kept the matter Secret, Let the Ship Sail, and the passengers go down to Chester by Land to go on Board. On Thursday Evening Which was the day the passengers Went, A Small party was Sent down to Chester. They Stayed there that night in Cogg [incognito] and see the passengers go on board next Morning. They then imediately pushed on board, Seized and Examined Mr. Carter who in a Little time told them that there were Several Letters from Doctr. Kearsly & Mr. Brooks, And one from Mr. Snowden, That he had the Charge of them, and was Concerned with them in the plan they had Concerted, But that the Letters were then in the Custody of a woman down in the Cabin, And that She had them Concealed in a pocket Sewed to the inside of her Shift-Tail, Where in fact they Soon after found them and Came back to Town (leaving Carter as they had promised Upon his Making a discovery of the Whole Matter on a Oath before Mr. Grayham at Chester) and then Seized the Authors. The Letters were to Lord Dartmouth and other Ministers of State, But under Cover to Misses McCawley. The Substance and design was pressing their Sending to Philadelphia five thousand Regulars, on Which Condition they would Engage five thousand more here to Join them, provided the Royal Standard Should be also Sent in, and Kearsly appointed to *bear* it, for that Great numbers of those who now wear Cockades & Uniform were hearty in the Ministerial Cause. That the Rest were a pack of Cowards for that he (Kearsly) had made above five thousand of them Run By Snapping a Single Pistol at them &c &c. They had with them for the use of the Ministry one of Joshua Fishers plans of Delaware Bay & River, whereon they had described the place Where the Chevaux Defreise's were fixed. Besides these and Many more Villinous Contrivances, they were takeing home the out-lines for a print to be Struck off in London, Shewing Kearsly's late Exhibition in the Cart, going through the Streets of Philadelphia with the Mob, many of Whom he undertakes particularly to discribe, to wit, Bradford &c. &c. many of whom were actually not there, and how he every now and then by Snapping his Pistol made them Run &c. His abuse of the Congress, Committees &c. (in his letters) is intolerable, Such as Rebels, Villians &c. After the Committee of Safety had Examined them and the Contents of the Letters, they Sent a Pilot Boat down the River to overtake the Ship, to bring up Carter, and to Search the Box of Letters and to bring all of them that they Supposed to be from, or to Suspicious persons. This Boat Returned Sunday afternoon, brought Carter and put him in Goal, and also brought a Number of Letters belonging to and wrote by other persons. The Committee of Safety has been Setting on these affairs all this day. But I have been so Closely Confined to Congress to day, that I don't yet know what they have done—or What others are accused.

It is now near Eight at night and Mr. John David the bearer of this Sets out tomorrow Morning, therefore Shall only Tell you that I am Tolerable well and disire my love to our families, and Conclude Yrs. &c. Caesar Rodney

P.S. I am grieved much for my Plow-horses which you say are Dead —But must bear it as well as I Can.

RC (DeHi).

[1] Thomas Rodney was elected a representative to the House of Assembly for the Three Lower Counties. Rodney, *Letters* (Ryden), p. 66n.

[2] Dr. John Kearsley, James Brooks, Leonard Snowden, and Christopher Carter were arrested by the Pennsylvania Committee of Safety for conducting correspondence with British officials inimical to American liberties. On October 10, some of their captured papers were turned over to John Dickinson "for the perusal of the Continental Congress." Dickinson reported October 14 that the issue had been placed before Congress, which "declined making any particular order respecting them" and referred the committee of safety to a congressional resolve of October 6, a decision the committee of safety interpreted as a call to continue the confinement of Kearsley and Brooks. *Am. Archives*, 4th ser. 3:1814–29, passim; and *JCC*, 3:280.

Secret Committee Contract

Philadelphia. Committee Chamber October 9th. 1775.

Be it rembered that it is agreed by & between the following persons to wit Philip Livingston, John Alsop and Francis Lewis of the city of New York, merchants,[1] and Samuel Ward, John Langdon, Silas Deane, Thomas Willing & Thomas M'Kean Esquires a Quorum of the Committee of Secrecy appointed by the Honble Continental Congress for the Thirteen United Colonies of North America that a voyage or voyages shall be forthwith undertaken for the speedy procuring fifty tonns of powder twelve brass six pounds cannon a thousand stand of good soldiers muskets & bayonets and two thousand good double-bridled gun-locks and in case all the powder mentioned cannot be obtained then as much salt-petre & sulphur as will make the quantity that may be deficient—that the vessel or vessels shall be chartered for the use of the continental Colonies afsd. and a skilful & prudent supercargo or supercargoes employed by the said Philip Livingston, John Alsop & Francis Lewis at the expence of the said Colonies and that the said supercargoes may be allowed five per-cent commissions—that thirty six thousand dollars continental currency shall be forthwith advanced to them the said Messrs. Livingston, Alsop & Lewis,[2] for which they are hereafter to render an Account to the United Colonies who are to bear the whole risk of the afsd. adventure and that the said Messrs. Livingston, Alsop & Lewis shall be allowed for their trouble five per cent commissions on the first cost of the afsd. articles or as much of them as shall be delivered. All the articles mentioned are to be put on shore in some safe and convenient place in some of the United Colonies to the Eastward of Chesepeake-Bay and notice of the place given as soon as conveniently may be to a Quorum of the Committee of Secrecy for the time being. Witness our hands the day & year aforesaid.

Phil. Livingston — Sam. Ward
Frans Lewis — John Langdon
John Alsop — Silas Deane
Thos. Willing
Tho M'Kean

MS (NHi). Written by McKean and signed by Alsop, Deane, Langdon, Lewis, Livingston, Ward, Willing, and McKean.

[1] This day Congress referred to the Secret Committee a letter of October 4 from the New York Convention enclosing a New York merchant's proposal for obtaining gunpowder from the French West Indies. See *Am. Archives,* 4th ser. 3:944; and *JCC,* 3:286. Since neither this contract nor the Secret Committee minutes of proceedings for this day mention the proposal, it is not known whether this contract was a direct outgrowth of that proposal. See "Journal of the Secret Committee," October 9, 1775. MH.

[2] The order authorizing the exportation of wheat and flour to the value of $36,000, signed by Samuel Ward, Thomas McKean, Thomas Willing, John Langdon, and Silas Deane, and certified by President Hancock on October 9, 1775, is in the Rufus King Papers, NHi. Two other papers located with this order also bear upon the transaction. A receipt signed by Philip Livingston indicates that on October 11 he received $18,711 from George Clymer, continental treasurer, and that the balance of the $36,000 was to be paid to John Alsop. A set of notes that were apparently written years later in connection with the settlement of old accounts, states that Livingston, Alsop, and Lewis chartered the sloop *Lucretia* with Cornelius Haight as master, who took a cargo of flour to the West Indies and shipped 388 kegs of powder from St. Eustatius in December 1775.

Samuel Ward's Diary

Octr. 9th. [1775]

A Letter from the Com[missary] relative to £500 advanced for Colo. Arnold & the Money orderd to be pd. accordingly.[1] Further Order for exchanging £20000 P[ennsylvania]C[urrenc]y for Genl.

Schuyler. Mr. Duane authorized to propose to the Comee. of Safety of this Province to borrow one Ton of Powder for New York. Letters from Genls. Schuyler & Montgomery read referred to a Comee., John Adams, John Rutledge, Mr. Chace, R Livingston & Mr. Deane.[2] The affair between Pennsylvania & Connect. farther deferred. The Delegates of Pennsylvania to send what hard Money the Treasrs have got to Genl. Schuyler by two of the light horse.

Recomd. to the provincial Convention of New Jersey to immediately raise two Battali[on]s of 8 Compa[nie]s each at continental Charge, each Co[mpan]y for a Year 68 Privates & Officers as recommended by Congress in the militia Bill, privates at 5 Doll[ar]s per m[ont]h & discharged at any time allowg. 1 Months Pay gratis, instead of bounty, 1 pr. Shoes, 1 pr. yarn stocking & a felt hat given each private. Pay of the Officers the same as that now in the contin[enta]l Army; if that be raised the officers of these Battalions to have the same.

MS (RHi).

[1] See Commissary General Joseph Trumbull's letter to Eliphalet Dyer of September 23 in *Am. Archives*, 4th ser. 3:778–79.

[2] For Schuyler's letters to Hancock of September 19 and 29, together with accompanying enclosures, see ibid., pp. 738–44, 839–41; and PCC, item 153, 1:140–65, 180–89. The committee appointed to respond to these communications brought in a draft reply on October 10, which Congress approved after some debate on the 11th and sent off over the signature of Hancock. See *JCC*, 3:284–85, 287–88; and Hancock to Philip Schuyler, October 11, 1775.

John Adams' Notes of Debates

Octr. 10. [1775]

Who shall have the Appointment of the Officers in the 2 Battallions to be raised in New Jersey?[1]

Sherman. Best to leave it to the Provincial Conventions.

Ward seconds the Motion.

Chace. This is persisting in Error in Spight of Experience. We have found by Experience that giving the Choice of Officers to the People, is attended with bad Consequences. The French Officers are allowed to exceed any in Europe, because a Gentleman is hardly entituled to the Smiles of the Ladies without serving a Campaign. In my Province, We want Officers. Gentlemen have recommended Persons from personal Friendships, who were not suitable. Such Friendships will have more Weight, in the Colonies.

Dyer. We must derive all our Knowledge, from the Delegates of that Colony. The Representatives at large are as good Judges and would give more Satisfaction. You cant raise an Army if you put Officers over the Men whom they dont know. It requires Time to bring People off from ancient Usage.

E. Rutledge. We dont mean to break in upon what has been done. In our Province we have raised our Compliment of Men in the Neighbouring Colonies. I am for it that We may have Power to reward Merit.

Ward. The Motion is intended for a Precedent. In the Expedition to Carthagena and Canada, the Crown only appointed a Lieutenant in my Colony. The Men will not enlist. When the Militia Bill was before Us. I was vs. giving the Choice to the Men. I dont know any Man in the Jerseys.

Duane. A Subject of Importance—a Matter of Delicacy. We ought to be all upon a Footing. We are to form the grand Outlines of an American Army—a general Regulation. Will such a Regulation be salutary? The public Good alone, will govern me. If We were to set out anew, would the same Plan be pursued. It has not been unprecedented, in this Congress. Mr. Campbell, Allen, Warner, were promoted here. We ought to insist upon it. We shall be able to regulate an Army better. Schuyler and Montgomery would govern my Judgment. I would rather take the opinion of Gen. Washington than of any Convention. We can turn out the unworthy and reward Merit. The Usage is for it.

Governors used to make Officers—except in Con. and Rhode Island. But We cant raise an Army? We are then in a deplorable Situation indeed. We pay. Cant We appoint with the Advice of our Generals.

Langdon. Looks upon this a very extraordinary Motion, and big with many Mischiefs.

Deane. It is the Peoples Money, not ours. It will be fatal. We cant sett up a Sale for Offices, like Lord Barrington.

E. Rutledge. The appointment hitherto has been as if the Money belonged to particular Provinces not to the Continent. We cant reward Merit. The Governor appointed Officers with Us.

Ross. My Sentiments coincide with those of the Gentlemen from N.Y. and C[arolina] and would go farther and appoint every Officer, even an Ensign. We have no Command of the Army! They have different Rules and Articles.

Jay. Am of opinion with the Gentleman who spoke last. The Union depends much upon breaking down provincial Conventions. The whole Army refused to be mustered by your Muster Master.

MS (MHi). Adams, *Diary* (Butterfield), 2:202–4.

[1] See New Jersey Delegates to the President of the New Jersey Congress, October 9, 1775.

John Adams to Abigail Adams

Octr. 10. 1775

I am much concerned least you should feel an Addition to your Anxieties, from your having so seldom heard from me. But I pray you to dismiss all Concern about me. I am happier far than I was before the Adjournment. My Health is better, and Business and Conversation are much more to my Taste.

The surprizing Intelligence We have in private Letters concerning the Director of the Hospital,[1] has made me more cautious of Writing than ever. I must be excused from writing a Syllable of any Thing of any Moment. My Letters have been and will be nothing, but Trifles. I dont cho[o]se to trust the Post. I am afraid to trust private Travellers. They may peep. Accidents may happen, and I would avoid, if I could, even Ridicule, but especially Mischief.

Pray, bundle up every Paper, not already hid, and conceal them in impenetrable Darkness. Nobody knows what may occur.

My Love to those who are dearest to us both. Send yours to the Care of the Gentleman whose Care has hitherto been successfull. Date them in Time, but not Place, and assume a new fictitious Name.

RC (MHi). Adams, *Family Correspondence* (Butterfield), 1:299.

[1] For a detailed narrative of the arrest, conviction, and imprisonment of Dr. Benjamin Church for carrying on "a criminal correspondence with the enemy," see Allen French, *General Gage's Informers, New Material upon Lexington & Concord. Benjamin Thompson as Loyalist & the Treachery of Benjamin Church Jr.* (Ann Arbor: University of Michigan Press, 1932), pp. 147–201. Church's conspiracy, which was described in Washington's October 5 letter to Hancock, was brought before Congress on October 13, and Dr. John Morgan was elected to succeed him as director general and chief physician of the Continental Army Hospital on October 17. *JCC*, 3:293–95, 297.

John Adams to James Warren

Dr Sir Philadelphia Octr. 10th 1775

Mr Jonathan Mifflin, a young Gentleman of this City, a Relation of our Friend the Quarter Master General will hand you this Letter.

I believe you will have enough of my Correspondence this Time, for it has certainly been filled with mere Impertenence and contains nothing of War or Politicks which are so agreable to your Taste.

Our Expectations are very Sanguine, of Intelligence from Schuyler that Canada is ours. Our Advices from England breath nothing but Malice, Revenge and Cruelty.

Powder, and Salt Petre are Still the Cry from one End of the Continent to the other. We must, and, God willing, We will have them.

I long to hear concerning our Friends in Boston. My Friends cannot be too particular. I want to know the Condition of every Individual. I want to know also every Event however minute which Turns up in our Camp or Lines. We have most formidable Descriptions of Gages Fortifications in Boston. Ninety Pieces of Brass Field Pieces from four to Eight Pounders have certainly been cast in the Tower for America, and Carriages, Wheelbarrows, Flat bottomed Boats &c I am &c

RC (MHi). In Adams' hand, though not signed.

Samuel Adams to James Warren

My dear sir Philada Octob 10 1775

Since my last, I have receivd Intelligence from London, that the British Ministry after having receivd the Advice of the Engagement on Bunkers Hill held various Councils on American Affairs and had resolvd to persevere in their Attempts to enslave us. 50 or 60 brass field pieces 6 & 9 pounders four thousand Stands of small arms with ammunition had been shipd from the Tower of London for Quebeck to arm the Canadians—five Regiments from Ireland viz 17th, 27th, 28th, 46th & 55th were orderd to Boston—4 Companies of the Train of Artillery are to go with the Ordnance & Stores to Quebeck. Several Ships of War were also orderd to America. What was intended for Quebeck were to sail in a fortnight from the Date of the Letter which was the 8th of August. The Regiments from Ireland were intended to be at Boston in October. The Parliamt was to meet in Octr and so soon, that a Sanction might be given as early as possible to the Measures that have been taken as well as others to be adopted. General Gage had been appointed Governor General of all North America but afterwards it was concluded that Leave should be given him to return home. This was to make Room for Genl Amherst who is to take the Command in the Spring with a promise of 20,000 Men—2000 Highlanders 3000 Irish Roman Catholicks and the rest, if they cannot be raisd in England, to consist of Hannoverians Hessians & other Germans. The Plan said to have been laid before Ministry last Spring which was to divide the Troops then sent out, a part of them to go to New York is now to be followed. General Gages Necessity then obligd him to alter that plan and to collect all his Troops together at Boston. Govr Carleton had orders to enter upon the New England Frontiers with the Canadians, and Tryon with the Forces at New York was to meet and cooperate with him. This it is said was the Design of his return to his Governmt. The Idea is not yet given up, and to facilitate the plan a Number of flat bottomd boats were to be constructed and so contrivd as when they touch the Shore, to throw down a platform that will land at once 6 Armed Men. They may be used to fire field pieces or Swivel Guns. When they are compleated they are to be taken to pieces and sent to Canada to be used on the Lakes. It was reported in England that the Officers just arrivd from Boston said, the Intention was to dispossess the Americans of Dorchester Neck which was all they thought of doing this Campain; supposing that by the Spring they should have Reinforcements sufficient to attempt any thing, especially as they concluded the Americans would be obligd from the Severity of the Winter to break up their Encampment, while the Soldiers would be in good Quarters in Boston. They also said that the officers were much disgusted with the Service, and that it was with the utmost difficulty the Soldiers were compelld to fight.

By late Accounts from the Northern Army things wear a promising Aspect there. Genl Schuylers Success will frustrate the designs of Ministry in Canada.

Letters have been intercepted here which discover a plot of which I have not now time to write you,[1] as the Bearer Mr Mifflin of whose going I was apprisd but a few Minutes ago is now waiting. I am impatient to hear the particulars of a report we have just heard concerning Dr. Church which astonishes me.

Be kind enough to forward the inclosd Letter. Excuse this indigested Account of Matters, wch however comes from good Authority and be assured that I am with due Regards to your good Lady and Friends, most affectionately yours S A

RC (MHi).

[1] A reference to Dr. John Kearsley's plot. See Caesar Rodney to Thomas Rodney, October 9, 1775.

Thomas Jefferson to Francis Eppes

Dear Sir Philadelphia, Oct. 10th, 1775.

I wrote to Patty on my arrival here, and there being then nothing new in the politcal way I inclosed her letter under a blank cover to you. Since that we have received from England news of much importance, which coming thro' many channels we beleive may be confidently relied on. Both the ministerial and provincial accounts of the battle of Bunker's hill had got to England. The ministry were determined to push the war with vigor, a measure in which they were fixed by the defeat of the Spaniards by the Moors. 90. brass cannon were embarked from the tower and may be hourly expected either at N. York or Boston. 2000 troops were to sail from Ireland about the

25th. Sep. These we have reason to beleive are destined for N. York. Commodore Shuldam was to sail about the same time with a great number of frigates and small vessels of war to be distributed among the middle colonies. He comes at the express and earnest intercessions of Ld. Dunmore, and the plan is to lay waste all the plantations on our river sides. Of this we gave immediate notice to our committee of safety by an express whom we dispatched hence last Friday, that if any defence could be provided on the rivers by fortifications or small vessels it might be done immediately.[1] In the spring 10,000 men more are to come over. They are to be procured by taking away two thirds of the Garrison at Gibralter (who are to be replaced by some Hessians) by 2000 Highlanders and 5000 Roman Catholics whom they propose to raise in Ireland. Instead of the Roman Catholics however some of our accounts say foreigners are to be sent. Their plan is this. They are to take possession of New York and Albany, keeping up a communication between them by means of their vessels. Between Albany and St. John's they propose also to keep open the communication; and again between St. John's, Quebec, and Boston. By this means they expect Gage, Tryon and Carleton may distress us on every side acting in concert with one another. By means of Hudson's river they expect to cut off all correspondence between the Northern and Southern rivers. Gage was appointed Governor General of all America; but Sir Jeffery Amherst consented afterwards to come over, so that Gage is to be recalled. But it [*is*] beleived Amherst will not come till the Spring. In the mean time Howe will have the command. The co-operation of the Canadians is taken for granted in all the ministerial schemes. We hope therefore they will all be dislocated by the events in that quarter. For an account of these I must refer you to Patty. My warmest affection to Mrs. Eppes. Adieu.

RC (ViU). Jefferson, *Papers* (Boyd), 1:246–47.

[1] See Virginia Delegates to the Williamsburg Committee of Safety, October 5, 1775.

Samuel Ward's Diary

[October 10, 1775]

10th. Some Accts. allowed. The Money sent to Genl. Schuyler. Answer to Genl. Schuylers Lettr. Reprted & referred. Appointmt of field officers Referred. To be resolved to morrow into a Comee. of the whole to take into Consideration the State of Trade.

MS (RHi).

Josiah Bartlett to Mary Bartlett

Philadelphia October 11th 1775. Directs numerous questions to his wife about friends and conditions in New Hampshire. Reports his recovery from inoculation for smallpox, "I Can now inform you that by the Goodness of God I am in a Good State of health Tho I have not Quite got my Strength up. I have no news to inform you of; you will See in the newspaper all the publick news."

RC (NhHi).

John Hancock to Philip Schuyler

Sir, Philada. Octr. 11th. 1775.

The Congress have considered your Letters of the 19th and 29th of Sepr. last, and directed me to assure you, that they are very sensible of the Difficulties under which you labour, and your unremitted Dilligence to remove such as may in any wise obstruct the public service. They most heartily lament the Loss of your Health, as well on your own, as on Account of the Public, but find some Pleasure in thinking that you are not without Consolation, when you reflect, that the Obligations of your Country are increased in Proportion to the Sacrifices you make to her Interest. Their Concern for the Public is greatly alliviated by the Abilities and Zeal of Genl. Montgomery, in which they cannot but place the highest Confidence.

The Congress see the Necessity of attending to the Situation of Canada, but trust that your Care and Prudence will render any Delegation from this Body unnecessary, at least for the present. What they expect from your Endeavours is, that the Canadians be induced to accede to an Union with these Colonies, and that they form from their several Parishes a Provincial Convention and send Delegates to this Congress. And as in the present unsettled State of that Country, a regular Election can hardly be expected, we must acquiesce in the Choice of such Parishes and Districts as are disposed to join us.

You may assure them that we shall hold their Rights as dear as our own, and on their Union with us, exert our utmost Endeavours to obtain for them and their Posterity the Blessings of a free Government, and that Security to their Persons and Property, which is derived from the British Constitution.

And you may further declare that we hold sacred the Rights of Conscience, and shall never molest them in the free Enjoyment of their Religion.

If our Arms should be crowned with Success, you will consult with your principal Officers about the Number of Troops that will be necessary for the Defence of Canada, and for the different Posts of Crown Point and Ticonderoga, and the best Method of procuring Men for those Services. If you should observe in the Canadians an Inclination to take up Arms, you may immediately, at the Expence of the Continent, raise a Regiment and appoint such officers as you conceive will be most agreeable to them, and serviceable to us.

The Congress will endeavour to attend to the Cloathing of your Troops, and approve of your Design to purchase Woolens at Montreal, which they sincerely hope it may be in your Power to accomplish. You may depend upon their Compliance with all Contracts made by you for the Supply of the Troops under your Command.

The Establishment of a Civil Government in Canada is a Subject of great Consequence, and requires the most deliberate Councils. The Temper, the Disposition and local Circumstances of our Brethen in that Colony must be known, before we can form a proper Judgment on so important a Question. You will endeavour therefore to collect the Sentiments of the most discreet and sensible among the principal Canadians and English on this Head, and communicate *their* opinion, with *your* Remarks to the Congress.

It is the Determination of this Congress at all Events to keep the Command of Lake Champlain. They would therefore have the most effectual Measures adopted for that Purpose; and if our Enemies should be expelled [*from*] Montreal, will exert their utmost Endeavours to secure the River St. Lawrence, and prevent by Batteries, Vessels, and every other Obstruction the ministerial Troops from regaining the Possession of that Town.

The Congress approve of the Presents made to the Coghnewagas, also of the Disposition of the Prisoners, and have borrowed one Ton of gun Powder from the Committee of Safety of this Colony, and directed it to be sent to the Provincial Convention of New York, with a Request to transmit to you the whole, or such a Part of it, as they can spare. Nails will be supplied you, by the Convention of New York, when they receive your Direction on that Head. They, together with the Committee of Albany, and the Governor of Connecticut will on Application, furnish such Carpenters and Blacksmiths, as you may want over and above what may be procured from among the Troops. As for the Artificers taken from thence, you will pay them the customary Allowance, if you think their Services entitle them to any Reward.

The Congress are pleased with the Mode in which you prepare to settle with and pay those, who took and garrisoned Crown Point, and desire that the Accounts may be transmitted to them as soon as possible.

Mr. Phelps will be considered as Deputy to Mr. Livingston for the

New York Department, and be paid as such at the Rate of forty Dollars per Month from his Entrance into the Service.

The Congress are greatly hurt at the Misconduct of a Part of the Troops, and hope they will take the earliest opportunity to obliterate their Disgrace.[1] It is their earnest Wish, that the strictest Discipline be observed. For, as on the one Hand, they are resolved to reward those, who deserve their Favour, so on the other, a Regard for their Country forbids them to overlook the offenses of such as neglect their Duty, or basely betray their Trust.

I cannot conclude without assuring you that the Congress are highly sensible of the Spirit, Activity, and Zeal, of Mr. James Livingston,[2] from which they cannot but promise themselves Advantages, that will be entitled to their earliest Recompence.

I have the Honor to be &c. J H Prest.

LB (DNA: PCC, item 12A). On the authorship of this letter, see Samuel Ward's Diary, October 9, 1775, note 2.

[1] For a brief discussion of the difficulties which Generals Schuyler and Montgomery experienced with the New England troops under their command, see Allen French, *The First Year of the American Revolution* (New York: Houghton Mifflin Co., 1934), pp. 425–27.

[2] James Livingston (1747–1832), a grain merchant situated by the strategic Richelieu River, was actively engaged in efforts to persuade Canadians to support the invading forces of Schuyler and Montgomery. Livingston raised a regiment of Canadian volunteers in November and December 1775 and commanded it until January 1781, receiving a colonel's commission from Congress on January 8, 1776. *DAB;* and Gustave Lanctot, *Canada & the American Revolution, 1774–1783,* trans. Margaret M. Cameron (Toronto and Vancouver: Clarke, Irwin & Co., 1967), pp. 63–66.

Samuel Ward's Diary

[October 11, 1775]

11th. Pennsylvania & Connect. to report to Morrow. Some Accts. allowed. Debate concrng field officers resumed & refer'd until the return of the Comee from Cambridge. Comee. for billeting &c.

MS (RHi).

Samuel Ward to Henry Ward

Dear Brother Philadelphia 11th Octr. 1775

I received yours of 3rd. inst. and very readily allow it to ballance our literary Accts. to that time.

Dr. Church, Who could have thought or even suspected it, a Man who seemed to be all Animation in the Cause of his Country, highly caressed, employed in several very honorable & lucrative Departments, & in full Possession of the Confidence of his Country, what a Complication of Madness & Wickedness must a Soul be filled with to be capable of such Perfidy, what Punishment can equal such horrid Crimes.[1] I communicated the Affair to the Massachusetts Delegates. They could hardly conceive it possible. They soon after recd. some Acct. of the Matter themselves. A Letter from Mr. Secry Reed says upon searching his Papers nothing amiss was found in them. His Friends from thence would infer his Innocence, he pretends that the Letters sent through Wallace were wrote to his Bror. in Law Fleming (late Partner with Mein) & contained Accts. favourable to our Cause. Such Letters as these might have been sent in every Week without Interruption, of course there could be no Occasion for that expensive roundabout & suspicious Way of Conveyance which he took. I am obliged to you for the circumstantial Acct. of the Matter as it throws Light on the Subject. How happy it is that He is discovered before he has done us any considerable Mischief.

The greatest that I am apprehensive of is that it may induce Suspicions & lessen that Confidence which is necessary to a cordial Union & our mutual Support, this ought carefully to be guarded against as fatal, and at the same Time the utmost Vigilance is necessary least we should be betrayed.

Our Letter to Govr. Cooke & my last to you contain most of the News, but since those I have seen one Letter from a faithful & very sensible Friend in England which gives us a most minute Acct. of affairs. The K—— says He, who out does Lord Mansfield himself in Dissimulation & Lust of Power is at the Head of the violent Measures pursued & planning; Councils are frequently called, various Conclusions formed but all agreeing in this to make an absolute Conquest of America. The K—— hath himself prevailed on Sir Jeffery Amherst to come over next Spring, has engaged him a Reinforcement of 20000 Men, 2000 of them Highlanders 3000 Roman Catholics the remaining 15000 to be Hanoverians & Hessians, the Plan of Operations much the same as in our Letter to Govr. Cooke. After giving us a very full Acct. of the Intentions of the Enemy, Our Friend in a most masterly Manner points out many very important Measures for our Defence some of which the Congress have already taken, the rest they will soon adopt I believe, some of them are of such a Nature I dont chuse to commit them to paper. The constant training of the Militia is one thing recommended another is that all the valuable Goods should be removed from Rhode Island least the Town should be surprized as Boston was; I hope this Sentiment from One in England who has the best Means of information will add such Weight to my frequent Applications upon that Subject as may secure every thing which it is in their Power to remove or defend. The People of New York have moved & are daily moving their Families & most valuable Effects into the Country. A very Strong Fortification is building on the Highlands about 45 miles above New York which it is said will effectually command the North River. Two Battalions are ordered by Congress to be immediately raised in the Jerseys for the Defence of that Post & the neighbouring Coasts in one Word all Hopes of a speedy Reconciliation are given over and We unanimously determine to push the War with the greatest Vigor.

We recd. Govr. Cooke's Letters of the 3d. and if any thing new turns up to Day We shall write by the Post, if not, We shall omit it for I am almost worn out with Attention; I am upon a standing Comee. of Claims which meets every Morning before Congress; and upon the Secret Comee. which meets almost every afternoon. These with a close Attendance upon Congress and writing many Letters make my Duty very hard; And I cannot get time to ride or take other Exercise but I hope the Business will not be so pressing very long. My affectionate Regards to our Friends. May God preserve them all. I am Most affectionately yours. Sam Ward

P.S. That Bundle & Letter for Nancy you will please to take care of & forward as directed.

RC (RHi).

[1] On this point, see John Adams to Abigail Adams, October 10, 1775, note 1.

John Adams' Notes of Debates

Oct. 12. [1775]

Report, on Trade, considered in a Committee of the whole.[1]

Lee. It has been moved to bring the debate to one Point, by putting the Q. whether the Custom houses shall be shut up, and the officers discharged from their several Functions. This would put N. York, N.C., lower Counties and Georgia upon the same Footing with the other Colonies.[2]

I therefore move you, that the C[ustom] Houses be shut, and the officers discharged. This will remove Jealousies and Divisions.

Zubly. The Measure, We are now to consider, extreamly interesting. I shall offer my Thoughts. If We decide properly, I hope We shall establish our Cause—if improperly, We shall overthrow it, altogether.

1st Prop[osition]. Trade is important. 2. We must have a Reconciliation with G.B. or the Means of carrying on the War. An unhappy day when We shall.

A Republican Government is little better than Government of Devils. I have been acquainted with it from 6 Years old.

We must regulate our Trade so as that a Reconciliation be obtained or We enable[d] to carry on the War.

Cant say, but I do hope for a Reconciliation, and that this Winter may bring it. I may enjoy my Hopes for Reconciliation, others may enjoy theirs that none will take Place.

A Vessell will not go, without Sails or Oars. Wisdom is better than Weapons of War. We dont mean to oppose G.B. merely for Diversion. If it is necessary that We make War, and that we have the Means of it, This Continent ought to know what it is about. The Nation dont. We ought to know what they mean to be about. We ought to have Intelligence of the Designs. K. of Prussia and Count Daune march'd and counter march'd untill they could not impose upon Each other any more. Every Thing We want for the War are Powder and Shot.

2d Thing necessary that We have Arms and Ammunition.

3. We must have Money. The Cont[inent']s Credit must be supported. We must keep up a Notion that this Paper is good for Something. It has not yet a general Circulation. The Mississippi Scheme in France and the South Sea Scheme in England were written for our Learning. An hundred Million fell in one day. 20 Men of War may block up the Harbour of N. York, Del[aw]are River, Cheasapeak Bay, the Carolinas and Georgia.

Whether We can raise a Navy is an important Question. We may have a Navy—and to carry on the War We must have a Navy. Can We do this without Trade? Can we gain Intelligence without Trade. Can We get Powder without Trade? Every Vessell you send out is thrown away. N. England where the War is may live without Trade. Money circulates there—they may live. Without Trade our People must starve. We cannot live. We cannot feed or cloath our People. My Resolution was that I would do and suffer any Thing rather than not be free. But I resolved not to do impossible Things.

If We must trade, We must trade with Somebody, and with Somebody that will trade with us, either with foreigners or G.B. If with foreigners, We must either go to them or they must come to us. We cant go to them if our Harbours are shut up. I look upon the Trade with foreigners as impracticable. St. Lawrence being open is a Supposition.

N. England People last War went to C[ape] Francois.

Spaniards are too lazy to come to Us.

If We cant trade with foreigners we must trade with G. Britain. Is it practicable. Will it quit cost. Will it do more hurt than good. This is breaking our Association. Our People will think We are giving Way and giving all up. They will say one mischivous Man has overset the whole Navigation. I speak from Principle. It has been said here that the Association was made in terrorem.

Gadsden. 2ds. Lees Motion, and affirms that We can carry on Trade from one End of the Continent to the other.

Deane. Custom house Officers discharged! Were they ever in our Pay, in our service. Let em stand where they are. Let this Congress establish what Offices they please. Let the others die. I think that all the Colonies ought to be upon a footing. We must have Trade. I think We ought to apply abroad. We must have Powder and Goods. We cant keep our People easy without.

Lee. The Gentleman agrees that all ought to be upon a Footing. Let him shew how this can be done without shutting the Custom-houses.

Jay. This should be the last Business We undertake. It is like cutting the Foot to the shoe, not making a shoe for the Foot. Let Us establish a System first.

I think We ought to consider the whole, before We come to any Resolutions. Now Gentlemen have their Doubts whether the N. Exportation was a good Measure. I was last Year, clear vs. it. Because the Enemy have burn'd Charlestown, would Gentlemen have Us burn N. York? Let us lay every Burden as equal on all the Shoulders that We can. If Prov[idence] or Ministry inflict Misfortunes on one, shall We inflict the same on all? I have one Arm sore—why should not the other Arm be made sore too? But Jealousies will arise. Are these reasonable? Is it politick? We are to consult the general Good of all America. Are We to do hurt to remove unreasonable Jealousies. Because Ministry have imposed hardships on one, shall We impose the same on all. It is not from affection to N. York, that I speak. If a Man has lost his Teeth on one side of his Jaws, shall he pull out the Teeth from the other that both sides may be upon a Footing? Is it not realizing the Quarrell of the Belly and the Members? The other Colonies may avail themselves of the Custom houses in the exempted Colonies.

Lee. All must bear a proportional share of the Continental Expence. Will the exempted Colonies take upon themselves the whole Expence. V. pays a sixth Part, the lower Counties an 80th—yet lower Counties may trade, V. not. The Gentleman exercised an Abundance of Wit to shew the Unreasonableness of Jealousies. If this ministerial Bait is swallowed by America another will be thrown out.

Jay. Why should not N.Y. make Money, and N. Jersey not. One Colony can cloath them.

McKean. I have 4 Reasons for putting the favoured Colonies upon a footing with the rest. 1st. is to disappoint the Ministry. Their design was insidious. 2. I would not have it believed by Ministry or other Colonies that those Colonies had less Virtue than others. 3. I have a

Reconciliation in View, it would be in the Power of those Colonies, it might become their Interest to prolong the War. 4. I believe Parliament has done or will do it for us, i.e. put us on the same footing. I would choose that the exempted Colonies should have the Honour of it. Not clear that this is the best Way of putting them upon a Footing. If We should be successfull in Canada, I would be for opening our Trade to some Places in G.B., Jamaica, &c.

J. Rutledge. Wonders that a Subject so clear, has taken up so much Time. I was for a general Non Exportation. Is it not surprizing, that there should so soon be a Motion for breaking the Association. We have been reproached for our Breach of Faith in breaking the Non Imp. I have the best Authority to say that if We had abided by a former Non Imp. We should have had redress. We may be obliged hereafter to break the Association, but why should We break it before We feel it. I expected the Delegates from the exempted Colonies would have moved to be put upon the same footing.

Dont like shutting the C. Houses and discharging the Officers—but moves that the Res[olution] be, that People in York, N. Car., Georgia and lower Counties dont apply to the Custom house.

Zubly. Georgia is settled along Savanna River, 200 miles in Extent, and 100 mile the other Way. I look upon it the Association alltogether will be the Ruin of the Cause. We have 10,000 fighting Indians near us. Carolina has already smuggled Goods from Georgia.

Chase. I will undertake to prove that if the Revd. Gentlemans Positions are true and his Advice followed, We shall all be made Slaves. If he speaks the Opinion of Georgia I sincerely lament that they ever appeared in Congress. They cannot, they will not comply! Why did they come here? Sir We are deceived. Sir We are abused! Why do they come here? I want to know why their provinc[ial] Congress came to such Resolutions. Did they come here to ruin America. That Gentlemans Advice will bring Destruction upon all N. America. I am for the Resolution upon the Table. There will be Jealousies, if N.Y. and the other exempted Colonies are not put upon a footing.

It is not any great Advantage to the exempted Colonies. What can they export that will not be serviceable to G.B. and the West Indies.

The exports of N. Car. are of vast Importance to G.B. If these Colonies are in Rebellion, will not their Effects be confiscated, and seized even upon the Ocean.

Arms and Ammunition must be obtained by what is call'd Smuggling. I doubt not We shall have the Supply. Leaving open N. York &c. will prevent our getting Arms and Ammunition.

Houstoun. Where the Protection of this Room did not extend, I would not set very tamely.

Chase. I think the Gentleman ought to take offence at his Brother Delegate.

Wythe. Agrees with the Gentleman from N. York that We dont proceed regularly. The Safety of America depends essentially on a Union of the People in it. Can We think that Union will be preserved if 4 Colonies are exempted. When N. York Assembly did not approve the Procedings of the Congress it was not only murmured at, but lamented as a Defection from the public Cause. When Attica was invaded by the Lacedemonians, Pericles ordered an Estate to be ravaged and laid waste because he tho't it would be exempted, by the Spartan King.

Nothing was ever more unhappily applied, than the fable of the Stomach and the Limbs.

Sherman. Another Argument for putting [*sentence unfinished*].

MS (MHi). Adams, *Diary* (Butterfield), 2:204–8.

[1] A continuation of the debate in the committee of the whole on "the state of the trade" of the colonies. *JCC*, 3:291.

[2] Great Britain had not yet included the ports of these colonies under the terms of the acts restraining American commerce. See John Adams' Notes of Debates, October 4, 1775.

John Adams to William Tudor

Dr sir Octr. 12. 1775

I have recd yours of the first of this Inst. and am glad to find you have me still in Remembrance.

I wrote you some time ago, and ventured to acquaint you with the appointment of fifty dollars a Month to the Judge Advocate for himself and his Clerk, to commence from his first Appointment. This I hope you recd. I feel more anxious about Letters than formerly as you may well imagine. The Times are so critical and there are so many Peepers, that one cant be too carefull. Indeed the horrid Story you allude to in yours of the surgeon &c is enough to make one jealous of every Body, but it must not have this Effect.[1] In the Reign of Charles the first, such Instances of Treachery and Infidelity, were not uncommon. I would fain hope however that this has turned out more favourably than was feared: yet from several private Letters received here by Gentlemen, I am Staggered. What shall We say? I think it very odd, however, that every Event which happens at the Camp should regularly come to Governers Ward or Hopkins, or to Coll Dyer or Mr Deane, before it comes to me. It is really astonishing. However hush Complaint.

The last Accounts from my Family were very disagreable—and yours mentions not a Word of it. I hope for the best but should be rejoiced to hear.

Three Battalions I believe will be raised in Pensilvania and the

Jersies for the Defence of New York.[2] News We have none, but such as you see in the Papers.

As you are now in the military Line of Life, I presume it will not be disagreable to have your Thoughts turned to military Speculations. I want to know what Books upon Martial Science are to be found in the Army, and whether, among the many young Gentlemen in the service, any of them are studious of the Principles of the Art. It is a shame for Youths of Genius and Education to be in the Army, without exerting themselves to become Masters of the Profession. If it is objected that Books are not to be had, Measures ought to be taken to procure them. To this End I wish to collect a perfect List of the best authors, and should be obliged to you if you would enquire and make up one for me—and at the same Time enquire whether the following are in the Possn. of any Body in the Army. Dalrymples military Essay. Saxes Reveries. History of Prussia. History of Frederic 3d. Le Blonds military Engineer. History of the late War. Mullers Works Eight Volumns. Maneuvres for a Battalion of Infantry, by Major Young. Military Guide, by Simes. Andersons Art of War. Prussian Field Regulations. King of Prussia's Advice to young officers. Playdells Field Fortification. Simes's Medley. Bellidore, worth all the rest.[3]

RC (MHi).

[1] The allusion is to Dr. Benjamin Church. See Adams to Abigail Adams, October 10, and Samuel Ward to Henry Ward, October 11, 1775.

[2] See *JCC*, 3:285–86, 291.

[3] Remainder of MS apparently missing.

John Adams to James Warren

Dr Sir Octr. 12. 1775

I would write often if I had any thing to communicate: But obligations of Honour forbid some Communications and other Considerations prevent others. The common Chatt of a Coffee house, is too frivolous for me to recollect or you to read. I have inclosed a Paper upon which I will make no Remark: But leave you to your own Conjectures.[1] Only I must absolutely insist that it be mentioned to nobody. It may gratify your Curiosity and give Some Relief to your Cares.

I most earnestly pray that all my Friends would exert themselves to furnish me with Intelligence of a particular Nature. I mean with a List of all the Depredations committed upon our Trade, a List of all the Vessells which have been taken by the Cutters, Cruizers &c the Names of the Vessells, Masters owners, Burthen of the ship the Nature of the Cargo's and the Value of both. Nothing will contribute so much to facilitate Reprizals, as an exact Account of our Losses and Damages.[2] I wish our General Ct. would take it up—and examine it thoroughly.

We have no Accounts nor Vouchers yet. Nor one Line from the Comtee. appointed to correspond with Us.

I am very happy—how it is I know not—but I am very happy.

RC (MHi). In Adams' hand, though not signed.

[1] Adams enclosed a plan to send armed ships to capture the powder stored on the islands of Antigua and St. Eustatius. *Warren-Adams Letters*, 1:135–36.

[2] On October 18, Adams was named to a committee appointed to prepare "a just and well authenticated account of the hostilities committed by the ministerial troops and navy in America since last March." *JCC*, 3:298–99.

John Hancock to the New Jersey Provincial Convention

Gentlemen: Philadelphia, October 12, 1775.[1]

Some late intelligence, laid before Congress, seems to render it absolutely necessary, for the protection of our liberties and safety of our lives, to raise several new Battalions, and therefore the Congress have come into the enclosed resolutions, which I am ordered to transmit to you.[2] The Congress have the firmest confidence that, from your experienced zeal in this great cause, you will exert your utmost endeavours to carry the said resolutions into execution with all possible expedition.

The Congress have agreed to furnish the men with a hunting-shirt, not exceeding the value of one dollar and one-third of a dollar, and a blanket, provided these can be procured; but these are not to be made part of the terms of enlistment.

I am, Gentlemen, your most obedient humble servant,

John Hancock, President.

P.S. By order of Congress, I forward you forty-eight commissions for the Captains and subaltern officers in the *New-Jersey* Battalions.

MS not found; reprinted from *Am. Archives*, 4th ser. 3:1223.

[1] Hancock wrote a similar letter this day to the Pennsylvania Committee of Safety, asking it to raise one battalion of troops for the Continental Army. Ibid., pp. 1766–67.

[2] These enclosures were congressional resolves of October 9 and 12, pertaining to the raising of two New Jersey battalions. Congress deemed it necessary to raise these forces in consequence of a letter from an unidentified correspondent in London asserting that the British were about to make an effort to seize control of New York City, Albany, and the section of the Hudson between them, so as to disrupt communications between New York and neighboring provinces. To frus-

trate this design Congress planned to add the New Jersey battalions to the American forces already in the Highlands in southern New York. Ibid., p. 1281; *JCC*, 3:285–86, 290–91; and John Adams' Notes of Debates, October 7, 1775.

Samuel Ward's Diary

[October 12, 1775]

12th. Capn. & other Comn. officers allowed while recruiting or on their March 2 2/3 doll[ar]s Billet, & the men while in quarters 1 Dollar per Week, while on March 1 1/3. Blanket & shirt allowed each Soldier if to be got not to be in the terms of enlistment.[1] The President to transmit blank Com[mission]s to the convention of New Jersey for the Officers ordered to com[man]d the Troops.

John Penn Esqr. a Delegate from No. Carolina arrived & took his Place accordingly.[2] Resolved into a Com[mitte]e of the whole for consideration of the State of the trade of the united Colonies. Mr. Ward reported that the Comee. had taken into their consideration according to the Order of the Day the State of the Trade &c.

MS (RHi).

[1] See *JCC*, 3:289.

[2] Penn was chosen by the North Carolina Provincial Congress on September 8 to take the place of Richard Caswell, who had resigned his seat in Congress to become the treasurer of the Southern District of North Carolina. William John Schmidt, "The North Carolina Delegates in the Continental Congress, 1774–1781" (Ph.D. diss., University of North Carolina, Chapel Hill, 1968), pp. 45–47.

Samuel Ward to Deborah Ward

My dearest Debby — Philadelphia 12th. Octr. 1775

Your Letter accompanying your Sisters was very acceptable. I shall always be pleased to receive Letters from you & write to you and though your Daddy does not always write a very good Letter the Correspondence probably will be no Injury to You. Your Aunts I imagine are with you before this Time, their Company I doubt not will be agreable and instructive. I could wish it was in my Power to give you & all the rest of my dear Tribe a better Education but when all that We have is called in Question by wicked men if We can but preserve Life Liberty & Property we shall be happy. You must endeavour to polish & improve each other.

Your dear Bror. Sammy I know no Way of writing to at present, as soon as I find any mode of conveying Letters I will let you know it.

My dear little [boys?] I hope they are prudent & industrious & take all possible Care of every thing, and would have them spend the

Evenings & as much time as they can spare in reading & writing. They have nobody to teach them cyphering but they have learnt so much that they can easily keep what they have got. They can improve in writing & we have many excellent Books which they may greatly improve their Minds by and I would wish you & Polly to read & write as much as possible. Dear little Betsey I hope does not run wild, she must be always clean neat decent & industrious. What time she can get to spare I wish her to spend in reading proper Books. When I shall see any of you God only knows. The Business before us is of such vast Importance, the Feild so large & the Answer from England to our Applications which may not be expected this month or more so very interesting that it is impossible for me to form any Judgment when I may return; probably not until some time in the Winter. You must all do the best you can to preserve our common Interest & make each other happy. As to the disposing of the Money I left a Memorandum for Mrs. Lamoine to be paid £5—law. She cant want it all & every now & then I will pay her some. I owed young Robert Stevens about 80 Dollars as I recollect. The Note Simon Pease has I would have that paid; your Bror. Greene you may get to do it for you, charge directly all Moneys you [. . . .][2]

RC (RHi).

[1] Ward also wrote a letter this day to his daughter Anna, expressing concern over her poor health. Ward, *Correspondence* (Knollenberg), pp. 101–2.

[2] Remainder of MS missing.

John Adams' Notes of Debates

Octr. 13. 1775

R. Livingston. Hopes the whole Matter will be putt off. Is willing as it seems the general sense, that all should be put upon a Footing.[1]

Gadsden. Hopes it will not be putt off. S. Carolina will be in the utmost Confusion if this matter is not decided. Let the Continent determine.

Stone. Can see no particular Inconvenience to Carolina. 2ds. the Motion of Mr. Livingston, for postponing the Question, and gives his Reasons. The Powder Committee must take Clearances. If they are allowed to take Clearances, and no other, then whenever they take a Clearance it will be known, that it is for Powder, and the Vessell will be watched.

Lee. I see very clearly, that the best Time for putting a Question is when it is best understood. That Time is the present. As to Powder, Time may be allowed for the Committee to clear Vessells.

J. Rutledge. Thinks this Motion extraordinary. This Subject has been under Consideration 3 Weeks. It is really trifling. The Committee may have Time allowed to clear Vessells for Powder. But I had rather the Continent should run the Risque of sending Vessells without clearances. What Confusion would ensue if Congress should break up without any Resolution of this sort. The Motion seems intended to defeat the Resolution entirely. Those who are against it, are for postponing.

Jay. We have complied with the restraining Act. The Question is whether we shall have Trade or not? And this is to introduce a most destructive Scheme, a scheme which will drive away all your Sailors, and lay up all your Ships to rot at the Wharves.[2]

MS (MHi). Adams, *Diary* (Butterfield), 2:208–9.

[1] A continuation of the debate in the committee of the whole on "the state of the trade" of the colonies. *JCC*, 3:291–92.

[2] For a further exposition of Jay's view on exportation, see John Jay to Alexander McDougall, October 17, 1775.

John Adams to Abigail Adams

Octr. 13. 1775. Consoles his wife on the death of her mother, Elizabeth Quincy Smith.[1] Concludes: "The Prospect before Us is an Ocean of Uncertainties, in which no pleasing objects appear. We have few Hopes, excepting that of preserving our Honour and our Consciences untainted and a free Constitution to our Country. . . . My Heart is too full of Grief for you and our Friends to whom I wish you to present my Regards, to say any Thing of News or Politicks. Yet the Affair of the surgeon general is so strange, and important an Event that I cannot close this gloomy Letter, without adding a Sigh for this imprudent unfortunate Man! I know not whether the Evidence will support the Word Treachery, but what may We not expect after Treachery to himself, his Wife and Children!"

RC (MHi). Adams, *Family Correspondence* (Butterfield), 1:300–301.

[1] Adams also wrote letters of sympathy and encouragement to his daughter, Abigail, and to his son, Thomas Boylston, on October 20, 1775. Adams, *Family Correspondence* (Butterfield), 1:304–5.

John Adams to Charles Lee

My dear Sir — Philadelphia Octr. 13. 1775

Your obliging Favour of the fifth Inst. I this Moment received, and give me Leave to assure you that no Letter I ever received, gave me greater Pleasure. In truth sir I have been under some Apprehensions, that a certain Passage, in a very unfortunate as well as inconsiderate Letter, might have made Some disagreable Impressions on your Mind.[1] I was indeed relieved in some Degree by accounts which I had from Gentlemen who knew your sentiments, especially such as were present when you first heard it read. The candid, genteel and generous Manner in which it was heard and animadverted on, gave me great Satisfaction. I had thought of writing you on the Subject, but was hindered by certain Notions of Delicacy perhaps as whimsical, as any Thing alluded to in that Letter. But I rejoice exceedingly, that this incident has induced you to write.

I frankly confess to you that a little Whim and Eccentricity, so far from being an objection to any one in my Mind, is rather, a Recommendation, at first Blush, and my Reasons are, because few Persons in the World, within my Experience or little Reading, who have been possessed of Virtues or Abilities, have been entirely without them; and because few Persons have been remarkable for them, without having Something at the same Time, truly valuable in them.

I confess farther that a Fondness for Dogs, by no means depreciates any Character in my Estimation, because many of the greatest Men have been remarkable for it; and because I think it Evidence of an honest Mind and an Heart capable of Friendship, Fidelity and Strong Attachments being Characteristicks of that Animal.

Your opinions of my Generosity, Valour, Good sense, Patriotism and Zeal for the Rights of Humanity, is extreamly flattering to me: and I beg leave to assure you, in the strongest Manner and I flatter myself that my Language and Conduct in public and private upon all occasions, notwithstanding the wanton Expressions in the intercepted Letter have demonstrated, that this opinion is reciprocal. Your Sincerity, sir, I never doubted, any more than I did my own, when I expressed or implied an opinion of your Attainments as a Schollar and a Soldier. Indeed I might have expressed a much higher opinion of these than I did, with the Same Sincerity. But enough of this.

At the Story of the Surgeon General I stand astonished. A Man of Genius, of Learning, of Family, of Character, a Writer of Liberty Songs and good ones too, a Speaker of Liberty orations, a Member of the Boston Committee of Correspondence, a Member of the Massachusetts Congress, an Agent for that Congress to the Continental Congress, a Member of the House, a Director General of the Hospital and Surgeon General. Good God! What shall We say of human Nature? What shall We say of American Patriots? Or rather what will the World say? The World however, will not be too severe. Indeed, Sir, We ought to expect, in a Contest like this, however we may detest, such Examples as this. History furnishes Instances more or less, in all Quarells like this. The D[octo]r's Brother Poet, Waller,[2] in the Struggle with a Stuart, was his Antitype. We cannot be too cautious of the Persons We entrust, in such Times as these: Yet We ought not to let our Caution degenerate into groundless Jealousy. There is a Medium between Credulity on one hand and a base suspicious Temper on the other from which We need not be induced to deviate, even in such Times as these, and by such Examples as the Drs.

The Nature of the Conspiracy and the Duration and Extent of it Seem as yet in much obscurity. I hope Time, and Care will bring the whole Truth to light that exact and impartial Justice may be done, if that is possible.

Before this Reaches you, a Comtee. from Congress will tell you News from hence. I wish, sir that I could write freely to you concerning our Proceedings. But you know the obligations I am under to be upon the Reserve: and the danger there would be as I know not the Carrier of this Letter, if I was at perfect Liberty. But this I must Say, that I See no danger of our "displaying Timidity." This Congress is more united, and more determined, than ever. And, if the petrified Tyrants would but send us their Ultimatum, which is expected Soon,[3] you would see Us, in Earnest.

As to confiscating Estates,[4] that is but a small Part of what will be done when We are engaging seriously.

You began upon a Subject, towards the Close of your Letter of infinite Importance; I read with avidity your Thoughts and was much chagrin'd that you gave me so few of them. The Intricacy and Multiplicity of the Questions involved in it, require more extensive Knowledge and a larger Mind than mine to determine them with Precision. There is so much Uncertainty too, that I believe no Man is capable of deciding with Precision; but it must be left to Time, Accident and Experience, to begin and improve the Plan of our Trade.

If We should invite "all the Maritime Powers of the World into our Ports," would any one of them come? At least, untill they should be convinced that We were able, and determined to fight it out with G. B. to the last? Are they yet convinced of this, or will they be very soon? Besides, if they should, Would it be Sound Policy in Us to admit them? Would it not be sounder to confine the Benefit and the Bargain to one or a few?

Is it not wiser to send our own Ships to all maritime Powers, and admit private adventurers from foreign Nations, if by any Means We can defend them against Cutters and Cruizers, or teach them to elude them. I have upon this Subject a System of my own but am not bigoted to it, nor to any other. You will oblige me vastly by your Sentiments at large.

RC (MHi). In Adams' hand, though not signed. Recipient identified from Lee's October 5 letter to Adams, which contains two phrases quoted by Adams. Charles Lee to John Adams, October 5, 1775, Adams, *Works* (Adams), 2:414–15n.

[1] In his famous July 24 letter to James Warren, which was captured and

published by the British, Adams had made an unflattering reference to Lee, who accepted the remark with grace.

[2] Edmund Waller (1606–87), Stuart poet and politician, who thrice reversed his political allegiance during the era of the Puritan revolution. *DNB.*

[3] Remainder of MS missing; continuation of the text supplied from *Warren-Adams Letters,* 1:138–39.

[4] Massachusetts had already moved to vest control of the property of loyalist emigrés in the hands of the town governments on June 21, 1775. *Am. Archives,* 4th ser. 2:1431.

John Adams to James Warren

Octr. 13. 1775

Yours of October 1 and 2d I received this Morning with the Letters inclosed. These were from my afflicted Wife, giving me Such a continued History of her Distresses, as has affected me too much to write you a long Letter.

The Misfortune, or what shall I call it of the Surgion General had been represented here in Several Letters in very glaring Colours untill one arrived from the secretary to the general, couched in Terms of more Temper and Candour. By your Account,[1] and indeed by the Letter itself it appears an unaccountable affair. Balaam praying for Leave to curse Israel, is the Emblem. A manifest Reluctance at hurting his Country, yet desirous of making a Merit, with the other Side —what shall We think! Is there reason to believe that other Letters have gone the same Way? I was so little acquainted with the World that I never heard a Suspicion to the Disadvantage of his Moral Character, untill I was lately with you at the Adjournment. I should scarcely have joined in a certain Recommendation, if I had heard before what I heard then—for Honour and Fidelity violated in Such gross Instances in private Life, are slender securities in public. Be not concerned about your Friends at the Congress—their Recommendations will not be discredited by this Event. Gentlemen here have behaved universally with the Utmost Politeness, upon this occasion. They say they pitty us, for the Suspicions that there is danger may arise among us of one another, and the Hurt to that Confidence in one another which ought to be—but any Man ought to be kick'd for a Brute that shall reproach Us in Thought, Word or Deed on this account.

Our Accounts from Schuyler's Army are as agreable as yours from Arnold. We are in hourly Expectation.

Rejoice to hear of your Successes by Sea. Let Cargill and Obrien be put into continental service immediately I pray.

We begin to feel a little of a Seafaring Inclination here. The Powder at Quebec, will place us all upon the Top of the House.

Your Letters are very usefull to me, and I cannot have too many, or too long.

I believe We shall take some of the twenty Gun ships before long. We must excite by Policy that Kind of exalted Courage, which is ever victorious by sea and land—which is irresistable. The Saracens had it —the Knights of Malta—the Assassins—Cromwells Soldiers and Sailors. Nay N. England men have ever had it hitherto—they never yet fail'd in an attempt of any Kind.

RC (MHi). In Adams' hand, though not signed.

[1] See James Warren to John Adams, October 1, 1775. *Warren-Adams Letters,* 1:121–23.

Samuel Adams to James Warren

My dear sir, Philadelphia Octob. 13th 1775

It is now more than a Month since we arrivd in this City. I have receivd but one Letter and for that I am much indebted to you. I thought our Assembly had appointed a Committee to transmit Intelligence to us. We hear nothing from them. Have they no Intelligence of Importance to send to us? If so, let them inform us even of that, and we will pay the Postage of their Letter. But surely it is of some Importance that we should know whether C[hurch] is a Traiter or not—that on the one hand we might joyn like disinterrested Patriots in execrating him, or on the other hand, in vindicating the Character of an unfortunate Friend. Our pride is sorely mortified when there are Grounds to suspect that so eminent a Countryman is become a Traiter. The Fool will say in his heart, there is no such thing in the World as publick Spirit—the most virtuous Citizen will be suspected of concealing his dishonest Designs under a Cloak of Zeal for his Country and the brightest Examples will lose their Influence.

I am very sollicitous that our Army, if it be practicable, should make a resolute Attack upon the Rebels before a Reinforcement to them shall arrive, which I think may be depended upon very soon. Genl Gage I understand is already gone for England. This verifies a part of the Intelligence which I gave you in my last Letter. Howe will remain in Command till the Spring when Amherst will come out as strong as they can make him. It is said that ——— usd his utmost Power of Dissimulation (and he is as great a Master of it as Mansfield or Hutchinson) to prevail on him to undertake the Command. Among the officers of the British Army, the Slavish Maxim "The Will of the Prince is Law" too much prevails. They will suffer the arbitrary and cruel Commands of their Sovereign to supercede the Dictates of Honor, Morality and Conscience. I fear there are few, if more than one Effingham to be found in Britain. I have thought there was more of the true principle of Honor in the British Army, than among any other publick Class. If this be a Truth it is a melancholly one, for it is greatly to be apprehended that there is not Virtue enough in the Nation to save it. We know by long Experience that there is not Virtue enough there to save America. Why then should America expect it from Britain. This fond Hope of a Change from violent to lenient Measures in Britain is the Rock which endangers the Shipwreck of America.

This Instant is arrivd an authentick Account of Dr Churchs Affair and a Copy of the Letter he had intended to send into Boston. To me it appears to be a very unintelligible Letter—I have not indeed thoroughly examind it—I have only heard it read. I do not recollect that it in any measure was calculated to expose the Weakness of our Army, which a Traitor would gladly have seizd the opportunity of doing, especially as he might have done it at that time with great Truth. The Union of Individual Colonies & of the Continental Congress, and their firmness and Resolution are picturd in high Colours; he informs of the Arrival of large Quantities of Gun powder at a time when he knew there was the greatest Scarcity, and was solliciting his Friends here to take every Method for providing as he expressed it that "unum necessarium." Other parts of his Letter wear a different Complection, such as his mentioning the Defeat of our Army at Bunkers Hill as "lucky," his attempting three times in vain to send in his Letter, the messenger in the third Attempt being taken up (which I do not recollect to have heard before) and the Manner in which this Letter was conceald. But I will quit this disagreeable Subject and conclude with assuring you that I am very affectionately, yours

S A

RC (MHi).

Samuel Ward's Diary

[October 13, 1775]

13th. Resolved into a Com[mitte]e of the whole & resumed the Consideration of Trade &c. Mr. Ward reported that &c. A Letter from Genl. Washington with Papers relative to Dr. Church &c.[1] Resolved that a swift sailg. [*vessel*] to carry 10 car[riage] Guns & a proportionable Number of Swivels with 80 men to be filled with all possible dispatch to cruize three months eastward for intercepting such Transports laden with warlike Stores & other Supplies for our Ene[mie]s & such other Purposes as the Cong[res]s may direct. A Com[mitte]e appointed to estimate the Expence & report a proper

Vessel. (Remainder of the Report referred to Monday next.) Memorials from New York & Phi[ladelphi]a Merchants relative to Tea; Mes[sr]s Rutledge, S. & J. Adams, Mr. Ward & Colo. Lee the Comee. to take into their consideration of the Memorials & report.[2]

MS (RHi).

[1] For Washington's letter to Hancock of October 5, together with accompanying enclosures, see PCC, item 152, 1:181–216; and *Am. Archives*, 4th ser. 3:956–63.

[2] See *JCC*, 3:294, 298, 353, 370, 388–89.

Samuel Ward's Diary

[October 14, 1775]

14th. Letters from Genl. Washingn again taken into Consideration; postponed to Monday. A Director Genl. of hospital &c to be chosen on Monday next. Affair between Connecticut & Pennsylvania referred until Monday. A Comee. was moved for by the first.[1]

MS (RHi).

[1] That is, moved by the Connecticut delegates. See *JCC*, 3:295.

Samuel Ward to Henry Ward

Philadelphia 15th Octr. 1775. Thanks his brother for accounts of the "affair of Dr. Church," and goes on to discuss Rhode Island affairs. "Poor Newport, the People are at last thrown into that distressed Situation which I have long foreseen. I wish more of them had taken my Advice & saved what they could seasonably. The Measures taken by the Depy. Govr. & Council I think were very judicious. We shall have one Advantage from this Maneuvre of Wallaces.[1] We shall know our Enemies & be able to treat them properly. The present State of the Colony appears to me to demand immediate and great Attention. If there be any thing that We can do here I hope We shall have timely Instructions." Considers the state of the conflict with Great Britain. "Our Enemies are now straining every Nerve; We in this Respect ought to imitate them. Suppose we should have occasion for 30000 Troops, the difference between 30s/ & 40s/ per Month would be £180000 law M[one]y per Year. Would We risque every thing dear to human Nature to save that paltry Sum to thirteen Colonies? Can any Man weight it against the Liberties of America. I hope you will attend to this Matter very closely. If We have good Troops I am not afraid of the Event, if We should suffer those we now have to be disbanded [. . .] up raw &

faithless men to fight a veteran Army strongly reinforced God knows what may be the Consequence."

RC (RHi). Abstracted from badly mutilated document.

[1] Capt. James Wallace, commander of H.M.S. *Rose,* was in charge of a squadron of British naval vessels which patroled Narragansett Bay, harassing American shipping and procuring supplies from local farmers for the British army. Early in October Wallace threatened to destroy Newport unless Rhode Island withdrew a force of fifteen hundred militiamen, which had been dispatched there by the provincial government to prevent his obtaining supplies for British troops in Boston. Although the militiamen retired from the town and Wallace did not bombard it, his threat to do so caused great alarm and triggered an exodus of townspeople into the surrounding countryside. William G. Roelker and Clarkson A. Collins, "The Patrol of Narragansett Bay (1774–76) by H. M. S. *Rose,* Captain James Wallace," *Rhode Island History* 9 (January 1950): 18–22.

Committee on Powder Report

[October 16? 1775][1]

The Committee appointed to enquire, what Powder has been Sent to the Army in the Northern Department, have attended that service and beg Leave to report

	Wt
That five Thousand Weight of Powder, sent from South Carolina, has been forwarded to the Said Army	5000
That Two Thousand one hundred and thirty six Pounds Weight have been forwarded to the Same Army from the City of Philadelphia	2136
That Seventeen hundred Weight have been forwarded from New York	1700
That Eight hundred Weight has been forwarded from Connecticutt	800
That Thirteen hundred Weight has been forwarded at another Time from the City of Philadelphia	1300
	10936
In Addition to which Two thousand Weight has been lately ordered to New York and from thence to the same Army	2000
	12,936

MS (MHi). In the hand of John Adams.

[1] This draft report was prepared by Adams sometime after October 16, when he, John Langdon, and Eliphalet Dyer were appointed to a committee "to enquire what quantity of powder has been sent to the northern army, and report by whom sent." *JCC,* 3:296. There is no indication in the journals when the committee made its report. See also John Hancock to the New York Provincial Convention, October 16, 1775.

Silas Deane's Proposals for Establishing a Navy

[October 16? 1775][1]

Estimate of the Expence of fitting for the Sea The following Shipps of Warr on a Three Mo. Cruize.

(Viz) One of 24 Gunns—9, 6, & 4 pounders with 200 Men, &c, &c.

	Dollrs.		
1 Captn.	20	per mo.	£7.10.0
Two Lieuts.	15 } 15 }	each do.	11. 5.0
1 Master	15	do.	5.12.6
Two Mates	12½ } 12½ }	each do.	9. 7.6
1 Boatswain	12½	do.	4.13.9
One Mate	10	do.	3.15.0
One Cook	10	do.	3.15.0
Two Mates—5 Dollrs each	10	do.	3.15.0
One Doctr.	15	do.	5.12.6
One Mate	10	do.	3.15.0
One Gunner	12½	do.	4.13.9
Two Mates—10 Drs. each	20	do.	7.10.0
One Capt. Marines	15	do.	5.12.6
One Armorer	10	do.	3.15.0
Officers 18	215		80.12.6
Men 182 @ 5 Drs	910		341. 5.0
200	1125		421.17.6
	3		3
Three Months Wages will be	3375		1265.12.6
Three Months provisions—say	2000		750. 0.0
24 Gunns & Carriages @ 50 Dr	1200		450. 0.0
20 Swivels @ 8 Drs	160		60. 0.0
60 best Muskets with long Bayonets—11 Drs	660		247.10.0
100 pr. pistols @ 10 Drs	1000		375. 0.0
200 Cutlasses @ 1 Dr	200		75. 0.0
10 Blunderbusses 10 Dr	100		37.10.0
2 Tonn of powder @ 800 Dollrs.	1600		600. 0.0
Stinkpotts, hand Granades & powder flask—say	500		187.10.0

Vessel fitted suppose	3500	1312.10.0
Amount of one Vessel of 24 Gunns	14295	5360.12.6
One ditto—ditto	14295	5360.12.6
Amount of Two Vessels of 24 Gunns for Three Mo. Cruize Carried Up	28590	£10721. 5.0
	Dollrs	
Amount Brt. Up.	28590	£10721. 5.0
One of 18 Gunns in the same proportion will Amount To—Nearest	10721	4020.10.6
Add one of the same Number of Gunns	10721	4020.10.6
One of 14 Gunns in the same proportion will Amount To	8339	3127. 2.6
Add one of the same Number of Gunns	8339	3127. 2.6
Suppose there be in Addition to these Four Shipps of Thirty Six Gunns each—built to draw but Twelve feet of Water. The Metal will be heavier but the No. of Men & value of Shipp will not rise in the same proportion. On the Scale of the Above they will Amount To Twenty One thousand 442 Dollrs. each. I will suppose them to Cost 25000 each then.		
4 Shipps of 36 Gunns each will Amount to	100,000	37.500. 0.0
	166,710	£62.516.11.0
Suppose I am short for sundry small articles and extra or incidental Charges to the Amt. of	13290	4983.15.0
	180,000	£67.500. 6.0

Total Amt. for fitting out on a Cruise of Three Months a Fleet of Ten Sail (Viz) 4 of 36 Gunns each
2 of 24 Gunns each
2 of 18 Gunns each
& 2 of 14 Gunns each

10

The Sailors wages are set at Five Dollars each, in Addition to which I propose that one third the Value of all prizes taken be shared between the Officers and Seamen.

The Enemy have not a Naval force Now on this Coast equall to the foregoing, if the Asia, Somerset, & Boyne be put out of the Question. These Three Shipps are ordered home and Forty Gunn Shipps and downward are to be employed on the American Station for the future. It is evident if they cruize in a Fleet they will not be formidable to Trade, and if single they will be liable to be attacked by an equall if not Superior force of the Continental fleet.

Connecticut has fitted out Two & Rhode Island Two, these joining with the Two from the Massachusetts and those which other Colonies & Individuals will fix for the Sea will go near, to form a Naval force equall if not Superior to what the Ministry will think of sending to America the Next season for they dream as little of Our meeting them, on the Sea as of Our invading Canada, and though their Naval power, & resources be ever so great in Brittain, they must inevitably be defeated the Next Campaign in America if We get early to Sea, these Shipps, and with them surprize, & intercept their Transports, or any considerable part of them, this effected, the distance between Us & Europe will put it out of their power to recover the blow, untill the season is over.

What will be the Loss to the Continent if these vessels should be so unfortunate as to make no prizes? I answer the Three Mo. Wages and provisions will Amount To nearest one Third of the Gross Sum or sixty Thousand Dollars, and the *ware & Tare* will make up Ninety or one half which is a large Computation—but if by means of this Force the Coastwise Trade only is protected to say Nothing of securing the introduction of Ammunition &c under their protection.

The Freight of Flour only to the Army will amount To a great part of the Sum, as every Barrel which they consume at present pays at least 12 Dollar Transportation more than if carried by Water. 40,000 Barrels transported will save Sixty Thousand out of the Ninety Thousand Dollars And other Articles will doubtless Amount to as much more. It is a fact that more than 40,000 Bls. of Flour have been consumed the present Season.

But the probability of Captures is much, in favor of the adventure.

The Transports unsuspecting danger will sail without Convoy. Every prize of this kind is of double Advantage—it weakens & disappoints the Enemy, strengthens & encourages Our Army.

It is good policy now to set on foot a Naval Force under proper Regulations, & the reasons for it are—

At least Ten Thousand Seamen are thrown out of employ in the Northern Colonies. These with their Owners, & the various mechanics, dependent on this extensive branch of Business cannot possibly long rest easy, in their present destitute, distress'd Situation, their Shipps rotting & their Families starving.

They will not revolt from the Cause but reprisal being justifiable as well by the Laws of Nature as of Nations, they will pursue the only Method in their power for indemnifying themselves, and Reprisals will be made. This will at best be but a kind of Justifiable piracy & subject to No Law or Rule, the Consequences may be very pernicious.

The first fortunate Adventurer will set many more on pushing their Fortunes.

Is it not more prudent, where the Loss can, at most, be so trifling to Turn this Spirit, this Temper, this Necessity of the Times down its right & proper Channel, and reduce it while in its infancy to Rule & Order before it become thro Want of Regulation, unmanageable? This will be, not only preventing, a Licentious roving, or piracy, but will be turning Our Enemies Weapons upon him.

Should private Adventurers take up the M[atter], every one will soon make his own Laws & in a few Years, No Law will govern, the mischief will grow rapidly & Our Own property will not be safe.

Such Adventures are already entered upon, Witness several Captures made by the provincials without order or direction.

This calls upon Us to be taken up & regulated at the first setting out. It will afterward be out of Our power. Our Coasts will swarm with roving adventurers, who if they forbear plundering of Us or Our immediate Freinds, may thro Necessity invade the property of the Subjects of those with whom We wish to stand well, & bring Accumulated Mischeif on these Colonies.

Can there be a scheme, or plan, by which, the above proposed, Naval Armament may be equipp'd, without burthening these Colonies, or interfering with their other important & Necessary Operations? I think there may, & therefore take leave to propose—

I. That a Committee of   persons skill'd in Maratime Affairs be Appointed to fitt for Sea with all possible dispatch the foregoing Vessels of Warr—that They have power to Commission proper persons to command the same and to Constitute such rules, Ordinances, & directions as they shall judge best for the well regulating such Naval force, subject to the revision, & Alteration, of the General Congress, or such board as they may hereafter appoint for that purpose—Also to give the several Commanders from Time to Time such Instructions for their Conduct as they shall judge Necessary Subject to the Controll of the Congress.

II. This Committee shall receive from the Continental Treasury the Sum of in Bills emitted solely for that purpose & made redeemable as hereafter provided for, and that sd. Committee receive after the rate of per Cent on the Sums by them disbursed, in executing said Trust for the Congress.[2]

III. These Vessels shall cruise, only to protect the Trade of these Colonies from the insults of Ministerial Cutters, & Shipps of Warr, & for intercepting, & seizing such Vessels as shall be employed to Transport Stores, or shall have Stores on board for the Ministerial Forces employed against these Colonies.

IV. The Neat [net] proceeds of all prizes after deducting the Shares of the Captors shall be by the Committee Accounted for to the Congress, by them to be applied toward sinking the Bills emitted for that purpose—all Convoy Mony, or [. . .] freight, shall be applied to the same purpose but of these the Officers & Seamen Shall have no Share. Whatever Stores, or Vessels, which on being found Useless for the present & shall be judged proper for Sale, they shall be sold for Gold, or Silver, or those Bills emitted for Naval purposes & the Neat Amount of the Sales shall be applied to discharge & sink the Sum first Granted for these purposes.

V. The Vessels of Warr already fitted out by any of these Colonies or Individuals or such as may hereafter be fitted out & shall join any part of the Fleet belonging to the Continent shall during their continuing with such Fleet or any part thereof be under the same Orders & Regulations as sd. Fleet are, & be subject to the Directions of the cheif Commander of the Continental Fleet then present, and all prizes taken, they or any of them present, & assisting shall be divided by the proportion of Gunns & Men in the respective Shipps or Vessels present.

VI. That the first Commissioned Captain be stiled Commodore and be considered as, & have the powers of a Commander in Cheif, under the Congress, or sd. Committee over sd. Fleet.

I have now run over the outlines of a Naval Establishment. The American Exchequer may have No Money to spare, for such an Adventure. That is not the Question. Is it Necessary, if so, let Us look for Ways, & Means. I would have the Money struck for the use of the Navy, be kept as a distinct affair, & the Bills be sunk, or discharged independant of other Concerns. If there should be any prizes they will help to pay off the Bills. The Sales of the Vessels, after the Cruize, if the Congress should not incline to keep it longer, in pay, will go farr in paying off the Bills. Suppose to make out The One half only, it is very probable, that selling, even at this discount with the Convoy Money, Freight & prizes, that the whole will be discharged. But in case this should fail & the whole at the end of Three Mo. be sunk, will not the forcing Our Enemy to keep their Naval force collected in a Fleet give such a free access to Vessels bringing the Stores We want, be an advantage adequate to this Sum? I think it will & more.

The Bills emitted should be paid off in three annual payments, and suppose to render the payment certain without burthening the public it be, by Three annual Lotteries, in which Case, whatever the Fleet may bring in, may be applied to the repairing of it, & increasing, if Necessary. This will take off all popular Objection in point of expences.

The Continent may be alarmed, at an additional expence, if a Navy be set on foot at Continental Charge, but a provision for sinking the Bills, by Lottery, will burthen no one, and it can be done with the greatest Certainty, by putting the Lottery, in effect, into Three Classes obliging the fortunate Adventurers in the first to receive a certain Number of Tickets in the Second in payment, in proportion To The Value of the prizes drawn, by which, a Sale will be insured, of so large a part of the next that the drawing will be punctually complied with.

MS (CtHi). In the hand of Silas Deane. Endorsed: "Estimate made At [Phila]delphia: Octo. 1775, which the American Navy [. . .] first begun."

[1] It seems probable that Deane had these proposals in mind when he wrote to Thomas Mumford on October 16 that he had been "directed by Congress to lay before them an Estimate of the Expence of a Naval Armament sufficient to Cope with the Cruisers, on this Coast." Deane was a member of the committee appointed on October 5 to prepare a plan for intercepting two British vessels and subsequently served as a member of the committee appointed on the 13th to prepare an estimate of the expense of outfitting two armed vessels for a three-month cruise. Congress had charged these committees with specific and rather limited tasks, but Deane took advantage of this opportunity to promote a plan for the establishment of a viable naval force. Although the press of other business consumed the attention of Congress on the 16th, Deane's proposals were probably included in the report of the committee "to prepare an estimate," which was read on the 17th, debated, and recommitted. On October 30 this committee, which came to be designated as the Naval Committee, was enlarged and authorized to outfit two additional vessels. Although the Naval Committee gradually acquired most of the functions suggested in Deane's proposal I, the overall thrust of his proposals was apparently too advanced for the majority of Congress at that time. See *JCC*, 3:277–80, 293–94, 297, 311–12; and Deane to Thomas Mumford, October 16? 1775.

[2] The only indication that Congress ever considered a separate emission of bills to fund naval operations was its resolution of November 8 which authorized the "Committee appointed to make an estimate . . . to contract for the making proper paper for a future emission of paper bills of credit." *JCC*, 3:342.

Silas Deane to Thomas Mumford

Dear Sir Philadelphia Octo. [16?] 1775[1]

Yours of the 3d I received this Moment, and am obliged to you, for the useful hints contained in it, as well as for your kind remembrance of Me. Sure I am you will not think Me Neglectful of you, when you consider my Situation. In a Word, distress'd as I am, at the prospects before Me & the cross, and untoward Accidents daily happening, I should well nigh go distracted were it not, that a continual Attention to Business, every hour of the Day, & Night, save those of Sleep, drive away reflection. Our People at Westmoreland have Conducted in a most shocking manner, so as to alarm this province & City to its very Center. A few Days before the adjournment of the Congress, in August, information was given that the Settlers under Connecticut, & those under Pensylvania had bickerings, & that there was danger of a Civil intestine dissention in that Quarter. After some Consultation on the Subject publicly in the Congress, & in private between the Delegates of the two Colonies in which some warmth was shown by individuals on both sides, We came to this Resolution that We would write to the Settlers under the different Claims to remain peaceably, on the Lands they had taken up, during the present Contest.[2] For my own part, I tho't that Our Letter would have such an effect, that I pledg'd myself, to the Congress, that the peace of the Colonies would receive no interruption, from that Quarter, for give me leave, in confidence to Tell you, that the indiscreet zeal of Col. Dyer did the Cause no service, and had, as I could plainly perceive, much hurt himself among The People of influence, interested in those Lands. The Col. meant well, but disputing on the Connecticut claim in all Companies, by means of artful & designing men, served to increase, & inflame the Apprehensions of the people. Mr. Sherman, & myself, pursued quite a different plan. For my own part, I avoided the dispute wholly and when forced upon it express'd my warmest wishes for a friendly Settlement. By this means I stood well with the more dispassionate, of the other party, when we left Philadelphia & I fondly hoped that my influence, with the settlers (to whom I had wrote in the most peremptory stile to keep quiet)[3] was such that I should have no Trouble from that Quarter.

Judd & Slumans expedition you have heard of, it is differently related, I will therefore pass no positive judgment on every particular, but on the whole, it was the most pernicious step they could have taken.[4] This whole province is alarmed, Judd & Sluman were a few Days since bro't under a strong guard to this City, and their Freinds denied all access to them at the first—& the people in this City thrown into such a Flame that Nothing but Col. Dyers character, as a Member of Congress, protected him for a few Days at first from per-

Silas Deane

sonal insult. The most opulent inhabitants of this City have lately become interested, under the Proprietaries in those Lands, they assembled, & fell to raising Money to employ an Armed Force to drive off all Our People without exception. Artful Enemies to the general Cause of America blew up the Flame, in hopes of breaking the general Union. I need not be more particular, to give you an Idea, of the distress which this Affair threw Me into, in a word I publicly, & sincerely condemned their Conduct. The Cheif Justice ordered them to procure Bail for their Appearance, with Sureties Freeholders of The province. This could not be procured, & they were committed. The Congress ordered the Delegates, of the two Colonies, to conferr & labor a Settlement, they did, but hitherto in vain, tho' I think the Storm subsides, and that a Temporary Settlement may be bro't about if rightly managed, which believe Me is a most delicate, as well as arduous task.[5] Sluman & Judd will probably think hard, of my censuring them, so severely as I have, but I have done it in Sincerity, Nor has anything they have said to Me, altered my Opinion. Tho' did I think otherways, I should be in no way of serving them, by attempting To justify them, while the Confidence which the Delegates of this Colony, & other cool persons here have in Me will enable Me I trust to help on the healing of this unhappy breach between the Two Colonies. Thus my Freind, you see the critical Situation into which this mad frolic of these Men has thrown Us, and indeed the very Union of the Colonies.

I have wrote many Letters into Connecticut, but have received few Answers. As to Commerce, it is my Opinion that it will be opened soon with all Foreign States but no decision has yet been had, the Congress early appointed a Committee on the Subject of which I was one. We made a Report, which is now under Consideration.[6] You shall early be informed of whatever it may be. You ask Me, when I shall return, which Question I am in no way of answering, but will give you my particular Situation. The Congress have appointed a Board of Claims, of which I am one, & cannot of course be able to return untill the Accts. of the Expences of this Campaign at least, are Settled. On this Business, We set every Morning. The Congress have also appointed a Secret Committee, for Supplying the Continent with certain Necessary Articles, of this I am one, and wish I could see You, or some other of my Connecticut Mercantile Freinds, here, as it would be in my power, to help them, & in theirs to serve their Country.[7] This hint is all I can give, on this head, & if you will come down, the Sooner, the better. A Naval Force is a favorite object of mine, & I have a prospect now, of carrying that point, having succeeded, in getting Our Connecticut, & the Rhode Island Vessels into Continental pay,[8] which motion I was seconded in beyond my expectations, and was further directed by Congress to lay before them an

Estimate of the Expence of a Naval Armament sufficient to Cope with the Cruisers, on this Coast.[9] This I shall lay before them this Day, and am of your Opinion, That N. London harbor is well situated for the rendevous of an American Navy, & my Freind, is it not worth while for N. London to labor to obtain the advantages of such a Collection of Navigation spending their Money there? I think it prudent, & adviseable, therefore for you or some other to come instantly down here, by which, You may undoubtedly procure, an advantageous employment for your Navigation. As to the Assembly choosing New Delegates, the Congress will not interfere, either in the Mode, or Time, agreeable to any Colony. I think however, it would be best, for the Assembly, to make a New Election, or at least To re-elect their Delegates annually. As to myself, I know not how I stand in their estimation, but make this my rule, to serve them chearfully, to the best of my Abilities, when called upon, and with equall Chearfullness to give place to better Men.[10] By what I have said above you will See I have no idle Time. My Compts. to all Freinds in Assembly—particularly to Mr. Hosmer, I wish he was here, & if You make a new choice he must be one. I have wrote to him a long Letter, and Several Short ones without any Answer. How does his Lead Works go on?

I am Sir Your most Obedt. & very Huml. Servt.

Silas Deane

P.S. Where is the Maccaroni, & how have you Succeeded, in procuring a most Necessary Article? Will it not be prudent, to Arm one half the Militia, with pikes of handles of about Ten feet in length, the heads Three square, with sharp stripps of Iron running down about One feet on the handle from the head to prevent The Enemy laying hold with their hands in the Action. Will a Battery, on Winthropps Neck, another on Mamecock, & a few Gunns on the heights on the [eastern] Shore secure that Harbor? How farr up the Nor[wich Ri]ver is their Sufficient Depth of Water for a [twenty] Gunnshipp?

RC (NN). Addressed: "To Thomas Mumford Esqr. of New London Now at the Genl. Assembly, New Haven."

[1] Deane dated this letter "Octo. 15th," but he also recorded in his diary: "Monday 15th at Congress." *CHS Bulletin* 29 (July 1964): 96A. Since he often misdated documents by one day and since he indicated in this letter that he intended to present a report to Congress "this day," Deane probably wrote this letter on Monday, October 16, rather than Sunday the 15th.

[2] See Connecticut Delegates to Zebulon Butler et al., August 2, 1775.

[3] See Deane to Zebulon Butler, July 24, 1775.

[4] See Eliphalet Dyer to Zebulon Butler, October 1, 1775.

[5] Unable to reach an agreement, the Connecticut and Pennsylvania delegates requested on October 14 that a new committee be chosen from among the delegates of the other colonies. The resulting committee, appointed October 17, deliberated periodically until December 20, when in accordance with their report Congress

resolved that both sides should cease hostilities and suspend further settlement of the disputed territory until a legal decision was forthcoming. *JCC*, 3:295, 297, 321, 439–40. See also Connecticut Delegates' Proposed Resolution, October 17? 1775.

[6] The report of the committee on trade, appointed September 22, was read October 2 and considered by the committee of the whole during most of October. On November 1 Congress resolved to continue prohibiting all exportation except that undertaken for the importation of arms and ammunition. *JCC*, 3:259, 268–69, 314.

[7] The Secret Committee soon contracted with Mumford to procure 50 tons of gunpowder. See Secret Committee Minutes of Proceedings, November 28, 1775.

[8] See the resolutions of October 5 reported by the committee "to prepare a plan for intercepting two vessels, which are on their way to Canada." *JCC*, 3:279.

[9] See Silas Deane's Proposals for Establishing a Navy, October 16? 1775, note 1.

[10] At the October session of the Connecticut Assembly Oliver Wolcott and Samuel Huntington were chosen to replace Deane and Eliphalet Dyer as delegates to Congress for the following year. *Am. Archives*, 4th ser. 3:1018–19. For a discussion of the motives behind Deane's defeat, which included disenchantment with Deane's restraint in pressing Connecticut claims in the Wyoming valley, see Christopher Collier, *Roger Sherman's Connecticut* (Middletown, Conn.: Wesleyan University Press, 1971), pp. 131–33. See also Deane to Elizabeth Deane, November 26; and Connecticut Delegates to Jonathan Trumbull, Sr., December 5, 1775.

John Hancock to the New York Provincial Convention

Gentlemen Philadelphia, Oct. 16, 1775.

By some late advices from General Schuyler, we understand that he is in great distress for want of powder.[1] And as so much depends on the success of that expedition—indeed as the safety of all America depends upon it—the Congress have unamiously agreed that the ton of powder forwarded to you last week from Philadelphia be, with all possible expedition, dispatch'd to General Schuyler. In the meantime the Congress will fall upon all the measures in their power to furnish you with what they possibly can.

You will please immediately to put this Recommendation in Execution.[2]

I am Gentlemen, Your most Obed. hum. servt.

John Hancock Presidt.

RC (N). Written by Charles Thomson, with last two paragraphs and signature by Hancock. *Journals of N. Y. Prov. Cong.*, 2:5. RC damaged; missing words supplied from Tr.

[1] This day, upon receiving an October 5 letter from General Schuyler declaring his inability to supply General Montgomery with gunpowder, Congress ordered the New York Provincial Congress to forward a ton of powder to Schuyler and appointed a committee to ascertain how much had already been sent to the northern army. This committee drafted a report, but there is no record that it was formally submitted to Congress. See PCC, item 153, 1:190–93; *Am. Archives*, 4th ser. 3:951–52; *JCC*, 3:295–96; and Committee on Powder Report, October 16? 1775.

[2] The New York Provincial Congress received this letter on October 18 and immediately decided to send the gunpowder requested to Schuyler. *Am. Archives,* 4th ser. 3:1291–92.

New York Delegates to the New York Provincial Convention

Gent: Philadelphia 16th Octr 1775

Four of your Delegates being absent on publick business, & another detained by ill health, we are at present reduced to five, less than which number are insufficient to form a representation, So that in case of sickness, or the necessary absence of anyone of us, our province remains unrepresented.

We submitt it therefore to your consideration whether a delegation of the power to three when the rest are absent, would not be advantagious to the colony?[1]

We beg to be favoured with your answer to this as soon as possible & have the honour to be with the greatest respect Your most Obt Hum Servants

Jas. Duane
Robt R Livingston junr
John Alsop
Henry Wisner
John Jay

RC (N). Addressed: "To the hon. the Provincial Convention of New York." Written by Robert R. Livingston, Jr., and signed by Livingston, Alsop, Duane, Jay, and Wisner.

[1] On October 20 the Provincial Congress refused to permit only three New York delegates to function as a quorum in Congress, but in view of the continuing problem of absenteeism in the New York delegation, the Provincial Congress reconsidered this decision and on December 21 resolved that when circumstances dictated as few as three or four delegates could represent the province in Congress. *Am. Archives,* 4th ser. 3:1298, 4:436.

Virginia Delegate to Unknown

October 16, 1775

What have I read in the Virginia papers to-day! That an officer and 13 men went into the town of Norfolk at noon-day, and took from thence, unopposed, an inhabitant of the place, and the printer's types.[1] Would this have been suffered in York! Not whilst there was a single man living to defend the poor captive. O, Sir! did you but know what I feel upon this occasion, you would sympathise with me.

Is it possible, says one, that they would suffer such a thing? Why you see it is possible, says another; for they have suffered it. Well, says a third, I would not have such a disgrace upon my colony for the whole world. Can you conceive a more unhappy state for a man of feelings? A man who has the honour of his country at heart? I tell them that the chief of the inhabitants are tories: Then why do you suffer such wretches to stay among you?

Ah! why do we suffer them indeed! It would not be permitted in any other colony on the continent, I am convinced. But what are we to do? The bulk of the inhabitants of Norfolk is composed of natives of North Britain; and all the world knows that the late Virginia convention have expressly exempted those men from the service of defending their country, or rather, they have granted them a privilege of doing all the mischief imaginable to the common cause of America. They say it is *inhuman,* it is cruel, it is barbarous, to make them take arms against their countrymen. Poor, mean tools of despotism! Brutus condemned his sons to death, because they supported tyranny, and Timoleon slew his brother, because he was a tyrant; but if these examples of patriotism are of too old a date for them to follow, let them look at many brave men, both English and Scotchmen, now on the continent, who have most ardently embarked in the common cause of freedom and mankind. They feel no *shocks to humanity,* but, warmed with the spirit of liberty, are ready to plunge the dagger into a tyrant brother.

It is high time for the test act to make its appearance among us. It is highly proper that the *worthy natives* of Britain should be distinguished from the others, and that every man should have the choice of joining us or not; but it is also reasonable, that those who will not join us should be forthwith sent out of the country; for who can trust a man in his neighbourhood whose principles are avowedly against the liberties of the people. It requires no great gift of prophecy to foretell, that if such men are suffered to live among us, whether natives of North or of South Britain, or of our own country, our plans and operations must forever be betrayed, which, in all probability, will prove the downfall of Virginia.

But there is another reason for the rapid progress which lord Dunmore makes in and about Norfolk: Without regular forces to support them, without minute-men, and the militia but badly armed, what are the poor, wretched inhabitants to do? They must either submit to the military government of lord Dunmore, or suffer the miseries of imprisonment, and the loss of property. Five thousand regular forces, with a few horse, would have prevented the disgrace of Norfolk and Princess Anne, and perhaps of the whole lower country. Those men are weak politicians who would sacrifice a wide extended coast to the mean consideration of saving a little public money.

MS not found; reprinted from the *Virginia Gazette* (Pinkney), November 2, 1775. Printed under the heading: "*Extract of a letter from a member of the continental congress to his friend in* Virginia, *dated* October 16, 1775."

[1] For more contemporary accounts of the September 30, 1775, raid on the office of John Hunter Holt, printer of the *Virginia Gazette or Norfolk Intelligencer,* by a band of British soldiers and sailors acting at the behest of Lord Dunmore, see *Am. Archives,* 4th ser. 3:847, 923. See also Richard Henry Lee to George Washington, October 22, 1775.

Samuel Ward's Diary

[October 16, 1775]

16th. Letter from provincial Congs. of New Jersies requesting the Lib[ert]y of appointing field officers to the two Battalions proposed. to be raised. Comee. appointed to answer it.[1] Letter from Genl. Schuyler enclosing Letters from Genl. Montgomery & others.[2] 200000 Dollars ordered to be sent to Genl. Schuyler under Direction of the Pennsylvania Delegs; a Ton of Powder to [*be*] sent from New York to Genl. Schuyler. A Comee. to consider of further Ways & Means for promoting the Manufacture of salt petre; the salt petre taken at Turtle Bay to be sent to the Powder Mills at New York.[3]

Mr. Randolph & Mr. Hopkins app[ointe]d to confer with Mr. McPharson. A Comee. to Inquire what quantity of Powder has been sent to Gen. Schuyler. The Order of the Day further referred.

MS (RHi).

[1] For the New Jersey Provincial Congress' letter to Congress of October 13, see PCC, item 68, fols. 15–18; and *Am. Archives,* 4th ser. 3:1050–51. The committee appointed this day by Congress to respond to this letter submitted a draft reply on October 25, which Congress approved only after inserting in it a key sentence about the appointment of regimental field officers. The letter was then sent over the signature of President Hancock. *JCC,* 3:295, 304–5; and Hancock to the New Jersey Provincial Congress, October 25, 1775.

[2] This day Congress received a letter from General Schuyler to Hancock of October 5, enclosing two letters of September 28 from General Montgomery to Schuyler as well as letters to Montgomery from Maj. Timothy Bedel of September 18, from James Livingston of September 27, and from Col. Seth Warner of September 27, 1775. See PCC, item 153, 1:190–209; and *Am. Archives,* 4th ser. 3:951–55, where Bedel's letter is incorrectly dated September 28.

[3] See *JCC,* 3:296.

John Zubly's Diary

[October 16, 1775]

16. Attended congress.[1] Joined in a Letter to Georgia Committee.[2]

MS (GHi).

[1] According to the brief entries in his diary, Zubly attended Congress each day this week, October 16–21, 1775.

[2] Not found.

Connecticut Delegates' Proposed Resolution

[October 17? 1775][1]

Whereas it is represented to this Congress, that some Disturbances have lately happened among the People inhabiting the Lands in Controversy between the Colony of *Connecticut* and the Proprietors of the Colony of *Pennsylvania,* which, unless speedily quieted, may interrupt the Harmony and weaken the Union of the confederated Colonies, when their united Efforts are necessary for the Defence of their common Rights and Liberties; and that the Peace of said Inhabitants cannot be preserved, nor Offenders duly punished there by the Civil Authority of the Colonies of *Connecticut* and *Pennsylvania,* or either of them, by Reason of their interfering Claims of Jurisdiction, and the Assembly of the Colony of *Pennsylvania* and the Delegates of the Colony of *Connecticut* have requested the Interposition and Advice of the Congress in the Premises.

Resolved that in the Opinion of the Congress, it is expedient for preserving the Peace of said Colonies that a *Temporary Line of Jurisdiction* be fixed between them, and therefore recommend for the present, and until there shall be a *legal* Settlement of said Controversy, or some other Regulation established, that the Colony of *Connecticut* confine the Exercise of its Jurisdiction (at the Place in Controversy) to that Part of a Township incorporated by the Assembly of that Colony by the Name of *Westmoreland,* that lieth East of a Meridan Line beginning at Latitude 41° North, at the Distance of 15 *English* Miles West from the East Branch of *Susquehannah* River, and from thence running North to the North Line of the Lands in Controversy. And that the Colony of *Pennsylvania* forbear to exercise Jurisdiction within those Limits, unless the South Limit of said Town include any of the Inhabitants who settled and hold under the Claim of the Proprietors of *Pennsylvania,* that then those Inhabitants remain under the Jurisdiction of *Pennsylvania,* and that all the Inhabitants, on said controverted Lands, be suffered peaceably to occupy the Lands now in their actual Possession.

Provided nevertheless, that nothing contained in this temporary Provision shall any way affect or prejudice the legal Title or Claim of either Party to any of the said Lands. And it is further recommended that all Persons who have been arrested only for attempting to enter upon and take Possession of any of the vacant or uncultivated Lands in Controversy, be forthwith released, and that all their Effects be restored to them. And that for the future all concerned carefully avoid whatever may tend to disturb the Peace, or interrupt the Harmony and Friendship that ought at all Times, and more especially the present, to subsist among all true Lovers of their Country.

MS not found; reprinted from *Pa. Archives,* 8th ser. 8:7320–21.

[1] The inability of the Connecticut and Pennsylvania delegates to come to an agreement on the subject of "the disputes between the people of the two colonies on the waters of the Susquehannah," led to the appointment on October 17 of a committee to take the controversy into consideration. *JCC,* 3:297. The committee then apparently heard representations from the Connecticut and Pennsylvania delegates, and in the course of its hearings received the following proposed resolution from the Connecticut delegates. Concerned that congressional adoption of the proposal would confirm Connecticut settlers in possession of a large tract of land in the area, representatives from the counties of Northumberland and Northampton submitted a memorial to the Pennsylvania Assembly on October 25 "to solicit Assistance . . . against the *Connecticut* Intruders." This memorial contained the proposed resolution. For the full text of the memorial and the response of the Assembly to the Northumberland and Northampton Counties' plea, see *Pa. Archives,* 8th ser. 8:7314–23, 7326, 7330–32.

Although the committee reported to Congress on November 4, the dispute remained an issue of continuing concern, and the congressional resolve of December 20, calling for an end to hostilities, seemed aimed at delay rather than decisive settlement of the conflict. See *JCC,* 3:321, 335–36, 377, 439–40, 453; and Silas Deane to Thomas Mumford, October 16? 1775.

John Hancock to the New York Provincial Convention

Gentlemen Philadelphia, 17th Oct. 1775.

As the Congress apprehend there may be a Design of an attack upon New York, I am directed by them to Desire you will give directions for the immediate Removal of all the Sulphur now in the city of New York to a place of greater safety at a distance from the City, and you will please to Inform Congress to what place you have ordered it.

I am gentlemen, Your most Obedt. servt.

John Hancock Presidt.

RC (N). *Journals of N.Y. Prov. Cong.,* 2:5. RC damaged; missing words supplied from Tr.

John Jay to Alexander McDougall

Dear Sir Phil. 17 Octr 1775

I am much obliged to you for your friendly Letter by Mr Fine—his Business will soon be determined. The Hint you give is by no means pleasing. I wish your apprehensions were without Foundation tho I have too good an opinion of your Discernment to entertain Hopes of your being mistaken. You will much oblige me by a few Lines now & then. I need not caution you to be careful by what Hands you send them.

Tho I lament your absence from the Scene of Action It gives me Pleasure to find you on a field which you should not quit with Precipitation. Prudence forbids my being explicit. Were I sure that this Letter would reach you unopened it would be a very long one.

Why you restrain Exports permitted by the association I know not.[1] The Sacrifice tho well intended is expensive. Your Seamen will forsake you. I should not be surprized if Necessity should add them to the Number of your Enemies.

No news yet as to the Effect of our Petition. God grant it may be a means of restoring the Peace & I may add the Prosperity of the Empire now rent by unnatural Convulsions. But we ought not to rely wholly on it, lest it prove a broken Reed & pierce us.

I am with great Sincerity your Friend & hble Servt

John Jay

RC (NHi).

[1] On October 13 the New York Provincial Congress, in response to a request from Nicholas Low for permission to ship flour out of the province, asked Congress if New Yorkers were barred from exporting goods to any place not mentioned in the "General Association." PCC, item 67, fols. 105, 108; and *Am. Archives,* 4th ser. 3:1286. The New York delegates provided a partial reply to this inquiry on October 26 by transmitting to the Provincial Congress a resolution of that date permitting limited commerce with the foreign West Indies, but a more complete answer was not forthcoming until November 1, when Congress reconfirmed the general ban on all exports from the colonies until March 1, 1776, without congressional approval, except for trade among the 13 colonies and the exchange of certain American goods for arms and ammunition from the foreign West Indies. See *JCC,* 3:308, 314; *Am. Archives,* 4th ser. 3:1309, 1315; and New York Delegates to Nathaniel Woodhull, October 26, 1775.

Robert R. Livingston, Jr., to John Stevens

Hond. Sir Philadelphia 17th Octr. 1775.

I have been a little uneasy at not hearing from you in answer to mine accompanying the money I sent you by the Waggon, which I hope came safe to hand. I have recd. a Letter from Polly this week, in which she informs me that she is well. I enclose you one from her. I propose if I can get leave to set off from this for New York & from thence home some time next week. If I can get so much time I will take you in my rout[e]. I have been very unfortunately circumstanced ever since I have been here, so many of my Colleagues being absent as not to leave more than a deligation, so that I could not gratify the wish I had of seeing you without leaving our Colony unrepresented. We are very solicitous about news from the Nor[th]ward where our army are very disagreeably stationed in a wet unhealthy country, so that their success must be speedy or their expedition will be defeated by sickness. Our accts. hitherto have been pritty favourable except that the folly of Allen urged him to expose himself with a handful of men before Montreal where he was taken & his party defeated with small loss. Tell John that his friend James Livingston is very active & gaining great honour by the assistance he lends us in Canada where he displays great bravery, & conduct. I sent by Mr. Allen a Letter to Genl Gates which I hope John recd. before he set out for Boston, if he is gone. If not I shall expect to be favour'd with his company to the manor. Present my Love to Mrs. Stevens & comps. to other friends at the valley & believe me to be Your Dutiful Son

Robt R Livingston

RC (NjHi). Addressed "To The Hon. John Stevens Esqr., Valley Lebanon."

Samuel Ward's Diary

[October 17, 1775]

17th. A Comee. appointed to consider & Report what is fit to be done in the disputes between Pennsylvania & Connecticut.[1] Some Accts. allowed. Letter from Govr. Cooke read.[2] Dr. Morgan chosen Director Genl. of the hospital in the Room of Dr. Church. President desired to write to the Convention of New York to desire that all the Sulphur in the City be removed to a place of Safety.

MS (RHi).

[1] See Connecticut Delegates' Proposed Resolution, October 17? 1775, note.

[2] This letter, dated October 9, has not been found. *JCC*, 3:297.

John Adams to James Warren

Dr Sir Octr. 18. 1775

The Letter of Dr [*Church*] is the oddest Thing imaginable. There are so many Lies in it, calculated to give the Enemy an high Idea of our Power and Importance, as well as so many Truths tending to do us good that one knows not how to think him treacherous. Yet there are several Strokes, which cannot be accounted for at least by me, without the Supposition of Iniquity. In Short I endeavour to Suspend my Judgment. Dont let us abandon him for a Traitor without certain Evidence.

But there is not So much Deliberation in many others, or so much Compassion.

The Congress declined entering into any Discussion of the Evidence, or any Determination concerning his Guilt, or the Nature of his offence. But in general they had a full Conviction that it was so gross an Imprudence at least, and was So Suspicious, that it became them to dismiss him from their Service, which they did instantly.

Yesterday they chose a Successor, Dr Morgan an eminent Surgeon of this City.[1] We, as usual had our Men to propose, Dr Hall Jackson and Dr Forster. But Dr Forsters Sufferings and Services—and Dr Jacksons great Fame, Experience and Merits were pleaded in vain.

There is a Fatality attends our Province. It Seems destined to fall into Contempt. It was destined that We should make Mistakes I think, in our Appointment of Generals, Delegates, Surgeons and every Thing else except Paymaster & Judge Advocate. I hope they will not turn Cowards, Traytors, nor Lubbers, if they do I shall renounce all.

Dr Morgan will be with you soon. He is Professor of Medicine in the Colledge here, and reads Lectures in the Winter. He is a Brother of Mr Duche and of our Mr Stillman. I may write you more particularly about him another Time.

Let me close now with a Matter of some Importance. Congress have appointed Deane, Wythe, and your Servant a Committee to collect a just Account of the Hostilities committed by the ministerial Troops and Navy, in America, Since last March; with proper Evidence of the Truth of the Facts related, the Number and Value of the Buildings destroyed by them, also the Number and Value of the Vessells inward and outward bound, which have been Seized by them, Since that Period, also the Stock taken by them from different Parts of the Continent.[2] We shall write to the Assemblies of New England and Virginia, at least, but we shall likewise write to many Individuals Requesting their Assistance and to you among others. I wish you would think a little and consult with others concerning this Business, for it nearly concerns our province to have it well done.

RC (MHi). In Adams' hand, though not signed.

[1] John Morgan (1735–89), Philadelphia physician and a founder of the medical school at the College of Philadelphia, was appointed "director general and chief physician of the Hospital" in place of Dr. Church on October 17. *DAB;* and *JCC,* 3:297.

[2] See *JCC,* 3:298–99, 307. See also Adams' letters to Abigail Adams and to William Cooper of October 19; and Committee on Hostilities to Nathaniel Woodhull, October 19, 1775.

Samuel Ward's Diary

[October 18, 1775]

18th. Report relative to the Tea read & postponed generally. Delegates from New Hampshire presen[te]d an Instruction from the provincial Congress for the Advice of Congress relative to their assuming Govern[t].; referred to Monday next.[1]

A Comee. appointed to collect a just & well authenticated Ac[coun]t of all Hostilities comm[itte]d since 1st March last by ministerial troops & Ships of War & of the Numbers & Value of houses burnt & Vessels taken.

MS (RHi).

[1] See *JCC*, 3:298.

John Adams to Abigail Adams

My Dear Octr: 19. 1775

It is some Time since I wrote you, and I have nothing, now, to write but Repetitions of Respect and Affection. I am anxious to hear from you. I hope, the Family is better, and that your Grief for the great Loss We have all sustained is somewhat abated. I hope your Father and Sister Betcy, are well, tho they must be greatly afflicted. Give my Love to Betcy, and let her know that I feel, most intimately for her, as well as for myself, and the rest. I consider the Stroke must fall heavier upon her, as it was nearer to her. Her Prosperity is near my Heart—I wish her every Blessing which she can possibly wish for herself.

Really it is very painfull to be 400 Miles from ones Family and Friends when We know they are in Affliction. It seems as if It would be a Joy to me to fly home, even to share with you your Burdens and Misfortunes. Surely, if I were with you, it would be my Study to allay your Griefs, to mitigate your Pains and to divert your melancholly Thoughts.

When I shall come home I know not. We have so much to do, and it is so difficult to do it right, that We must learn Patience. Upon my Word I think, if ever I were to come here again, I must bring you with me. I could live here pleasantly if I had you, with me. Will you come and have the small Pox here? I wish I could remove all the Family, our little Daughter and Sons, and all go through the Distemper here. What if We should? Let me please myself with the Thought however.

Congress has appointed Mr. Wythe, Mr. Deane and me, a Committee to collect an Account of the Hostilities committed by the Troops and Ships, with proper Evidence of the Number and Value of the Houses and other Buildings destroyed or damaged, the Vessells captivated and the Cattle, Sheep, Hogs &c. taken. We are about writing to all the general assemblies of New England, and to many private Gentlemen in each Collony to assist Us in making the

Collections.[1] The Gentlemen with me are able Men. Deane's Character you know. He is a very ingenious Man and an able Politician. Wythe is a new Member from Virginia, a Lawyer of the highest Eminence in that Province, a learned and very laborious Man: so that We may hope this Commission will be well executed. A Tale of Woe it will be! Such a scene of Distress, and Destruction and so patiently and magnanimously born. Such a Scene of Cruelty and Barbarity, so unfeelingly committed. I mention this to you my dear, that you may look up and transmit to me a Paper, which Coll. Palmer lent me containing a Relation of the Charlestown Battle, which was transmitted to England by the Committee of Safety. This Paper I must have, or a Copy of it.[2]

I wish I could collect from the People of Boston or others, a proper Set of Paintings of the Scenes of Distress and Misery, brought upon that Town from the Commencement of the Port Bill. Posterity must hear a Story that shall make their Ears to Tingle.

Yours—yours—yours—

RC (MHi). Adams, *Family Correspondence* (Butterfield), 1:302–4.

[1] See Committee on Hostilities to Nathaniel Woodhull, this date.

[2] This "Relation" was prepared under the direction of the Massachusetts Committee of Safety and forwarded to England in a letter of Joseph Palmer to Arthur Lee, July 25, 1775. Both the narrative and the letter of transmittal are printed in *Am. Archives,* 4th ser. 2:1373–76. Adams received at least two copies. Adams, *Family Correspondence* (Butterfield), 1:304n.

John Adams to William Cooper

Dear sir Philadelphia Octr. 19. 1775

I have but a Moment to inform you[1] that Congress have appointed a Committee, to collect an account of the Hostilities committed by the Army and Navy, with authentic Evidence of the Facts—the Number and Value of the Buildings destroyed—the Vessells inward and outward bound, captivated or Seized and the Stock taken from any Part of the Continent.

You will be informed in a more regular Manner and from better Authority very soon. Mean Time I beg you would do every Thing in your Power to forward this Business which is of great Moment, and let me beg the favour of you to send me a Copy by Post or the first Conveyance of the account which was sent from Authority in our Province of the Charlestown Battle, to England.

My Love to all Friends, your excellent Brother especially and believe me to be your Friend &c John Adams

[*P.S.*] The Bearer is Captain Mordecai Gist, a Gentleman of Character and an officer of Merit, in Maryland.[2]

RC (MHi).

[1] William Cooper (1721–1809), Boston town clerk, secretary of the Massachusetts Committee of Safety, and a member of the provincial assembly, was elected speaker pro tempore of the House of Representatives on September 29, 1775. *Appleton's Cyclopaedia of American Biography;* and *Am. Archives,* 4th ser. 3:1433, 1446. In his December 5 response to Adams, Cooper informed him that "a Committee of both Houses of which I am one has been appointed in consequence of the Committee of Congresses letter being laid before them, and a circular letter is to be forwarded to the Selectmen & Committees of Correspondence in the several towns where hostilities have been committed, that we may be able to furnish your Committee with a collected account of the damages sustained in those towns." Adams Papers, MHi.

[2] Mordecai Gist (1742/43–92), Baltimore merchant and captain of the Baltimore Independent Company. By 1779 he had become a brigadier general in the Continental Army. *DAB.*

John Adams to Joseph Palmer

Dr Sir Octr. 19. 1775

Before I left Watertown a Committee of both Houses was appointed to enquire after Virgin lead and leaden ore, and the Methods of making Salt, who were to transmit their Discoveries to me. Another Committee was appointed, to correspond with your Delegates, here and communicate to them the earliest Intelligence of all Things necessary for us to know.

We have never received a letter from Either of those Committees, but are in constant Hope and hourly Expectation of Letters from both.

There is another Thing of great Importance, which I earnestly wish may be furnished us, if practicable immediately, I mean Some accounts and Vouchers or at least Some Representation of the Expenses which our Province has subjected itself to in the common Cause, that We may endeavour to obtain a Reimbursement, before the Continental Treasury shall be exhausted, which I fear will be Sooner than any one can imagine.

Congress has appointed a Comtee to collect a Narration of the Violences and Depredations, the Rapine and Plunder of the Army and Navy, with affidavits to support it, for the Information of this Generation and all Posterity. This Comtee. will write to your general Court and to you particularly very soon requesting your assistance. Pray send me by the first Post Copy of the account of the Charlestown Battle, which was sent to England by the Comtee. of Safety.[1] I forgot to bring it with me and have wanted it very much.

We are in hourly Expectation of being overwhelmed all at once, with Floods of Intelligence from England, Quebec, St. Johns, Cambridge, and twenty other Places. But at present it is as dead as Midnight.

A Transport is ashore at Egg Harbour, with Soldiers. They have drowned their Powder and Arms as the Mohacks did The Tea.

My Compliments to the Family & all Friends. Yours

RC (M-Ar). In Adams' hand, though not signed. Tr (DLC). RC incomplete; first three paragraphs supplied from Tr.

[1] Joseph Palmer soon sent Adams a copy of the "Account of the Battle of Charlestown" and reported in detail the activities of the provincial committee on lead. Joseph Palmer to John Adams, October 31, and November 11, 1775, Adams Papers, MHi.

John Adams to James Warren

My dear sir Octr. 19. 1775

It was the latter End of August that I left you. All September has run away, and 19 days in Octr.—and We have had no regular Intelligence from Watertown or Cambridge. Your Goodness I acknowledge. But there was a Committee of both Houses appointed, to correspond with your Delegates; and We were to be informed of every Thing that occurr'd in Boston, Cambridge, Roxbury, Watertown &c especially of every Thing which passed in Either House. But have never received a single Letter not even a Scratch of a Pen from this Comtee. or any Member of it, unless you are one, which I dont know that you are. Should be glad to hear if this Committee is all defunct or not.

I have, in almost every Letter I have written, to any of my Friends, entreated that We might have accounts and Vouchers Sent us, that We might obtain a Reimbursement of Some Part at least of the inordinate Expence that has fallen upon Us—But have received No Answer from any one, concerning it. I wish to be informed, however, what the Difficulty is, that lies in the way, if We cannot have the Accounts &c. The Continental Money goes away so fast, that I greatly fear We shall have none left in the Treasury, before We get the Proper Evidence and Information to obtain a Reimbursement for our Province.[1] Dollars go but little Way in Maintaining Armies—Very costly Commodities indeed. The Expence already accrued will astonish Us all, I fear.

Congress has appointed a Comtee., Deane, Wythe & your servant, to collect a Narration of Hostilities, and Evidence to prove it—to ascertain the Number and Value of the Buildings destroyed, Vessells captivated, and Cattle plundered &c every where. I hope We shall tell a true Story, and then I am sure it will be an affecting one. We shall not omit their Butcheries nor their Robberies nor their Piracies. But We shall want Assistance from every Quarter. I want the Distresses of Boston painted by Dr Coopers Pencil—every Thing must be Supported by Affidavits. This will be an usefull Work for the Information of all the Colonies of what has passed in Some—for the Information of our Friends in England—and in all Europe, and all Posterity. Besides it may pave the Way to obtain Retribution and Compensation, but this had better not be talked of at present. The Committee will write to the Assemblies, and to private Gentn. No Pains or Expence will be Spared. I hope to render the Execution of this Commission compleat. It concerns our Province very much.

RC (MHi). In Adams' hand, though not signed.

[1] Although the committee to prepare the Massachusetts accounts was instructed on September 30 to draw up a letter for the Continental Congress, four weeks elapsed before the letter was sent. See *Am. Archives,* 4th ser. 3:1446; and Perez Morton to the Continental Congress, October 25, 1775, PCC, item 65, fols. 59–67.

John Adams to James Warren

Dr Sir Octr. 19th. 1775

What Think you of an American Fleet?[1] I dont Mean 100 ships of the Line, by a Fleet, but I Suppose this Term may be applied to any naval Force consisting of several Vessells, tho the Number, the Weight of Metal, or the Quantity of Tonnage may be small.

The Expence would be very great—true. But the Expence might be born and perhaps the Profits and Benefits to be obtained by it, would be a Compensation. A naval Force might be created, which would do something. It would destroy Single Cutters and Cruisers—it might destroy small Corvets or Fleets of these like Wallaces at R. Island and Ld Dunmores at Virginia—it might oblige our Enemies to sail in Fleets—for two or three Vessells of 36 and twenty Guns, well armed and manned might attack and carry a 64 or a 70 or a 50 Gun Ship.

But, there is a great objection to this. All the Trade of Pensylvania, the Lower Counties, a great Part of Maryland and N. Jersey Sails in between the Capes of Delaware Bay—and if a strong Fleet should be posted in that Bay, Superior to our Fleet it might obstruct all the Trade of this River. Further the Trade of Virginia and the rest of Maryland floats into Cheasapeak Bay between the Capes of Henry and Charles where a Fleet might Stop all. Besides Virginia and Maryland have no Navigation of their own nor any Carpenters to build ships. Their whole Trade is carried on in British Bottoms by British, most of it by North British Merchants.

These Circumstances distinguish them quite from New England, where the Inlets are innumerable and the Navigation all their own.

They agree that a Fleet would protect & secure the Trade of New England but deny that it would that of the Southern Colonies.

Will it not be difficult to perswade them then to be at the Expence of building a Fleet, merely for N. England. We are Speculating now about Things at a Distance. Should We be driven to a War at all Points, a Fleet a public Fleet as well as privateers might make prey enough of the Trade of our Enemies to make it worth while.

RC (MHi). In Adams' hand, though not signed.

[1] On October 3, 1775, the Rhode Island delegates had laid before Congress their instructions from the Rhode Island Assembly containing a proposed resolution calling for the creation of an American fleet. Although debate on the issue began October 7, Congress subsequently repeatedly deferred action on the Rhode Island request, and eventually it became merged with proposals to arm vessels for intercepting Canadian supply ships. *JCC*, 3:274–75, 277, 293–94, 297, 311–12. See also John Adams' Notes of Debates, October 7 and 30; Naval Committee to Silas Deane, November 7; and Samuel Ward to Henry Ward, November 16 and December 14, 1775.

John Adams to James Warren

Dr sir Octr. 19. 1775

I want to be with you, Tete a Tete, to canvass, and discuss the complicated subject of Trade. I Say nothing of private Consultations or public Debates, upon this important Head.

When I write you Letters you must expect nothing from me but unconnected Scraps and broken Hints. Continual Successions of Company allow me Time only to Scrawl a Page of Paper, without Thought.

Shall We hush the Trade of the whole Continent and not permit a Vessell to go out of our Harbours except from one Colony to another? How long will or can our People bear this? I Say they can bear it forever. If Parliament should build a Wall of Brass, at low Water Mark, We might live and be happy. We must change our Habits, our Prejudices, our Palates, our Taste in Dress, Furniture, Equipage, Architecture &c. But We can live and be happy. But the Question is whether our People have Virtue enough to be mere Husbandmen, Mechanicks & Soldiers? That they have not Virtue enough to bear it always, I take for granted. How long then will their Virtue last? till next Spring?

If We Stop all Trade, G. B., I. and W. I. will not be furnished with any Thing.

Shall We then give Permission for our Vessells to go to foreign Nations, if they can escape the Men of War? Can they escape the Men of War? How many will escape in Proportion? If any Escape, will they not venture to Britain, Ireland, and W. I. in defyance of our Association? If they do not, will not the British Dominions furnish themselves with our Produce from foreign Ports, and thereby avoid that Distress, which We expect will overtake them? Will not the W. I. Islands especially, who cannot exist without our Provisions for 6 Months, unless Glov[er and?] Walker were ignorant.

If We should invite other maritime Powers, or private Adventurers from foreign Nations to come here, Will they venture? They run the risque of escaping Men of War, and the Dangers of an unknown Coast. Maps and Charts may give Strangers a confused Idea of the Geography of our Country and of the Principal Inlets of Harbours, Rivers, Creeks, Coves, Islands &c but without skillfull Pilots, the danger of Shipwreck will be 10 to one.

This vast object is never out of my Mind. Help me to grapple it.[1] The W. I., Barbadoes particularly, begin We are told here, by a late Vessell to be terrified out of their wits.

RC (MHi). In Adams' hand, though not signed.

[1] Warren subsequently expressed sympathy for Adams' wish for an almost total stoppage of American trade but reluctantly conceded that "the temper and genius of the people, [*and*] the long habits they have been used to," would require Congress to allow such trade "as will not endanger the success of your [*Congress'*] commercial measures." James Warren to John Adams, November 5, 1775. *Warren-Adams Letters,* 1:176–77.

Samuel Adams to James Warren

My dear sir Philade Octob 19 1775

This Letter will be deliverd to you by Capt Gist,[1] a gentleman who I am well informd is meritorious in his endeavors with others in the Colony of Maryland to inspire the Inhabitants there with Military Virtue. You will excuse the Freedom I take in recommending him to your Notice. It is for the Sake of my Country.

Our Affairs are at this Moment in a critical Situation. I am impatient to hear from Schuyler and Arnold. By Accounts receivd last Evening from Quebeck, the Lt Governor of that Colony (Carleton being absent) had raisd a Number of Companies of Canadians to defend the Country. There was however no Expectation of an Expedition to Quebeck at that time viz the 28th September.

"Tis not in Mortals to command Success." If we fail we may yet console our selves, in reflecting that we have done all that was in our power to save our Country—voluisse sat est. I am in haste Yours affectionately S A

RC (MHi).

[1] See John Adams to William Cooper, this date, note 1.

Committee on Hostilities to Nathaniel Woodhull

Sir, Philadelphia, 19 Oct. 1775.

The continental congress having been pleased to appoint us a committee for collecting an account of the hostilities committed by the ministerial troops and navy in America since last March, with proper evidence of the truth of the facts related, the number and value of the buildings destroyed, and of the vessels inward and outward bound seised by them as nearly as can be ascertained, and also the stock taken by them from different parts of the continent, as you may see by the resolve inclosed; we entreat the assistance of the convention of your colony in this business, that we may be enabled to perform what is required of us in the manner and with the expedition the congress expects; and, to that end, that you will be pleased to furnish us with the necessary materials, sending to us clear distinct full and circumstantial details of the hostile and destructive acts, and the captures or seisures and depredations, in your colony, and accurate estimates of the loss and damage, with the solemn examinations of witnesses, and other papers and documents officially authenticated.[1]

We are, Sir, Your obedient humble servants,

Silas Deane

John Adams

George Wythe

RC (OClWHi). Written by Wythe and signed by Adams, Deane, and Wythe. Addressed: "The Honoble. Nathaniel Woodhull Esqr., President, & the Convention, New York."

[1] Congress appointed this committee on October 18 and on the 26th ordered "that the resolution of 18 Inst. respecting the obtaining a well authenticated account of the Hostilities committed by the ministerial troops and navy, be published in the news papers." *JCC*, 3:298–99, 307. The committee sent a similar letter this day to the New Hampshire Committee of Safety and apparently wrote other provincial governing bodies and prominent individuals, but after this early flurry the committee's activities lapsed. *Am. Archives*, 4th ser. 3:1105; and Committee on Hostilities to James Warren, October 24, 1775. Jonathan Trumbull, Sr., responded for Connecticut on March 25, 1776. *Am. Archives*, 4th ser. 5:149–65. John Adams received several replies from Massachusetts. Joseph Palmer to John Adams, October 31, and November 11; Samuel Cooper to John Adams, November 6; and Elbridge Gerry to John Adams, November 11, 1775, all in the Adams Papers, MHi. See also John Adams to James Warren, October 18, 1775, and his letters to Abigail Adams, William Cooper, and Joseph Palmer, this date.

Benjamin Franklin to Richard Bache

Dear Son Cambridge Head Quarters, Oct. 19. 1775

We hear you have had an Alarm at Philada. I hope no ill consequences have attended it. I wonder I had no Line from you.[1] I make no doubt of our People's defending their City & Country bravely, on the most trying Occasions.

I hear nothing yet of Mr. Goddard, but suppose he is on the Road. I suppose we shall leave this Place next Week. I shall not return in Company with the other Delegates, as I must call for my Sister, and we shall hardly be able to travel so fast, but I expect to be at Philada. within a few Days of them.[2]

There has been a plentiful Year here as well as with us. And there are as many chearful Countenances among those who are driven from House and Home at Boston or lost their All at Charlestown, as among other People. Not a Murmur has yet been heard, that if they had been less zealous in the Cause of Liberty they might still have enjoy'd their Possessions. For my own Part tho' I am for the most prudent Parsimony of the publick Treasure, I am not terrified by the Expence of this War, should it continue ever so long. A little more Frugality, or a little more Industry in Individuals will with Ease defray it. Suppose it 100,000 £ a Month or 1,200,000 £ a Year. If 500,000 Families will each spend a Shilling a Week less, or earn a Shilling a Week more; or if they will spend 6 pence a Week less and earn 6 pence a Week more, they may pay the whole Sum without otherwise feeling it. Forbearing to drink Tea saves three fourths of the Money; and 500,000 Women doing each threepence Worth of Spinning or Knitting in a Week will pay the rest.* I wish nevertheless most earnestly for Peace, this War being a truly unnatural & mischievious one; but we have nothing to expect from Submission but Slavery, and Contempt. I am ever Your affectionate Father B. F.

[*P.S.*] Love to dear Sally & the Children.[3]

*How much more then may be done by the superior Frugality & Industry of the Men?

RC (RBrHi).

[1] Richard Bache (1737–1811), a Philadelphia merchant who had married Franklin's daughter Sarah (Sally) in 1767, was a member of the Philadelphia committee of correspondence, a deputy postmaster in 1775, and Franklin's successor as postmaster general, 1776–82. *DAB*.

[2] Franklin wrote a brief letter to his sister on October 16 reporting that he had arrived at Cambridge with two other delegates "last Night," expected to stay "about a Week," and planned to take her home with him on his return to Philadelphia. Carl Van Doren, ed., *The Letters of Benjamin Franklin and Jane Mecom,* American Philosophical Society, *Memoirs,* vol. 27 (Princeton: Princeton University Press, 1950), pp. 163–64.

[3] For the continuation of this letter, see Franklin to Richard Bache, October 24, 1775.

Samuel Ward's Diary

[October 19, 1775]

19th. A Petition from Messrs. Sears & Randal relative to Tea refer'd a fortnight.[1] Some Accts allowed. Report from Com[mitte]e for consid[erin]g the best M[ean]s for supplying the Army read: Order to Capt. Sears for 30000 Doll[ar]s in Accts. of the flour supplyed by him. Comee. appointed to confer with Capt. McPharson reported. Orderd that a Letter be wrote to Genl. Washington recommendg. him to the Genl. to whom he is immediately to repair.[2] The provincial Convention of New York desired to transmit to this Congress copies of any proceedings of their['s] upon a Letter from Govr. Tryon or of the Mayor & Aldermen.[3]

MS (RHi).

[1] See *JCC*, 3:300, 319, 330.

[2] See *JCC*, 3:300, 301.

[3] See *JCC*, 3:300; and John Hancock to the New York Provincial Congress, October 20, 1775.

Samuel Ward to Mary Ward

My dearest Polly Philadelphia 19th Octr. 1775

I have the Pleasure of your Letter of 11th and am thankfull that you are all tolerably well and free from the sad Distresses which involve the maritime towns. The poor people of Newport I believe wish they had seasonably taken my Advice and secured their Effects in the Country and abandoned the Town. Govr. Cooke has done every thing in his Power for the common Defense; it is vastly happy that Sessions resigned & We have the Place filled with so good a man as Mr. Cook; I wish you would have wrote Me more particularly how Hunter & others escaped & who they are that have openly taken that detestable Part; the most particular Accts. of every thing of public Importance as well as of the State of the Family I shall always be glad of.

Before this I imagine you must have recd. several other Letters for I have wrote by Post & otherwise not less than five or six to some of you. As to the Cheese you have got from Block Island you must get it home & take good Care of it until you can sell it. Thompson's & Blevins I would weigh & mark carefully & let them take good Care of it until you can sell it. Some Market may present at Stonington Harbor or your Uncle or Bror. Greene may help you to one. In the mean time see that it is well saved; keep Plenty of the best for ourselves. My last was to Debby. I mention'd the hogs & many other things in it. You must lay in 2500 lb of Pork, either buy hogs & fat or engage good Pork enough to make up with what you fat yourselves; that Quantity, if it be possible to do it without Cash you will, if not you must give it.

I would not sell any more Wheat at 5/3. Indeed I dont think you ought to sell any at all unless you have taken in some Quantity, for your Family is large & may be larger, for if any of our worthy distressed Friends should seek shelter with you I would receive them kindly at a reasonable Rate. I want to know what has become of the Freebodys, your Aunt Vernon & other particular Connect[ion]s.

It is high Time your Harvest was on the way we used to do dig Potatoes a Day's & husk a load at Night is the best Way but you must do the best you can My dear; after Harvest I would by all Means look for Seaweed & get up as much as possible, if you can secure it over the Beach we may cart across the Ice in the winter or scow it across, may be you can hire Capt. Babcocks Scow until we can build one. You must learn to do without Me for I shall be very little with You. I wish to know how you manage the marsh. The Fence against Dodge ought to be done up & all your young Cattle & spare Horses turned on. Eldridge may pick Bay berries & watch them too; they must be wartered at the Island & confined on the Island every Night, in the Morning driven towards the west End of our Beach. The Bayberries will help pay for his Time but if there are none, the keeping so many Creatures will richly pay it. He might take a bush hook & clear up that Island with a Cedar Tree on it & if he is faithful I will make him some present for extraordinary Trouble.

We have no News here but what you will see in the Papers sent with my last, there is no other Prospect but of War. We are taking the most vigorous Measures to bring things to a happy Issue. Remember Me to all the Family & our Friends. May Heaven preserve you all. I am Your very affect. Father Sam Ward

RC (RHi).

John Adams' Notes of Debates

Oct. 20. [1775]

Deane.[1] Their Plunder only afforded one Meal of fresh meat for the privates. All the rest was reserved for the Officers and their Friends among the Inhabitants. I would have Traders prohibited from importing unnecessary Articles, and from exporting live Stock, except Horses.

Gadsden. If we give one leave when there is 100 who have an equal Right, it will occasion Jealousy. Let each Colony export to the Amount of so many thousand Pounds, and no more.

Chase. We have Letters, from Guadaloupe, Martinique and the Havanna that they will supply us with Powder for Tobacco.

Gadsden. France and Spain would be glad to see G.B. despotic in America. Our being in a better State than their Colonies, occasions complaints among them, Insurrections and Rebellions, but these Powers would be glad We were an independent State.

Chase. The Proposition is for exporting for a special Purpose, importing Powder. I would not permit our Cash to go for Rum. Live Stock is an inconsiderable Part of our Cargoes.

I dont wish to intermix any Thing in this debate. I would restrain the Merchant from importing any Thing but Powder &c.

Molasses was an Article of importance in the Trade of the Northern Colonies. But now they cant carry on the African Trade, and the Rum is pernicious. If you give a Latitude for any Thing but Arms and Ammunition, We shant agree what Articles are necessary and what unnecessary. Each Colony should carry on this Trade, not individuals. I would not limit the Quantity of Ammunition to be imported by each Colony. An 100 Ton a Colony would supply the W. Indies mediately and the Army and Navy. 20 Ton would be a considerable Adventure for a Colony. Debts are due from the B[ritish] W. India Islands to the Inhabitants of these Colonies. I am not for permitting Vessells to go in Ballast and fetch Cash. I wish to import Cash from every Place as much as possible.

Deane. It cannot be done with secrecy or dispatch. I rather think it would be as well to leave it to Traders.

Zubly. It is of great Weight that there be no favourites.

Dyer. There will be such continual Applications to the Assemblies, by their Friends among the Traders, it will open a compleat Exportation. It would compleatly supply the W. Indies.

Jay. We have more to expect from the Enterprise, Activity and Industry of private Adventurers, than from the Lukewarmness of Assemblies. We want French Woolens, Dutch Worsteds, Duck for Tents, German Steel, &c. Public Virtue is not so active as private Love of Gain. Shall We shutt the Door vs. private Enterprise.

Lee. The Gentleman may move for those Things as Exceptions to the general Rule.

Randolph. We are making Laws contradictory in Terms. We say nobody shall export and yet Somebody shall. Against all Rule.

Lee. It is a common Rule in making Laws, to make a Rule and then make a Proviso for special Cases.

Dyer. The Rule and the Proviso are passed at once in the same Act, 'tho. If I give my Voice for an Unconditional Proposition, what security have I that the Condition or Proviso will be added afterwards. The greatest Impropriety, in the World.

Chase. Both Sides are right, and it arises from this, that one Proposition is to be made public the other kept secret. We have very little Confidence in each other.

Zubly. If half the Law is to be public and the other half secret, will not half the People be governed by one half and the other half by the other. Will they not clash?

Jay. Least your Produce falls into the Hands of your Enemies, you publish a Law that none go from the Continent. Yet to get Powder, We keep a secret Law that Produce may be exported. Then comes the Wrangles among the People. A Vessell is seen loading. A fellow runs to the Committee.

Lee. The Inconvenience may arise in some Measure, but will not the People be quieted, by the Authority of the Conventions. If We give public Notice, our Enemies will be more active to intercept Us. On the Contrary the People may be quieted by the Committees of Safety.

Wythe. The only Persons who can be affected by this Resolution are those, whom on the other side the Water will be called Smugglers. Consider the danger these Smugglers will run—lyable to seizure by C. House officers, by Men of War at Sea, and by Custom house officers in the Port they go to. What can they bring. Cash, Powder, or foreign Manufactures. Cant see the least Reason for restraining our Trade, as little can be carried on. My Opinion is We had better open our Trade altogether. It has long been my Opinion, and I have heard no Arguments vs. it.

Zubly. We cant do without Trade. To be, or not to be is too trifling a Question for many Gentlemen. All that Wise Men can do among many Difficulties, is to choose the least.

Stone. Cannot agree to the Proposition made by the gentleman from Maryland. Not for binding the People closer, than they are bound already. The Proposition is the same with that which was made that our Vessells should be stopp'd and foreigners invited to come here for our Produce and protect their own Trade. This appears to be a destructive System.

It was a laborious Task to get America into a general Non Exportation to G.B., I., and W. Indies.

Shall We now combine with Britain, to distress our People in their Trade, more than by the Association. People have look'd up to this, and are unwilling to go further. The restraining Bill a most cruel, unjust, unconstitutional Act: Yet We are going to greater Cruelties than they. We are all to be in the same Circumstances of Poverty and Distress. Will the West Indies be supplied by a circuitous Trade. I think not. How can the West Indies get Supplies from France, Holland or Spain? The whole Produce will not be carried. It is said the Men of War will take the Produce. This Argument will operate against exporting for Powder. The Army will be supplied. It is impossible to prevent their getting Supplies at least of Bread. It appears to me, this is not a temporary Expedient, but will have a perpetual Influence. It is a destructive, ruinous Expedient and our People never will bear it. Under the faith that your Ports would be kept open to foreigners, People have made Contracts with foreigners. You are giving a Sanction to the Act of Parliament, and going further. Under such a Regulation We never can exist.

I would export Produce to foreign W. Indies, or any where for Powder. But the Mode of doing it, will defeat it. The Assemblies never will turn Merchants successfully. I would have private Adventurers give Bond, to return Powder, or the Produce itself.

Chase. Differs from his Colleague. A different Proposition from that for restraining our People and inviting foreigners. This Proposition invites your People.

If you carry on your Exports, without the Protection of a foreign Power you destroy America.

If you Stop Provisions and not other Produce you create a Jealousy. If you export Provisions and not other Produce you create a Jealousy. Dont think the Risque will prevent Supplies to the W. I. Islands.

We must prevent em Lumber as well as Provisions. Great Quantities will be exported, notwithstanding the Risque. All the fleet of B. cannot stop our Trade. We can carry it all on. We must starve the W. I. Islands and prevent em exporting their Produce to G.B. There will be great Quantities of Provisions and Lumber exported. It will enhance the Expence to carry em to Spain or France first and thence to the W. Indies, but the Price will be such that the W. Indies will get em. I hold it clearly We can do without Trade. This Country produces all the Necessaries, many of the Conveniences and some of the Superfluities of Life. We cant grow rich. Our Provisions will be cheap. We can maintain our Army and our Poor. We shant loose our Sailors—The Fishermen will serve in another Capacity. We must defend the Lakes, and Cities.

Merchants will not grow rich—there is the Rub. I have too good an opinion of the Virtue of our People to suppose they will grumble.

If We drop our commercial System of Opposition We are undone. We must fail. We must give up the Profits of Trade or loose our Liberties.

Let the Door of Reconciliation be once shutt, I would trade with foreign Powers and apply to them for Protection.

Leave your Ports open, and every Man that can will adventure. The Risque will not prevent it.

It was strongly contended at the first Congress that Trade should be stopp'd to all the World, that all Remittances should cease. You would have saved a civil War if you had, but it could not be carried —the Gentleman from S. Carolina could not prevail to stop our Exports to B., I. and W.I.

Our Vessells will all be liable to Seizure—our Trade must be a smuggling Trade. Yet We can trade considerably, and many Vessells will escape. No Vessell can take a Clearance. Many Vessells will go out unless you restrain them. All America is in suspence. The common sense of the People have pointed out this Measure. They have stopped their Vessells.

Lee. We possess a fine Climate and a fertile Soil. Wood, Iron, Sheep &c. We make 11. or 12,00000 thousand[2] Pounds Worth of Provisions more than is necessary for our own Consumption. Dont think it necessary to combat the Opinion of some Gentlemen that We cannot live without Trade

Money has debauched States as well as Individuals, but I hope its Influence will not prevail over America vs. her Rights and dearest Interests.

We shall distress the W. Indies so as immediately to quit Coin for Corn. 4 Millions go yearly from the W. Indies to B. and a Million at least returns. If our Provisions go from these Shores, then they will go where the best Price is to be had. W. Indies and our Enemies will get em.

If it was not proper a year ago, it may be now. This Proposition is not perpetual. When We get Powder We may make ourselves strong by sea and carry on Trade.

J. Rutledge. A Question of the greatest Magnitude that has come before the Congress. If it is necessary to do without Trade our Constituents will submit to it. The Army will be supplied with Flower from England, where it is now cheaper than here. But they would be supplied here, if they were to demand it, upon Pain of destroying our Towns. W. Indies are supplied and have laid up Stores, and some of them have been raising Provisions on their own Lands. It will bear hard upon the Farmer as well as the Merchant. Dont think the Reasons the same now as last Year. It would then have destroyed the Linen Manufactory, and the W.I.—but now they have had Notice of it they are prepared against it.

MS (MHi). Adams, *Diary* (Butterfield), 2:209–13.

[1] A continuation of the debate in the committee of the whole on "the state of the trade" of the colonies. *JCC*, 3:301–2.

[2] Adams probably meant to write eleven or twelve hundred thousand.

John Adams to James Warren

Dear Sir Octr. 20. 1775

Can The Inhabitants of North America *live* without foreign Trade?

There is Beef and Pork, and Poultry, and Mutton and Venison and Veal, Milk, Butter, Cheese, Corn, Barley, Rye, Wheat, in short every Species of Eatables animal and Vegetable in a vast abundance, an immense Profusion. We raise about Eleven hundred Thousand Bushells of Corn yearly more than We can possibly consume. The Country produces Provisions of all Kinds, enough for the sustenance of the Inhabitants, and an immense Surplusage.

We have Wood and Iron in plenty. We have a good Climate as well as a fertile Soil.

But Cloathing. If instead of raising [*a*] Million Bushells of Wheat for Exportation, and Rice, Tobacco, naval Stores, Indigo, Flaxseed, Horses, Cattle, &c, Fish, oyl, Bone, Potash &c, &c, &c, the Hands now employed in raising Surplusages of these Articles for Exportation, were employed in raising Flax and Wool, and manufacturing them into Cloathing, We should be cloathed comfortably.

We must at first indeed Sacrifice Some of our Appetites. Coffee, Wine, Punch, Sugar, Molasses, &c and our Dress would not be so elegant. Silks and Velvets & Lace must be dispensed with. But these are Trifles in a Contest for Liberty.

But is there Temperance, Fortitude and Perseverance enough among the People to indure Such a Mortification of their Appetites, Passions and Fancies? Is not the Merchantile Interest comprehending Merchants, Mechanicks, Labourers So numerous, and So complicated with the landed Interest, as to produce a general Impatience and Uneasiness, under Restrictions So Severe?

By a total Cessation of Commerce, sh[all?] [. . .] away our Mariners? Will they not go, [. . .] martime Nations, the French, the Spaniards, the Dutch? or which is worse will they not go to England, and on Board of British Men of War?

Shall We not lose a large Property in Navigation which will rot by the Wharves?

On the other Hand if We give Liberty [*to*] Trade, will not most of our Vessells be Seized? perhaps all but those of the Tories who may be priviledged.

RC (MHi). In Adams' hand, though not signed.

John Adams to James Warren

Dr sir Octr. 20. 1775

The Bearer of this is John McPherson Esq.[1] He is a Genius—an old Sea Warriour, Nine or ten Times wounded in Sea Fights.

He has a son in the Service—Aid de Camp to Schuyler—a very sensible Man.

Of Mr McPhersons Errand to the Camp ask no Questions and I will tell you no false News. It will make a Noise, in Time—but for the present for Gods sake let not a Word be said.

I hope all our Friends who have opportunity will shew him Respect.

RC (MHi). In Adams' hand, though not signed.

[1] For a discussion of Macpherson's mission, see John Adams' Diary, September 18, 1775.

Samuel Adams to Elizabeth Adams

Dear Betsy Philadelphia Octob 20 1775

I have not yet receivd a Letter from you, altho' it is more than seven Weeks since I left you. I do not mean to chide you, for I am satisfied it is not your Fault. Your Want of Leisure or opportunity to write to me, or perhaps the Miscarriage of your Letters, is certainly a Misfortune to me, for the Receipt of them would serve to alleviate my Cares.

I have wrote you several times since my Arrival here. In my last I gave you a particular Account of our latest Intelligence from England, which I rely u[pon as] it came from a Correspondent whose C[onnec]tions have always afforded him the opportunity of giving me the earliest and best advice.

The Affairs of our Country are at this Moment in the most Critical Scituation. Every Wheel seems now to be in Motion. I am so fully satisfied in the Justice of our Cause, that I can confidently as well as devoutly pray, that the righteous Disposer of all things would succeed our Enterprises. If he suffers us to be defeated in any or all of them I shall believe it to be for the most wise and gracious Purposes and shall heartily acquiesce in the Divine Disposal. It is an unspeakeable Consolation to an Actor upon the publick Stage, when, after the most careful Retrospect, he can satisfy himself that he has had in his View no private or selfish Considerations, but has ever been g[uided] by the pure Motive of serving his Country, and delivering it from the rapacious Hand of a Tyrant.

I am exceedingly anxious to hear from our Northern and Eastern

Armies. Much, I was going to say, All depends upon the military Virtue of Schuyler and Arnold. If they do what they can, it will be as [much as] in Reason their Country ought to expect f[rom them.] Mortals cannot command Success. Should they succeed (God grant they may!) the plan which our Enemies have laid for the Destruction of the New England Colonies, and in the Event of all the rest, will be defeated.

Pray, my dear, let me hear from you soon. I am greatly concernd for your Security & happiness, and that of my Family. I wrote my Daughter yesterday. Pay my particular Regards to Sister Polly. Tell my Domesticks individually that I remember them. I pray God to bless you all. S A

RC (NN).

Samuel Adams to William Heath

My dear Sir Philadelphia Octob 20 1775

Should I acknowledge to you that I can give no good Reason why I have not written to you before this time, I am apt to believe you would be as much at a Loss on your Part to apologize to me for your Omissions. Believe me my Friend, my Friendship for you which has always been sincere, is not in the least abated. Your Letters to me will meet with the most grateful Reception, I beg you therefore to improve every opportunity of writing.

I wish I could inform you of some things which I believe it would be for the common Good that some Individuals should know, but I am bound by the Ties of Honor to keep them secret, and such an Obligation I am sure you will allow me to hold sacred.

The Affairs of our Country are at this Moment in the most critical Scituation. I wait with the utmost Impatience, to hear from Genl Schuyler and Coll Arnold. I was going to say that all depends upon their Success. If they do all that is in their Power, it will be as much as their Country can in Reason expect from them. Mortals cannot command Success. I wish, if it be practicable, that our Army would make some bold push upon the Rebels, but I trust to the Wisdom of our Generals. While I am writing (in the Lobby) I am informd that a Ship is just arrivd from London. If I shall hear any important News before I shall be obligd to close this Letter I will insert it.

The Bearer of this Letter Mr Josiah Hart and his Companion Mr John Folwell are the Sons of wealthy Farmers in this Colony, and Friends to our Cause. They command Military Companies in the County in which they live, and are going to visit the Camp for Improvement. They are not dressed like Fops, but as they are recommended to me as young Men of Merit I dare say you will show them due Respect. The Father of Mr Hart, is reputed to be a singular Friend to our Colony. I am now in haste and can add no more than that I am your affectionate Friend Samuel Adams

RC (MHi). Addressed: "To Brigadier General Heath at the Camp in Cambridge."

Silas Deane's Diary

[October 20, 1775]

Friday—19th [*i.e.* 20th]. At Congress on Navl. Affrs. Com[mitte]e.[1] Exp[ense]s 1s. 6d.

MS (CtHi). *CHS Bulletin* 29 (July 1964): 96A.

[1] That is, the committee appointed on October 13 to estimate the cost of fitting out armed vessels. *JCC*, 3:294, 311.

John Hancock to the New York Provincial Congress

Gentlemen Philadelphia, 20th Octo. 1775

A Letter appearing in the New York paper of 16th Inst. said to be wrote by Governor Tryon to the Mayor of New York, expressing, "That this Congress had recommended it to the Provincial Congress to seize, or take up the officers of that Government, and particularly himself by name."[1]

I am Directed by this Congress to Request that you will immediately send them a genuine Copy of the Letter above mention'd, together with a Copy of any order or proceeding of yours, or of the Mayor & Corporation in Consequence of the said Letter of Governor Tryon.[2]

I am Gentlemen Your most Obedt hum Servt.

John Hancock President

RC (N). *Journals of N. Y. Prov. Cong.*, 2:5. RC damaged; missing words supplied from Tr.

[1] For Governor Tryon's letter of October 13 to Mayor Whitehead Hicks of New York City, see *Am. Archives*, 4th ser. 3:1052.

[2] For the New York Provincial Congress' reply of November 2 to Hancock's request, see PCC, item 67, fols. 129–30; and *Am. Archives*, 4th ser. 3:1314–15. The enclosures which accompanied this reply are in ibid., pp. 1052–54.

Samuel Ward's Diary

[October 20, 1775]

20th. Letter to Genl. Washington relative to Capt. McPharson read & approved,[1] three hundred Dollars orderd to be advanced to him. Resolved into a Comee. of the whole. Mr. Ward reported that the Comee had taken into Consideration the matter referrd to them but having come to no Resolutions desired Leave to sett to morrow which was granted.[2]

MS (RHi).

[1] Hancock's letter to Washington of this date is in *JCC*, 3:301.

[2] The "matter referred to them" was the state of American trade. *JCC*, 3:301–2.

John Adams' Notes of Debates

Octr. 21. [1775]

Zubly.[1] We cant do without Powder, Intelligence, Druggs. Georgia must have an Indian War, if they cant supply the Indians. The Creeks and Cherrokees are in our Province. We must have Indian Trade. Four Millions have been spent in 6 Months. We have been successfull. But We have gain'd little. All the Power of G.B. it is true, has gained very little. N. England has been at great Expence, so has N. York. Pensylvania has spent hundred thousand Pounds of their Money to fortify their River. Virginia as much. N. Carolina a great deal. S. Carolina have issued a Million.

18 Millions of Dollars is an enormous Sum of Money. Whenever your Money fails, you fail too. We are to pay Six Millions, now, 12 Millions more presently, and have no Trade. I would bear the Character of a Madman, or that of an Emissary of Lord North, rather than believe it possible to pay 18 Millions of Dollars without Trade. Can We make bricks without Straw? We can live upon Acorns, but will We?

Wythe. The Rule that the Question should be put upon the last Motion that is made and seconded—this is productive of great Confusion in our Debates—6 or 7 Motions at once.

Commerce, whether we consider it, in an Economical, a moral, or political Light appears to be a great Good. Civility and Charity, as well as Knowledge are promoted by it. The Auri Sacra Fames is a fine Subject for Philosophers and Orators to display themselves upon. But the abuse of a Thing is not an Argument vs. it. If the Gentleman was possessed of Philosophers Stone or Fortunatus's Cap, would he not oblige the Continent with the Use of it.

Why should not America have a Navy? No maritime Power, near the Sea Coast, can be safe without it. It is no Chimæra. The Romans suddenly built one in their Carthaginian War. Why may We not lay a Foundation for it. We abound with Furs [Firs], Iron ore, Tar, Pitch, Turpentine. We have all the materials for construction of a Navy. No Country exceeds us in Felicity of Climate or Fertility of Soil. America is one of the Wings upon which the British Eagle has soared to the Skies. I am sanguine, and enthusiastical enough to wish and to hope, that it will be sung that America inter Nubila condit. British Navy will never be able to effect our Destruction. Before the days of Minus, Natives round the Archipelago carried on piratical Wars. The Moors carry on such Wars now, but the Pillars of Hercules are their Ne Plus ultra. We are too far off, for Britain to carry on a Piratical War. We shall sometime or other rise superiour to all the difficulties they may thro in our Way. I wont say there is none that doeth good in Britain, no not one, but I will say she has not righteous Persons enough to save their State. They hold those Things honorable which please em and those for just which profit em.

I know of no Instance where a Colony has revolted and a foreign Nation has interposed to subdue them. But many of the Contrary. If France and Spain should furnish Ships and Soldiers, England must pay them! Where are her Finances. Why should We divert our People from Commerce and banish our Seamen.

Our Petition may be declared to be received graciously, and promised to be laid before Parliament. But We can expect no success from it. Have they ever condescended to take Notice of you. Rapine, Depopulation, Burning, Murder. Turn your Eyes to Concord, Lexington, Charlestown, Bristol, N. York—there you see the Character of Ministry and Parliament.

We shall distress our Enemies by stopping Trade. Granted. But how will the small Quantities we shall be able to export, supply our Enemies. Tricks may be practised.

If desire of Gain prevails with Merchants so does Caution against Risques.

Gadsden. I wish We could keep to a Point. I have heard the two Gentlemen, with a great deal of Pleasure. I have argued for opening our Ports, but am for shutting them untill We hear the Event of our Petition to the King, and longer untill the Congress shall determine otherwise. I am for a Navy too, and I think that shutting our Ports for a Time, will help us to a Navy. If We leave our Ports open, warm Men will have their Ships seized, and moderate ones will be favoured.

Lee. When you hoist out a Glimmering of Hope that the People are to be furnished from abroad, you give a Check to our own Manufacturers. People are now everywhere attending to Corn and Sheep and Cotton and Linen.

Chase. A Glove has been offered by the Gentleman from Georgia and I beg leave to discharge my Promise to that Gentleman to answer his Arguments.

My Position was this—that that Gentlemans System would end in the total destruction of American Liberty. I never shall dispute self evident Propositions.

The present State of Things requires Reconciliation, or Means to carry on War. Intelligence We must have. We must have Powder and shot. We must support the Credit of our Money.

You must have a Navy to carry on the War. You cant have a Navy says the Gentleman. What is the Consequence? I say, that We must submit.

G.B. with 20 ships can distroy all our Trade, and ravage our sea Coast—can block up all your Harbours—prevent your getting Powder. What is the Consequence? That We should submit. You cant trade with nobody, you must trade with Somebody. You cant trade with any Body but G.B.—therefore I say We must submit. We cant trade with foreigners, the Gentleman said. The whole Train of his Reasoning proved that We must break our whole Association as to Exports and Imports. If We trade with G.B. will she furnish us with Powder and Arms.

Our Exports are about 3 Millions. Would B. permit us to export to her, and receive Cash in return? It would impoverish and ruin G.B. They will never permit a Trade on our Side without a Trade on theirs!

Gentn. from N. York, would not permit Tobacco and Naval Stores to be sent to G.B.—nothing that will support their naval Power or Revenue. But will not this break the Union? Would 3 Colonies stop their Staple when the other Colonies exported theirs.

1500 Seamen are employed by the Tobacco Colonies—125 Sail of British Ships.

But you may drop your Staple, your Tobacco. But it is difficult to alter old Habits. We have a great Number of female Slaves, that are best employed about Tobacco. N.C. cannot, will not give up their Staple.

The Gentleman from G. was for trading with G.B. and all the World. He says We cant trade with any Nation but Britain, therefore We must trade with B. alone.

What Trade shall we have, if We exclude B., I., W.I., British and foreign. Eastern Provinces may carry it on with a small Fleet, if their Harbours were fortified. S[outhern] Colonies cannot. Eastern Colonies cant carry on their Trade to that Extent without a naval Power to protect em not only on the Coast but on the Ocean, and to the

Port of their Destination. The same force, that would assist the Eastern Colonies, would be of little service to us in summer Time. It must be a small, narrow and limited Trade.

The best Instrument We have is our Opposition by Commerce. If We taken into Consideration G.B. in all her Glory—Commons voted 18.18.20 milions[2] last War, 80,000 seamen, from her Trade alone. Her strength is all Artificial—from her Trade alone.

Imports from G.B. to the united Colonies are 3 Millions per annum—15 Millions to all the World—1/5th. 3/4 is british Manufactures.

A Thousand british Vessells are employed in American Trade. 12 Thousand Sailors—all out of employ. What a Stroke! I dont take into view I[reland] or W. Indies.

Colonies generally indebted about one years Importation. The Revenue of Tobacco alone half a Million, if paid. N[orth] Britain enter less than the Quantity and dont pay what they ought. It employs a great Number of Manufacturers. Reexported abroad is a Million. It is more. 80,000 Hdds are reexported and pays British Debts. The Reexport employs Ships, Sailors, Freight, Commissions, Insurance.

Ireland. The flaxseed 40,000£ st. Linen brought 2,150000£ from I. to England. Yard 200,000. Ireland can raise some flaxseed, but not much.

W. Indies. Glover, Burk, and other Authors. They depend for Indian Corn and Provisions, and Lumber, and they depend upon Us for a great Part of the Consumption of their Produce. Indian Corn and Fish are not to be had but from the Colonies, except Pilchards and Herrings. Jamaica can best provide for her Wants, but not entirely. Ireland can send em Beef and Butter but no Grain. B. can send em Wheat, Oats not Corn, without which they cannot do.

Stop Rum and Sugar, how do you affect the Revenue and the Trade?

They must relax the Navigation Act to enable foreign Nations to supply the W. Indies. This is dangerous as it would force open a Trade between foreigners and them.

Britain can never support a War with Us, at the Loss of such a valuable Trade.

Affrican Trade dependent upon the W. India Trade.—700,000£.

25,000 Hdds. of Sugar are imported directly into these Colonies and as much more, from Britain, manufactured.

Jamaica alone takes 150,000£ st. of our Produce.

National Debt 140,0000,[3] ten Millions the Peace Establishment. 20 Million the whole Current Cash of the Nation. Blackstone. I never read any Body that better understood the subject. For the State of the Revenue, He calculates the Taxes of Ireland and England.

Taxes of B. perpetual and annual. Funds three—the Aggregate, general and South Sea. Taxes upon every Article of Luxuries and Necessaries. These funds are mortgaged for the civil List 800,000 as well as the Interest of the Debt.

MS (MHi). Adams, *Diary* (Butterfield), 2:213–17.

[1] A continuation of the debate in the committee of the whole on the "state of the trade" of the colonies. *JCC*, 3:302.

[2] Adams probably meant 18 or 20 million.

[3] Adams may have meant 140 million.

John Adams to William Tudor

Dear Sir Octr. 21. 1775

Mr. John Folwell and Mr Josiah Hart of Warminster in the County of Bucks in the Colony of Pensilvania, will be the Bearers of this Letter. Each of them is a Captain of a Company of Militia, in their Country which is no small Degree of Honour and Elevation here. The Father of one of them, Mr Joseph Hart, has been induced by a generous Sympathetic Disposition to take much Pains in collecting Money and other Donations for the poor Bostonians, and his Character and Influence in his Country have enabled him to do it with success. These Travellers are visiting your Camp, in order to acquire military Knowledge and Experience, that their Country may have the Benefit of it whenever opportunity shall present.[1]

I wish therefore that you would befriend them as far as the laborious avocations of your office will admit, by introducing them to such Persons and conducting them to such Places, as will be most likely to promote their honest design.

Hope your Health is restored and confirmed.

The Continental association is most rigidly and sacredly observed, throughout the Continent in all material Branches of it. Not a vessell puts to Sea any where.

We have a Report of a Cutter or Transport on shore at Egg Harbour—proper Persons are gone to take Care of her, and see that no body suffers and nothing be lost.

Pray write me your successes, and your Dissappointment. Boston, Cambridge, Roxbury, the Sources of Intelligence, and Watertown [. . .] every Circumstance from these Places has Use. My Respects to your Parents. &c.

My dear Mrs Adams has gone through severe Tryals Since I left her—I tremble for her—But hope She is in Circumstances less disagreable than she was. Pray write to her, if you cant visit her. She wants some thing to divert her Melancholly Thoughts.

RC (MHi). In Adams' hand, though not signed.

[1] Adams wrote a similar letter of introduction to Abigail Adams on this date. See Adams, *Family Correspondence* (Butterfield), 1:309.

John Adams to James Warren

Dear Sir Octr. 21. 1775

I believe I shall surfeit you with Letters, which contain nothing but Recommendations of Gentlemen to your Attention, especially as you have so many important affairs to take up all your Time and Thoughts.

But the Bearers are Gentlemen, who come so well recommended to me that I could not refuse my self the Pleasure of giving them an opportunity of Seeing my Friend Warren, of whom you must know I am very proud.

The Name of one of them is John Folwell, the other Josiah Hart, each of them a Captain of a Company of Militia in the County of Bucks in this Province. Mr Joseph Hart the Father of one of them has exerted himself with much success in procuring Donations for Boston.

These Travellers visit the Camp from the best Motive that of gaining Knowledge in the military Art by Experience—that their Country may have the Use of it, whenever there shall be an opportunity.

You will greatly oblige them by giving them a Letter to General Thomas, and by introducing them to such Persons and Places as will best answer the honest and usefull End they have in View.

I could wish them as well as other Strangers introduced to H. Knox and young Josiah Waters, if they are any where about the Camp. These young Fellows if I am not mistaken would give strangers no contemptible Tale of the military Knowledge of Mass. M[en] in the sublimist Chapters of the Art of War.

Salt Petre is certainly making in considerable Quantities in several Places. I wish to know what success Dr Whiting has.

You wonder, that certain *Improprieties* are not felt. Well you may. But I have done finding fault. I content myself with blushing alone, and mourning in secret, the Loss of Reputation our Colony Suffers, by giving such *Samples* of her Sons to the World. Myself, remember the worst Sample of all. Pray change it.

RC (MHi). In Adams' hand, though not signed.

John Adams to James Warren

Dear sir Octr. 21. 1775

We must bend our Attention to Salt Petre. We must make it. While B. is Mistress of the sea, and has so much Influence with foreign Courts, We cannot depend upon a Supply from abroad.

It is certain that it can be made here because it is certain that it has been formerly and more latterly. Dr Graham of White Plains in the Colony of New York told me, that he has made Some thousands of Pounds Weight, many years ago, by Means of a German servant whom he bought and found to be good for nothing else.

Messrs De Witte, one of Windham, the other of Norwich, have made a considerable Quantity, a sample of which has been shewn me by Coll Dyer, and they have made a large Collection of Materials for making more.

Mr Wisner of New York informs me that his son has made a Quantity of very good, by the Method published by the Continental Congress.

Two Persons belonging to York Town in this Colony have made one hundred and twenty Weight, have recd the Premium and are making more.

A Gentleman in Maryland made some last June from Tobacco House Earth.

Mr Randolph our venerable President, affirms to me that, every Planter almost in that Colony, has made it from Tobacco House Earth. That the Proscess is so simple that a Child can make it. It consists in nothing but making a Lixivium from the Earth which is impregnated with it, and then evaporating the Lixivium. That there is certainly discovered in Virginia a vast Quantity of the Rocks of Salt Petre. That there are Salt Petre Rocks he says all Chemists & Naturalists who have written Agree. And that he was informed by many Gentlemen in Virginia, cautious, incredulous Men, of strict Honour and Veracity, that they have been to see the Rocks and tryed them and found them, by Experiment to be the very Rock of Salt Petre.

The old Gentn. in Short, who is not credulous nor inthusiastical but very steady, Solid, and grave, is as sanguine and confident as you can conceive, that it is the Easiest Thing in the World to make it, and that the Tobacco Colonies alone are sufficient to supply the Continent forever.

Every Colony My Friend must set up Works at the public Expence.

I am determined never to have Salt Petre out of my Mind but to insert some stroke or other about it in every Letter for the future. It must be had.

RC (MHi). In Adams' hand, though not signed.

Francis Lightfoot Lee to Landon Carter

My dear Col. Philadelphia Octr. 21st 1775

I received your Letter with great pleasure tho contrary to your expectation it paid postage to the *hated* Post office. As the constitutional post now goes regularly, we may with a safe conscience say how d'ye to each other.[1] It gives me concern to hear that you are withdrawing from public business;[2] upon my word, this is not a time for men of abilities with good intentions to be only spectators, if we cant do all the good we cou'd wish, let us at least endeavour to prevent all the mischeif in our power. Your good friend Ld. Dunmore is endeavouring to raise all the powers on earth to demolish poor Virginia. We have advice, that at his earnest sollicitation a fleet may be expected this fall to ravage our defenceless plantations & burn our little Towns. And we have lately discovered a plot of his & Conolly's, which is to be executed in the following manner. Conolly despairing of getting up the Country through Virga. or the Carolinas, is to go to St. Augustine from thence to the Creeks & Cherokees, and through all the tribes to Detroit; by general Gage's commission he is to have the Garrison & Cannon of that place, & the assistance of the French at that settlement. With all these he is to form an army in the spring, & march to Pitsburgh, from thence to Alexandria, proclaiming freedom to all servants that will enlist; there he is to be join'd by Dunmore with the fleet & troops from England & march through the Country. He has Captains commissions from Dunmore for Cornstalk & White Eyes. We have given the earliest intelligence of these schemes to our Com. of safety, & hope with their endeavours assisted by the Carolinas & Georgia, that Conolly may be intercepted this fall or winter.[3] Our military operations this campaign have been very languid, from the want of powder, but we still hope, our success in Canada will be such, as to cut a figure for the first essay. Such measures have been taken, as give us good reason to expect a plentifull supply of that necessary article before the next spring; and then we shall be in readiness to receive the very warm attack, which from all our advices, the Ministry are preparing for us. But least we shou'd fail in being supply'd from abroad, every man shou'd exert himself in making saltpetre. Your several plantations wou'd furnish a good deal, & you know the process is easy. With plenty of powder, the Victory is surely ours.

Octr. 22d. Here I was interrupted yesterday evening by an express for Doct. Shippen to our worthy speaker. He went out to dine with Mr. Hill and while at dinner was suddenly seized with a dead palsy, and this morning we are inform'd that he died last night.[4] You knew his Virtues & will lament the loss of the friend and Patriot. I am so concern'd that I cant think of politicks.

My best respects to my good friend Mr. Carter.[5] I have got a man at work to make his wool cards, & we are in possession of Miss Betsy's musick, which shall be sent by the first opportunity. Mrs. Lee joins me in every good wish to Mrs. Carter & Miss Lucy. We have no doubt of Miss Lucy's happiness in the married state, as so much depends upon herself, & knowing the worth of Mr. Colston. Remember me to all friends. When I shall see them, God knows. Believe me my dear Col. your sincerely affect. friend & respectfull Servant

Francis Light. Lee

RC (ViHi).

[1] Although this is the first of Lee's extant letters written from Philadelphia, his congressional service commenced on September 11 when he arrived there to begin a term to which he had been elected on August 15 in place of Richard Bland. His claim against Virginia, dated Philadelphia, August 11, 1776, included £762–15s–0 for "attendance on Congress from Sepr. 8, 1775, to Aug. 10th. 1776 inclusive being 339 days at 45s each day" and £11–10s–0 for "travelling to Philadelphia 230 miles at 1d a mile." NNPM.

[2] Landon Carter (1710–78), Virginia planter, member of the House of Burgesses, 1752–68, and chairman of the Richmond County Committee, 1774–75, was so incensed by some recently adopted militia regulations in Virginia that he threatened to resign his office as county lieutenant in charge of the Richmond militia, although he did not actually carry out his threat until early in 1776. Jack P. Greene, ed., *The Diary of Colonel Landon Carter of Sabine Hall, 1752–1778,* 2 vols. (Charlottesville: University Press of Virginia, 1965), 1:3–8, 2:937–39.

[3] For an account of Dr. John Connolly (1743?–1813) and his abortive plan to raise a force of loyalists and Indians in the backcountry to oppose the American cause, see *DAB,* Supplement one; and Paul H. Smith, *Loyalists and Redcoats: A Study in British Revolutionary Policy* (Chapel Hill: University of North Carolina Press, 1964), pp. 15–18.

[4] For comments on Peyton Randolph's death and funeral, see Robert Treat Paine's Diary, October 22; John Adams' second letter to James Warren, October 23, 1775; and *JCC,* 3:302–4.

[5] Presumably Robert Wormeley Carter (1734–97), Landon's eldest son, who had been Lee's colleague from Richmond County in the House of Burgesses and at recent Virginia conventions. Louis Morton, "Robert Wormeley Carter of Sabine Hall," *Journal of Southern History* 12 (August 1946): 350–51.

Samuel Ward's Diary

[October 21, 1775]

21. According to the Order of the Day the Congress again resolved itself into a Comee. of the whole in Order &c. Mr. Ward reported as above.[1]

MS (RHi).

[1] See Ward's Diary, October 20, 1775.

Richard Henry Lee to George Washington

Dear Sir, Philadelphia 22d October 1775

I thank you for your obliging favor of the 13th[1] and I assure you that no Man living approves the vigorous measures you mention more than myself. Great bodies, you know, move slow; and it is as sure, that the most palpable and glorious events may be delayed, and the best causes finally lost by slow, timid, and indicisive counsels. We must be content however to take human nature as we find it, and endeavor to draw good out of evil. You will, no doubt, have heared of the disgraceful conduct of our Norfolk, in suffering Lord Dunmore, with a few men to take away their printing press! It happened when the good men of that place were all away, and none but Tories & Negroes remained behind. Virginia is much incensed and 500 men are ordered immediately down to Norfolk. I expect, by every Post, to hear of the demolition of that infamous nest of Tories.[2]

By a Vessell in 20 days from Quebec, which I believe brings us later intelligence than you had from thence when the last Express left Camp, we learn that the D[eputy] Governor had 12 Companies of Canadians in training, and that they were generally on their guard. But the same acco[unt] says, the Government was so suspicious of the attachment of its Troops, that they were trusted with no more than 4 rounds of Cartridge. This still gives us some hopes of success on that quarter. Before this reaches you will have heared of Collo. Allens unlucky, and unwise attempt upon Mt. Real, nor have we, from the last accounts much prospect of success from St. Johns. The Ministerial dependance on Canada is so great, that no object can be of greater importance to North America than to defeat them there. It appears to me, that we must have that Country with us this winter cost what it will. Colo. Stephen writes me from Fort Pitt, that the Indians on that quarter come slowly in to the Commissioners, and that they evidently appear to be waiting the event of things in Canada, when they will surely, according to custom, join the strongest side. We have so many resourses for powder, that I think we cannot fail of getting well supplied with that most necessary article.

Remember me, if you please, to Gen. Gates, and to all my acquaintances with you.

I am, with great esteem and sincerity, dear Sir Your affectionate and obedient servant. Richard Henry Lee

P.S. Monday morning. 'Tis with infinite concern I inform you that our good old Speaker Peyton Randolph Esqr. went yesterday to dine with Mr. Harry Hill, was taken during the course of dinner with the dead palsey, and at 9 oClock at night died without a groan. Thus has

American liberty lost a powerful Advocate, and human nature a sincere friend. R. H. L.

RC (DLC).

[1] Not found.

[2] See Virginia Delegate to Unknown, October 16, 1775.

Robert Treat Paine's Diary

[October 22, 1775]

Fair. Heard Mr. Duché PM. This Evning the honble Peyton Randolf Esqr. late President of the Congress died Suddenly of a parylitick fit at the house of Mr. Henry Hill near Schuylkill [. . .]

MS (MHi)

John Adams to Abigail Adams

Octr. 23. 1775

Yesterday yours of Octr. 9th. came to Hand. Your Letters never failed to give me Pleasure—the greatest Pleasure that I take, is in receiving them. And altho every one, which has yet come to Hand is replete with melancholly Tidings, yet I can truly say I never was so earnest to receive them. I rejoice in the happy Principles and the happy Temper, which apparently dictated them all.

I feel myself much affected with the Breach upon the Family. But We can count a Mother, a Brother, an Aunt, and a Brothers Child among the slain by this cruel Pestilence. May God almighty put a stop to its Rage, and humble us under the Ravages already made by it.

The sorrows of all our Friends on the Loss of your Mother are never out of my Mind. I pray God to spare my Parent whose Life has been prolonged by his Goodness hitherto, as well as yours that survives.

The tremendous Calamities already felt of Fire, Sword and Pestilence, may be only Harbingers of greater still. We have no security against Calamities here—this Planet is its Region. The only Principle is to be prepared for the worst Events.

If I could write as well as you, my sorrows would be as eloquent as yours, but upon my Word I cannot.

The unaccountable Event which you allude to has reached this Place and occasioned a Fall.[1] I would be glad however that the worst Construction might not be put. Let him have fair Play—tho I doubt.

The Man who violates private Faith, cancells solemn Obligations, whom neither Honour nor Conscience holds, shall never be knowingly trusted by me. Had I known, when I first voted for a Director of an Hospital, what I heard afterwards when I was down, I would not have voted as I did. Open barefaced Immorality ought not to be so countenanced. Tho I think, a Fatality attends us in some Instances, yet a divine Protection and favour is visible in others, and let us be chearfull whatever happens. Chearfullness is not a sin in any Times.

I am afraid to hear again almost least some other should be sick in the House. Yet I hope better, and that you will reassume your wonted Chearfullness and write again upon News and Politics. Send your Letters to Warren for Conveyance. I wont trust any other.

RC (MHi). Adams, *Family Correspondence* (Butterfield), 1:311–12.

[1] Adams is alluding to Benjamin Church. See Adams to Abigail Adams, October 10, 1775, note.

John Adams to James Warren

Dear Sir Octr. 23. 1775

Yours of the 12th instant came to Hand Yesterday. Thank you and your good Lady, for your kind Condolance, on the Loss of an excellent Mother,[1] a Loss which is and ought to be more particularly affecting because there is Reason to fear that her kind Exertions for the Relief my Family when in great Distress contributed to her Catastrophe. I dread to hear further from my Family least a pestilential Infection should have seized Some other Branch of it—But will hope for better Things.

I dont Think you negligent, my Friend, having had too much Experience of your Care & attention. I only thought it my Duty to omit no oppertunity to press for accounts &c. I wish my other Friends were as little chargeable with Negligence as you.

I want to know a Thousand Things. What are the Prices of European and West India Goods. How the Non Exportation is observed. How the Prices of Provisions. Whether there is any Prospect of keeping any Trade alive and what.

You will receive a Letter from a Comtee,[2] whose Business it is to prepare a compleat Narration of the War—at least of the Murders, Robberies, Piracies, Treasons, Felonies, Villanies &c of the Army and Navy. Mr Wythe who is one, is a Virginian, a Lawyer of high Rank at the Bar, a great Schollar, a most indefatigable Man and a staunch Virginian, to all appearance.

You will observe the Vote limits Us to last March. This was done without design & I dont intend to be so limited and therefore I hope the two Houses will appoint a Committee upon a larger Scale and collect Facts at least from the Port Bill i.e. the time when it took Place. I hope neither Time, Trouble nor Expence will be spared upon this occasion, that an Account of the Expence will be kept by the Province, and altho I have no authority to say it will be paid yet I believe it will by the Continent.

Compliments to Mrs Warren—tell [*her*] I had rather have received a Letter than a Promise of one tho that is valuable.

RC (MHi). In Adams' hand, though not signed.

[1] Abigail Adams' mother, Elizabeth Quincy Smith. See John Adams to Abigail Adams, October 13, 1775.

[2] See Committee on Hostilities to James Warren, October 24, 1775.

John Adams to James Warren

Dear Sir Octr. 24. [*i.e.* 23] 1775

I have only Time to acquaint you that Yesterday, that eminent American, and most worthy Man The Honourable Peytonn Randolph Esqr our first venerable President, departed this Life in an Apoplectic Fit. He was seized at Table having but a few Moments before set down with a good deal of Company to dinner. He died in the Evening, without ever recovering his senses after the first Stroke.

As this Gentleman Sustained very deservedly One of the first American Characters, as he was the first President of the united Colonies, and as he was universally esteemed for his great Virtues and shining Abilities, the Congress have determind to shew his Memory and Remains all possible Demonstrations of Respect.[1] The whole Body is to attend the Funeral, in as much Mourning as our Laws will admit. The Funeral is to be tomorrow. I am the more pleased with this Respect on Account of an Impropriety, which you know was unfelt.[2]

This venerable Sage, I assure you, since he has stood upon the same Floor with the rest of Us has rose in the Esteem of all. He was attentive, judicious and his Knowledge, Eloquence, and classical Correctness shewed Us the able and experienced Statesman and Senator, whereas his former station had in a great Measure concealed these and shewed Us chiefly the upright and impartial Moderator of Debate.

You would have wondered more at the Want of [Sensi]bility which you remarked if you have [been] here and seen, the Difference.

Mr Randolph was as firm, stable and consistent a Patriot as any here—the Loss must be very great to Virginia in Particular and the Continent in general.

I sometimes wonder that a similar Fate does not befall more of the Members. Minds so engaged and Bodies so little exercised are very apt to fall.

This goes by Mr Gawen Brown.

RC (MHi). In Adams' hand, though not signed. Although Adams dated this letter October 24, 1775, his statements on Peyton Randolph's death and funeral indicate that he probably wrote it on October 23.

[1] Congress on October 23 resolved to attend the funeral and to "continue in Mourning for the space of one month." A committee was appointed "to superintend the funeral." *JCC*, 3:302–3.

[2] A reference to John Hancock's continuing as president when Randolph returned to Congress in September. See John Adams to James Warren, September 19, 1775.

Samuel Adams to Elbridge Gerry

My dear Sir Philadelphia Octob 23 1775

I am much obligd to you for your Favor of the 9th Instant which I receivd by the Post. I shall make the best use of it. It affords me Intelligence of Importance, which I have already communicated to a few confidential Friends.[1] I hope you will continue to write to me by every opportunity. The Bearer of this Letter Mr. Gawen Brown, has this moment informd me that he setts off early tomorrow Morning for Cambridge, the place of his Residence, and it being now Evening, I can only tell you at present that I will write you more fully by the next opportunity. I am with great Esteem, your affectionate Friend

Saml Adams

[*P.S.*] Yesterday Peyton Randolph Esqr one of the Virginia Delegates was Seizd with an Apoplectict Fit and died in a few Hours. My regards to all Friends. I beg the favor of you to forward the inclosd by some speedy and safe hand.

RC (NNPM).

[1] Gerry had reported on the expenses of the army at Cambridge, efforts to outfit privateers, prospects for manufacturing powder and arms, and the organization of militia units. He urged Congress to "fit out a heavy ship or two, and increase them as circumstances shall admit." Gerry to Samuel Adams, October 9, 1775, Austin, *Life of Gerry*, 1:115–19.

Committee of Conference Minutes of Proceedings

[October 23–24, 1775]

The Delegates[1] now proceeded to confer with General Washington as well on sundry Matters mentioned in his Letters to the Congress upon which no Order had been made as also upon other Matters occurring in the Course of this Business, viz

First. In the new Establishment of the Army should the General Officers be allowed Regiments & the Field Officers Companies.

Agreed in the Negative unanimously.

Secondly. The Affairs of the Hospital require a Director Genl. if Doctr. Church is unworthy of continuing in that office. Lt. Col. Hand (late a Surgeon in the Army) & Dr. Foster are the only two who have made Application for the office to the General.

Agreed that this be referred wholly to the Congress.

Thirdly. In what Light are Vessels which are made Captures of with their Cargoes to be considered? That is, what Part is to be assigned the Captors in the Pay of the Continent & whose Vessels are fitted out at the publick Expence & how is the Residue of the Cargo & Vessel to be disposed of?

The Instructions given by the General to the armed Vessels now out being considered were approved, except that 1/3 of the whole Capture be allowed the Officers & Men with any Reserve.

4. What is to be done with Prisoners taken in Transports by Vessels either in the Continental Pay or others? Are they to be detained as Prisoners or released; if the former what Distinctions are to be made between those taken by the Continental Vessels & others. In Respect to the Generals Cognizance of them is meant?

Agreed. That all Persons taken in Arms on Board any Prize be deemed Prisoners at the Disposal of the General as well such Prizes as are taken by Vessels fitted out in the Pay of the Continent as others.[2] That all Vessels employed merely as Transports & unarmed with their Crews be set at Liberty upon giving Security to return to Europe—but that this Indulgence be not extended longer than to the 1st. of April next.[3]

5th. In what Manner are Prisoners to be treated? What Allowance made them & how are they to be cloathed?

Agreed that they be treated as Prisoners of War but with Humanity & the Allowance of Provisions to be the Rations of the Army—that the Officers being in Pay should supply themselves with Cloaths, their Bills to be taken therefor—the Soldiers furnished as they now are.[4]

6. Suppose Troops should be landed at New York; is it expected that any Part of the Army before Boston be detached while the ministerial Troops remain there?

Agreed that the Number of Men in the new Army being calculated to oppose the Army at Boston it is not expected that the General should detach any Part of it to New York or elsewhere, unless it appears to him necessary so to do for the common Safety.[5]

7. Ought not Negroes to be excluded from the new Inlistmt especially such as are Slaves. All were thought improper by the Council of Officers.

Agreed That they be rejected altogether.[6]

8th. How often should the Troops be paid. The General Officers were divided upon this Point. Some were for a Payment per Month, others every 3 Months?

Agreed that they be paid monthly.[7]

9th. Are the Rations which have been allowed the Officers & have issued, an Account thereof given the Congress & now laid before the Committees agreeable?

Agreed that the present Allowance be continued as being usual & necessary.[8]

10. Is it adviseable to propose an Exchange of Prisoners? Should any of the Officers & Soldiers in the Army or Navy now in our Power be given up for any except the Officers & Soldiers of the American Army?

Agreed that an Exchange will be proper Citizens for Citizens, Officer for officer of equal Rank & Soldier for Soldier.[9]

11. A Proposition has been made in Behalf of Ensign Moland to go & reside among his Friends in Pennsylvania giving his Parol—would this be disagreeable.

Agreed: That under all Circumstances it is best he should remain where he is.[10]

12. Artificers of different Sorts have been employed on the best Terms they could be got, but may nevertheless appear high—none having less than 1/ extraordinary for every Day they work. Some have £4.10 per Month & with great Difficulty got on those Terms. Is this agreeable?

Agreed that it is & that the General go on upon the present Agreement, as being the best that can probably be made.[11]

13. The Riffle Companies have exceeded their Establishment in Point of Numbers, but have nevertheless been paid as they had no more Officers than were allowed by Congress: is this right?

Agreed that the General pick out from each Company such as are not Marksmen & dismiss them in such Manner as will be safest, with an Allowance of Pay to go home, if they do not Chuse to Enlist into other Corps[12] & in the mean Time that all receive their Pay.[13]

14. Very unhappy Disputes prevail in the Regiment of Artillery, Col. Gridly is become very obnoxious to that Corps & the General is informed that he will prove the Destruction of the Regiment if continued therein—what is to be done in the Case?

Agreed. That as all Officers must be approved by the General, if it shall appear in forming a new Army, that the Difference is irreconcilable, Col Gridly be dismiss'd in some honourable Way, & that the half Pay which he renounced by entering into the American Army ought to be compensated to him.[14]

15. Artillery of different kinds will be wanted, how is it to be got & where?

Agreed That what can be spared from New York & Crown Point be procured.[15]

16. Engineers are also much wanted where can they be got.

Agreed to recommend to the Congress Henry Knox Esqr. & Lieut Col. Puttnam who have Skill in this Branch, as Assistant Engineers with suitable Pay, & Rank as Lieut. Colonels, The present Pay of Assistant Engineers being deemed too small.

17. Several Indian Chiefs of the St. Francis, Penobscot, Stockbridge & St. John's Tribes have been to offer their Services & told they would be called for when wanted & dismiss'd with Presents. Ought they to be called if a Necessity for them should appear, & is the giving them Presents proper?

Agreed That these Indians or others may be called on in Case of real Necessity, & that the giving them Presents is both suitable & proper?[16]

18. Would it not be adviseable to have Expresses posted along the Roads at different Distances (Persons of Character) for the Purpose of conveying early & frequent Intelligence?

Agreed that such a Regulation is highly necessary, but that the Mode of carrying it into Execution be left to the Congress.[17]

19. Lead & Flints are much wanted where & in what Quantities can they be had?

Agreed. That as much Lead as can be spared from the Northern Department & is wanted here should be sent down from Ticonderoga & all other Supplies of these Articles attended to.[18]

20. Several issuing Commissaries & Clerks are necessarily employed under the Commissary General, For which no Provision is made. Several Assistant Quarter Masters are also employed in order to discharge that Duty. A Clerk is & allways has been necessary to assist in the Office of the Adjutant Genl. What Pay should be allowed them?

The Commissary being sick & unable to explain the Duty of these Commissaries, Clerks &c Agreed that he draw up a Memorial to the Congress stating the Ranks, Duties &c. of the several Officers under him, that the Quarter Master General do the same to enable the Congress to fix the Proportion of Pay to be allowed them. That these Memorials be first shewn to the General & by him Transmitted to the Congress.

21. Six Vessels (armed) are now fitted out & fitting upon the best Terms to intercept the Enemys Supplies will this be agreeable to the Congress?

Agreed that the Committee approve of the Scheme & will recommend it to the Congress.[19]

October 24th. 1775

The Committee proceeded in their Conference on the Generals Queries, viz

1. When the Army receives such Supplies of Powder as to be enabled to spare some to the Country how & upon what Terms is it to be done?

Agreed. That it be sold to them at a reasonable Price.[20]

2d. Tents, if the Army should have Occasion to take the Field, will be indispensably necessary for the Officers & Men, how are they to be provided & are the Officers to be allowed any?

Agreed. That it be recommended to the Honl. Congress to pay an early Attention to this Article & if the Pay of the Officers is not considerably increased that Tents be allowed them.

The General informed the Committee that he had given particular Orders that all the Tents now in Use should be carefully pack'd up in proper Places during the Winter.

The Council of War lately held having in Consequence of an Intimation from the Congress deliberated on the Expediency of an Attack upon Boston & determined that at present it was not practicable. The General wishes to know how far it may be deemed proper & adviseable to avail himself of the Season to destroy the Troops who propose to winter at Boston by a Bombardment when the Harbour is block'd up, or in other Words whether the Loss of the Town & the Property therein are to be so considered as that an Attack upon the Troops there should be avoided when it evidently appears the Town must of Consequence be destroyed.

The Committee were of Opinion this is a Matter of too Much Importance to be determined by them, therefore ref[er] it to the Congress.

The General now requested that the Committee would represent to the Congress the Necessity of having Money constantly & regularly sent, & that some Regulation upon this Head should be made as soon as possible.

Also That the Congress would be pleased to establish or recommend it to the Legislature of this Province to establish some Court for the Tryal & Condemnation of Vessels taken from the Enemy, so that they may be distinguished from those of a different Character & all Abuses prevented as much as possible.

MS (DNA:PCC, item 33). In the hand of Joseph Reed and endorsed by Reed: "A true Copy of the Minutes of the Conference held by the Delegates from the Continental Congress with General Washington. Jos. Reed, Secy. Head Quarters, Cambridge Octr. 24, 1775."

[1] On September 30, Benjamin Franklin, Benjamin Harrison, and Thomas Lynch were appointed a committee to confer with General Washington and representatives of the New England colonies as a consequence of Washington's September 21 letter which was read in Congress the 29th. See Washington, *Writings* (Fitzpatrick), 3:505–13. Instructions to the committee, subsequently known as the Committee of Conference, were drafted by a separate committee of five and approved by Congress on October 2. A conference attended by the three delegates, General Washington, and eight representatives of the New England colonies was held at Cambridge October 18–22, after which Franklin, Harrison, and Lynch met separately with Washington October 23–24 to discuss the subjects covered in these "Minutes." These were enclosed with a letter of October 24 from the Committee of Conference to President Hancock, read in Congress November 1, and subsequently considered and acted upon in several sessions from November 4 to December 22, 1775. The minutes of the meetings that took place October 18–22 are in *Am. Archives*, 4th ser. 3:1156–61. Proceedings of Congress pertaining to the Committee of Conference from September 29 to December 22, 1775, can be traced through the journals. *JCC*, 3:264–66, 270–71, 313–14, 318, 320–25, 328, 330–34, 398–402, 423, 425, 442, 444–45.

[2] In the margin at this point of the MS the word "agreed" appears in the hand of Josiah Bartlett. Apparently this copy of the minutes was used to indicate the response of the full Congress as the delegates in November debated and acted upon the preliminary decisions made by the Committee of Conference when various propositions were originally discussed wtih Washington at Cambridge. All similar notations, additions, and changes of phraseology, also in the hand of Bartlett, are duly noted below.

[3] "Transports Refer'd to Com[mitte]e." "Report made."

[4] "Agreed."

[5] "Agreed."

[6] "Refer'd."

[7] "Agreed."

[8] "Agreed & Sent."

[9] As Reed wrote it, this sentence originally read: "Agreed that an Exchange will be proper, Citizens for Citizens, but not Officers & Soldiers of the regular Army for Citizens." The last clause was lined out, however, and Bartlett completed the sentence as it is printed here, adding also the word "Agreed" at the end of the statement.

[10] "Agreed."

[11] "Agreed."

[12] This clause was inserted by Bartlett.

[13] "Agreed."

[14] Richard Gridley was replaced by Henry Knox on November 17. *JCC*, 3:358–59. See also John Adams to Abigail Adams, June 18, 1775, note.

[15] "Agreed."

[16] "Agreed."

[17] "Refer'd to Com[mitte]e of three."

[18] "Determin'd."

[19] "Agreed."

[20] "Agreed."

Thomas Cushing to William Cooper

Dear Sir Philadelphia Octr. 23. 1775

I received yours of the 24th September on the 21st Instant & not before, What has delayed its passage here I cannot say. I wrote you the beginning of this month but have not as yet been favoured with an Answer. Wish our Freinds would write us more frequently.

I am obliged to you for the Enquiry you made at Dedham for a House for me, should be glad to Govern my self by the Opinion of the County as to the place of Holding the Probate, provided at this difficult time I can be accomodated with such a place as will be agreable to them.[1] If I had been so happy as to have seen you before I left Watertown, I doubt whether it would have been proper for me to have signed any blank Letters of Administration or Letters of Guardianship, before I had my Commission & more than a month before by law I could have entered upon the discharge of the office I was appointed to, for, if you will recollect, you will find that, by the Law that was made by the General Court upon this Occasion, none of the new appointments were to take place till after the 20 of September last. This matter I considered before I left Watertown or else should certainly have seen you previous to my departure and have Signed the Papers you mention, which I am sensible, could it have been done with any Propriety, would have been for the ease of the County.

I am most Surprized that any Persons among us should just now think of dividing the County, especially at this very critical time when we have so many other matters of the greatest magnitude to Engage our Attention; such a thing was never attempted in any other County without first notifying every Town in the County of such an Intention. Can the Inhabitants of Boston (the Shire Town whose Interest it so nearly affects) in their present distressed dispersed State attend to a Question of such Moment, Certainly not, & will the Inhabitants of the other Towns in the County take the advantage of this their distress? or if they would, will the General Court attend to them at such a time? Certainly not. Whenever a Bill for determining What offices are incompatable with each other shall be brought into the House, I hope it will be considered with great attention and due deliberation. There are many difficulties attending such a Measure which at first View may not be thought of. I hope we shall not run from one Extream to another. I sincerely wish the Court may be directed to such a Conduct as may tend Effectually to Strengthen our happy Constitution & be for the lasting benefit of the Government.

I am Glad to find General Washington is fitting out some Vessells of War, this is a Necessary Measure as our Enemies are dayly pirating our Vessells. I have frequently Urged it here. As to the Establishment of Courts of Admiralty, that will come on of Course, but it will not do to urge it *here* at present.

I cannot as yet form any judgment When I shall be able to return, many Interesting and important Matters demand my attention &

presence here. As therefore I shall be necessarily detained here for some time, I have no objection that, during my absence, you should take Guardian and Administration Bonds, in particular Cases where you may find it necessary, and I doubt not you will take Special Care & Caution that in all such Cases the Bondsmen are good & sufficient. Let me know whether it is necessary for me to return home immediately. Our Late President Mr Randolph dyed yesterday of the Palsy, he is to be buried to morrow, he was a worthy Character, he was sinsible, a Gentleman of an even Temper and of sound Judgement; he dyed engaged in a good Cause. My Freind Let us follow his Example, Let us persevere in Supporting this good Cause. Let us Act with Zeal not Rashness, let no attachment to Persons, Parties or factions lead us from the Path of Duty, but let us be Calm, firm, steady & unwearied in our Endeavors to serve our Country. In this way Heaven will smile upon our exertions & I doubt not the Good Lord will Send us glorious Deliverance.

I congratulate you upon your late promotion a[s] Speaker, [. . .] My Freind is honoured & meets with the approbation of his Countrymen. I partake of the pleasure & am always highly gratified.

I conclude Dr Sir with the greatest Esteem & [. . .] Yr Freind & Servt

Tho Cushing

RC (MHi).

[1] Cushing simultaneously held the offices of: "for the County of Suffolk, Chief Justice of the County Court, Justice of Probate, Justice of the Peace and of the Quorum, Special Justice of the Pleas, and Justice throughout the 'colony'." Ellen E. Brennan, *Plural Office-Holding in Massachusetts, 1760–1780* (Chapel Hill: University of North Carolina Press, 1945), p. 112.

James Duane to Robert Livingston

My dear and honourd Sir, Philad 23d Octob. 1775

Be pleased to accept my best Thanks for your kind Letter of the 4th Instant. I sincerely Join with you in dreading a Seperation from Great Britain which can be acceptable to very few. If all wisdom is not banished from the King's Councils the petitions of America can no longer be disregarded; and I must flatter myself that the last from our Congress being altogether unexceptionable, even to the most despotic Court, will produce a Conference and Accommodation on a constitutional and permanent basis.

I thank you for the Intelligence from Lieut Thomas which is more particular in some Respects than the Congress Accounts. I suppose Genl Montgomerie can shelter his Troops at Montreal whenever he pleases, and by changes and frequent Reliefes, will be able to keep the Field as long as is necessary for the Capture of St John's, which I agree with you cannot be supplied in the manner the Canadian Prisoners represent.

I hoped before this to have had some Subject for a Letter; but we have no News from England but what the Prints furnish, and the whole amounts to no more than Surmise and Conjecture. If Administrations was disposed to Peace, I think they woud come to no Conclusion without the advice of Parliament, in Support of whose usurped Authority this cruel and unnatural war has been prosecuted. I therefore expect nothing decisive till their next Sessions. In the meantime I hope the winter will put a Stop to the Ravages of the King's Ships which are employed in carrying on a pitiful predatory war against defenceless Towns and Coasts, disgraceful to the British Fleet. As to the Army they are confined in narrow Limits and kept in a State of Inaction by a Superior Power; so that no danger is to be apprehended from them without a very great Reinforcement.

Upon the whole the Aspect of American Affairs is as favourable as we had any Reason to expect, tho we must all deplore the precious Blood which has been shed by Englishmen and Countrymen during this horrid Conflict.

I am still undetermined how to dispose of my Family this winter. Over myself I fear I shall have little Command. My dearest Polly seems desirous that we should fix in New York for the Improvement of our Children. But that unhappy City is in too much danger and Confusion to Justify such a Measure, at least it so appears to me. At all Events I shall endeavour to be with my Family in a few weeks for I grow very impatient under such tedious Seperations. Some certain Account from England (which we have Reason daily to expect) of the probable Fate of our Petition will determine my Conduct.

Adieu my dear and honourd Sir. Present my dutiful Regards to Mamma and every branch of the Family and believe ever Your Affectionate & dutiful Son & very obedient Servant Jas Duane

RC (NHpR: Livingston-Redmond Collection deposit).

Virginia Delegates to the Williamsburg Committee of Safety

Gentlemen Philadelphia 23d Octr. 1775

Among General Washington's last inclosures to Congress, was the deposition, a copy of which is now sent for your information.[1] Comparing this with the last intelligence we had the honor of sending you, Lord Dunmores inimical system against Virginia seems to be pretty fully explained. To frustrate this part of his Lordships plan, will it not be highly expedient to intercept Majr. Connelly & his papers in his passage thro the Indian Country, or to have him arrested whilst in his Winter quarters? It is not improbable but that this may be effected, by offering reward to Men of proper spirit, enterprize, and knowledge of the Country & Indian nations thro which this wicked Agent proposes to pass. We submit to you Gentlemen the prudence of sending a copy of this deposition to the Committee of Safety in N. C., with a request that they will detach a few Runners on this useful errand. We expect the same application will be made to S.C. & G. by their Delegates in Congress.

FC (MH). Unsigned draft in the hand of Richard Henry Lee.

[1] Undoubtedly William Cowley's affidavit, describing John Connolly's plan to organize the western Indians and the French in the Illinois country for a spring invasion of Virginia, which was enclosed in Washington's letter to Congress of October 12. *Am. Archives*, 4th ser. 3:1037–39, 1047–48. See also Francis Lightfoot Lee to Landon Carter, October 21, 1775.

Samuel Ward's Diary

[October 23, 1775]

23rd. Resolved to attend the funeral with a mourning crape round the left Arm, to be continued a month.[1] Mr. Middleton, Mr. Hopkins & Mr. Chase appointed to superintend the funeral & to request Mr. Duchee to preach a funeral discourse. New appointment of the Delegs. of the lower Counties, their credentials presented & approved.

MS (RHi).

[1] Robert Treat Paine's diary for this date reads: "Fair. I went to Congress. They Adjd. on Acct. of the death of Mr. Randolph." MHi. John Zubly wrote in his: "Peyton Randolph Esq. having suddenly died yesterday Congress adjourned. Went to see Mr. Schlatter." GHi.

John Adams to James Warren

Dear Sir Octr. 24. 1775

When it is said that it is the Prerogative of omniscience to Search Hearts, I Suppose it is meant that no human Sagacity can penetrate at all Times into Mens Bosoms and discover with precise Certainty the secrets there: and in this Sense it is certainly true.

But there is a Sense in which Men may be said to be possessed of a Faculty of Searching Hearts too. There is a Discernment competent to Mortals by which they can penetrate into the Minds of Men and discover their Secret Passions, Prejudices, Habits, Hopes, Fears, Wishes and Designs, and by this Means judge what Part they will act in given Circumstances for the future, and see what Principles & Motives have actuated them to the Conduct they have held, in certain Conjunctures of Circumstances which are passed.

A Dexterity and Facility of thus unravelling Mens Thought and a Faculty of governing them by Means of the Knowledge We have of them, constitutes the principal Part of the Art of a Politician.

In a Provincial Assembly, where We know a Mans Pedigree and Biography, his Education, Profession & Connections, as well as his Fortune, it is easy to see what it is that governs a Man and determines him to this Party in Preference to that, to this system of Politicks rather than another &c.

But here it is quite otherwise. We frequently see Phenomena which puzzle Us.

It requires Time to enquire and learn the Characters and Connections, the Interests and Views of a Multitude of Strangers.

It would be an exquisite Amusement, an high Gratification of Curiosity, this same Mystery of Politicks if the Magnitude of the Interests & Consequences did not interest us sometimes too much.

RC (MHi). In Adams' hand, though not signed.

Committee of Conference to John Hancock

Sir Cambridge Octo. 24. 1775

We arrived at this place on the 15 and shoud have proceeded immediately to perform the Duty imposed by the Congress, but the President of the Congress of New Hampshire was detained by the Illness of his Family from attending. After waiting two days for him it was determined to call in General Sullivan to represent that Colony. The president joined us next day, and we have been constantly employed in the Consideration of the many important Matters with which we are charged, all of which we hope will be finished today.

We enclose you a Copy of the several Determinations[1] of this meeting on those Heads on which the Governors of Rhode Island and Connecticut, the Council of this Province, the President of the Congress of New Hampshire, together with the General, were directed to be consulted, by which you will see that they were unanimously of Opinion, not only that any Reduction of pay was absolutely impracticable but that a bare proposal of this Nature woud cause such Discontents, if not Mutinies as woud perhaps prove the Ruin of the Army. We are sorry to find this Opinion too much confirmed, by the Difficulty that occurs in prevailing on the Troops of Connecticut to inlist for the month of December only, according to the Directions of Congress.

Under these Circumstances we thought it our Duty to consent that the General shoud immediately proceed to a new Inlistment of the present Army for the next year without waiting for the Directions of Congress, being convinced by the Opinion, not only of the Gentlemen we were directed to consult, but of every Officer we conversed with on the subject, that every Moments delay was big with Danger. We have however reserved, in the terms of the new Inlistments a Right in Congress to disband at Pleasure, without mentioning the Months additional pay Voted the Soldiers in Case they had listed at 5 dollars per month.

Last night we received the Melancholy Account of the burning the Town of Falmouth, by some Ships sent for that Purpose by Admiral Graves, the commanding officer of which declared he had Orders to destroy every Seaport between that and Boston. It is easy to conceive what Effects this must produce in this Camp, every Soldier who came from Falmouth insistg. on leave to go and take care of his Family and to find a place for them where they may be covered from the inclemency of the approaching Winter. Indeed tis too reasonable a Request to be refused. Shoud the Same Fate fall to the share of many such Towns, tis easy to foretell what must happen to the Army especially shoud it happen before the new Army is inlisted. This we hope will not only excuse our conduct, but induce Congress to hasten their Deliberations upon this matter.

One more Reason for dispatch is that Men may much more probably inlist before, than after they feel the hardships of a Winter Campaign.

Upon examining the Journals of assembly it appears that the Men raised in the Years 1758 & 1759 by this Colony received fourteen pounds bounty & had thirty six Shillings per month pay, which as their Engagements were for Six Months only, was much higher Terms than the present when no other Bounty is allowed than a Coat to each Man.

We are with great Respect Sir your most Obedt.

Tho Lynch

B Franklin

Benj Harrison

RC (DNA:PCC, item 33). Written by Lynch and signed by Lynch, Franklin, and Harrison. Endorsed by Charles Thomson: "Letter from Comee. of Conference. Cambridge 24 Octr. 1775. Recd & read Novr. 1. With 2 reports from said Comee."

[1] See Committee of Conference Minutes, October 23–24, 1775, note 1.

Committee on Hostilities to James Warren

Sir Philadelphia Octr. 24. 1775

The Congress has resolved, that a just Account of the Hostilities committed by the ministerial Army and Navy in America, Since the month of March last, be collected, with proper Evidence of the Facts; the Number and Value of the Buildings destroyed, the Vessells whether inward or outward bound, Seized or captivated and the Stock of all kinds, plundered, in any Part of the Continent, as you will see by an authenticated Copy of the Resolution, here inclosed.[1]

It is apprehended that little need be said to shew the Utility of this Measure. It may be necessary for our Justification, in the Judgment of the People of Great Britain, and foreign Nations; the Information of the Colonies and the Use of History, not to mention any other Purpose.

Our Distance here, from the Scenes of Violence makes it necessary for us to apply to several Assemblies, as well as private Gentlemen for Assistance; and from your Character it is presumed, you will chearfully yeild us all the Aid in your Power.

It will be requisite that every Fact be supported by Affidavits, authenticated by the highest Authority of the Place, where they shall be taken.

Our Apology for giving you this Trouble, is the manifest Utility of it, to the common Cause of the Colonies, in these Times of public Distress and Danger. We Subscribe ourselves, with great Respect, Sir, your most obedient and very humble Servants.

Silas Deane

John Adams

George Wythe

RC (MHi). Written by Adams and signed by Adams, Deane, and Wythe.

[1] The committee sent nearly identical letters to Ezra Stiles, October [18?], DLC, to Elbridge Gerry, October 24, NjR, and to Samuel Cooper, October 25, 1775, a draft of which is in the Adams Papers, MHi. For a further discussion of the committee's actions and responses to it, see Committee on Hostilities to Nathaniel Woodhull, October 19, 1775.

Benjamin Franklin to Richard Bache

[October 24, 1775]

P.S. Oct. 24. We propose setting out homewards tomorrow. Here is a fine healthy Army, wanting nothing but some Improvement in its Officers, which is daily making.

This Letter should have gone by last Post, but was left by Accident. You may publish the Part of it that is mark'd mentioning no Name.[1] We have just receiv'd Alarm of the burning of Falmouth Casco Bay; and are assur'd that Orders are come over to burn, ravish and destroy all the Sea Coast; such is the Government of the best of Princes! If the People of Philadelphia, to be more at their Ease in defending the City should think fit to remove their Families, and some of their Goods, do you after taking Care of Sally and the Children, remember to secure my Account Books and Writings which are in the Glass Desk and two Trunks in my Library. I hope too that the Library may be Sav'd; but we must run all Risques, that being to[o] bulky to be remov'd.

RC (RBrHi). A continuation of Franklin to Richard Bache, October 19, 1775.

[1] It cannot now be determined what portion of the letter Franklin marked for publication.

Thomas Jefferson to Francis Eppes

Dear Sir Philadelphia, Oct. 24, 1775.

Since my last, we have nothing new from England or from the camps at either Cambridge or St. John's. Our eyes are turned to the latter place with no little anxiety, the weather having been uncommonly bad for troops in that quarter, exposed to the inclemencies of the sky without any protection. Carleton is retired to Quebec, and though it does not appear he has any intimation of Arnold's expedition, yet we hear he has embodied 1,100 men to be on his guard. A small vessel was the other day cast away on the Jersey shore (she was one of the transports which had some time ago brought over troops to Boston), on board of which were a captain, with his subordinate officers and marines, amounting to 23 in all, and also a Duncan Campbell, who was going to recruit men at New York for General Gage, he having some time before undertaken the same business in the same place, and actually carried off 60 men. The marines and their officers were all taken immediately, except their captain and the recruiting gentleman; these pushed off in a little boat, and coasted it to Long Island, where they got on board a sloop which was to have sailed in an hour, when the party sent after them came upon them. They were brought to this city this morning, the marines having been here some time.[1] Our good old Speaker died the night before last. For the particulars of that melancholy event I must refer you to Patty. My affections attend Mrs. Eppes. Adieu. Th. Jefferson

MS not found; reprinted from Jefferson, *Papers* (Boyd), 1:248–49.

[1] The Pennsylvania Committee of Safety's examination of Duncan Campbell and his instructions from General Gage were read in Congress on the 25th and ordered to be published. *JCC*, 3:305–6.

Samuel Ward to Henry Ward

Dear Bror. Philadelphia 24th. Octr. 1775

Since my last We have had the Honor of a Letter from the Depy. Govr. which was immediately read in Congress.[1] As soon as any Resolutions are formed upon the Subject We shall transmit them to his Honor; I was very desirous of obtaining a Resolution of Congress so as to have forwarded it to the Assembly at the insuing Session but could not obtain it.

Not a Word from Europe since my last, the Vessels which have arrived having had long Passages. This Morning one Duncan Campbell at first an half pay Officer lately promised a Comp[an]y Comm[an]d who married in this Province & setled in Dutchess County in N. York was brought before the Comee. of Safety of this Province. He and one Sims [Symes] a Lieut. under him & a Serjeant & about twenty Privates were on Board a Transport from Boston which was cast away at Little Egg Harbor, they were going to N. York to enlist Men for Genl. Howe. The Wretch had sometime ago enlisted 60 men & carried them to Boston, & had engaged a Number of others in the County he lived in. It is said that he has £1500 in Cash with him. A Parcel of Guns & Powder they have thrown over board. The Guns we hope to get again. If any further particulars transpire before I close this you shall have them.

Dr. Kearsley is sentenced to close Imprisonment by the Comee. of Safety in the back Counties & this Morning a Guard sett out with him accordingly his Confinemt. to continue during the present Contest with Great Britain.

On Sunday Evening our late worthy President Mr. Randolph died very suddenly, he dined at one Mr. Hills three Miles out of Town, soon after Dinner he was taken with a choaking & one Side of his Face was distorted & about eight He expired. The Congress determined yesterday to go into mourning (as permitted by our Association) appointed a Comee. to wait on Mr. Duchee & request him to preach a funeral Sermon & the Comee. to give all proper Directions in concert with his Friends & Lady for the funeral Service & We shall all walk as Mourners.[2]

Be good enough to give Me in your next a most particular Acct. of the State of our Colony. I want to know where Sister Vernon Mr. Redwood, Ellerys, Freebody & many others of our Friends are & what is like to become of the People in general and who put themselves under Protection of the Men of War; every thing of Importance done at the Assembly you will naturally communicate, & the Proceedings at the Conference at Cambridge with your Sentiments upon such measures as you think best for us to pursue in Congress I shall be glad of.

With Regard to the Voyage proposed by the Depy. Govr. I have wrote to his Honor twice by Order of the Secret Comee. of which I am Chairman and every thing necessary upon our Part is ready & I hope the Voyage is undertaken before this time.[3]

I have seen the Examinations of Capt. Campbell, his Lieut. & some Marines, the Privates swear or at least say but I think swear that the Capt & officers promised them 200 Acres of good cultivated Land each out of the forfeited Estates, Campbell denies this. His Instru[ction]s from Genl. Gage which I have also seen amongst other Things direct him to encourage the *Scotch & other Nations* to enter into the Kings Service; the Regiment to which he belongs is 72d now raising called the royal fensible Americans; proper Regard to all Friends Yours most affectionately Sam Ward

RC (RHi).

[1] On October 17 Congress read an October 9 letter from Rhode Island Deputy Governor Nicholas Cooke which apparently is no longer extant. *JCC*, 3:297.

[2] This day Robert Treat Paine recorded in his diary: "Fair Cool. Rode to German Town. P.M. the funeral Peyton Randolf Esqr. attended in the most respectable Manner & a Sermon preached at Christs Church by Mr. Duche." MHi.

[3] See Ward to Nicholas Cooke, October 5, 1775, note.

John Zubly's Diary

[October 24, 1775]

Tuesday, 24. Bought a horse. Attended the funeral of Mr. Randolph. Mr. Duche preachd. Col. 4:5. Wrote to Mr. Caldwell. A Separation from the Parent state I wd. dread as one of the greatest evils & should it ever be proposed [*will*] write pray & fight against it. Some good Men may desire it but good Men do not always Know what they are about. I have more than a little thought on this Matter, & being borned & bred in a Commonwealth should not be unacquainted with republican Govt. but wish never to see the day when the Issue whether we ought to Separate Shd be agitated. Hints of this Kind arm our friends & Enemies in G. B. against us & are pernicious in the highest degree. I would rather enlarge than retract my Vote. There is a lack of Confidence in America which allarms me. We are too haughty to look unto God & all our publick papers rather talk of presenting Law to a Conquered people than defending ourselves under great disadvantages against one of the greatest forces of the universe.

MS (GHi).

John Adams' Diary

Octr. 25th. 1775. Wednesday.

Mr. Duane told me at the Funeral of our late virtuous and able President that he, Mr. Duane, had accustomed him self to read the Year Books. Mr. De Lancey who was C[hief] J[ustice] of N. York he said advised him to it, as the best Method of imbibing the Spirit of the Law. De Lancey told him that he had translated a Pile of Cases from the Year Books, altho he was a very lazy Man.

Duane says that Jefferson is the greatest Rubber off of Dust that he has met with, that he has learned French, Italian, Spanish and wants to learn German.

Duane says, he has no Curiosity at all—not the least Inclination to see a City or a Building &c.

That his Memory fails, is very averse to be burthened. That in his Youth he could remember any Thing. Nothing but what he could learn, but it is very different now.

Last[1] Evening Mr. Hewes of N. Carolina, introduced to my Namesake and me, a Mr. Hog from that Colony,[2] one of the Proprietors of Transylvania, a late Purchase from the Cherokees upon the Ohio. He is an associate with Henderson who was lately one of the Associate Judges of N. Carolina, who is President of the Convention in Transylvania.

These Proprietors have no Grant from the Crown nor from any Colony, are within the Limits of Virginia and North Carolina, by their Charters which bound those Colonies on the South Sea. They are charged with Republican Notions—and Utopian Schemes.

MS (MHi). Adams, *Diary* (Butterfield), 2:217–18.

[1] The remainder of this entry was erroneously printed under the date September 28, 1775, in Burnett, *Letters*, 1:210.

[2] James Hogg (1729–1805) was a proprietor of the Transylvania Company, a North Carolina land company which intended to establish a new colony west of the Alleghenies between the Cumberland and Kentucky Rivers. He arrived in Philadelphia on October 22 with a memorial from the proprietors of the company to the Continental Congress requesting that Transylvania be added to the United Colonies and that Hogg be recognized as Transylvania's delegate to Congress. Although he held informal discussions with several delegates, Hogg was apparently discouraged, especially by the Virginians, from making a formal presentation to Congress. Hogg's report to the proprietors on his mission to Philadelphia and the minutes of the proprietors' proceedings of September 25, 1775, which includes the

memorial Hogg was to submit to Congress, are in *Am. Archives,* 4th ser. 4:543–46, 553–55. For an account of Hogg and the Transylvania Company, see Archibald Henderson, "The Transylvania Company, Study in Personnel," pt. 1, *The Filson Club History Quarterly* 21 (January 1947): 3–21. See also Silas Deane to James Hogg, November 2, 1775. Joseph Hewes and William Hooper probably took their seats at this session of Congress for the first time on October 23, since it is clear from Hogg's report that they arrived with him in Philadelphia on Sunday, October 22. See *Am. Archives,* 4th ser. 4:544.

John Adams to James Warren

Dear Sir Octr. 25th. 1775

Upon the Receipt of the Intelligence of Dr [*Church's*] Letter, Dr Morgan was chosen in his Room.[1] This Letter is intended to be sent by him, and therefore probably will not go in ten days.

John Morgan, a Native of this City, is a Doctor of Physick, a Fellow of the Royal Society at London; Correspondent of the Royal Academy of Surgery at Paris; Member of the Arcadian Belles Lettres Society at Rome; Licentiate of the Royal Colledges of Physicians in London and in Edinburgh; and Professor of the Theory and Practice of Medicine in the Colledge of Philadelphia.

This Gentleman Served an Apprenticeship of six or seven years under Dr John Redman, an eminent Physician in this City, during which Time he had an opportunity of Seeing the Practice of all the eminent Physicians in this City, as he attended at the Hospital, and for one year made up the Prescriptions of all. After this he devoted himself four Years to a military Life, and went into the service as a Physician and surgeon to the Troops raised by this Colony; after this he went abroad, and Spent five years in Europe, under the most celebrated Masters in every Branch of Medicine, and visiting the principal Cities and Seats of Science in Great Britain, Holland, France and Italy.

This Gentleman in 1765, delivered a Discourse upon the Institution of Medical Schools in America,[2] at a Commencement, which was published with a Preface, containing an Apology for attempting to introduce the regular Mode of practising Physic in Phyladelphia.

Every Winter Since he has read Lectures to the Students at the Colledge as a Professor &c.

He and our Revd Chaplain Mr Duche, who is now promoted to be Recter of the three United Episcopal Churches in this City, married two sisters. Mr Stillman of Boston, the Antipædobaptist Minister married Dr Morgans Sister.

The Dr's moral Character is very good. Thus much sir I thought myself well employed in Writing to you, who have a Curiosity after

Characters. I wish I could give a Loose to my Pencil and draw Characters for your Inspection, by the Dozen. But Letters dont always go safe.

Dr Morgan sir, deserves particular Honour and Respect, wherever he goes.

RC (MHi). In Adams' hand, though not signed.

[1] John Morgan was appointed on October 17. *JCC*, 3:297.

[2] John Morgan, *A Discourse Upon the Institution of Medical Schools in America* . . . (Philadelphia: William Bradford, 1765).

John Adams to James Warren

Dear sir Octr. 25th. 1775

Governor Ward of Rhode Island has a son about five and twenty years old who has been so far carried away in the Absence of his Father, with a Zeal for his Country as to inlist into the Artillery as a private.[1] He never Said a Word to the Governor about [*it*], or he would have had a Commission. A younger Brother, who solicited of his father Permission to enter the service, was made a Captain. Now it is a Pity, that this young Gentlemans Patriotism should not be encour[a]ged and rewarded, and it is a greater Pity that an Elder Brother should be a private soldier in an Army where his younger Brother is an officer and a Captain—and a greater Pity still that a Governor of a Province and a worthy Member of the Continental Congress, and the Constant Chairman of our Committee of the whole House, should have a deserving son in the Army in the Ranks, when Multitidues of others in Commissions have no such Pretentions.

I wish you would mention this Matter at Head Quarters and see if any Thing can be done for him. The Governer had no Expectation I believe that I should interest myself in this Matter, but the Fact coming accidentally to my Knowledge, I determined to write about it immediately, and I knew not how to set this Thing in Motion.

I write every Thing to you, who know how to take me. You dont Expect Correctness nor Ceremony from me. When I have any Thing to write and one Moment to write it in I scratch it off to you—who dont expect that I should digest these things, or reduce them to correct Writing.[2] You must know I have not time for that.

RC (MHi). In Adams' hand, though not signed.

[1] Charles Ward (1747–?) was subsequently commissioned an ensign in the Massachusetts Line, Twenty-fifth Continental Infantry, January 1, 1776. Ward, *Correspondence* (Knollenberg), pp. 187, 214. See also James Warren to John Adams, November 14, 1775, *Warren-Adams Letters*, 1:185.

[2] Adams wrote a third letter this day to Warren describing a method of making

saltpetre "from the Air" and asking if commissions had been obtained by James Cargill and Jeremiah O'Brien. John Adams to James Warren, October 25, 1775, *Warren-Adams Letters,* 1:163–64.

Josiah Bartlett to Mary Bartlett

My Dear Philadelphia October 25th 1775

I had the pleasure this morning to Receive yours of the 13th of this month informing me that you & the Rest of my family were well altho Molly & Ezra had been Sick. I hope you will take good Care of your & the familys health as nothing will give me greater pain than to know any of you were Dangerously Sick in my absence. I am by the Goodness of God in a Good State of health; have got my Strength and have not so much of the Headach as usual. When I Shall be able to Return I Cannot inform you But am in hopes I Shall be at home Sometime in December. I Expect it will be very Difficult going Such a jorney in the winter; As Soon as Business will admit you may be asured I Shall Return with all Speed.

I Begin to fear I Shall Soon want Exercise as we are obliged to Set Every Day Except Sunday from 9 in the morning till near 4 in the afternoon and by that time we have Dined or Supped Call it which you please it is night and So have no time for Riding out.

Last Sunday Mr Randolph member of Congress from Virginia & late President of the Congress was taken at table with an Apoplexy & Died in a few hours and was yesterday Buried attended by the Congress, the Assembly of this Province, the ministers of all Denominations in this City, 3 Regiments Consisting of about 2000 men in their Regimentals with Drums muffled &c and it is thought 12 or 15 thousand other Inhabitants; in Short it is Supposed to be much the greatest funeral that Ever was in America. I hope you will take particular Care to lay in wood and other necessaries for winter to make you Comfortable and if in want of money apply for the money Due from the Town as I mentioned. Remember my Love to all the Children, and tell Polly I Received her letter and Shall be very Careful not to Bring home the Small Pox to my family as Col. Moulton Did to his. I think my Self & Cloaths Clear of it at this time. Remember me to all friends. I wrote you 3 times already this month viz the 4th the 10th & 14th all which I hope you have Received. Yours &c

Josiah Bartlett

P.S. Give my Regards to Mr. Thurstain. Fryday night 27th. This Letter Sealed to be Sent tomorrow morning; am now well.

RC (NhHi).

John Hancock to the New Jersey Convention

Gentlemen, Philada. Octr. 25. 1775

The Congress having taken into Consideration your Letters of the 13 & 14 Inst.[1] have directed me to inform you, that they are of Opinion, the Public Service makes it necessary that the Jersey Battalions be levied with all possible Expedition: but as the Congress are waiting the Return of their Committee from Camp in Order to establish permanent Regulations for all the continental Forces, they for the present incline to suspend a Determination on the Question about the Appointment of Regimental Field Officers.[2]

The public Exigencies will not admit of Loans from the Continental Treasury to any Colonies. The Congress however hope that this will not disable you from supplying yourselves with Arms & Ammunition, in doing which it is not doubted, you will fall upon such Means, as will be most for the Ease and Safety of the Colony without hazarding the Emission of Paper Currency.

From some Expressions in your Letter of the 14th Inst the Congress apprehend it is the Intention of your Convention to take into Constant Pay 4000 Minute Men. But as this will be a very heavy Expence, and more, it is apprehended, than any one Colony can afford, we hope you will well weigh & consider such a Measure before you adopt it. With Respect to Provisions for Minute Men, the Congress have made none; conceiving that the several Colonies will make proper Provisions for them where necessary, or when they are called into actual Service, except when they are taken into the Continental Service, in which Case they will be entitled to the same Pay, as other Continen[t]al Troops. I am &c J H Prest.

LB (DNA: PCC, item 12A). Written by a committee of Congress and sent over Hancock's signature. *JCC*, 3:295, 304–5.

[1] For these letters, see PCC, item 68, fols. 15–19; and *Am. Archives*, 4th ser. 3:1050–51.

[2] Congress added this paragraph to the letter after the committee's draft was read and debated. *JCC*, 3:305. For Congress' final action on the appointment of field officers for the New Jersey battalions, see William Livingston to William Alexander, November 8, 1775.

Secret Committee Minutes of Proceedings

Committee Chamber Octr. 25th. 1775 Philadelphia

At a meeting of the Committee. present. Saml. Ward, John Langdon, Silas Deane, John Alsop, & Thos. McKean Esqrs. a Quorum of sd. Committee.

A Contract enterd into between Alexander Gillon[1] of Charlestown, S. Carolina Mercht. of the one part, & the sd. Committee of Secrecy on the other part as follows to wit The sd. A. Gillon doth agree & promise for himself, his Executors & Administrators to charter & purchase, as soon as possible, a sufficient number of Ships or other vessels for the exporting & carrying as much of the produce or manufactures of the province of S. Carolina aforesd. or of some other of the aforesd. U[nited] Colos. as can be procurd for twenty thousand pounds sterlg. money of G. Britain,[2] to Holland or other European market, agreeble to the association & there to sell the same And he doth hereby engage to purchase the produce or manufactures aforesd. at the lowest price that he can & to the amount of twenty thousand pounds lawful money aforesd. & the same to ship as soon as possible, but at all events before the first day of Jany. next, to some part of Holland, & that he will proceed with the same personally & sell or cause to be sold, the said produce & manufactures for the highest & best prices that can be obtaind for the same, & that he will lay out & expend the nett proceeds of all the sd. Adventure in purchasing at the lowest rates of the best quality two hundred tons of Gunpowder, cheifly pistol powder, twenty four brass field peices (6 pounds), four thousand double bridle gunlocks & a thousand stand of good Soldiers muskets & bayonets, & in case the whole of the powder cannot be procurd then as much saltpetre & sulphur as will make as much powder as may be deficient.[3] As by the sd. Con[tra]ct &c fol. 8 &c &c &c.

MS (MH).

[1] Alexander Gillon (1741–94), prominent Charleston, S. C., merchant of Dutch birth, was a member of the South Carolina Provincial Congress, 1775–76, and was appointed commodore of the South Carolina navy in 1778. D. E. Huger Smith, "Commodore Alexander Gillon and the Frigate South Carolina," *South Carolina Historical and Genealogical Magazine* 9 (October 1908): 189–92; and *DAB*.

[2] The Secret Committee advanced Gillon $45,000 on October 27, 1775. See Secret Committee Account, September 27, 1775–August 26, 1776.

[3] For additional information pertaining to Gillon's contract, see Secret Committee Minutes of Proceedings, July 18 and August 8, 1776.

Samuel Ward's Diary

[October 25, 1775]

25th. A Letter from Gn Washington 30th Sepr., two from Govr. Trumbull, & one from convention of N. York read.[1] An Answer to the Convn. of N. Jersey reported, the matter of field officers referred to the return of the Comee., & the Convn. desired to raise the Battalions with all speed. Some Accts. allowed. Ins[truction]s from Gen. Gage to Capt. Campbell read & ordered to be published. Examination of Campbell & others read & copies to be sent to Convention of N. York with recommendation to them to seize [*Mr. Grant*].[2]

Mr. Hewes added to the Comee of Claims.[3]

MS (RHi).

[1] See *JCC*, 3:304; PCC, item 152, 1:175–78, item 66, fols. 37–38, item 67, fol. 121; and *Am. Archives*, 4th ser. 3:852–54, 988, 1082, 1118.

[2] See *JCC*, 3:306.

[3] Silas Deane's diary entry for this date reads simply: "Wednesday 25th at Congress, at Com[mitte]e on Susquehannah affrs." *CHS Bullentin* 29 (July 1964): 96A.

Benjamin Franklin to Joseph Greenleaf

Sir, Head Quarters, Cambridge, Oct. 26. [17]75

I intended to have called upon you yesterday at Watertown,[1] but was prevented by other Business.

Mr. Goddard, appointed Riding Surveyor to the General Post-Office, is on his Way, settling the Post Offices from Philadelphia Eastward. He will probably be here in a few days, and has Instructions for Regulating everything relating to them. I think it will be right for the Committee to receive and pay all to the End of the last Quarter; and let the present Quarter, commencing with this Month, be on Account of the General Post Office. I should be glad however to know from you, the *Amount* of the Receipts, and of the Disbursements, while the Offices were under the Direction of the Committee; which if you please you may send me at your convenient Leisure.

I am very respectfully, Sir, Yours & the Committees, Most obedient huml Servant B Franklin

[*P.S.*] I do not recollect that I received the Letter you mention to have sent me in August last. I return homewards this day.

RC (PPAmP).

[1] Joseph Greenleaf (1720–1810), of Abington, Mass., had moved to Boston in 1771 where he subsequently established himself briefly as a printer and was elected a selectman of the town. On May 15, 1775, Greenleaf was appointed to the committee "for establishing post offices and post riders," to which Franklin refers below, and in 1776 he became chairman of the Massachusetts Committee of Safety. James E. Greenleaf, *Genealogy of the Greenleaf Family* (Boston: Frank Wood, 1896), pp. 77–78, 195; and *Journals of each Provincial Congress of Massachusetts in 1774 and 1775, and of the Committee of Safety . . .*, ed. William Lincoln (Boston: Dutton and Wentworth, 1838), p. 224. Franklin evidently took advantage of his trip to Cambridge to examine into postal affairs wherever the opportunity offered. According to Silas Deane's diary, Deane "gave Docr. Franklin a Memorandum of the post Office," whose nature was not recorded, just before Franklin left Philadelphia on October 4. *CHS Bulletin* 29 (July 1964): 96A.

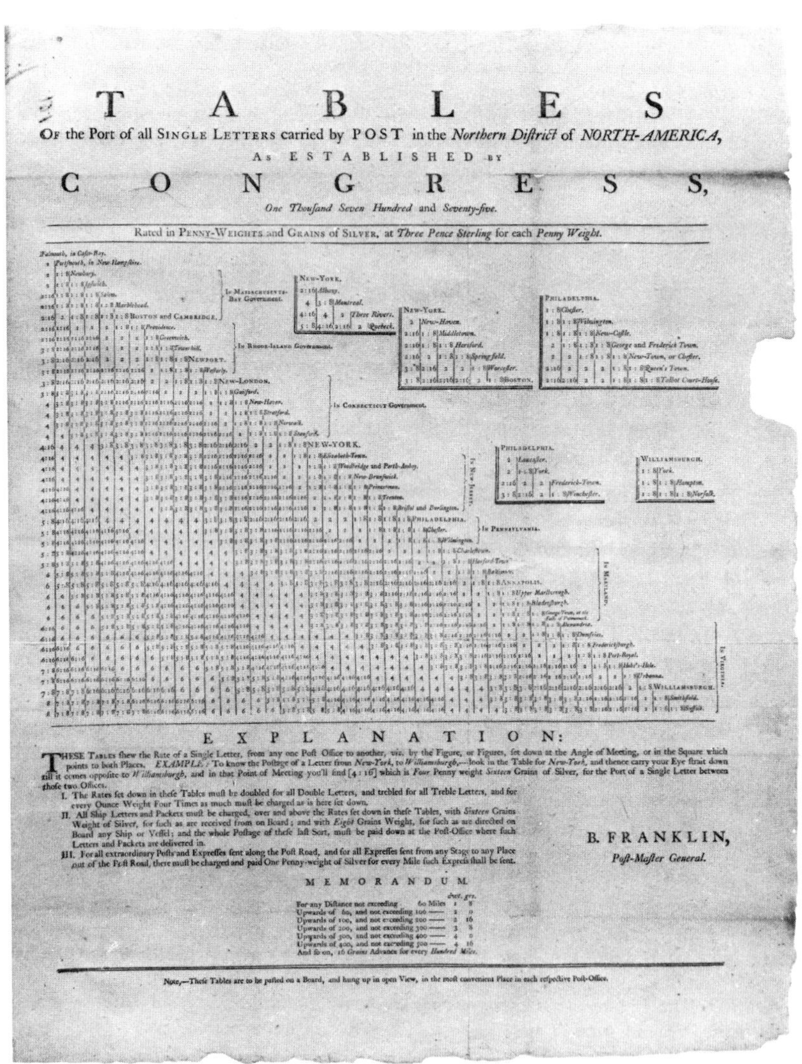

TABLES

Of the Port of all SINGLE LETTERS carried by POST in the *Northern District* of *NORTH-AMERICA*,

AS ESTABLISHED BY

CONGRESS,

One Thousand Seven Hundred and *Seventy-five.*

Rated in PENNY-WEIGHTS and GRAINS of SILVER, at *Three Pence Sterling* for each *Penny Weight.*

Falmouth, in Casco-Bay. — *Portsmouth, in New Hampshire.* — *Newbury.* — *Ipswich.* — *Salem.* — *Marblehead.* — BOSTON and CAMBRIDGE. (IN MASSACHUSETTS-BAY GOVERNMENT.) — *Providence.* — *Greenwich.* — *Tower-hill.* — NEWPORT. — *Westerly.* (IN RHODE-ISLAND GOVERNMENT.) — NEW-LONDON. — *Guilford.* — *New-Haven.* — *Stratford.* — *Norwalk.* — *Stanford.* (IN CONNECTICUT GOVERNMENT.) — NEW-YORK. — *Elizabeth-Town.* — *Woodbridge and Perth-Amboy.* — *New-Brunswick.* — *Princetown.* — *Trenton.* (IN NEW JERSEY.) — *Bristol and Burlington.* — PHILADELPHIA. — *Chester.* — *Wilmington.* (IN PENNSYLVANIA.) — *Charlestown.* — *Harford Town.* — *Baltimore.* — ANNAPOLIS. — *Upper Marlborough.* — *Bladensburgh.* — *George-Town, at the Falls of Patowmack.* — *Alexandria.* (IN MARYLAND.) — *Dumfries.* — *Fredericksburgh.* — *Port-Royal.* — *Hobb's-Hole.* — *Urbanna.* — WILLIAMSBURGH. — *Smithfield.* — *Suffolk.* (IN VIRGINIA.)

NEW-YORK.				
2:16	*Albany.*			
4	3:8	*Montreal.*		
4:16	4	2	*Three Rivers.*	
5:8	4:16	2:16	2	*Quebeck.*

NEW-YORK.						
2	*New-Haven.*					
2:16	1:8	*Middletown.*				
2:16	1:8	1:8	*Hartford.*			
2:16	2	1:8	1:8	*Springfield.*		
3:8	2:16	2	2	1:8	*Worcester.*	
3:8	2:16	2:16	2:16	2	1:8	BOSTON.

PHILADELPHIA.							
1:8	*Chester.*						
1:8	1:8	*Wilmington.*					
1:8	1:8	1:8	*New-Castle.*				
2	1:8	1:8	1:8	*George and Frederick Town.*			
2	2	1:8	1:8	1:8	*New-Town, or Chester.*		
2:16	2	2	2	1:8	1:8	*Queen's Town.*	
2:16	2:16	2	2	1:8	1:8	1:8	*Tolbot Court-House.*

PHILADELPHIA.				
2	*Lancaster.*			
2	1:8	*York.*		
2:16	2	2	*Frederick-Town.*	
3:8	2:16	2	1:8	*Winchester.*

WILLIAMSBURGH.			
1:8	*York.*		
1:8	1:8	*Hampton.*	
1:8	1:8	1:8	*Norfolk.*

EXPLANATION:

THESE TABLES shew the Rate of a Single Letter, from any one Post Office to another, *viz.* by the Figure, or Figures, set down at the Angle of Meeting, or in the Square which points to both Places. *EXAMPLE:* To know the Postage of a Letter from *New-York*, to *Williamsburgh*,—look in the Table for *New-York*, and thence carry your Eye strait down till it comes opposite to *Williamsburgh*, and in that Point of Meeting you'll find [4 : 16] which is *Four* Penny weight *Sixteen* Grains of Silver, for the Port of a Single Letter between those two Offices.

I. The Rates set down in these Tables must be doubled for all Double Letters, and trebled for all Treble Letters, and for every Ounce Weight Four Times as much must be charged as is here set down.

II. All Ship Letters and Packets must be charged, over and above the Rates set down in these Tables, with *Sixteen* Grains Weight of Silver, for such as are received from on Board; and with *Eight* Grains Weight, for such as are directed on Board any Ship or Vessel; and the whole Postage of these last Sort, must be paid down at the Post-Office where such Letters and Packets are delivered in.

III. For all extraordinary Posts and Expresses sent along the Post Road, and for all Expresses sent from any Stage to any Place out of the Post Road, there must be charged and paid One Penny-weight of Silver for every Mile such Express shall be sent.

B. FRANKLIN,
Post-Master General.

MEMORANDUM.

		dwt.	*grs.*
For any Distance not exceeding	60 Miles	1	8
Upwards of 60, and not exceeding 100	——	2	0
Upwards of 100, and not exceeding 200	——	2	16
Upwards of 200, and not exceeding 300	——	3	8
Upwards of 300, and not exceeding 400	——	4	0
Upwards of 400, and not exceeding 500	——	4	16

And so on, 16 *Grains* Advance for every *Hundred Miles.*

Note,—These Tables are to be pasted on a Board, and hung up in open View, in the most convenient Place in each respective Post-Office.

Postage Rates, 1775

John Hancock to the New York Provincial Congress

Gentlemen
Philada. 26th Octo. 1775.

A transport with two Officers & a number of marines having been cast away on the coast of New Jersey near Brigantine Beech, the captain, Officers & a number of the men were taken prisoners & brought to this place, where they have been examined by the Committee of Safety of this province. By order of the Congress I inclose you a copy of their examination, by which you will see the dangerous practices the officers have been engaged in, & it is not doubted but you will take effectual measures to put a stop to them.[1]

It is intimated that there is one Grant in Dutchess County now employed in raising recruits. The Congress expect you will inquire into this matter & if possible secure the said Grant.[2]

It being represented to the Congress that a large quantity of blankets & shirts remain in the King's stores in New York, the Congress came to the following Resolution: "That it be recommended to the Convention of New York immediately to take possession of the said blankets & shirts & forward so many of them as may be necessary, to General Schuyler for the use of the army under his Command."[3]

I am Gentlemen Your most Obedt. Servt.

John Hancock, Presidt.

RC (N). Written by Charles Thomson and signed by Hancock. *Journals of N. Y. Prov. Cong.*, 2:5. RC damaged; missing words supplied from Tr.

[1] The "dangerous practices" in question were the efforts of Capt. Duncan Campbell and one Lieutenant Symes to recruit volunteers in New York for Lt. Col. Allan Maclean's battalion of provincials in the British army, on which see *JCC*, 3:305–6; and *Am. Archives*, 4th ser. 3:1311–14.

[2] On this point, see *Am. Archives*, 4th ser. 3:1322–23.

[3] A band of New Yorkers had seized some royal stores on October 9, but the next day the Provincial Congress, fearing that the seizure would lead to the naval bombardment of New York City, ordered the goods returned. Fear of British retaliation was still strong when news of this resolve of Congress reached New York, and consequently the Provincial Congress refused to carry it out. Ibid., pp. 1322–23; and William H. W. Sabine, ed., *Historical Memoirs from 16 March 1763 to 9 July 1776 of William Smith . . .* (New York: Colburn & Tegg, 1956), pp. 241–42.

John Jay to Sarah Jay

My dear Sally
Ph. 26 Octr 1775

I am much obliged to you for your kind Letter by this Stage. The Bundle came safe to Hand, and Claas says he thanks you for it.

I was in Hopes you had received some of my Letters at the Time yours was written, and am at a Loss to account for their being so long on the way.

Since Mr. Ph. Livingston & Mr. Lewis left us, the number of our Delegates here does not exceed that which is necessary to represent the Province, so that I shall not be able to leave this Town a Day till one of those Gentlemen return. Coll. Morris has not yet returned from Fort Pitt. I saw Mrs. Lawrence the Day before Yesterday, she presents her Love &c. to you & your Sisters. The Weather thank God! grows cold, and from this circumstance alone you may know that I am well. I shall be happy if it agrees as well with you, but cant help fearing it will prevent your having as much Exercise as I believe would be useful to you.

Mr. Fine who is to be the Bearer of This Letter has just called for it, and is now waiting.

Adieu my Dear Sally. Believe me to be most affectionately Yours

John Jay

RC (NNC).

John Jay to Alexander McDougall

Dear Sir Ph. 26 Oct 1775

I have recd. your Letter by Mr Clough and you may rely on my paying due Attention to your Recommendation.

Mr. Fine has a Letter from us to your Convention inclosing a Resolve of Congress enabling them to ship on their Account Provisions &c. to the Foreign West Indies for the Purpose of purchasing ammunition &c.[1] Under this Resolve I apprehend you may avail yourself of Mr. Fine's Contract by taking it upon yourselves & allowing him such Commissions as will be nearly adequate to the Proffits he expects from the Voyage.[2] I have not informed him of the Purport of the Resolve, thinking it more prudent to refer to the Convention.

I am Sir your Frd. & hble Serv John Jay

RC (NHi).

[1] See *JCC*, 3:308; and New York Delegates to Nathaniel Woodhull, this date.

[2] Although an inference may be drawn from Jay's remarks that Fine, an otherwise obscure individual, had been granted a contract for procuring gunpowder by the Secret Committee, there is no record of such a transaction in the committee's minutes of proceedings. In any event the New York Provincial Congress appointed a committee to consult with Fine about obtaining gunpowder from the foreign West Indies, but the result of its meeting with him is not recorded. *Am. Archives*, 4th ser. 3:1315.

New Hampshire Delegates to William Whipple

Sr. Philad 26th Octob 1775

Your favor, in Committee of the 12th Instant[1] is now before us in answer to which we Say that General Washington had laid the affair of the flower ship, before the Congress, some days before your favor Came to hand, but nothing has been concluded. We urged, that the Ship and her Cargo belonged to the Colony as she was taken by our men in Provincial pay; and not by Continental forces; That we had Suffer'd and were still Suffering many losses by the taking of our Ships inward and outward bound; and that before the takeing of this flower ship. As soon as this matter is settled shall inform you.[2]

We were greatly Rejoyced to hear that the Batteries are in Such Readyness, as we have expected to hear that Portsmouth was Canonaded. Cap[tain] George Hastin[g]s (who built a Ship at Kennebeck last year and loaded with Masts at Portsmouth) is now here, haveing been cast away on the Jersey shore, in a Transport from Boston, bound to New York, with Cap[tain] Duncan Chambel, & Leiut Simes, and Number of men, who were imploy'd to Inlist Scotchmen in the Back parts of New York to Reinforce the Ministerial Army. They are all Close Prisoners, Except Cap[tain] Hastin[g]s; a quantity of goods &c is Saved out of the Ship.

I saw Cap[tain] Hastings Yesterday and as I was Aquainted with him he ventured to informe me, that when he saild from Boston, 4th Instant, Cap[tain] Mowatt (Scotchman) with three Armied Transports, were almost Ready to go round to Portsmouth, for the purpose of burning the Town, therefore (for God sake be ye ready).

You mention Powder; there is a Secret Committee for Procuring that Article, of which Mr. Langdon is one;[3] every Precausion is takeing for Ample Supplies, but as the whole Continent is to be Supplied, as well as the two Armies, it makes it uncertain when [*we*] can send you any. We beg leave here to Suggest, that the greatest Attention should be paid to the use of powder, that no Cannon be fired unless drove to the last extremity.

We were Sorry to See that you Intended to emitt more paper money but as Genl. Washington's Requisition Demanded it, [*it*] must be done. The House is now Crouded with Motions, otherwise should have moved for a grant of a Certain Sum to our Colony, which would have answer'd our purpose without emittg; shall do it first oppertunity, but fear the want of our Acct. will prevent the grant.[4]

We Some time Since made motion for the Regulation of our Civil Government, and this day a Committee is Appointed to Consider the Motion and Report thereon; Could have wished for a Petition from our Congress Settg forth all the Reasons &c had been Transmitted us, which would have help'd the matter much.[5]

Committee has been appointed to Collect the Depredations Committed by the Sons of Tyranny thro' the Continent which you'll hear from. We are with Respect your most obt. Servt

Josiah Bartlett

John Langdon

P.S. Inclosed is Resolution of Congress Respectg Powder.[6]

RC (Nh-Ar). Written by Langdon and signed by Bartlett and Langdon.

[1] See *N.H. Provincial Papers*, 7:624.

[2] General Washington's letter of October 5 referring the issue of the *Prince George* to Congress was read in Congress on October 13. *JCC*, 3:293. The original was endorsed by Charles Thomson: "That part of this letter wch relates to the capture of a vessel in N. Hampshire referred to the Comee appointed to bring in regulations for prizes." PCC, item 152, 1:181–87. Washington later agreed to divide the flour with the New Hampshire Committee of Safety. George Washington to the Committee of Safety of New Hampshire, October 15, 1775, Washington, *Writings* (Fitzpatrick), 4:30–31. Congress finally established rules for the seizure of ships and cargoes on November 25, 1775. *JCC*, 3:371–75.

[3] See *JCC*, 2:253–55.

[4] Congress authorized a grant of $40,000 to New Hampshire on December 4, 1775. *JCC*, 3:403.

[5] See *JCC*, 3:307; and New Hampshire Delegates to Matthew Thornton, October 2, 1775. See also New Hampshire Delegates to Matthew Thornton, November 3, 1775.

[6] See *JCC*, 3:308.

New York Delegates to Nathaniel Woodhull

Sir Philad. 26 Octr. 1775

We have the pleasure of enclosing you[1] a resolve passed this day in Congress, which we hope will enable our Province to provide ammunition with Certainty & Dispatch.[2]

You will easily perceive the Propriety of keeping it as secret as the Nature of the Business will admit; and we have particular Reasons for wishing that the Vessels intended for this Voyage may be soon dispatched.

We have declined informing Mr. Fine of the purport of this Resolve, thinking it more prudent to refer the whole to your Discretion. It will not be long before you will be made acquainted with the Sentiments of the Congress respecting the general State of Trade.[3] As to a certain necessary article,[4] it is not as yet to be procured here.

We are Sir with the greatest Respect the Convention's & Your very hble Servts.

Robt. R. Livingston junr

Jas Duane

John Jay

RC (N). Written by Jay and signed by Jay, Duane, and Livingston. *Journal of N. Y. Prov. Cong.*, 2:18. RC damaged; missing words supplied from Tr.

[1] Nathaniel Woodhull (1722–76), Suffolk County, N. Y., farmer, militia officer, and assemblyman, was at this time president pro tempore of the New York Provincial Congress and brigadier general in the Long Island militia. *DAB*.

[2] See *JCC*, 3:308.

[3] See John Jay to Alexander McDougall, October 17, 1775, note.

[4] Presumably gunpowder, the shortage of which in New York was a recurring theme in the correspondence between the Provincial Congress and the New York delegates. *Am. Archives*, 4th ser. 3:1269, 1272, 1279, 1292.

Samuel Ward's Diary

[October 26, 1775]

26th. Resolvd. that the Resolution of 15th July relative to giving Prov[ision]s or other American Produce for Powder be prin[te]d in hand Bills & sent throug[hou]t Europe & foreign W. Is.

Convention of New York to take into their Cus[tod]y Blankets, Shirts &c & send such of them as may be necessary for Genl. Schuylers Army to him. A Comee. appointed to take into consideration the Letter from N. York orderd to report an Answer. An Express orderd to Virginia to inquire into the Matter of rock Salt Petre & bring Samples.[1] A Comee. (J. Adams, J. Rutledge, Mr. Ward, Colo. Lee, Mr. Sherman) appointed to take into their Consideration the Instruction to the Delegates of N. Hampshire & report their Opinion thereon. The Resolution for obtaining well authenticated Accts. of hostilities &c order'd to be printed in the Newspapers, then resolvd. into a Comee. of the whole. Mr. Ward reported a Resolution that it be recommended to the Assemblies &c to export to the foreign W. Indies on Acct. & Risque of the Colonies r[e]spectively Provisions or other Produce except horned Cattle, Sheep, hogs & Poultry for the Importation of Arms & Ammunition for their several Colonies.

MS (RHi).

[1] In response to this resolution, Thomas Jefferson this day wrote to Thomas Lynch of Bedford County, Va., and joined with the other Virginia delegates in a joint letter to Lynch requesting mineral samples and an assessment of the prospects for successful exploitation of the saltpetre deposits reported to be located in southwestern Virginia. Neither of the letters to Lynch has been found, but Lynch's responses are in the Jefferson Papers, DLC, and are printed in Jefferson, *Papers* (Boyd), 1:261–64.

John Adams' Notes of Debates

1775. Octr. 27.[1]

R. R. Livingston.[2] Cloathing will rise tho Provisions will fall. Labourers will be discharged. One Quarter Part of R. Island, N. York, and Pensylvania depend upon Trade, as Merchants, Shopkeepers, Shipwrights, Blockmakers, Riggers, Smiths, &c. &c. &c.

The 6 Northern Dollars [Colonies] must raise 9 millions of Dollars to support the Poor.

This Vote will stop our Trade for 14 months, altho it professes to do it only to the 20th of March. For the Winter when the Men of War cannot cruise upon the Coast is the only Time that We can trade.

Wealthy Merchants, and monied Men cannot get the Interest of Money.

More Virtue is expected from our People, than any People ever had. The Low Countries did not reason as We do about speculative opinions, but they felt the oppression for a long Course of Years, rich and poor.

Zubly. Concludes that the Sense and Bent of the People, is vs. stopping Trade by the Eagerness with which they exported before the 10th. of September.

We cant get Intelligence, without Trade. All that are supported by Trade, must be out of Business.

Every Argument which shews that our Association will materially affect the Trade of G.B. will shew that We must be affected too, by a Stoppage of our Trade.

G.B. has many Resources. I have bought 2 Barrells of Rice in Carolina for 15s. and Negro Cloth was 3s. instead of 18d.

The W. Indies will get supplies to keep soul and Body together.[3] The ingenious Dutchmen will smuggle some Indian Corn from America.

Is it right to starve one Man because I have quarelled with another. I have a great Scruple whether it is just, or prudent. In Decr. 1776, We shall owe between 20 and 30 Millions of Money.

J. Rutledge. Am for adhering to the Association and going no further. The Non Export. in Terrorem—and generally agreed.

The Consequences will be dreadfull, if We ruin the Merchants.

Will not the Army be supplied if Vessells go from one Province to another.

We may pass a Resolution that no live Stock shall be exported.

MS (MHi). Adams, *Diary* (Butterfield), 2:219–20.

[1] These notes are the last of a series for the period October 4–27 that Adams kept covering debates in the committee of the whole on "the state of the trade" of the colonies. The issue continued to be debated, however, and a committee report of October 31 was adopted by Congress on November 1. *JCC*, 3:307–8, 312, 314–15.

[2] For a more complete text of Livingston's speech, see Robert R. Livingston, Jr.'s Notes for a Speech in Congress, this date.

[3] On the previous day Congress had resolved to recommend that the provincial governments authorize limited exportation of provisions to the West Indies "as

they may deem necessary for the importation of arms, ammunition, sulphur, and salt petre." *JCC*, 3:308.

Francis Lewis to Jabez Huntington

Sir New York 27 October 1775

As a Member of the Continental Congress, it was by them thought expedient, that I should proceed to this City in order to purchase necessarys for the Troops at Cambridge, agreeable thereto. I have sent by the bearer Twenty Packages to your address as specified in the inclosed receipt, reffering him to you for payment of the freight, as Mr. Vandervoort informs me that you transact the public business at Norwich.[1]

I must intreat you to forward these goods as soon as possible by land, to the address of Major Mifflin Quar. Masr. General at the Camp at Cambridge. I shall also advise Major Mifflin thereof by Post.[2]

I have the Honor to be, Sir Your very Humble Servt,

Frans. Lewis

MS not found; reprinted from Burnett, *Letters*, 1:242.

[1] Jabez Huntington (1719–86), Norwich, Conn., merchant, was a member of the Connecticut Council of Safety and a lieutenant colonel of militia. *DAB*.

[2] Although Lewis, John Alsop, and Philip Livingston had contracted with the Secret Committee on October 9 to supply arms and ammunition to the colonies, the present letter clearly refers to Lewis' work as a member of a committee appointed on September 23 to provide the Continental Army with £5000 sterling worth of woolen goods. Burnett's conjecture that Lewis was acting in behalf of the Secret Committee when he wrote this letter is therefore probably incorrect, since it is apparent from the journals that the committees were separate and distinct bodies. See Burnett, *Letters*, 1:242n.2; *JCC*, 3:260, 281; and Secret Committee Contract, October 9, 1775.

Robert R. Livingston, Jr.'s Notes for a Speech in Congress

[October 27, 1775][1]

Motion [*to continue nonexportation is*] part [*of the*] general system.

Limitation to *March*—when apparent [*we can*] only trade in winter—enemy [*can*] prevent [*us*] in summer.[2]

Arguments against Trade [*are*] general—hardly believe serious.

Inconveniences from stopage [*of*] trade.

III. Objects.

I. Enable our own people to bear Burthens & to render them willing to carry on war.

II. To procure means [*of*] war.

III. To impoverish, weaken enemy.

I. May be laid down as a principle, that all circumstances being alike, those support war longest who have most superfluous wealth. Those avoid it who feel more injuries from war than [*they have*] reason [*to*] expect from submission.

Consider effect [*of nonexportation*] on wealth [*of the*] people.

1st. Reduction of price of produce to 1/2 value—Price [*of*] Labour must fall same proportion.

This no inconvenience if [*it*] stood alone, because labour & subsistance bear same proportion to each other.

3 Things to be consider'd:

1. Tho labour cheap yet vent for produce small—farmer discharge labourers.

2d. Cloathing dearer than before—thereafter [*when*] produce falls 1/2, necessaries purchased [*rise in*] same proportion: value of cloathing, salt &c. is as 1 to 2; the farmer [*would*] pay 2/3 of income.

3. Burthen still heavier on labourer who [*in*] genl. being maintained by farmer, worked for cloathing & triffle for pleasure of family. [*With his*] wages diminished 1/2, necessaries except food raised 1/2, [*it is*] impossible [*that he*] can cloath himself at all.

2d. People [*who*] subsist by trade: Merchants, ship builders, Rope & sailmakers, Sailors, Smiths, Millars, labourers employed [*at*] Furnaces, carriers by land & water—in New York, Pensylvania, Rode Island make about 1/4 of the whole—other Colonies North [*of*] Pensylvania 1/8—so that have upwards [*of*] 225,000 [*plus*] 75,000 [*or*] 300,000 people besides labourers out of employ who must be supported. All these must be supported by farmer whose income [*is*] already diminished 2/3.

May be said [*that these*] may be employed. How? Not in culture, Lands less cultivated now than before. Not manufactures—always worked up all materials; of course [*there are*] hands to do it without them.

Consider rigor [*of*] climate, delicate life, many [*of*] these [*do*] not think 30 dollars [*a*] year extravagant for subsistance. 9,000,000 [*dollars*]. This tax must be raised immidiately on 7 Colonies & those [*the*] poorest.

Mass.ts part general system.
limitation to march—when apparent only trade in winter—enemy prevent in summer—
Arg.t ag.d trade gen.l—hardly believe serious—

2d Inconveniences from stopage trade.

III. Objects
1 enable our own people to bear burthens & to render them willing to carry on war—
II. to procure means war.
III. to impoverish weaken enemy—

I May be laid down as a principle. That all circum=stances being alike. those support war longest who have most superfluous wealth—
Those avoid it who feel more injuries from war than reason expect from submission—

Consider. effect on wealth. people—
1st Reduction of price value of produce to 1/2 value—Price Labour must fall same proportion—
This no inconvenience if stood alone be=cause labour & subsistance bear same pro=portion to each other—
3 things to be consider'd
1. tho labour cheap yet vent for produce small—farmer discharge labourers
2. Cloathing dearer than before—therefore produce falls 1/2 necessaries purchased same proportion value of cloathing &c. is as 1 to 2 the farmer pay 2/3 of mon

Robert R. Livingston Notes

May be said some [*of*] these [*colonies are*] rich; support themselves & others.

Deny. Riches [*of*] northern colonies consists [*of*] stock in trade, money at interest, Land rents.

1st. No use. 2nd. Interest money can not be paid when trade stoped, nor can principle be recovered—suits [*at*] law stoped, of course credit, & with it circulation [*of*] cash. 3d. Landlord cannot expect rent of people taxed 2/3 of whole estate.

So that this resolution [*to continue nonexportation*] anihilates all property.[3]

II. Inquire whether war with all these pressures [*is*] not more greivous than any they expect from ⟨*peace*⟩ submission. If it is they chuse lesser evil.

[*The people*] felt no oppression—found [*they*] grew wealthy under dominion [*of*] parliment. Yet spirit [*of*] liberty excited wonderfully. Hopes boyed up, now see serious. We ourselves thought virtue shd. not be tried. [*If we would*] not tax 3,000,000 when in affluence, how expect 7 Colonies [*to*] bear weight [*of*] 9,000,000 [*dollars*], besides burthen of war & a total loss besides of 2/3 of property?

Add to this [*that the*] value [*of*] commodities on hand [*which*] amount to ,[4] operate as a bridle on possessors. Horses, wheat &c. which could sell £30, now but 15; as much under influence as if £15 given him to desert cause.

People know too that on submission storm [*would*] burst only on leaders; That oppressions [*would*] not [*be*] heavy at least for time.

[*People*] already alledge dispute [*is*] about property; they have none.

No instance [*in*] history [*that a*] people reduced [*to*] this situation maintained war. Revolt [*in the*] Low Countries not paralel, grivously opressd religion—governmt felt many years—body [*of the*] people felt as much as rich.

During war [*the Dutch*] carried on trade—grew rich.

Case nearest ours—commotion [*in the*] year 1640.[5]

Their people soon tired [*of*] governmt of republick, Tho' trade most flourishing state, meerly on acct. [*of*] taxes. Petition [*and*] commotions shew inclinations, army necessary to subject them. Restoration matter [*of*] genl. satisfaction.

Calculate from northern colonies these inconveniences, not so much felt southwd. Trade [*in the South is*] carried on English bottoms—no Seamen, no merchants, but few factors. No ship builders—various mechanicks employed in that business—few carriers but negroes.

Planters live on estates, cultivation [*of*] which with great number [*of*] hands easily procure food & clothing sufficient for whites. Blacks go naked till 14—of course may till 50.

Not wonder therefore some [*of*] them stickle measure which judging own climate is but temporary inconvenience.

Hope [*they*] change sentiments when [*they*] take view [*of the*] northern ones.

Whether [*we can*] obtain means [*of*] war [*if*] this takes place.

1st. Wants sufficiently obvious. Operations [*of*] armies checked by it. Citys defenseless. Coast lyable to be ravaged.

Second. Exception with respect [*to*] them but these [*will*] not answer purpose—2 reasons:

(1st) Because publishes wants to our enimies—make [*them*] more vigilant.

(2d) Few merchants engage when bound at all events to return [*with*] military stores. May so happen [*these*] cannot be got at port sent—then voyage frustrated. If trade left at large, they always indeavour to get them because yield most proffit—adventure because shd [*they*] fail [*to obtain*] that cargo [*they would*] still not return empty.

Has been said that if [*we had*] open ports none but eastern colonies trade—own advantage—rejoice at it. Tho' they joined sentiment that our enjoying advantage [*was*] not hurtful [*to the*] rest [*of the*] provinces, [*it*] wd excite jealousy in theirs.

Yet persuaded own Constituents think as to wish them advantages ten times greater. Besides every Colony [*has*] chance during winter of sliping out.

3d Objection. impossibility [*of*] obtaining navy. [*Nonexportation*] banishes seamen, who not only [*are*] lost but become enimies—forced by necessity into British service.

[*Given*] these considerations [*we*] Must Trade.

III. Meathods proposed. 1st. Invite forreigners. 2d. Trade with all the world except G. B. & I. 3d. Export immediately to G. B. & Ireland except tobacco & lumber.

I. Invite forreigners. 2 Inquiries.

1st. Whether foreigners at large or particular nations?

2d. Whether temporary expedient or lastg Basis of our trade?

If at large no national object. Still less so if only temporary expedient. Not expect merchants [*to*] alter course [*of*] trade & turn [*into* a] chanel which expect soon [*to be*] stoped & in which expect many rivals.

If then must trade [*with a*] particular power, inquire who shall be! Holland, Portugal unable to protect us. [*Would*] Spain regardless of her own trade consider new one as object? Suffered all staples to decay, mismanagement—weak, unenterprizing—war already on hand.

Only remaining power France.

1st. How [. . . .][6]

1st. Is [*it*] not very doubtful whether she [*France*] will trade with us, considering low state [*of her*] finances, weakness [*of the*] present monarchy, And late conduct?

Gent. asserts she must; for want [*of*] grain which [*she can*] get no where else. Our exports of grain to France do not make a 110th part of her consumption. Our exports to her never amounted 1,000,000 [*bushels*]—her consumption 150,000,000.

So [*France*] not forced [*to trade for*] those. As many advantages [*would*] result [*to*] her from trade, may possibly think [*it*] worth her notice.

But private adventurers never undertake this. Before govermt interposes, must settle Terms. Must at least be permanent at all events.

Have Gent. turned thoughts to what terms shall be?

Have fix'd time? Considered whether trade may not become monopoly? Whether she can supply us with woollens without getting them from England? Whether this [*might*] not defeat our non importation? True, this [*would be a*] loss [*to*] G. B., but have [*gentlemen*] considered whether greater loss [*might*] not fall on us?

Have made any provision for our shipbuilders, sailors &c. or must [*these*] be a burthen?

But this evident & this measure not to be adopted till treaties settled—nor they entered into till [*the French*] agree to break with Great Britain.

II. Trade with foreigners at large [*in our*] own bottoms. This more advantagious because still imploy our own hands. Retain Sailors.

Still has its disadvantages.

1st. Vessels liable to capture. By which means [*Britain*

would] receive our commodities on a cheap lay.

2d. West Indies would be supplied from foreign West Indies.

3d. British goods would be lodged at foreign ports. Thus non importation, in which our chief strength, [*would*] be defeated.

4th. When our trade [*is*] witheld, Briton [*would*] be under necessity of fetching some commodities from Northern nations [*which she*] now gets of us. This [*would*] afford vent to goods [*she*] usually send to us.

May [*be*] said no purchasers.

Mistake. Both Dutch & English send woollens up Baltick. Of course price must be nearly equal. If so then a small reduction in price [*would*] enable English to undersell Dutch. That reduction would [*be*] made. For as [*Britain*] must fetch commodities from there, [*she*] must either send vessels empty and loose freight outward, or by sinking whole profit, make freight.

May be said This was done when [*she*] traded with us—of course [*her prices*] could sink no lower.

Not fact. When same good imported [*by Britain*] from America that [*she would now*] get from Northern nations, & at rather a cheaper rate—profit to the mercht trading with them was on his outward entries—only took their commodities to make a freight. Now reverse.

So [*it is*] clear By non exportation agreement we defeat non importation. Leave [*British*] manufactures & merchants [*in the*] same state they were, subjecting indeed [*that*] nation to a loss, but too small to be early felt. That made up by captures.

If Then [*a*] mode can be fallen upon that can prevent these inconveniences, preserve our non importation inviolate, sure prejudice or hard words shd. not prevent a cool examination of it.

This did myself honour to mention. As was recd. cooly, [*I*] shd. have passed over had [*I*] not been called upon.[7] Now endeavour to defend.

III. Export immediately to G.B. & Ireland except tobacco ⟨& *Lumber*⟩, but not import. These evident advantages.

1st. If our exports equal [£] 2,500,000 we must drain [*Britain*] anualy of that some [*sum*]. Effect this [*would*] have on G.B. when considered [*that her*] current cash not more than [£] 2,000,000. Besides employing hands, enriching country, [*it would*] enable [*us*] to pay whole expense [*of the*] war.

Enables [*us to*] purchase what [*we*] want [*to*] carry on war. Cheaper, less risk. For vessel would be safe from here to England then have money with which [*to*] trade [*with*] any foreign nation. Landings little danger [*if*] any, numerous inlets on coast.

This would give us intelligence of Movements of our enimies.

Would reserve our seamen.

Objections.

1st. That prohibition [*of*] tobacco [*exports*] would create disgust [*in*] 2 Colonies. [*For*] my own part [*I have a*] higher opinion [*of their*] virtue than [*to*] think so. Principles on which prohibited might be explained. Lands [*which*] raise tobacco [*are*] fit [*for*] any grain. Female negroes not employed, but will they be employed if trade totally stoped? If not, were disadvantage.

2d. That many things exported by us manufactured in England & reshiped. Have shewn [*that if Britain*] did not get [*them*] from Colonies, [*they would*] be procured from elsewhere—& in return for them manufactors. *Iron.* But even if not, [*the*] value of those as well as home consumption [*would be*] paid us in specie.

3d. Number hands employed in reshiping. But surely more employed [*by*] us in shiping—not only same but what they consume too.

4th. Flax seed [*to*] Ireland not so important as [*we*] imagine. [*They could*] procure [*it*] from Holland [*as they*] formerly did. Whole value [*£*] 40,000. Idle [*to*] think [*they*] could not manufacture [*for*] want of it.

5th. West Indies—provision Shiped not reshiped there.

Gent did not think much weight in argument when [*he*] supposes trade [*would*] be so ruinous to G.B. that she would prohibit it.

Worth trying. Perhaps interest [*of*] individual [*would*] over rule publick good.

Find [*that Britain*] does carry on some trades where ballance [*is*] against her—East Indies.

[*During the*] last non importation against [*Britain, we*] exported to her.

Probable [*we would*] enjoy advantage at least [*for*] some

time when [*Britain*] prohibited exportation [*of*] specie, which [*is the*] most probable meathod [*Britain would*] take [*to*] stop it. Purchase forreign bills answer same purpose.

Gent went far into non importation & disadvantages Britain laboured from. [*I*] agree [*with that*] sentiment, & [*am*] so far [*from*] wishing to break it that I mention this [*as the*] only mode to preserve [*non importation*] in full force.

Breach association. But if [*non exportation is*] founded in error, shd. be revoked. Not at present. Let people feel want [*of*] trade, which [*they will*] do in few weeks, then grant.

MS (NHi). In the hand of Robert R. Livingston, Jr. Although an effort has been made to preserve the cryptic character of Livingston's notes, editorial insertions have been added to make them more intelligible and several abbreviations have been expanded without brackets. (For the first page of these notes, see illustration.)

[1] John Adams' Notes of Debates for October 27 clearly demonstrate that this day, in the midst of a debate on a motion to continue a ban on all exports not specifically approved by Congress, Livingston delivered a speech in the committee of the whole based on these notes. Livingston forcefully opposed the motion, but notwithstanding his effort, Congress decided on November 1 to prohibit until March 1, 1776, virtually all non-congressionally sanctioned exports from the colonies. See John Adams' Notes of Debates, this day; and *JCC*, 3:308, 314.

[2] For an expanded version of the cryptic notes in this paragraph, see John Adams' Notes of Debates, this date.

[3] See above, note 1.

[4] Blank in MS.

[5] An allusion to the English Revolution.

[6] At this point in the MS two pages are missing.

[7] Presumably a reference to Livingston's remarks in Congress on October 3, on which see John Adams' Notes of Debates for that date.

Samuel Ward's Diary

[October 27, 1775]

27th. A Report from the Comee appointed to take into their Consideration a Letter from N. York was read. The Congress then resolved itself into a Comee. of the whole. Mr. Ward reported that they had come into no Resolutions &c.[1]

MS (RHi).

[1] See *JCC*, 3:308.

John Adams to Abigail Adams

My dear Octr. 28. 1775

The Fall of Dr. Ch[urc]h, has given me many disagreable Reflections, as it places human Nature itself in a Point of bad Light, but the Virtue, the sincerity, the Honour, of Boston and Massachusetts Patriots in a worse. What shall We say of a Country which produces such Characters as Hutchinson and Church? However to turn my Attention from this detestible Subject to another more agreable. Congress has appointed instead of Church, Dr. Morgan of this City whose Character I will pourtray for your Satisfaction.

The Gentleman appointed Director and surgeon general of the Hospital, is John Morgan M.D. Fellow of the Royal Society at London; Correspondent of the Royal Academy of Surgery at Paris; Member of the Arcadian Belles Lettres Society at Rome; Licentiate of the Royal Colledges of Physicians in London and in Edinburgh; and Professor of the Theory and Practice of Medicine in the Colledge of Philadelphia.

This Gentleman was one of the first who received their Education in the Colledge in this City, and served an Apprenticeship of six Years with Dr. John Redman an eminent Phisician, here, during one whole Year of which he put up the Prescriptions of all the Phisicians who attended the public Hospital here, who were all eminent. After this the Dr. entered the Army and served four Years under Generals Moncton, Forbes and Stanwix, where he had an entensive Practice, in the Army among all Kinds of Diseases. Five years after, he left the Army he spent in Europe,[1] under the most celebrated Masters in every Branch of Medicine. During this Period he visited the principal Cities and Seats of Science in Great Britain, Holland, France and Italy.

Returning from his Travels, he was chosen Professor of Medicine in the Colledge in this City, where he has constantly read Lectures every Winter, and for many Years practiced among the Citizens.

Dr. Morgans moral Character is very good, and his manners are civil, decent, and agreable. He married a sister of the Lady of our Chaplain, Mr. Dushe, who is new Rector of the three united Churches in this City. A sister of the Doctors is married to Mr. Stillman the Antipaedobaptist lately in Boston, now in this Place.

Thus I hope We shall hear no Complaint that this Place is not now well filled.

Jealousy and Envy spare nobody. Some have whispered that the Dr. is a little Visionary in Theory and Practice. But all agree that he is attentive, vigilant and laborious for the good of his Patients in a great Degree, and he is said to be a pious Man.

RC (MHi). Adams, *Family Correspondence* (Butterfield), 1:314–16.

[1] Adams apparently meant that after he left the army Morgan spent five years studying medicine in Europe.

John Adams to James Warren

Dr sir Octr. 28? 1775[1]

Our Association, against Importations and Exportations, from and to G Britain, Ireland and the British West Indies, if We consider its Influence, upon the Revenue, the Commerce, the Manufactures and the Agriculture of the Kingdom, is a formidable Shield of Defence for Us. It is Shearing of its Beams that Luminary, which, in all its Glory might dazzle our feeble Sight.

But a Question arises, whether, our Association against Exportations, can be observed, so as to have its full Effect, upon Britain, Ireland and the West Indies, unless We extend it further? We have agreed not to export to B., I. and the W. Indies. Parliament has made an Act that We Shall not export to any other Place, So that Trade is entirely stopped. But will not a Smuggling Trade be opened? That is will not Adventurers push out Vessells against the Act of Parliament! If they do, when the Vessells are once at Sea, will they not go to the Place where a Famine price is to be had. The Spirit of Commerce is mercenary and avaricious, and Merchants will go where the Scarcity is greatest, the Demand quickest and the Price highest.

What Security then can we have that Merchants will not order their Vessells to the West India Islands, British or foreign, to Ireland or even to Great Britain, in Defyance of our association?

Besides is there not reason to apprehend, that the concealed Tories of whom there are many in every Colony, and especially in every maritime Town, will Send their Vessells to sea, on purpose to be taken by the Enemy and sent to Supply the Army and Navy in America. It is true, their Vessells would be forfeited, and seized and condemned no doubt but they might be pleased with this, and would easily obtain hereafter Compensation or Retribution for this meritorious Sacrifice, from the Ministry.

In Short may not our association be wholly evaded and eluded, if We dont draw it closer?

My own opinion upon these great Questions I may possibly give you sometime or other. But I wish to have yours.[2]

RC (MHi). In Adams' hand, though not signed.

[1] It appears from the RC that Adams superimposed a five or eight upon a four. From the substance of his comments to Warren it seems probable that they were

written soon after the debate of October 27 on nonexportation. See Adams' Notes of Debates, October 27, 1775.

[3] In a November 14–15 letter Warren counseled Adams: "I think the Association can't be too close drawn. We had better have no trade than suffer inconveniences from the interested tricks of Tories, or even merchants, who pretend to be well-principled, and yet are governed by interest alone." *Warren-Adams Letters*, 1:185.

John Hancock to Nathaniel Woodhull

Sir Philadelphia, 28th Octr. 1775.

Your Letter of the 17th inst. has been laid before the Congress and I am directed to Acquaint you, that they Approve of your immediately Raising a Company of matrosses, to consist of Sixty Eight Privates.[1] They prefer that Number, as it is the fixed Establishment of the Companies in the Continental Service. You will please to Appoint & forward the List of the officers proper to Command them, & their Commissions shall be made out and Sent you. The Congress Desire you will inform them when this Company shall be Completed; and they will Take under Consideration your proposals for Raising a larger Number.

Inclos'd is the Resolution of Congress.[2]

I am Gentlemen Your most Obedt hum. servt.

John Hancock President

RC (N). *Journals of N. Y. Prov. Cong.*, 2:7. RC damaged; missing words supplied from Tr.

[1] In Woodhull's October 17 letter to Congress, the New York Provincial Congress had provided the estimate that eventually four companies of matrosses would be required to man the fortifications then under construction in the Highlands but conceded that for the present only one company was needed. See PCC, item 67, 1:109–15; and *Am. Archives*, 4th ser. 3:1290.

[2] See *JCC*, 3:309.

Samuel Ward's Diary

[October 28, 1775]

28th. The Comee. of Saf[e]ty of Phila. laid before Congress the Examinations of Capn. Campbell &c ordered to be confined in Gaol by the Direction of the Comee.,[1] the Officers to be allowed 10/ Pa. Currency a Day the privates 7/6. A Comp[an]y Matrosses ordered to be raised in the Province of N. York. Some Accts. allowed. Mr. Wythe, Mr. Pain, Mr. Humpheys added to the salt petre Comee. Five of the Comee. of Claims to be a Quorum for the future.

The Inspectors of the Press to delivr. the Proof Sheets & sheets of the continental Bills to the cont. Treasu[rer]s & they to deliver one to the Delegs. of each Colony to be lodged with the provincial Treasr. & retain the rest in their Hands.

MS (RHi).

[1] On this point, see also John Hancock to the New York Provincial Congress, October 26, 1775.

John Adams to Abigail Adams

Octr. 29. 1775

I cannot exclude from my Mind your melancholly Situation. The Griefs of your Father and Sisters, your Uncles and Aunts, as well as the remoter Connections, often croud in upon me, when my whole Attention ought to be directed to other Subjects.

Your Uncle Quincy, my Friend as well as Uncle, must regret the loss of a beloved Sister, Dr. Tufts my other Friend I know bewails the loss of a Friend, as well as an Aunt and a sister, Mr. Cranch the Friend of my youth as well as of my riper Years, whose tender Heart sympathizes with his fellow Creatures in every Affliction and Distress, in this Case feels the Loss of a Friend, a fellow Christian, and a Mother.

But alas what avail these mournfull Reflections. The best Thing We can do, the greatest Respect We can show to the Memory of our departed Friend, is to copy into Our own Lives, those Virtues which in her Lifetime rendered her the Object of our Esteem, Love and Admiration. I must confess I ever felt a Veneration for her, which seems increased by the News of her Translation.

Above all Things my dear, let us inculcate these great Virtues and bright Excellencies upon our Children.[1]

Your Mother had a clear, and penetrating Understanding and a profound Judgment, as well as an honest and a friendly and a charitable Heart.

There is one Thing however, which you will forgive me if I hint to you. Let me ask you rather, if you are not of my opinion? Were not her Talents, and Virtues too much confined, to private, social and domestic Life. My Opinion of the Duties of Religion and Morality, comprehends a very extensive Connection with society at large, and the great Interest of the public. Does not natural Morality, and much more Christian Benevolence, make it our indispensible Duty to lay ourselves out, to serve our fellow Creatures to the Utmost of our Power, in promoting and supporting those great Politicial systems, and general Regulations upon which the Happiness of Multitudes depends. The Benevolence, Charity, Capacity and Industry which exerted in private Life, would make a family, a Parish or a Town Happy, employed upon a larger Scale, in Support of the great Principles of Virtue and Freedom of political Regulations might secure whole Nations and Generations from Misery, Want and Contempt. Public Virtues, and political Qualities therefore should be incessantly cherished in our Children.

RC (MHi). Adams, *Family Correspondence* (Butterfield), 1:316–17.

[1] In another letter to Abigail this day, Adams dilated upon the capabilities of human nature and "the virtues and powers to which men may be trained, by early education and constant discipline." "It should be your care, therefore," he urged, "and mine, to elevate the minds of our children and exalt their courage; to accelerate and animate their industry and activity; to excite in them an habitual contempt of meanness, abhorrence of injustice and inhumanity, and an ambition to excel in every capacity, faculty, and virtue." Adams to Abigail Adams, October 29, 1775, Adams, *Family Correspondence* (Butterfield), 1:317–18.

John Adams to Abigail Adams

Octr. 29. 1775

There is, in the human Breast, a social Affection, which extends to our whole Species. Faintly indeed; but in some degree. The Nation, Kingdom, or Community to which We belong is embraced by it more vigorously. It is stronger still towards the Province to which we belong, and in which We had our Birth. It is stronger and stronger, as We descend to the County, Town, Parish, Neighbourhood, and Family, which We call our own. And here We find it often so powerfull as to become partial, to blind our Eyes, to darken our Understandings and pervert our Wills.

It is to this Infirmity, in my own Heart, that I must perhaps attribute that local Attachment, that partial Fondness, that overweening Prejudice in favour of New England, which I feel very often and which I fear sometimes, leads me to expose myself to just Ridicule.

New England has in many Respects the Advantage of every other Colony in America, and indeed of every other Part of the World, that I know any Thing of.

1. The people are purer English Blood, less mixed with Scotch, Irish, Dutch, French, Danish, Sweedish &c. than any other; and descended from Englishmen too who left Europe, in purer Times than the present and less tainted with Corruption than those they left behind them.

2. The Institutions in New England for the Support of Religion, Morals and Decency, exceed any other, obliging every Parish to have a Minister, and every Person to go to Meeting &c.

3. The public Institutions in New England for the Education of

Youth, supporting Colledges at the public Expence and obliging Towns to maintain Grammar schools, is not equalled and never was in any Part of the World.

4. The Division of our Territory, that is our Counties into Townships, empowering Towns to assemble, choose officers, make Laws, mend roads, and twenty other Things, gives every Man an opportunity of shewing and improving that Education which he received at Colledge or at school, and makes Knowledge and Dexterity at public Business common.

5. Our Laws for the Distribution of Intestate Estates occasions a frequent Division of landed Property and prevents Monopolies, of Land.

But in opposition to these We have laboured under many Disadvantages. The exorbitant Prerogatives of our Governors &c. which would have overborn our Liberties, if it had not been opposed by the five preceding Particulars.

RC (MHi). Adams, *Family Correspondence* (Butterfield), 1:318–19.

Samuel Adams to Elbridge Gerry

My dear Sir Philadelphia Octob 29 1775

I wrote to you a few days ago by young Mr Brown and then duly acknowledgd your Letter of the 9th Instant.

You tell me that a Committee of both Houses of Assembly is appointed to bring in a Militia Bill.[1] I am of your Opinion that this Matter requires great Attention and I wish with you to see our Militia formd not only into Battallions but also Brigades. But should we not be cautious of putting them under the Direction of the Generals of the Continent, at least until such a Legislative shall be established in America as every Colony shall consent to.

The Continental Army is at present very properly under the Direction of the Continental Congress. Possibly if ever such a Legislative should be formd, it may be proper that the whole Military Power of every Colony should be under its absolute Direction. Be that as it may, will it not, till then, be prudent, that the Militia of each Colony should be under the Direction of its own Legislative which is and ought to be the sovereign uncontroulable Power within its own Limits or Territory. I hope our Militia will be always prepard to aid the Forces of the Continent in this righteous Opposition to Tyranny. But it is your natural Strength which ought to be under your own Direction & employd for your own Safety. It is a Misfortune to a Colony to become the Seat of War. It is always dangerous to the Liberties of the People to have an Army kept up among them over which they have no Controul. There is at present a Necessity for it. The Continental Army is kept up in our Colony for our Security. But History affords us abundant Evidence of established Armies making themselves the Masters of those Countries which they were designd to protect.

It is now in the Power of our Assembly to establish many wholesome Laws & Regulations which could not be done under the former Administration of Government. Bad Men may be kept out of places of publick Trust. The utmost Circumspection I hope will be used in the Choice of Men for publick officers. It is to be expected that some who are void of the least Regard to the publick, will put on the Appearance & even speak boldly in the Language of Patriots, with the sole purpose of getting the Confidence of the publick & securing the Loaves and Fishes for themselves or their Sons. Men who Stand Candidates for publick posts should be critically traced in their Views and Pretensions, and tho' we would despise mean & base Suspicions, yet there is a Degree of Jealousy which is absolutely necessary in this degenerate State of Mankind and is indeed at all times to be considerd as a political Virtue. It is in your power also to prevent a Plurality of Places incompatible with each other being vested in the same Persons. This our Patriots have loudly and very justly complaind of in times past, and it will be an everlasting Disgrace to them if they suffer the practice to continue.[2] Care, I am informd, is taking to remedy this Evil with as little Inconvenience as possible, but it is my opinion that the Remedy ought to be deep & thorough. After every other Consideration, Virtue is the surest Means of securing the State. Our brave Ancestors laid an excellent Foundation for the establishing and perpetuating virtuous Principles in the Country, when they created a publick Seminary of Learning, even before they had cut down the Woods in Cambridge, and they early made Laws for the Support of Grammar Schools. A better Foundation could no Men lay. I hope you will improve the Golden opportunity which you now have of restoring the ancient Purity of Manners in our Country. Every thing that we esteem valuable depends upon it. For, Freedom or Slavery, says an admired Writer, will prevail in a Country according as the Disposition and Manners of the Inhabitants render them fit for the one or the other.[3]

FC (NN).

[1] The controversy over remodeling the militia in Massachusetts is discussed in Stephen E. Patterson, *Political Parties in Revolutionary Massachusetts* (Madison: University of Wisconsin Press, 1973), pp. 128–32. See also, Samuel Adams to James Otis, November 23, 1775.

[2] For an analysis of plural officeholding among "our Patriots," see Ellen E. Brennan, *Plural Office-Holding in Massachusetts 1760–1780* (Chapel Hill: University

of North Carolina Press, 1945), pp. 107–35.
[3] For the continuation of this letter, see Adams to Gerry, November 4, 1775.

John Adams' Notes of Debates

1775. Octr. 30th. Monday.

Ross. We cant get Seamen to man 4 Vessells. We could not get Seamen to mann our Boats, our Gallies.[1]

Wythe, Nelson, and Lee for fitting out 4 Ships.

MS (MHi). Adams, *Diary* (Butterfield), 2:220.

[1] These remarks were made during debate over a resolution to arm two more vessels in addition to the two approved on October 13. Congress adopted the resolution, and Adams was one of four delegates added to the committee charged with implementing the plan. *JCC,* 3:311–12.

Samuel Ward's Diary

[October 30, 1775]

30th. Four armd. Vessells order'd to be fitted out; a Comee. for that Purpose [*chosen*]. Recom[mendatio]n of provinl. Cong[res]s of New Jersey for field Officers referred.

MS (RHi).

John Zubly's Diary

[October 30, 1775]

30. Attended Committee & Congress. Spent the Evening agreably with Mr. Kirkland the Indian Missionary.

MS (GHi).

Thomas Jefferson to John Page

Dear Page[1] Philadelphia Oct. 31. 1775.

We have nothing new from England or the camp before Boston. By a private letter this day to a gentleman of Congress from General Montgomery we learn that our forces before St. John's are 4000. in number besides 500. Canadians the latter of whom have repelled with great intrepidity three different attacks from the fort. We apprehend it will not hold out much longer as Monsr. St. Luc de la Corne and several other principal inhabitants of Montreal who have been our great enemies have offered to make terms. This St. Luc is great Seigneur among the Canadians, and almost absolute with the Indians. He has been our most bitter enemy. He is acknowledged to be the greatest of all scoundrels. To be assured of this I need only mention to you that he is the ruffian who when during the last war Fort William Henry was surrendered to the French and Indians on condition of saving the lives of the garrison, had every soul murdered in cold blood. The check which the Canadians received at first is now wearing off. They were made to beleive we had an army of 15,000 men going there. This put them in high spirits. But when they saw Montgomery with but 2700 they were thunderstruck at the situation they had brought themselves into. However when they found even this small armament march boldly to invest St. John's and put a good face on the matter they revived, and the recruits since have contributed to inspirit them more.

I have set apart nearly one day in every week since I came here to write letters. Notwithstanding this I have never received the scrip of a pen from any mortal breathing.[2] I should have excepted two lines from Mr. Pendleton to desire me to buy him 24. lb of wire from which I concluded he was alive. I speak not this for you from whom I would not wish to receive a letter till I know you can write one without injury to your health. But in future as I must be satisfied with information from my collegues that my country still exists, so I am determined to be satisfied also with their epistolary communications of what passes within our knowledge. Adieu Dear Page.

DELENDA EST NORFOLK[3]

RC (NN). Jefferson, *Papers* (Boyd), 1:250–51.

[1] John Page (1744–1808), Virginia planter, burgess, and councilor, was a member of the Virginia Committee of Public Safety. He became lieutenant governor of Virginia in 1776 and was later elected a United States Representative and governor of Virginia. *DAB.*

[2] Although Jefferson was understandably upset by the lack of personal correspondence from his friends, Edmund Pendleton, chairman of the Committee of Safety, kept the Virginia delegates informed on major public developments at home. Pendleton's letters of October 15 to Richard Henry Lee and of October 28 to the Virginia delegates are printed in Edmund Pendleton, *The Letters and Papers of Edmund Pendleton*, ed. David J. Mays, 2 vols. (Charlottesville: University Press of Virginia, 1967), 1:120–21, 124–25.

[3] A reference to Lord Dunmore's use of Norfolk as a base for his naval operations against coastal towns.

Samuel Ward's Diary

[October 31, 1775]

31st. Letters from G. Schuyler read,[1] resolvd into a Comee. of the whole. Mr. Ward repor[te]d a certain Resol[utio]n & desired leave to sett again. Report referred. Resolve of the assem[bl]y of Pennsylvania presented & referred to Friday.

MS (RHi).

[1] The journals record the receipt this day of letters from General Schuyler of October 6, 13, 14, and 19, but these were not all written by Schuyler nor were all the Schuyler letters which arrived this day included in this list. To begin with, Congress actually received letters from Schuyler to Hancock of October 13, 14, and 20, as well as from Schuyler to General Wooster of October 19. See PCC, item 153, 1:210–13, 222–25, 230–33, 238–41; and *Am. Archives,* 4th ser. 3:1065–66, 1093–95 (where the October 13 letter is misdated October 18), 1107, and 1124. In addition, Schuyler sent enclosures of letters he received from General Montgomery of October 6, 9, and 13, and from Wooster of October 19. See PCC, item 153, 1:214–21, 226–27, 234–37; and *Am. Archives,* 4th ser. 3:1095–97, 1107–8. Thus Burnett's lengthy note about the dates of Schuyler's letters can be ignored, since it rests on the erroneous assumptions that the letters mentioned in the journals under this date were all written by Schuyler and that the Schuyler letters in *Am. Archives* are correctly dated. Burnett, *Letters,* 1:245n.

John Adams to James Warren

Dr sir Octr. 1775

What think you of a North American Monarchy? Suppose We should appoint a Continental King, and a Continental House of Lords, and a Continental House of Commons, to be annually, or triennially or Septennially elected? And in this Way make a Supreme American Legislature? This is easily done you know by an omnipotent Continental Congress. And when once effected, His American Majesty may appoint a Governor for every Province, as his Britannic Majesty used to do, and Lt Governor and secretary and judge of Admiralty. Nay his Continental Majesty may appoint the Judges of the supream Courts &c too—or if his American Majesty should condiscend to permit the provincial Legislatures, or assemblies [*to*] nominate two three or four Persons out of whom he should select a governor, and 3 or 4 Men for Chief Justice &c out of whom he should choose one, would not this do nicely?

To his Continental Majisty, in his Continental Privy Council, Appeals might lie from all Admiralty Cases, and from all civil Causes [possessed?] at least, of a certain Value, and all Disputes about Land, that is about Boundaries of Colonies, should be settled by the Continental King and Council, as they used to be by the British K. and Council. What a magnifient System?[1]

I assure you this is no Chimera of my own. It is whispered about in Coffee Houses, &c and there are [*those*] who wish it.

I am inclined to think it is done, as one Artifice more to divide the Colonies. But in vain. It would be very curious to give you an History of the out a Door Tricks for this important Evil of dividing the Colonies. Last Fall the Quakers and Antipædobaptists were conjured up to pick a Quarrell with Massachusetts;[2] last Spring the Land Jobbers were stimulated to pick a Quarrell with Connecticutt for the same End. The Quakers and Anabaptists were hushed and abashed, or rather the reasonable conscientious Part of them were convincd in one Evening. The Land Jobbers will meet no better success.

RC (MHi). In Adams' hand, though not signed. Adams failed to specify the day on which he wrote this letter, and its content is too general to support speculation on its precise date.

[1] Adams' discussion of the augmentation of the powers of Congress is strongly suggestive of the 8th, 9th, and 10th paragraphs of Silas Deane's Proposals to Congress, November ? 1775.

[2] See John Adams' Diary, October 14, 1774, note.

Samuel Chase to the Maryland Council of Safety

Gentlemen Philadelphia November 1st. 1775

The Congress have directed the enclosed Resolutions,[1] and Papers to be transmitted to You. I submit to your Consideration whether it would not be proper to communicate Copies to the Committee of Observation of each County, and request their diligent attention and steady Execution of the Resolves, and if Annapolis cannot be defended it would not be adviseable to remove the public Records and Loan office.

I am Gentlemen with Regard and Respect Your Obedt. Servant

Saml. Chase

RC (MdAA).

[1] Undoubtedly the resolutions of November 1 on nonexportation. *JCC*, 3:314.

John Hancock to the Speaker of the Massachusetts Assembly

Sir Philadelphia Nover. 1st. 1775

I have only Time to Inform you that I have the Directions of Congress to Transmitt to your Assembly the Inclos'd Resolutions pass'd by them,[1] and to desire that you will not make them more publick than the nature of them Requires.

I am Sir Yours and the Assembly's Most Obediant Humble, Servt.

John Hancock President

Tr (M-Ar). Endorsed: "Letter from the President respecting our Exports: & Imports: refering to the Restraining Act."

[1] See *JCC*, 3:314.

Samuel Ward's Diary

Novr. 1. [1775]

Letter from G. Washin[gto]n containg. an Acct. of burning Falmouth &c read.[1] Copies to be forwarded to the several Colonies by the Delegates. A Letter from the Comee. with Copies of their Proceedings.[2]

The Report of the Comee. of the whole order'd that no Provisions be exported &c, New York & the other excepted Colonies to take no Advantage of such Exceptions, No Rice to be shipped, that no live stock (necessary Sea Stores at the discretion of the Comee. of Safety & Horses excepted) to be exported or waterborn except in Bays, Rivers & Sounds.

MS (RHi).

[1] On October 18 a British naval squadron, commanded by Lt. Henry Mowat and acting under express orders from Admiral Samuel Graves, destroyed most of Falmouth (now Portland, Maine) in retaliation for the town's having fired upon a British naval vessel the previous August. Clark, *Naval Documents*, 2:324–26, 471, 487–89, 500–502. Washington's letter to Hancock of October 24 and the accompanying enclosures describing this incident are in PCC, item 152, 1:241–50; and *Am. Archives*, 4th ser. 3:1151–55.

[2] That is, the committee to confer with General Washington. See Committee of Conference to John Hancock, October 24, 1775; and *Am. Archives*, 4th ser. 3:1156–63.

Samuel Ward to Deborah Ward

My dearest Debby Philadelphia 1st Novr 1775

Your Letter 25th was very acceptable. The Difficulties and Disorders in the Business and Family I dont so much wonder at as I have been so much from home this last year & when at home have been so much engaged in Matters which prevented my taking that Care of my Family & affairs which I could wish but surely my little dear Children cannot so soon forget their Duty to God, to their Father, their Country, Family, Friends & to themselves; They are young but old enough to consider that He who gave them Being & whose Goodness supports, comforts & preserves them every moment Deserves their highest affection & their most chearful Obedience. Again a kind most indulgent Father ever ready to do them all the Service in his Power at the Risque of his Life, at the Expence of many of the Amusements & Pleasures of this World must be entitled to their warmest Affection, Gratitude and Duty. Their Country also has a Right to their best Services and if they spend their time idly instead of being usefully employed in Business or in improving their own Understandings they will be only a Burthen to the Community and never capable of doing any great Good; their Sisters, Brothers and Friends have a Right to expect all the Good in their Power to do them but if they contract vicious or idle Habits They will not be able to do Good to any, and lastly upon their own Behaviour depends their present & future Happiness. They much want a good School, proper Company & the Care of a kind watchful Parent or Parents; all these and every thing else that would have a Tendency [*to*] make them wise, good & happy they should have if it was in my Power to obtain them for my Children, but instead of murmuring because We have not every Wish gratified let us make the best Improvement of what We have. What inconceivable Distress many Parts of the Continent feel. Let us thank God that We have a comfortable Retreat where it is probable our Enemies will not be able to reach Us, what We may be called to do or suffer I cannot at present say but the Cause in which We are engaged is good. The great Author of our Beings made us free, tamely to suffer ourselves to be enslaved would be to spurn at his Bounty and quit that noble Rank of free and rational Creatures which He designed us for and degrade Ourselves almost to the Level of the brute Creation; This our Duty obliges us to shun at the Hazard not only of many of the Comforts of Life but even of Life itself.

I wrote so fully upon Business lately that it is not necessary to add much now. I mentioned the Quantity of Pork which you must lay in. I hope the Hogs & Cattle are well fed & no Waste made; your Flax should be rolled before this time; if it is not done already let it be done as soon as possible. Linens of all kinds will be scarce and very dear; make therefore & take in all you can at a moderate Rate. Besides the Manufacture of Wool mentioned when at home there should be one good fine p[iece] Broadcloth made for Me & your Brothers and a p[iece] good Duray also for Summer with proper linings for each. I wish to know what state your manufacturing is in. With Regard to Molasses I dont think you'l get it under 1/6 per Gall. If you can get right good for that I would take one hhd more but you must not sell at 48/ a Gallon; 2s/ law. would be as little as you can afford. If you can get Rum do get 1 Hhd at least for People will be unwilling to do without it; if you have no Prospect of getting any be sure to keep plenty for yourselves for a good while. Be sure to keep plenty of Salt for your own Use & Wine also. Pins are not to be had save at a most extravagant Price: if you have none to use I will buy a few if I see any Way to get them home; I'l see if I can buy any black handkerchiefs. One of the p[iece]s of Bandannois missing I sent to Providence by one Mr. Dabney who lives near your Uncle Ward, write to him & he will see that you have it. The other p[iece]s I sent to Norwich by one Mr. .[1] Mr. Benjm. Clarke may contrive to get it some how or other for you without much Trouble or Expence if you write to him soon about it.

We have no late News from England, by the last. We have nothing to expect but War and I think We are in a Way to carry it on with the greatest Success. Gentlemen who a few months since could not bear the Idea of War now chearfully concur with us in the most spirited Measures. The Expedition against St. Johns in Canada has always gone on heavily but upon the whole I think We shall take it and by the best Accts. from Colo. Arnold He had got near Quebec without any Opposition, the Canadians were very friendly, there were no Soldiers in Quebec & few or no Guns mounted on the Walls, the Troops were in good Health & high Spirits & expected to take the Place easily. I have never heard from your Bror. since he was at Fort Weston 24th Sepr. The Congress has ordered two Battalions to be raised in New Jersey, one in this Province, two were lately raised by Consent of Cong[res]s in No. Carolina, & to Morrow I expect So. Carolina will be allowed to raise two Battalions at the Expence of the Continent.[2] In one Word my Dear We are determined to spare neither Men nor Money; May God of his infinite Goodness direct & Prosper all our Measures & in his own due Time restore Peace, Liberty & Safety to this Continent.

I would gladly write to your Aunts but I am engaged in a Comee. in the mornings always & often in an Evening which with attending constantly upon Congress leaves Me little or no Time for necessary Relaxation & Exercise; I am obliged to them for their kind Remembrance of Me in your Letter. Give my most affectionate Regards to them, to all your Brothers & Sisters, to my Family & Friends. I am My dearest Your most affece. Parent

Sam Ward

P.S. Since writing the above two Ships have arrived from London. They bring over amongst other Things a Proclamation dated 23rd Augst last for suppressing Rebellion & Treason in the Colonies.[3] We are all declared to be Rebels in effect tho not in express Terms, this has a most happy Effect here for those who hoped for Redress from our Petitions now give them up & heartily join with us in carrying on the War vigorously. May God bless you all.

RC (MWA).

[1] MS blank.

[2] On November 4 Congress resolved to raise three battalions for the defense of South Carolina. *JCC*, 3:325.

[3] On August 23, 1775, the king issued a proclamation declaring the colonies in rebellion and calling upon his loyal subjects to assist him in quelling it. *Am. Archives*, 4th ser. 3:240–41.

John Adams' Proposals for an Expedition to Nova Scotia

[November 2–10? 1775][1]

Proposals.

That two Battallions of Marines be raised consisting of one Coll, two Lt Colls, two Majors &c (officers as usual in other Regiments) that they consist of five hundred Privates each Battalion, exclusive of officers.

That particular Care be taken that no Persons be appointed to office or inlisted into Said Battalions but Such as have actually Served in the Merchant Service as Seamen, or so acquainted with maritime Affairs as to be able to serve to advantage by Sea, when required.

That they be enlisted and commissioned to be held for and during the present War, between G. Britain and the Colonies, unless regularly dismissed by orders of the Congress.

That they be distinguished by the Name of the 1st and 2d Battalion of American Marines.

That a Sufficient Number of Vessells be taken up, and provided at Newbury Port, or Portsmouth by the 1st day of December next for transporting Said two Battalions and three Months Provisions, and other Necessaries.

That Said two Battalions be raised and marched to Said Place of Rendezvous, by the 1st of December, and in Case they are not easily raised or there is likely to be delay, that the General Draught out of the Forces under his Command to make up, any such Deficiency, of those who have been employed at Sea if Such are to be had.

That Said Battalions shall be armed in the following Manner vizt, a light Fusee, fitted for Slinging—a large Hatchet with a long Handle, and a Spear, with thirty two Rounds per Man of Ammunition.

That a Number of Men be immediately Sent into Nova Scotia, to inform themselves of the Temper and Disposition of the Inhabitants of that Colony with respect to the Present Struggle between G. B.

and these Colonies, and how far, they may be willing or able to take an active Part in the present Dispute.

That two Swift Sailing Boats be employed constantly to ply between Minas and Portsmouth or Newbury to bring Intelligence of the State and Situation of the Province, in general but most minutely of every Thing respecting the Town and Harbour of Hallifax.

That as soon as the Said two Battallions shall be arrived, at either of Said Ports and the Situation of that Colony and the Town of Hallifax shall be known the Said Battallions embark for Minas and make their Voyage with all possible Dispatch.

That previous to their Arrival, Horses and Carriages be privately engaged for their Use, and that on their Landing they immediately make a forced March for Hallifax and possess themselves of that Town and of the naval and other Stores there and if practicable of the Shipping.

Note. Coll Arnolds Expedition was Supposed in Boston to have been against this Place, which caused the General to Send thither Shipps, and Troops, but not enough to make Resistance to two Such Battallions. Further the Country are intirely in our favour, a few Scotch Traders and renegade Tories excepted.

Should this Expedition by any Accident be found impracticable, these would be two Battallions of the utmost Service, being capable of Serving either by Sea or Land.

Should the Expedition Succeed, the Consequences will be of the utmost Importance, nothing less than the greatest Distress, if not the Utter Ruin of the ministerial Navy in America. The Naval Stores in that Place are Said to be of vast Value, the Docks and Barracks and yards cost the Nation more than one Million Sterling, and is the only Place at which Shipps of War can refitt in America.

These Battalions Should consist of Ten Companies each of fifty privates in a Company. The Reason for this is, that in fitting out any Ship of War one of these Companies would compleatly man a Small Vessell and two of them make a large Proportion of Marines for the largest.

Should this Expedition Succeed, which it most unavoidably will, if prudently managed, the Destruction of the Docks and Yards, and the Stores, which may be brought off, will be an immense affair, and a Retreat can even be made with Safety.

But if a Ship or two of Warr should be taken, in the Harbour, of which you may be certain, and the Place by Reinforcements held, untill a force Superiour can be brought from G. B. it will unavoidably destroy, and defeat every operation of our Enemy for the next Campaign, as all their Transport Ships may by a few Armed Vessells from this Port be intercepted before they can have Intelligence to avoid them.

MS (MHi). In the hand of John Adams.

[1] On November 2 Adams was appointed to a committee to consider a petition from "the Inhabitants of Passamaquaddy in Nova Scotia . . . [who] applied to the Congress to be admitted into the association of the North Americans, for the preservation of their rights and liberties." It is not known when the committee submitted its report, but the journal entry for November 9 states that Congress "resumed" consideration of it, and the following day three resolutions were passed in consequence of the committee's report. Because these resolutions clearly reflect the substance of Adams' "proposals"—the third resolution repeats much of the phraseology of his first four paragraphs—it is probable that Adams played a key role in drafting the committee's report. *JCC*, 3:316, 343–44, 348. For the effort that was made to determine the feasibility of an expedition to Nova Scotia, see John Hancock to George Washington, November 10, 1775, note.

Silas Deane to James Hogg

Thursday morning, 2d Nov. 1775.

Sir, You have, in the foregoing,[1] the outlines of the policy of the Connecticut government, in as concise a view as I could; the great and leading principles of which will, I conceive, apply to any new state; and the sooner they are applied the better it will be for the health and prosperity of the rising community.

An equal and certain security of life, liberty and property; an equal share in the rights of legislation, and an equal distribution of the benefits resulting from society; with an early attention to the principles, morals and manners of the whole, are the great first principles of a good government, and these well fixed, lesser matters will easily and advantageously adjust, as I may say, themselves. I am far from thinking our system is entirely fit for you, in every point. It has grown up and enlarged itself, as we have grown. Its principal features are worth your attending to; and, if I had leisure, would point out, more particularly, which part I think you might adopt immediately, what additions are necessary, and why some parts should be rejected. But I will, if possible, give you, after your perusal of this, the general heads of what, from my little reading and observation, I think to be the most simple, and, consequently, the best plan of government.

I am, Sir, yours, S Deane

[*P.S.*] Two laws, I see, I have run over without noting upon: the one is, for punishing vagabonds, by setting them to hard labour. The other, for the punishment of theft, which you may think too light, but I think too severe; or, in other words, I would avoid infamous punishments, such as cropping, branding, whipping, &c., and substitute hard labour in their stead.

MS not found; reprinted from James Hall, *Sketches of History, Life, and Manners, in the West*, 2 vols. (Philadelphia: Harrison Hall, 1835), 2:233–34.

[1] "The foregoing," containing a lengthy summary of Connecticut's charter and early settlement, and Deane's views on policies essential to the regulation and development of new colonies, was reprinted from Hall's *Sketches* in *Am. Archives*, 4th ser. 4:556–58. Hogg's response of November 16 to Deane's letter is in *Collections of the Connecticut Historical Society*, 2 (1870): 318–19. For Hogg's activities, see also John Adams' Diary, October 25, 1775, note 2.

Francis Lewis' Memorandum on Clothing

[November 2–10? 1775][1]

Memo. for Mr Alsop

Clothing &c to be purchased by resolve of Congress for the Northen Army vizt

3ms.	Felt Hatts	to be purchased	at New York
3ms.	Caps	do.	at do.
3ms.	pair Buckskin Breeches	1ms. or 1300	at do. at 3 dollars
3ms.	pair Shoes	2ms.	at do. abt. 6/9 or 7/.
3ms.	Wastcoats		
300	Watch Coats for Sentrys of Duffills or Tearnoughts.		

N.B. as some of the above articles will be purchased here as they are packd up we shall forward them by the Amboy Stage to your address. Upon their arival at New York you will cause them to be forwarded to Albany addressed to the Commissy Genl. for that Departmt. As I have already directed my son to purchase many of the above Articles at New York please to consult him who will assist you all he can, let me know what is procured at New York that we may govern ourselves here.

There is some pieces of Strouds in Curtensius's hands that were bought of Wharton; I think they may be sent. I bought two Bales of Blanketts of Hayman Levy to send to Cambridge; if not sent that way, those should go also to Albany.

If the Number of shoes could not be Compleated I think it wd be adviseable to send up some Packs of Deer Lether for Maukasons.

MS (NHi). Endorsed by John Alsop: "Francis Lewis' Mem[orandum] for Cloathing &ca. & Garret Ketellas's accot of Same. Decr. 1775."

[1] On November 2 Congress appointed John Alsop, Lewis, and Roger Sherman a committee to procure various articles of clothing for General Schuyler's army. *JCC*, 3:317–18. Lewis subsequently sent Alsop, who had gone to New York on committee business, the above memorandum. Although Alsop apparently endorsed this document "Decr. 1775," in fact this date probably refers to the Ketellas "accot." mentioned in this endorsement rather than to Lewis' memorandum, as there is good reason to believe that Lewis composed the latter sometime before November 10, because on that date Congress decided to send the clothing to Schuyler by way of Dobbs Ferry, instead of first shipping it to Alsop in New York City, as Lewis envisaged in his memorandum. *JCC*, 3:344. That Lewis wrote his memorandum early in November is also indicated by his letter to Alsop of November 19, wherein

he lists as having already been purchased in Philadelphia some articles of clothing which his memorandum had called for Alsop to buy in New York. See also Lewis to Alsop, November 19, 21, 25, 28, 30, and December 2, 5, 10, 1775.

Samuel Ward's Diary

[November 2, 1775]

2d. Some Accts. allowed. The Comee. for fittg. out armed Vessells authorizd. to draw for money agree with officers &c., one third of all transports to be given the Men who take them & one half of all Vessells of War.

Petition from Passamaquidy. referred to a Comee.[1]

The Delegates to transmit their Cols. the resolutions relative to trade. Memorial of Comee. Safety of Pinnsylva orderd to lye on the Table.[2] Report of Mr. Bedford muster master [*and*] a Petition from J[ohn] Rains of Bermuda read, ord. to lye. Upon readg. Letters from Gens. Schuyler, Montgy. & Mr. Living[sto]n,[3] a Comee. of three appointed to repair to Genl. Schuyler &c; a Comee. appoind. to draw up Instructions for them. 3000 felt hats, stock[ing]s &c ordered to be purchased & sent to Gen. Schuyler & sold to the Soldiers at prime cost &c. A Comee. to purchase them, Mr. Alsop, Mr. Lewis, Mr. Shearman. Business increased so fast could not go on with the Min[ute]s.

MS (RHi).

[1] See John Adams' Proposals for an Expedition to Nova Scotia, November 2–10, 1775, note.

[2] For this memorial, see the proceedings of the Pennsylvania Committee of Safety for November 1 and 2, 1775, in *Am. Archives,* 4th ser. 3:1831–32.

[3] For the letters from Generals Montgomery and Schuyler presumably referred to here, see Ward's Diary, October 31, 1775, note. Commissary Walter Livingston's letter to Robert R. Livingston, Jr., of October 18, received by Congress on October 30, is in PCC, item 78, 14:15–18.

Samuel Ward to Henry Ward

Dear Bror. Philadelphia 2d Novr. 1775

Your Favour from Cambridge was very acceptable. Poor Newport I have done and offered every thing in my Power to serve them; May Heaven direct them to such Measures as may be for the best.

Your Concern for Powder is very natural. The Quantity wanted must be very great though not so much as you mention, I will however move to have our Orders enlarged tho I was fully satisfied with the Quantity we were directed to contract for until I recd. your Letter. The leaden Mines in Connecticut are opened, proper Buildings are erecting, vast Quantities of Oar are got out & will soon be smelted & the Gentn. of that Colony tell me they can furnish the whole Continent very soon. The other Resolutions recommended by you I shall move in Congress at a convenient Time.

The Evening before last two Ships arrivd from England. The Advices which they bring (amongst which is a Proclamation for suppressing Rebellion & Sedition) are of immense Service to [us]. Our Councils have been hitherto too fluctuating; one Day measures for carrying on the Ware was adopted, the next nothing must be done that would widen the unhappy Breech between G. B. & the Colonies; as these different Ideas have prevailed our Conduct has been directed. Had We at the opening of the Congress in May immediately taken proper Measures for carrying on the War with Vigor We might have been in Possession of all Canada undoubtedly & probably of Boston. Thank God the happy Day which I have long wished for is at length arrived. The southern Colonies no longer entertain Jealousies of the northern, they no longer look back to G. Britain, they are convinced that they have been pursuing a Phantom and that their only Safety is a vigorous determind Defence. One of the Gentn.[1] who has been most sanguine for pacific measures & very jealous of the N.E. Colonies addressing Me in the Stile of Bror. Rebel told me he was now ready to join Us heartily. We have got says He a sufficient Answer to our Petition; I want nothing more but am ready to declare Ourselves independent, send Ambassadors &c & much more which Prudence forbids me to commit to Paper. Our Resolutions will henceforth be spirited, clear and decisive. May the supreme Govr. of the Universe direct & prosper them. The Pleasure which this Unanimity gives Me is inexpressible. I consider it as a sure Presage of Victory, My Anxiety is now at an End. I am no longer worried with contradictory Resolutions but feel a calm chearfull Satisfaction in having one great & just Object in View & the Means of obtaining it certainly by the divine Bl[essing].

I am concerned that I have recd. no Answer from the Depy. Govr. to my Letters wrote him by Order of the Secret Comee. The Voyage was unanimously approved of, and as I wrote him that they might immediately proceed & the money to be advanced should at any Time be ready for his order I hope they have sailed but wish to know as soon as possible.[2]

The Necessity of importing Powder occasioned the inclosed Resolution to be taken.[3] You will deliver it to the Depy. Govr.; it will not be unnecessarily communicated to any. I designed to have draughted a Letter to his Honor & communicated it to my Collegue but am so incessantly engaged could not get Time to do it by this Post but hope to do it by next.

The necessity of withholding Supplies from the Army in Boston, & from the W. Indies appears so great that I beleive no Exportation will be allowed from the united Colonies except from Coly. to Colony & for the purpose of procuring Arms & Ammunition;[4] I am not at Liberty to transmit the Proceedings but thus [Far] I think my Duty to the Colony obliges me to write least the Merchts. should make Contracts to their Injury. You will communicate this only to the Depy. Govr. & such Gents. as you think proper for the present, next Week I imagine We may transmit to the Coly. a particular Acct. of the matter. My best Regards to our Friends. I am Your most affece. Bror.

Sam Ward

RC (RHi).

[1] Samuel Chase. See Ward to Henry Ward, February 19, 1776.

[2] On this point, see Ward to Nicholas Cooke, October 5, 1775.

[3] Probably the resolution of November 1 on nonexportation. See *JCC*, 3:314.

[4] Since Congress had already passed a resolution to this effect, Ward's hint that it might do so in the future appears to have been a subterfuge to evade the injunction about keeping congressional proceedings secret, a matter that seems to have concerned him as he composed this entire paragraph. See also the resolves of this date pertaining to the publication of Congress' decision, *JCC*, 3:316–17.

John Zubly's Diary

[November 2, 1775]

Thursday, 2. Attended Committee & Congress. Heard of the late Arrival of Capt. Bunner at Savannah whom I had given over as lost. Dined with Col. Dickenson. (NB. Nov. 1. had an Evng. Conversation with F. [. . .] & Shewed him my Plan.)[1] Joined in a Letter to Committee of Safety.[2]

MS (GHi).

[1] Francis Dana, who had just returned from a visit to Philadelphia, told Ezra Stiles in April 1776 that Congress had rejected a proposal by Zubly to send another petition to England. See Ezra Stiles, *The Literary Diary of Ezra Stiles . . .*, ed. Franklin B. Dexter, 3 vols. (New York: C. Scribner's Sons, 1901), 2:10; and Zubly to Archibald Bulloch and John Houstoun, November 10, 1775, note 1.

[2] This letter, not found, probably transmitted the resolves of November 1 concerning trade. See *JCC*, 3:314–15.

New Hampshire Delegates to Matthew Thornton

Philada 3d Novr. 1775

Sr

This Serves to Inclose a Resolve of the Congress Relative to Civil Government for the Colony of New Hampshire by which you'll see they Recommend such a form, as shall be agreable to a free Representation of the People, in short Such a government as shall be most Agreable to the Province. The Arguments on this Matter (being the first of the Kind as we had no Charter) were Truely Ciceronial, the eminent Speakers did honour to themselves and the Continent; Carried by a very great Majority.[1]

The Power is ample and full, even to the Choice of governor, if the Colony should think it Necessary but that, we humbly Conceive worthy of Consideration. You'll See that the government is Limited to the Present Contest to ease the minds of Some few persons, who were fearful of Independance, we tho't it Advisable not to oppose that part too much, for once we had taken, any Sort of government, nothing but Negotiation with Great Britain can Alter it.

We would here beg leave to Suggest whether a government Somewhat Similar to the Massachusetts would not be best—a free Representation of the Province tho' not too many as they may be increased at any Time, but it would be hard to Diminish; those Representatives to Chose a Council, of proper number; Say 15; these two Branches to Act in all Cases whatever and not to Proceed so far as govenor at Present, tho' the Door may be left open for that purpose. We throw out these hints with great Submission to the Honbl. Convention.

We think [*we*] can say (without boasting) [*we*] have done our duty in this matter, by paying constant Attention, for a long time, not only in the House but in Private Conversation with Members, to clear up any doubts they might have on this head. We can't help Rejoiceg to see this as a ground work of our government, and hope by the Blessing of Divine Providence, never to Return to our former Despotick State.

Inclosed is also Resolves Respectg. Trade which we had orders to Transmitt.[2]

We have Also the Pleasure to inform you that an express has Just Arrived from St. John's, with Advice that our men has taken the fortress at Chamble,[3] and have Sent the Standard Coulours of the Seventh Regiment to this Congress, took Six Tons of Powder, and many Valuable Stores, abt. 100 Prisoners, hope to have Possession of St. John's Soon. Mr. Langdon Expects to Set out in five days for Canada, being one of a Committee for that Place.[4] We are your most obt. Servt

John Langdon

Josiah Bartlett

[*P.S.*] The Sooner government is Set abt. the Better.

RC (Nh-Ar). Written by Langdon and signed by Bartlett and Langdon.

[1] For the action of Congress, see *JCC*, 3:319. John Adams later recorded a lengthy account of the debates on this issue in his autobiography. Adams, *Diary*

(Butterfield), 3:354–57. See also New Hampshire Delegates to Matthew Thornton, October 2, 1775, note 2.

[2] The resolutions passed on November 1. *JCC*, 3:314–15.

[3] Robert Treat Paine noted in his diary for November 3 that "news came that Chamble was taken by Majr. Brown 19th Ulto." MHi.

[4] On November 2 John Langdon, Robert Treat Paine, and Eliphalet Dyer were appointed a committee "to repair to the northward, to confer with Genl. Schuyler, and pursue such instructions as may be given them in charge by the Congress." Congress adopted instructions for the committee on November 8. *JCC*, 3:317, 339–41. Langdon's assumption that the committee was "to go to Canada" is of interest because there is no mention of Canada in the resolution passed by Congress creating the committee, and instructions for the committee were not adopted until November 8. The report of the committee to prepare those instructions is also a matter of some mystery, for Secretary Thomson's journal entry for the eighth states that "the Congress then resumed the consideration of the instructions," indicating that they had already been reported and considered although there is no other indication that they actually were. Since Thomson's manuscript journal entry for November 6 is an incomplete one, perhaps the space left for continuing the entry was to be devoted to the report of the committee appointed to prepare instructions for Langdon's committee. See *JCC*, 3:317, 320, 339; and PCC, item 1, 1:140.

New York Delegates to the New York Provincial Convention

Gentlemen Philadelphia, 3d Nov. 1775.

On perusing our Credentials we find the Continuance of our Delegation unlimited. As this appears to us an omission of great Importance we think it our Duty to apprize you of it, and hope that no Delicacy with Respect to us may influence you to decline a new appointment.

We have been informed that Compensation for our Expences & Loss of Time is under your Consideration,[1] and as we presume an Account of the Provision made by the other Colonies for their respective Delegates would be agreable to You, We take the Liberty of subjoining it.

Georgia	£100 Sterling to each Delegate per Month
South Carolina	£300 Ster. to each for the last Congress
North Carolina	500 Currency to each per Year
Virginia	a half Joh[ane]s[2] to each per Day
Maryland	40/to each per Day[3]
Pensylvania	20/ to each per Day besides the Allowance to such of the Members as come from the Counties
New Jersey	

Connecticut ....3 Dollar to each per Day for Loss of Time & all their Expences, allowing each Delegate 2 Horses & a Servt.
Rhode Island ......Exactly the same as Connecticut
Massachusetts ......All their Expences as above & two Dollars per Day
New Hampshire ....All their Expences as above & half a Guinea per Day

We are, sir, with the greatest respect, the Congress's and Your hble. servts.

Robt. R. Livingston Junr. Jas. Duane
Frans. Lewis John Alsop
Henry Wisner John Jay
Wm. Floyd

RC (N). Written by Jay and signed by Jay, Alsop, Duane, Floyd, Lewis, Robert R. Livingston, Jr., and Wisner. FC (NNC). In Jay's hand, though not signed. *Journals of N. Y. Prov. Cong.*, 2:18–19. RC damaged; missing words supplied from FC and Tr.

[1] On December 15, the Provincial Congress decided to recompense the New York delegates four dollars a day for their service in Congress. *Am. Archives*, 4th ser. 4:414–15.

[2] "The name by which the Portuguese *dobra de quarto escudos*, or *peca* of Johannes or João V (1703–50), a gold coin of the value of 6,400 reis, or about 36s. sterling (also commonly called João), was known in the British American Colonies." *OED*.

[3] In the RC of this letter, badly damaged by fire, the term "Proc." follows at this point, indicating that the Maryland allowance was calculated in proclamation money.

John Zubly's Diary

[November 3, 1775]

3. Attended Committee & Congress. [ ][1] in express & most formal terms disclaimd ——— ⟨to⟩ ——— & declared for [sepa?] ration—because we must [fight?] a [w]ing [. . . .]

⟨*seconded that Congress* [. . . .]⟩

Z[ubly] warmly opposed—appealed to Protes[tatio]n on 1st Reflect[ion]— & sd if Breach of [pe]ace & Separat[ion] was the Sense of [Congre]ss—it was time for [Zubly?] to take h[imsel]f away.[2]

C[hristopher] G[adsden] & cried agreed agreed. Sd that A[ccomodation?] was their ——— but now no more, & very overbearing. Declard every Man at liberty to Speak of that. I said & claimd the same Liberty. N[olo] C[ontendere].

MS (GHi).

[1] This entry provides no evidence on the identity of this speaker.

[2] November 9 was Zubly's last day in Congress. See Zubly to Archibald Bulloch and John Houstoun, November 10, 1775.

John Adams to Abigail Adams

Novr. 4. 1775

Have but Yesterday received yours of Octr. 21.

Your Letters of the following Dates I have received. Septr. 8. and 10. 16. 29. Oct. 1. 9. 21. 22.[1] These Letters and indeed every Line from you, gives me inexpressible Pleasure, notwithstanding the melancholly Scenes discribed in most of them of late.

I am happy to learn that the Family is in Health once more, and hope it will continue.

My Duty to my Mother. I wish she would not be concerned about me. She ought to consider that a Dissentery can kill as surely as a Cannon. This Town is as secure from the Cannon and Men of War as the Moon is. I wish she had a little of your Fortitude. I had rather be kill'd by a Ball than live in such continual Fears as she does.

I cant write so often as I wish: I am engaged from 7 in the Morning till 11. at Night.

Two Pair of Colours belonging to the Seventh Regiment, were brought here last night from Chambly, and hung up in Mrs. Hancocks Chamber with great Splendor and Elegance. That Lady sends her Compliments and good Wishes. Among an hundred Men, almost at this House she lives and behaves with Modesty, Decency, Dignity and Discretion I assure you. Her Behaviour is easy and genteel. She avoids talking upon Politicks. In large and mixed Companies she is totally silent, as a Lady ought to be—but whether her Eyes are so penetrating and her Attention so quick, to the Words, Looks, Gestures, sentiments &c. of the Company, as yours would be, saucy as you are this Way, I wont say.

But to resume a more serious subject. You ask me to write to your Father and sister, and my Heart wishes and longs to do it, but you can have no Conception, what there is to prevent me. I really fear I shall ruin myself for Want of Exercise.

RC (MHi). Adams, *Family Correspondence* (Butterfield), 1:319–20.

[1] All are printed in Adams, *Family Correspondence,* volume one.

Samuel Adams to Elbridge Gerry

Novr 4th. [1775]

My Time is so little at my own Disposal that I am obligd to improve a Moment as I can catch it to write to a Friend. I wish I was at Liberty to communicate to you some of our Proceedings, but I am restraind, and though it is painful to me to keep Secrets from a few confidential Friends, I am resolvd that I will not violate my Honor. I may venture to tell you one of our Resolutions which in the Nature of it must be immediately made publick, and that is to recommend to our Sister Colony N Hampshire to exercise Government in such a form as they shall judge necessary for the preservation of peace and good order, during the Continuance of the present Contest with Britain.[1] This I would not have you mention abroad till you see it publishd or hear it publickly talkd of. The government of the N England Colonies I suppose will soon be nearly on the same Footing, and I am of opinion that it will not be long before every Colony will see the Necessity of setting up Government within themselves for Reasons that appear to me to be obvious.

Yesterday the Congress was presented with the Colours of the 7th Regiment taken at Fort Chamblee which was a few days ago surrenderd to Major Brown—*One hundred & twenty four Barrels of Gun powder*. May Heaven grant us further Success.[2] I am your affectionate Friend

S A

FC (NN). A continuation of Adams to Elbridge Gerry, October 29, 1775.

[1] See New Hampshire Delegates to Matthew Thornton, November 3, 1775.

[2] General Schuyler's account of the capture of Fort Chambly was read in Congress on November 4. *JCC*, 3:320.

Samuel Adams to James Warren

My dear sir, Philada Nove 4th 1775

I thank you heartily for your very acceptable Letter of the 23 of October by Fessenden. It is very afflicting to hear the universal Complaint of the Want of that most necessary Article Gunpowder, and especially in the Camp before Boston. I hope however that this want will soon be supplied, and God grant that a good Use may be made of it.

The Congress yesterday was presented with the Colors of the Seventh Regiment, taken in Fort Chamblee which is surrendered to Major Brown. The Acquisition of 124 Barrils of Powder gives a happy Turn to our Affairs in that Quarter the Success of which I almost began to despair of.

The Gentlemen who have lately returned from the Camp may, *perhaps all* of them entertain a favorable opinion of our Colony. I may possibly be partial in saying, not more favorable than it deserves. Be that as it may, the Congress have judgd it necessary to continue the Establishment of the Mens pay, and to enlarge that of the Captains & Leiutenants.[1]

In Addition to the Continental Army four new Battalions are to be raisd viz three for the Defence of South Carolina and one for Georgia.[2] These with 1000 Men before orderd for North Carolina, with the Assistance of provincial Forces it is hoped will be sufficient to defend the three Southernmost Colonies.

It is recommended to N Hampshire to form a Government to their own liking, during this Contest—and S Carolina is allowd to do the same if they judge it necessary.[3] I believe the Time is near when the most timid will see the absolute Necessity of every one of the Colonies setting up a Government within itself.

No Provisions or Produce is to be exported from any of the united Colonies to any part of the World till the first of March except for the Importation of the Unum necessarium[4] and for Supplys from one Colony to another, under the Direction of Committees, and a further Exception of live Stock under the last Head, and Horses are allowed to be sent to the foreign West Indies. We shall by the Spring know the full Effect of our Nonexportation Agreement in the West Indies. Perhaps Alliances may then be formed with foreign Powers, and Trade opened to all the World Great Britain excepted.

You will possibly think I have set my self down to furnish a few Paragraphs for Edes & Gills paper, and what is more that I am betraying the Secrets of Congress. I confess I am giving my Friend as much Information as I dare, of things, which are of such a Nature as that they cannot long be kept secret, and therefore I suppose it never was intended they should be. I mention them however in Confidence that you will not publish them. I wish I was at Liberty to tell you many of the Transactions of our Body but I am restraind by the Ties of Honor, and though it is painful to me, you know, to keep Secrets, I will not violate my Honor to releive my self or gratify my Friend.[5] But why have I told you so trifling a Story, for which I cannot forgive my self till I have askd forgiveness of you. We live in a most important Age, which demands that every Moment should be improvd to some serious Purpose. It is the Age of George the Third; and to do Justice to our most gracious King, I will affirm it as my opinion, that his Councils and Administration will necessarily produce the grandest Revolutions the World has ever yet seen. The Wheels of Providence seem to be in their swiftest Motion; Events succeed each other so rapidly that the most industrious and able Politicians can scarcely improve them to the full purpose for which they seem to be designd.

You must send your best Men here; therefore recall me from this Service. Men of moderate Abilities, especially when weakend by Age are not fit to be employed in founding Empires.

Let me talk with you a little about the Affairs of our own Colony. I perswade my self my dear friend, that the greatest Care and Circumspection will be used, to conduct its internal Police with Wisdom & Integrity.

The Eyes of Mankind will be upon you, to see whether the Government, which is now more popular than it has been for many years past, will be productive of more Virtue moral and political. We may look up to Armies for our Defence, but Virtue is our best Security. It is not possible that any State should long continue free, where Virtue is not supremely honord. This is as seasonably as it is justly said by one of the most celebrated Writers of the present time. Perhaps the Form of Government now adopted may be permanent. Should it be only temporary, the golden opportunity of recovering the Virtue and reforming the Manners of our Country should be industriously improvd. Our Ancestors laid an excellent Foundation for the Security of Liberty, by setting up in a few years after their Arrival, a publick Seminary of Learning; and by their Laws, they obligd every Town consisting of a certain Number of Families to keep & maintain a Grammar School. I should be much grievd if it should be true as I am informd, that some of our Towns have dismissd their Schoolmasters, alledging that the extraordinary Expence of defending the Country renders them unable to support them. I hope this Inattention to the Principles of our wise forefathers does not prevail. If there should be any Danger of it, would not the leading Gentlemen do eminent Service to the Publick, by impressing upon the Minds of the People, the Necessity & Importance of encouraging that System of Education, which in my opinion, is so well calculated to diffuse among the Individuals of the Community, the Principles of Morality, so essentially necessary for the Preservation of publick Liberty. These are Virtues & Vices wch. are properly called *political*. "Corruption, Dishonesty to ones Country, Luxury and Extravagance tend to the Ruin of States." The opposite Virtues tend to their Establishment. But "there is a Connection between Vices as well as Virtues, and one opens the Door for the Entrance of another." Therefore "Every able Politician will guard against other Vices," and be attentive to promote every Virtue. He who is void of virtuous Attachment in private Life, is, or very soon will be void of all Regard to his Country. There is seldom an Instance of a Man guilty of betraying his Country, who had not before lost the feeling of moral Obligation in his private Connection. Before C——h was detected of holding a criminal Correspondence with the Enemies of his Country, his Infidelity to his Wife had been notorious. Since private & publick Vices, though not always apparently, are in Reality so nearly connected, of how much Importance, how necessary is it, that the utmost pains be taken by the Publick to have the Principles of Virtue early inculcated on the Minds even of children, and the moral Sense universally kept alive, and that the wise Institutions of our Ancestors for those great Purposes be encouraged by the Government for no People will tamely surrender their Liberties, nor can they easily be subdued, where Knowledge is diffusd and Virtue preservd. On the Contrary, when People are universally ignorant & debauchd in their Manners, they will sink under their own Weight, without the Aid of foreign Invaders.

There are other things which, I humbly conceive, require the most serious Consideration of the Legislative. We have heretofore complaind, and I think justly, that bad Men have too often found their Way into places of publick Trust. "Nothing is more essential to the Establishment of Manners in a State, than that all Persons employd in Places of Power and Trust by Men of *exemplary* Characters. The Publick cannot be too curious concerning the Character of publick Men." We have also complaind, that a Plurality of Places incompatible with each other have sometimes been vested in one Person. If under the former Administration there was no Danger to be apprehended from vesting the different Powers of Government in the same Persons, why did the Patriots so loudly protest against it? If Danger is always to be apprehended from it, Should we not by continuing the Practice, too much imitate the degenerate Romans, who upon the Fall of Julius set up Augustus. They changd indeed their Masters, and when they had destroyd the Tyrant sufferd the Tyranny to continue. Tell me how a Judge of Probate can consistently sit at the Council Board and joyn in a Decision there upon an Appeal from *his own* Judgment. Perhaps, being personally interested in *another* Appointment, I may view it with a partial Eye.[6] But you may well remember that the Secretary of the Colony declind taking a Seat at the Council Board, to which he had been elected *prior* to his Appointment, until, in the House of Representatives he had publickly requested their Opinion of the Propriety of it, and there heard it explicitly declared by an eminent and truly patriotick Member as his opinion, that as the Place was not then as it formerly had been, the Gift of the Crown but of the People, there was no Impropriety in his holding it. The rest of the Members were silent. Major H——y [Joseph Hawley] has as much of the Stern Virtue and Spirit of a Roman Censor as any Gentleman I ever conversd with.

The Appointment of the Secretary and his Election to a Seat at the Board were both made in the Time of his Absense from the Colony, and without the Solicitation of any of his Friends that he knew of—most assuredly without his own. As he is resolved never wittingly to disgrace himself or his Country, he still employs his Mind on the Subject, and wishes for your candid and impartial Sentiments.

I fear I have trespassd on your Leisure, and conclude with assuring you that I am with sincere Regards to Mrs Warren Your very affectionate Friend[7]

S A

RC (MHi). FC (NN).

[1] Congress passed several resolves on November 4 based on the report of the Committee of Conference. *JCC*, 3:321–25.

[2] These measures were adopted on November 4. *JCC*, 3:325–26.

[3] *JCC*, 3:319, 326–27.

[4] After "except for" in the draft of this letter Adams wrote "the Importation of Arms and Ammunition."

[5] The next 11 lines of the RC have been inked out, apparently by Warren. The excised material, almost totally unreadable, is not in Adams' draft.

[6] Samuel Adams was both secretary and member of the Massachusetts Council. See Samuel Adams to Elbridge Gerry, October 29, 1775, note. See also Thomas Cushing to William Cooper, October 23, 1775.

[7] For the continuation of this letter, see Adams to Warren, November 7, 1775.

Rhode Island Delegates to Nicholas Cooke

Sir: Phila 4 Nov 1775.

We deferred an answer to your Honor's last letter hoping to have obtained the Resolves of Congress upon the Interesting Subjects contained in it.[1] We laid it before Congress. Business has since been very pressing, but we shall embrace the first favorable opportunity of obtaining the proper Resolves and shall transmit them as soon as possible.

We have no news from England since the arrival of the Ship which brought the Pro[clamation] for suppressing Rebellion and Sedition. We have the pleasure to assure you Sir that this has a most happy Effect upon the affairs of America. Gentlemen no longer expect a Redress of Grievances from Petition, etc. They now speak out plainly and cheerfully enter into the most liberal spirited and decisive measures. We congratulate you Sir upon the happy Reduction of Fort Chamblee. The Paper containing the Articles of Capitulation, List of Stores, etc., we have enclosed. There is no doubt but we have possession of St. John's before this time

The Congress has taken into consideration the state of the trade of the United Colonies. We enclose you an Extract of their proceedings.[2] We are sensible of the vast Importance of Trade to our Colony but when we consider the invaluable privileges for which we are contending, We are sure that the Virtue of our Constituents will with pleasure sacrifice a temporary Commerce to the salvation of their Country.

The moment that our Ports can be opened with a Prospect of Success to the Merchts. and with safety to the Liberating of America we shall use our utmost Influence to restore to the Colony all the Benefits of a free and extensive commerce. We are with very great Regards, Sir Your most obedient and very humble Servts.

Step Hopkins

Sam: Ward

P.S. The Paper does not do justice to Majr. Livingston and 300 Canadians who were with Majr. Brown and assisted in taking the Fort.[3]

I am concerned that I have recd. no answer to my Letters to your Honor relative to the proposed Voyage; I hope the Vessel is gone for Winter approaches fast and it is of the last Importance for us to obtain Powder before Spring. The inclosed Advertisement I would wish sent to the Foreign West Inds. and other money Places.[4]

Your most obedient S. Ward

MS not found; reprinted from Ward, *Correspondence* (Knollenberg), pp. 117–18.

[1] Apparently not extant. The latest preceding letter from Cooke now available, dated October 10, 1775, is surely not the document referred to here. Ward, *Correspondence* (Knollenberg), pp. 98–99.

[2] See *JCC*, 3:314–15.

[3] Fort Chambly, captured October 18, 1775.

[4] Evidently in connection with Congress' resolution of October 26. *JCC*, 3:308.

John Zubly's Diary

[November 4, 1775]

Saturday, 4. Attended Committee & Congress. Declared my Doubts as to [. . .] a Battalion & wishd it referrd to C[onventio]n of G[eorgia].[1] Mr. C[hase?] opposed—[. . .] some friends of [. . .] proposed it wait but were overruld by some not friendly [. . .] Motion it [. . . .][2]

Dind with Isr[ael] Pemberton—going [way?] of moderate Men [. . . .][3] Quite indisposed took a Vomit.

MS (GHi).

[1] Congress resolved this day to keep a battalion in Georgia at the Continental expense. *JCC*, 3:325.

[2] Approximately eight words indecipherable.

[3] Approximately seven words indecipherable.

John Adams to Elbridge Gerry

Dear sir Philadelphia November 5. 1775

I am under Such Restrictions, Injunctions and Engagements of Secrecy respecting every Thing which passes in Congress, that I cannot communicate my own Thoughts freely to my Friends, So far as is necessary to ask their Advice, and opinions concerning questions which many of them understand much better than I do.

This however is an inconvenience, which must be Submitted to for the sake of Superiour Advantages.

But I must take the Liberty to say, that I think We shall soon think of maritime affairs, and naval Preparations. No great Things are to be expected at first, but out of a little a great deal may grow.

It is very odd that I, who have Spent my days in researches and Employments so very different, and who have never thought much of old Ocean, or the Dominion of it, should be necessitated to make such Enquiries: But it is my fate, and my Duty, and therefore I must attempt it.[1]

I am to enquire what Number of seamen may be found in our Province, who would probably inlist in the service, either as Marines, or on board of Armed Vessells, in the Pay of the Continent, or in the Pay of the Province, or on board of Privateers, fitted out by Private Adventurers.[2]

I must also intreat you, to let me know the Names, Places of abode, and Characters, of such Persons belonging to any of the seaport Towns in our Province, who are qualified for officers and Commanders of Armed Vessells.

I want to be further instructed, what ships, Brigantines, schooners &c are to be found in any Part of the Province, which are to be sold or hired out, which will be suitable for armed Vessells—what their Tonnage, the Depth of water they draw, their Breadth, their Decks, &c, and to whom they belong, and what is their Age.

Further, what Places in our Province, are most secure and best accommodated for Building new Vessells, of Force in Case a Measure of that Kind Should be thought of.

The Committee have returned, much pleased with what they have seen and heard, which shews that their Embassy will be productive of happy Effects. They say the only disagreeable Circumstance was that their Engagements, Haste, and constant Attention to Business was such as prevented them from forming such Acquaintances with the Gentlemen of our Province as they wished. But as Congress was waiting for their Return before they could determine upon Affairs of the last Moment, they had not Time to spare.

They are pretty well convinced I believe of several important Points, which they and others doubted before.

New Hampshire has leave to assume a Government and so has South Carolina but this must not be freely talked of as yet, at least from me.

New England will now be able to exert her strength which a little Time will shew to be greater than either Great Britain or America imagines.

I give you Joy of the agreable Prospect in Canada. We have the Colors of the seventh Regiment as the first fruits of Victory.

RC (NHpR). In Adams' hand, though not signed.

[1] For Adams' later recollections of his services in the establishment of the American navy, see Adams, *Diary* (Butterfield), 3:342–51. See also Adams' Notes of Debates, October 7, 1775.

[2] For a list of persons suitable for naval command which Adams later compiled, see ibid., 2:221–22. Gerry promised Adams a list of persons and places as soon as a committee could be organized "for obtaining the Facts from the Maritime Towns." Gerry to Adams, December 4, 1775, MHi. See also Adams to James Warren, this date. Gerry subsequently communicated this request to the Massachusetts House of Representatives, which voted on December 11 to send a printed request for this information to the seaport towns. *Am. Archives,* 4th ser. 4:1332–33.

John Adams to John Trumbull

My dear sir Novr 5. 1775

I take an opportunity by this Express, to thank you for McFingal, a Poem which has been Shewn me within a few days.[1] It is excellent, and perhaps the more so for being misterious. It wants explanatory Notes as much as Hudibras. I cant conjecture the Characters either of Honorius or McFingal.

Am Sorry to learn that We are likely to loose some of our best Men. We may have better in their stead for ought I know but We shall certainly loose good ones.

There is scarcely a more active, industrious, enterprising and capable Man, than Mr Deane, I assure you. I shall sincerely lament the Loss of his services. Men of such great daring active Spirits are much Wanted.

I shall think myself much obliged to you, if you would write me. I want to hear the great Politicks and even the Small Talk of your Colony.

For my own Part I feel very enthusiastic at Times. Events which turn up every day are so new unexpected and surprising to most Men, that I wonder more Heads are not turn'd than We hear of. Human Nature Seems to be employed like Sampson, taking Hold of the Pillars of Tyranny and pulling down the whole building at a—Lunge I believe is the best Word. I hope it will not, like him bury it self in the Ruins, but build up the wisest and most durable Frames for securing its Happiness. But Time must determine.

I am, sir, with much Esteem your Friend

RC (NjP). In Adams' hand, though not signed.

[1] John Trumbull (1750–1831), Connecticut poet and jurist, was a former law student of John Adams. Trumbull, who wrote the first canto of his mock epic "M'Fingal" in the fall of 1775, had it published early in 1776 with a 1775 imprint. This highly satirical account of British officers and officials was expanded and republished after the war. *DAB*.

John Adams to James Warren

Dear Sir Novr. 5. 1775.

The Committee have returned, and I think well pleased with their Reception as well as with what they saw and heard. Impressions have been made upon them either by the New England Gentlemen, or at Head Quarters, much to the Advantage of our Cause, I assure you. Their Return has contributed much to Harmony and Unanimity, in all smaller Matters, in the great material Questions there was enough of them before.

I am under great obligations to you for your Attention to me. Shall answer your Letters as soon as time will admit, but I assure you, I am very busy.

I am obliged to trouble you with Enquiries concerning Subjects which you understand very well and I know nothing of.

I want to know what is become of the Whalemen, Codfishers, and other Seamen belonging to our Province and what Number of them you imagine might be inlisted into the Service of the Continent, or of the Province, or of private Adventurers, in Case a Taste for Privateering and a maritime Warfare should prevail. Whether you think that two or three Battalions of Marines could be easily inlisted in our Province.

What Ships, Brigantines, Schooners, suitable for armed Vessells might be purchased or hired, and at what Prices in our Province, what their Burthen, Depth of Water, Length of Keel, Breadth, hight between Decks, Age &c and to whom they belong.

What Places are most suitable that is safest and best accommodated for building new Vessells, if any should be wanted—and what shipwrights may be had, and in what Time Vessells compleated.

But above all, what Persons, their Names, Ages, Places of abode and Characters, may be found in our Province who might be qualified to serve as Commanders and officers &c.[1]

These are necessary Enquiries, and I am very ill qualified to make them, yet to tell you a secret in Confidence, it has become my Duty. There is a Disposition prevailing to spare no Pains or Expence in the necessary Defence of our Rights by Sea or Land.

The News you will see in the Papers, give you Joy of the good Prospect to the Northward.

New Hampshire has Permission to establish what Form of Government they like best, and so has S. Carolina and so will every other Colony which shall ask for it which they all will do soon, if the Squabble continues.

New England will now be able to exert her Strength and if I ken it right, it will be found to be that of a full grown Man, no Infant.

Who expected to live to see the Principles of Liberty Spread and prevail so rapidly, human Nature exerting her whole Rights, unshackled by Priests or Kings or Nobles, pulling down Tyrannies like Sampson, and building up, what Governments the People think best framed for human Felicity.

God grant the Spirit, success.

My best Respects to your good Lady, will write her as soon as possible.

RC (MHi). In Adams' hand, though not signed.

[1] For Warren's response, see his letter of November 14–15. *Warren-Adams Letters*, 1:181–86.

Josiah Bartlett to Mary Bartlett

My Dear Philadelphia Novr the 6th 1775

Tho I wrote to you the 27th of last month I Cant help writing by Every opertunity to let you know that I am well for if hearing from me gives you & my Children half the Satisfaction that hearing from you & them Does me I Shall not think much of the trouble of writing. I have been now above 2 months from home & had but 2 Letters from you Tho I have wrote you 7 or 8 before this.

I hope you & the family are all in Good hea[l]th. If I was within 100 miles So as to Come home once in a month or two & see you and Return I Should be very Glad but must tarry till the Congress rises and as there is So much Business before us, I know not when that will be. I have some hopes I may be able to Return next month; if not I fear I shall be obliged to tarry till Spring as I fear it will be impossible to Return in the winter with Safety if Business should permit it. I Shall Do Every thing in my Power to Return as soon as I Can with propriety.

If I find I Cannot Return till Spring I Shall write you largely what I would have done as to my affairs at Home & Shall order you money for that purpose. However I have some hopes to be at home my self. I hope you will take proper Care against winter both for Cloathing & other things for your self & family and Shall leave it to your Discretion.

Remember my Love to all the Children from Polly to Sally and tell them all to behave well that I may have a good account of them at my Return.

Tell Peter if he Behaves well that I Shall Remember him when I Return.

We have Just Received an account of the taking Fort Chamble & of the Burning of Falmouth and that the villains Design attacking Portsm[outh]. If they do I hope our people will give them a proper Reception.

Remember me to all friends. I am yours &c

Josiah Bartlett

P.S. Gidion George is well.

RC (NhHi).

Stephen Hopkins to Esek Hopkins

Dear sir Philadelphia Novr. 6. 1775

You will perceive by a Letter from the Committee,[1] dated yesterday, that they have pitched upon you to take the Command of a Small Fleet, which they and I hope will be but the Beginning of one much larger.[2]

I Suppose you may be more serviceable to your Country, in this very dangerous Crisis of its affairs, by taking upon you this Command than you can in any other Way. I should therefore hope that this will be a sufficient Inducement, for you to accept of this offer.

You[r] Pay and Perquisites will be such as you will have no Reason to complain of. Such officers and Seamen as you may procure to come with you, may be informed, that they will enter into Pay from their first engageing in this service, and will be intituled to share as Prize, the one half of all Armed Vessells, and the one Third of all Transports that shall be taken.

You may assure all with whom you converse that the Congress increase in their Unanimity, and rise Stronger and Stronger in the Spirit of opposition to the Tyrannical Measures of Administration. I am your affectionate Brother Step Hopkins

RC (CSmH). Written by John Adams and signed by Hopkins.

[1] That is, the Naval Committee, on which see Naval Committee to Silas Deane,

Detail from John Trumbull's painting *The Declaration of Independence, 4 July 1776,* 1786-1820. Courtesy of the architect of the Capitol.

Pencil sketch by John Trumbull, 1791. Fordham University Library, New York.

Stephen Hopkins
For a discussion of the two portraits, see the list of illustrations, p. xxv.

November 7, 1775, note 1. The committee's letter to Hopkins of November 5 has not been found.

[2] Esek Hopkins (1718–1802), Rhode Island sea captain and privateer in the French and Indian War, was offered command of the fledgling Continental Navy on November 5 by the Naval Committee, of which his brother, Stephen, was a member and sometime chairman. Congress granted his commission as commander in chief on December 22, 1775, an office he held until March 1777, when he was relieved of it for unsatisfactory performance of duties. *DAB;* and *JCC*, 3:443, 7:204.

John Langdon to Ammi Ruhamah Cutter

Dear Sr. Philad. 6th Nov. 1775

Your kind favor of 22d Octob is now before me,[1] am much Obliged for your Friendly hint Respectg my ship, as I've been at a loss for some time, whether to Trust the money in London, tho' my Brother will be on the Spot who will take all proper Steps;[2] as it happens I owe them no money, but most heartily wish I had twenty thousand of theirs, in my hands, it all should go most freely for the good of Lux.

The more than Savage Cruelty of that haughty Scotchman Mowatt, Shocks every Idea, none but his Abandon[ed] Masters could have tho't of such wanton Cruelty. No, not even the grand enemy to mankind, with all his band of infernal Spirits, as described by Milton could have been more Cruel. Heaven Grant, if *He* should Arrive at Portsmouth, that one of our thirty two pounders Winged with fate, may hurl him head long to the place he Deserves.

Am much obliged for your being so Particular in your letter. Shall send the Copy of Mowatt's Letter with Extracts from yours, to the press; have shewn them to most of the Congress, who are greatly pleased with the Conduct of New Hampshire, as they have been for some time much Concern'd for our fate. We take every opportunity to lay our Spirited Advices before the Congress which gives wait [weight] to the Colony, which I may say Stands as fair, with the Congress as any on the Continent. I have no Doubt of the True Spirit of my fellow Country men, and Citizens, and that their heads will be Cover'd in the day of Battle, and the more so when I see, with pleasure men of Sense and influence give their assistance. In short I've no other Idea, but to Come off Victorious "for thrice is he Armed who has his q[u]arrell *Just* and *he's* but Naked tho locked up in Steel whose Concience with Injustice is Corrupted."

The Colonies Seem more and more united and Determined to make a vigorous Defence.

Have the Pleasure to inform you that, have obtaind, after paying Close Attention, a Resolution of Congress to take Some Sort of Government, Duri[n]g these Disputes, which I've inclosed to our

Convention.[3] Also that we have the Rigimental Coulours of the Seventh Regiment hung up in Congress which was Taken at Chamble which place was taken by our Troops, with all Six Tons of Powder, Provisions, arms in Considerable quantity. I have the Honour of being Appointed one of a Committee to go to Canada,[4] to Regulate some matters there but as the Season is so far Advanced had some hope to get off but fear shall not. Expect to set off in few days. My kind Respects to your Family and all Friends and Beleive to be with great Respect Your Friend and Hbl. Servt. Jno. Langdon

RC (PHi).

[1] Ammi Ruhamah Cutter (1735–1819), Portsmouth, N. H., physician and justice of the peace, former minor merchant and large landowner, had been a political intimate of Gov. John Wentworth. He later served as physician general of the eastern department, 1777–78. Shipton, *Harvard Graduates*, 13:220–25.

[2] Woodbury Langdon (1738?–1805), prominent Portsmouth merchant and member of the provincial assembly, 1774–75, had sailed for London on September 9, 1775. After two years of largely mysterious activity in both London and France (where he apparently aided brother John's commercial connection with Silas Deane), he returned to New York, where he was confined at the urging of Gov. John Wentworth. He escaped in late December, 1777, reestablished himself in New Hampshire, and eventually represented that province in Congress in 1779. *DAB;* and Lawrence S. Mayo, *John Langdon of New Hampshire* (Concord, N. H.: Rumford Press, 1937), pp. 88–89, 155–68.

[3] See New Hampshire Delegates to Matthew Thornton, November 3, 1775.

[4] See ibid., note 4.

Robert Treat Paine to William Whiting

Sr Philada. Novr. 6th. 1775

I recd. yr. letter of Octr. 6th in which you give me an Account of your progress in making Salt-petre.[1] I hope before this time you have had a good Account of working up the Meeting House Earth at G. Barrington; it is to little purpose that we make Experiments if we do not carry it to large practice; we want *great quantitys* of Salt petre, & not barely to know that we are able to make it, *shot* we have known a long time, & I think we are wholly inexcusable if do not turn out very large quantitys of *Salt petre* by the Spring of the Year. We have Specimens of exceeding fine Petre brought us here from many parts of this Colony, New Jersey & other places & nothing is clearer than that numbers of People in different places are able to make it. The grand Matter is to propagate the making it in large Quantitys. I was in great expectation that the Resolves of the Congress on this Subject would have produced good Effects in the Tobacco Colonies, but on Enquiry I find that the Convention of Virginia did not take any steps to carry it into Execution (having many

Matters before them). Maryland voted a Sum of money but appointed no operators. The Congress very justly alarmed at the astonishing inattention of the Colonies to this most essential Matter, have Appointed Another Comittee to devise Ways & Means to promote this Manufacture.[2]

I have the honour to be one of this Cmttee, & great pains have we taken about it, we have not yet determined how, but we have under Consideration to send certain Germans who are here, & who have given Specimens of their skill, into the Tobacco Colonies to carry on the manufacture there. The great Works of this City have made no Salt petre valuable, the House of Assembly of this Colony have the matter under Consideration.

I hope Something Great will be done in New England—& this Sr. brings me to what I have principally in veiw in writing Vizt. there Laying a foundation for a great quantity of Salt petre next Spring. There are two matters to be attended to forthwith, the first is to Search out & work up all the impregnated Materials that are now on hand or to be found & At the Same time to provide mix & duly dispose suitable materials for impregnation in as large quantitys as possible. I hope this matter is not neglected—immediate Care must be taken—sheds must be prepared over dry Land & the Materials must not be put very thick if made in Beds under Sheds, for if they are thick or deep the Air will not impregnate it through. It is generally thought best that the Stuff should be made into Walls or fences as they call them, some such are made in this city & they talk much of making many here. An easy method of making these fences is this. Let the Stuff be properly mixed & Cut Straw be mixed with it to make it stick together, then let your Walls be made about 15 or 18 inches at bottom, abt. 5 feet high & tapering to the top to about 4 or 5 inches thick in Order to make it Stand while forming let peices of Joyce or Poles be cut of a Suitable length & set in this Manner with the ends on the Ground & little Stakes Stuck against the ends into the Ground. A number of Such pairs of Joyce must be set at convenient distance ranging as you intend the Wall shall go, rough boards are to be put on the inside of these Joyce frames so that when the dirt is put between them it may be kept up & so as you raise your Dirt you put more boards till you get to the Top, ramming the Dirt as you go along Sufficient to keep it from falling & yet not so hard as to prevent the Air from entering. These Walls should be covered with boards or straw so as to prevent the Rains from washing the sides. The Germans I have consulted on this Matter are of Opinion that if proper Materials are now put up in a judicious manner they will be so impregnated in 6 months as to yeild largely. Therefore at all events Materials must be forwith provided in as large a manner as possible.

Sr. it [*is*] my opinion that unless we exert our selves in this Matter & have some tollerable Success it is very uncertain whether every thing else we can do will Avail as much, & if we are successful in this matter in my Opinion every thing else favourable will come of Course.

I hope you Correspond with yr. Brethren of the Salt petre Cmttee & also with other well disposed Active Salt petre Makers in any place that you know of, spurring them on to lay up proper materials in a proper manner. Pray shew this to Major Hawley, Mr. Gerry & other persons who are desirous to promote this matter.

Give my Regards to all Friends. The Express is waiting & I must Subscribe yr. friend & hble Sert. R T Paine

RC (MHi).

[1] William Whiting (1730–92), Great Barrington, Mass., physician and representative to the Provincial Congress, 1774–76, was a member of a legislative committee named in mid-1775 to seek practical methods of making saltpetre. Charles J. Taylor, *History of Great Barrington, Massachusetts* (Great Barrington: Clark W. Bryan & Co., 1882), pp. 273–75; and *Am. Archives*, 4th ser. 2:1460, 1462. Whiting's letter to Paine, dated October 6, 1775, is at MHi.

[2] Paine, Charles Humphreys, and George Wythe were appointed to the "salt petre committee" on October 29. *JCC*, 3:310–11.

Roger Sherman to Jonathan Ingersoll

Sir Philadelphia Novr. 6th. 1775

I received Your letter of the 30th of October. Would request you[1] to use your best discretion on my behalf in Securing and recovering the money due on the Several notes which I put into Your hands, and You may rest Assured that You Shall not Suffer by any loss which may happen, and I will See that Justice be done the Assignee So far as is in my power.

I dont know when I can come home, or have opportunity to attend to my own private affairs.

There has been Several Addresses to General Gage from Some persons in Boston, on his leaving that place, lately published here. John Simson is a subscriber of one of them, wherein is this remarkable paragraph: viz, "We cannot forbear to express our Sentiments, that could a restoration to quiet and good Order have been effected in this Province by the influence of personal character, a gentleman of Your Excellency's *Established reputation* for *Candour* & *Justice,* for *moderation,* and an *obliging disposition,* invested at the Same time with the *Supreme Military Authority,* could not have failed to have Secured it." General Gage's treatment of the Unhappy Sufferers in Boston will Evidence how well he deserved this Character! If the aforesaid Subscriber is your client, you would do well to consider whether consistent with Duty or Safety You can continue to do Business for or correspond with Such a Traitor to his Native Country. I remain Yours to Serve Roger Sherman

RC (CtNhHi).

[1] Jonathan Ingersoll (1747–1823), New Haven, Conn., lawyer and nephew of Jared Ingersoll, later served in the assembly and as lieutenant governor of Connecticut. Franklin B. Dexter, *Biographical Sketches of the Graduates of Yale College,* 6 vols. (New York: Henry Holt and Co., 1885–1919), 3:187–88.

Samuel Adams to Elizabeth Adams

My dear Philada. Novr 7th 1775

My last Letter to you I Sent by young Mr Gawen Brown who left this place about a fortnight ago. I know not how many I have written. I wish you would send me the Dates of those you have receivd in your next.

My Son informs me in a late Letter, that you were about removing to little Cambridge. I am exceedingly pleasd with it, because I am sure you could not be comfortable in your house at Dedham in the cold Season. When we shall return to our Habitation in Boston, if ever, is uncertain. The Barbarity of our Enemies in the Desolations they have wantonly made at Falmouth and elsewhere, is a Presage of what will probably befall that Town which has so long endur'd the Rage of a merciless Tyrant. It has disgraced the Name of Britain, and added to the Character of the Ministry, another indelible Mark of Infamy. We must be content to suffer the Loss of all things in this Life, rather than tamely surrender the publick Liberty. The Eyes of the People of Britain seem to be fast closed; if they should ever be opened they will rejoyce, and thank the Americans for resisting a Tyranny which is manifestly intended to overwhelm them and the whole British Empire. Righteous Heaven will surely smile on a Cause so righteous as ours is, and our Country, if it does its Duty will see an End to its oppressions. Whether I shall live to rejoyce with the Friends of Liberty and Virtue, my fellow Laborers in the Common Cause, is a Matter of no Consequence. I will endeavor by Gods Assistance, to act my little part well—to approve my self to Him, and trust every thing which concerns me to his all-gracious Providence.

The Newspapers will give you an Account of the Surrender of the Garrison at Fort Chambly to Major Brown of the Massachusetts. The Colors of the 7th Regiment were taken there and were brought to the Congress on Fryday last.

I wrote to my Daughter not long ago. I hope she has receivd the Letter. Remember me to her and to Sister Polly and all other Friends.

You will believe, my dear Betsy, without the Formality of my repeating it to you, that I am, most affectionately, your S A

RC (NN).

Samuel Adams to James Warren

November 7th, [1775]

Your kind Letter of the 26 of October by Coll Read was brot to me last Evening.

Our Friend Mr J A and my self were highly entertaind with the Papers inclosd in your Letter to him. It is wonderful to me that there should be any Difficulty about the Expulsion of Church. I intend to write to you by Doctr Morgan who will leave this City in a few days. Adieu S A

RC (MHi). A continuation of Adams to Warren, November 4, 1775.

John Hancock to George Washington

Sir Philadelphia 7th Novr. 1775

I am suddenly Call'd upon by the Congress to Dispatch an Express to you, which gives me time only to Inform you that the Congress having Taken into consideration the Report of the Committee appointed to Confer with you, have come to severall Resolutions, which by their order I here Inclose.[1] They have not yet gone thro' the Report, when Acted upon, the Resolutions they may Adopt will be Transmitted you by Express.

Your Letter of the 30th ulto. No 11, just Rec'd & laid before Congress, but I am Directed not to Detain the Express.[2]

I have the Honour to be with the utmost Respect Sir Your most Obedt Servt John Hancock Presidt

RC (DLC).

[1] Hancock sent Washington a wide variety of resolutions relating to the Continental Army which Congress adopted on November 4 and 6. *JCC*, 3:321–25, 328, 330–35. Although the latter resolves appear in the journals with the entry for November 7, Congress actually approved them the preceding day, a conclusion supported by both Secretary Thomson's journal entry for the sixth and the date of his attestation to the copy of these resolves enclosed in this letter from Hancock. *JCC*, 3:328; and Washington Papers, DLC.

[2] Washington's letter to Hancock of October 30 is in PCC, item 152, 1:255; and Washington, *Writings* (Fitzpatrick), 4:55–56.

Thomas Jefferson to Francis Eppes

Dear Sir Philadelphia Nov. 7. 1775

We have no late intelligence here except of the surrender of Chambly, with 90. prisoners of war, 6 1/2 tons of powder, 150 stands of arms and some other small matters. The acquisition of this powder we hope has before this made us masters of St. John's, on which Montreal and the upper parts of St. Laurence will of course be ours. The fate of Arnold's expedition we know not as yet. We have had some disagreeable accounts of internal commotions in South Carolina.

I have never received the scrip of a pen from any mortal in Virginia since I left it, nor been able by any enquiries I could make to hear of my family. I had hoped that when Mrs. Byrd came I should have heard something of them, but she could tell me nothing about them. The suspense under which I am is too terrible to be endured. If any thing has happened, for god's sake let me know it. My best affections to Mrs. Eppes. Adieu.

RC (ViU: Thomas Jefferson Memorial Foundation deposit). Jefferson, *Papers* (Boyd), 1:252.

Naval Committee to Silas Deane

To Silas Deane Esqr. Philadelphia November the 7th 1775

You are desired to repair immediately to the City of New York, and there purchase a Ship suitable for carrying 20 nine pounders upon one deck, if such a Ship can there be found. Also a Sloop, suitable to carry ten guns, which we would choose should be Bermudian built if such a one can be had. If you succeed in purchasing both, or either of these Vessels, you will use all possible expedition to procure them to be armed and equipped for the Sea. For this purpose you will apply to, and employ such persons as can carry this business into the most speedy execution. Should there be danger in fitting these Vessels at New York from the Kings ships, you may then send the Vessels eastward thro the Sound to New London or Norwich in order to be armed and fitted. Should this be the case you will repair immediately to the place where the Ships are to be fitted, and there use every means in your power to procure this to be done with the utmost expedition. For the Colony of Connecticut you are to procure powder for both these Vessels, and such other Military Stores as can there be had. You will procure the Cannon and other Stores at New York or any other place where it can be done in the best and most expeditious manner. You will also procure Officers and Men suitable for these Vessels. As soon as these Vessels can possibly be fitted for the Sea, you will order them immediately into Delaware Bay. You will by every opportunity give us the most exact intelligence of all your proceedings by conveyances the most safe and secure that can be obtained. You are empower'd to draw on Governor Hopkins for such sums of money as may be necessary for the above business.

Step Hopkins Joseph Hewes
Christ Gadsden John Adams
Richard Henry Lee Jno. Langdon

P.S. In the course of your Journey at New York, or elsewhere you are to employ proper Persons to engage experienced and able-bodied seamen to man the ships now fitting out who must repair to Philadelphia with all possible dispatch.[1]

RC (CtHi). Written by Lee and signed by Lee, Adams, Gadsden, Hewes, Hopkins, and Langdon.

[1] This committee, created October 13 and enlarged October 30, came to be designated the Naval Committee, although often described in the journals as "the committee for fitting out armed vessels." For its origin and development to early 1776, when its functions were absorbed by what came to be called the Marine Committee, see *JCC*, 3:277–78, 293–94, 311–12, 364, 376, 378–87, 395–97, 420, 425–28, 4:90, 186; and Adams, *Diary* (Butterfield), 3:342–50. Deane, himself a member of the Naval Committee, went to New York but failed to accomplish his mission. See Naval Committee to Deane, November 16; and Deane to Elizabeth Deane, November 26, 1775. For other aspects of the committee's work, see also John Adams to Elbridge Gerry, November 5; Stephen Hopkins to Esek Hopkins, November 6; Richard Henry Lee to George Washington, November 13; and Samuel Chase to John Adams, November 16, 1775.

Samuel Ward to Henry Ward

Philadelphia 7th Novr. 1775. Mentions progress of the American invasion of Canada, and alludes to efforts then under way in Congress to secure the establishment of a Continental Navy. "Our Instruction relative to a Fleet has never been under Consideration yet. I expect in a Day or two to have it determined. I am heartily glad We did not press the matter at first as We have a much better Prospect of carrying some decisive Measure now than at the opening of the Session."[1]

Abstracted from mutilated RC (RHi).

[1] For the instructions to Ward and Hopkins from the Rhode Island Assembly calling for the creation of an American fleet, which were laid before Congress October 3, 1775, see *JCC*, 3:274.

Christopher Gadsden

William Livingston to William Alexander

My Lord 8 Novr. 1775

Yesterday the officers for the 2 Jersey Battalions nominated by the Provincial Convention were appointed by the Congress, & to facilitate your obtaining some superior rank, I thought it best to say nothing about the priority of the date in the respective Commissions.[1] These were accordingly all dated the 7 Instant. This morning I moved the Matter, & urged the necessity of the measure from this fact but the thing was not relished, & therefore the date of the other Commissions was changed into 8th. The moment I received the Commissions I made it my Business to procure an express but have not yet been able to get one. I have not yet received your Letter, nor my Surtout [*overcoat*] which I greatly want. I am your most humble Servt Wil. Livingston

RC (NHi).

[1] William Alexander (1726–83), a merchant and New Jersey officeholder whose claim to the title of 6th Earl of Stirling had been disallowed by the House of Lords, was appointed colonel of the First New Jersey Battalion by Congress on November 7 and subsequently rose to the rank of major general in the Continental Army. Alexander's wife Sarah was William Livingston's sister. *DAB;* and *JCC,* 3:335.

Robert Treat Paine's Diary

[November 8, 1775]

I was appointed a Cmttee wth R R Livingston & John Langdon Esqr to go to Canada.[1]

MS (MHi).

[1] Although the initial appointments to the committee were made on November 2, Robert R. Livingston, Jr., was named this day to replace Eliphalet Dyer, who "on account of his indisposition, excused himself from going to the northward." Simultaneously Congress adopted a lengthy list of instructions for the committee. *JCC,* 3:317, 339–41.

Secret Committee Minutes of Proceedings

Philadelphia. Committee Chamber Nov. 8 1775

At a Meeting of the Commee. of Secrecy, Present Saml. Ward [ ].[1]

A Contract was enterd into Between Nathaniel Shaw jun.[2] of New London in the Colony of Connecticut Mercht. of the one part, & the sd. Committee of the other part as follows vizt. That a voyage or voyages shall be undertaken forthwith for the speedy procuring thirty five tons gunpowder, or in case any part of the gunpowder cannot be had, as much saltpetre with a proportionate quantity of Sulphur as will make the quantity deficient—As by the sd. Contract copied into the Register fol. 13 & &c &c.

At a meeting of the Committee of Secrecy, present Saml. Ward, Thos. Willing, Benjn. Franklin, Thos. McKean, Josiah Bartlett. A Contract was enterd into between John Langdon of the town of Portsmouth in the Colony of New Hampshire Mercht. of the one part & the sd. Commitee. of the other part—That a voyage or voyages shall be forthwith undertaken for the speedy procuring twenty five tons of good gunpowder, or in case any part of the gunpowder cannot be had as much Saltpetre with a proportionate quantity of Sulphur as will make the quantity that may be deficient.

See Reg[iste]r fol. 15 &c.[3]

MS (MH).

[1] One-half line left blank in MS. For the delegates who attended this meeting of the committee, see the third paragraph.

[2] Nathaniel Shaw, Jr. (1735–82), a leading Connecticut merchant in the West Indian trade, was a member of the New London Committee of Correspondence, 1774–78, and in 1776 became an agent for naval supplies for the Connecticut Council of Safety and a prize agent for the Continental Congress. *DAB*. For information about Shaw's execution of this contract, see Samuel Ward to Nathaniel Shaw, December 13, 1775; and David Mumford to Silas Deane, January 10, 1776, *Collections of the Connecticut Historical Society*, 23 (1930): 13–15.

[3] For the sums advanced on these contracts, see Secret Committee Account, September 27, 1775–August 26, 1776.

John Dickinson's Proposed Instructions

[November 9? 1775][1]

Gentlemen,

The Trust reposed in You, is of such a Nature, and the Modes of executing it may be so diversified in the Course of your Deliberations, that it is scarcely possible to give You particular Instructions respecting it.

We therefore, in general, direct You, that You or any four of You meet in Congress the Delegates of the several ⟨*British*⟩ Colonies now ⟨*setting in Congress*⟩ assembled in this City, and any such Delegates ⟨*that of the said Colonies that*⟩ as may meet in Congress next Year; that You consult together on the present critical & alarming State of public Affairs; that You exert your utmost Endeavours to agree upon & Command such Measures, as You shall judge to afford the best Prospect of obtaining Redress of American Grievances, and restoring that Union & Harmony between Great Britain & the Colonies so essential to the Wellfare & Happiness of both Countries; & that You take especial Care to avoid all proceedings that may have any Tendency to render a Reconciliation between them, impracticable; We hereby strictly enjoining you, that You in Behalf of this Colony, dissent from and utterly reject any propositions, should such be made, that may cause or lead to a Separation from our Mother Country, a Change of the Form of Government, or the Establishment of a Commonwealth.

You are ordered to make Report of your proceedings to the Assembly of this province at their next Session.

MS (PHi). In the hand of John Dickinson.

[1] The congressional decisions of November 3 and 4 to advise New Hampshire and South Carolina to take steps to create new provincial governments were opposed by several delegates who viewed them as barriers to future negotiations and as steps leading to separation from Britain. Such also was the fear of many Pennsylvania assemblymen, who, led by John Dickinson, moved quickly to prevent the Pennsylvania delegation in Congress from supporting similar measures in the future. On November 4, the Pennsylvania Assembly had selected a new slate of delegates, which now included Andrew Allen and Robert Morris in the place of George Ross and Thomas Mifflin, and on the seventh, a committee of eight headed by Dickinson (the only delegate to Congress named to the committee) was appointed to draft instructions for the delegates. There can be little doubt that Dickinson actually drafted the instructions prepared by this committee or that the present document was the draft submitted to the assembly and adopted on November 9. See *Pa. Archives,* 8th ser. 8:7347, 7350, 7352–53.

The assembly's action was also part of a larger campaign, for on November 28 the New Jersey Assembly adopted nearly identical instructions for their delegates in Congress. *Am. Archives,* 4th ser. 3:1857. But since the New Jersey instructions were coupled with a move to submit a separate petition to the king, the action of New Jersey elicited still another congressional response in which Dickinson was centrally involved. Thus on December 4 Congress resolved that "it will be very dangerous to the liberties and welfare of America, if any Colony should separately petition the King or either house of Parliament," and appointed a committee consisting of Dickinson, John Jay, and George Wythe to "confer" with the New Jersey Assembly. *JCC,* 3:404. Apparently Dickinson was the key appointee on the committee, since as author of the Pennsylvania instructions he could allay fears that the congressional mission was simply another unwarranted move to intervene in the internal affairs of the colonies. Certainly Dickinson played the dominant role before the New Jersey Assembly on December 5 when the committee was invited to speak to the house, and the effort was rewarded when the assembly immediately thereafter resolved against submitting their own petition to the king. See Notes on Delegates' Remarks to the New Jersey Assembly, December 5, 1775.

Notwithstanding the original purpose of the Pennsylvania instructions, however, Congress on December 4 passed a resolution encouraging Virginia to reorganize its government that was cast in language almost identical to the resolves pertaining to New Hampshire and South Carolina passed on November 3 and 4. *JCC,* 3:403–4. For the comments of two delegates who expressed apprehension that the Pennsylvania instructions would have an undesirable effect, see George Ross to James

Wilson, November 17, 1775, note 2; and Samuel Chase to John Adams, December 8, 1775.

John Hancock to James Bowdoin, Sr.

Sir, Congress Chamber 9 Novr. 1775 Philada.

I am exceeding Glad to find by the Report of our Committee of Conference[1] that your health was so Establish'd as to be able to attend the Publick Business, I hope soon to hear of your perfect Recovery.

I have the pleasure to inform you that your Son Mr. James Bowdoin[2] Arriv'd last Eveng in this City from London, and this morning Breakfasted with me, he is in good health, and proposes in a few days to Set out for Cambrige. I Congratulate you on his Arrival. No Answer to the Congress Petition, the King Refusing to Receive it on the Throne; that we must work out our own Salvation.

I Beg my best Respects to your good Lady, & am with Respect, Sir Your Most Obedt Servt, John Hancock

RC (MHi).

[1] Bowdoin was one of the Massachusetts leaders who met with the congressional Committee of Conference in Cambridge on October 18–22, 1775. *Am. Archives*, 4th ser. 3:1156.

[2] James Bowdoin, Jr. (1752–1811), who had been studying at Christ Church, Oxford, and traveling in Europe. *DAB*.

John Hancock to George Clymer and Michael Hillegas

Congress Chamber, 9th Novem'r, 1775. Requests Continental Treasurers Clymer and Hillegas to pay $3,000 to the Philadelphia Committee of Safety as "an advance for the use of the Battalion now raising."

Abstracted from *Am. Archives*, 4th ser. 3:1839.

John Hancock to the New York Provincial Convention

Gentlemen Philadelphia, November 9, 1775

Your several letters lately Rec'd, have been laid before the Congress; those that Respect the Fort in the Highlands have been Acted upon, and I here Inclose you the Resolutions of Congress thereupon which you will please to put in immediate Execution.[1] As soon as Congress have Determin'd upon the other matters mention'd in your Letters, the Result shall be Communicated to you, as I am Directed to forward immediately by Express the Inclos'd, I have not Time to Add, but that I am with Respect, Gentlemen Your most Obedt servt.

John Hancock Presidt.

RC (N). *Journals of N. Y. Prov. Cong.*, 2:7. RC damaged; missing words supplied from Tr.

[1] On November 6 Congress received letters from the New York Provincial Congress of October 27, and November 2 and 3, 1775. See PCC, item 67, fols. 125, 129–30, 135; and *Am. Archives*, 4th ser. 3:1205–6, 1314–15, 1323. Congress thereupon appointed a committee to consider these letters, whose report led to the adoption on November 8 of a series of resolves concerning the fortification of the Highlands in New York. *JCC*, 3:327, 337–39.

Joseph Hewes to James Iredell

Dear Sir: Philadelphia, 9th November, 1775

When I came here and had conversed with the Massachusetts delegates, I found it a difficult matter to get a letter sent to the Commissioners in Boston. I was informed no letter was suffered to go in till its contents had been examined by a committee, and that letters wrote by persons they thought disaffected, were sometimes stopped, though the contents were only business or compliments. Under the circumstances, I thought it prudent to open your letter, and put it under cover to Gen. Washington, at the same time requesting the favor of him, after he had read its contents, to send it into Boston, and to permit an answer to return the same way. I have not yet received an answer from him, but am in hopes it will not be long before I have that honor.[1] I could think of no better way to get you an answer from the Commissioners. If I have done wrong I must rely on your goodness to excuse it. I can say but little on the score of politics—the present appearance is much against us and our cause. We have had no accounts from England later than the 26th of August. We are told our Petition will be disregarded; that we shall be declared rebels, and our estates confiscated; we are threatened with ships of war, troops, Russians, Hanoverians and Hessians. God knows how it will end. Some officers from Gen. Gage's army have been detected in enlisting men in the Province of New York to go to Boston; some of these recruits have been examined on oath, and declared that each of them was promised two hundred acres of land, not in the woods, but cleared cultivated land with houses thereon, that they were to be put in possession at the end of the war, when the rebels were subdued, which they were taught to believe would soon happen. We are in daily expectation of further intelligence from England, several vessels being expected here; the last ships that have arrived brought the king's proclamation. You will see it in the newspapers; it is remarkable those ships brought very few letters from private persons—it would seem as if the proclamation had deterred our friends from writing on the subject of politics. My best compliments to the ladies, and believe me to be, with much esteem, Dear Sir, Your most obedient humble servant, Joseph Hewes

MS not found; reprinted from Griffith J. McRee, *Life and Correspondence of James Iredell, One of the Associate Justices of the Supreme Court of the United States*, 2 vols. (New York: D. Appleton and Co., 1857–58), 1:265–66.

[1] Hewes' letter to Washington has not been found, and there are no extant letters from Washington to Hewes before 1779.

Joseph Hewes to Samuel Johnston

Dear Sir Philadelphia 9th Nov. 1775

It is now I imagine near three Weeks since your Provincial Council broke up and I take it for granted you have sent an express with the account of your deliberations to your Delegat[es] here. We expect it dayly and are Anxious for its Arival.[1] I hope you have fallen on some method to furnish your Soldiers with Arms and Amunition, those Articles are very scarse throughout all the Colonies.[2] I find on enquiry that neither can be got here, all the Gunsmiths in this Province are engaged and cannot make Arms near so fast as they are wanted. Powder is also very Scarse notwithstanding every effort seems to have been exerted both to make and import. The Congress exert every Nerve to put the Colonies into a proper state of defence, four Regiments are ordered to be raised on Continental Pay for the defence of South Carolina and Georgia.[3] It is expected the two Regiments with you will be continued and kept up the same as other parts of the Army. One Regiment is now raising in this Province and Two in New Jersey on the same establishment. Twenty thousand Men are to be kept up near Boston and Five thousand on the Lakes, Canada &c, The whole Army to be enlisted to the 31st of December 1776 unless discharged sooner by Order of Congress. The Pay of the Captains, Lieutenants and Ensigns is increased, they are now allowed as follows, a Captain 26 2/3 Dollars, a Lieutenant 18 Dollars, an Ensign 13 1/3 Dollars per Calendar month. The Rations allowed the Soldiers thro' the whole Army you have as follows,

One pound of Beef or 3/4 lb of Pork, or 1 lb of Salt Fish per day each Man.

1 lb of bread or Flour.

3 pints of Peas or Beans per Week or Vegetables in proportion, rating Peas or Beans at 6/ per Bushel.

1 pint of milk per man per day or at the rate of 1/72 of a Dollar per pint.

1/2 pint of Rice, or one pint of Indian meal per man per week.

One quart of Spruce Beer or Cyder per man, or 9 gallons of Molasses per Company of 100 Men per week.

3 lb. of Candles to 100 men per week for guards.

24 lb of Soft Soap or 8 lb. hard Soap for 100 men per Week.[4]

I doubt not you will find it Necessary to come into a new agreement with your Commissaries, for it will be but Just and right to give your Soldiers the same allowance that is given to those in other places. It is also recommended that all the Soldiers be put into some Uniform, that the Public purchase the Cloth and have it made up and that it be discounted out of each Mans Pay, at the rate of 10/ per month. The Soldiers near Boston we are told are well pleased with this regulation.

Several other matters which together with some Ships and Vessels that are fitting out at the Charge of the Continent will enhance our expences amazingly, by which you may Judge we have but little expectation of a reconciliation. I can assure you from all the accounts we have yet received from England we have Scarsely a dawn of hope that it will take place.

Mr. Middleton and Mr. Rutledge two of the Delegates for South Carolina set out for that Province on Sunday last. They intended thro' Halifax and carried a Letter for you from the President inclosing a resolution respecting Trade.

I have enclosed some News papers in A Letter to Mr. Smith, to them you must look for News. I hope all your Family are in good health, my Complements to them, you and they have always the best wishes of Dear Sir your mo. Obedt. hume. Servant

Joseph Hewes

[*P.S.*] Nov. 10th. Since writing the above, a Ship Arived from London and brings papers to 12th Septemr. No answer is to be given to the Petition of the Congress as the King did not receive it on the Throne, Parliament prorogued to the 26th Octo.

RC (Nc-Ar).

[1] Johnston had already written separate letters to Hewes and to the North Carolina delegates on November 5. Clark, *Naval Documents*, 2:898–99.

[2] On this point, see Hewes to Johnston, November 26, 1775.

[3] Congress resolved on November 4 to maintain "at the continental expense" three battalions for the defense of South Carolina and one for that of Georgia. *JCC*, 3:325. This action was probably prompted by the request of the South Carolina Council of Safety, in their September 18 letter to the South Carolina

delegates, for "an Army of Observation & General Officers to Command all our forces, at the general charge of the Colonies." *South Carolina Historical and Genealogical Magazine* 1 (October 1900): 285–90. Having been informed that Congress had "granted 1000 Men to North Carolina," the council asserted that South Carolina's weaker position required even greater defensive measures, "without which Carolina & Georgia will be involved in such difficulties as may & probably will greatly injure the common Interests of America."

[4] Congress adopted the preceding regulations about the pay and rations of the Continental Army on November 4. *JCC*, 3:322.

New York Delegates to the New York Provincial Congress

Gentlemen— Philad. 9th Novemr. 1775.

The Congress have taken the resolution to appoint a commander of the fortress in the Highlands, with the rank of colonel, and Wednesday is fixed for that purpose. As it must be of moment that this command should be vested in a person of abilities, and in whom the inhabitants place confidence, we wish you would name three or four gentlemen who are competent for the trust, and we shall endeavour to get one of them preferred.

You will however be pleased to observe that as these works are erected at a Continental expense, the Congress claim an absolute right to appoint the officers.[1]

We have the honour to be, With the greatest respect, gentlemen, Your most obedient humble servants,[2]

Jas. Duane,

Robt. R. Livingston, Junr.

MS not found; reprinted from *Journals of N. Y. Prov. Cong.*, 2:107.

[1] On the appointment of a commander for the fortifications in the Highlands, see New York Delegates to the New York Provincial Convention, January 5, 1776, note 1.

[2] Governor Tryon of New York somehow obtained an FC of this letter (containing some minor variations from the present text), written by James Duane and directed to Abraham Yates, then president of the New York Provincial Congress. On the verso of this FC is the following note in an unidentified hand: "The [. . .] Batterys in the hi[gh] lan[d]s is to be Strongly fortifyed with all expedition [. . .] on each Side of the River, as I hord [*heard*] them Say this Day. The above Letter is Yates's own writing." James Brattle, a former servant of Tryon's who was employed as Duane's valet at the time of this letter, occasionally sent the governor intelligence reports about the proceedings of Congress, including some of Duane's own correspondence. But since this document is clearly in Duane's hand it is unlikely that Brattle would have forwarded it to Tryon with a covering note ascribing it to Yates, unless perhaps a third person was a party to Brattle's activities, and added a hastily written endorsement with an attribution prompted by the appearance of Yates' name on the document. In any event, Tryon forwarded

the FC in a letter of December 7 to the Earl of Dartmouth. See PRO: C.O. 5, 1107:11, 29. For further information about Brattle, see Clark, *Naval Documents,* 2:1051n, 3:698–700; and Christopher Marshall, *Extracts from the Diary of Christopher Marshall, Kept in Philadelphia and Lancaster during the American Revolution, 1774–1781,* ed. William Duane (Albany: Joel Munsell, 1877), pp. 56–57.

John Hancock to Nicholas Cooke

Philadelphia Novr 10th 1775. Requests Governor Nicholas Cooke of Rhode Island to forward to the New York Committee of Safety one ton of "some Powder . . . lately Arriv'd in your Colony."

Abstracted from *Proceedings of the American Antiquarian Society,* new ser. 36 (1926): 286.

John Hancock to the New York Provincial Congress

Philadelphia, 10th November, 1775. Informs Provincial Congress that the "committee to purchase clothing for the army in the northern department" will ship supplies of clothes the following day which "are ordered to be sent by land to Dobs ferry, where you are requested to have a boat ready to take them in and transport them immediately to Albany."[1]

Abstracted from *Journals of N. Y. Prov. Cong.,* 2:7.

[1] See *JCC,* 3:317–18, 342, 344.

John Hancock to Philip Schuyler

Sir Philadelphia 10 Novr. 1775

The Congress have taken into Consideration your several Letters and the Accounts received from Canada,[1] and have appointed three of their own Body a Committee to repair immediately to Ticonderoga and confer with you & to execute several Matters agreeable to Instructions given them, a Copy of which I here inclose.[2]

The gentlemen propose setting out on their Journey to Morrow Morning,[3] to whom beg leave to refer you for every Thing passing here and have only Time to add my sincere Wishes for the perfect Restoration of your Health and that I am with the utmost Respect & Esteem Sir Your most obedient Servant

John Hancock president

Tr (NN).

[1] For the letters of Schuyler alluded to by Hancock, see Samuel Ward's Diary, October 31, 1775, note 1.

[2] For the Committee to the Northward, appointed on November 2, and their instructions, adopted on November 8, see *JCC*, 3:312, 317, 339–42; and New Hampshire Delegates to Matthew Thornton, November 3, 1775, note 4. This committee received additional instructions on November 11 and, after conferring with Schuyler at Ticonderoga later in the month, submitted a report to Congress in December which laid the basis for adoption of an extensive series of resolutions early in January 1776. See Committee to the Northward Minutes of Proceedings, November 30, 1775; and *JCC*, 3:350, 446–52, 459; 4:38–40, 43–45.

[3] Robert Treat Paine's diary entry for November 12 reads: "At 11 oClock Set out with Mr. R. R. Livingston & Mr. Langdon. Rode to Bristol & din'd, thence to Trenton by 7 oClock." MHi.

John Hancock to George Washington

Sir Philadelphia Novr. 10th 1775

By order of Congress I have the Honour to forward you the Inclos'd Resolutions this moment come into. The suddeness of this order and your Zeal for the Service supercedes all necessity of Recommending this measure to your particular Notice, have only to Add that Congress leave the Appointment of the persons to you.[1]

A Variety of Business has Occurr'd, which has prevented a final Determination upon the Report of the Committee of Conference, as soon as perfected, the Result shall be Transmitted you.

I have the honour to be with the utmost Respect and Esteem, Sir Your most Obedt servt. John Hancock President

RC (DLC).

[1] Hancock sent Washington three resolves adopted by Congress this day, the first and second of which directed the general to send two spies into Nova Scotia "to enquire into the state of that colony" and to decide whether it was feasible to dispatch an American raiding party there, and the third authorized him to raise two battalions of marines. Congress passed the first two resolves in response to the reception on November 2 of a petition from the Committee of Safety of Passamaquoddy, Nova Scotia, asking for admission to the Association, and Washington reacted to them by sending Aaron Willard and Moses Child to Nova Scotia to ascertain the disposition of the inhabitants and to investigate the state of the defenses there. Since Gov. Francis Legge of Nova Scotia had imposed martial law upon the province, however, Willard and Child were unable to penetrate farther than Campobello, no more than 30 miles into the colony. As a result, when they reported back to Washington in February 1776 that a large majority of Nova Scotians were sympathetic to the American cause and that the colony itself was only lightly defended, Washington accepted their account sceptically and submitted it to Congress in the same spirit. *JCC*, 3:316, 343–44; *Am. Archives*, 4th ser. 4:1148–50; and Washington, *Writings* (Fitzpatrick), 4:99–100, 112–13, 331. See also John Adams' Proposals for an Expedition to Nova Scotia, November 2–10? 1775.

John Zubly to John Houstoun and Archibald Bulloch

Gentlemen [November 10? 1775][1]

I am Setting off for Georgia greatly indisposd. You will doubtless reach home before me tho You should not depart these ten days. In Case of my first Arrival I think not to make any Report to our Council of Safety till we are all present.[2]

I have left my Case with Spirits at my Lodgings (having a smaler one) which I advise you to take with you well filled if You do not mean to drink whiskey &c by the Way. It will either suit You or Messr Habersham.

Should I arrive before You I will not fail to acquaint Your friends but I can only travel slow.

I wish You a pleasant Journey & am, Your very humble Serv.

J.J. Zubly

RC (NN).

[1] Zubly's diary—which for November 6 through 9 contains little more than brief entries confirming his attendance at Congress—indicates that on November 10 he "sat of[f] from Philada. on my return [*to Georgia*]." GHi. According to a tradition among Georgia historians, which apparently first appeared early in the 19th century in the work of Hugh McCall and since then has been repeated with variations by several scholars and antiquarians, Zubly left Philadelphia under a cloud. As "the time for independence drew near," McCall maintained, Zubly, dismayed by Congress' drift towards separation from Great Britain, wrote a letter to Georgia Governor James Wright charging Congress with nefarious designs. Then, when accused by Samuel Chase of carrying on a treasonous correspondence with Wright, Zubly denied the charge but left Congress as Chase was preparing to present incriminating evidence against him. Congress, McCall went on to say, thereupon dispatched John Houstoun to follow Zubly back to Georgia and counteract any unfavorable reports that Zubly might attempt to spread there. Hugh McCall, *The History of Georgia, Containing Brief Sketches of the Most Remarkable Events up to the Present Day,* 2 vols. (Savannah: Seymour & Williams, 1811–16), 2:89–90.

In striking contrast to this sensational account of Zubly's departure is the utter lack of comment on his returning home among the surviving contemporary documents. Furthermore, there is no tangible evidence confirming the existence of Zubly's alleged letter to Wright and no indication in the governor's published correspondence that he ever received information about Congress from Zubly. *Collections of the Georgia Historical Society* 3 (1873): 209–44. On the other hand, Ezra Stiles recorded an account of Zubly's departure sufficiently similar to McCall's to have been the origin of the version preserved in the work of so many Georgia historians. According to Stiles, Francis Dana told him in April 1776, on the basis of conversations Dana had had with some delegates on a recent visit to Philadelphia, that Zubly had been motivated to leave both by Congress' drift toward independence and its refusal to support his proposal to send yet another petition to Great Britain. And Dana also mentioned a rumor supposedly then current that Zubly had been detected in a correspondence with South Carolina Governor William Campbell, which although allegedly initiated after Zubly's return to Georgia, may well have been the source of the tradition of his letter to Wright that gained acceptance in the 19th century. Ezra Stiles, *The Literary Diary of Ezra Stiles . . . ,* ed. Franklin B. Dexter, 3 vols. (New York: C. Scribner's Sons, 1901), 2:10.

Although there is a suspicious coincidence between the adoption by Congress on November 9 of a stringent secrecy resolution, which Zubly did not sign, and his departure from Philadelphia on the following day, it is tempting to dismiss McCall's account. Certainly this letter of November 10 to his colleagues suggests that he left amicably; and subsequent traditions that Houstoun was hastily sent off to follow him to protect against any mischief Zubly might create when he arrived home alone are seemingly belied by the fact that Zubly expected Bulloch and Houstoun to leave Philadelphia soon and even thought that they might reach Georgia before him.

[2] Both Zubly and Bulloch attended the council of safety on December 19 and presented the November 4 resolution about raising a battalion in Georgia. *The Revolutionary Records of the State of Georgia,* ed. Allen D. Candler, 3 vols. (Atlanta: Franklin-Turner Co., 1908), 1:77; and *JCC,* 3:325.

John Adams to Henry Knox

Dr sir Philadelphia Novr 11. 1775

I had the Pleasure of a Letter from you[1] a few days ago and was rejoiced to learn that you have at last determined to take a more important Share than you have done hitherto in the Conduct of our military Matters. I have been impressed with an opinion of your Knowledge and Abilities in the military Way for several years, and of late have endeavoured, both at Camp, at Watertown and at Philadelphia, by mentioning your Name and Character, to make you more known, and consequently in a better Way for Promotion.

It was a sincere opinion of your Merit and Qualifications, which prompted me to act this Part and therefore I am very happy to be able to inform you, that I believe you will very soon be provided for according to your Wishes, at least you may depend upon this that nothing in my Power shall be wanting to effect it.

It is of vast Importance, my dear Sir, that I should be minutely informed of every thing which passes at the Camp, while I hold a Place in the Great Council of America: and therefore I must beg the Favour of you to write me as often as you can by safe Conveyances. I want to know the Name, Rank, and Character of every officer in the Army. I mean every honest and able one, but more especially of every officer, who is best acquainted with the Theory and Practice of Fortification and Gunnery. What is comprehend[ed] within the Term Engineer? and whether it includes skill both in Fortification and Gunnery—and what skillfull Engineers you have in the Army and whether any of them and who have seen service & when and where. I am sir your very humble Sert John Adams

[*P.S.*] I want to know if there is a compleat set of Books upon the military Art in all its Branches in the Library of Harvard Colledge and what Books are the best upon those Subjects.

RC (MHi).

[1] Henry Knox (1750–1806), Boston bookseller, was appointed colonel of artillery on November 17, 1775, and after serving as a general officer during the war he became secretary at war in 1785. *DAB;* and *JCC,* 3:359.

Thomas Lynch to Philip Schuyler

My dear Sir Phila. Novr. 11. 1775

I owe you my best thanks for the Part you have taken in ascertaining the true State of the Connecticut Regiments. I had seen Governor Trumbull, who shewed me your first Letter, in which you mentiond that 500 of Hinmans were to proceed to Canada. I told him that Colo Dyer had misinformed that I said that I did not imagine, there were more than two or three Hundred Men of Hinmans who were there, properly armed & ready for Service; and being asked where the Rest were, I answered I did not know any thing about them, only that they were not at the Camp, & told the Govr further that I was glad to hear so many had joined the Army since I left it, so that I went farther in my Guess than I find by your Letter was fact.[1]

I am very sorry to find they fell so short of your & general Montgomery's opinion on the Article of Courage. I pity, from my soul, that brave gentleman, his Feelings must have [*been*] truely acute when he saw them running away from themselves.

We wait in a State of the most anxious suspence for Accounts of the total Reduction of Canada and their accession to our League.

I beg our most respectful Compliments to you, your Family and Friends particularly Mr Mon[t]gomery, Mr Campbell &c. Your affece & sincere Tho Lynch

RC (NN).

[1] For an account of General Schuyler's difficulties with Col. Benjamin Hinman, commander of the Fourth Connecticut Regiment, see Schuyler's letters to Gov. Jonathan Trumbull of October 12 and 13, 1775, in *Am. Archives,* 4th ser. 3:1033–35, 1054; and Benson J. Lossing, *The Life and Times of Philip Schuyler,* 2 vols. (New York: Sheldon & Co., 1860–73), 1:340–43.

Samuel Ward to Henry Ward

My dear Bror. Philadelphia 11th Novr. 1775

A Ship arrived from London on Thursday. Our Petition you see the Fate of in the Letter published in the Paper I sent Govr. Cooke last Evening. Passengers assure us that the Hanoverians refuse to come to America, that Administration is determined to push their Measures at all Events, that 20000 Troops are to be sent over in the

Spring, four or five Regiments this Fall, that Terms of Accommodation that is the Terms upon which they are willing to receive Us & our Posterity for their Slaves are to be committed to the General & that they will treat with us no other Way; The King has carried Sir Jeffery Amherst out in his Coach seven Mornings running but can't prevail upon him to take the Command in America, that Genl. Monckton hath nobly refused said he would never engage in such an infamous Cause. Orders are given to open all Letters at the post Offices & stop such as contain any American Intelligence. The People disapprove the Introduction of foreign Troops; the Parliament setts 26th Octr., Ministry was collecting its Forces to carry every Measure with a high hand. Opposition was rallying its Friends in Order to make a vigorous Stand. A Letter from a Gentn. of high Character whose Intelligence hath ever been good says that Ministry was putting Arms into the Hands of all who would receive them, English, scotch, irish, roman catholics, Hessians, Hanoverians &c, and that fifty Men of War are to destroy all our maritime Towns & interdict our Trade. If Administration succeeds they are determined another Letter says to extirpate the New England Colonies. An Army from Canada & the 20000 men from England they suppose capable of doing this, these Threats will not intimidate one brave Man but animate all in their Country's Cause and blessed be God We are in his all gracious Hands & not in those of a Ministry fit to serve a Nero only. To Be or not to be is now the Question; every private View, Passion & Interest ought to be buried. We are embarked in one common Bottom. If She sinks We all perish; if She survives the Storm, Peace & Plenty (the offspring of Liberty) and every thing which will dignify & felicitate human Nature will be the Reward of our Virtue. Oh my Brother This is not the Cause of the Colonies & of Britain only but of human Nature itself, and that God who is the Author of Nature, the Friend of Mankind and who hath so remarkably preserved & prospered these Colonies will still continue his all gracious Protection to which I most devoutly recommend You, my Friends & my Country.

I am Yours most affectionately Sam Ward

RC (DLC photostat).

John Adams to Abigail Adams

My dear Novr. 12. 1775

I am often afraid you will think it hard that I dont write oftener to you. But it is really impossible. Could I follow the Inclinations of my Heart I should spend half my Time, in this most agreable and pleasing Employment: But Business presses me so close that I am necessitated to mortify my self. From 7 to ten in the Committees and from six to ten in the Evening in the same, and from 10 to four in Congress. Many Letters to write too upon Business.

As to News, you have every Thing in the public Papers, which I am not now under the strongest Ties of Honour, Virtue and Love of my Country to keep secret, and not to divulge directly or indirectly.[1]

I am most earnestly desirous to come home, but when I shall get Leave I know not.

I long to write to your Excellent Father and sisters, but cannot get Time. You must have observed, and so must all my Friends that every Letter I write is scratched off in the utmost Haste.

How do you like Dr. Franklyn? He tells me he called at the House and saw you, and that he had the Pleasure of dining with you at his Friend Coll. Quincys. This gave me great Pleasure because I concluded from it that my dear and most worthy sisters Cranch and Betcy were better.

RC (MHi). Adams, *Family Correspondence* (Butterfield), 1:326.

[1] A new secrecy resolution, requiring "that every member signify his consent to this agreement by signing the same," had been passed by Congress on November 9. *JCC*, 3:342–43.

John Adams to John Thomas

Sir Philadelphia Novr. 13th 1775

I am much obliged to you for two Letters, one by the Committee; the other dated Novr. 1.[1]

The subject of the first is not yet determined in Congress, but I have no doubt your Desires will be complied with.

As soon as I recd the last I waited on Dr Morgan and shewed your Letter, together with one from Mr Gorden and a very sensible one from Dr Hayward relative to the same subject. Mr Aspinwall was known to Dr Morgan, and well esteemed. Of this Gentleman I knew nothing but by Character. Dr Hayward I knew personally and highly esteemed.

I hope, that neither Aspinwall nor Hayward will be removed, but it will depend much on the Representations of Dr Morgan, which I dare say will not be against Either of them. No doubt he will think two surgeons necessary at Roxbury, and represent accordingly and then Congress will probably establish them.

You may depend upon the little in my Power at all Times, to assist Merit and promote the service.

As Congress has made the Passage of Letters free, I hope to receive more frequent Intelligence from my Friends for the future, and you may be assurd sir, that every Line from you will be peculiarly acceptable to, sir your most obedient sert John Adams

[*P.S.*] The Sum total of all Intelligence from England is that the first Man is "unalterably determined, Let the Event and Consequences be what they will, to compell the Colonies to absolute Obedience." Poor deluded Man!

RC (MHi).

[1] Two letters of John Thomas to Adams, dated October 24 and November 1, 1775, are in the Adams Papers, MHi. Among the topics discussed in the first letter are suitable candidates for engineering and artillery officers. In the second, Thomas recommended Dr. William Aspinwall for a future position in the hospital department.

Josiah Bartlett to the New Hampshire Committee of Safety

Gentn Philadelphia Novr 13th 1775

Enclosed I transmit to you the Letter Directed to the Speaker of our House of Assembly. I Suppose it Came from England Sent by the agents who presented the late Petition of Congress; By it you will be able to Guess what will be the fate of that Petition.[1] I also Send you a Duplicate of the vote of Congress Concerning our Civil affairs, the first Copy of the vote was sent Novr 6th. Yesterday Capt Langdon Set off on his Jorney to Canada so that I am left here alone to act in Behalf of our Colony, I Don't Expect him here any more During this Session of the Congress.

When the Congress will rise I Cant Say But fear it Cant till winter, if it can before Spring.

The affair of the Ship taken at Portsmouth has not been considered by Congress, by reason of urgent Business, But I Expect soon that that & several other captures will be taken under consideration & some General rules adopted, when any thing is Determined on it, will inform you by the first oppertunity.[2]

I am Directed by the Congress to Send you the Inclosed Resolves for making Salt Petre and I would Earnestly Recomend the puting them in practice.[3] It appears from Several Experiments in this Colony that the Surface of the Earth that has been for some years kept from the rain will produce Salt petre. The floor of a meeting House being taken up, the Earth under it produced one pound from Every Bushel; under Barns stables &c much more. There appears to be no more art in making it, than in making pot ash. When the Liquor is properly Boiled and put into pans to Cool, it Shoots & Sticks to the Bottom & Sides very Beautifully, the Liquor may then be Easily Drained off and Either Boyled over again or put on another mash.

Tho probably the Continent will be well Supplied with Powder in the Spring yet it is best by all means to put it out of the power of our Enemies to Defeat us of the necessary article, by Supplying our Selves and if we have a Double or treble Quantity, it will be no Damage, and in future Save our Cash from being Sent abroad after it.

I am Gentlemen your friend & Humble Servt

Josiah Bartlett

RC (Nh-Ar).

[1] Although this letter has not been found, it was probably a copy of Richard Penn and Arthur Lee's September 2, 1775, letter reporting the refusal of George III to receive and answer Congress' petition. Copies of this letter sent to the speakers of the Pennsylvania and New Jersey assemblies are printed in *Am. Archives*, 4th ser. 3:1792, 1851–52.

[2] See New Hampshire Delegates to William Whipple, October 26, 1775, note 1.

[3] The resolves of July 28 and November 10, which Congress directed the delegates to make public. *JCC*, 2:218–19, 3:345–48. Apparently Bartlett also enclosed copies of three November 4 resolves pertaining to arms, deserters, and General Washington's power to impress materials for military transportation. See *N. H. Provincial Papers*, 7:643–44.

John DeHart to the New Jersey Assembly

Gentlemen of the Genl. Assembly
of the Colony of New Jersey Elizth. Town Novemr. 13 1775

Your resolution of the 24th of January past having appointed me with others to attend the Continental Congress of the Colonies then intended to be held at Philadelphia in May following with Instructions to propose and agree to every Constitutional measure for the accommodation of the unhappy differences then subsisting between our Mother Country & the Colonies, In obedience to the said resolution with the other Gentlemen I attended the said Congress but have not been able by any reasonable and constitutional measure to obtain that accommodation so ardently wished for by the House. On the contrary his Majesty seemeth to have turned a deaf Ear to all the supplications of his Loyal Colonists and his Ministers & Parliament have denounced vengeance against all those in America who refuse absolute submission to Acts of Parliament in all Cases whatsoever and have caused the Blood of Numbers of his Majestys most Loyal American subjects to be Spilled which with other arbitrary and Barbarous Actions hath compelled the Colonies to Arm in their Own defence and hath brought them to the verge of a Civil War with the parent State so that all prospect of procuring an accomodation by constitutional Measures seemeth to be nearly at an end.

The peculiar Circumstances of my family hath prevented me from attending the Congress for Sometime past and the same Still continuing renders it uncertain when I shall be able to attend. This and other reasons needless to be mentioned induces me earnestly to desire and request that the Honourable House will now be pleased to appoint another to attend the Continental Congress in my Stead.[1] I am Gentlemen your most Obliged & most Obedient hum servt

John DeHart

RC (NjMoHP).

[1] About this time James Kinsey also sought permission from the New Jersey Assembly to resign his seat in Congress. DeHart and Kinsey both insisted to the assembly that they wanted to leave Congress only because their service there had become a source of great personal inconvenience to them, but Gov. William Franklin of New Jersey dismissed this explanation and asserted that their resignations were "generally attributed to Apprehension of Danger." Whatever the truth of the matter, the assembly accepted their resignations on November 22 and on the same day authorized any two of New Jersey's three remaining delegates to represent the province in Congress. However, after taking into consideration the difficulties that might arise from requiring the presence of two delegates in Philadelphia, the assembly decided on November 30 to allow any one of them to constitute a quorum in Congress. DeHart was reelected to Congress in February 1776, but in June 1776, in the midst of debates on independence, he again resigned "on account of the situation of his family and affairs." *JCC*, 3:396–97; *Am. Archives*, 4th ser. 3:1852–53, 1860, 4:1592, 6:1618; and *N. J. Archives*, 10:680–81.

Richard Henry Lee to George Washington

Dear Sir, Philadelphia Novemr 13th 1775

I must beg leave at the beginning of this letter to apologise for any incorrectness as I write in great haste. Indeed the hurry of business is such here with many of us, that we have little time for the ordinary offices of life.

You may be assured that I will do Colo. Read [Reed] all the service that I can in the way you desire.[1] We have a Ship here in 6 weeks from London, that brought the original letter of which the inclosed is a copy.[2] Tis from a well informed, sensible friend, and may be relyed on. All the other letters from London join in confirming it to be the fixt determination of K and Court to leave undone nothing that they can do, to compel implicit obedience in America. One very sensible letter that I have seen, mentions that Gen. Amherst had recommended (& 'twas said it would be executed) to remove the Army this winter from Boston to Long Island, in order to get amply supplied by ravaging N. Jersey, N. York, and Rhode Island. Should this be attempted, I suppose you will be furnished with an opportunity of giving them a genteel parting salute. And besides, I should suppose that a winter favorable for us, would expose them to ruin from a timely, strong attack, of superior numbers on that naked Island. It seems that immense stores of Indian goods are sent to Canada in order to bribe the Indians to an early and vigorous attack on all our frontiers next Spring. God grant that Colo. Arnolds success and Montgomeries may frustrate this diabolical part of their infernal plan against the common natural rights of Mankind!

We hoped here that the surrender of Chamble, with the military stores there obtained, would speedily procure the reduction of St. Johns, but no accounts are yet come of this wished event. After Lord Dunmore, supported by the North British Tories, had long committed every outrage at Norfolk unopposed, our people not having Arms or ammunition until lately; his Banditti at length attempted Hampton, where they met with the chastisement you will see described in the part of Dixons paper inclosed.[3] The Lieutenant Wright there mentioned has been since found dead on the Shore, a bullet having been placed in his body before he jumpt over board. We have not yet heard the consequence of their next intended attack, but it seems a very heavy Cannonade was heared there the next day. If the Devil inspired them to come on shore, I make no doubt but we shall have a good account of them. I have a very particular reason for entreating that you will inform me by return of Post, what number, and what strength of Armed Vessels could possibly be procured from the ports where you are, to be in Delaware Bay, if Congress should desire it by the middle or last of December at furthest. Two or 3 Vessels of tolerable force, issuing from hence, may affect a stroke or two of great consequence to us at that Season. We have certainly 4000 weight of powder, and a very considerable quantity of Oznaburgs arrived in Virginia from Statia for the use of our little Army consisting of about 2000 men now at Williamsburg & Hampton.

Be pleased to let Gen. Lee see the letter from England.

I heartily wish you every happiness and all the success the goodness of your cause deserves & I am, with great esteem dear Sir Your affect. friend and obedient Servant. Richard Henry Lee

[*P.S.*] Congress has ordered 500,000 dollars to you soon as they can be signed.[4]

The Continental and Virginia Commissioners have just concluded a treaty of firm friendship with the Ohio Indians and those of the Six Nations that inhabit near that Quarter. We have taken the most effectual measures, by sending Runners from all the Southern provinces into the Indian Nations thro which he proposes to pass to arrest and secure Ld. Dunmores wicked Agent Conelly.[5]

RC (DLC).

[1] Washington had requested Lee's aid in obtaining postponements of legal cases in Philadelphia involving Joseph Reed, the general's secretary. Washington, *Writings* (Fitzpatrick), 4:52. See also Thomas Lynch to Washington, this date.

[2] Dated "Septr. 4th 1775," this letter reports British plans to augment their military forces in America and comments on the king's proclamation against the American rebellion and his refusal to receive the petition of the united colonies. Washington Papers, DLC.

[3] This account of the action at Hampton, Va., October 26–27, is from the *Virginia Gazette* (Dixon and Hunter), October 28, 1775.

[4] See *JCC*, 3:352.

[5] See Francis L. Lee to Landon Carter, October 21, and Virginia Delegates to the Williamsburg Committee of Safety, October 23, 1775.

Thomas Lynch to George Washington

My dear Sir

Phila Nov 13. 1775

In consequence of your Favr. By Colo Read [Reed] I applied to the Chief Justice who tells me the Supreme Courts were lately held and that it will be some time before their Term will return,[1] that he knows of no Capital Suit now depending and that it [*is*] very easy for Colo Read to manage matters so as not to let that prevent his Return to you. I am sure Mr Chew is so heartily disposed to oblige you and to serve the Cause, that nothing in his Power will be wanting. I fear however that you will be sometime in want of your Secretary, as I did not find him in hast to return when I mentioned to him what is just now related. He doubtless has many private affairs to transact. The Loss must be greatly increased by Mr Randolphs absence who I hear came to Town last Night.

I am happy to inform you that Congress has agreed to every Recommendation of the Committee and have gone beyond it in allowing the additional pay to the officers.[2] I rejoice at this but cant think with Patience that pityfull wretches who stood cavilling with you when entreated to serve the next Campaign shoud reap the Benefit of this addition. They will now be ready enough but hope you will be able to refuse them with the Contempt they deserve and to find better in their Rooms. Coud not some of the Gentlemen at Camp inlist the New England Men who have been perswaded to leave you, Frazier told me he coud. It woud be a Capital Point to convince the World that it is not necessary to have bad Officers of that Country in order to raise Men there. I can scarce bear their Tyranny.

I have a Letter from undoubted authority that assures me, that the Destruction of the Parliamentary Army in America will certainly produce Peace and by another that the Seizing Quebec will produce the same Effect. I have no doubt America stands now indebted to her General for the One & will before the Return of Spring for the other. Mistake me not, I have not altered my mind a jot since I left you. I mean not to anticipate your Determinations, but only to approve your Design to hover like an Eagle over your Prey, always ready to Pounce [*on*] it when the proper Time comes; I have not forgot your Proposition relative to that City; I try to pave the way for it, and wait for the Season as you do.[3]

No appearance of Peace unless produced by necessity on the part of the Enemy, every human feeling seems to have forsaken them. Fear and Interest only are listened to.

We hear Seven Tonns of Powder are arrived at Rhode Island & as many at Portsmouth, I hope tis true as it will possess us of advantagious grounds & begin the Enemys Destruction. It is suspected in England Howes Army will give you the slip [*and*] land at Long Island; which God of his infinite mercy grant. We wait with impatience to hear of the total reduction of Canada.

Your Virginians we hear have drubbed L[ord] D[unmore], killed & took 50 Men and sank one of his Vessells. May all such Vilains so perish.

A Mr. Richd. Hare, Brother to the Porter Brewer, sailed in the Transport for Quebec. As you have or must take him let me recommend him to your Civilities while with you, and to send him to his Friends here. His Brother boards Miss Willing on them.

The Articles of War has all the amendments as reported.[4] You will inforce them. You will not now suffer your Officers to sweep the Parade [*with*] the Skirts of their Coats or bottoms of their Trowsers, to cheat or to mess with their Men, to skulk in battle or sneak in Quarters. In short being now paid they must do their Duty & look as well as act like Gentlemen. Do not bate them an Ace, my Dear General, but depend on every Support of your Friends here. I have strove to keep two Battallions now raising in the Jerseys and one here quite disengaged that they may be ready on a call to join you, shoud those you have desert you. I have not been quite unsuccesful.[5] The Winter is our own, Boston will not during that season be reinforced; at least we have reason to think so.

I want the Return I desired from Gates exceedingly. Complts to him, Lee, Putnam, Mifflin &c.

'Tis so dark I cant read this Letter over or I woud save you the trouble of decyphering it. Dear Sir your most Obedt. Serv

Tho Lynch

[*P.S.*] Ought not that Spirit of Independance and of Seperation from all other authority, which appeared in the case of Capt. Dyer to [be?] abolished. Will it be right to keep your Negroes for wood cutters?

RC (DLC).

[1] For an explication of the various references to Joseph Reed in this paragraph, see Washington, *Writings* (Fitzpatrick), 4:123–24. See also Richard Henry Lee to Washington, this date, note 1.

[2] For congressional action on the report of the Committee of Conference, see *JCC*, 3:321–25, 331–34.

[3] On October 24 Washington had consulted with the Committee of Conference about the expediency of a proposal to drive the British army from Boston by subjecting the city to bombardment at a time of year when the harbor was frozen. The committee, mindful of the potential cost in human life and property damage which this plan entailed, hesitated to approve it and instead referred the matter to Congress, where it was decided on December 22 to allow Washington to attack Boston "in any manner he may think expedient, notwithstanding the town and the property in it may thereby be destroyed." See Committee of Conference Minutes, October 24, 1775; and *JCC*, 3:423, 442, 444–45.

[4] See *JCC*, 3:331–34.

[5] To judge from Secretary Thomson's deletion of an entry in the journals, Congress apparently approved and then rescinded, on November 7, a resolution to transfer to the Highlands in New York two battalions recently raised in New Jersey. Since it then decided three days later to send only six companies of this force to the Highlands, Lynch might well have accounted this a success of sorts for his efforts in Washington's behalf. See *JCC*, 3:335, 345.

Roger Sherman's Memorandum of a Conversation

Philadelphia Nov 13th 1775

Mr. James Dean Says that on his passage from Albany to New York on board Capt Legrange's Vessel He heard one Leach a merchant from Schenectady Say, that he Sold some provision to Mr. Walter Livingstone Commissary in the Northern department, for the use of the Army, that Mr. Livingstone produced a Receipt for him to Sign for £24 more than the Sum he was to receive, that he refused to Sign it alledging that it would be unjust, that Mr. Livingstone replied that if he had his due it could be no damage to him and that he would not pay him unless he Signed the receipt. Mr. Leach Said, he Still refused to Sign it, & told the Commissary that he would complain to Congress: but after Some further altercation he told Mr. Livingstone that for one half the extra Sum he would Sign the receipt, which was complied with and the articles of his account altered to correspond with the receipt. Flour was altered from 16/6 to 18/ per Ct., the price of Peas increased to 9d per Bushel and 3d added to the price of each flour Barrel. Mr. Leach mentioned at the Same time another Instance wherein Mr. Livingstone demanded & took a receipt for £8 more than he paid for Some Service done for the public that amounted to about £50. Mr. Leach's due was £200, he Signed a receipt for £224. Captain Legrange & his wife & Mr. James Dean Indian Interpreter were present on board the Vessel and heard the discourse aforesaid.[1]

MS (MWA). In the hand of Roger Sherman, and endorsed by Sherman: "James Dean's Information."

[1] Deane undoubtedly brought these damaging allegations about Commissary Livingston to Sherman's attention because of Sherman's appointment on November 2 to a committee to obtain clothing for General Schuyler's army, but no evidence has been found to indicate that Sherman took any action in response to them. *JCC*, 3:317–18. For an account of Livingston's activities as commissary, emphasizing inefficiency rather than corruption in the northern department, see Victor L. Johnson, *The Administration of the American Commissariat during the Revolutionary War* (Philadelphia: University of Pennsylvania, 1941), pp. 111–24. See also Samuel Adams to Joseph Trumbull, August 3, 1776.

Samuel Ward to Catharine Greene

My dearest Daughter Philadelphia 13 Novr. 1775

I have the Pleasure of your Letter by Dr. Franklin and am thankfull that you & your Family are well.[1] Your first Letter I recd. soon after it was wrote and answered it by the first Opportunity, whether I wrote by Post or a private Hand I cannot remember, But tho it may be unseasonable with Regard to the Advice you asked I promise Myself it will not be unwelcome whenever it arrives. I should often write to You but I am often engaged in Committes Morning & Evening that my Time is so taken up that I cannot indulge myself the Pleasure of writing to you & my other Children so often as I wish. Mr. Greene gave me some Encouragement that he would write to me, a good long Letter would be very acceptable and I shall probably stay here long enough to give you both Opportunities of writing to me. Some Gentlemen think We may at Christmas adjourn until Spring, others think We must sett the whole Winter, affairs grow every Day more serious. May divine Wisdom direct all our Measures.

By the last Ships We have Letters of 9th & 10th Sepr. They all agree in this that the Administration is determined to push their Measures at all Events. One Letter says the King in a Conference which he lately had with a Person of Rank told him that he was unalterably determined let the Consequence be what it would to reduce the Colonies to absolute Obedience. For this Purpose 50 sail of Men of War & 20000 land Forces are to be sent over in the Spring, our maritime Towns to be destroyed & all Commerce interdicted. In one Word those Wicked Madmen are calling not upon Heaven but upon every other Power to assist them in destroying Us. There is now and then a timid Wretch who is frightend with these terrible Denunciations of Vengeance but I have the vast Pleasure to see that instead of intimidating they highly animate, instead of dividing they most strongly unite the People in general and the Congress in particular. We are now all or very nearly all of one Mind, the only Question is how We shall best defend all Parts of the Continent & most effectually distress and annoy our Enemies. Many very important Plans are under Consideration, others will be taken into consideration very soon and from the Spirit with which Measures are now planned & pursued I have no Doubt but by the divine Blessing We shall be able to reduce our Enemies to Reason and establish the Rights and Liberties of this Country upon an equitable advantageous & permanent Basis.

What Fortifications you have at Greenwich I dont know but I wish if they are not sufficient to defend[2] the Town that the People would immediately erect such Works as will defend it against the most savage Enemies for such under the sacred name of Christians the once glorious Name of Englishmen & the endearing Appellation of Brethren We have now to fight. Many Measures are taken by Congress to get a sufficient Quantity of Powder but I fear some of them may fail. The Want of that Article alone may ruin Us; every Measure therefore ought to be taken to obtain it. I hope Mr. Greene & the Com[pan]y may be able in the Course of this Winter to serve the Country in this important Matter without Injury to their private Fortunes. The General Assembly is authorized by Congress to send out Vessels loaded with any produce except horned Cattle, Sheep, hogs & poultry to the foreign West Indies for Powder. If the Comp[an]y has a swift small Vessel I doubt not but the Depy. Govr. would employ them, or if they have Cash or good Bills they may send on their own Acct. for Powder, they cant export produce unless on the Colonys Acct.

I wish Mr. Greene may acquaint your Uncle Greene & the People of Greenwich that every Expectation of an Accommodation is entirely over that our only Safety is under God in a brave Defence of our Lives & Property that they may take every possible Measure for their Defence. Happily We have this Winter to prepare in, the Prize for which We are contending is every thing dear to human Nature, no Time is to be lost, may Heaven direct & prosper us all.

My affectionate Regards to Mr. Greene, to your Uncles Greene & Hubbart, to your Aunt & all their Families & all your Bros. and Familys. I am My dearest Child Your very affece. Parent.

Sam Ward

P.S. The few Lines added by Nany gave me the highest Pleasure. May Heaven grant her again the wise Prayer of Horace "a sound Mind & a sound Body that She may enjoy herself & continue a Blessing to Us all." We have late News from Arnold. He was at Point Levy opposite to Quebec with his detachment all well, the French had been very helpful, Genl. Carleton & Guy Johnston at Montreal that I hope Arnold has met little or no Resistance. I expected to hear St. Johns was taken before now.[3]

RC (MWA). RC (RHi). These two fragments are parts of the same letter.

[1] Catherine Ward Greene (1752–82), Ward's third eldest daughter, was the wife of Christopher Greene (1748–1830), the younger brother of Gen. Nathanael Greene. Ward, *Correspondence* (Knollenberg), pp. 45n.25, 216.

[2] At this point the MWA RC ends, and the rest of the text is taken from the RHi RC.

[3] Congress officially received word of the surrender of St. Johns on November 15, although the messenger who brought these tidings actually arrived in Philadelphia on the previous day. *JCC*, 3:353; and John Adams to Joseph Ward, November 14, 1775.

John Adams to Samuel Osgood

Novr. 14. 1775

I was yesterday favoured with your agreable Letter by Captn. Price, for which as well as a former Letter I acknowledge myself much obliged to you.[1]

In such a Period as this, Sir, when Thirteen Colonies unacquainted in a great Measure, with each other, are rushing together into one Mass, it would be a Miracle, if Such heterogeneous Ingredients did not at first produce violent Fermentations. These ought to be expected, and prepared for by every Man concerned in the Conduct of our Councils or Arms.

I hope the Generals will act with Discernment and Integrity in Seperating those officers who are to be discharged from the rest. But the Reduction of the Regiments cannot be avoided. Our Province had so many more officers than other Colonies in Proportion to their Number of Men, that altho the Congress excused it for the Time passed, in Consideration of the Confusion and Distress of our affairs when the Troops were raised, yet they will not consent that the Inconvenience should continue, now there is Leisure to correct the Error.

I am much concerned at Times on Account of the Pay of the Privates. It is thought here to be very exorbitant—and many Gentlemen are under great Concern about the Consequences. The Expence of the War will accumulate upon the Colonies a Debt, like that of our Enemies. And we have no Funds out of which even the Interest can be paid and our People are not used to Taxes upon the Luxuries, much less upon the Conveniences and Necessaries of Life.

I shall always be obliged to you for Information, which at this distance is much wanted. You may write [*with*] the Utmost Freedom to me, the minutest Partic[ulars]. I shall make no use of such Freedoms to your disadvantage, [. . .] may improve them to the Benefit of the Public. Be carefull however of your Conveyances.

My respectfull Compliments to General Ward and all his Family. I am with much Respect your very huml sert John Adams

RC (NHi).

[1] Samuel Osgood (1748–1813), Andover, Mass., merchant and member of the Provincial Congress, was aide-de-camp to Gen. Artemas Ward, 1775–76, and a delegate to Congress, 1781–84. *DAB*.

John Adams to William Tudor

Dear Sir Novr. 14. 1775

I received your kind Letter of the 28th of Octr. but yesterday.[1] It was such a Letter as I wish all my Friends would write me, as often as possible—that is it was long, full of Intelligence, well written and very entertaining.

I lament the Dishonour which falls upon the Colony by the mean, mercenary Conduct of some of her Servants. But in all Events I hope no Instance of Fraud or Peculation will be overlooked, but Strictly and impartially punished, untill every Rascall is banished from the Army, whatever Colony may have given him Existence.

It behoves the Congress, it behoves the Army to Shew that nothing but a rigid inflexible Virtue, and a Spotless Purity Character, can preserve or acquire any Employment.

Virtue, my young Friend, Virtue alone is or can be the Foundation of our new Governments, and it must be encouraged by Rewards, in every Department civil and military.

Your Account of the Drs. Defence at the Bar of the House is very entertaining.[2] I should have formed no Idea of that Hearing if you had not obliged me, with an Account.

I think with the Candid, that Contempt is due to him for his Timidity and Duplicity. But I cannot wholly acquit him of something worse. He mentions in his Letter his having in a former Letter given his Correspondent a Hint of the Design against Bunkers Hill. Now I never can be clearly freed from Jealousy, untill I see that Letter. The *Hint* he mentions might [have] occasioned [our?] Loss of that Post, and of all the Li[ves] which were destroyed on the 17th of June. However I have hitherto kept my Mind in Suspense.

I wish you would let me know who Bellidore is.[3] What Countryman, and in what Language he wrote—what was his station, Employment and Character.

We must make our young Genius's perfect Masters of the Art of War, in every Branch. I hope America will not long lie under the Reproach of not producing her own officers and Generals, as England has done a long Time.

[*P.S.*] Wearing an Uniform and receiving Pay is not all. I want to see an Emulation among our young Gentlemen, which shall be the most perfect Master of all the Languages and Arts which are subservient to Politicks and War. Politicks are the Science of human Happiness and War the Art of Securing it. I would fain therefore have both perfectly understood.

RC (MHi). In Adams' hand, though not signed.

[1] Tudor's letter is in the Adams Papers, MHi.

[2] Benjamin Church's account of his defense in the Massachusetts House of Representatives, October 28, 1775, and the official records of that meeting are in *Am. Archives,* 4th ser. 3:1479–87.

[3] Bernard Forest de Belidor (1697–1761), French mathematician and artillery expert, published several works on artillery, engineering and fortifications. *Biographie Universelle, Ancienne et Moderne* (Paris: Michaud frères, 1811–62).

John Adams to Joseph Ward

Sir, Philadelphia, Nov'r 14, 1775.

I had yesterday the pleasure of your letter of the 4th inst. by Captain Price, for which, as well as a former kind letter, I heartily thank you.[1]

The report you mention, that Congress have resolved upon a free trade, is so far from being true that you must have seen by the public papers before now that they have resolved to stop all trade untill next March. What will be done then time will discover. This winter I hope will be improved in preparing some kind of defence for trade. I hope the Colonies will do this separately. But these subjects are too important and intricate to be discussed in a narrow compass, and too delicate to be committed to a private letter.

The report that Congress has resolved to have no more connections, &c., untill they shall be indemnified, for the damages done by the tyranny of their enemies, will not be true perhaps so soon as some expect it. Verbal resolutions accomplish nothing. It is to no purpose to declare what we will or will not do in future times. Let reasoning Men infer what we shall do from what we actually do.

The late conduct, in burning towns, so disgracefull to the English name and character, would justify anything, but similar barbarity. Let us preserve our temper, our wisdom, our humanity and civility, though our enemies are every day renouncing theirs. But let us omit nothing necessary for the security of our cause.

You are anxious for Arnold. So are we, and for Montgomery too, untill this day, when an express has brought us the refreshing news of the capitulation of St. Johns—for Arnold I am anxious still—God

grant him success. My compliments to Gen. Ward and his Family.
I am with respect, Your very humble servant, John Adams

MS not found; reprinted from *The Literary World*, 11 (September 18, 1852) : 179. Addressed: "To Joseph Ward, Esq., Secretary to General Ward, Roxbury."

[1] Joseph Ward (1737–1812), Newton and Boston schoolmaster and patriot newspaper essayist, was major and aide-de-camp to Gen. Artemas Ward, 1775–76, and later served as commissary general of musters, 1777–78, and commissary general of prisoners, 1780–83. *JCC*, 7:252, 16:366; and Francis Jackson, *History of the Early Settlement of Newton* (Boston: Stacy and Richardson, 1854), pp. 509–51.

Samuel Adams to James Warren

Dear sir, Philade Nove 14 1775

I wrote to you a few days ago by Fessenden and then promisd to write you again by Dr Morgan who is so obliging as to take the Care of this Letter.[1] The Dr. though not yet arrivd to the Age of forty has long sustaind the Character of learned and is very eminent in the Profession of Physick and Surgery, and I dare say will fill the place to which he is appointed with Dignity. You will find him to be an agreable Acquaintance.

I have not time to write you a long Letter and indeed if I had I ought not to do it, for I believe my last effectually tried your Patience. I will only tell you that, an Account is just come from Virginia, that Dunmore had landed a Number of Men in Hampton whereupon a Scuffle ensued, with the Loss of fifty on his Side, besides the sinking of one of his Tenders. We wait with Impatience for a Confirmation of this Story.

I am in haste Your affectionate Friend S Adams

RC (MeHi).

[1] Dr. John Morgan had been appointed director general of the hospital on October 17. *JCC*, 3:297. See John Adams to James Warren, October 18, 1775, note 1.

Silas Deane to Thomas Mumford

Dear Sir New York Novr. 14th. 1775

I received your's per your Brother just as I was leaving Philadelphia for this place.[1] The Money may be had, and I have in the Course of Our Contracting made a reserve, for the Quantity of that Necessary Article referr'd to in yours, which your Freinds have engaged. It will be best for you to be present with the Committee on making the Contract,[2] but if you can by no Means attend, send instantly the most Circumstantial Account of your proposals & designs.

The Terms most suitable to The Committee are, for you to take up the Vessels, and load them, on Commissions, at risque of the Continent. Your Neighbor contracted in this way,[3] and though I have not the strongest Faith in him, yet I should have appeared singular, had I refused him the Chance, which others obtained, & Mr Alsop was in his favor in the Committee. No Time is to be lost in this Affair. I shall compleat The Business I came here upon,[4] in Two Days more, & then return to Philadelphia. Is there a single Deck'd Vessel in your Neighborhood which will carry Sixteen Gunns? If there is write Me. Can you contract for a Shipp that shall Carry Thirty Nine-pounders to be off the Stocks in March next? This hint will enable you to judge of my Business here, and that you may possibly be of Service to yourself, & Country by coming down to Philadelphia.

I am my Dear sir Yours Silas Deane

RC (Robert J. Sudderth, Jr., Lookout Mountain, Tenn., 1973).

[1] Mumford's letter to Deane of October 19, 1775, is in *Collections of the Connecticut Historical Society* 23 (1930): 11–12.

[2] For the Secret Committee's contract with Mumford, see Secret Committee Minutes of Proceedings, November 28, 1775.

[3] A reference doubtlessly to the Secret Committee's contract with Nathaniel Shaw, Jr., November 8, 1775.

[4] See Naval Committee to Deane, November 7, 1775.

Thomas Lynch to Richard Montgomery

Sir Phila Novr. 14 [1775]

I shoud not break in upon the many weighty Considerations that must always employ your Mind but to request your good offices for a Mr. Richd Hare, who embarked for Quebec in the Transport, we so eagerly wish to meet with. Shoud he come into your hands, be good enough to help him forward to his Friends at this Place, with as many Conveniences as may be.

Mr. Livingston will carry you all the News, except perhaps the opinion of our Friends in England, that the total reduction of Canada this Winter must certainly produce Peace in the Spring.

Ld Dunmore is said to have got a Beating & to have lost one Ship & 50 men, by the Virginian[s].

I wish you success, only in proportion to your Merit. I desire no more & will be contented with no Less for then Canada all Canada is ours. Sir your most Obedt Servt Tho Lynch

RC (PRO: C.O. 5, 1107). Addressed: "To The honble Brigadier General Richd. Montgomery at St. Johns in Canada." Lynch's letter was intercepted by the British and enclosed by Gov. William Tryon of New York in a letter to Lord Dartmouth of December 7, 1775.

John Adams to Abigail Adams

Novr. 15th. 1775

This I suppose will go by Mr. James Bowdoin who has just arrived here from London. He has been very obliging in communicating to me Pamphlets and News Papers in which last I find that some Parts of Novanglus have been retailed out there and have brought on a Battle in the public Papers between Hutchinson and Pounal.[1] Mr. Bowdoin has been to Italy, Holland, France and England and is returned an honest and warm American. He says to his Astonishment, he found the great American Controversy better understood, and the Consequences of it more clearly foreseen in France than in England.

RC (MHi). Adams, *Family Correspondence* (Butterfield), 1:326–27.

[1] For a discussion of this point, see Adams, *Family Correspondence* (Butterfield), 1:327n.2.

John Adams to Richard Henry Lee

Dear Sir Philadelphia Novr 15th. 1775

The Course of Events, naturally turns the Thoughts of Gentlemen to the Subjects of Legislation and Jurisprudence, and it is a curious Problem what Form of Government, is most readily & easily adopted by a Colony upon a Sudden Emergency. Nature and Experience have already pointed out the Solution of this Problem, in the Choice of Conventions and Committees of Safety. Nothing is wanting in Addition to these to make a compleat Government, but the Appointment of Magistrates for the due Administration of Justice.

Taking Nature and Experience for my Guide I have made the following Sketch,[1] which may be varied in any one particular an infinite Number of Ways, So as to accommodate it to the different Genius, Temper, Principles and even Prejudices of different People.

A Legislative, an Executive and a judicial Power, comprehend the whole of what is meant and understood by Government. It is by ballancing each one of these Powers against the other two, that the Effort in human Nature towards Tyranny can alone be checked and restrained and any degree of Freedom preserved in the Constitution.

Let a full and free Representation of the People be chosen for an House of Commons.

Let the House choose by Ballott twelve, Sixteen, Twenty four or Twenty Eight Persons, either Members of the House, or from the People at large as the Elections please, for a Council.

Let the House and Council by joint Ballott choose a Governor, annually, triennially or Septennially as you will.

Let the Governor, Council, and House be each a distinct and independant Branch of the Legislature, and have a Negative on all Laws.

Let the Lt. Governor, Secretary, Treasurer, Commissary, Attorney General and Solicitor General, be chosen annually, by joint Ballott of both Houses.

Let the Governor with Seven Councillors be a Quorum.

Let all officers and Magistrates, civil and military, be nominated and appointed by the Governor, by and with the Advice and Consent of his Council.

Let no officer be appointed but at a General Council, and let Notice be given to all the Councillors, Seven days at least before a General Council.

Let the Judges, at least of the Supreme Court, be incapacitated by Law from holding any share of the Legislative or Executive Power, Let their Commissions be during good Behaviour, and their Salaries ascertained and established by Law.

Let the Governor have the Command of the Army, the Militia, Forts &c.

Let the Colony have a Seal and affix it to all Commissions.

In this Way a Single Month is Sufficient without the least Convulsion or even Animosity to accomplish a total Revolution in the Government of a Colony.

If it is thought more beneficial a Law may be made by this new Legislature leaving to the People at large the Priviledge of choosing their Governor, and Councillors annually, as soon as affairs get into a more quiet Course.

In Adopting a Plan, in some Respects Similar to this, human Nature would appear in its proper Glory asserting its own moral Dignity, pulling down Tyrannies, at a single Exertion and erecting Such new Fabricks, as it thinks best calculated to promote its Happiness.

As you was the last Evening polite enough to ask me for this Model, if such a Trifle will be of any service to you, or any gratification of Curiosity, here you have it, from, sir your Friend and humble servant

John Adams

RC (ViU).

[1] This "Sketch" may have been the origin of Adams' later pamphlet, apparently published at Lee's request, *Thoughts on Government: Applicable to the Present State of the American Colonies* (Philadelphia: John Dunlap, 1776), which was originally drafted in the form of letters to William Hooper, John Penn, Jonathan D. Sergeant, and George Wythe. See Adams, *Diary* (Butterfield), 3:331–32n; Adams, *Works* (Adams), 4:185–93; John Adams to John Penn, March 19–27? 1776; and John Adams to James Warren, April 20, 1776.

John Adams to Samuel Osgood

Sir Novr. 15. 1775

The true Cause why General Frie has not recd from me, any particular Intelligence, is that the Matter has been hitherto Suspended, and that I am under Such Engagements of Secrecy, that I could not in Honour acquaint him with any Thing that has pass'd in Congress.[1]

As Soon as I arrived in Philadelphia, I made it my Business to introduce General Fries Name and Character into Conversation in every private Company where it could be done with Propriety, and to make his long services and Experience known. But I found an Interest making in private Circles in Favour of Coll. Armstrong of Pensilvania, a Gentleman of Character, and Experience in War, a Presbyterian in Religion, whose Name runs high for Piety, Virtue and Valour. What has been done in Congress I must be excused from Saying, but nothing in my Power has been omitted, to promote the Wishes of our Colony or the Honour and Interest of General Frie. It is Sufficient to say, that nothing has as yet been determined. But it will be settled soon. And let it be decided as it may, every good American will acquiese in the Decision.

New England, as you justly observe is the Nursery of brave and hardy Men, and has hitherto Stemmed the Torrent of Tyranny, and must continue to do it, but the other Colonies are making rapid Advances in the military Art, and We must be cautious that we dont hold our own Heads too high, and hold up invidious Distinctions. The other Colonies are capable of furnishing good Soldiers, and they Spare no Pains to emulate New England herself.

You observe that no Tory Province has been So contemned as ours. There may be some ground of Complaint, but have not our People aimed at more Respect than was their due? No other Colony I am fully sensible could have borne the shock as ours has done and it is possible that this Circumstance may have made our People expect more than their due.

It is certainly true that some of our Southern Brethren have not annexed the Same Ideas to the Words Liberty, Honour and Politeness that we have; but I have the Pleasure to observe every day that We learn to think and feel alike more and more.

I am Sorry that the Committee did not dine with General Ward, but am convinced there was no unfriendly Design. The Gentlemen politely told me that the only disagreable Circumstance in their Journey was that they had not Time to cultivate an Acquaintance with Gentlemen in Camp and at Watertown, as they earnestly wished.

Am very Sorry for General Wards ill State of Health, and that this has made him entertain Thoughts of resigning. I cannot think that the Acceptance of the Invitation from the Connecticutt officers, was pointed, or intended as a Slight to General Wards. Perhaps the Connecticutt gentn. might send a Card, which General Ward might omit —or it might be mere Inadvertence or Accident. *A Card is an Engine of vast Importance in this World.* But even if it was designed it is not worth regarding. These Little things are below the Dignity of our glorious Cause, which is the best and greatest that ever engaged the human Mind.

It has been an inexpressible Mortification to me, to observe in So many Instances, the attentions of Gentlemen in high Departments both civil and military, to the little Circumstances of Rank and Ceremony; when their Minds and Hearts ought to have been occupied, by the greatest objects on this side of Heaven.

I have been sufficiently plagued with these Frivolisms myself, but I despise them all, and I dont much revere any Man who regards them.

I wish you to write me often and with Freedom. But you must not be too punctilious in waiting for my answers for I assure you I have more things to do than I am fit for, if I had three Hours where I have one.

I am &c John Adams

[*P.S.*] Your first Letter to me is now before me.

RC (NHi).

[1] Joseph Frye (1712–94), Fryeburg, Mass., storekeeper and veteran of both King George's and the French and Indian Wars, was appointed a major general of Massachusetts militia in 1775. *DAB.* On September 21, 1775, Congress had deferred action on the selection of a brigadier general after evenly dividing between Frye and John Armstrong, Sr. Ultimately Congress appointed Frye a brigadier general on January 10 and named Armstrong to the same rank on March 1, 1776. *JCC,* 3:257, 4:47, 181.

James Duane to Alexander McDougall

Sir Philad. 15t Nov 1775

Upon an Occasion which I shall be at Liberty to mention when we meet, a member took notice in Congress of your not having Joind your Regimen[t] when it was in actual Service and which he conceivd to have been your indispensible Duty. I recollect that in August you told me you proposed to proceed with the last Detachment and that your Stay so long was necessary to forward the Business. I afterwards understood, but indistinctly, that you had been requested to remain in New York by the provincial Convention as it was thought your presence was useful. I mentiond these Circumstances adding that there cou'd be no doubt but that you woud be able to explain

the Reason for not proceeding with the Regiment to the Satisfaction of the most Scrupulous. After informing you of the fact advice must be superfluous as you must immediately see the propriety of getting General Schuyler at a convenient time to report to the Congress the motives of your remaining in Convention instead of taking the Field. I woud not wish this to be done by way of Excuse but in the ordinary Course of Business when the Returns are forwarded.[1] I am Sir your very huml Sert
Jas Duane

RC (NHi).

[1] McDougall, then a colonel in the First New York Regiment, had not joined his troops in the invasion of Canada because John Jay and Philip Schuyler had convinced him that his attendance at the New York Provincial Congress was more important to the revolutionary cause than his presence on the battlefield. Roger J. Champagne, "New York's Radicals and the Coming of Independence," *Journal of American History* 51 (June 1964): 33–34.

Stephen Hopkins to Ruth Hopkins

Beloved Ruth Philadelphia Novr. 15. 1775

This only serves to enclose you an Order on the General Treasurer for Eighty Pounds that was granted me by the Assembly in August last. You will receive this Money for the purchasing of Beef, Pork, Butter, Cheese, Hay, Wood and every other Necessary for the Family. I am in very good Health as your Mother also is wishing we might return to you. When that will be Heaven only Knows.[1]

Step Hopkins

RC (PHi).

[1] Earlier this day Hopkins had written a letter of condolence to Ruth on the occasion of the disappearance at sea of her husband, Hopkins' youngest son, George. "Long Ago Should I have Wrote You," Hopkins began, "had I known how to Write, or what to Say: A feeling Father Mourning for the loss of a hopeful Son, how Can I write Comfortably to a beloved Daughter deprived of a tender Husband." NjHi.

Samuel Adams to James Bowdoin, Sr.

Sir, Philadel. Nove 16 1775

I embrace this opportunity of writing to you by your Son, whose unexpected Arrival from London the last Week gave me much Pleasure. He seems in a great Degree to have recoverd his Health, and I dare say it will be still more satisfactory to you to find, that he is warmly attachd to the Rights of his Country and of Mankind. Give me Leave to congratulate you, and also to express to you the Joy I feel on another Occasion; which is, that your own Health is so far restord to you, as to enable you again, and at so important a Crisis, to aid our Country with your Council. For my own part, I had even buried you, though I had not forgot you. I thank God who has disappointed our Fears; and it is my ardent Prayer that your Health may be perfectly restord and your eminent Usefulness long continued.

We live my dear Sir, in an important Age—An Age in which we are called to struggle hard in Support of the publick Liberty. The Conflict, I am satisfied, will the next Spring be more severe than ever. The Petition of Congress has been treated with insolent Contempt. I cannot conceive that there is any room to hope from the virtuous Efforts of the People of Britain. They seem to be generally unprincipled and fitted for the Yoke of arbitrary Power. The opposition of the few is feeble and languid—while the Tyrant is flushd with Expectations from his Fleets and Armies, and has, I am told, explicitly declared, that, "Let the Consequences be what they may, it is his *unalterable* Determination, to *compel* the Colonists to *absolute* Obedience."

The Plan of the British Court, as I was well informed the last Winter, was to take Possession of New York, make themselves masters of Hudsons River and the Lakes, cut off all Communication between the Northern and Southern Colonies, and employ the Canadians upon whom they greatly relyd, in distressing the Frontiers of New England. Providence has smiled upon our Northern Expedition. Already St Johns is reducd, and if we gain the Possession of all Canada this Winter, of which there is a fair Prospect, Their Design, so far as it respects this Part of their Plan, will be totally frustrated.

I will not further trespass upon your Time. If you can find Leisure, a Letter from you will exceedingly oblige me, for you may believe me when I assure you that I am with the greatest Esteem, your Friend, and very humble Servant, S A

RC (MHi).

Samuel Chase to John Adams

My Dear Sir. Baltimore Town. Nov. 16th. 1775

I am well assured that a Supply of Powder is arrived at Statia, so writes Captain Waters on 10th October. A Dutch Vessell bound to Surrinam has contracted with a Captain of this place for twenty five Tons, if he comes for it by Xmas.

I have seen several of the principal Gentn. here.[1] They are wishing for the Destruction of Lord Dunmore and his fleet. Inclosed You receive the Terms on which two Vessells can be procured here. The first I am well assured is very reasonable. The province have 15 6-pounders, and the Merchants here will furnish a Ton of Gunpowder for that Expedition. If either of the vessells should be accepted, write to Robert Alexander Esqr. of this Town.

My Compliments to your worthy Colleagues Yr. obedt. Sevt.

S Chase

RC (MHi).

[1] Adams was appointed on October 30 to the committee to prepare armed vessels "for the protection and defense of the united Colonies," which gradually assumed the status of a standing committee and had recently dispatched Silas Deane to New York to purchase vessels for that purpose. *JCC,* 3:311–12; and Naval Committee to Silas Deane, November 7, 1775. Apparently Chase, who had been elected by Anne Arundel County as a delegate to the Maryland Convention scheduled to convene December 7, was also to procure information for the committee and to dispatch his findings to Adams for its use. In a second letter written nine days later, Chase repeated his belief that a brig could be obtained at Baltimore at a reasonable price. "The Owner is waiting your Answer," he continued. "I therefore beg You to send the Determination of the Committee to Mr. Robert Alexander of that Town." Chase to John Adams, November 25, 1775, MHi. See also Benjamin Harrison to Wilson Miles Cary, December 10, 1775.

Joseph Hewes to Samuel Johnston

Dear Sir Philadelphia 16 Nov 1775

Since I wrote last several ships have arived from England and brought accounts to the 14th of September. They also brought Letters for a number of Persons inimical to our cause; many of these Letters have been opened by the Committee of Safety by which we find the Ministry are determined to carry on the War against American Rebels with the utmost Vigor. I saw a Letter from a Member of Parliament to Docr. Franklin mentioning that Gen. Haldiman had been Closeted by the King who was very particular in his enquiry what sort of people the Americans were, how did they Collect an Army together, how furnish them with arms & amunition, how Cloath, pay & Victual them &c. To these and a great number of questions of the like kind he received such Answers as gave him great uneasiness. It seems the Reduction of America is a favourite plan of his own; he has declared he will pawn all the Jewels of his Crown in order to effect it. You will see by the papers our Troops have taken Fort Chamblee and St. Johns in Canada. We expect Montreal & Quebec are ours by this time. Some of the late Letters from London mention a Number (say 5000) of Troops will be immediately sent to make a diversion in the Southern Colonies. From all the Accounts I have seen I think it would be very imprudent to discharge any of your Soldiers, Congress seems to be very well satisfied that they are raised. There are no Arms nor any Powder to be got here. You may be supplied with some Powder from South Carolina, Arms you must get in your own Province if possible. You must encourage the making of them; pray do not discharge either of your Regiments till you hear further from your Delegates.

I am in haste Dr Sir Your very huml Servant

Joseph Hewes

N.B. The packet for M Smith was to have gone by a return express from Charlestown but he went to[o] high up the Country. If Smith is not with you when it reaches you pray open it.

RC (DLC).

Naval Committee to Silas Deane

Sir Philadelphia 16th Novr. 1775

We received yours of yesterday and observe the Contents,[1] and think if you can procure two Vessells that are properly capable of carrying sixteen six pounders each, and can be procured on reasonable terms and fitted, either in New York or Connecticut, in such manner as they may be able to enter Delaware Bay with proper Arms, Ammunition and stores for four months, and manned with good seamen and Landmen within one month from this time, we advise you to purchase them and equip them.[2]

If you should purchase and undertake to equip these Vessels, give us notice by the first opportunity that we may govern ourselves accordingly.

By order of the Committee I am Sir Your humble servant

Step Hopkins

RC (CtHi). Written in a clerical hand and signed by Stephen Hopkins.

[1] Not found.

[2] See Naval Committee to Deane, November 7, 1775.

Samuel Ward to Henry Ward

Dear Bror. Philadelphia 16th Novr. 1775

I am obliged to You for your Favor of the 7th. The judicious and decisive Conduct of the General Assembly does great Honor to the Colony. I had that Part of your Letter containing those Proceedings read in Congress; they were highly approved.[1] Mr. Adams, Colo.

Dyre & others observed afterwards to me that We had sett them all a noble Example.

I hope Mr. Cooke is in the Chair before this Time, present my most affectionate & respectful Congratulations upon the Occasion. I hope some Gentleman who is a zealous Friend to the Liberties of his Country and who hath Sense & Spirit enough to see and pursue her true Interests at all Hazards supplies his Place.

I could have wished that the Colony instead of another Emission had directed Us to apply to Congress for the Sum wanted though the Accts. were not ready.[2] Connecticut did so & obtained it and We should without Doubt have been allowed what We wanted. I fear too great a Flood of Bills may affect their Credit and of all things We should be most careful to keep up the Credit of our Money. While that is done We can raise any Supplies for the common Defence, without it We should be vastly embarrassed.

The Gentn. who may attend with the Accts. of the Comee. of Safety I shall be most heartily glad to see and they may spend their Time here very agreably but I must confess I can have no Idea of the Accts being so intricate as to make it absolutely necessary that they should at this advanced Season take so much Trouble but it will answer this good End if there should be any Money in the Treasury to pay us with they can take it home with them perhaps in a cheaper Manner than We could find it. The Treasury is almost empty but another Emission will be made soon.

I most cordially congratulate You upon the happy Reduction of St. Johns, the Papers give you most of the particulars. Genl. Montgomeries Letter says that he was immediately setting out for Montreal and mentioning the Repulse of Carleton he adds that He beleives it to be his last Effort (No News of Arnold). A Committee with Powers nearly similar to those given the Comee. which was at Cambridge is sett out for Ticonderoga & Canada, the Gentn. are Mr. Langdon, Mr. Robt. R Livingston & Mr. Paine. They have some Instructions relative to the particular Situation of the Canadians besides those concerning the Troops.

Mr. Hopkins & Lady are very well. I have seen many Letters from England since my last; they all agree in the Acc[oun]ts I then gave you. In a Conference which the King had with a Person from America He told him that he was unalterably determined let the Consequence be what it would to compel the Colonies to absolute Obedience. Thank God his Power does not equal his Obstinacy & Pride. Our Instructions for an American Fleet has been long upon the Table; when it was first presented it was looked upon as perfectly chimerical, but Gentn. now consider it in a very different Light. It is this Day to be taken into Consideration & I have great Hopes of carrying. Dr. Franklin, Colo. Lee, the two Adams & many others will support it; if it succeeds I shall remember your Idea of our building two of the Ships; Duty calls Me away. Proper Regards to all. Your most affece. Bror. Sam Ward

RC (RHi).

[1] Henry Ward's letter of November 7 has not been found, but the proceedings of the Rhode Island Assembly for the session of October 31, which were apparently described in his letter, are in John R. Bartlett, ed., *Records of the Colony of Rhode Island and Providence Plantations in New England,* 10 vols. (Providence: A. Crawford Greene, 1856–65), 7:375–408.

[2] The Rhode Island Assembly had resolved "that £20,000, lawful money bills, be immediately printed," to help pay off the province's public debt. Ibid., p. 389.

John Hancock to Walter Livingston

Sir, Philada. Novr. 17th. 1775

The Congress having resolved that the Prisoners taken at Chambly and St. Johns be sent to the Towns of Reading, Lancaster & York in the Colony of Pennsylvania; and having issued Orders to the Officer who has the Charge of conducting them to march them by the nearest Road to the Town of Reading in said Colony, and to apply to you for Provisions for Subsistance on their March, I am directed to order you to supply them agreeably to the Rations given to the Continental Army.[1]

I am further to direct you, if the Prisoners agree to it, to send the Women, Children and Baggage by Water to Amboy, from thence to be sent across to Borden-Town, and from thence by Water to Philada.; from which last Place they will be sent to join the Garrison in the Towns allotted them—this being judged, the safest, cheapest, and most commodious Way of conveying them.

Should the Express not meet the Party with the Prisoners, please to take the Letter, and deliver it to the Commanding Officer, on his Arrival with the Prisoners at Albany.[2] I am &c J. H. Prest.

LB (DNA: PCC, item 12A). Addressed: "To Walter Livingston Esqr. Deputy Com[missary] General."

[1] Hancock wrote this day to the officer in charge of the British prisoners who surrendered to American forces at Chambly and St. Johns, directing him "to march the Prisoners under your Command by the nearest Way to Reading in the Colony [*of Pennsylvania*]; and for their Subsistance on their March, you are to apply to the Commissary General." *Am. Archives,* 4th ser. 3:1588; and *JCC,* 3:358.

[2] Hancock also sent a letter this day to the Committee of Safety at Trenton, the destination of the British commissioned officers taken at Chambly, enclosing a congressional resolve of this date directing that these officers "be put on their parole of honour" to remain in the vicinity of Trenton and to "carry on no

political correspondence whatever, on the subject of the dispute between Great Britain and these Colonies." *Am. Archives*, 4th ser. 3:1588; and *JCC*, 3:359.

George Ross to James Wilson

Dear Wilson Reading 17th Novr. 1775

I am extreamly sorry I did not see you before I left Philada.[1] My going by Chester occasioned my Missing you on the Road.

I can't help saying Heaven seems to Smile on & favour the great Cause of Liberty. Our Successes have been equal to our most sanguine hopes And I think nothing but our own misconduct can prevent our Triumphing over the Enemies of America. I fear the late Instructions to the Delegates will have very fatal consequences; pray tell me what is generally thought of them.[2]

A Reason seems necessary to be given why I did not write to you by your messenger to Fort Pitt. The real truth is I did write but the Boy went off without my knowledge. I thought & still think the Congress did not use you or Mr. Morris well by not sending an Answer but we could get nothing done with the Gent. of Virginia. I beg to hear from you & shall be impatient for a letter.

Mr. Broadhead whose spirit you know as well as General Character wants to have an appointment in the Battalion now raising as a field officer.[3] He will wait on you. If you think him a proper person shall be glad you will afford him your friendship. I am with great sincerity Your Affect Friend & Hble Servt. Geo. Ross

P.S. Mr. Hartley requested you would Interest yourself in his behalf should an opportunity offer to procure him an Appointment, of the Rank of a Field Officer.[4] You know him to be an Early & Active Associator.

RC (PHi). Addressed: "To James Willson, Esquire, Philada. Per favour of Col. Broadhead."

[1] Ross, who divided his time between Congress and the Pennsylvania Assembly during the latter's October–November 1775 session, was not reelected to Congress on November 4. *Pa. Archives*, 8th ser. 8:7347.

[2] See John Dickinson's Proposed Instructions, November 9, 1775; and Samuel Chase to John Adams, December 8, 1775.

[3] Daniel Brodhead (1736–1809) of Reading, deputy surveyor-general of Pennsylvania, received a lieutenant colonel's commission in Miles' Pennsylvania Rifle Battalion in March 1776, was active in the 1776 and 1777 campaigns, and eventually played a prominent role in military operations on the western frontier. *DAB*.

[4] Thomas Hartley (1748–1800), who was commissioned lieutenant colonel in the Sixth Battalion of the Pennsylvania Line, January 10, 1776. *DAB*. Ross later wrote a letter to Franklin recommending Hartley. Ross to Benjamin Franklin, December 10, 1775, MA.

John Adams to Abigail Adams

November 18. 1775[1]

Your kind Letter of the 5th. Inst. came to Hand yesterday by Captain McPherson. I admire your skill in Phisiognomy, and your Talent at drawing Characters, as well as that of your Friend Marcia from whom at the same Time I received several important Characters, which you shall one day see.

I agree with you in your sentiments that there is Reason to be diffident of a Man who grossly violates the Principles of Morals, in any one particular habitually.[2] This sentiment was conveyed to Us in one of the Paradoxes of the ancient Stoicks, that "all sins were equal," and the same Idea is suggested from higher Authority, He that violates the Law in any one Instance is guilty of all. I have no Confidence in any Man who is not exact in his Morals. And you know that I look upon Religion as the most perfect System, and the most awfull Sanction of Morality.

Your Goodness of Heart, as well as your sound Judgment will applaud me for using the utmost Caution in my Letters. But if you could see me, and observe how I am employed you would wonder that I find Time to write to any Body. I am very busy and so is every Body else here.

I hope to be with you at Christmas, and then to be excused from coming here again, at least until others have taken their Turns.

The late Appointment you mention gives me many very serious Thoughts.[3] It is an Office of high Trust, and of vast Importance at any Time: But of greater at this, than any other. The Confusions and Distractions of the Times, will encumber that Office with embarrassments, expose it to dangers and Slanders, which it never knew before. Besides I am apprehensive of other Difficulties. Mr. [William] Cushing has been on that Bench, and was my senior at the Bar. Will he accept under another? Mr. Paine too has taken an odd Turn in his Head of late, and is so peevish, passionate and violent that he will make the Place disagreable, if he does not think better of it. Mr. Cushing, Mr. Serjeant [Sargeant] and Mr. Read are very able Men, and Mr. Paine might be so if he was undisturbed in his Mind. But the Unhappy Affair in his Family, his Church and Town, appears to me to have affected his Mind too much. It is a melancholly Thought to me, because I have ever had a Friendship for him. I am really sorry that he has exposed his Character and Reputation so much of late as he has done, by certain Airs he has given himself, and it has many Times, in the beginning of the summer, when I was in an ill state of Health made me unhappy. But since the Adjournment, I have avoided Altercation with him, and this I shall continue to do.

That Ambition and Avarice reign every where as you observe, is

George Ross

most true. But I hope that Preferment will follow Merit, after our Affairs get into a more settled Course.

Remember me to all.

When you said that Kissing goes by Favour, you did not explain the Particulars I wish you had. But all Censure and Clamour at this Time must be avoided and discountenanced as much as possible.

I should be glad to be informed, whether the Appointment of me, that you speak of, appears to be to the satisfaction of the People or not.

RC (MHi). Adams, *Family Correspondence* (Butterfield), 1:327–28.

[1] Congress did not meet on November 18, the only Saturday it failed to sit while in session before February 3, 1776. *JCC*, 3:359. No explanation accompanied this decision—and Adams' letter to Abigail, which is silent on the point, is the only document found that was written by a delegate on this date—but see Caesar Rodney to Thomas Rodney, November 27, 1775, note 1.

[2] Dr. Benjamin Church's apostasy stimulated Adams to several discussions on this subject.

[3] Adams accepted an appointment as chief justice of the Massachusetts Superior Court of Judicature a few days later, but never took his seat on the bench. He resigned the post early in 1777. See Adams to Perez Morton, November 24, 1775; and Adams, *Works* (Adams), 3:23–25. Adams' fears that his appointment might arouse jealousies among more senior members of the bar proved to be well founded. See Robert Treat Paine to Joseph Palmer, January 1, 1776.

Francis Lewis to John Alsop

Dr Sir Phila. 19 Novemr. 1775

I have been favored with both your Letters of 15th & 17th Inst.[1] From the little encouragemt given me in your former relative to your procuring the necessary supplys for the Northen Army, induesed me to exert my faculties for procuring all I could here and consequently encreased the orders but your last letter informs me that you have engaged a large quantity at New York both which will I fear greatly exceed the quantity order[ed] by Congress. Therefore I think it would be advisable not to forward more to Albany than wd (with what I have sent from hence, engaged & sent from New York) compleat the order of Congress for that department; at foot you have a list of what I sent from New York, what have sent from hence and what more is to be sent from hence.

As a member of the Committe for the Army supplys at Cambridge, we have directions for several articles to be there, so that such arti[c]les as appears more in quantity engaged than is ordered for the Northen Army, may be apply'd to the Cambridge supply. Indeed the two Jersey Battalions will be glad to take any overpluss that may be; must observe this to you that at Cambridge they are sup-ply'd with shoes & stockings in the vicinage. I had directed Hayman Levy to engage several articles which he informs me has done, of which I apprehend my son did not inform you. I shall pay Mr. Ph. Livingston £250 on your Accot. and Send you some Dollars but must call upon the Treasuary to enable me.

My son will shew you a list of what articles Colo. Mifflin request the Committee to supply the Army in his department by which you'l judge of what may be stoped from the Northen Supplys now at New York. Be carefull we dont exceed our orders.

Thursday last I sent from hence in two Waggons for Dobbs Ferry Ten Casks & Eight Bales of Cloathing Markd N. These are the Goods we purposed sendg via Amboy but Congress would not risque it that way therefore order'd it by land to Dobbs Ferry. We shall send off another Waggon load on Tuesday next. You'l please to give directions that an Albany sloop be sent to Dobb's Ferry in order to take these Goods on board and to return a Receipt of the Packages.

Our Congress is greatly decreased in Number. Our Coloney, the Jerseys & Georgia have not been represented since you left us and other Colonies occasionaly so that business goes on heavily. I have lately purchased sixty one Pieces of Yorkshire Cloth; pray would it not be best sending those Cloths to Nw York and have them made up there according to Col. Mifflins directions. If you think so let me know per first. I am, Dr Sir your very Humble Servt

Frans Lewis

Resolve of Congress for Northen Departmt.

3 ms. Felt. Hatts .. Supplyed from hence .... 800 hatts .. more bespoke
3 ms. Worsted Caps .... none
3 ms. pair Buckskin Breeches .... 600 pr.
3 ms. pr. Shoes .... 1000 pr.
3 ms. pr. Yarn stockgs. .... 3384 pr.
3 ms. warm Wastcoats .... suppose .... 1000.

Course Woolen Goods vizt Strouds, Tearnots, Duffills &c. which are allready sent up in Bales to the amount of abt. £600.

P.S. As Mr Hayman Levy who brings you this has allready procurd for me several Articles believe you'l find him usefull if you shd think fitt to imploy him.

I have sent y[ou] by Mr Levy Thirty two Sheets at 118 Dollars each is 3776 Dollrs. Please acknowledge the receipt.

RC (NHi). Addressed: "To John Alsop Esqr per Mr Levy—New York."

[1] Not found. See Francis Lewis' Memorandum on Clothing, November 2–10? 1775, note.

Thomas Lynch to Ralph Izard

Dear Sir: November 19, 1775.

Having much to say to you, I begin, before I certainly know how this is to reach you.[1]

I had your favor by a young gentleman whom I shall take every opportunity to endeavor at least to serve. I think it is abundantly his due.

You have had accounts of the battle at Bunker's Hill; the loss on the part of the Regulars, is near the truth; on the other, greatly exaggerated[. . . .][2]

You wonder, with many others, that an Army so superior as ours, have not recovered Boston—and demolished the little Army of *Rebels* therein. You know, Boston. Recollect my friend that it is surrounded by the sea, except a very narrow causeway—that the enemy is master of the sea—that this only entrance by land is fortified to the utmost extent of art—work within work—defended by Cannon, and rendered impassable by deep diches—that the whole city is commanded by two steep, and high hills, each of which is fortified on the ascent, and a little Citadel at the top, with guns that reach everywhere. Recollect that thirty-two Battalions of choice British Troops, (or half her Army) occupy those works—that this Army has every advantage that Arms, Artillery, and plenty of ammunition can give. Add their being under the best Officers Britain can boast—and add, that our men are young Soldiers, and want that steadiness necessary to the attack of Trenches with bare Musketry—which long discipline alone can give. Consider that the business of the Enemy is to subdue America, and while they are imprisoned in Boston, their errand stands still—that they are every day perishing by disease, want, and desertion—all which must increase as winter cuts off their resources by sea—and I mistake if you will not own, that our Generals act wisely in not risking a repulse, or loosing a number of brave men in obtaining *that*—which a little time must give them, without loss, and make total and conclusive when it happens.

Should Howe, be driven to his ships in summer, he will easily land in some other part, and begin new trouble. Ice prevents all this.

Be assured, that our strength at Boston, by means of Fortifications, is such as leaves no doubt of our security. I wish the strength of Howe's Army, joined to all that we are threatened with next year, were to try an attack there—and that the fate of the War depended on the event. I should think fifty thousand men would inevitably be defeated in such an attempt. I have been lately at Cambridge, and speak from what I have seen. I have also, very lately, been at our Camp on the Lakes.

Have we not, my dear sir, great reason to bless God, for all his abundant mercies, on this occasion. Consider America, lulled in a long state of peace, and security. Where were we to look for Armies —more especially for Generals—attacked suddenly, and under cover of friendship, and protection, by the most powerful nation in the world, who, not content with her superiority of strength, calls in all other nations to her assistance, uses art—as well as force—to provoke attacks from our neighbours, calls in Savages to ravage our frontiers, to massacre our defenceless women and children, offers every incitement to our Slaves to rebel and murder their masters, ravage and burn our unfortified sea-coast. Behold, on the sudden, this distressed, unprepared people roused—behold Armies raised—and still more strange—under the command of veteran Officers, not only securing our Enemy from ravaging our country, but carrying War into every place where an Enemy can be found.

The people so earnestly pressed to attack us, refusing every act, every force; our Indians keeping up peace, against all acts used to detach them from us, by lies, calumnies, and interest. Our Slaves remaining faithful—against the promise even of liberty, dearest—best —of all rewards. Behold two entire British Battalions, for the first time in her history prisoners of war—besides those in Boston—nay, what is still stranger—the coast of New England—scoured by Privateers—unmolested, and supplies to the army cut off. Could our most sanguine hopes, have gone so far last spring? Yet blessed be God all this is the case.

Abused—belied—discarded—destroyed—with a rage, and malice altogether unknown, to civilized, or even barbarous nations' of this day—can it be credited—that America still languishes for reconciliation? Thus impregnable–thus prosperous, in every attempt–that she rises not a single jot in her terms of accommodation—that she even in sight of her unoffending towns, now in ashes—demands not restitution—nor reimbursement? Surely our worst enemies, must confess —that of all people we are the most placable, mild, and forgiving. That this is the case, you may be sure—no new demand would be made on our part. Peace and reconciliation, upon the one condition, we have ever asked it, viz.: Restitution of Rights, would be received as the greatest blessing.

I objected when our last petition was before Congress—that using such lowly, and humiliating expressions, would produce, in narrow minds, an opinion of our weakness. I was not mistaken. I find that thought in papers and letters from the other side—as if boasting were a proof of anything but the bully[. . . .]

From all this you will find such a departure from every rule of war, among even barbarous states, as very little entitle them to such terms, as you will observe them receive from our gallant General, in the enclosed Capitulation—every article of which is religiously observed on our side.[3]

Let them boast of their greatness—of the arts of Kingcraft, of Policy—be it ours, to be faithful, humane, and affectionate to our prostrate Foes. Let us treat them like the Individuals, of a Nation, with whom we do not consider ourselves at war—but rather as Defenders from Tyranny and Oppresion. Should the Slaves of those Monsters, add Injury to oppression, I hope we shall always act, like brave, humane, and Polite Victors.

It gives me great pleasure to be able to enclose you an account of the reduction of Montreal[4]—and the greater part of Canada[. . . .]

Pray remark that no rejoicings have been permitted, though the advantages we have gained are so important—even the consideration of their having been obtained with so little Blood, has not been sufficient, to make us forget, that we were conquering our Brethren—let them blush who have forgotten this.

I wish Britain would adopt the measure—of calling a Convention of Delegates, from the Assemblies of each Colony—by act of Parliament. I shall readily adopt the measure, we quarrel not about words.

While you are at home, can't you send us ship loads of Powder; Our Saltpetre does not come in fast enough; 'twill fetch a great price, and be a very beneficial Trade, to France, Holland, or any other Nation, who will get valuable returns, in Provisions for their West Indies.

If you meet with inaccuracies you'll pardon them in so long a letter, from one who really has not an hour in the day at his own disposal[. . . .]

I fear I shall stay here all winter. I will not desert the Assembly here, while it lasts, be the season ever so disagreeable, or my stay inconvenient.

I shall be always happy in your Friendship and correspondence, and shall certainly answer every letter I receive, which was not the case of that, sent before the last.

My family's most respectful compliments, attend you, and yours. You know the hand of Dear sir, yours sincerely and Affectionately.

P.S. I was in hopes, we should have availed ourselves of your abilities, and Integrity. Don't suspect I asked it. Could you sound, and find out, the sentiments of those who have the power to help us, particularly of those, who could send us necessaries, for war, and coarse goods, in exchange for our Productions. No Custom House dare touch them, and Men-of-War are easily avoided, the Trade would be amazingly profitable.

Ten of the Troops from Ireland are arrived; there has been a dreadful storm, which is said to have destroyed many of the Transports, with almost the whole Fish, and Fishery of Newfoundland.

Howe's Army must be very weak, for they suffered Lee to take possession of Cobble Hill, a few days ago—which being within half cannon shot, of their lines, and commanding Lechmere's Point, where they last landed, gave them as good an opportunity as they could wish, of forcing our Army to a Battle, on equal terms—this Point being full as near, and as much exposed to their Artillery, as ours; strong necessity urging them also, want of Provisions, having brought on scurvy, and other dreadful diseases, and their lines thinning every day, by death, and desertion, all could not bring them out. Deserters say there is much discontent among the men, and that the Officers are obliged to lie, in order to quiet them, by assuring them, of an immediate Reinforcement of three thousand Men, when they know, none such is coming.

I had the pleasure of entertaining the Commanding Officer of St. John's yesterday, and of ordering the disposition of two Regiments of British Troops. While we are called, and treated as Barbarians, their prisoners have every indulgence possible. In this, may we always be their superiors.

The ways are at this season, so impracticable, that we have no late accounts from Quebec.

Gun-lock makers, in any number, skilful Saltpetre makers, and Powder makers, would be very acceptable—they are to be got in Germany.

MS not found; reprinted from Ralph Izard, *Correspondence of Mr. Ralph Izard of South Carolina, from the Year 1774 to 1804; with a Short Memoir*, ed. Anne Izard Deas (New York: Charles S. Francis & Co., 1844), pp. 151–59.

[1] Izard was in England when this letter was written.

[2] Ellipses here and below in Deas Tr.

[3] Doubtless a reference to the Articles of Capitulation agreed upon between General Montgomery and Maj. Charles Preston for the surrender of St. Johns on November 2.

[4] Lynch's references here to an account of the reduction of Montreal—which was read in Congress on November 29—and in the postscript below to the taking of Cobble Hill—which occurred on November 23—suggest that a considerable period elapsed between the time he began and the time he completed this letter, or that Deas constructed this text from more than one document.

Francis Lightfoot Lee to Landon Carter

My dear Colonel Philadelphia Novr. 20 1775

I wrote to Col. Tayloe two or three days agoe, from whome I suppose you have had the news, and intended by Mr. Colston to answer your last letter; but an express from the Camp last night having brot fresh intelligence I take the advantage of tomorrow's post to communicate it to you. The transports from Ireland with five Regiments compleat have arrived at Boston, a fishing boat with 6 muskets took a schooner belonging to the fleet loaded with provisions for the officers, in her were many letters by which we learn that the Roman Catholic Lords, Bishops & Gentry are extreamly active in procuring recruits; the Protestants very averse to the business, many recruiting parties driven out of their towns, and even the lower class of Catholics show great dislike to it, but with the high premiums given by the Popish towns &c many recruits are raised, & it is expected as many will be raised as will compleat the number entended for the next campaign, which they say is 22,000. 5,000 Hanoverians are to garrison Gibralter & Port Mahon, the British regiments there to go to England & Ireland. I will not anticipate your reflection upon these infamous proceedings of the Ministry, but I think he must be blind indeed who does not see the design of establishing arbitrary Government in America; and unworthy the name of man, who does not oppose it, at all hazard. The establishment of Popery will no doubt, be the reward of the exertions of the Roman catholics. We do not think the whole of these raw Irish will make a dinner for our troops. Our only fear is the want of ammunition, but we hope to be releived from that before next spring. Our cutters have taken two more of their caitering Vessels, one loaded with wood the other with provisions. 600 of the enemy made a sally out of Boston to carry off some cattle but a few of our men quickly repulsed them, with the loss of two of their men. We have heard of Arnolds being in Canada & recd. with open arms by the inhabitants, so we expect that Quebec & of course the whole Province is ours by this time. So much for news.

I am glad to find that amidst all the breeches button making in Virga. & in spite of the Cholic you keep up your spirits; & therefore hope you have defeated all the party schemes in Richmond. Lord Dunmore seems to be a little quiet since the taste of Virga. prowess at Hampton; we expect that Col. Woodford will keep him to his good behaviour at Norfolk. Pray remember me to all my friends, present my best respects to my friend Mr. Carter & his Lady, & believe me allways yr. aftn. hble Sert Francis Lightfoot Lee

RC (ViHi).

Thomas Jefferson to Francis Eppes

Dear Sir Philadelphia Nov. 21. 1775.

After sealing my last letter to you we received an account of the capture of St. John's which I wrote on the letter. What I there gave you was a true account of that matter. We consider this as having determined the fate of Canada. A Committee of Congress is gone to improve circumstances so as to bring the Canadians into our Union. We have accounts of Arnold as late as Octob. 13. All well and in fine spirits. We cannot help hoping him in possession of Quebec as we know Carleton to be absent in the neighborhood of Montreal. Our armed vessels to the northward have taken some of the ships coming with provisions from Ireland to Boston. By the intercepted letters we have a confirmation that they will have an army of four or five and twenty thousand there by the spring. But they will be raw teagues. 3000. are lately arrived there. I have written to Patty a proposition to keep yourselves at a distance from the alarms of Ld. Dunmore. To her therefore for want of time I must refer you and shall hope to meet you as proposed. I am Dr. Sir with my best affections to Mrs. Eppes Your friend & servt., Th: Jefferson

Reprinted from Jefferson, *Papers* (Boyd), 1:264.

Francis Lewis to John Alsop

Dr Sir Phila. 21 Novemr. 1775

I wrote you Yesterday per Express to which reffer you. Last night (and not before) I obtained an Account of the Cost of such Articles as our Agent here bought up for the use of the Northen Army, of which is an Inclosed Copy which I must desire you would forward with the utmost expedition possible to the Commissary at Albany. The Inclosed Invoice is very incorrect but time will not permit me to new modle it.

You'l please to write Mr Walter Livingston. The inclosed points out the quantity & first cost of the several Articles and that it behoves him to have them carefully examined by the Invoice and the more so as this very Agent of ours (Aeroyd) has been deficient 6 p[iece]s of Coating in a parcell of Woolens sent to Cambridge as appears by the Quater Masr. General's return to the Committee. You'l also advise Mr Livingston after examining the several Articles that he make a return thereof to our Committee, and that in supplying the Troops he add to the first cost a sufficiency to reimburse Congress for the cost, Commissns. & all other incident charges. You'l also observe that the persons charge whom we imploy'd is not yet assertained.

Pray let me know as soon as possible the quantity and amount of the Cloathing engaged by you, and those Articles that (from both places) appear to be more than the quantity limitted for the Northward, I think should be retained for the Troops at Cambridge. I am Dr. Sir. Your very Humbl Servt Frans Lewis

[*P.S.*] We have no news here.

RC (NHi).

Robert Morris and John Dickinson to Oswell Eve

Sir Philada. Novr. 21st 1775

I am requested by some Honorable Members of the Congress to recommend the bearer hereof Mr. Paul Revere to you.[1] He is just arrived from New England where it is discovered they can manufacture a good deal of Salt Petre in Consequence of which they desire to Erect a Powder Mill & Mr. Revere has been pitched upon to gain instruction & Knowledge in this branch. A Powder Mill in New England cannot in the least degree affect your Manufacture nor be of any disadvantage to you. Therefore these Gentn & myself hope You will Chearfully & from Public Spirited Motives give Mr. Revere such information as will inable him to Conduct the bussiness on his return home. I shall be glad of any opportunity to approve myself.

Sir Your very Obed Servt. Robt Morris

P.S. Mr. Revere will desire to see the Construction of your Mill & I hope you will gratify him in that point.

Sir,[2]

I heartily join with Mr. Morris in his Request; and am with great Respect, Your very hble Servt. John Dickinson

RC (MHi) . In the hand of Robert Morris.

[1] Oswell Eve, former sea captain and Philadelphia merchant who had returned to Pennsylvania in 1773 after five years residence in the West Indies, operated a powder mill at Frankford. *PMHB* 5 (1881):19–20.

[2] This and the remainder of the document is in Dickinson's hand.

Robert Treat Paine to Philip Schuyler

Dear Sr Albany Novr. 21st. 1775

This day I arrived here in Company with Mr. Langdon who together with Mr. Robert R. Livingstone are a Committee from the Congress to repair to you & Consult divers matters me[n]tioned in your Letters to the Congress.[1] Mr. Livingstone is not arrived here, but proposed to join to morrow night, after which we shall make all dispatch possible. Mean while We thought it proper to inform you thus far by this Express, who goes so soon to morrow that we have not time to enlarge. We have brought with us blank Commissions for the New Army to be raised.

We congratulate you on the Success of our Army & hoping the restoration of your health I am your most Obedient hble Servt.

Rob Treat Paine

RC (MH).

[1] Paine noted in his diary for this day: "Rode 8m to Miller's & Breakfasted. Thence to Albany 12m. The rode very rutty, much [. . .] & hard frozen & considerable snow & Ice. Arrived at 1 o Clock. Went to Widow Vernon Tavern but the officers & soldiers that were taken at St. John's being in Town we could not be entertained there. We dind there & I went to Mr. John [Guys?] [. . .] & lodged. This Evening Capt. Livingston arrivd here from Montreal & brought news that it was taken by our Troops. Wrote general Schuyler by an Express going to him from General Washington that we were on our way to visit him." MHi.

Samuel Ward to Henry Ward

Dear Bror. Philadelphia 21st Novr. 1775

Yesterday We had a Number of Letters (taken on Board the Transport from Ireland) to the officers in Boston read in Congress. The Writers of some of them freely condemn our Enemies, assure their correspondents that the People at large heartily wish Us Success & some even say that it is Time for Ireland to follow our Example. There is great Reluctance to the Service; additional Bounties are given by the leading roman Catholics. Other Letters say that the People of both England & Ireland in general are against Us, that many who have supported our Interest until the Proclamation came out have now changed Sides, but tho' these Letters vary in that Respect They all agree that the King is determined let the Consequence be what it will to reduce us to Submission. I am vastly pleased to find that our Friends in England give us such good Intelligence. The five Regiments which I lately wrote You might be expected this Fall came out with this Transport & are chiefly or by this time wholly arrived & that the 20000 men are to come in the Spring & the Men of War is confirmed in these Letters. If We can but get Arms and Ammunition I have no Doubt but We shall give a good Acct. of them and I think We have a good Prospect. Many Vessels are out on the Merchts. Acct. some on the several Colonies and others on Acct. of the Continent and great Encouragement hath been given & a Person well acquainted in Germany with the manufacture of Salt Petre is employed by Congress to go down immediately to Virginia & sett up very extensive Works but as every possable method will be made us[e] of for interupting these Supplies I hope the Merchts in Providence have or will immediately take the most speedy & effectual Methods for obtaining large Supplies. I think they ought to import Lead by all Means for allowing We succeed in getting it out of the Conn[ecticu]t Mines which is by no Means absolutely certain yet, the land Carriage would cost almost as much as the lead would abroad. Arms also will be wanted for We must undoubtedly encrease our Army very considerably. Happily for America the Congress will chearfully adopt the most vigorous Measures & pursue them with the utmost Spirit; that Timidity and Fluctuation of Counsels which a Hope of Reconciliation induced have done Us infinite Mischief. One of the above referred to Letters says that Ministry concluded from our Petition that the Congress found themselves too weak to carry on Opposition & took a Resolution to exert their whole Force to crush us at once. Many of Us expected this would be the Consequence of those measures but Thanks be to God We are not like to be again haunted with that evil genius And the Sin of Fear is now intirely banished from amongst us.

By Letters from Camp I find there is infinite Difficulty in reinlisting the Army. The Idea of making it wholly continental has induced so many Alterations disgusting to both officers & men that very little Success has attended our recruiting Orders. I have often told the Congress that under the Idea of new modelling I was afraid We should destroy our Army. It is expected that an Attack will be made upon our Lines on the Arrival of all the Reinforcements. A Reduction of the Army, or a Want of Powder or Arms may be fatal, You are much nearer the Camp than I am & may be better acquainted with the Difficulties. Southern Gentlemen wish to remove that Attachment which the Officers & men have to their respective Colonies & make them look up to the Continent at large for their Support or Promotion. I never thought that Attachment injurious to the common Cause but the strongest Inducement to People to risque every thing in Defence of the whole upon the Preservation of which must depend the Safety of each Colony. I wish therefore not to eradicate but regulate it in such a Manner as may most conduce to the Protection of the whole. I am not a little alarmed at the present Situation of the Army, I wish your utmost Influence may be used to put things upon a proper Footing and must beg Leave through you to recommend the matter to the immediate Attention of the Governor. There is no Time to be lost.

We have been so vastly hurried that the building a Navy hath not been taken into Consideration yet but it will be done in a Day or two I think.

Proper Regards to all. Your very affece. Bror. Sam Ward

P.S. Do write Me very particularly the State of the Army.

RC (RHi).

Silas Deane to Samuel B. Webb

Dear Saml Philadelphia Nov. 22d. 1775

I have not wrote you for some time past, merely thro' the multiplicity of Business in which I have for some time since been engaged. I have seen Col. Read who is much Your Friend and if the Office You referr to should be established I have no doubt of procuring you the Birth.[1] I hear that Mr. Chester intends returning, but I do not advise you to accept his place for if you can be appointed Genl. Gates's Deputy & assistant Secretary it will place you at head Quarters under the Generals Eye, in the best Company for improving in knowledge & good breeding and be in a genteel Station, as well as a good one for any future advancement. You are Now entered on the Military Course, & are fortunate in Your First office, & Connections. Every thing hereafter depends on Yourself, and as I must advise You to pursue that track, for Life, I must urge You To improve every leisure moment in reading the best Treatises on Warr & histories of Seiges &c also that you slip no Opportunity of being present at and acquainting yourself with every Military Operation of any Consequence, and that You now keep a Journal not for entering down Trifles as they may daily occur but of every Operation of Consequence with Your own Observations on it at the Time, and afterward of the Event. Also now enter all the regulations for an Army, such as their Rations, Cloathing, Arms, &c, &c, which you may find of vast Service in future to you, in your military Departments. How long the present unnatural Warr may last is dreadfully uncertain, but should it close within a year, or two, you may as well lay the first Rudiments of Military knowledge, as To introduce You with *eclat* into any other Service, for Warr will continue in one part of the World, or another, untill the Millennium arrive, & that is not, nor will soon I imagine.

As to Mr. Simpson I am sorry for his Situation and wish his Character stood fairer in the Country than it does,[2] many People in the Country asserting that he was unnecessarily Subservient To Genl. Gage, & that party, and therefore I fear he will Suffer in his Interest as Confiscations are You see begun in Rhode Island. I shall probably see You as soon as I am dismiss'd from this Place which by the Influence of some of my Freinds will take place in January. I am in haste Dear Sam Yours Affectionately Silas Deane

[*P.S.*] Mrs. Deane has paid me a Visit, & I returned as farr as N. York in her Company being sent there on Business of the Congress, which happened in my Way. Your Brother was with me, & I returned but Yesterday. You must Send Me an Acct. of the Number, & force, of the Armed Vessels, now Cruising to the Eastward. I want it for public purposes.

RC (CtY).

[1] Webb was appointed an aide-de-camp to Washington on June 21, 1776. Washington, *Writings* (Fitzpatrick), 5:165. See also Joseph Reed to Webb, November 26, 1775, and January 16, 1776. Webb, *Correspondence* (Ford), 1:120, 126.

[2] John Simpson, Boston loyalist, was the husband of Webb's sister Sarah. Webb, *Correspondence* (Ford), 1:119.

John Jay to Ibbetson Hamar

Philadelphia November 22, 1775. "Your letter enclosing one for Mr. Duer was delivered to me.[1] I am much obliged to him for affording me an opportunity for the exercise of humanity and for putting it in my power to give you evidence of the benevolent principles on which we wish the present and unnatural contest may be conducted. He will be pleased to communicate the enclosed resolution of Congress to the Committee of Trenton,[2] it being necessary that before your departure they should be satisfied of your having obtained permission and give them the parole of honor usual on similar occasions. I would advise you to go the shortest Road to Mr. Duer's and avoid staying longer at any place on the way than may be necessary. The Congress will attend to your request of leave to visit the city but have as yet come to no determination.[3] Be assured sir that if upon future occasions it should be in my power to contribute to your ease and happiness you may without the least reserve command any services I can consistently render you."

MS not found; abstracted from extract in *Kenneth W. Rendell Catalog,* no. 92 (1974), p. 27.

[1] Lt. Ibbetson Hamar of the Seventh Regiment of Foot, or Royal Fusiliers, had been taken prisoner at Chambly on October 17 and had been paroled by General Schuyler to Trenton along with other commissioned officers from his detachment. *A List of the General and Field-Officers, As they Rank in the Army; of the several Regiments of Horse, Dragoons, and Foot, on the British and Irish Establishments* (London: J. Millan, 1775), p. 61; and John Hancock to Walter Livingston, November 17, 1775, note 2.

[2] See *JCC,* 3:359.

[3] On November 24 Congress granted Lieutenant Hamar "leave to reside with" William Duer near Saratoga. *JCC,* 3:367.

John Jay to Joseph Stopford

Philadelphia November 22, 1775. "The letter from Mr. Duer to Mr. Livingston and myself which you were so kind as to forward came duly to hand.[1] Mr. Livingston is out of town, but I have not the least doubt of his readiness to join with me in paying the greatest attention to Mr. Duer's recommendation. The dictates of benevolence added to the reluctance with which we have been drawn into this controversy will ever lead me to regret the necessity which has placed us in our present relation to each other, and to abate the rigors of war by every good office common to brethren and fellow subjects. Be pleased sir to present my compliments to the other government [*New Jersey*] and with them be persuaded that I will at all times readily adopt and promote any measures which may be agreeable to you and not inconsistent with the interests of the colony."

MS not found; abstracted from extract in *Kenneth W. Rendell Catalog*, no. 92 (1974), pp. 27–28.

[1] Maj. Joseph Stopford, commander of the detachment of the Seventh Regiment of Foot, or Royal Fusiliers, which had surrendered at Chambly on October 17, was at this time on parole in Trenton. *A List of the General and Field-Officers, As they Rank in the Army; of the several Regiments of Horse, Dragoons, and Foot, on the British and Irish Establishments* (London: J. Millan, 1775), p. 61; and Jay to Ibbetson Hamar, this date, note 1.

John Adams to James Otis, Sr.

Sir Philadelphia Novr. 23. 1775

I had the Honour of your Letter of Novr. the Eleventh,[1] by Express, and am very Sorry to learn that any Difference of Sentiment has arisen between the two Honourable Houses, respecting the Militia Bill, as it is so necessary at this critical Moment, for the public Service.[2]

If I was of opinion that any Resolution of the Congress now in Force was against the Claim of the Honourable House, as the Honourable Board have proposed that We shall lay the Question before Congress I should think it my Duty to do it; But it appears to me that Supposing the two Resolutions to clash, the last ought to be considered as binding, and as, by this, it is left in the "Discretion of the Assembly either to adopt the foregoing Resolutions, in the whole or in Part, or to continue their former, as they on Consideration of all Circumstances shall think fit," I think it plain, that the Honourable Board may comply with the Desire of the Honourable House if, in their Discretion they think fit.

I am the more confirmed in the opinion, that it is unnecessary to lay this Matter before Congress, as they have lately advised the Colonies of New Hampshire, and one more, if they think it necessary, to establish such Forms of Government, as they shall judge best calculated to promote the Happiness of the People.

Besides the Congress are so pressed with Business, and engaged upon Questions of greater Moment that I should be unwilling, unless in a Case of absolute Necessity to interrupt them by a Question of this Kind, not to mention that I would not wish to make known so publickly and extensively, that a Controversy had so soon arisen, between the Branches of our new Government.

I have had frequent Consultations with my Colleagues, since the Receipt of your Letter, upon this Subject; but as we are not unanimous,[3] I think it my Du'y to write my private sentiments as soon as possible. If Either of my Colleagues shall think fit to propose the Question to Congress, I shall there give my candid opinion, as I have done to you.

I have the Honour to be, with great Respect to the Honourable Board, Sir, your most obedient and very humble Servant.

John Adams

RC (NNPM).

[1] For this letter from James Otis, Sr. (1702–78), president of the Massachusetts Council, see *Am. Archives*, 4th ser. 3:1531.

[2] The conflict between the Massachusetts House and Council over their authority to appoint militia officers is discussed in Stephen E. Patterson, *Political Parties in Revolutionary Massachusetts* (Madison: University of Wisconsin Press, 1973), pp. 128–32. Adams also discussed this topic in his November 25 letter to Joseph Hawley.

[3] See Samuel Adams to James Otis, Sr., this date; and Massachusetts Delegates to the Massachusetts Council, November 24 and 29, 1775.

Samuel Adams to James Otis, Sr.

Sir Philadelphia Novr. 23d. 1775

Having very maturely considerd your Letter of the 11th of November, written in the Name and by order of the Honble. the Council of Massachusetts Bay,[1] and directed to the Delegates of that Colony,[2] I beg Leave to offer it as my opinion that the Resolve of Congress pass'd on the 9th July [June] last,[3] must be superceded by the subsequent Resolve of the 8th of July following,[4] so far as they appear to militate with each other.

By the last of these Resolves, the Conventions, or Assemblies of the several Colonies annually elective, are at their Discretion either to adopt the Method therein pointed out for the Regulation of their Militia either in whole, or in part, or to continue their former Regulations, as they on Consideration of all Circumstances shall think fit. It therefore seems to me manifest, that the Honble. Council are under no Restraint from yielding to the Honble. House a Voice with them in the Choice of the Militia Officers in the Colony.

I am prevaild upon to believe that this is the sense of the Congress; because they have lately recommended it to the Colony of New Hampshire to set up and exercise Government in such Form as they shall judge to be most conducive to the Promotion of Peace and good

Order among themselves, without laying them under Restrictions of any kind.

As the Honble. Board have been pleasd to direct us to give our opinion *with* or *without* consulting our Brethren of the Congress,[5] I hope I shall be justified, after having conferr'd with my Colleagues on the Subject, in declining on my part to have the Matter laid before Congress, for Reasons which were of Weight in my Mind; and indeed I am of opinion, that the Congress would not chuse to take any Order of that Kind, they having diverse times of late declin'd to determine on Matters which concern'd the internal Police of Individuals[6] of the United Colonies.

It is my most ardent Wish, that a cordial Agreement between the two Houses may ever subsist, more especially in the Establishment of the Militia, upon which the Safety of the Colony so greatly depends.

I am with all due Regards to the Honorable Council Sir Your most Humble Sert. Samuel Adams

Tr (M-Ar). FC (NN).

[1] See John Adams to James Otis, Sr., this date. Samuel Adams had previously expressed his views of the controversy in his October 29 letter to Elbridge Gerry.

[2] Adams had added "and consulted with my Colleagues" in the FC.

[3] Adams' draft reads "on the 9th June last, relative to establishing Civil Government." See *JCC,* 2:83–84.

[4] Adams probably meant July 18, when resolutions governing the establishment of militia were passed. *JCC,* 2:187–90.

[5] Adams had added "as we shall judge best" in his draft.

[6] "Either" instead of "individuals" in Adams' draft.

Josiah Bartlett to Nathaniel Folsom

Sir Philadelphia Novembr. 23d 1775

When I left New Hampshire I was in hopes to have been favored by my friends, who had the care of publick affairs; with frequent accounts of Every thing of a public nature transacted in the colony. You must be Sensible that besides my anxious Desire of Knowing every thing that Relates to welfare of the Colony; it is highly necessary as your Delegate that I should be well & Early informed of all its publick affairs; somethings that perhaps you would think of little consequence would have been of great Service if I had been informed of them. Every other Delegate Every week Receives Regular accounts from their Congresses, Committes of Safety & private Gentlemen, so as to be able to give a particular account of their Respective Colonies; while I Know but very Little of our Colony affairs Since I left it.

The Publick papers have informed us that Portsmouth has been threatned by the Tools of tyranny and that the Colony had Exerted themselves for its Defence. I want to be informed what is Done, what Batteries, how many Guns mounted, what No. of men constantly Kept there; what No. of men has been employed about Building the Batteries &c whither the Inhabitants have moved out their Effects; whither the province is making more paper Bills, if so how much & when Redeemable. Whither a new Convention is Called, and when to meet. Whither a new Committe of Safety is appointed, and if so who are the members. How the people like the Resolve of the Congress concerning Civil government, and what is done in consequence of it. Whither the Colony has undertaken to procure themselves any Powder. Whither any Salt petre is made or any body Engaging in that Business. Whither the fire arms voted by the covention are made. Whither the people in General are peacable & orderly or not. I should be very Glad to be informed of these and of Every other public affair, as soon & as often as possible, and hope that you and my other friends will frequently write to me. If it does no other good (that is if Some of the letters should not convey me any material public intelligence) it will at least give me great pleasure to hear from my friends in our Colony, while (as I Expect) I am confined here the Ensuing winter.

In order to Encourage intelligence being conveyed to & from the Delegates while the Congress is Sitting, they have ordered that all letters from & to them be carried post free as you will see by the publick prints.

I hope our Colony will omit nothing in their power to put themselves in a good State of Defence for unless good providence interpose, I Believe the ministry will use their greatest Efforts the spring and Summer coming to Subdue us to Slavery. Thus it appears by the latest & best account.

If we can Stand our ground one year more I make no doubt things will turn to our minds.

Capt Langdon went off to Ticonderoga the 12th Inst so I am left here alone in behalf of our Colony & I am obliged to attend constantly otherwise the Colony will have no vote. We frequently leave off so late as to Scarcly to Dine by Day light. I am in good Health; hope this will find you & your family so too. Remember me to all friends. I am Sir your friend and Servant Josiah Bartlett

P.S. Please to inform me how the Gentlemen at Portsmouth behaved in the late Surprize there and Excuse my incorrectness & Blotings as I have not time to Copy it and write in haste by Candle light.

J B

RC (PHi).

Committee to the Northward to John Hancock

Sr Albany Novr. 23 1775

We arrived the 16th in the Evening at New Winsor, having been detained part of a day by Rain. The morning following we rowed down the River about 8 miles to the Fortress in the Highlands where we spent the day in making such Observations as we thought would be of most use to the Congress, & wish our time would have permitted us to render them more perfect without interfering with the other commissions with which we have been honoured.[1]

We found the fortress in the care of Messrs Bedlow, Greenal & Lawrence whom the Convention of New York had appointed Commissioners to Superintend the Work wch. was carried on under the direction of Mr. Romans, agreeable to his plan presented to the Congress.

The Garrison consisted of 100 men, being the remainder of two companys, from which drafts were made to compleat those that were sent up to the Northward while they continued recruiting. Exclusive of these there were at the fortress 27 Carpenters, 16 Masons, 2 Smiths & 59 Labourers, a Clerk & a Steward.

We must own that we found the fort in a less defensible Scituation than we had reason to expect, owing chiefly to an injudicious disposition of the labour which has hitherto been bestowed on the Barracks, the Blockhouse & the South West Curtain. This, Mr. Romans assured us, would be finished in a week & would mount 14 Cannon, but when Compleated we consider as very insufficient in itself to answer the purpose of defence, tho it is doubtless Necessary to render the whole fortification perfect, but as it is the least useful it should have been the last finished. It does not command the Reach to the Southward, nor can it injure a Vessel turning the West point, & after She has got round, a small breeze or even the tide will enable a ship to pass the Curtain in a few minutes. The principal Strength of the fortress will consist in the South Bastion on which no labour has as yet been bestowed; a Vessel turning the Point is immediately exposed to its fire. The Platform of this will be raised 57 feet above high Water mark, when Compleated, which gives it an elevation of about 11 degrees above the guns of a Vessell at the West point, Supposing she carries them 12 feet above the surface of the Water, According to Mr. Romans Account.

On this Bastion it is proposed to mount 11 Large Cannon. The block house is finished & has 6 4 pounders mounted in it, & is at present the only Strength of the fortress. The Barracks Consist of 14 Rooms, each of which may contain 30 men, but they are not yet Compleated for want of Bricks with which to run up the Chimneys.

The fortress is unfortunately commanded by all the Grounds about it, & is much exposed to an attack by Land, but the most Obvious defect is that the Grounds on the West point are much higher than the Fortress behind which point an Enemy may land without the Least danger. In order to render this Post impassable it seems necessary that this Place Should be Occupied & batteries thrown up on the opposite Shore, where they may be erected with little expense as the Earth is Said to be pretty free from stone. This will indeed render our Works very extensive, but we fear nothing Short of this will be sufficient to avail us of the winding of the River.

Mr. Romans informs us of a place about 4 miles lower down the River, which is free from the inconveniency we have mentioned & where the elevation is much greater. Had we had more time we should have gone & examined it.

We would submitt to the Congress whether it may not be proper to send Some persons better versed in these matters than we are, to take An Accurate Survey of the highlands, & to pitch on those Spots on which Batterys may be most cheaply, expeditiously & advantagiously raised.

We found at the fortress

8	9 pounders &	6 Carriages
42	6 pounders &	18 Carriages
16	4 pounders &	4 Do.
5	3 pounders	
101	9 pound Shot	
180	6 pound Do.	
140	4 Do. Do.	
43	double Leaded 6 lb. shot	
19	Do. 4 lb. Do.	
	Cannon Cartridges	
400 of	9 lb.	
400 of	6 lb.	
88 of	4 lb.	
185 lb. of	Match	
100 lb.	Muskett ball	
100 lb.	Grape Shott	
170 lb.	Powder	

These are all the particulars which our short stay at the fort enabled us to collect. We offer our own sentiments in matters with which we are so little acquainted with the greatest diffidence, & submitt them implicitly to the Congress but cannot help wishing when we consider the importance of the object, that they would take the opinion of those who are capable of giving them more useful information.

We congratulate you & the Congress on the happy success of our

Arms & remain with the greatest Respect your & their most Obedient humble Servants Robt R Livingston Junr

Rob Treat Paine

John Langdon

P.S. We purpose to set out to morrow for Ticonderoga.

RC (DNA: PCC, item 78, vol. 14). Written by Paine and signed by Livingston, Langdon, and Paine.

[1] Paine had made this notation on his visit to the incomplete fort at West Point. "Went to Breakfast with George Clinton Esqr. at his Seat 1/2 a mile off. Thence went in a Barge belonging to the post down to the Fort on the Highlands 7 a.m. Cold fair day, Wind NE. Viewed the Fort & Scituations & P.M. returned & was set on shore on the East side of the River & lodged at Carpenters. Very Cold coming up high wind & ice made on Oars." Robert Treat Paine's diary, November 17, 1775, MHi.

John Hancock to John Hulbert

Sir, Philada. Novr. 23d 1775

After you have stationed the Men under your Command in the Fort in the Highlands on Hudson's River, and given the necessary Directions to your inferiour officers, you have the Leave of Congress, agreeably to your Application to be absent from your Post fourteen Days,[1] at the Expiration of which Time, you are to return to your Duty in the Forts on Hudson's River. I am Sir &c J.H. Prest.

LB (DNA: PCC, item 12A).

[1] This may have been a slip of the pen by the clerk who maintained Hancock's letterbook since Congress had granted Hulbert only 10 days leave. *JCC*, 3:364.

Samuel Ward to Henry Ward

Dear Bror. Philadela. 23d Novr. 1775

I promised myself a Letter from You by last Post & a particular Acct. of the Proceedings of the Assembly but am sadly disappointed. Dont fail another Post whilest I am here if it be possible to avoid it, Should you ever be from all your Connections Months together youl know the Pleasure of receiving Letters from them.

If Gentlemen have not already sett out for this City with the Accts of the Comee. of Safety I should advise their deferring the Journey a little while as there is no Money in the Treasury. Orders are given for making Paper for another Emission which I think will be about two Millions of Dollars,[1] if they are on the Journey we will do the best We can.

I want to know what Effect the Stoppage of Trade has in our Colony, whether any Powder or Arms have lately arrived and in [. . .] Thing of Importance to the common Cause.

Nothing of Importance since mine of last Tuesday. My Concern for the Army hangs heavy upon Me. If they are but well supplied with good Arms & Ammunition and reconciled to the new Regulations or will continue under the old chearfully in the Service I shall not fear a Battle. Be full in your next upon this Head. Adieu My dear Bror. Sam Ward

RC (RHi).

[1] The committee on the treasury brought in their report on November 24, and Congress resolved on November 29 to emit $3 million in bills of credit. *JCC*, 3:369, 390.

John Adams to Perez Morton

Sir Philadelphia Novr. 24. 1775

I had the Honour of receiving your Letter of the Twenty Eighth of October last, by Mr Revere, in which you acquaint me that the Major Part of the Honourable Council,[1] by Virtue of the Power and Authority, in and by the Royal Charter of the Massachusetts Bay in the absence of the Governor and Lieutenant Governor lodged in them have seen fit to appoint me, with the Advice and Consent of Council, to be a Justice of the Superiour Court of Judicature, &c. for that Colony, inclosing a List of the Honourable Gentlemen, who are to hold Seats on the Same Bench, and requesting me to Signify in Writing my acceptance or Refusal, of Said Appointment as Soon as might be.[2]

I am deeply penetrated, sir, with a Sense of the high Importance of that office, at all times difficult, but under those Distresses in which our Country is involved, exposed to greater Hazards and Embarrassments, than were ever known, in the History of former Times.

As I have ever considered the Confidence of the Public the more honourable, in Proportion to the Perplexity and Danger of the Times, So I cannot but esteem this distinguished Mark of the Approbation of the honourable Board, as a greater Obligation than if it had been bestowed at a Season of greater Ease and Security. Whatever discouraging Circumstances, therefore may attend me, in Point of Health, of Fortune or Experience I dare not refuse to undertake this Duty.

Be pleased, then to acquaint the Honourable Board, that as soon as the Circumstances of the Colonies, will admit an Adjournment of the Congress, I Shall return to the Honourable Board and undertake, to the Utmost of my Ability, to discharge the momentous Duties, to which they have seen fit to appoint me.

Although I am happy to see a List of Gentlemen appointed to the Bench, of whose Abilities and Virtues I have the highest Esteem, and with whom I have long lived in Friendship; yet the Rank in which it has pleased the Honourable Board to place me, perplexes me more than any other Circumstance but as I ought to presume that this was done upon the best Reasons, I must Submit my private opinion to the Judgment of that honourable Body, in whose Department it is to determine.

With the most devout Wishes for the Peace and Prosperity of the Colonies, and of the Massachusetts Bay in particular and with the greatest Respect to the Honourable Board I am, sir, your most obedient, humble servant John Adams

RC (M-Ar).

[1] Perez Morton (1750–1837), Plymouth and Boston, Mass., lawyer, was deputy secretary to the Council of State, 1775–76. Adams, *Family Correspondence* (Butterfield), 1:141n.

[2] For a discussion of Adams' acceptance of the post of chief justice of the Massachusetts Superior Court, see John Adams to Abigail Adams, November 18, 1775, note 3.

Benjamin Harrison to Unknown

[Philadelphia, November 24, 1775][1]

The confederation is an article mentioned in your letter.[2] Let me give you a state of that matter: In the last congress, it was observed by a gentleman, with whose extensive knowledge and abilities the world is well acquainted, that when we set out originally upon the plan of a commercial opposition, an instrument was formed by which the colonies were bound to stand by one another, till certain ends were obtained. This was the association; that Great Britain had now rendered an opposition by arms necessary, in which case he thought there should be also some bond of union, in writing, that each colony might know how far it stood engaged, and for what purposes, and how far it had a right to rely on its sister colonies. He therefore introduced a form of confederation, to be moulded into any shape thought proper, and merely to set the thing a-going. I do not recollect whether it was read or not, but I well remember that the congress refused to enter into any consideration of it, to send it to the conventions for their approbation, to have it printed for public perusal, to have any entry made in their journals of such a paper being offered, or in any manner to make any order which should imply either approbation or disapprobation of it; it was simply permitted to lie on the table, from which it followed, that if gentlemen thought proper to say anything about if afterwards, it was to be on their own authority individually, and not as proceeding by the order, or even the desire, of congress. Since this, not a word has ever passed in congress upon it, nor had we heard any thing without doors till Mr. Inglis informed us such a paper had been solemnly laid before a neighbouring convention for them to say whether they would accede to or reject it in the lump, it being said that the alteration or diminution, even of a letter would not be admitted; that in the lump they chose to decline it;[3] and that the thing began to make some noise in Virginia. This is the whole I know of it. Though I might not approve of the confederation proposed, perhaps, as it stood (for really I do not remember what it was) yet I am ready openly to declare to the world it is my opinion we ought to be bound together by some treaty of alliance, or confederacy, in which the objects of the war should be defined, the terms of closing it delineated, and the colonies of the union bound to each other to contribute their respective force to obtain these objects, and when these objects were attained, that any one colony should have a right to say they would go no farther.

MS not found; reprinted from the *Virginia Gazette* (Pinkney), December 13, 1775, under the heading: "Extract of a letter from a gentleman in Philadelphia to his friend in this city [Williamsburg], dated November 24."

[1] Worthington C. Ford published this letter in the *Nation,* 48 (March 28, 1889): 261–63, with a brief essay inviting further study of the Articles of Confederation which Franklin proposed July 21, 1775, because of the paucity of evidence available on the subject. Ford deduced the identity of the author from the fact that Richard Henry Lee and Harrison were the only Virginia delegates who were in Philadelphia in both July and November and his assumption that the letter's moderate tone did not fit Lee's radical views. It is possible, of course, that the author was not a Virginian, but in the absence of other evidence Ford's conjecture invites no challenge.

[2] A letter to the Virginia delegates of November 11 from the Virginia Committee of Safety but written by Edmund Pendleton contains the following query: "What is become of the Confederation? We are told some Copies are in the Colony and condemned, whilst we can say nothing on the Subject, being strangers to its contents." It is a reasonable conjecture that the recipient of the letter printed above was one of the six members of the Virginia Committee who signed the letter of November 11, although Pendleton himself may be a more likely candidate than Richard Bland, Carter Braxton, Dudley Digges, John Page, or John Tabb. See Edmund Pendleton, *The Letters and Papers of Edmund Pendleton, 1734–1803,* ed. David J. Mays, 2 vols. (Charlottesville: The University Press of Virginia, 1967), 1:129.

[3] The North Carolina Provincial Congress had rejected the proposed articles on September 4, 1775. *Am. Archives,* 4th ser. 3:196. See also Silas Deane's Proposals to Congress, November ? 1775, note 1.

Richard Henry Lee to Henry Tucker

Sir, Philadelphia 24th of Novr. 1775.

As the contents of the inclosed paper concerns our common Countries, I have thought it my duty as a Delegate to Congress from Virginia to inclose it to you by the first opportunity.[1] As Salt is now much wanted in Virginia and the Country has been favored with a plentiful crop the last season, it will be very convenient for both Countries that your Island furnish that article quickly as possible, and to the full amount permitted by the resolution of Congress. The restraining Act of Parliament of the last Session does not interfere with you in this business, yet it will be prudent to make use of quick sailing Vessels, and if a few guns & men are put on board to keep off the small Tenders in Chesapeake Bay, that are every now & then committing Acts of piracy, they might be of service. It will be the most safe to run immediately up York, Rappahanock, or Potomack, as the Men of war generally lye in Hampton road or about Norfolk. The Committee of Safety sits constantly, and means will be taken to give all possible dispatch to your business in Virginia.

I write in great haste, and[2]

FC (ViU). In the hand of Richard Henry Lee.

[1] The "inclosed paper" was doubtless a copy of congressional resolutions of November 22 on trade between the "united colonies" and Bermuda. *JCC*, 3:362–64. For additional information about Henry Tucker and relations between Congress and Bermuda, see Thomas Jefferson to St. George Tucker, June 10, 1775, note 1.

[2] Remainder of MS missing.

Massachusetts Delegates to the Massachusetts Council

Gentlemen Philadelphia Novr. 24, 1775

Mr Revere the Express informs us this morning he is setting out for home, so that by his return we are not able to give you any advice with respect to the subject of your Letter of the 11th Instant;[1] the determination of the Question, referred to in that Letter, either one way or the other so nearly affects the Interest of & will be so important in its consequences to the Colony we have the honor to represent, that we dare not venture our opinions what would be the sentiments of Congress upon such a measure as the House proposes and therefore are clearly of opinion the matter ought to be laid before the Congress & their sentiments taken upon the same, but we have been so crouded with the consideration of so many interesting & important matters since Mr Reveres arrival that there has been no opportunity for this as yet, and therefore must defer at present giving you the advise you request. Your application for Money is now under the consideration of a Committee of Congress. We conclude with great respect, Your Honors most obedient humble Servts.

John Hancock

Thos. Cushing

Tr (M-Ar).

[1] The Massachusetts delegation was divided over the Massachusetts Council's November 11 request for advice on the "altercation" between the council and House of Representatives over the right to appoint militia officers. As a result Hancock and Cushing wrote this letter and one of November 29 to the Massachusetts Council, and John Adams and Samuel Adams wrote individually to James Otis, council president, on November 23, 1775. As John Adams explained: "after taking a great deal of Pains with my Colleague your Friend Mr Cushing, I could not get him to agree with the rest of Us in writing a joint letter." John Adams to Joseph Hawley, November 25, 1775. Robert Treat Paine, the remaining Massachusett's delegate, was then in New York with the committee sent to confer with General Schuyler. For additional references on this issue, see John Adams to James Otis, November 23, 1775.

Roger Sherman to Volkert P. Douw

Sir Philadelphia Novr. 24th. 1775

I Suppose the President has transmitted to you the resolutions of the Congress on the Several matters mentioned in Your letter.[1] I would only inform You That in Settling Mr. Deans account of past Services and expences, nothing was allowed him on account of what he paid of Mr. Spencer's expences who travelled with him among the Indians, but as you mentioned nothing of it in your letter, that matter was left to be settled between him and Mr. Spencer, or by the Commissioners.

Mr. Dean Informed that said Spencer had Sometime past been employed as a blacksmith among the Indians and that Some of them were desirous that he Should come and reside among them again, that he understands their language which is a material circumstance in favour of employing him if he is otherwise qualified & willing to undertake, but that is left with the Commissioners. It is important that who ever are employed among them Should be persons of a good Moral Character, friendly to American libertys and to the Missionaries that reside among them. I have no doubt but that the Commissioners will pay due attention to every thing in their department which may conduce to the public good. Mr. Timothy Edwards of Stockbridge is appointed a Commissioner instead of Major Hawley who declined the Service.[2] I am Sir with due regards Your humble Servant

Roger Sherman

FC (MHi). Addressed: "Mr. Volcart P. Dow."

[1] Volkert P. Douw, mayor of Albany from 1761 to 1770, had been appointed an Indian commissioner for the northern department by Congress in July 1775. *JCC*, 2:183; and Joel Munsell, ed., *Collections of the History of Albany from its Discovery to the Present Time, with Notices of its Public Institutions, and Biographical Sketches of Citizens Deceased*, 4 vols. (Albany, N. Y.: J. Munsell, 1865–71), vol. 1, passim. Douw wrote Hancock a letter on November 6 requesting guidance on several issues concerning relations with the Iroquois; and on November 11 Congress read this letter and appointed a committee to report on it consisting of Sherman and four other delegates. This committee thereupon submitted a report, most of which Congress approved on November 23. *JCC*, 3:350, 365–66; and *Am. Archives*, 4th ser. 3:1372–73.

[2] See *JCC*, 3:368.

John Adams to Joseph Hawley

My dear Sir Philadelphia Novr. 25. 1775

This afternoon at five O Clock, I received your kind Letter of November the 14 dated at Brookfield, which was the more agreable because such Favours from you short as this is are very rare.

You tell me, Sir, "that We shall have no Winter Army, if our Congress dont give better Encouragement to the Privates than at present is held forth to them" and that "there must be some small Bounty given them, on the Inlistment."

What Encouragement is held forth, or at least has been, I know not, but before this Time no doubt they have been informed of the Ultimatum of the Congress. No Bounty is offered—40 shillings lawfull Money Per Month, after much Altercation, is allowed.[1] It is undoubtedly true, that an opinion prevails among the Gentlemen of the Army from the Southward, and indeed throughout all the Colonies, excepting New England, that the Pay of the Privates is too high and that of the officers too low. So that you may easily conceive the Difficulties We have had to surmount. You may depend upon it, that this has cost many an anxious Day and Night. And the Utmost that could be done has been. We cannot Suddenly alter the Temper, Principles, opinions or Prejudices of Men. The Characters of Gentlemen in the four New England Colonies, differ as much from those in the others, as that of the Common People differs, that is as much as several distinct Nations almost. Gentlemen, Men of Sense, or any Kind of Education in the other Colonies are much fewer in Proportion than in N. England. Gentlemen in the other Colonies have large Plantations of slaves, and the common People among them are very ignorant and very poor. These Gentlemen are accustomed, habituated to higher Notions of themselves and the distinction between them and the common People, than We are. And an instantaneous alteration of the Character of a Colony, and that Temper and those Sentiments which its Inhabitants imbibed with their Mothers Milk, and which have grown with their Growth and strengthened with their Strength, cannot be made without a Miracle. I dread the Consequences of this Disimilitude of Character, and without the Utmost Caution on both sides, and the most considerate Forbearance with one another and prudent Condescention on both sides, they will certainly be fatal. An Alteration of the Southern Constitutions, which must certainly take Place if this War continues will gradually bring all the Continent nearer and nearer to each other in all Respects. But this is the Most Critical Moment, We have yet seen. This Winter will cast the Die. For Gods Sake therefore, reconcile our People to what has been done, for you may depend upon it, that nothing more can be done here—and I should shudder at the Thought of proposing a Bounty. A burnt Child dreads the fire. The Pay of the officers is raised, that of a Captain to 26 dollars and one third per Month, Lts and Ensigns in Proportion—Regimental officers not raised.

You then hint, "that if Congress should repeal or explain away the Res. of 18 July respecting the appointment of military officers, and vest the Council with the sole Power, it would throw the Colony into Confusion and end in the Distruction of the Council."

The Day before Yesterday I wrote a Letter to the Honorable Board in answer from one from their President by order to us upon that Subject, which Letter Revere carried from this City yesterday Morning. Therein I candidly gave my opinion to their Honours that our Resolution was clear and plain, that the Colony might Use their own Discretion, and therefore that they might yield this Point to the House—and that the Point was so plain that I did not see the least occasion for laying the Controversy before Congress.[2] But my dear Friend I must take the Freedom to tell you that the same has happened upon this occasion which has happened on a thousand others, after taking a great deal of Pains with my Colleague your Friend Mr Cushing, I could not get him to agree with the rest of Us in writing a joint Letter, nor could I get him to say what opinion he would give if it was moved in Congress. What he has written I know not. But it is very hard to be linked and yoked eternally, with People who have either no opinions, or opposite Opinions, and to be plagued with the opposition of our own Colony to the most necessary Measures, at the same Time that you have all the Monarchical Superstitions and the Aristocratical Domination, of Nine other Colonies to contend with.

FC (MHi).

[1] For Congress' resolution that the pay of privates "be the same as in the present army," see *JCC,* 3:322. A resolution specifically denying reenlistment bounties was passed on November 30. *JCC,* 3:393.

[2] Adams had noted on the back of Hawley's November 14 letter: "Recd this Letter at Dinner 4 o Clock Saturday November 25, 1775. Yesterday Morning i.e.

Fryday Novr. 24. Paul Revere went off from this Place with my Letter to the Board, in which I gave it as my opinion that the Council might give up the Point in Dispute with the House about the appointment of Militia officers, and that the Resolution of Congress mentioned in this Letter was so clear that We need not apply to that Assembly for any Explanation." Joseph Hawley to John Adams, November 14, 1775, MHi. See John Adams to James Otis, and Samuel Adams to James Otis, November 23; and Massachusetts Delegates to the Massachusetts Council, November 24 and 29, 1775.

John Adams to Mercy Warren

Madam Philadelphia Novr. 25. 1775

I had the Pleasure of yours of Novr. 4th Several Days ago.

You know Madam, that I have no Pleasure or Amusements which has any Charms for me. Balls, Assemblies, Concerts, Cards, Horses, Dogs, never engaged any Part of my attention or Concern. Nor am I ever happy in large and promiscuous Companies. Business alone, with the intimate unreserved Conversation of a very few Friends, Books, and familiar Correspondences, have ever engaged all my Time, and I have no Pleasure no Ease in any other Way. In this Place I have no opportunity to meddle with Books, only in the Way of Business. The Conversation I have here is all in the ceremonious, reserved, impenetrable Way. Thus I have Sketched a Character for myself of a morose Philosopher and a Surly Politician, neither of which are very amiable or respectable, but yet there is too much truth in it—and from it you will easily believe that I have very little Pleasure here, excepting in the Correspondence of my Friends, and among these I assure you Madam there is none, whose Letters I read with more Pleasure and Instruction than yours. I wish it was in my Power to write to you oftener than I do,[1] but I am really engaged in constant Business of seven to ten in the Morning in Committee, from ten to four in Congress and from Six to Ten again in Committee. Our Assembly is scarcly numerous enough for the Business. Every Body is engaged all Day in Congress and all the Morning and evening in Committees. I mention this Madam as an Apology for not writing you so often as I ought and as a Reason for my Request that you would not wait for my answers.

The Dispute you mention between the House and Board I hope will be easily settled. Yet I believe the Board acted with great Honour and Integrity and with a wise Design and a virtuous Resolution to do nothing that should endanger the Union.

But I am clear that it is best the two Houses should join in the Appointment of officers of Militia, and I am equally clear that the Resolve of Congress was intended to leave it to the Discretion of the Colony to adopt such a Mode as should please themselves, and I have done myself the Honour to write these sentiments to the Board, who were pleased to write to us upon the occasion. Am obliged to you for your Account of the state of Things in Boston, I am ever anxious about our Friends who remain there and nothing is ever more acceptable to me than to learn what passes there.

The Inactivity of the two Armies, is not very agreable to me. Fabius's Cunctando was wise and brave. But if I had submitted to it in his situation, it would have been a cruel Mortification to me. Zeal and Fire and Activity and Enterprize Strike my Imagination too much. I am obliged to be constantly on my Guard—yet the Heat within will burst forth at Times.

The Characters drawn in your last entertained me very agreably. They were taken off, by a nice & penetrating Eye. I hope you will favour me with more of these Characters. I wish I could draw a Number of Characters for your Inspection. I should perhaps daub on the Paint too thick—but the Features would be very strong.

The General is amiable and Accomplished and judicious and cool; You will soon know the Person and Character of his Lady.[2] I hope She has as much Ambition, for her Husbands Glory, as Portia & Marcia have, and then the Lord have Mercy on the Souls of Howe and Burgoyne & all the Troops in Boston.

FC (MHi).

[1] Adams had written a brief note to Mrs. Warren on October 31 acknowledging the receipt of her letter of October 12–14, 1775, but adding little more than a conventional wish for her well-being. MHi.

[2] Martha Washington had arrived in Philadelphia on November 21, where her presence touched off a commotion over the propriety of a ball scheduled in her honor for November 24. Although political leaders in the city convinced Mrs. Washington not to attend because it "would be very disagreeable at this melancholy time," at least one delegate registered his dissatisfaction with the decision. "Col. Harrison came to rebuke Samuel Adams for using his influence for the stopping of this entertainment, which he declared was legal, just and laudable." Christopher Marshall, *Extracts from the Diary of Christopher Marshall, Kept in Philadelphia and Lancaster during the American Revolution, 1774–1781*, ed. William Duane (Albany: Joel Munsell, 1877), pp. 51–53.

Francis Lewis to John Alsop

Sir Phila. 25 Novmr. 1775

I wrote you by Express, Mr Levy &c. to which am without an answer. I now inclose you two receipts for two Waggon Loads of Cloathing who went off from hence for Dobb's Ferry the 23 & 24 Inst. These are for Genl. Schuylers Army. In the first of these Waggons I sent Four Bales directed for Colo. Mifflin and ordered the Waggoner to leave them with Mr. Jona. Hampton at Eliza. Town with a letter directed to him as Chairman of their Committee requesting them to forward those Bales to you & you'l please apply to have them forwarded via Norwich for Cambridge.

You have also inclosed two Invoices of the Goods bought & sent from this place for Genl. Schuylers Army Amountg to £5279.2.6 Pensila. Currency or Dollars 14077 2/3ds. on which we have broker[a]g[e] & Waggon hire yet to pay. Shall endeavor to send you 3 or 4000 Dollars by first convenient if have so much remaining.

Pray get the Convention *or whom else* to send a trusty person to receive these two Waggons load of Clothg a[t] Dobb's Ferry and that a sloop be immediate let [*and*] sent to convey them to Albany.

I think it would not be adviseable to Send any more cloathing &c to the Northward, but that what you have now engaged be sent to the Army at Cambridge as that orders is not Compleated espectialy in the Article of Buckskin Breeches. We have nothing new here, business goes on heavily for want of more members attending. Mr. P. Livingston confined to his Room for several days with a Cold. I am Dr Sir Your very Humble Servt. Frans. Lewis

P.S. It will be necessary to forward these Invoices with the Goods to Mr. Walter Livingston. With the Invoices is annexed the different Packages.

RC (NHi).

Edward Rutledge to Thomas Bee

My dear Bee. Novr. 25 1775

I should have done myself the Pleasure of writing you by Return of the Express but was so ill at that time, that I found it impossible. I am now much better, tho' still greatly distressed with a Cough which I see no Prospect of getting rid of until I lead my Course to a warmer and better Climate. So much for myself. Letters from Genl. Washington a few days since inform us of the arrival of Troops from Ireland, the Number is not known but it is guess'd at 2000, or 2500. It is the opinion of himself & officers that Howe will soon attack him. I wish he may; if our people behave like Men, success will, nay must attend us. Some time last Summer, the officers at Boston fitted out a large Schooner from that place & dispatched her to Ireland for a Supply of Tongues, Wine &c. On her Return a few Days ago, she was intercepted by one of our armed Vessels in Continental pay, and brought into Harbour with all her Grog & an abundance of Letters from Gentn. in Ireland to their Friends in Boston. These Letters were open'd &

have afforded much Amusement & some Intelligence. We find by them that Administration are determined at all Events to attempt the Reduction of America, that Boston will be made strong by 22 or 25000 Men in the Course of this Winter & the Spring—that Lord Kinmare has added to the King's Bounty that of 10/6 per Man for all who shall inlist under Major Roche—that the City of Corke has followed the Example but more extensively, that Lord Bellamount has the Direction of the Recruiting parties in that part of the Kingdom—that the Roman Catholic Priests have been applied to to stimulate their Flocks against us, which they have promised to do, if the Regiments to be raised be officer'd by Gentn. of their religious p[ers]uasion—in short that all the Powers of Hell are to be let loose upon us. On the other Hand, Intelligence by the same Conveyance inform us that all the Whigs in the Kingdom a very few Excepted are warmly interested in our Cause, that the common people are not less well affected, that several Towns have resolved not to permit any officers to recruit amongst them, & have destroyed the Drums of those who have been hardy enough to attempt it, & that the Dislike to the Service is so great & so general that those employed therein meet with little or no Success.

So much for Irish Politics. You Will no Doubt 'eer this reaches you hear of our having taken Chambleé & St. John's. We should have wrote to the Commee upon the Subject, but waited for more particulars. We have received no farther Accounts from that Quarter; but are in daily Expectation of hearing of the Fall of Montreal & Quebec. In the last of those places I am told there is great Abundance of what we want very much—powder & military Stores. I have that Expedition much at Heart I must confess, for I really think & have thought for a long Time, that America will be saved in Canada. It may put Reconciliation at a greater Distance 'tis true, as his Majesty will find just difficulty to persuade himself to part with arbitrary power tho' it were established but in an Acre of Ground; however it will make the Cure radical whenever it is effected, & really we have lived in so unsettled a Condition for such a length of Time that I would now wish to fight it fairly out & either establish a Connection consistent with the Principles of Liberty & placed upon a permanent Basis, or have nothing more to do with them. The latter I think most likely to be the case. The Distruction of our Towns in the wanton Manner in which it has been affected, a mode of Warfare (as I have already expressed it) totally exploded amongst civilized Nations, give us little Reason to think that they will attempt to make Peace. Indeed if it is not soon set about, it will be all in Vain even to wish for it hereafter. The Minds of People will be so warmed by the Acts of Cruelty hitherto exercised & daily committing against them that they will not wish for a Connection with Men of such savage Disposition.

Pray make my Respects where due. God bless you. In Haste, Yrs truly
Edward Rutledge

RC (MH).

Silas Deane to Elizabeth Deane

My Dear Philadelphia Novr. 26th 1775

Your's of the 22d recd. last Night, every thing which happens to so near a Freind is interesting how ever unimportant to the rest of the World. I therefore rejoice at your safe return, & at your finding the Families in so good a Situation to whom my warmest remembrance, & Congratulations to the New parents.

Thos. Mumford Esqr. arrived here Night before last, & his Brother as usual, sticks by the Stuff. Col. Dyer increases in fretfullness with the severity of the Weather, and brother Roger sets off tomorrow to pay a Visit to Connecticut before the New Delegation are seated.[1]

Things are in just the same Train as when You left Us, & consequently I am quite willing to quit my Station to abler Men, & who they are, the Colony knows, or ought to know best.[2]

I did not leave New York untill Saturday Morng. and then with the Mortification of effecting Nothing.[3] Was thrown into the most wretched Situation, at those two little Ferries, which took Us not Five Minutes to cross, took Me Near as many Hours. The wind & Tide conspiring against Us, carried Us quite down into the Bay, & in short I was glad to get on Shore at any Rate, or any where, after well nigh perishing with the Cold. At Elisabeth Town where We dined on Sunday, I dined & found my Freind Jay waiting for Me. He took a Seat with Me, & we had as agreeable a Journey, as the badness of the Roads and Weather would admit of, saving that at Woodbridge Where we lodged, Somebody finding out that I had Two loose Coats (for I bot. Me a New one in New York) very civilly borrowed my old One, without troubling Me with any Questions about the matter or debating which he should take, he also borrowed a P[air] of Shoes & Buckles & some other Trifles of Mr. Jay, & has not call'd on either of Us since. Thus You see, it is in Vain for Me, to think of having more than One Coat at a Time, were I provident enough to lay in so small a Stock which you know I am not in general.

I del[ivere]d your billet & pattern to Mrs. Trist, who thanks You for your Commission, which w[he]n Executed will report.

Beleive me my Dear my long & thorough acquaintance with the Genius of Our Assembly prevents my being surprized at any sudden Whim they take, or uneasy at any of their Resolutions so farr as they respect myself individually. On a review of the part I have acted on the public Theatre of Life, an examination of my own Genius & Disposition, unfitt for Trimming, Coasting, & intrigues with the populace, I have greater reason to wonder how I ever became popular at all. What therefore I did not expect, I have Too much Philosophy to be in distress at loosing. I only wish that my Freinds felt as easy, on this Occasion as myself; if they knew what fatigues I have undergone, & the disagreeable prospects before Me, as to public Affairs, they could wish Me here only in Confidence that my Abilities might be of service to the public, rather than to myself, but of this The Supreme Assembly are best Judges, & to them I submit sincerely praying, that the Consequences which I think I foresee, necessarily flowing from this measure may be averted. I am surprized that Knight should abuse Me in the manner he has done, cost what it will procure a supply elsewhere. I should be sorry that you or my Freinds should manifest any uneasiness on my being superceded, for they who effected it will find, & that soon, the mischeif intended, recoil on them to their Shame & disgrace, or I am greatly mistaken, and at present God knows I wish the worst of them no other punishment, than a Consciousness of the low, envious, jealous, & sordid motives by which they are actuated; as on the other hand one of the greatest pleasures I enjoy is a Consciousness of the rectitude of my intentions & Conduct, & the pleasing Reflection of being Superior to such Motives & those actuated by them. I have wrote a Long Lettr. and on a review it is too much about myself, I will write of something of more importance in my Next. My Compliments to all Freinds. I am my Dear Your Affectionate Husband S Deane

RC (CtHi).

[1] Roger Sherman's accounts indicate that he claimed reimbursement for 184 days for two terms of service during the period May 3—December 2, 1775. Since Sherman was apparently in Philadelphia from May 10 to August 2 and September 10 to November 27, 1775, his claim included approximately 20 days for travel. See Roger Sherman's Memoranda Book, DLC.

[2] The Connecticut Assembly had decided not to return Deane to Congress. See Deane to Thomas Mumford, October 16, 1775, note 10.

[3] Deane had been in New York on committee business. See Naval Committee to Deane, November 7 and 16, 1775.

Joseph Hewes to Samuel Johnston

Dear Sir Philadelphia 26th Nov. 1775

The Congress have had sundry Petitions before them from the Inhabitants of Bermuda seting forth the distressed state of that Island for want of Provisions and have had an estimate of the quantity consumed for several years past. They have come into a resolution to supply them.[1] I send it you herewith and desire you will lay a copy of it before the Provincial Council and the Committees of the Sea Ports &c. I have wrote to you sundry times since I came here but have not been so fortunate as to hear a single word from Edenton since I left it.

By some intercepted Letters we find the British Ministry are determined to reinforce their Army at Boston with 22,500 Men, which are to be sent over with all possible expedition. Five Regiments each 700 men are already arived, the remainder will be out early in the Spring, of this matter we have pretty good intelligence. It is thought we shall have Occasion for all the Men we can raise so that you must not discharge your Troops till you hear further from our Body. Tho. Persons wrote to Penn that you intended to disband them at your next meeting. We have had that matter under consideration, a Committee was appointed to consider it, and will report perhaps to morrow. I have not seen the report but am told the purport of it is that your two Regiments shall be kept in pay till December 1776 unless discharged sooner by Order of Congress and that it is recommended to you to fall upon every method in your power to get Arms & Amunition for them.[2] The latter you may be supplied with at Charles Town, I have done all I could to purchase Some of both here, but cannot as yet get any of either, if I could have done it I should have had an Order of Congress on the Treasurer here for money to have paid for them. If the Order from Congress should not reach you before you set of[f] for the next meeting of your Council you must prevent the disbanding of your Soldiers. I ought not to call them your Soldiers, the Continent consider them theirs and the Congress mean to give Orders Accordingly. Tho. Persons also wrote Penn that a person had purchased lately near 200 hhd of Tobacco in Bute & Granville, which he hinted was intended to be Shipped in Violation of the association, He also mentions that people in general are dissatisfied with the proceedings of the Convention at Hillsborough and are dayly falling off from the American Cause, for other matters of News I refer you to the Bearer Mr. Houston who is one of the Georgia delegates to whom I doubt not you will shew every Civility.

I am respectfully Dr Sir your mo. Obed. hum Serv

Joseph Hewes

RC (CtY: Pequot Library deposit).

[1] See *JCC*, 3:362–64.

[2] On November 5 Samuel Johnston, president of the North Carolina Provincial Congress, had written both to Hewes and to the North Carolina delegates informing them that the province was desperately in need of arms and ammunition for the two battalions which it had raised pursuant to a congressional resolve of June 26, 1775, in anticipation of their eventually being taken into Continental service. When Johnston's letters arrived in Philadelphia is unknown, but on November 24 Congress appointed a committee to consider the condition of North Carolina. The

committee's report of November 27 led Congress to adopt a series of resolutions on the following day, incorporating the two North Carolina battalions into the Continental Army and making other provisions and suggestions for her defense. *JCC,* 2:107; 3:368, 387–88; and Clark, *Naval Documents,* 2:898–99.

John Jay to Nathaniel Woodhull

Sir Philad. 26. Novr. 1775

I have the honor of transmitting to you the enclosed Resolutions of Congress relative to the Island of Bermuda.

We have not yet had the Pleasure of hearing that you had made a House, and are not without some anxiety on that hand.[1] In a few days we shall write to you, collectively, and should be glad frequently to be informed of the State of the Province.

The New England Exploit is much talked of, and Conjectures are numerous as to the Part the Convention will take relative to it.[2] Some consider it as an ill Compliment to the Government of the Province, and prophesy that you have too much christian Meekness to take any notice of it. For my own Part I dont approve of the feat, and think it neither argues much wisdom or much Bravery. At any Rate, if it was to have been done, I wish our own People and not Strangers had taken the Liberty of doing it.

I confess I am not a little jealous of the Honor of the Province, and am persuaded that its Reputation cannot be maintained without some little Spirit being mingled with its Prudence.

I am Sir with Respect & Esteem Your most obt. Servt

John Jay

RC (N). Tr (MH). RC damaged; missing words supplied from Tr.

[1] The New York Provincial Congress, although scheduled to reconvene November 14, was unable to muster a quorum until December 6. *Am Archives,* 4th ser. 3:1751.

[2] On November 23 a group of Connecticut men led by Isaac Sears, a New York radical leader, had gone to New York City and destroyed the press and seized the type of James Rivington, the staunchly loyalist printer of *Rivington's New York Gazeteer.* The Provincial Congress, after some debate, issued a mild protest about this incident to Governor Trumbull of Connecticut on December 12. Ibid., 4:393, 400–402; and Bernard Mason, *The Road to Independence. The Revolutionary Movement in New York, 1773–1777* (Lexington: University of Kentucky Press, 1967), pp. 53–60.

Richard Henry Lee to George Washington

Dear General Philadelphia 26th Novr. 1775

As Mr. Custis can furnish you with an exact account of our affairs in Virginia, it will be unnecessary for me to say any thing on that subject. Proper persons will certainly and presently be appointed, under proper regulations, to determine on sea Captures. I heartily congratulate you on the surrender of St. Johns. That of Montreal must, I think, quickly follow, because it is quite defenceless and because the far greater part of the Canadians are surely on our side. If Colo. Arnold meets with success at Quebec, we shall be in a fine posture to receive our enemies next spring. I have been strongly inclined to think that the design of this last reenforcement to Boston, is intended for something decisive this fall. Their credit, their necessities, and many other considerations seem to render an attempt on yr. lines probable. I make no doubt but the most effectual guard will be taken to render this attempt fatal to its Authors. It is impossible that vice can so triumph over virtue, as that the Slaves of Tyranny should succeed against the brave and generous Assertors of Liberty, and the just rights of humanity.

We expect every day to hear from England, but no intelligence has come from thence since I wrote you last.

I heartily wish you a happy meeting with your Lady who leaves this place tomorrow for Cambridge.

I am, with, singular esteem, dear Sir Your most affectionate and obedt. Servant Richard Henry Lee

P.S. We have sent a Committee to Canada to invite Delegates here and to settle the affairs of that Army.

RC (DLC).

Andrew Allen to Jasper Yeates

Philada. Novr. 27th. 1775. Discusses a financial matter in which he hopes Yeates[1] can obtain a judgment if there is otherwise no prospect for a settlement, and concludes: "We have nothing particular stirring here, but wait impatiently for Accounts from Canada. May they be such as we wish."

RC (PHi).

[1] Jasper Yeates (1745–1817), Lancaster, Pa., lawyer, and chairman of the Lancaster committee of correspondence in 1775–76, was appointed commissioner for Indian affairs in the middle department on July 4, 1776. *DAB;* and *JCC,* 5:517.

Josiah Bartlett to the New Hampshire Committee of Safety

Gent. Philadelphia Noveme 27th 1775

Being in great haste when I sealed my last Letter to you, I inadvertently omitted the enclosed Letter from the Agents, nor was I sensible of the Omission till I found it among my papers last *Saturday*.

The Enclosed Resolves I am directed by Congress to transmit to you.[1]

I should be very glad to be informed of all the Circumstances of our Publick Affairs. I think that a particular knowledge of them would often be of very great advantage. But as I now hope I shall set out for New Hampshire in a fortnight or three Weeks,[2] I expect I shall not be able to hear from [*you*] after you receive this till my return, unless contrary to my present hopes I shall be detained here for the Winter.

I am Gentlemen your friend and humble Servant,

Josiah Bartlett

Tr (DLC).

[1] Probably the resolves establishing rules for the disposition of naval prizes adopted on November 25. *JCC*, 3:371–75.

[2] Bartlett expressed the same hope to his wife this day. "If Contrary to my present hopes I should not be able to Return this winter which I shall know in 10 or 15 Days I shall send George home with letters to you," he added. "Remember me to all friends. I am sorry to hear the Town is Still Divided about ministerial affairs." Bartlett to Mary Bartlett, November 27, 1775. NhHi.

John Hancock to George Clymer and Michael Hillegas

In Congress, November 27, 1775. Requests Continental Treasurers Clymer and Hillegas to pay $3,000 to the Pennsylvania Committee of Safety "for the pay of the Battalion raised by order of the Congress in this Colony, the said Committee to be accountable for the expenditure of said sum."[1]

Abstracted from *Am. Archives*, 4th ser. 3:1847.

[1] See *JCC*, 3:377.

John Hancock to the New York Provincial Congress

Philadelphia, November 27, 1775. Requests Provincial Congress "to furnish the troops raised in New Jersey, for the defence of New York, with as many fire arms as your Colony can conveniently spare," and "to send them to Lord Stirling, who commands the forces in the Jerseys."[1]

Abstracted from *Am. Archives*, 4th ser. 3:1760.

[1] See *JCC*, 3:376.

Robert R. Livingston, Jr., to John Jay

Dear John Fort George 27 Nov 1775.

I am now on the borders of Lake George where we have been detained this day & part of yesterday by a head wind & extream severe wheather. It is almost impossible to conceive the difference we found in the climate in half a miles riding. After we got over the mountain, within the reach of the woods that close from the lake it was like leaping from Octr. to Decr. We hope to leave this tomorrow & have prepared tinder boxes & axes for an enca[m]pment on the shore, as we can hardly expect as they tell us to get over in one day & hope to experience the pleasure of laying on hemlock beds. They laugh at us here for having brought but one blanket with us, but we hope to make it up in fire. This morning & part of yesterday I employed in going over the ground where the French received the first check from Sir Wm Johnston, & this afternoon I went over the remains of Fort William Henry, & the French lines part of which are still visible. No fort could have been more unfortunately scituated as it is commanded by almost all the grounds about it, yet it appears that the defence must have been prety gallant, since the approaches were begun at a distance yet they held out till they got within twenty yards of the fort, every gun but one of which was dismounted. You remember how the capitulation was violated & the horrid Slaughter of those brave fellows by the Indians under the command of Le Corne. I could hardly stir a step with[out] imagining that I walked over the grave of some unfortunate victim to the ambition of princes. We have little hopes of getting farther than Ticonderoga, as the lake is already frozen to Crown Point, & the cold of last night & this day have I dare say extended it not a little.

We met upon the road great numbers of the Connecticut Troops, most of whom as we are informed have gone home. It give[s] me great pleasure to find that Montgomerry has contrived to gain the affection as well of the New England Troops as our own. They speak of him in the highest terms. You cannot conceive at the distance you are, the difficulties he & his troops have had to struggle with, difficulties which I am amazed they should ever get over. By the last accounts we have from Montreal, we hear that Montgomerry had ordered a battery to be raisd at the mouth of the Sorrel & got a Gondola from the lake into the river St. Lawrence by which means he has stoped nine vessels loaded with stores from going down, & I am in great hope they will be taken. Carleton is said to have escaped by land to Quebeck, where we hear he has about 700 men chiefly of the Royal Emigrants (in which [. . .] Stephen Watts is inlisted) & they are employed below Quebeck in distressing the inhabitants who are favourable to us. Arnold we hear is at Point Levi waiting for assistance from Montgomerry who writes me that he will go down immediately if he can get his men to follow him in which we hear he is like to succeed. He proposes to secure the channel below Quebeck & advises that some able genl. be sent to take the command, and recommends Lee as he expects a pretty severe attack in the spring. I wish he would stay himself as I know [*no*] person of more prudence & conduct in our service, but I believe he finds that the provision made for a second in command, will not support one at the head of an army. He says nothing of this to me but express[es] a warm desire to return to his farm & mill.

I hope you have seen Harry. I have great satisfaction in the commendation he receive[s] from all who have served with him. Both his Colo & lieutenant Coll have resigned, so that I hope he will receive the rank to which he was before entitled, & has now earned. If he is still with you I pray you to take him by the hand, you will find amidst his roughness, many good qualities.

There is one subject on which I wished to speak to you had I had the pleasure of seeing you. They talk of sending the new levies to Boston, I think we should by no means consent to it, for many reasons that I dare not commit to paper, but which will suggest them selves to you. If you are not tired of politicks I would just mention to you that under the notion of soldiers baggage there are two compleat suits of cloathing at Montreal for each Soldier which have never yet be[en] unpacked. Now I have great doubt, whether by the capitulation they can be entitled to these & If they are, whether they may not be purchased of the soldiers for our Northern army at a cheap rate, indeed we may afford to pay well for them as the transportation will amount to nearly their value. If the Congress should take any order with respect to this matter, I should be glad if they would send off an express to stop them here. Hitherto I have only asked your attention to those matters which your love of your country makes it your pleasure to attend to. I could wish to detain you by the less important concerns of private friendship, which I never feel so strongly as when absence & solitude acquaint me with the movements of my own heart, but Pain[e] already considers me as impolite. Let me hear from you, & direct to the care of Walter Livingston at Albany. God bless you & remember me to any lady you think fit. Farewell. Yours Most Sincerely Robt R Livingston junr

P S I just hear [*it is*] doubtful whether Carlton has escaped. His vessels have made too fruitless attempts. Montgomerry has marched to join Arnold, most of our troops enlist. All those that Wo[o]ster had with him stay [*and*] amount to about 300.

RC (NNC).

Naval Committee to Dudley Saltonstall

Sir, Philadelphia Novr. 27th. 1775

The Congress are now preparing two Ships and two Brigantines to be fitted out as soon as possible to cruise against our common enemy. They have thought of you as a proper person to take the command of one of those ships as Captain.[1] If you enter into this service, which we take to be the service of your country, You will give us the earliest information and repair to Philadelphia as soon as your affairs will possibly admit and bring with you as many officers and seamen as you can procure at New London and between that place and Philadelphia. Those who may not be able to come with you, leave proper persons to encourage and conduct along after you.

If money should be necessary for the performance of this service you may draw on Mr Eleazer Miller, Merchant in New York who has money in his hands for that purpose.

In a day or two after you receive this, you will receive by the Messr. Mumfords the Conditions and encouragement offered to the Seamen.

We are Sir Your humble servants, Signed by Order of Comme.

Step Hopkins Silas Deane

John Adams Christ. Gadsden

Joseph Hewes

RC (MdAN). Written in a clerical hand and signed by Adams, Deane, Gadsden, Hewes, and Hopkins.

[1] Dudley Saltonstall (1738–96), privateersman in the French and Indian War and subsequently commander of merchant vessels, was offered this commission by the Naval Committee at the instance of his brother-in-law, Silas Deane. Saltonstall accepted the committee's offer on December 7 and became commander of the *Alfred*, the flagship of Esek Hopkins' tiny fleet. Adams, *Diary* (Butterfield), 3:350; Clark, *Naval Documents*, 2:1324; and *DAB*.

Caesar Rodney to Thomas Rodney

Nov. 27th. 1775.[1] Warns his brother to "give Strick orders to your people" to be careful of the chevaux-de-frise in the Delaware River. Reports that Mrs. Washington, Mrs. Gates, Mrs. Lewis, and "Collo. Custis & his Lady . . . all of Virginia set out from here this morning for the Camp at Cambridge" amid great pomp. "We have certain intelligence that there are 2500 or at least 2000 troops landed at Boston from Ireland, and it is thought by many that, with this reinforcement they will make a push to get out by attacking our lines

—If they should attempt it, I hope our Brave American Boys (Who have been hitherto fortunate) will give us a good account of them."[2]

Tr (DLC). Addressed: "Thomas Rodney Esq. in Dover Kent County." Copied from the original in possession of Stan V. Henkels for Edmund C. Burnett. *Stan V. Henkels Catalog,* no. 1328 (May 25, 1923), lot 134; and Rodney, *Letters* (Ryden), pp. 68–69.

[1] Rodney apparently also wrote to his brother during the previous week. Although only a transcript of his postscript to that letter survives, it was probably written the week of November 19, since November 18 was one of the rare Saturdays that Congress did not meet. "Last Friday Eveng the congress adjourned till Monday & on Saturday Morng Mr. Hancock & I went in his carriage to Trenton on a party of pleasure a relaxation from business. We were accompanied by Mr. Livingston of New York, & Mr Hooper of North Carolina. We returned on Sunday Eveng. At Trenton I heard a high character (from the inhabitants) of Capt Caldwell, as the bravest officer they had seen. It seems, the men in going up by water had all got drunk; & when they got to Trenton, kicked up a riot." Tr (DLC).

[2] For the continuation of this letter, see Rodney to Thomas Rodney, November 29, 1775.

James Duane to the New York Provincial Convention

Gentlemen Philad 28t Noveme 1775

I have the Honour of transmitting to you the enclosed Resolutions of the Congress in obedience to their Order.[1]

Our Letter on the Subject of the Fortress on Hudson's River remains unanswered. It is of so much Importance that our Colony should be satisfied of the Fidelity & abilities of the officer to whom this Command is entrusted that we wait impatiently for your Recommendation, flattering ourselves that it will have it's full weight. We have procured an Order in your favour for 50000 Dollars agreeable to the Request of the late Congress, and as soon as the Bills are signed, which has been unaccountebly protracted by the Gentlemen who undertook this Business, the money will be forwarded.[2]

I have the Honour to be with the greatest Respect Gent. Your most Obedient hume Servant Jas Duane

P.S.[3] The Resolution referred to in the enclosed Extracts is in the press and will speedily [*be*] published among other acts of Congress. 500 weight of powder is now forwarded; it was borrowed from Pensylvania by the Congress with difficulty.[4]

RC (NN). RC (N).

[1] Duane sent the Provincial Congress two congressional resolves of November 4, one on the manufacture of firelocks and the other on the harboring of deserters, and one of November 10 on the production of saltpetre. *JCC,* 3:322–23, 324–25, 347–48; and *Am. Archives,* 4th ser. 3:1760.

[2] In response to complaints by the Provincial Congress that it had insufficient money on hand to meet projected military expenditures, Congress resolved on November 11 to send $50,000 "to be accounted for by said convention [*congress*]." *JCC*, 3:352; and *Am. Archives*, 4th ser. 3:1300.

[3] This postscript was separated from Duane's letter when it was removed from the New York State Library and remains there among the papers of the New York Provincial Congress.

[4] Congress had resolved on November 8 to request the Philadelphia Committee of Safety to send 500 pounds of gunpowder to New York for use in the fortifications in the Highlands. *JCC*, 3:338–39.

Francis Lewis to John Alsop

Dr Sir Phila 28 Novemr. 1775

I have your favor of 24 Novmr. before me. I should think it advisable not to send any more Articles to the Northen department as I am convinced in my own mind we have exceeded the quantity order'd by Congress; would therefore advise the remainder upon hands be forwarded to Colo. Mifflin as the order for that department is not compleat. I shall send off the last Waggon Ld. from hence for that department tomorrow. In my former I sent you an abstract of Col. Mifflins requisition from hence; have only sent him abt. £3500 Currency from hence; what has been allready sent from Nw York my son & Hayman Levy will give you the amount. The order you know for that departmt was for £5000 sterlg. What I shall send from hence tomorrow will be chiefly Hatts, Breeches & a few shoes.

Att foot you have a list of the Articles allready sent to the Northen department.

Ld Dunmore has had a skirmich with 150 Virginians whom he put to the rout & took some prisoners. I am Dr Sir Your very Humble Servt.

Frans Lewis

P.S. I give you joy of the surender of Montreal. As they will there get Cloathing sufficient I think it would be advisable to order all the Clothing that is att Albany for the Camp at Cambridge.

Sent from Phila. to the Northen Troops.

Mittled Stockings	3402	pair
Felt Hatts	770	
Woolen Caps	156	
Leather Breeches	578	pair
Shoes	670	pair
Wastcoats	2695	
Watch Coats	379	

RC (NHi).

Secret Committee Minutes of Proceedings

Philadelphia Committee Cham[be]r Nov. 28 1775

At a Meeting of the Comee. of Secrecy Present Saml Ward, Benjamin Franklin, Thos. Willing, Josiah Bartlett & Francis Lewis Esqrs. A Contract was enterd into between Thos. Mumford of N. London in the Colony of Connecticut Mercht. of the one part, & the sd. Commee. of the other part.[1]

That a voyage or voyages shall be forthwith undertaken for the speedy procur[in]g of fifty tons of good gunpowder or in case any part of the gunpowder cannot be had, then as much Saltpetre &c.

MS (MH).

[1] The Secret Committee's order of November 28 authorizing Mumford to export wheat or other produce to the value of $15,000, which was signed by Ward, Franklin, Willing, Bartlett, and Lewis, and countersigned by President Hancock and Governor Trumbull, is listed in *G. A. Baker Catalog,* no. 15 (October 24, 1938), item 87, along with the contract between Mumford and the committee, item 88. According to the Secret Committee Account, September 27, 1775–August 26, 1776, Mumford received an advance of $28,500. For correspondence pertaining to this contract, see Silas Deane to Thomas Mumford, October 16? and November 14, 1775; and Mumford to Deane, October 19, 1775, *Collections of the Connecticut Historical Society* 23 (1930): 11–12.

Thomas Jefferson to John Randolph

Dear Sir Philadelphia Nov. 29. 1775

I am to give you the melancholy intelligence of the death of our most worthy Speaker which happened here on the 22d of the last month. He was struck with an Apoplexy, and expired within five hours.

I have it in my power to acquaint you that the successes of our arms have corresponded with the justice of our cause. Chambly and St. John's have been taken some weeks ago, and in them the whole regular army in Canada except about 40. or 50. men. This day we receive certain intelligence that our General Montgomery is received into Montreal: and expect every hour to be informed that Quebec has opened it's arms to Colo. Arnold who with 1100 men was sent from Boston up the Kennebec and down the Chaudiere river to that place. He expected to be there early this month. Montreal acceded to us on the 13th. and Carleton set out with the shattered remain[s] of his little army for Quebec where we hope he will be taken up by Arnold. In a short time we have reason to hope the delegates of Canada will join us in Congress and complete the American Union as far as we wish to have it completed. We hear that one of the British transports is arrived at Boston, the rest are beating off the coast in very bad weather. You will have heard before this reaches you that Ld. Dunmore has commenced hostilities in Virginia. That people bore with every thing till he attempted to burn the town of Hampton. They opposed and repelled him with considerable loss on his side and none on ours. It has raised our country into perfect phrensy. It is an immense misfortune to the whole empire to have a king of such a disposition at such a time. We are told and every thing proves it true that he is the bitterest enemy we have. His minister is able, and that satisfies me that ignorance or wickedness somewhere controuls him. In an earlier part of this contest our petitions told him that from our king there was but one appeal. The admonition was despised and that appeal forced on us. To undo his empire he has but one truth more to learn, that after colonies have drawn the sword there is but one step more they can take. That step is now pressed upon us by the measures adopted as if they were afraid we would not take it. Beleive me Dear Sir there is not in the British empire a man who more cordially loves a Union with Gr. Britain than I do. But by the god that made me I will cease to exist before I yeild to a connection on such terms as the British parliament propose and in this I think I speak the sentiments of America. We want neither inducement nor power to declare and assert a separation. It is will alone which is wanting and that is growing apace under the fostering hand of our king. One bloody campaign will probably decide everlastingly our future course; I am sorry to find a bloody campaign is decided on. If our winds and waters should not combine to rescue their shores from slavery, and General Howe's reinforcement should arrive in safety we have hopes he will be inspirited to come out of Boston and take another drubbing: and we must drub you soundly before the sceptered tyrant will know we are not mere brutes, to crouch under his hand and kiss the rod with which he deigns to scourge us.

Edmund passed thro' this city on his way to Williamsburgh to see whether his presence might be of service in settling his uncle's affairs. He was in perfect health, and will return again to the camp at Cambridge. My compliments to Mrs. Randolph and the young ladies and beleive me to be Dear Sir Your's &c.

FC (DLC). Jefferson, *Papers* (Boyd), 1:268–70.

Francis Lightfoot Lee to a Friend in London

Dear Sir, Philadelphia Novr. 29th. 1775

This Letter I hope will find you perfectly recover'd from your Virginia fever, & the fatigues of the Voyage. I have not been in Virga.

since we parted, & have not been able to hear any thing of your affairs. While the present distractions continue you will not expect I dare say to receive much in the remittance way, however I have written to Esqr. Lee to push your principal creditors, & remit what he can get from them. I have paid Doctor Fauntleroys acct here, for which I have drawn on Mr. Lee. As the difference between the Ministry & America is not likely soon to be settled, I suppose the price of tobo. will be high in London this winter, by which means you will make a saving voyage. If you can find an opportunity, shall be glad to receive acct. sales & acct. current. Is it high treason to correspond upon mercantile business?[1] Poor old England how is it degraded! You will see the news in the public papers. Mrs. Lee joins me in wishing you & our friends on Tower Hill, health & happiness.[2]

Francis Light. Lee

RC (ViHi).

[1] An allusion to the king's proclamation of August 23, 1775, forbidding correspondence with those in rebellion in North America. *Am. Archives,* 4th ser. 3:240–41.

[2] For the continuation of this letter, see Lee to a Friend in London, December 11, 1775.

Richard Henry Lee to Catherine Macaulay

Dear Madam, Philadelphia 29th Novr 1775

As a good *Christian* properly attached to your native Country, I am sure you must be pleased to hear that North America is not fallen, nor likely to fall down before the *Images* that the King hath set up. After more than ten years abuse and injury on one side, of modest representation on the other; Administration at length determine to try if the sword cannot affect, what threatening Acts of Parliament had in vain attempted; that is, the ruin of the just rights and liberty of this great Continent. Lexington, Concord, and Bunkers Hill opened the tragic scene; and clearly proved to the whole world that N. America had no reliance but on its own virtue in Arms. The battle of Bunkers Hill, tho followed by strong reenforcements, has not enlarged the prison of the Ministerial Army many paces. After the clearest proofs that the Quebec Act was going to be carried into effect by marching an Army of Canadians &c. into these Colonies, and when every attempt had been made to bring the Savages on the defenceless women and Children along our extensive frontiers; it became high time, on principles of self preservation, to avert the meditated [Evi]l. The war was therefore sent into their own Country having first, by proper Agents and Memorials, explained to the Inhabitants of Canada and to the Indians, the views and objects of the United Colonies. Success, equal to the justice of the cause, has followed this undertaking. With indefatigable zeal 3000 Men crossed Lake Champlain and laid siege to Fort St. Johns, which place, as the key to Canada, had been made very strong by Govr. Carlton, and garrisoned with 500 regular Troops and 100 Canadians. During this siege, a detachment from the Army pierced further into the Country, invested and took Fort Chamble (between St. Johns & Montreal) that was garrison'd by about 80 Regulars. Gen. Carleton having by this time collected 800 Men, marched to the relief of St. Johns, when 600 of the Am. Troops met and defeated him. This was presently followed by the surrender of St. Johns, with all the Garrison prisoners of war, and there they found a plentiful supply of military stores. A rapid march to Montreal was next made, and yesterd[ay] brought the account of the surrender of that Town [*to*] General Montgomerie on Monday the 13th instant upon condition that the people should quietly enjoy their religion and not be molested in their property. Gen. Carleton had escaped down the St. Laurence with 2 or 3 Vessels, but it was expected he would fall into the hands of Collo. Arnold, then at Quebec, to which place he had penetrated with 1000 men by the rivers Kenebec and Chaudiere. No doubt is entertained here, but that this Congress will be shortly joined by Delegates from Canada, which will then complete the union of 14 provinces. Thus have the evil machinations of an unprincipled Administration been turned greatly to the honor and security of the people they meant to ruin. The proclamation that followed the receipt of so humble a petition has determined the Councils of America to prepare for defence with the utmost vigor both by Sea & Land. Altho' upon the former of these elements, America may not at first be in condition to meet the force of G. Britain, yet as Hercules was once in his Cradle, so, time and attention will, under the fostering hand of Liberty, make great changes [in] this matter. The knowing Ones are of opinion that by next Spring so many Armed Vessels will be fitted out as to annoy our enemies greatly, and to afford much protection to the Trade of North America. It is wonderful what great benefits have already been obtained by the infant efforts of some Colonies in this way. Whilst this Country abounds in Wood, iron & Artisans, whilst a soil and Climate fitted for the abundant production of Hemp is possessed by an industrious people, strength on the sea cannot long be wanting. The Congress has ordered a suspension of all exportation for a certain time. This looks like ruin to the West Indies. The almost infinite distress that these Islands will feel in a short time is realy shocking to human[it]y, but in this case, charity must begin at home, and the liberties of North America be at all events secured.

The animation and perseverance that the spirit of Liberty and resentment furnishes was well displaid in the seige of St. Johns. Twas a wet cold season, and the Men thinly clothed, the ground so low & wet on which they were placed, that they were compelled to lay heaps of brush, and weeds on the Top of the brush, that they might sleep out of the water at night. In this horrid situation they vigorously pressed the seige for 47 days, when the Garrison surrendered prisoners of war.

Lord Dunmores unparallelled conduct in Virginia has, a few Scotch excepted, united every Man in that large Colony. If Administration had searched thro the world for a person the best fitted to ruin their cause, and procure union and success for these Colonies, they could not have found a more complete Agent than Lord Dunmore.

We regret not having heared from England since early in September, but our Congress disregarding this, are proceeding with vigor, perseverance, and judgement in effecting the great purpose for which they were appointed.

You know the Writer of this letter Madam, and therefore it is as unnecessary to sign it, as it would be to assure you of his affection and esteem for your whole self, and all your connections. We hope all are well at St. Bees and that proper care will be taken there in this tempestuous Season.

The last Post produces a proclamation from Ld. Dunmore declaring Liberty to the Slaves and proclaiming the Law martial to be the only law in that Colony—And all this he says is done "in virtue of the power and authority to me given by his Majesty."[1] Is it possible that his Majesty could authorize him thus to remedy evils which his Lordship himself had created? I would have inclosed you a copy of this curious proclamation, had I not feared it would too much increase the size of this packet.

The inhumanity with which this war (unprovoked as it has been on this side) is prosecuted, is realy shocking. A few days since, in the midst of winters [. . .] that northern climate, did Gen Howe turn out of Boston between two & three hundred Women and Children without even the necessaries of life. Some of them died on the water side before their hospitable Countrymen could relieve them. This cruelty is the more unpardonable, as these unhappy people have been by violence detained in Boston until now, contrary to the faith of a most positive agreement entered into between the Town & Gen. Gage.

The inclosed printed papers will shew you Madam how successful the cause of liberty has been in Canada. No doubt is entertained of Quebec & Govr. Carleton having fallen into the hands of Gen. Mongomerie & Colo. Arnold. A Valuable Artillery Store Ship is just fallen into our hands and the Stores are at our Camp at Cambridge.

The Ship is the Nancy I think.

FC (ViU).

[1] Dunmore's proclamation of November 7, 1775, is printed in *Am. Archives,* 4th ser. 3:1385.

Robert R. Livingston, Jr., to Richard Montgomery

Dear Genl Ticonderoga 29th Novr 1775

I arrived here yesterday with two Gent from the Congress as a committee to settle the arrangment of the money & if necessary to go over to you.[1] But we find that your foresight & Genl. Schuylers has anticipated our instructions. I believe we shall leave you to manage what you have so prosperously begun, I shd. almost say finished. I long to take you by the hand & to talk over with you the ennumerable fatigues & difficulties which I see from your letter to the Genl to me that you have sustained.[2] I assure you that I have most sincerely simpatized with you, however I would have you comfort your[self] with the approbation of the continent which you most heartily have. If heaven shd. again bless us with peace, these very troubles will be sources of pleasure, as our friend Virgil expresses it "Forsan Hæc meminise juvabit." But I am restrained from coming over to you by reasons of which Schuyler approves & which I am sure will be very satisfactory to you when I shall have an opportunity of mentioning them. I do not care at present to trust any thing to paper which I would not chuse to let the world see. I wish to heaven you could so contrive it in your new arrangement of Officers as to leave of[f] those who are unworthy to command. I know it is difficult but it is necessary. A certain battallion is so exceedingly ill officered that I shd. be sorry to see it continued especially with the rank it now holds. I should be glad to hear in what manner you have settled this. Coll Wyncoop tells me that you have purchased cloathing for the troops that have reenlisted without making any deduction from their pay. This is exceeding the terms prescribed by the congress & I am fearful will create some difficulty. You see by the instructions sent you by Genl. Schuyler that the men who were at the taking of St. Johns, Montreal & Ticonderoga will be entitled on their reenlistment to two months pay. If you have not published this I believe it would be best to say nothing of it & lay outt that money in cloathing. I shall talk to the genl. & my Colleagues on that head when you shall hear from me again. We have little good news from England, every thing looks as if they were resolved to push us hard next summer. If we have but the means of defence I shall not be apprehensive of any thing they can do, I can not however help lammenting that we shd.

be forced to by the mad policy of a few bad men to continue a war that must be ruinous to those whom we wish to consider as friends.

I do not know how to approve or blame your Desire of quiting the service. Your country still wants you, nor do I know how your loss will be supplied, & yet the sacrifice you must make is such as can hardly be borne by a man of any sensibility or feeling, heaven direct you to what is best.

As for the politicks of our province it still moves in the same rascally channel in which it has hitherto run. When I last heard from New York the tories were loud presuming upon a miscarriage in Canada. What alteration your success has made I am unable to say. I have much to say but am called down to see Capt. Gordon who is below. I shall either continue this or write to you again as I have opportunity, but least the post shd. go too early I will stop here & remain Most Affectionately my Dr Sir Yours &c.

Robt R Livingston junr

RC (NHpR:Livingston-Redmond Collection deposit). Addressed: "Brigadier Genl Montgomerry, Montreal."

[1] See Committee to the Northward Minutes of Proceedings, November 30, 1775.

[2] Presumably a reference to Montgomery's letter to Livingston of November 1775, on which see *Am. Archives,* 4th ser. 3:1638–39.

Massachusetts Delegates to the Massachusetts Council

Gentlemen Philadelphia Nov. 29 1775

We wrote you on the 24 Instant that we thought the matter in dispute between the two Houses ought to be laid before the Congress and their Sentiments taken upon it, but for various reasons, too many now to enumerate, this has not as yet been done;[1] however we have consulted the members of the Congress individually and upon conversing with them, we find that in general they are extreamly desirous we should Conform, in all Governmental Matters, as near as possible to the Spirit & Substance of our Charter, and it is their Opinion that, when the Resolutions of the 18 July last was passed it was the intention of the Congress, not to superceed the resolve of the 8 of June last, but to leave such Governments as were competent to the Business to model and regulate their Militia agreable to their several Constitutions as prescribed by their respective Charters. However, they said as it appeared from our representation of matters, that our House of Representatives had conceived otherwise of this Matter & had Claimed a right to a Voice, with the Council, in the choice of militia officers & that if the dispute was Continued it could throw the Colony into a Ferment; and considering also that at this critical Juncture our Militia might be suddenly wanted and it was therefore highly expedient & necessary it should be immediately settled & regulated, it was their Opinion that it would be adviseable for the Council, during the present exigency of our affairs, to gratify the House of Representatives in this Claim but not by any means any further to deviate from the Charter. Thus we have collected and advised you of the Sentiments of the members of the Congress in general, which we doubt not will be some aid to you in your deliberations & determinations upon this Important Subject, and were we present we should Vote Agreable to this Advise.

We Conclude with great Respect Your Honor's most obedient humble Servs John Hancock

Thomas Cushing

[*P.S.*] Mr Hancock writes your Assembly on publick matters.[2]

RC (M-Ar). Written by Cushing and signed by Hancock and Cushing. Endorsed: "In Council Decr 12th 1775. Read & ordered that an attested Copy thereof be sent down to the Hon. House. Perez Morton, Dpy Secy."

[1] See John Adams to James Otis, November 23; Samuel Adams to James Otis, November 23; and Massachusetts Delegates to the Massachusetts Council, November 24, 1775.

[2] Probably John Hancock to the Massachusetts Assembly, December 2, 1775.

Caesar Rodney to Thomas Rodney

Wednesday Novm. 29th. 1775

You will find in this days paper an account of the surrender of Montreal to General Montgomery on the thirteenth instant, the Congress has (as yet) Received no express but expect one every hour as the account is generally believed,[1] Mr. Livingston being a man of Carrector, Brother to a Member of the Congress and brother-in-law to General Montgomery.

Pray take care to have both your & My business in Such order as to receive as little damage as possible in your absence particularly, take care that all the Chimneys be swept clean. I am with my love to all my friends Yours Caesar Rodney

P.S. Remember to bring up one of Caesar's frocks that I may have his Uniform made and as you come by land I desire you would inform yourself what State our Money printing is in. I shall want to know.

Tr (DLC). A continuation of Rodney to Thomas Rodney, November 27, 1775.

[1] This day Congress received General Schuyler's November 18 letter informing them of the fall of Montreal. *JCC*, 3:389.

Committee of Secret Correspondence to Arthur Lee

Sir, Phila 30 Novr 1775

We have the honor to be appointed by the Congress a Committee of Correspondence with the friends of America on the other side of the———.[1] Our institution is with design to preserve secresy, & thereby secure our friends, who we suppose may be endangered and alarmed by the late proclamation.[2] It is considered as of the utmost consequence to the cause of Liberty, that an intercourse should be kept up, and we shall be obliged by your sentiments of the most probable and secure method of effecting it. If any should be certainly resolved on which you may think much concerns America to be apprised of, we shall consider it within the power of our appointment to pay the expence of an Express Boat, if you can provide one under proper cautions.

We are Sir your most obd. servants.[3]

Tr (ViU). In the hand of Richard Henry Lee.

[1] John Dickinson, Benjamin Franklin, Benjamin Harrison, John Jay, and Thomas Johnson were appointed on November 29 to correspond "with our friends in Great Britain, Ireland, and other parts of the world." *JCC,* 3:392. Additional information on the selection of the committee is available in the autobiography of John Adams, who reported that soon after it was formed John Jay came to him to apologize for his "being omitted in the Choice of the two great Secret Committees of Commerce and Correspondence." "He said in express terms," Adams explained, " 'that my Character stood very high with the Members, and he knew there was but one Thing which prevented me from being universally acknowledged to be the first Man in Congress, and that was this, there was a great Division in the House, and two Men had effected it, Samuel Adams and Richard Henry Lee, and as I was known to be very intimate with those two Gentlemen, many others were jealous of me.' " Adams, *Diary* (Butterfield), 3:340–41.

[2] On November 13 Congress appointed a committee consisting of Richard Henry Lee, William Livingston, and James Wilson to respond to "sundry illegal ministerial proclamations that have lately apppeared in America." The committee's report, a "declaration" focusing upon the royal proclamation of August 23, 1775, was submitted on November 29, adopted on December 6, and subsequently distributed in the form of a broadside. See *Am. Archives,* 4th ser. 3:240–41; and *JCC,* 3:353, 392, 409–12, 513.

[3] Lee added the following note at the bottom of this document, probably sometime after September 29, 1779, when William Carmichael was elected secretary to the minister plenipotentiary to negotiate a treaty with Spain. See *JCC,* 15:1127. "Copy of a letter from the Committee of Secret Correspondence to Dr. Lee soon after the first institution of this Committee—its members then were Mr. Harrison, Dr. Franklin, Mr. Dickinson, Mr. Johnson, Mr. Jay. The correspondence here requested was entered upon by Dr. Lee, and one of his dispatches being committed to the care of Mr. Carmichael, he with Mr. Deane in concert opened, and detained this dispatch for two years and made use of its contents to create enemies to Dr. Lee. Dr. Franklin knew of this proceedure and expressed not his disapprobation, but on the contrary continued the patron, friend, and intimate of Mr. Deane. The Congress being made thoroughly acquainted with this whole proceedure, instead of censuring the authors of an injury done to their pledged faith, were not only

silent, but rewarded Mr. Deane, and advanced Mr. Carmichael to an office of high trust."

Committee to the Northward Minutes of Proceedings

30 Nov. 1775

Minutes of a Conference with Genl. Schuyler[1]

The opinion 3000 Troops necessary in Canada for the spring that those who may remain this winter be sufficient till spring.

About 200 of the New England Troops have reinlisted.

About 1000 of New York in Canada what number will reinlist unknown.

Coll. Easton & Coll. Beadle are still in Canada but on their way home.

Warner with the Green Mountain boys returned.

Livingston, Arnold has carried in about 600 men.

That 4 companies will be necessary at the two Posts of Ticonderoga & Fort George.

Genl. Schuylers Opinion that at least 3000 men shd be in Canada before the Ice breaks up. That there are about 1900 there now including Arnolds, many of whom he imagines will relieve.

That 2 regiments be immediately raised including 4 Comps. that are now recruiting & the Officers sent to recruit in whatever province the Congress may direct.

Directions with respect to provisions already given we having a sufficientcy till spring in Canada.

That resolutions with respect to the bounty already executed.

That the fortifications at Ticonderoga be repaired but that some not be done this winter. Tho if men could be procured the timber might be prepared at a much cheaper rate than in the spring. That a communication shd be opened between Johansburgh & Fort Ann by which means the fortress may be most easily reinforced & supplied. That no Fortress need be erected at Crown Point.

That few arms can be procured in the way that is proposed. Those that were in the hands of the New York Troops belong to that province. When they are stoped credit must be given.

Canadian Regiment already set on foot.

Tun of powder to be sent down tomorrow. Cannon cannot be moved till the lake is froze.

That Genl. Montgomerry from the 1st Letter of the Congress & the necessity of the case was induced to reinlist the Troops. What arrangement he has made of the forces is unknown to us. That Genl. Schuyler has wrote to him to transmitt it as soon as possible.

That Genl. has already ordered the officers who do not chuse to reinlist to return their [names?].

To mention Capt. Lamb.

Beding—Barrack Master—regimental paymaster—Conductor of Attillery.

MS (N). In the hand of Robert R. Livingston, Jr.

[1] The Committee to the Northward (Livingston, Langdon, and Paine), drawing upon information obtained from several on-site inspections and discussions such as this one with General Schuyler, submitted a report to Congress on December 23. *JCC*, 3:446–52. On January 8–9, 1776, Congress adopted several resolutions based on that report and the recommendations of another committee appointed to respond to Schuyler's letters. *JCC*, 3:424, 436, 455, 456, 459, 4:38–40, 43–45. See also John Hancock to Philip Schuyler, November 10, 1775, note 2.

Committee to the Northward to Richard Montgomery

Sir Ticonderoga 30th Novr. 1775

The Congress having done us the honour to Appoint us as a Committee to Confer with the General and yourself on the measures Necessary to be taken for the reinlistment of the Army, as also to Conciliate the affections of the Canadians and to remove as far as in us lay every Objection that the good people of that Province might have to a Union with the thirteen Colonies, who are Strugling in the Glorious Cause of freedom, We arrived here a few days Since in prosecution of that design; but are extreamly happy to find that General Schuyler and yourself have in a Great measure by your prudence and foresight anticipated our business, and renderd a Journey into Canada in some measure unnecessary at present which indeed we rather decline on Account of the Advanced season of the year and the improbability of your being able to lend us any assistance, while the enemies of the Natural Rights of man continue their hostilities against our fellow Subjects in that Province, and Confine your Attention to those Military opperations which are Necessary to procure their Relief.

We cannot help however expressing the ardent wishes of the Congress that you would Cherish the first dawnings of liberty among a people, who have early testified their sense of its Value if we may be Admitted to Judge from the Assistance they afforded you in repelling its enemies. That you would assure them that the Honble. the Congress have thro us declared that they hold their Rights as dear as their own, and that on their Uniting with them they will exert their utmost endeavours to procure, for them and their posterity the blessing of a free government and that Security to their property and persons which is derived from the British Constitution—that they hold Sacred the rights of Conscience, and will never disturb them in the free enjoyment of their Religion.[1]

The Honb. Congress Recommend it to you to use your utmost endeavours to procure a free meeting of the people in their several Parishes, out of whom to Chuse a Provincial Convention who will form such Rules and regulations as the present exigencies may render Necessary for their Province. From this body they hope that delagates will be chosen to meet and Cooperate with them in such measures as they shall think Necessary for their mutual Security against the unjust Violences of an arbitrary ministry. If the unsettled state of the Province should Prevent a free and full Representation of the whole Colony, yet the Honb. the Congress will Acquiess in the Choice of Such Towns, Parishes and districts, as may think it proper to send deputies—or if previous to their meeting in Congress they should have any Difficulties which it is out of your power to remove, a Committee of Congress will at any time when the Communication is more open be ready to meet and Confer with them on the Subject at Albany, Montreal, or any other place, which they May think proper to appoint. We need not mention to you the propriety of punishing in the Severest manner any of our Troops, who should so far forget the duty that they owe to us and our worthy Allies, as to offer the least injury either to their property or Persons. We know not your Arrangement of the Army, but Presume you have not in the distribution of Commissions over looked the Merrit of those who deserve well of their Country, nor Sufferd them to be Advanced who have merrited its Censure.

General Schuyler has inclosed our last instructions which will shew you the Design of the Congress with Respect to Quebeck but which from your letter we find you have already in some measure Anticipated. He also gives you our Sense with Respect to the Clothing and bounty to the Troops, in the management of which we must rely upon your prudence and doubt not that the Congress will make good any engagements to which you may have found it Necessary to enter. The other Subjects of our Conference with the General, some of which are mentioned to you in his letter and others wanting the Sanction of Congress we think it unnecessary at present to trouble you with. The post being just abt to Depart we cannot enlarge. If any other opportunity should offer, we may write you again before we leave this.

We Congratulate you upon the happy Success of our Arms and hope shortly to hear that your prosperous endeavours has left no footing to our enemies in that Country from which they hoped to draw the most effectual supplies.

We Remain with the greatest Respect Your most Hbl Servts

Rob. R. Livingston

Rob. T. Paine

Jno Langdon

Tr (DNA: PCC, item 166). Endorsed by Charles Thomson: "Decr. 23. A Letter and Report of the committee appointed to repair to Ticonderoga & Confer with Genl. Schuyler. Read Decr. 23. 1775—referred to Mr. Dickinson, Mr. McKean, Mr. Wythe, Mr. Hooper, Mr. Jefferson, Mr. Langdon." FC (DLC). In the hand of Robert R. Livingston, Jr., though not signed.

[1] The following phrases were crossed out in Livingston's draft: "Tho the power of Government being now in a great measure dissolved in that province it will be necessary to take some measures to prevent the evils that may arise from confusion & anarchy but as the congress wish not presume to interfere in the internal policy of any province but leave that solely to the management of its own members." DLC. Montgomery's political plans for Canada are discussed in Gustave Lanctot, *Canada & the American Revolution 1774–1783*, trans. Margaret M. Cameron (Toronto: Clarke, Irwin & Co., 1967), pp. 94–96.

John Hancock to Richard Montgomery

Sir, Philada. Novr. 30th 1775

I am directed by the Congress to transmit you their Thanks for your great and signal Services in the Expedition committed to your Command against the British Troops in the Province of Canada.[1]

The Reduction of St. Johns and Montreal they esteem of inexpressible Advantage to the united Colonies, and the most mortifying Contravention to the ministerial System of enslaving the extensive Territory of Canada. It cannot therefore fail of reflecting singular Lustre on the Character of a General so issentially instrumental in preserving that Liberty, by the Abolition of which, a corrupt Parliament intended to annihilate every Appearance of Freedom in America. Nor, are the Humanity and Politeness, with which you have treated those in your Power less illustrious Instances of Magnanimity, than the Valour, by which you reduced them to it. The Congress, utterly abhorrent from every Species of Cruelty to Prisoners, and determined to adhere to this benevolent Maxim, till the Conduct of their Enemies renders a Deviation from it indispensible necessary, will ever applaud their Officers for beautifully blending the Christian with the Conqueror; and never, in endeavouring to acquire the Character of the Hero, to lose that of the Man.

The Victories already gained in Canada afford us a happy presage of the Smiles of Providence on the farther Designation of the Continental Arms in the North, and will in all Probability greatly facilitate the entire Reduction of the deluded Malignants in that Province to Liberty. These, Sir, are Exploits so glorious in their Execution, and so extensive in their Consequences, that the Memory of Genl. Montgomery, will doubtless be of equal Duration, with the Remembrance of the Benefits derived from his Command.

At the same Time that the Congress rejoice with you in the Success of their Arms under your more immediate Direction, they cannot avoid expressing their Concern at the Intimation you give of your Intention to retire from the Service.[2] They are sensible that the Loss of so brave and experienced an officer will be universally regretted as a Misfortune to all America. But they still hope, that upon reconsidering the Matter, the same generous and patriotic Motives, which first induced you to take so capital a Part in opposing the unprovoked Hostilities of an unnatural Enemy, will prompt you to persevere in the Cause, and to continue gathering fresh Laurels, till you find our Oppressions reduced to Reason, and America restored to her constitutional Liberties. I am &c J.H. Prest.

LB (DNA: PCC, item 12A).

[1] On November 29 Congress received letters from General Montgomery to General Schuyler of November 13 and from Schuyler to Hancock of November 18 announcing the capitulation of Montreal, and on the following day it appointed a committee to draw up letters of thanks for them and for Gen. David Wooster, who also held a command in the northern department. *JCC*, 3:389, 393; PCC, item 153, 1:294–301; and *Am. Archives*, 4th ser. 3:1595–96, 1602–3. This committee presented to Congress on December 12 draft letters to Montgomery, Schuyler, and Wooster, "which were read and approved, and *Ordered* . . . to be transmitted." Although these letters were not submitted to Congress and approved until December 12, and although they were copied into Hancock's letterbook after letters of December 8, all three were dated November 30, 1775. It seems probable that the committee actually wrote them on the 30th and that the subsequent delay between their composition and submission to Congress was due to the press of more urgent business. See *JCC*, 3:424; and PCC, item 12A, 1:26–29.

[2] Montgomery had intimated a wish to resign from his command in his letter to Schuyler of November 13, 1775. See *Am. Archives*, 4th ser. 3:1602–3.

John Hancock to Philip Schuyler

Sir, Novr. 30th. 1775.[1]

It is with the utmost Satisfaction that the Congress received your Information of the Surrender of Montreal, & the general Success which has attended the American Arms in the Province of Canada.

They are sensible of the various Obstacles you had to encounter, and have unanimously resolved that your Conduct, Attention, and Perseverance, merit the Thanks of the united Colonies, which I have now the Pleasure of presenting to you.

The Congress hear with Concern your Request of Leave to retire.[2] They regret the Injuries your Health has sustained in the Service, and beg you will not insist on a Measure, which would at once deprive America of the future Benefits she expects from your Zeal and Abilities, and rob you of the Honor of compleating the glorious Work you have so happily & successfully begun.

You have hitherto risen superior to a Thousand Difficulties in giving Freedom to a great and an oppressed People. You have already reaped many Laurels, but a plentiful Harvest still invites you. Proceed therefore, and let the Footsteps of Victory open a Way for Blessings of Liberty, and the Happiness of well ordered Government to visit that extensive Dominion.

Consider that the Road to Glory is seldom strewed with Flowers, and that when the black and bloody Standard of Tyranny is erected in a Land possessed by Freemen, Patriots cease to remain inactive Spectators of their Country's Fall.

Reflect, Sir, that the Happiness, or Misery, of Millions yet unborn, is now to be determined; and remember that you will receive an honourable Compensation for all your Fatigues, in being able to leave the Memory of illustrious Actions, attended by the gratitude of a great and free People, as a fair, a splendid, and a valuable Inheritance to your Posterity. I am &c

LB (DNA: PCC, item 12A).

[1] On the date of this letter, see Hancock to Richard Montgomery, this date, note 1.

[2] In a letter to Hancock of November 18, 1775, General Schuyler had expressed a wish to retire from his command at the end of the current Canadian campaign. See PCC, item 153, 1:294–301; and *Am. Archives,* 4th ser. 3:1595–96.

John Hancock to David Wooster

Sir, Philada. Novr. 30th 1775[1]

That a conscious Pleasure arises from Patriotism, your Experience must have already evinced to you. Your Brethen in America, on whose Behalf that Patriotism has been exerted, will not with-hold that Accession of Pleasure which you ought to receive, from their just and grateful Applauses.

I am directed by the Congress to transmit to you the Thanks of the united Colonies for the very important Assistance which you have contributed in reducing St. Johns, and spreading the Banners of Freedom over the greatest Part of Canada.

I am &c. J.H. Prest.

LB (DNA: PCC, item 12A).

[1] On the date of this letter, see Hancock to Richard Montgomery, this date, note 1.

Francis Lewis to John Alsop

Dr Sir Phila. 30, Novemr. 1775

As the major part of the Forces Commanded by Genl. Montgomery are now in Kennady where they will remain the Winter where we learn they will be compleatly cloathed and upon better terms than by those provided from hence, I shd therefore think it advisable to stop all articles of Cloathing that are not sent off from Albany or even Fort George and order them to be sent to the Camp at Cambridge where they will be usefull, but if they are sent on the other quarter they will not be there received in the course of the Winter.

Pray in your next advise me with the quantity & cost of what has been engaged at Nw York for the Northen department, for the 20000 dollars Warranted for that purpose is allready swallow'd up here and not sufficient therefore must move for a second Warrant.

The S[ecret] Committee have in all their Contracts hitherto given their honor for the security of those Vessels as may be seized &c which the Owners are satisfied; I do not think it wd. look well in us to require further securities than our Neighbours. We should be all upon an equal footing.

If can get a Waggon shall this day or tomorrow send to Powles [Paulus] Hook ferry 500 lb. of powder for the use of the fortification in the Highlands, there will be also in the same Waggon some Breeches & Hats for the Troop at Cambridge, pray let there be a carefull person to receive. I am Dr. Sr. Yours &c Frans Lewis

RC (NHi).

Secret Committee Minutes of Proceedings

Philadelphia Comm[itt]ee Chambr Nov. 30th. 1775

At a meeting of the C[ommittee] of S[ecrecy] present Saml. Ward, Benjn. Franklin, Silas Deane, Philip Livingston, Josiah Bartlett, Francis Lewis. A Contract was enterd into between Saml. Mifflin & George Clymer Esqrs. of the City of Philadelphia Merchts. & the sd. Committee.[1]

That a voyage be immediately undertaken to some proper port or ports in Europe for the speedy procuring of twenty tons of good gunpowder, or if Gunpowder cannot be had, as much salt petre with 15 lb of Sulphur to every hundred weight thereof, as will make that quan[t]ity, five hundred stand of good arms & three thousand good plain double bridled gunlocks for the use of the U[nited] C[olonies].

MS (MH).

[1] According to the Secret Committee Account, September 27, 1775–August 26, 1776, Mifflin and Clymer received an advance of $7,500.

Silas Deane's Proposals to Congress

Proposals &c [November ? 1775][1]

1st. The Colonies on this Continent (viz.) New Hampshire, Massachusetts Bay, Rhode Island, Connecticut, New York, New Jersey, Pennsylvania, Delaware, Maryland, Virginia, North Carolina, South Carolina, & Georgia, will enter into a mutual Confederation for the defence of their Liberties and immunities against all invaders or Violators thereof whatever and shall be bound to each other, for defending to the last extremity the privileges of the whole, & of each separately.

2d. No Treaty, or proposal of Accommodation with those with whom they are, or may be, Contending shall be entered into, or made, but by, & with the Consent, of the whole in General Congress, by their Delegates assembled.

3d. A General Congress shall be held, at least once Annually forever, to consist of delegates, elected by the several Houses, of Assembly in the several Colonies, which Congress shall convene for the first Time each Year on the 5th Day of September unless sd. 5th Day fall on Sunday in which case on the Day next following.

4th. To preserve an equall Representation the Number of Souls, in each Colony, shall be taken Annually, and the Accts thus fairly taken and properly attested, transmitted to the Secretary of the General Congress.

5th. To every Twenty five Thousand Souls one Voice, or Delegate, shall be allowed, in general Congress from each Colony respectively.[2]

6th. In determining on Supplies of Men, or Money, and in passing Accts. Laid before them & other Concerns of a Lesser Nature there must be a Majority of Numbers represented in Congress, independant of particular Colonies, as for instance on a question of Supply, Three Delegates from one Colony vote, Two for, & one against, the Numbers stand Fifty and Twenty five Thousand, or Two & one for that Colony & so on thro' the whole the Majority of the whole taken.

7th. In determining on Warr, or peace, on the privileges of the Colonies in General, or of any one in particular, there must be, in order to make a Vote, a Majority both of Colonies, and Numbers shall be Necessary.

8th. Each Colony shall in every respect, retain its present mode of internal police & legislation, excepting that no house of Assembly shall sit longer than Three Years, or less than one, before a New Election shall take place. That they shall sit on their Own Adjournments—That where the Governors are Now appointed by the Crown, they shall be appointed by the General Congress during good Behavior & The same with respect to Leiut. Governors. Councellors now appointed by the Crown as well as Judges & other Officers in the

Royal Appointment in Royal Governments shall be elected by the Representatives of the People in their General Assembly, and so elected, to hold their Offices during good Behavior. In the Charter & proprietary Governments the same Course as at present.

9th. Any Councellor, Judge, or other Officer, elected by such Assembly and afterward by them displaced, if he think himself injured, may appeal to the General Congress, who shall have the final Cognizance in such Cases.

10th. All disputes between different Colonies, which they cannot agree to determine otherways, shall be referr'd to the General Congress and their Judgment to be final in all such Cases.

11th. That the first place, for assembling such Congress shall be at Philadelphia, & on the 5th Day of September A.D. After which, it shall be, in the power of sd. Congress, to adjourn, to such Time & place as shall be agreeable to them, & to alter the place of their first Annual Meeting as Time & Circumstances shall require.

12th. The Militia, of the several Colonies, shall remain under the direction of their respective Legislatures who are to take their more general Instructions from sd. Congress. But all Forces whither by Land, or Sea, called into Actual Service shall be under the Directions of the Congress.

13th. The Congress shall have power of Appointing their Secretary, or Secretaries, and all other Continental Officers, who shall not hold their respective Commissions, during the pleasure or during the sitting of that Congress but during good Behavior & shall be liable to be removed by any subsequent Congress for misbehavior in Office and for No other Cause.

14th. There shall be one Currency, or Rate of Money, thro the whole of the Colonies, and in Those, where the Governor has the power at present, of a Negative on the Acts of Assembly, such Governor shall transmit all Acts pass'd to the Next Congress to be by them approved or rejected.

15th. No Government, Charter or proprietary, shall have the power of laying any Duty, excise, or Custom on any Wares, or Merchandize; but when such is necessary, in any Government or Colony, the Assembly shall by their Delegates apply to the General Congress therefor.

16th. The avails of all duties, custom, or excise laid on any Wares, Merchandize or Commerce which shall be Collected shall be paid into The Treasury of the United Colonies.

MS (CtHi). In the hand of Silas Deane.

[1] Interest in a plan of confederation, which had been stimulated by the proposed "Articles of Confederation" Franklin submitted to Congress on July 21st, was renewed in the autumn of 1775 and briefly bubbled to the surface in Congress again on January 16, 1776. At the time of the August adjournment of Congress,

several delegates had returned home with copies of Franklin's plan, and in North Carolina they were submitted to the provincial congress and formally rejected. Elsewhere they seem to have been only the subject of informal discussion, although leaders in several provinces apparently expected the subject of confederation to be reintroduced in Congress, and Connecticut, to judge from Governor Trumbull's correspondence, expected her delegates to submit draft Articles of Confederation for debate. In their letter of December 5th to Trumbull, Deane and Dyer mentioned the subject in the context of their receipt of his letters of November 18 and 25, 1775. "The draught of Articles of Confederation we have not as yet been able to lay before the Congress," they explained, "Business of every kind, & from every Quarter thickening fast at this Season." See Edmund C. Burnett, *The Continental Congress* (New York: Macmillan Co., 1941), pp. 91–92; Benjamin Franklin's Proposed Articles of Confederation, July 21, 1775; *N. C. Colonial Records,* 10:175–79, 264; Connecticut Delegates to Jonathan Trumbull, December 5, 1775; and Samuel Ward to Henry Ward, December 31, 1775.

No positive evidence has been found to establish when Deane wrote the "Proposals" printed here, but the subject of his ninth paragraph suggests a preoccupation with his failure to be renamed to another term in Congress. Although it seems logical that the governor's letters may have been the occasion for Deane's renewed interest in a confederation, he may well have composed the document at an earlier date. It is less likely that the proposals were of later composition, since Deane learned in mid-November that he had not been reappointed to another term as a Connecticut delegate, and he was subsequently extremely busy with other matters before Congress up to his last day in attendance, January 16, 1776, the day the delegates rejected an effort to fix a time "for considering the Instrument of Confederation formerly brought in by a Comee." Although Secretary Thomson made no mention of the subject in the journals from July 21, 1775, to June 7, 1776, a committee report of December 24, 1775, includes Franklin's plan in a list of items of unfinished business. See Richard Smith's Diary, January 16, 1776; and *JCC,* 3:454–56.

[2] This proposal for proportional representation, a principle generally opposed by small state delegates, plus other features designed to augment the power of Congress (such as those contained in his 8th, 9th, 10th, 14th, and 15th proposals), mark Deane as a man early preoccupied with practical problems of centralized administration and sympathetic to a surprisingly strong Continental authority. It seems unlikely, therefore, that this document was the "draught of Articles of Confederation" Deane and Dyer referred to in their December 5th letter to Trumbull, or that it reflects Dyer's or Sherman's views, although Connecticut herself would not be affected by Deane's most daring suggestions in his 8th and 14th proposals. More concerned with their local autonomy, Deane's Connecticut constituents were traditionally suspicious of such sentiments, and knowledge of his views on the subject may also have played a small part in the Connecticut Assembly's refusal in October to reappoint him to another term in Congress.

Joseph Hewes to Samuel Johnston

Dear Sir Philadelphia 1st Decembr 1775

I have wrote to you several times lately and have nothing new to communicate, but what you have in our Joint Letter[1] and the papers therewith sent. We have mentioned the calling a Convention in January, but unless you think it absolutely necessary I could wish it might be put of[f] till May when in all probability we shall have it in our power to lay before you a compleat Journal of our proceedings of the last Congress, as also of the present, this I think necessary, as it will be much better to take up our proceedings in one View than by detached pieces, and it will never do to harrass our people by calling them too often to meet in Convention.

However these matters must rest on your own Judgement and discretion. I wish I could inform you when we shall adjourn, some say about Christmas, others, not till Spring. I am inclined to think with the former; for we grow tired, indolent, Captious, Jealous and want a recess. These only discover themselves now and then, in general we are pretty unanimous and friendly. No plan of Seperation has been offered, the Colonies will never agree to any till drove to it by dire necessity. I wish the time may not come too soon. I fear it will be the case if the British Ministry pursue their present diabolical Schemes. I am weary of politicks and wish I could retire to my former private Station (to speak in the language of J[osiah] Child) a pence and farthings Man.

My Compliments to your [family?] and be assured that I am with great esteem Dear Sir your most obedt huml Servt

Joseph Hewes

P.S. The bearer, Wm Chew who is sent express to receive from you Sixty dollars which you [. . . .] to N. Carolina, if he does not find you at Edenton he is to have 6 pence per Mile, and all [. . .] paid for any distance that he may go out of to find you after he gets to Edenton.

RC (NN). Tr (DLC). Burnett, *Letters*, 1:266–67. RC fragmentary; missing words supplied from Tr.

[1] Not found.

John Hancock to the Commander of the Pennsylvania Battalion

Sir Congress Chamber Decr. 2d. 1775.

I am directed by Congress to order you immediately to send, keep, and continue, until further Orders, such and so large a Guard of the Batallion under your Command, as you shall think proper, for guarding and secure keeping the Vessels and Stores on the Wharves of Messrs. Willing & Morris, and Mr. Cuthbert in the City of Philada.[1]

I am &c J.H. Prest.

LB (DNA: PCC, item 12A). Addressed: "To the Officer commanding the Batallion raised in Pennsylvania."

[1] Congress dispatched a guard to these wharves to protect four ships of the Continental Navy then being outfitted there. See *JCC,* 3:396; and Clark, *Naval Documents,* 2:1236.

John Hancock to the Massachusetts Assembly

Gentlemen Philadelphia December 2, 1775

The inclosed Resolutions I transmit to you by order of Congress;[1] your attachment to the common cause and great zeal to promote the public Service renders any further recommendation unnecessary. Your Letter with the Accounts inclosed I duly laid before Congress and the Letter with its Inclosures is under the consideration of a Committee, when they report & Congress determine, you shall be acquainted with the Result.[2]

Being much engaged in dispatching Expresses, have not time to add, but that I am with real esteem Gentlemen Your most Obedt. Servant John Hancock Presidt.

[*P.S.*] I have just received your Resolution for the extension of our time,[3] it is very uncertain when Congress will adjourn, you will therefore please to take such order as you shall judge best.

Tr (M-Ar).

[1] On December 1 Congress directed that the New England colonies be informed of its resolutions on pay for the Continental Army and asked to promote the recruiting service. *JCC,* 3:394.

[2] On November 16 Congress had received a letter of October 25 from the Massachusetts General Court, accompanied by a list of military expenditures amounting to approximately £133,000, for which the province was seeking compensation. Congress immediately appointed a committee to examine these claims and on December 4 approved the payment of $443,333 to Massachusetts. *JCC,* 3:356, 402–3; PCC, item 65, fols. 59–74; Hancock to the Massachusetts Assembly, December 23, 1775; Massachusetts Delegates to the Massachusetts Assembly, January 1, 1776; and *Am. Archives,* 4th ser. 3:1473–74.

[3] The Massachusetts General Court had decided on November 10–11 to extend the term of service of the Massachusetts delegates from December 31, 1775, to January 31, 1776. *JCC,* 3:404–5.

John Hancock to Jonathan Trumbull, Sr.

Sir, Philada. Decr. 2d. 1775

The Congress having found it necessary to send Com[missioner]s to the Northward to consult with Genl. Schuyler, among other Things have instructed them, to use their best Endeavours, to induce the Men to re-inlist for one year from the first of Jany. next in the Continental Service: and for the Encouragement of the Connecticut

Troops, who have not been mustered by the Deputy Muster Master Genl., They have given Directions, that such as reinlist be paid all Arrears that may be due to them according to the Rolls to be sent by you.[1]

You will be pleased therefore as soon as possible to transmit to Genl. Schuyler by Express, the Rolls of such of your Colony as are employed in that Department, ascertaining how long the Men have been in the Service.

I enclose you the Resolutions of Congress respecting the Disposition of the Officers taken at St. Johns; by which you will perceive they are to be stationed in the lower Parts of Lebanon and Windham, and to be upon their Parole, and under certain Restrictions therein mentioned, which you will please to order to be executed, and when effected, transmit me a Copy signed by each Officer to be laid before the Congress.[2]

I am directed by Congress to inform you, that no Bounty is to be allowed the Soldiers on Re-inlistment: but the Genl. is directed to pay such Soldiers, as will reinlist for the succeeding year, their Wages for the Months of October, November, and December, and also to advance to them one Month's Pay. And I am ordered to recommend to you to promote the recruiting Service in the present Army, as well as in the particular Colony.[3] I have the Honour to be &c

JH Prest.

LB (DNA: PCC, item 12A).

[1] See *JCC*, 3:394.

[2] See *JCC*, 3:359.

[3] See *JCC*, 3:393–94.

John Hancock to George Washington

Sir Philadelphia Decemr. 2. 1775

Your severall Letters from the time the Committee left the Camp to the 19th of November inclusive being duly Rec'd, were laid before Congress, on which, as well as on the Report from their Committee, they have Come to sundry further Resolutions, which I have the honour to inclose you.[1] The money order'd is getting ready and will be forwarded with all possible Expedition. The Congress have Resolved to make a further Emission of Three Million of Dollars, which I hope will be finished, & such supplies forwarded as will Answer your Exigencies and enable you for the future to pay the Army Monthly, and fulfill your other Engagements.

I have nothing further in Command from Congress.

Yesterday we Rec'd Advice by an Express from the Committee of

Frederic in Maryland, that Conolly & three associates were taken prisoners and are now in Confinement in that County. By his Examination taken and the Papers found with him, the Deposition of his Servant, which you Transmitted to Congress, is fully Confirm'd.[2]

This Day we Receiv'd Advice from Northampton in Virginia, that Lord Dunmore has Erected his Standard at Norfolk, proclaim'd Martial Law, invited the Negroes to Join him, and offer'd them Freedom, for which purpose he has issued a proclamation from on board the Ship where he Resides; and that Two Counties have been obliged to Submitt to him. However I hope such measures are taking as will speedily and effectually Repel his Violences and secure the peace & safety of that Colony.

The Committee have just brought in their Report on the Vessell taken by the People of New Hampshire. As soon as the Congress have come to a Determination thereon I shall do myself the pleasure of Transmitting it to you. In the mean while with sincere & hearty wishes for your Safety, Happiness & prosperity, I have the Honor to be, Sir, Your most Obedt hum servt. John Hancock President

[*P.S.*] I forward you severall Commissions for the officers of the Arm'd Vessells, also a Number of printed Articles for the Regulation of the Army as Amended; for the Recommendation of Mr Crafts & Trott to be Appointed officers in the Regiment of Artillery, and the Steps to be pursued with Respect to the Release of Mr. Ethan Allen, I beg leave to Refer you to the Resolves Inclos'd.

I inclose you a Commission for Henry Knox as Colonell of the Regimt. of Artillery. The Inclos'd Accott. of Advances to the Rifle Companies you will please to order the Pay Master to deduct from their Pay agreeable to the severall Charges.

Please to forward the Inclos'd Letters.

RC (DLC).

[1] Washington's letters to Hancock of October 24 and 30, and November 2, 8, 11, and 19, are in PCC, item 152, 1:241–42, 255–56, 259–62, 275–86; and Washington, *Writings* (Fitzpatrick), 4:40–41, 55–56, 58–59, 71–75, 81–84, 99–102. Hancock, in turn, sent Washington congressional resolves of November 25 on prize cases, of November 30 on raising two battalions of marines, of December 1 on the recruitment and pay of the Continental Army, and of December 2 on a host of matters relating to the Army. *JCC*, 3:371–75, 393–94, 398–402.

[2] See *JCC*, 3:394; and Francis Lightfoot Lee to Landon Carter, October 21–22, 1775, note 3.

William Hooper to Samuel Johnston

My dear Johnston Philada. Dec 2 1775

I have been so much engaged in scribbling to you in your honourable political Capacity that I have left nothing to say to you as a private Gentleman. I cannot however so far forget you as a friend, as not to assure you that I hold you in the most affectionate Remembrance.

From newspapers & private Letters we are assured that next Summer will be a bloody one. The Sovereign has declared (we hear) that he will pawn the Jewels of his Crown or humble America. Indians, Negroes, Russians, Hanoverians & Hessians are talked of as the Instruments to accomplish this blessed purpose. But under God, If we have virtue We may be free. Let every man say he will be free and act as if he wished it & We may defy the threats of the minister.

I beg leave to recommend to your particular Care a packet for Geo & Thos Hooper. Pray forward it by a safe and expeditious Oppty.

Remember me in the most respectful manner to your Lady & Sisters. Tell my good friend Iredell that I have exhausted all I have to say in the Letter w[ritte]n to the Council & must refer him to that Newspapers for politicks. I kiss his Hand. Mr Jones, Charlton & Smith have my best Wishes.

Adieu, Believe me to be Yours truly Wm Hooper

RC (DLC).

Francis Lightfoot Lee to Robert W. Carter

Dear Sir, [December 2, 1775]

We have had nothing new since the reduction of Montreal, which I suppose you must have heard of. It is supposed Arnold must be in possession of Quebec by this time. If he shou'd be too weak to effect it Montgomerie will join him from Montreal. At all events we have got the most valuable part of Canada, as it cuts off all communication with the Indians, & prevents inroads on our fronteers. It wou'd give me infinite pleasure, if our affairs to the Southward wore as favorable an Aspect; it will require very vigorous efforts, to put a stop to the proceedings of Lord Dunmore. We are extremely alarm'd by an express from the Comtee. of Northhampton County to Congress[1] informing that he has issued a Proclamation, declaring military Law in Virga. & offering freedom to all servants & slaves, who shall repair to the King's standard which he has erected; that the inhabitants of Norfolk & Princess Ann Counties have taken an Oath to oppose, to the last drop of their blood, any of their countrymen who shall come in arms into their Counties. The Comtee. asks for assistance, being apprehensive that their people from their exposed situation, & the number of their slaves, will thro fear be induced to follow the example of the other two Counties. We have got the Proclamation. I have been thus full least the letters from Northhampton to our Comtee. of safety shoud be intercepted; which they were apprehensive of. This intelligence gives great concern to all the real friends of America; & subjects your countrymen, to the sneers of its disguised Enemies, & the lukewarm. Fatal consequences may follow if an immediate stop is not put to that Devil's career.

I shoud think a sufficient force of Militia or Minute men, shou'd immediatly be sent to drive him & his adherent on board the ships; the estates of the inhabitants of Norfolk, or elsewhere, who have taken arms agst. the Country shoud be sequesterd for its defence, the proclamation burnt by the hangman, & heavy penalties inflicted on those who disperse them thro' the Country. The patroles shou'd be very diligent. Will it not be necessary for the convention by a short Ordinance, to establish the present Laws and Judges? It wou'd contribute more than anything to the quiet & safety of the people, & security of our commerce in the spring, if the Convention[2] wou'd exert themselves in fitting out small armed Vessells, to prevent small tenders from infesting the bay, & rivers; if it cannot be done in Virga. they might be procured here. Probably Virga. might spare powder for this purpose, but without very bad fortune we shall soon have it in. It is inconceivable what good effects have been produced from such a measure to the Northward, not a tender dares to come from under the Guns of the large ships; & the Vessells employ'd by the Army in Boston to procure wood & provisions are every day falling into our hands. There are small guns in several parts of Virga., a few at Hobb's Hole & Col. Fauntleroys. The furnaces shoud be set to casting them. God prosper your deliberations. Yr. afft. friend

Francis Light. Lee

RC (ViHi).

[1] A letter of November 25 from Samuel S. McCroskey, chairman of the Northampton County Committee, was received and read in Congress on December 2. See *JCC*, 3:395; and *Am. Archives*, 4th ser. 3:1669–71. In response to this request for assistance, which emphasized the vulnerability of this peninsular Eastern Shore county to Dunmore's naval raids, Congress immediately directed "the Committee for fitting out armed vessels" to plan an attack on Dunmore's ships in Chesapeake Bay and dispatched Benjamin Harrison to Maryland to prepare "two or three armed vessels" for destroying enemy ships there. Simultaneously the Northampton letter was referred to a committee whose proposals to dispatch three Pennsylvania companies to Northampton County and to encourage the people of Virginia to reorganize their provincial government were approved by Congress on December 4. See *JCC*, 3:395–96, 403–4; Richard Henry Lee to the Northampton Committee, December 5; and Benjamin Harrison to Wilson Miles Cary, December 10, 1775.

[2] Robert W. Carter was representing Richmond County at the Virginia Convention that convened in Richmond on December 1. *Am. Archives*, 4th ser. 4:76.

Francis Lewis to John Alsop

Dr Sir Phila. 2d Decemr. 1775

Upon perusing your letter of 29 Ulto. I find that we have greatly exceeded the quantity of Clothing for the Northen Troops.[1] You must remember your first letter to me of the 15th ulto. implyed a Doubt of your procuring any quantity & the season being far advanced induced Mr. Sherman & myself to extend our orders here, and thereupon persons were employd to contract for the articles, which could not be recalled when your letter of the 17th came to hand. However as the orders for Cambridge are not near compleated, pray stop what is at Nw York & Albany (at least) and direct them to be forwarded to Cambridge.

We have this day Sent off 500 l[bs] of Powder under the care of Mr. Burden the proprietor of the Burden Town & Amboy Stages, he engages to deliver it to your order at New York and insures the risque of seizures. Please to advise the Convention hereof. I am Sir Your very H[umble] Servt. Fran Lewis

RC (NHi).

[1] Alsop's letter to Lewis of November 29 has not been found, but a letter of that date written by Alsop to James Duane was intercepted by the British and enclosed by New York Governor Tryon in a communication to Lord Dartmouth of January 5, 1776. In this letter Alsop told Duane: "It gives me satisfaction to hear that No. Carolina delegates have similar instruct[ion]s To those of Pensylvania. I have spoke to Mr. Woodhull about ours. He tells me that he expects To morrow to make a Convention, and thinks it wou'd be proper for our delegates at Philada. to write them a letter requesting the same, for he told me if they were asked for, he Thought they shou'd be given. He thought also that the Convention woud be prety able to give The Sentiments of the people, which as far as I can learn are intirely against Confederat[ion] or independency but ardently wish [for] a reconcilliation free from Taxation. If you agree to write such a letter you may send opend [. . .] I think it might no[t] be Amiss to hint or point out some part of them agreeable to our sentiments, but this [*I*] Submit to your better Judgment. If you do this I presume you will not want a Copy of the Last Instructions from McKesson, otherwise Let me know.

"It is hard to say what is doing among us. Matters are kept very Secret when violence is intended. No doubt you heard of Messrs. Sears, Sam Browne & John Woodward['s] expedition. Last week at the head of about 80 Conn[ecticu]t horse men, armed with Bayonets fixd, [*they*] rode up to Rivingtons, Carried off his Types, and return'd very speed[il]y back to Conn[ecticu]t and on their returne Seized parson Seabury, the Mayor of WestChester & Judge Fowler and Carried them along with them. I think it a high insult upon our City and yet I fear if a Similar attempt shou'd be made, it wou'd not be opposed. Tho all most every body condemns it, none are to Stand forth. Really my friend it is time Affairs were brought to Some, or in a way of Settlemt. Otherwise the prospect is Very gloomy indeed. I hope no farther push will be made for any person so violent to Comand the Fort on Hudsons River; if it Shou'd pray oppose it. Our friend Doct. Jones has promised to write you. Perhaps he may be more intelligent than I am, for I have been so confin'd to business Since I have [*been*] home that have not the proper oppty yet [*to*] know of the politicks of our City."

In addition, attached to Alsop's letter is a note, presumably in the hand of an otherwise unidentified British official, stating: "In a letter from Mr. Alsop to Mr. Duane since this [*Alsop*] mentions that he believe[s] the N Yorkers would be Glad to make up matters on humble Terms." For Alsop's letter to Duane and the attached note, see PRO: C.O. 5, 1107:132–33.

Rhode Island Delegates to Nicholas Cooke

Sir Philadelphia 2d Decr. 1775

Since our last We have the Honor of two Letters from You. Genl. Hopkins has arrived very well, his accepting the Command of the Fleet gives universal Satisfaction. Capt. Whipple is not yet arrived. We are a little embarrassed about the Vessel, the Comee. informs us that the Colony considers her as belonging to the Continent & in their Service & propose to be repaid for her & the Wages of the People. If so will not refusing to let her cooperate with the Fleet wherever destined frustrate the Design of repayment for her & past Services. We wish your Honors farther Directions on this Head & hope they may arrive before there is a Necessity of coming to any Resolution about it, but if not We shall advise Capt. Whipple to follow his Instructions.[1]

The Congress is acquainted with the Difficulties of reinlisting the Troops and is taking measures for promoting that Service & wish the Colony will afford the General all proper Assistance in compleating the Levies.

We are heartily glad that the Chair is filled[2] and beg Leave to present our most sincere & respectful Compliments of Congratulation upon the Occasion and from the happy Experience We have had of Your Integrity & public Virtue We doubt not but all the Powers with which you are invested will be exerted for the Preservation of the Liberties of your Country. We are With very great Regard your most obedt. & very hble Servts.

S. Hopkins

Sam Ward

P.S. Lord Dunmore has issued a Proclamation which We have just seen requiring all Persons Capable of bearing Arms to repair to his Majts. Standard erected in Norfolk upon the Penalty of being declared Rebels. He hath offered Freedom to all Slaves belonging to those he calls Rebels that will take up Arms against the Country & hath forbad the Payment of all Taxes & Quitrents until Peace is restored & is taking every Measure to debauch the People. He has of all Sorts about twelve hundred.

RC (PHi). Written by Ward and signed by Ward and Hopkins.

[1] Abraham Whipple (1733–1819), naval officer and son-in-law of Esek Hopkins, was serving at this time as commodore of Rhode Island's two-ship navy. In this

capacity Whipple was currently engaged in transporting to Philadelphia some men recruited by Hopkins to serve in the Continental Navy and was under orders from Governor Cooke, upon completion of this mission, either to place himself under Hopkins' command or to return to Rhode Island, depending upon Congress' decision to station a Continental fleet off the New England coast. On December 22, two weeks before sailing orders were issued for the fledgling American fleet, Whipple accepted a commission in the Continental Navy as captain of the *Columbus*. *JCC*, 3:443; Clark, *Naval Documents*, 2:1092–93; and *DAB*.

[2] A reference to Cooke's recent assumption of the office of governor of Rhode Island. David S. Lovejoy, *Rhode Island Politics and the American Revolution, 1760–1776* (Providence: Brown University Press, 1958), p. 183.

Samuel Ward to Henry Ward

Dear Bror. Sabbath Day 11 oClock [December 2, 1775][1]

For Fear the Post should go out I was shorter than I designed; a very long Debate hath been held relative to reinlisting the Army. I proposed & urged every thing in my Power to get a Bounty given the Soldiers but could not prevail. The Southern Gentn. insist upon it that let the Event be what they will they would not give it & even Conn[ecticu]t & Hampshire voted against it but afterwards it was resolved to pay the Men the Arrears & one Months Pay Advance & write to the Colonies to assist Genl. Washington in compleating the Lines. The News from Virginia you have principally in the Govrs. Letter. It is alarming & if it had arrived before the Resolve against a Bounty would I think have helped Us in that Question; I shall endeavour to improve that & every other Circumstance to obtain every Encouragm[ent] to our People to inlist. Lord Dunmore has proclaimed martial Law, the apprehending Conolly & his Assistants must check his Lordships Progress. Dont fail to write & particularly with Regard to the Army.

The Committee of Princess Ann County in Virginia have wrote to the Congress for Troops as they are remote from the rest of the Colony: the Letters are now reading. Lord Dunmore has proposed an Oath to the People of this County to abjure American Proceedings &c and a Form of Association. [Such?] Parts if any of this Letter as you may think may intimidate or injure you'l not read publickly.

S W

[*P.S.*] The County where Ld. Dunmore is now exerting himself is separated from the rest of the Colony by Chesapeak Bay.

RC (RHi).

[1] The date assigned this letter rests upon a reference—"When I wrote you yesterday"—in Ward's letter to Henry of December 3. This conclusion is also supported by the fact that December 2 was a Saturday, which Ward, as a Sabbatarian Baptist, observed as the sabbath.

John Adams to Abigail Adams

My best Friend Decr. 3. 1775

Yours of Novr. 12 is before me. I wish I could write you every day, more than once, for although I have a Number of Friends, and many Relations who are very dear to me, yet all the Friendship I have for others is far unequal to that which warms my Heart for you. The most agreable Time that I spend here is in writing to you, and conversing with you when I am alone. But the Calls of Friendship and of private Affection must give Place to those of Duty and Honour, even private Friendship and Affections require it.

I am obliged by the Nature of the service I am in to correspond with many Gentlemen both of the Army and the two Houses of Assembly which takes up much of my Time. How I find Time to write half the Letters I do, I know not, for my whole Time seems engrossed with Business. The whole Congress is taken up, almost in different Committees from seven to Ten in the Morning—from Ten to four or sometimes five, we are in Congress and from six to Ten in Committees again. I dont mention this to make you think me a Man of Importance because it is not I alone, but the whole Congress is thus employed, but to apologise for not writing to you oftener.

Indeed I know not what to write that is worth your reading. I send you the Papers, which inform you of what is public. As to what passes in Congress I am tied fast by my Honour to communicate Nothing. I hope the Journal of the session will be published soon, and then you will see what We have been about in one View, excepting what ought to be excepted.

If I could visit the Coffee Houses, in the Evening and the Coffee Tables of the Ladies in the Afternoon, I could entertain you with many smart Remarks upon Dress and Air, &c. and give you many sprightly Conversations, but my Fate you know is to be moping over Books and Papers, all the Leisure Time I have when I have any.

I hope I shall be excused from coming to Philadelphia again, at least untill other Gentlemen have taken their Turns. But I never will come here again without you, if I can perswade you to come with me. Whom God has joined together ought not to be put asunder so long with their own Consent. We will bring Master Johnny with Us, you and he shall have the small Pox here, and We will be as happy, as Mr. Hancock and his Lady. Thank Nabby and John for their Letters, and kiss Charles and Tom for me. John writes like an Hero glowing with Ardor for his Country and burning with Indignation against her Enemies. When I return I will get the sulky back to New Haven, and there leave it to be repaired, to be brought home by the first Post after it is done.

[As to coming home, I have no Thoughts of it—shall stay here till the Year is out, for what I know. Affairs are in a critical state and important Steps are now taking every day, so that I could not reconcile it to my own Mind to be absent from this Place at present.

Nothing is expected from the Commissioners, yet We are waiting for them, in some Respects. The Tories, and Timids pretend to expect great Things from them. But the Generality expect nothing but more Insults and Affronts. Privateering is licensed and the Ports are wide open. As soon as the Resolves are printed, which will be tomorrow, I'le send them.

I have had a long Conversation with He seems to be in a better Temper, and I live on Terms of Decency and Civility with him and he with me. And I am determined to live so. Have lived in more Decency with him and another, since my last Return than ever, at least than since last August when the sin of Precedence was committed. Theres the Rub. But what cant be cured must be endured.

RC (MHi). Adams, *Family Correspondence* (Butterfield), 1:331–33.

[1] Although this letter has been published twice essentially as it appears here (in *Family Correspondence* and in Charles Francis Adams, ed., *Familiar Letters of John Adams and His Wife Abigail Adams,* pp. 126–28), the portion in brackets is not part of the original manuscript but was simply attached to the December 3 letter by Charles Francis while preparing the *Familiar Letters*. It appears that this section is the final page of a missing letter Adams wrote on April 6, 1776. Thus, Abigail's letter to John of March 16, 1776, containing an inquiry about "the Expectation of commissioners," is endorsed "answed April 6th. 1776." See Adams, *Family Correspondence* (Butterfield), 1:359–60. Furthermore, several passages from these concluding paragraphs support an April rather than a December date. On December 8 Adams asked leave to return home, a fact difficult to square with his assertion that he had "no Thoughts" of returning; Congress did not license privateering and open the ports until March 23 and April 6, 1776, respectively; and the person with whom Adams had recently conversed but whose name he left blank was undoubtedly Robert Treat Paine, who was not in Philadelphia in December 1775.

John Adams to James Warren

My dear Sir Philadelphia Decr. 3. 1775

I have only Time to acquaint you that Congress have ordered the arrears of Pay to be discharged to the Soldiers and one Months Advance Pay to be made, No Bounty nor any Allowance for Lunar Months.[1]

I have a Thousand Things to say—But no Time. Our Army must be reconciled to these Terms, or We shall be ruined for what I know. The Expences accumulating upon the Continent are so vast and boundless that We shall be bankrupt if not frugal.

I lately had an opportunity, suddenly, of mentioning two very deserving officers, Thomas Crafts Junior who now lives at Leominster and George Trot who lives at Braintree to be, the first a Lt Coll the second a Major of the Regiment of Artillery under Coll Knox. These are young Men under forty, excellent officers, very modest, civil, Sensible, and of prodigious Merit as well as Suffering in the American Cause. If they are neglected I shall be very mad, and kick and bounce like fury. Congress have ordered their Names to be sent to the General, and if he thinks they can be promoted without giving Disgust and making Uneasiness in the Regiment, to give them Commissions.[2] Gen. Washington knows neither of them. They have too much Merit & Modesty to thrust themselves forward and solicit, as has been the Manner of too many. But they are excellent officers, and have done great Things both in the political and military Way. In short vast Injustice will be done if they are not provided for. Several Captains in the Artillery Regiment were privates under these officers in Paddocks Company. Captain Crafts who is I believe the first Captain, is a younger Brother to Thomas. I believe that Burbeck, Mason, Foster &c would have no objection.

The Merit of these Men from the Year 1764 to this day, has been very great tho not known to every Body. My Conscience tells me they ought to be promoted. They have more Merit between you and me than half the Generals in the Army.

RC (MHi). In Adams' hand, though not signed.

[1] Congress reached these decisions on November 30, December 1, and 2. *JCC*, 3:393–94, 400.

[2] On December 2 Congress had resolved that Thomas Crafts, Jr., and George Trott be appointed to a new regiment of artillery, if Washington "shall judge them proper, and . . . the appointment of them will occasion no disturbance and disgust in the regiment." *JCC*, 3:399. Ultimately Crafts served as colonel of a Massachusetts artillery regiment, 1776–78, while Trott declined a commission as major in the same regiment. Massachusetts, Secretary of the Commonwealth, *Massachusetts Soldiers and Sailors of the Revolutionary War*, 17 vols. (Boston: Wright & Potter Printing Co., 1896–1908), 4:67, 16:64–65.

Samuel Ward to Henry Ward

Dear Bror. Philadela. 3rd Decr. 1775

When I wrote you yesterday I was not so well acquainted with the affairs of Virginia as I am now. Last Evening a Comee. (of which I am a member) appointed to take into Consideration the State of that Colony &c met. We had all the Virginia Delegates with Us and the Letters from the Comee. of Northhampton County with the Proclamn. & new Oath of Allegiance & an Association of Lord Dunmores planning before us. From the whole it appears to me that Norfolk & Princess Anne Counties lying on the South Side of Chesapeak Bay & forming the Northeast part of that Colony on the Southside of the Bay have been so far debauched & intimidated by Lord Dunmore who has been vastly active & politic that they have not been able to check his Operations. Having full Scope He hath exerted every influence derived from Authority, Coercion, Flattery & Corruption, hath offered Freedom to all indented Servants & Negroes who would join him & in this Way hath got about 1200 Men with him, is about to open Trade to the interdicted Ports, and has greatly alarmed the other Counties on that Bay. The Committee of Northhampton County lying on the other side of Chesapeak Bay & being unconnected with the rest of the Colony has wrote to the Congress for Aid. They assure Us that the People are well disposed but have neither Arms nor Ammunition and being two or three hundred miles remote from that Part of the Colony which can give them assistance they are afraid that Lord Dunmore will be able to force great numbers in that And the adjoining County of Awcomack into his Service & get large Quantities (half a million of Bushs.) of Wheat for Exportation to our Enemies. When the Situation of these Counties is considered the Character of the Colony ought no more to be affected by what is past there than that of our Colony should be by the imprudent Conduct of some People in Newport, indeed by all Accts. which I can get there is not half the Number of Tories in Proportion to their Numbers that We had last Spring, and that those People are Men of true Courage their whole History evinces. The Comee. has not yet reported but concludes to recommend a sufficient Force to be sent into those two Counties to protect our Friends & cover our Association until measures can be taken for effectually reducing Ld. Dunmore & his associates.

I enclose you a Curiosity a Jamaica Gentn. who was in London gave my worthy Friend lately from thence a Copy from which I took this, the whole is finely done & the last Line I think ought to be the motto of every American.

I have this Moment recd the Favors of Messrs. Nichs. & Jno. Brown addressed to Us jointly.[1] The Sentiments do great Honor to the Authors, they recommend Matters of vast Importance, make my most respectful Compliments And let them know that as soon as Mr. Hopkins & I can confer upon them We shall with great Pleasure acknowledge their Favors in a particular manner. It is very unhappy that We lodge apart. We are both much upon Comees. and our Time is so taken up that We have no Opportunities scarcely of consulting each other.

This Day I shall enjoy myself highly. Next to the Pleasure of being at home is that of seeing our Friends when abroad; Govr. Hopkins, his Bror. & Son, the Comee. for Accts[2] & Capt. Whipple all do me the Favor to dine with Me; never did I expect the Pleasure of seeing so many of my Countrymen on this Side Rhode Island. I shall be happy if the afternoon proves as agreable to them as I am sure it must be to Me. I expect them every Moment and therefore must conclude.

Your very affece. Bror. Sam Ward

[*P.S.*] No News since my last.

RC (RHi).

[1] See the letter of November 21, 1775, from Nicholas Brown (1729–91), a Providence merchant, to the Rhode Island delegates, in Clark, *Naval Documents,* 2:1090–92. The letter to the delegates from John Brown (1736–1803), Nicholas' brother (and likewise a Providence merchant, but at this time in Philadelphia to arrange the sale of surplus candles), has not been found. *DAB;* and James B. Hedges, *The Browns of Providence Plantations, Colonial Years* (Cambridge: Harvard University Press, 1952), pp. 221–22.

[2] That is, the Rhode Island Committee of Accounts, which was then in Philadelphia seeking compensation for various military expenditures made by the provincial government. Congress authorized the appropriation of $120,000 for this purpose on December 12, although not without first disallowing several claims put forth by Rhode Island. See *JCC,* 3:406, 408, 425; and John R. Bartlett, ed., *Records of the Colony of Rhode Island and Providence Plantations in New England,* 10 vols. (Providence: A. Crawford Greene, 1856–65), 7:411.

Josiah Bartlett to Mary Bartlett

My Dear Philadelphia Decembr 4th 1775.

Yesterday I Received yours of the 17th Instant and have the Satisfaction to be informed you are well (Except Colds). I am well tho I have lately had Something more of my old headach than I had for Sometime after I got well of the Small pox. I had that Distemper So very favorable that no person would Suspect I have had it by my looks; have but a few pock in my face & them So Small as not to be Seen unless Carefully looked for.

When I Shall be able to return I Can inform you no more than when I wrote you last; Some news of Governor Dunmores Behavior in Virginia will I See Detain me here longer than I was in hopes of.[1] However Still hope I Shall be able to Set out from hence by Christmas if not Sooner. Of this one thing you may be assured that as Soon as I Can return with propriety I shall immediately Set out, for I am Sure you cannot be more Desirous of Seeing me than I am of Seeing you & the family. But as providence has Called me here I Cannot Return (and I Believe you would not Desire I Should) till the Business will permit me to do it with honor. In the meantime whither I return Soon or not before Spring (which must in a great Measure Depend on what news we Receive) I hope and trust kind providence will order all things for the best, that our lives & healths may be preserved and we brought to See Each other again in health & Safety.

Let us Endeavor to make our lives as Comfortable as we Can and be Contented with the allotments of providence.

I have wrote you Every week last month & Shall Continue to write Every week while I tarry here be it longer or shorter. Hope not to write you from hence above once or twice more. As to my affairs at home I must leave them to your Direction till my return. Hope if you want any advice or assistance the Neighbors will not be backward. Give Peter a particular Charge to take good Care of the Cattle & not to waste the hay, and Encourage him to behave well till my Return.

Give my Compliments to Mr Thurstin & to all that ask after me. Remember my love to all the Children: I think a good Deal of them all, particularly poor Ezra; hope he is as well as when I left you otherwise think you would have wrote to me.

Tell my Daughters I Reced their letter & that I want to See them as much as they Do me. I Believe the account of the rising in England is not to be Depended on. Doctr Church is not to be Brought here at present but Confined in Conecticut till further order. I Believe no very great number of Regulars will be Sent from England this fall but think they may be Some Expected in the Spring. I hope the news they mention of the Gentleman at Exeter is not true. I Shall be very Sorry if it is. In haste I still Remain yours Josiah Bartlett

P.S. George is well. The weather here is Cold & the ground froze.

RC (NhHi).

[1] See Francis Lightfoot Lee to Robert W. Carter, December 2, 1775.

Josiah Bartlett to the New Hampshire Committee of Safety

Gentn Philadelphia Decembr 4th 1775

Yesterday I Received yours of the 21st Ultmo Requesting the Congress to grant a Sum of money to our Colony towards what we have advancd on account of the Continent.[1] I took the oppertunity this morning to lay the Same before Congress, who have voted us the Sum of forty Thousand Dollars as you will See by the inclosed Extract from their minutes.[2] I fear it will not be ready in less than three or four weeks from this time, as all that has been Emitted is Expended, and Several grants, previous to ours, made on the next Emission, which was ordered by Congress near a month ago. But the Committe has been retarded for want of proper paper; they now Say they Shall begin in a few Days. If the Congress Should not rise before the money is ready (which is at present uncertain) I will use my best Endeavors to Send it as Soon as possible by Some Safe Conveyance. Perhaps I may Send it to Cambridge and inform you that you may Send for it there. If the Congress Shall rise before it Can be procured I will to [*sic*] give orders to have it Sent as Soon as may be; unless by tarrying a short time I can bring it with me.

I am Gentn with great Respect your very Humble Servant

Josiah Bartlett

RC (Nh-Ar).

[1] See William Whipple to the New Hampshire Delegates, November 21, 1775, PCC, item 64, fols. 1, 4; and *N. H. Provincial Papers*, 7:672.

[2] *JCC*, 3:403.

Committee of Congress to Edward Motte

Sir Philada. Decr. 4th. 1775

The Congress have fixed upon the Towns of Reading, Lancaster, York and Carlisle for the Quarters of the Officers & Soldiers taken Prisoners at St. Johns, and have given us Directions to have them properly distributed in those Places.[1] We have thought proper therefore to order One hundred and twenty of the 7th Regiment to be stationed at York & the Remainder of that Corps to proceed on to Carlisle. The 26th Regiment Artillery & Engineers will of Course be divided in Lancaster & Reading and as there are Barracks at Lancaster capable of containing at least One hundred & fifty men you will forward that Number to that Place & leave the Remainder at Reading. You will inform the respective Committees of these Towns of the Purport of these Directions & apply to them to prepare the Quarters for the Troops and afford you all other necessary Assistance.

We are your hble Servts.

Tho Lynch
Andw Allen
Frans Lewis } Committee of Congress

P.S. The Officers are to be quartered with their respective Corps.

RC (ICHi). Addressed: "Capt. Mott."

[1] *JCC*, 3:404. The disposition of the British officers taken prisoner at St. Johns continued to occupy the attention of the committee and Captain Motte during the next several weeks. See *JCC*, 3:429, 433–35, 461–62, 4:17, 25.

John Jay to Alexander McDougall

Dear Sir Philad. 4 Decr. 1775

The Congress have at Length determined against the Tea holders, a measure in my opinion neither just or politic.[1] The objections offered to the Prayer of the Petition were merely ostensible & consequently frivolous. I fancy you may easily discern the Hinge on which this strange Decision turned. There is no Tea southward of the Place but what has paid Duty. &c. &c.

I mentioned to the Congress this morning, the anxiety which some of the Chambly officers expressed to you, relative to the Separation of that Garrison. On examining the Articles we find nothing to warrant their Construction, and consequently the Congress do not think proper to alter that arrangement. If those Gent. had any assurances from the General that the Garrison should remain together or in any other way were led to consider that as one of the Terms of Capitulation, I wish to be made acquainted with it. Your observations on the faith of Treaties are founded in Policy as well as Justice, and I am confident the Congress on being informed of any Errors of that Kind would most readily correct all Mistakes.[2]

The late valorous Expedition against Rivington, gives me Pain. I feel for the Honor of the Colony, and most sincerely hope they will upon this occasion act a Part that may do some little Credit to their Spirit as well as Prudence.

Would it be possible for you to furnish the Jersey Troops with any Arms? Remember your Accounts—several other Colonies are now pressing a Settlemt of theirs. The sooner ours are liquidated the better.

I hope your Convention will soon tell us whether they mean to make any & what Provision for us. Unless something of this Kind is soon done, I must return, my Finances being exhausted, and my Absence from Home pulling it out of my Power to collect money.

I am Dear Sir your Friend & hble Servt John Jay

[*P.S.*] Be so kind as to give the enclosed to young Hamilton.

RC (NHi).

[1] On November 28 Congress had rejected a committee report which, to judge from Jay's remarks in this letter, apparently favored granting the pleas of certain New York and Philadelphia merchants for a partial lifting of the ban on the consumption and sale of tea after March 1, 1775. *JCC*, 2:235; and 3:294, 298, 353, 370, 388–89.

[2] For the situation of British officers taken at Chambly, see John Hancock to Walter Livingston, November 17, 1775.

Massachusetts Delegates to Samuel Purviance, Jr.

Sir Philadelphia 4 Decembr 1775

We acknowledge the Receipt of your Letter of the 27th Novemr. wrote by Order of your Committee upon the Subject of Permitts for

Shipping Provisions to New England;[1] In Reply to which we observe, that the New England Colonies stand constantly in need of Supplies of Bread, Flour & Corn from your Country, more especially the Colony of the Massachusetts Bay, where the Continental Army are now fixed. The Exportaticn of the Articles before mentioned ought to be under a very strict Regulation to prevent any Misapplication of what may be intended for our Friends there.[2] We submit it to your Consideration, whether it would not be adviseable to require either a Certificate from Some Committees of Inspection in those Governments, and where such Certificates cannot be conveniently obtained, and the People applying for such Permitts are Residents of New England, or if your Colony to require the Shipper or the Master of the Vessell, in which the Provisions are to be exported, to give Bond, that they shall be landed or delivered to our Friends in those Governments, and to Oblige the Master to make Oath, that he will use his best Endeavours, that they shall be so landed and delivered.

We are with great Respect Your most hume Servts.

John Hancock Thomas Cushing

Samuel Adams John Adams

Tr (DLC).

[1] The November 27 letter of the Baltimore Committee of Safety has not been found, but it was written in response to a request from Joshua Hilton "to load his Sloop with Flour, &c., for New England." *Am. Archives,* 4th ser. 4:1732.

[2] This excess caution, despite the great need for provisions in Massachusetts, reflected fears in Congress that shippers might use intercolonial trade as a cover for forbidden overseas trade. With particular regard to Maryland, Congress had specifically declined to give Samuel and Robert Purviance permission to export wheat to foreign ports after the Association deadline. See John Adams' Notes of Debates, September 27, 1775; and *JCC,* 3:264. Subsequently, the Baltimore Committee of Safety began to issue permits for exportation of provisions to New England. *Am. Archives,* 4th ser. 4:1733–34, 1737–38.

Samuel Adams to James Warren

My dear Sir Philada. Decr. [5?] 1775

Mr Jonathan B. Smith, who has the Command of a Party orderd to guard and escorte a Sum of Money to your office, will deliver to you this Letter. He is a Gentleman of Merit, and a Friend to our common Cause. Your Friends here have been treated with Civility, and I dare say you will esteem him worthy of your particular Notice.

It will afford you Satisfaction to be informd that Congress has granted £133,000 to the Colony of Massachusetts Bay in part of their Account to be exhibited, to be paid out of a new Emission already orderd to be made, for which the Colony is to be accountable.[1]

We go on here by Degrees, though not with the Dispatch I could wish. Gentlemen seem more and more to enlarge their Views, and we must be contint to wait till the Fruit is ripe before we gather it.

A few days ago we had Intelligence from Virginia that their Governor Lord Dunmore had landed a Party of Regulars who, joynd by a Number of Volunteers, had attackd and defeated a Number of Provincials. His Auxiliaries consisted of the Inhabitants of Norfolk, a Town inhabited by Scotch Tories, and such weak & timid People as they prevaild upon to joyn them. Lord Dunmore has issued a Proclamation, calling upon the People to resort to the Kings Standard or be deemd Traitors, and declaring the indented Servants and Negroes belonging to Rebels, who will joyn him free. He has also in the same Proclamation declared his Determination to execute Martial Law, thereby tearing up the Foundations of civil Authority & Governmt in the Colony. The Congress, taking this under Consideration, have recommended to the Colony of Virginia the setting up and exercising civil Government, in like Manner as N Hampshire and South Carolina.[2]

I hope the Dispute between the two Houses relating to the Establishment of the Militia, has before this time subsided or settled. The Council wrote us a Letter upon the Subject, directing us to give our opinion of the Sense of Congress on the two Resolves referrd to, either with or without consulting our Brethren as we should think best. I had Reasons of weight in my own Mind against requesting the formal Determination of Congress; Mr J[ohn] A[dams] was of the same Mind. Mr C[ushing] was of a different opinion, nor would he agree with us in writing an Answer joyntly. We therefore wrote seperately, and, if you think it worth while, you may read our Letters which I suppose are in the Council Files.

I intreat you my Friend to joyn with your Compatriots in our Colony, in inspiring our Assembly with publick Spirit. There are Persons not far from you who watch for opportunities to disgrace the Colony in this Regard. I hope they will never give just Occasion to say "I cannot describe the egregious Want of publick Spirit which *reigns* here." It is exceedingly mortifying to me to hear such Paragraphs read. If I ever shall have the inexpressible Pleasure of conversing with you, I will candidly tell you *who* has written in this Stile. This much I can now assure you, that one at least of these Letter writers is not a mean Person. I have many things which I wish to say to you with Regard to the internal Police of our Colony but I have not Leisure now to write. You have Scilla and Charybdis to avoid. You cannot but be perplexd. I feel for you. You have need of the Grace of Patience, and (though it has been long said that I have fallen out with the word) I will add *Prudence* too. Persevere in that which your heart has ever been so warmly engagd in, the Establishment of a

Government upon the Principles of Liberty, and sufficiently guarding it from future Infringements of a Tyrant. I will only add, there may be Danger of Errors on the Side of *the People* which may be fatal to your Designs. Adieu S A

RC (MHi). Adams did not indicate the day he wrote this letter, but internal evidence suggests that it was written soon after December 4.

[1] On December 4 Congress approved a payment of $433,333 to Massachusetts. *JCC,* 3:403. See also John Hancock to the Massachusetts Assembly, December 2, 1775, note 1.

[2] The issue of effective civil government was brought before Congress on December 2. Congress subsequently ordered three companies from Pennsylvania to march into Northampton County and recommended that the Virginia convention, "if they think it necessary, establish such form of government as in their judgment will best produce the happiness of the people." *JCC,* 3:395–96, 403–4.

Connecticut Delegates to Jonathan Trumbull, Sr.

Sir Philadelphia Decemr. 5th. 1775

Your's of the 18th & 25th Ulto are before Us. The draught of Articles of Confederation we have not as yet been able to lay before the Congress, Business of every kind, & from every Quarter thickening fast at this Season.[1] We obtained a Com[mitte]e to hear the dispute between the Colony, and Mr. Penn, who reported, but the Delegates of this province opposed the acceptance of it, & finally the most we could obtain was such Orders, as we hope will prevent further hostilities, and a recommitment of the Report,[2] since which have not had Opportunity of being heard again before the Committee, but have a prospect of obtaining releif so farr as to have the prisoners *Judd & Sluman* discharged. This affair, sufficiently troublesome at any Time, has giv'n Us inconceivable Trouble in Our situation. We have advanced Money for their support, which has been, & still is, very expensive, but conclude the Colony, or Company will reimburse Us. The Com[mitte]e of Messrs. Deane, Adams, & Wythe, desire as early an Acct. as can be procured of the Damages done by the Enemy to the Inhabitants of Connecticut.[3]

Mr. Sherman left Us sometime since & you may probably have a Letter from him while in Connecticut.

Could any of Mr. Chesters conduct be surprising We should repress our wonder that a Letter wrote & Delivered him early in October should not come to hand untill the 24th Ulto., but his conduct here, respecting the unhappy Dispute Between Our Colony & Mr. Penns, has freed Us from being surprized at any thing he may hereafter say, or do on this Subject.

The Accompts inclosed in yours of the 25th We have only had Time to look at & without particular examination observe That altho it may be very proper, that The Continent should be acquainted with the distresses, & expenditures of each Colony, yet we are in doubt as to the propriety of laying in The expence of holding Assemblies, & sending Delegates to Congress, as a Charge to the Continent and are apprehensive such a Claim would rather do Us harm than otherways as no such Demand has been made by any other Colony. This Acct. is filed No. 12. The Acct. No. 13 will we conceive want explanation, how farr the expresses or post Riders were employed meerly in the Continental, & how farr in the service of individuals.

The Accompts No. 5 & No. 10 relate to Arms & Ammunition. The first we conceive (for the particulars are not before Us) is for the supply of those Articles on the Soldiers entering the Service, the latter is said to be in order to *replace Loss of Arms, Blankets &c.* These being gross Charges, will want explanation (Viz) whither the Colony agreed to furnish the Soldiers on enlisting with Arms & Blankets over & above their Wages, also whither these Charges were any part of them for Cloathing. The Acct. No. 9 requires we conceive, a very different stating, as the Board of Claims will not pass such General Charges as those for the Money advanced for Powder, Lead &c without knowing first what Quantity of those Articles they have actually received. Having but this Moment received Your last Favor And The express going out this Day must defer saying anything more particular on these Accts. at This Time, observing that as the Rhode Island Accts. are Now under examination We can in a day or Two, be more explicit, as the mode in which they are pass'd will form a precedent for Ours. But at the same Time inform you, that as several Colonies, this in particular, have been at large, & heavy expences, not only in training their Militia but in arming themselves both by Sea, & Land, without making any Charge that we have as yet heard of to the Continent therefor, We conceive that it will not be prudent to urge the Claim No. 11, for special Attendance &c in pursuance of the Act of Octo. 1774, nor shall We unless specially directed lay it in. This Colony have now in the River fourteen Armed Galleys, with near Seven Hundred Men on board and We are informed by their Committee of Safety which has sat daily for the last Six Mo. that their expences have amounted to more than Fifty Thousand pounds which they expect to bear as a Colony Charge, should they alter their Opinion the expence of Our Armed Vessels might then be urged for with greater propriety. Indeed We considered it a probable method, to have them appl[ie]d for, to get them into Continental Service, but your honor will remember That at the Time they were applied for, they were reported to be unfitt for the Eastward Service. The Congress are Now fitting out with all possible dispatch a Number of

Armed Vessels, and though the Committee have engaged the Number already ordered yet it is Our Opinion, more especially Mr. Deane's who attends that Board, That if the *Minerva* shall be judged Staunch, & fitt for Service, That She may be employed by the Congress. Wish your honor to write on this subject in your Next. As the Season advances, and Our Fleet must sail soon, Capt. Whipple has joined them, this Day, and is taken into Continental Service. Your motion for Cannon shall be laid before Congress tomorrow and We shall take the earliest Opportunity of giving you the Result.[4] Mr. Kirkland, & Mr. Deane are employed, and every thing respectg. the Indians appears favorable. It will be best that Mr. Wolcott take pains to go to the bottom of the Suspected Wickedness of one of his Collegues,[5] as he will stand on his defence, & may require a public Tryal.

We wish to know when the Assembly will be convened, as We trust, they will give Us an Opportunity of reporting Our proceedings to them, and rendering up that Trust committed to Us, and in Our absence taken from Us, before we had compleated it, for reasons unknown to Us, in the most public, as We are conscious to Ourselves We can in the most honorable manner. At a Time like this, when every man of Sensibility, & patriotism is *"feelingly alive all oer,"* when all that he can expect to save out of the general wreck of the Times is a Consciousness of having done every thing in his power to save his Country and render it happy, and a Character among his Countrymen correspondent therewith, We must be stupidly negligent to Ourselves, & Our immediate posterity affected by Our Characters, should We silently pass by the strongest Censure pass'd on Us by implication, in the late New Appointment—A Censure in the Face of the whole Continent, and which if unexplained will be forever considered as Such, though they will, which is Our cheif happiness, never find ground, or Cause *in Our Conduct*. Phlegmatic people may reason as they feel on the occasion; dark, envious, & designing persons, whither outdoors or in, may gloss it over to suit their Views. We trust neither set will prevent Our having a public opportunity of giving an Account of the Manner in which we have executed so farr as We have been permitted the all important Trust committed to Us, which is the only favor we wish for, or ask.

A dangerous Storm is gathering in the South, Lord Dunmore having proceeded to the black, & dreadful extremity of putting, as farr as is in his power into execution the execrable planns of ministry, by proclaiming Liberty to the Slaves in Virginia. Shall be able to write You more at large in Our Next on this Subject. The Naval Committee will be in want of Seamen & Marines; if therefore the Briga[ntine] in Colony Service will on refitting bear a Survey, and can be warranted sound, and Staunch for Service, Mr. Deane thinks the Naval Committee would employ her to bring round Seamen & Stores to this place, but this must be resolved on immediately as before hinted.

Respecting the Colony Accts., We cannot consider Ourselves at Liberty to lay them in partially without Your Orders, & for Reasons above we are convinced that exhibiting them as sent Us, would prejudice the Colony, particularly the Charge for training the Militia since Octo. 1774, The Charge for the Lead Mines and the general Charge of Monies advanced Mr. Sherman, Mr. Shaw &c. The importance of the Harbor of New London, the ease, & certainty of fortifying it with the great advantages resulting therefrom to the Continent in General, to the Colony in particular, have not escaped Our Notice, but with all Submission We suggest whither the Charge already incurred in that department had not better be omitted for the present untill the Continent will take it up generally. In everything that relates to the above, wish to have Your earliest Commands; in executing which We shall ever exert the Utmost of Our abilities, & hope to your Satisfaction. We are &c.

FC (CtHi). In the hand of Silas Deane, and endorsed by Deane: "Copy of a Lettr To Govr. Trumbull, Decr. 5th 1775."

[1] See Silas Deane's Proposals to Congress, November ? 1775.

[2] See Connecticut Delegates' Proposed Resolution, October 17? 1775, note.

[3] See *JCC*, 3:298–99; and Committee on Hostilities to Nathaniel Woodhull, October 19, 1775.

[4] On November 22 the Connecticut Council of Safety resolved that Congress be requested to send cannon recently captured from the northern posts to New London for its protection. There is no indication in the journals that Congress formally considered this motion. J. H. Trumbull and Charles J. Hoadly, eds., *The Public Records of the Colony of Connecticut* . . ., 15 vols. (Hartford: Case, Lockwood & Brainard Co., 1850–90), 15:181.

[5] Turbutt Francis (1740–97), an Indian commissioner for the northern department who was personally involved in western land investment in Pennsylvania, was thought to be responsible for introducing the Susquehannah issue into the treaty negotiations with the Indians at Albany in August 1775. For the involvement of Francis in this affair, see Oliver Wolcott to Philip Schuyler, January 22, 1776; and *Susquehannah Co. Papers*, 6:348–49, 416–20, 7:11–12, 24–28.

Notes on Delegates' Remarks to the New Jersey Assembly

[December 5,1775]

Notes of What Mr Dickinson, Mr Jay & Mr Wythe Said before the House of Assembly of New Jersey.[1]

The Parts Scored are the Very Words.

Mr Dickinson began with informing the house, that the Congress were Alarmed at the Reports of the House going to Petition the

King, said *That the Congress had taken the Matter into their Serious Consideration.* The result was that he and his Collegues, *Were Deputed to wait on the House.* He then began with the first Congress, sd. Their first Meeting was to appease the disorders *from Oppressive Acts of Parliaments.* Their *Most humble Petition & Declaration of Rights. Which was Approuved by all America particularly by This House, Which Adopted in great part the Very Words.* But the Congress Petition was Rejected and Britain Prepared for warr. Said She had been thought to believe *we were a Rope of sand and would not fight.* To Divide us the Resolution of the 20th February, was sent out, *Which the Congress Rejected, Pensilvania Rejected, & this House in a Most Manly manner in their Excellent address to their Governor.* In the Spring Genl Gage sent a Detachment to Lexington which, *without Cause put to Death Some Americans* but in the end they *were forc'd Shamefully to Retreat.* When the New Congress Met [*there was*] a General ferment in the Colonys *and a universall Union.* Said *had the Congress then Drawn the sword & thrown away the Scabbard all lovers of Liberty, all honest and Virtuous Men Would have applauded them,* but they Again Presented a humble Petition, sent it by the Honourable Mr Penn (which he would not have us beleive was Rejected, because no Answer; said it was not received on the Throne, Therefore No answer expected; The Conduct of Parliament and administration the only Answer) but said *it was Necessary to Convince Great Britain that we would fight, and were not a Rope of Sand, therefore An Army was formed, Expedition against Canada &c Success Attend every Where.* Said *The Savages who were to be lett loose to Murder our helpless wives & Children were our friends. The Canadians fought in our Cause,* and Canada, from thence Armys were to over run us, *is Conquered in as few Months as it took Britain Years.* Said *we have nothing to fear but from Europe 3000 Miles distant, but a Country so United Cannot be Conquered.* He said, *The Eyes of all Europe are upon us.* Untill *This Controversy the Strength & Importance of this Country was not known,* The Nations of Europe look with *jealous eyes on the Struggle.* Brittain has *Natural enemys France & Spain. Should we be unsuccessfull in the Next Campaign France will not sitt Still & Suffer Britain to Conquer.* He then braged of our Success & Courage, said *Nothing would bring Great Britain to reason but our Unity & Bravery, That all Great Britain wanted was to procure Separate Petitions,* which we Should avoid, it would *break our Union* we would be *a Rope of Sand.* Repeated as if to frighten us, That *Neither Mercy nor Justice was to be Expected from Great Britain.* He then Complimented the House on their former Petition and *Noble Answer* to the Governor, in their address on the Resolution of the 20th of February, and intreated us not to *Petition* but rest *on our former Petition and that of*

United America. He spoke near three quarter of an hour.

Mr Jay said that Mr Dickinson had been so full little was left for him, but said that we had *Nothing to expect from the Mercy and Justice of Britain: Petition Now not the Means, Vigor and Unanimity* the *only Means*. That the Petition of *United America* presented by the Congress ought to be *Relyed on, others Unncessary,* and *hoped the House would not think otherwise*. He Spoke ten or twelve minutes.

Mr Wythe to the same purpose about 8 minutes.

MS (PRO: C.O. 5, 1107). Enclosed in Gov. William Tryon to Lord Dartmouth, February 11, 1776. Another copy of these notes (together with several other documents) was enclosed in Gov. William Franklin's letter of January 5, 1776, to Lord Dartmouth, which was intercepted by William Alexander and sent to Congress on January 6. Richard Smith noted that this intercepted copy of the "Notes of the Speeches" was in the hand of Cortlandt Skinner, although it cannot be determined from Smith's comment whether Skinner was the person who originally took the notes in the assembly. See Richard Smith's Diary, January 9, 1776; and *Am. Archives*, 4th ser. 4:586–87.

[1] When the New Jersey Assembly convened on November 15, 1775, Gov. William Franklin, appealing to latent conservatism in the province, mounted a serious effort to sever New Jersey from the vanguard of colonial resistance to Great Britain. Strengthened by the recent receipt of four petitions from New Jersey citizens expressing fears that the province was on the road to independence, conservatives in the assembly succeeded in passing resolutions instructing New Jersey's delegates in Congress to oppose "any propositions . . . that may separate this Colony from the Mother Country, or change the form of Government thereof." Cast in language nearly identical to resolutions passed on November 9 by the Pennsylvania Assembly, and approved in concert with a motion calling for New Jersey to submit its own petition to the king, the New Jersey resolutions appeared as part of a broader movement to curb the influence of Congress on provincial government. However, the prospect of a petition by a single colony was viewed by patriot leaders as a threat to American unity. When the house appointed a committee to draft a petition to the king, which was reported and read on December 1, news of the maneuver was sent to Philadelphia, and on December 4 Congress appointed a committee of three "to confer" with the New Jersey Assembly, inasmuch as "in the present situation of affairs, it will be very dangerous to the liberties and welfare of America, if any Colony should separately petition the King or either house of Parliament." The delegates selected—John Dickinson, John Jay, and George Wythe—immediately hurried to Burlington and were admitted to the assembly on the fifth, just as the house was about to resume debate on the petition, which had had a second reading the preceding day. Permitted to present their arguments to the assembly sitting as a committee of the whole, the delegates effectively presented their case and convinced the assembled legislators that under the circumstances their petition would be ill-advised. Subsequently the house unanimously resolved: "That as a Petition is already before His Majesty, to which the House has received no answer, and hoping that it will effect the good purposes intended, in the opinion of this Committee the present Petition ought to be referred; and that the Committee of Correspondence do instruct the Agent [*Dennis DeBerdt in London*] to solicit an answer to the said former Petition." See *JCC*, 3:404; *Am. Archives*, 4th ser. 3:1857, 1863–65; *Pa. Archives*, 8th ser. 8:7353; and Larry R. Gerlach, "Revolution or Independence? New Jersey, 1760–1776" (Ph.D. diss., Rutgers University, 1968), pp. 624–30. For Governor Franklin's account of the

episode, along with another copy of the notes on the delegates' speeches, see *N. J. Archives*, 10:676–78, 689–91. See also John Dickinson's Proposed Instructions, November 9? 1775.

Richard Henry Lee to the Northampton Committee

Gentlemen Philadelphia 5th Decr. 1775

I have the honor to inclose you a resolve of Congress in answer to your application for assistance.[1] The three companies therein ordered will march in a few days, and I hope will be sufficient, with the assistance of the good and virtuous Men of Northampton, to secure the peace of your county, and prevent any lapse from the great Continental system so well laid, and so necessary for securing the just constitutional rights and Liberty of North America.

I have the honor to be Gentlemen your most humble servant,

Richard Henry Lee

RC (PHC).

[1] See *JCC*, 3:395, 403–4; and Francis Lightfoot Lee to Robert W. Carter, December 2, 1775.

Francis Lewis to John Alsop

Dr. Sir In Congress Phila. 5 Decemr 1775

I have but just time to acknowledge the receipt of yours of yesterday and to acquaint you that I have obtained a resolve of Congress for transporting the Clothing &c from Albany by land to Cambridge.[1] It is probable there might not be more shoes than is wanted to the Northward; you will regulate that accordingly. I can say nothing more on the Vessells' Security 'till [I?] see Mr. Livingston who is not in the House at present; shall consult him & write you by next Post. In haste I am Sir Your H Servt Fra Lewis

P.S. Please to send the inclosed by the Packet.

RC (NHi).

[1] See *JCC*, 3:407–8.

Secret Committee Minutes of Proceedings

Philadelphia Com[mittee] C[hamber] Decr. 5. 1775

At a meeting of the C[ommittee] of S[ecrecy] present Saml. Ward, Benjn. Franklin, Silas Deane, Phil. Livingston, Josiah Bartlett,

Francis Lewis. A Contract was enterd into between J. Chevalier & Peter Chevalier of the City of Philadelphia Merchts. of the one part & the sd. C[ommittee] on the other part.

That a voyage be immediately undertaken, to some proper port or ports in Europe for the speedy procuring of twenty tons of good gunpowder or if the Gunpowder cannot be had, as much salt petre with a proportion of 15 lb of Sulphur to every hundred weight of Salt petre as will be sufficient to make that quantity of Gun Powdr., one thousand stand of good Arms, three thousand good plain double bridled gunlocks & twenty tons of Lead.[1]

MS (MH).

[1] John and Peter Chevalier received an advance of $11,500 from the Secret Committee, but their ship the *Two Brothers* was captured by the British on December 26 and condemned as a prize. See Secret Committee Account, September 27, 1775–August 26, 1776; Secret Committee Minutes of Proceedings, April 9 and July 18, 1776; and Clark, *Naval Documents,* 3:1121.

Richard Henry Lee to George Washington

Dear Sir, Philadelphia 6th Decr. 1775

The inclosed letter from Colo. Pendleton came to hand two days ago, and as it will save a good deal of unnecessary writing, I send it to you.[1] The proclamation there alluded to, we have seen. It proclaims martial law thro Virginia and offers freedom to all the Slaves, calling their Masters rebels &c. It seems this unlucky triumph over Hutchings with his less than half armed Militia, so dispirited the miserable wretches in that neighborhood, that many have taken an oath of Ld. Dunmores prescribing, reprobating Congress, Committees &c. Long before this, Colo. Woodford with 800 good men, must be arrived in those parts, and I make no doubt has forced his Lordship on board his Ships again. All this would have been prevented, if our troops could have crossed James River in proper time, but they were obstructed & forced to march high up by the Men of War, and indeed, such is the nature of our water intersected Country, that a small number of men provided with Naval force, can harrass us extremely. I have good reason to hope that in a few weeks the state of things in Virginia will be greatly altered for the better. I thank you for your list of Armed Vessels, but at present no use can be made of them.[2] I hope some of them will be fortunate enough to meet with prizes eastward. I had not heared of your improvements on the Kanhawa being destroyed, and unless Mr. Lund Washington has received very accurate information on this head, I am yet inclined to doubt it, because I see in the treaty lately concluded with all the Ohio Indians, they first inform the Commissioners of the Kanhawa fort being burnt by some of their rash young men, but they promise to punish the offenders and prevent repetition of the like offenses. They are very precise in their information, and mention only the Fort as well as I remember. I hope therefore that your property may yet be safe. This treaty with the Indians is the more likely to last as Connelly, with his little Corps of Officers, are now in close custody in Maryland, having been arrested there, as they were stealing thro the Country to Pittsburg, from whence they were to proceed to Detroit, and with the Troops in those Western parts, Indians &c. he was to have done wonders. This wonderful Man is now in close jail. I congratulate you on the surrender of Montreal, and from Gen. Mongomeries letter giving account of that event, I think we have room to expect that Quebec is fallen before now. A Committee of Congress some time since sent to Canada, have direction to raise a Regiment in that Country, to invite Delegates to this Congress, and to give the strongest assurances of protection to their Civil & Religious rights. I am glad to hear of your getting Cobble hill & I hope it will prove useful to you. We are told that your enemy troops are very uneasy on Bunkers hill. God grant that their uneasiness may increase to their ruin. No accounts yet from England, but Ships are daily expected. I am, with much esteem, dear Sir Your affectionate and obedient Servant

Richard Henry Lee

RC (DLC).

[1] See Edmund Pendleton to Lee, November 27, 1775. Edmund Pendleton, *The Letters and Papers of Edmund Pendleton,* ed. David J. Mays, 2 vols. (Charlottesville: University Press of Virginia, 1967), 1:132–33.

[2] Washington had enclosed this list in his November 27 letter to Lee. Washington, *Writings* (Fitzpatrick), 4:116–17.

Robert R. Livingston, Jr., to John Jay

Dr. John Albany 6 Dec 1775

I wrote to you on my first arrival at Lake George & hoped to have found a Line from you here on my return. My disappointment has not however so angered me as to prevent my appologizing for you, of which this second letter is a proof. I most sincerely congratulate you upon our amazing success in Canada. If you knew the Obstacles we have had to strugle with you would think it little short of a miracle. Tho' as you will find by the letters you will receive herewith the matter is far from being ended, as the base desertion of the troops in the hour of victory, has left us much inferior to the enemy and I could wish that no attemp[t] was made upon Quebeck till the freezing of the lake admitted of our sending in a reinforcement, since there is no dependance to be placed upon the Canadians, & the first ill success

IN CONGRESS.

DECEMBER 6, 1775.

WE the Delegates of the Thirteen United Colonies in North America have taken into our moſt ſerious conſideration a Proclamation iſſued from the Court of St. James's on the Twenty-Third day of Auguſt laſt. The name of Majeſty is uſed to give it a ſanction and influence; and, on that account, it becomes a matter of importance to wipe off, in the name of the people of theſe United Colonies, the aſperſions, which it is calculated to throw upon our cauſe; and to prevent, as far as poſſible, the undeſerved puniſhments, which it is deſigned to prepare for our friends.

We are accuſed of "forgetting the allegiance which we owe to the power that "has protected and ſuſtained us." Why all this ambiguity and obſcurity in what ought to be ſo plain and obvious, as that he who runs may read it? What allegiance is it that we forget? Allegiance to Parliament? We never owed—we never owned it. Allegiance to our King? Our words have ever avowed it—our conduct has ever been conſiſtent with it. We condemn, and, with arms in our hands—a reſource which Freemen will never part with—we oppoſe the claim and exerciſe of unconſtitutional powers, to which neither the Crown or Parliament were ever entitled. By the Britiſh Conſtitution, our beſt inheritance, rights, as well as duties, deſcend upon us: We cannot violate the latter by defending the former: We ſhould act in diametrical oppoſition to both, if we permitted the claims of the Britiſh Parliament to be eſtabliſhed, and the meaſures purſued in conſequence of thoſe claims to be carried into execution among us. Our ſagacious anceſtors provided mounds againſt the inundation of tyranny and lawleſs power on one ſide, as well as againſt that of faction and licentiouſneſs on the other. On which ſide has the breach been made? Is it objected againſt us by the moſt inveterate and the moſt uncandid of our enemies, that we have oppoſed any of the juſt prerogatives of the Crown, or any legal exertion of thoſe prerogatives? Why, then, are we accuſed of forgetting our allegiance?—We have performed our duty: We have reſiſted in thoſe caſes, in which the right to reſiſt is ſtipulated as expreſsly, on our part, as the right to govern is, in other caſes, ſtipulated on the part of the Crown. The breach of allegiance is removed from our reſiſtance as far as tyranny is removed from legal government.

It is alledged that "we have proceeded "to an open and avowed rebellion." In what does this rebellion conſiſt? It is thus deſcribed——"Arraying ourſelves in hoſtile "manner to withſtand the execution of the "Law, and traiterouſly preparing, ordering "and levying war againſt the King." We know of no laws binding upon us, but ſuch as have been tranſmitted to us by our anceſtors, and ſuch as have been conſented to by ourſelves or our repreſentatives elected for that purpoſe. What laws, ſtampt with theſe characters, have we withſtood? We have indeed defended them; and we will riſque every thing, do every thing, and ſuffer every thing in their defence. To ſupport our laws, and our liberties eſtabliſhed by our laws, we have prepared, ordered, and levied war: But is this traiterouſly, or againſt the King? We view him as the Conſtitution repreſents him: That tells us he can do no wrong. The cruel and illegal attacks, which we oppoſe, have no foundation in the royal authority. We will not, on our part, loſe the diſtinction between the King and his Miniſters: Happy it would have been for ſome former Princes, had it been always preſerved on the part of the Crown!

Beſides all this we obſerve, on this part of the proclamation, that "rebellion" is a term undefined and unknown in the law. It might have been expected, that a proclamation, which, by the Britiſh conſtitution, has no other operation than merely that of enforcing what is already law, would have had a known legal baſis to have reſted upon. A correſpondence between the inhabitants of Great-Britain and their brethren in America produced, in better times, much ſatisfaction to individuals, and much advantage to the public. By what criterion ſhall one, who is unwilling to break off this correſpondence, and is, at the ſame time, anxious not to expoſe himſelf to the dreadful conſequences threatened in this proclamation—by what criterion ſhall he regulate his conduct? He is admoniſhed not to carry on correſpondence with the perſons now in rebellion in the colonies. How ſhall he aſcertain who are in rebellion, and who are not? He conſults the law to learn the nature of the ſuppoſed crime: the law is ſilent upon the ſubject. This, in a country where it has been often ſaid, and formerly with juſtice, that the government is by law and not by men, might render him perfectly eaſy. But proclamations have been ſometimes dangerous engines in the hands of thoſe in power. Information is commanded to be given to one of the Secretaries of State of all perſons "who ſhall be "found carrying on correſpondence with "the perſons in rebellion, in order to bring "to condign puniſhment the authors, perpetrators or abettors of ſuch dangerous de"ſigns." Let us ſuppoſe, for a moment, that ſome perſons in the colonies are in rebellion, and that thoſe, who carry on correſpondence with them, might learn, by ſome rule, which Britons are bound to know, how to diſcriminate them: Does it follow that all correſpondence with them deſerves to be puniſhed? It might have been intended to appriſe them of their danger, and to reclaim them from their crimes. By what law does a correſpondence with a criminal transfer or communicate his guilt? We know that thoſe who aid and adhere to the King's enemies; and thoſe, who correſpond with them in order to enable them to carry their deſigns into effect, are criminal in the eye of the law. But the law goes no farther. Can proclamations, according to the principles of reaſon and juſtice and the conſtitution go farther than the law?

But, perhaps, the principles of reaſon and juſtice and the conſtitution will not prevail: Experience ſuggeſts to us the doubt: If they ſhould not, we muſt reſort to arguments drawn from a very different ſource. We, therefore, in the name of the people of theſe United Colonies, and by authority, according to the pureſt maxims of repreſentation derived from them, declare, that whatever puniſhment ſhall be inflicted upon any perſons in the power of our enemies for favouring, aiding or abetting the cauſe of American liberty ſhall be retaliated in the ſame kind and the ſame degree upon thoſe, in our power, who have favoured, aided or abetted, or ſhall favour, aid or abet the ſyſtem of miniſterial oppreſſion. The eſſential difference between our cauſe and that of our enemies might juſtify a ſeverer puniſhment: The law of retaliation will unqueſtionably warrant one equally ſevere.

We mean not, however, by this declaration, to occaſion or to multiply puniſhments: Our ſole view is to prevent them. In this unhappy and unnatural controverſy, in which Britons fight againſt Britons and the deſcendants of Britons, let the calamities immediately incident to a civil war ſuffice. We hope additions will not, from wantonneſs be made to them on one ſide: We ſhall regret the neceſſity, if laid under the neceſſity, of making them on the other

Extract from the Minutes,

CHARLES THOMSON, *Sec.*

PRINTED by J. DUNLAP.

Congressional Resolution of December 6, 1775

will convert them into enemies, in which case with the assistance of Carleton we may be easily cut off. But the people that compose our army think so much for themselves that no general dare oppose their sentiments if he was so inclined. You can not conceive the trouble our generals have had, petition, mutinies & request to know the reason of every maneuvre without a power to suspend or punish the offenders, the strongest proof of which is that Montgomerry was under a necessity to reinstate Mott in order to quiet his men. Lamb is a good officer but so extremely turbulent that he excites infinite mischief in the army. A few days ago he promoted a petition & remonstrance upon the subject of some indulgence that was shewn to one or two officers who had families in Canada & were permitted to visit them on their parol[e]. It was couc[he]d in such terms that Montgomerry immediately resigned the command but on their making a proper appology reassumed it.

You can form no judgment of the impositions on the publick by the Officers & troops of the New England Colonies—I speak this in confidence & without prejudice. A great number of troops have been raised but when ordered upon duty tho they had recd. pay the whole season for doing nothing they dwindled down to a handful whole companies falling sick at once & yet full muster rolls being returned. You ask why this is not punished! The Offenders form the court martial & tho it may seem incredible yet mutiny, disarming the centries, & endeavouring to resque Offenders from the guard is punished only by a fine of 6/. Many of our own Officers are little better. However I am pleased to find that our troops have continued in Canada & have on all occasions behaved with spirit if we except the regiment raised in New York, who together with Waterburies regt. ran away at the first landing of which you have had an account. The rest of our Troops were not there accept [except] one or two companies who behaved well. Contrive if possible to introduce Gent. into the army. Genl. Prescot is now here, he is the author of all the cruelties agt. Walker & Allen in Canada, a man demented so low as to break the windows of the Barracks with his own cane. Montgomerry resented his conduct so highly as to refuse to see him or any of the Officers of his party. The Officers taken at St Johns we hear are gone with their men, notwithstanding an express direction to Capt. Mott of Connecticut who had the charge of them to separate them. This shd. by all means be done as they have it in idea to keep up the regiment which it would be very absurd to permit. You judging from the climate of Philadelphia may wonder we did not proceed to Canada but if I had been so inclined We should have met with many obstructions, besides that Canada is not yet in a state to negotiate, especially as we could derive no assistance from Montgomerry who was going down to Quebeck.

But my strongest objection was that your Committee is by no means adapted to the manners of the people with whom they are to deal & I am persuaded would not greatly raise the reputation of the congress, nor answer any good purpose among that polished people.

You brought us into this scrape, pray get us out, chuse men who have the address to conciliate the affections of their fellow mortals, & send them up in February. I will accompany them in my private capacity, as I wish to make the jaunt. If it lays in your way to serve Harry I know you will do it. Let me hear from you soon. The Express waits. Present my Comps. to Duane & [. . .]; they both owe me a letter. Farewell, Yrs Most Affly Robt R Livingston junr

RC (NNC).

Silas Deane to John Trumbull

Dear Sir Philadelphia Decr. 7th 1775

I wrote you a long Lettr. from N. York 14th inst.[1] to which have received No answer. This gives Me some little Uneasiness as I express'd my Tho'ts with the Freedom used between Freinds and though the World might without prejudice to Me, or mine, see every Word, yet having fell on suspicious Times I wish my Letters may go only to Those I wish to See[2]

RC (MiD-B). Addressed: "To John Trumbull Esqr., Attorney at Law, New Haven."

[1] Perhaps in response to Trumbull's letter of October 20. *NYHS Collections* 19 (1886): 86–90. Deane had been in New York on November 14 but returned to Philadelphia on November 21. See Deane to Thomas Mumford, November 14, and to Samuel Webb, November 22, 1775.

[2] Remainder of MS missing.

Caesar Rodney to Thomas Rodney

Sir Philadelpa. Thursday Decr. 7th 1775

On Wednesday week last I Recd your letter by Mr Sparron, but not till after the Post left town, and Yesterday Recd your second by Mr. Shee. I am Extreemly Sorry that Betsey has been and Continued to bee so ill when you last wrote. God grant Shee may get better. I hope Shee Will, But Shall be impatient till I hear that Shee has. I went to See Missrs Vining the other day for the first time Since I Came up, and Shee let me know that in Consequence of her having heard that you intended to Come up for her, She had Sent all her things to Appoquimmiack by the Shallop, that Shee had hardly left a Change of Cloaths, and if you Should not Come did not know What She Should do.

You say you are much oblidged to me for Communicating to you the Surrender of Montreal, But not Satisfied Desire that by the next oppertunity I would further [. . . .][1] taken it or not, and if not taken by Arnold, to accomplish it himself, if Possible. Montgomery intended to set out imediately after the taking Montreal & nothing can have prevented but the want of a Sufficient number his men *Willing* to go, Which was verry little doubted when the last Express left there.

In my last letter I told you that it was generally believed that 2000, or 2500 men had landed at Boston as a reinforcement to General Howe. This has since been frequently Contradicted and last night I saw Capn. Blewer (Robinson's partner) who left our Camp yesterday week and has brought letters from the general to the Congress. Capn. Blewer's account and all the accounts by him say there are but 450 arrived. That they now have in Boston and at Bunckers Hill about 7000, and that upward of 1000 of them are now in the Hospitals. That they are verry much distressed for fresh provissions and that the *Scurvy* has got among them. These accounts add that General [. . . .][2] Putnam Commanded the detachment that took possession of this place, that he had mounted Eight peices of Cannon there, four of them 24 and 18 pounders, and that they were takeing possession of Litchmare's point when he Came away, and beginning to fortify, Which when done would Command Charlestown ferry. I think it is something Extra-ordinary that they Should suffer our people to go on in this way without firing at them. However it is supposed by some that they have a general attack upon our lines in Contemplation. Time will unriddle the Mistery.

I have got my Blank Deeds and Books relative to the New Loan office nailed up in a Box and put on board Capt Bell's Shallop and Should be glad you would have good Care taken of them When they arrive.

When I finished the last above parragraft I was oblidged to go to Congress and had not been there more than two hours [. . . .][3] but Expect him tomorrow. He had got as far as Albany, and a Quick passage of a boat from Allbany to Elizabeth-Town to Lord Stirling and an Express from him to the Congress has brought us the News before Arnold's Express Could arrive. We have also got Intelligence (by letter) from General Montgomery that the party he sent down the Sorell has intercepted General Carlton and his Vesshels and that he (Montgomery) has since joined the party and got Carlton and his Veshells between them and Montreal, and Expects in a few days to have him & his fleet in possession.

It Seems Lord Pitt is gone home.

I have put on board of Bell five casks of fine new [gro]wn pippins. Be pleased to have good Care taken of them. They are marked C.R. black, on the heads of the Cask. Remember me to all my friends, and believe me Yrs. &c Caesar Rodney

RC (DeHi).

[1] MS torn; nine lines missing. Remaining fragments indicate a discussion of the possible capture of Quebec.

[2] MS torn; 10 lines missing.

[3] MS torn; eight lines missing. Fragments deal with Arnold's arrival at Quebec.

Samuel Chase to John Adams

Dear Sir Annapolis Decr. 8th. 1775.

I am obliged to You for your Letter of 2nd Instant.[1] I intirely agree with You in Sentiment as to the Propriety, nay the Necessity of assuming and exercising all the Powers of Government.[2] Our Convention only met yesterday afternoon. I shall, if possible, induce our People to set the Example, & first take Government.[3]

We have no News here worthy of your Notice. I cannot but intreat your Correspondence. If any Thing material occurs, pray inform Your affectionate and Obedient Servant Saml. Chase

[*P.S.*] I beg to be remembered to Mr S. Adams and your Brethren.

RC (MHi).

[1] Not found.

[2] Adams and Chase were among the strongest proponents of such action, and both had been directly involved in the congressional decisions of November 3 and 4 to advise New Hampshire and South Carolina to establish "such a form of government, as . . . will best produce the happiness of the people, and most effectually secure peace and good order . . . during the continuance of the present dispute." *JCC*, 3:319, 327. As members, respectively, of the committees to advise New Hampshire and South Carolina, Adams and Chase had no doubt previously discussed their views on the subject, one which Adams wrote on at length in his autobiography. And in a previous letter to Adams, Chase had denounced the Pennsylvania Assembly for reacting to the November 3 and 4 resolves by instructing its delegates on November 9 to dissent from "any Propositions . . . that may cause . . . a Change of the Form of this Government." "I am alarmed," Chase wrote from Maryland, "at the Instructions to the Deputies of Pennsylvania. I heartily condemn them. I think them ill timed, timorous and weak. They were not drawn by Men fit to conquer the World and rule her when she's wildest. How are they received by the Members of Congress? They suit the Palates of the persons instructed, and were probably drawn by themselves. But I may censure too vastly. I am young and Violent." Adams, *Diary* (Butterfield), 3:354–58; *Pa. Archives*, 8th ser. 8:7353; and Chase to John Adams, November 25, 1775, MHi. In surmising that the Pennsylvania instructions "were probably drawn by themselves," Chase was more right than he knew, for they were indeed the work of John Dickinson. See John Dickinson's Proposed Instructions, November 9? 1775.

[3] For the proceedings of the Maryland Convention, which continued in session until January 18, 1776, but refused to follow Chase's advice and instead explicitly instructed the Maryland delegates to oppose measures that might lead to independence, see *Am. Archives,* 4th ser. 4:711–72, especially 738–40.

John Hancock to Certain Colonies

Sir, Philada Decr 8 1775

On the second Inst. I forwarded to you by Order the Resolutions of the Congress, directing such Soldiers as will reinlist to be paid their Wages for the Months of October, Novr. and December, and moreover one Month's pay in Advance; and desiring you to exert your utmost Endeavours to promote the recruiting Service in the Army, as well as in your particular Colony.

By Letters since that from the General, the Congress are informed that from the 19th to the 28th of Novr. not more than 2540 reinlisted, and that only 966 had reinlisted before that Time. The Situation of the Genl. and Army is the more alarming, as Genl. Howe is well apprized of this Matter, and will, no doubt, on the first favourable opportunity, avail himself of the information. I need not inform you what Pain the Congress feels at this Want of Public Spirit and Backwardness in the Soldiers to reinlist: nor need I paint to you the dreadful Consequences that must ensue, should the Lines be abandoned, and the General deserted at a critical Moment. I am therefore desired to forward to you the enclosed Resolution of Congress[1] and to request you to exert yourselves in Defence of our Common Liberties by affording the Genl. all the Aid in your Power, and to comply with his Request for the Assistance of the Militia, whenever he may find it necessary to apply for it.

I have the Honor &c. J.H. Prest.

LB (DNA: PCC, item 12A). In the hand of Charles Thomson, and addressed: "To the Council of Massachusetts Bay, President of the Convention of New Hampshire, and governor of Rhode Island & Connecticut."

[1] The resolution in question, which was adopted by Congress on December 7, clarified a resolution of November 4 empowering Washington to call out New England militiamen under certain circumstances. *JCC,* 3:324, 414.

John Hancock to the Frederick County Committee of Inspection

Gentlemen, Philada. Decr. 8th 1775

Your Letter of the 24th of Novr. last being recd. was laid before

Congress; and I am directed to inform you, that the Congress highly approve your Conduct and Vigilance in seizing Cameron, Smith and Conally.[1]

I do myself the Pleasure of enclosing you a Resolution of Congress respecting the Place of their Confinement, and I am directed to desire you in Pursuance of said Resolution to send the Prisoners under Guard to Philada.[2]

I am Gentlemen &c J.H. Prest.

LB (DNA: PCC, item 12A).

[1] On December 1 Congress had received the November 24 letter from the Frederick County Committee, together with enclosures outlining the plot of John Connolly and his associates to rally the backcountry to the British cause. *JCC*, 3:394; and *Am. Archives*, 4th ser. 3:1660–62.

[2] See *JCC*, 3:415.

John Hancock to George Washington

Sir, Philada. Decr. 8. 1775

This will be delivered to you by Mr Jonathan [Bayard] Smith a gentlemen of this city who with two others is charged with 500,000 dollars for the use of the army under your command.[1]

I have the honor to be Sir Your obedient humble Servt

John Hancock Presidt

[*P.S.*] I shall Dispatch an Express this Day to you by order of Congress in Consequence of your Letter of 28th ulto.

RC (DLC). Written by Charles Thomson and signed by Hancock.

[1] See *JCC*, 3:394. This day Hancock also wrote a letter of recommendation "to the Committees of Pennsylvania, New Jersey, New York, Connecticut, and Massachusetts Bay,". requesting them to provide "fresh Horses or any other Assistance" to Smith and his traveling companions. DLC, Jonathan B. Smith Papers.

John Hancock to George Washington

Sir, Philada December 8. 1775

Your letter of the 28 of November by Captn Blewer being received was immediately laid before Congress.[1]

By my letter of the 2d instant, which I hope you will in due time receive, you will perceive the Congress have in a great measure prevented[2] your wishes, having written to New York and given orders to General Schuyler to supply you with and forward with all possible expedition what cannon can be spared. They have also directed Genl. Schuyler to make diligent search for lead, and retaining so much as may be wanted there to send the remainder to your camp. However it is hoped the gentlemen you have sent will expedite that business. By order of Congress I forwarded a commission for H. Knox, who is appointed Colonel of the regiment of Artillery. The Congress also have relieved your difficulties with respect to the two battalions of marines, having ordered that the raising them out of the army be suspended. It is the desire of Congress that such a body of forces may be raised, but their meaning is that it be in addition to the army voted. And they expect you will think of proper persons to command that corps & give orders for inlisting them wherever they may be found.

The Congress are sensibly affected with your situation and regret the backwardness in the troops to reinlist. In addition to what I had the honor of transmitting you the 2d Instant, they have desired me to inclose you a copy of a resolution passed yesterday and to write to the council of Massachusetts Bay, the Convention of New Hampshire and the Governors of Rhode Island & Connecticut, acquainting them with the present state of the army and enclosing copies of the resolutions of this Congress relative to your being empowered to call forth the militia of those governments on any emergency and requesting those colonies to exert themselves in defence of our common liberties by affording you all the aid in their power and to comply with your request for the assistance of the militia whenever you may find it necessary to apply for it.[3]

The Gentlemen with the money set out today. I hope the arrival of this will relieve some of your difficulties and that the payment of the arrears & the months advance, which you are empowered to offer will induce many to reinlist, who seem not to be attracted by nobler motives.

By letters received yesterday we learn that Col. Arnold after a fatiguing march had reached Canada, where he was well received by the inhabitants, that on the 14 of November he had reached Point Levi & was preparing to pass the river that night, that notwithstanding his being deserted by Col. Enos, he had great hopes of gaining possession of Quebec, as both the English & Canadian Inhabitants were well affected to our cause; that Carlton with the ships under his command was stopped in her passage down the river by a fort in our possession at the mouth of Sorrel & some row gallies, and that General Montgomery was preparing to attack him from Montreal but of these matters you will doubtless be more fully informed by an express which we understand was dispatched to you from Ticonderoga.[4]

I have the Honor to be with much Esteem, Sir Your most obedt huml sevt. John Hancock Presidt.

[*P.S.*] Please to Send the Inclos'd for Portsmo[uth] by Express, and order the Inclos'd for Massachusetts Assembly to be delivered.

RC (DLC). Written by Charles Thomson and signed by Hancock.

[1] Washington's letter to Hancock of November 28, 1775, which Congress received on December 6 and considered the following day, is in PCC, item 152, 1:291–98; and Washington, *Writings* (Fitzpatrick), 4:120–23.

[2] Used here in the sense of "anticipated." *OED*.

[3] See *JCC*, 3:324, 414; and John Hancock to Certain States, this date.

[4] On December 7 Congress received letters of November 22 and December 6 from General Schuyler and Colonel Alexander, respectively, together with enclosures describing the progress of Arnold and Montgomery in the invasion of Canada. PCC, item 153, 1:342–49, item 162, 2:348–51; and *Am. Archives*, 4th ser. 3:1633–36, 4:202–3.

John Jay to Alexander McDougall

Dear Sir Philad. 8 Decr 1775

Accept my Thanks for your Letter of the 6th Inst. which I recd. Yesterday. It gave me great Satisfaction to find you had at Length made a Convention. My Apprehensions on that Head occasion'd much anxiety, and am still grieved that the People of our Province have so little Firmness as to be duped by the artifices of men whose views are obvious, & of the Rectitude of whose Intentions there have long been Reason to doubt.

The printed Paper inclosed in your Letter is alarming and that for the Reasons you suggest. It is a Piece of Finesse difficult to obviate, considering the Temper of the Province. The Conduct proper to observe on the occasion turns so much on Circumstances that it is difficult at this Distance to advise what would be best.

To declare absolutely against having any more Assemblies would be dangerous, because the People are too little informed to see the Propriety of such a Measure. And yet the Reasons you urge for supplying their Place by Conventions are very forceable.

If an Assembly of proper Members could be formed, it would give me little Uneasiness. For then should Lord Norths Proposition be laid before them, it would be in their Power to reduce Administration to a disagreable Dilemma. My Plan in that Case would be to assure the Governor of their Desire of seing Peace between Britain & the Colonies reestablished, and of their Readiness to declare their Sentiments respecting Lord North's Proposal, whenever his Majesty would be pleased to direct some mode of hearing the joint Proposals and offers of his American Subjects. That hitherto the Petitions both of Assemblies & Congress had remained unanswered, & therefore that they must decline attempting to signify their Sentiments on the Subject till such Time a Way for them being heard was opened. That they had no Reason to expect that his majesty would pay greater attention to their Desires when signified by a Governors Letter to a

Secretary of State, than he had done to their Petitions. That the faith of the Ministry had not be[en] kept with the Colony, for that a former assembly had been invited to petition, and after being drawn into that measure were neglected. That they were determined to share the fate of their Neighbours, and tho disposed to Reconciliation, were determined to defend their Liberties.

The Jersey Troops are ordered to proceed to your Town as fast as they can procure Arms & Barack Necessaries.

I hope Mr. Hamilton continues busy, I have not recd. Holts paper these 3 months & therefore cannot Judge of the Progress he makes. Adieu, yours most sincerely[1] John Jay

RC (NHi).

[1] Jay also wrote a brief letter this day to his wife Sarah in which he expressed pleasure at the news that she was in good health. "The very uncertain State of my Letters," he also commented, "leads me to be cautious & Reserved. I am sorry to find myself under this Restraint, & should be happy if it was consistant with Prudence to write with as much Freedom as I think." N.

Thomas Lynch to George Washington

Dear Sir Decr. 8. 1775

Your Favour by Captn Blewer gives me infinite Concern not less on yours than on the Account of the Continent.[1] Providence favours us everywhere, our success in every operation excedes our most sanguine expectations and yet when God is ready to deliver our opressors into our hands, that Men cannot be found willing to receive them, is truely surprizing.

With grief & shame it must be confessed that the whole Blame lies not with the Army; youl find your hands streightened instead of strengthened. What the Event will be, it is impossible to foresee, perhaps it is only intended to force the Continent into Their own terms and to shew that neither Generals or Congress shall be permitted to controul the Army, perhaps to mortify the Favourties of Congress. Be this as it may Resolution & Firmness ought to Rule our Councils, a step yielded to improper & intemperate demands may be irretrievable.

I shall not take upon me to advise, tis as improper as needless. Your Riflemen, Negroes & deserters may in proper passes defend your artillery, Ammunition & Stores. Shoud your Lines be deserted, & the glorious golden opertunity of ending the War be lost, let not Hope be lost also. We have in the York Papers an account of your having taken an invaluable Transport & you have doubtless heard of Arnolds arrival at Quebec, I hope both may end as we wish, the Addition of Arms and Ammunition in the Transport according to Report must be most important to you. O! had you but an Army.

My best Compliments to your Lady and Family and to all my Acquaintances in the Camp. I told Gen Gates, Mifflin and others I shoud be much obliged to them coud they send me a good Drummer, they have forgot me.

One of our Members of Congress sets out today for N.E.[2] Whether his intents be wicked or not I doubt much he shoud be watched. Ship news that the Floridas being taken, but tis not credited, if true I have no doubt but tis with the Consent of our Court. God give you Health & Spirits to controul all opposition.

Your sincere Friend & most huml Servt. Tho Lynch

[*P.S.*] Command me freely whenever you please.

RC (DLC).

[1] Apparently Lynch was upset by passages in Washington's letter to Hancock of November 28, 1775, describing difficulties encountered in trying to enlist men "for the continuance of the War." Washington, *Writings* (Fitzpatrick), 4:121–22.

[2] John Adams. See John Adams' Diary, December 9, 1775.

North Carolina Delegates to Elihu Spencer

Reverend Sir Philadelphia 8th Decer. 1775

Mr. Livingston is so obliging as to cover this. We rely upon his friendship to apologize for the freedom we assume in thus abruptly introducing ourselves to your acquaintance.

In the present unhappy controversy between Great Britain and the Colonies it is the particular misfortune of North Carolina that in a very populous part of that Province there is seated a body of Men who not only refuse to become active in support of those rights and privileges which belong to them in common with the rest of the inhabitants of that Colony, but from the temper of mind which these people discover at present, there is some reason to apprehend that they might be led by any designing tool of Administration to pursue measures hostile to the friends of America and which might eventually involve them and us in a Melancholy scene of bloodshed. Those from whom these disagreeable consequences are principally to be apprehended are of the number of those who some years Ago were concerned in the Insurrection and from thence got the appellation of Regulators. To these however it is not confined, much pains has been taken to disseminate this disaffection. It prevails, we are informed, among the Highlanders and we much fear is too general in the back parts of North Carolina. It probably has its source in ignorance and want of information with respect to the nature of the dispute and the rectitude of those who advocate the American side of the question.

We know that the education of most of these men have been religious, that they look to their Spiritual pastors with great respect and

Robert Treat Paine

that truths from their mouths come with redoubled influence upon their minds; could one or more of this persuation be prevailed upon to exert his good offices to give them information and Stimulate them to their duty the most beneficial consequences would result. With this in contemplation the Continental Congress has resolved "that it is necessary that two Ministers of the Gospel should be applied to to go immediately amongst the Highlanders and Regulators in the Colony of North Carolina for the purpose of informing them of the nature of the present dispute between Great Britain and the Colonies and that the Gentlemen to be employed be allowed Forty dollars each per month for their Services and that the delegates of the said Colony be impowered to apply to and procure persons for this purpose."[1]

Under this Sanction and from the warmest testimonies of Mr Livingston and the reverend Mr. Duffield in favour of yourself and Mr McWhorter we are induced to apply to you both, earnestly requesting your patriotick aid and assistance to effect the desirable purpose which the Congress have in View by means of the above resolve.[2]

As you are well acquainted with the genius of the back inhabitants of our Province the task will be rendered easy to you and be assured that every thing in our power shall be exerted to make the Mission agreeable to you and to give Success to your endeavours. At the same time you will have the satisfaction of doing a signal Service to the friends of liberty in that Country and to America in general. With the expectation of hearing from you by the first oppertunity permit us to Subscribe ourselves Revd. Sir with great respect, your obd. hum Serts.

FC (NcU: Hayes Collection microfilm). Unsigned, though in the hand of Hewes and obviously intended for the signatures of all the North Carolina delegates.

[1] A resolve that Congress had adopted on November 28. *JCC*, 3:388.

[2] Elihu Spencer (1721–84), pastor of the Presbyterian church in Trenton, N. J., and Alexander McWhorter (1734–1807), pastor of the Newark Presbyterian Church, both of whom had had missionary experience in North Carolina during the mid-1760's, accepted an assignment from Congress to persuade disaffected North Carolinians to support the American cause. The two ministers spent approximately four months in North Carolina early in 1776 working on this task; and although the fruits of their labors are unclear, Congress eventually paid each of them $261 for their efforts. *JCC*, 3:438, 6:898–99; and William B. Sprague, *Annals of the American Pulpit; or Commemorative Notices of Distinguished American Clergymen of Various Denominations . . .*, 9 vols. (New York: Robert Carter & Brothers, 1857–68), 3:165–69, 208–15.

Robert Treat Paine's Diary

[December 8, 1775]

Above 100 Sachems & Warriors of the Onandaga, Oneiado, Mohawk & Tuscarora Tribes mett at Albany in Treaty. The Cmttee of

Congress & Comittee & Corporation of Albany mett with them; Genl Schuyler & Mr. Dough [Douw] were the only Com[missione]rs present.[1] The Indians gave each of the Comttee names, vizt. Mr. Livingston, Terogha of the Oneida; Mr. Langdon, Sanghradow one of the Mohawk, & my Self, Currewashee, meaning good news given by the Onandaga; they made a Speech & adjourned, to Monday next. Dind with some of Cmttee of Albany at Vernons & went in Evning to General Schuyler's & lodged. Snowed in the Evning.

MS (MHi).

[1] Congress' efforts to neutralize the Iroquois in the summer and fall of 1775, including overtures made at this conference at Albany, are discussed in Barbara Graymont, *The Iroquois in the American Revolution* (Syracuse: Syracuse University Press, 1972), pp. 62–85.

Edward Rutledge to Ralph Izard

My Dear Sir: Philadelphia, December 8, 1775.

I should have wrote you frequently, and fully, had I had the least reason, to imagine that you would have been in England at this day. But your own letters, and general report induced me to believe, that immediately upon your return to London, you would have prepared for a voyage to your Native Country—to act, and suffer in the Common Cause.

Let this then be my apology for silence—unmerited entirely on your part, and far from intentional offence on mine. Permit me to add further, that your residing abroad, at least for a time, will, in my opinion, be of more service than returning to America.

You will receive by this conveyance a proclamation issued by Lord Dunmore—tending in my judgment, more effectually to work an eternal separation between Great Britain and the Colonies, than any other expedient, which could possibly have been thought of.

Indeed my Friend, however chimerical such an Event may appear, to the feeble understanding of a deluded people, it seems to be not very far distant—if the Administration, continue their wicked projects, nor in itself is it at all impracticable.

I cannot, however, without much anxiety look forward. If all connection with your Island, shall but once be put an end to, we must bid adieu, at least for a number of years, to Ease, and Happiness. We launch as it were into an unknown Ocean—and engage in a Business to which we are entire strangers.

If, on the other hand, we fondly continue our Connection—at a time when every Engine of Oppression is raised against us—our Executive will be so weak—foreign Powers, will be so unwilling to assist us—the Demon of Anarchy, will lay such fast hold upon us—that we may at last fall a prey to those sons of Darkness on your side of the Atlantic.

Tell me then, I beseech you, (before it is too late) what are the sentiments of the English Nation—are the people of that Country determined to force us, into Independence? Or do they really imagine, that we are so void of the Feelings of Humanity, and so insensible to the calls of Reason as willingly to submit to every Insult—to every Injury? Do they expect that after our Towns have been destroyed—our Liberties repeatedly invaded—our women and children, driven from their Habitations—our nearest Relatives sacrificed at the Altar of Tyranny, our Slaves emancipated for the express purpose of massacreing their Masters—can they, I say, after all their injuries, expect that we shall return to our former connection with a forgiving, and cordial Disposition.

Surely if the Administration had consulted their friends, the Bishops, they could have informed them, that Christian charity—however strongly enjoined in Holy Writ—has seldom, if ever, extended so far in practice. Speaking for myself, I freely confess, that I feel such high Resentment for the unmerited—and indiscriminate cruelties committed against the Inhabitants of this Country—that I do not believe I shall ever forget—or ever forgive them; and so determined am I on being free that I will even quit my Native Country without a sigh—if the Genius of Liberty shall loose her Influence. That, however, I trust will never be the case.

America, indeed, appears to be the natural clime, for Freedom—and she seems to spread her powers still wider and wider[. . . .][1]

How truly vain must be the expectations of those, who wish to subjugate us, when we consider, that wanting every sinew of War, we have been able to resist—and baffle—their wicked attacks.

Let them reflect that America engaged in this contest, without Arms—Ammunition—Officers—or money. We shall, however, soon have a sufficient quantity of the two first articles—to do Mr. Howe's business for him—in the course of the winter[. . . .]

This session may determine the Fate, of a great Kingdom—unless the Parliament improve the opportunity now offered them, they may loose forever their American Colonies. May God grant them Wisdom to discover—and Virtue to pursue such measures—as may best tend to the Establishment of Peace, and Happiness [. . . .]

You must take this as I write it, for we are so closely engaged in Business, that we have hardly time to eat and drink, what with attention in the House, and committees.

I shall write to A[rthur] L[ee] in a few days. With much sincerity and affection, I am, my dear sir, Your friend.

MS not found; reprinted from Ralph Izard, *Correspondence of Mr. Ralph Izard of South Carolina, from the Year 1774 to 1804; with a Short Memoir,* ed. Anne Izard Deas (New York: Charles S. Francis & Co., 1844), pp. 164–68.

[1] Ellipses here and below in Deas Tr.

John Adams' Diary

1775. Decr. 9th.

Having Yesterday as[ked and] obtained Leave of Congress to go home, this Morning I mounted, with my own Servant only, about twelve o Clock, and reached the red Lyon about two where I dine. The Roads very miry and dirty, the Weather pleasant, and not cold.[1]

MS (MHi). Adams, *Diary* (Butterfield), 2:223–24.

[1] Adams' account with Massachusetts as a delegate to Congress for August–December 1775 is in Adams, *Diary* (Butterfield), 2:168–71.

James Duane to Cornelius Duane

Dear Brother Philad. 9th Decem. 1775

When I assure you that I have spent but one Night at home since the beginning of May, and that to comply with the Injunctions of my Countrymen I have been obliged to sacrifice all domestic Happiness and my private affairs—and if you add to the account the nature of the Business in which I am engaged, I hope you'l find some apology for my Inattention to you.[1]

I have given Mr. Gaine an order on a Friend in New York for the money you ask and directed him to forward it with this letter. In what specie it is I know not, but if Continental Currency is of so little Esteem in your Neighborhood I hope at my Request he will exchange it should my friend pay him in that Currency. Here it can be exchanged for Gold. Indeed no body would Be safe In questioning its Validity and very few I believe are disposed to do it.

I can form no opinion when the Congress will rise. Their proceedings down to the 1st of August are published which will be some gratification to your curiosity. I long impatiently to be released from an expensive and distressing affair, and hope soon to obtain my Quietus. My friends are importunate for my continuance in it while there is any Prospect of Reconciliation; but this is at present too distant and uncertain to Give me Encouragement, or keep up my spirits while I suffer a painful exclusion from the society of my Family and Friends.

Be pleased to present my respectful compliments to my worthy

Friends the Judge and Colonel and their Ladies and believe me to be, Dr Cornelius, Your Affectionate brother, Jas. Duane.

MS not found; reprinted from *Southern History Association Publications* 7 (1903): 176–77.

[1] Cornelius Duane (1736–81), an unsuccessful New York merchant, was one of Duane's younger brothers. Edward P. Alexander, *A Revolutionary Conservative. James Duane of New York* (New York: Columbia University Press, 1938), pp. 10, 13, 42.

Benjamin Franklin to Charles William Frederic Dumas

Dear Sir, Philadelphia, 9 December, 1775.

I received your several favors, of May 18th, June 30th, and July 8th, by Messrs. Vaillant and Pochard;[1] whom if I could serve upon your recommendation, it would give me great pleasure. Their total want of English is at present an obstruction to their getting any employment among us; but I hope they will soon obtain some knowledge of it. This is a good country for artificers or farmers; but gentlemen of mere science in *les belles lettres* cannot so easily subsist here, there being little demand for their assistance among an industrious people, who, as yet, have not much leisure for studies of that kind.

I am much obliged by the kind present you have made us of your edition of Vattel. It came to us in good season, when the circumstances of a rising state make it necessary frequently to consult the law of nations. Accordingly that copy, which I kept, (after depositing one in our own public library here, and sending the other to the College of Massachusetts Bay, as you directed,) has been continually in the hands of the members of our Congress, now sitting, who are much pleased with your notes and preface, and have entertained a high and just esteem for their author. Your manuscript *"Idée sur le Gouvernement et la Royauté"* is also well relished, and may, in time, have its effect. I thank you, likewise, for the other smaller pieces, which accompanied Vattel. *"Le court Exposé de ce qui s'est passé entre la Cour Britannique et les Colonies," &c.* being a very concise and clear statement of facts, will be reprinted here for the use of our new friends in Canada. The translations of the proceedings of our Congress are very acceptable. I send you herewith what of them has been farther published here, together with a few newspapers, containing accounts of some of the successes Providence has favored us with. We are threatened from England with a very powerful force, to come next year against us.[2] We are making all the provision in our power here to oppose that force, and we hope we shall be able to defend ourselves. But, as the events of war are always uncertain, possibly, after another campaign, we may find it necessary to ask the aid of some foreign power.

It gives us great pleasure to learn from you, that *toute l'Europe nous souhaite le plus heureux succès pour le maintien de nos libertés*. But we wish to know, whether any one of them, from principles of humanity, is disposed magnanimously to step in for the relief of an oppressed people; or whether, if, as it seems likely to happen, we should be obliged to break off all connexion with Britain, and declare ourselves an independent people, there is any state or power in Europe, who would be willing to enter into an alliance with us for the benefit of our commerce, which amounted, before the war, to near seven millions sterling per annum, and must continually increase, as our people increase most rapidly. Confiding, my dear friend, in your good will to us and to our cause, and in your sagacity and abilities for business, the committee of Congress, appointed for the purpose of establishing and conducting a correspondence with our friends in Europe, of which committee I have the honor to be a member, have directed me to request of you, that, as you are situated at the Hague, where ambassadors from all the courts reside, you would make use of the opportunity that situation affords you, of discovering, if possible, the disposition of the several courts with respect to such assistance or alliance, if we should apply for the one, or propose the other. As it may possibly be necessary, in particular instances, that you should, for this purpose, confer directly with some great ministers, and show them this letter as your credential, we only recommend it to your discretion, that you proceed therein with such caution, as to keep the same from the knowledge of the English ambassador, and prevent any public appearance, at present, of your being employed in any such business; as thereby we imagine many inconveniences may be avoided, and your means of rendering us service increased.

That you may be better able to answer some questions, which will probably be put to you, concerning our present situation, we inform you, that the whole continent is very firmly united, the party for the measures of the British ministry being very small, and much dispersed; that we have had on foot, the last campaign, an army of near twenty-five thousand men, wherewith we have been able, not only to block up the King's army in Boston, but to spare considerable detachments for the invasion of Canada, where we have met with great success, as the printed papers sent herewith will inform you, and have now reason to expect the whole province may be soon in our possession; that we purpose greatly to increase our force for the ensuing year, and thereby we hope, with the assistance of a well disciplined militia, to be able to defend our coast, nothwithstanding its great extent; that we have already a small squadron of armed vessels to protect our coasting trade, who have had some success in taking several of the enemy's cruisers, and some of their transport vessels and store ships. This little naval force we are about to augment, and expect it may be more considerable in the next summer.

We have hitherto applied to no foreign power. We are using the utmost industry in endeavouring to make saltpetre, and with daily increasing success. Our artificers are also everywhere busy in fabricating small arms, casting cannon, &c.; yet both arms and ammunition are much wanted. Any merchants, who would venture to send ships laden with those articles, might make great profit; such is the demand in every colony, and such generous prices are and will be given; of which, and of the manner of conducting such a voyage, the bearer, Mr. Story, can more fully inform you; and whoever brings in those articles is allowed to carry off the value in provisions, to our West Indies, where they will probably fetch a very high price, the general exportation from North America being stopped. This you will see more particularly in a printed resolution of the Congress.

We are in great want of good engineers, and wish you could engage and send us two able ones, in time for the next campaign, one acquainted with field service, sieges, &c., and the other with fortifying of seaports. They will, if well recommended, be made very welcome, and have honorable appointments, besides the expenses of their voyage hither, in which Mr. Story can also advise them. As what we now request of you, besides taking up your time, may put you to some expense, we send you for the present, enclosed, a bill for one hundred pounds sterling, to defray such expenses, and desire you to be assured that your services will be considered, and honorably rewarded, by the Congress.

We desire, also, that you would take the trouble of receiving from Arthur Lee, agent for the Congress in England, such letters as may be sent by him to your care, and of forwarding them to us with your despatches.[3] When you have occasion to write to him to inform him of any thing, which it may be of importance that our friends there should be acquainted with, please to send your letters to him, under cover, directed to Mr. Alderman Lee, merchant, on Tower Hill, London; and do not send it by post, but by some trusty shipper, or other prudent person, who will deliver it with his own hand. And when you send to us, if you have not a direct safe opportunity, we recommend sending by way of St. Eustatia, to the care of Messrs. Robert and Cornelius Stevenson, merchants there, who will forward your despatches to me. With sincere and great esteem and respect, I am, Sir, &c. B. Franklin.

Philad. Dec. 12. 1775.

[*P.S.*][4] We the underwritten, appointed by the American Congress a Committee of Foreign Correspondence, having perused the above

Letter, written at our Request, do approve and confirm the same.[5]

Was signed John Dickinson

John Jay

Reprinted from Benjamin Franklin, *The Works of Benjamin Franklin . . .*, ed. Jared Sparks, 10 vols. (Boston: Hilliard, Gray, and Co., 1836–40), 8:162–67. Extract with postscript, in the hand of Dumas (The Hague, Algemeen Ryksarchief: C. W. F. Dumas Collection).

[1] Dumas' draft of the first of these letters, bearing his endorsement "17 May 1775, Minute de ma Lettre à Mr. B. Franklin," is in DLC, C. W. F. Dumas Collection; his letter of June 30 is in PPAmP, Franklin Papers. Charles William Frederic Dumas (1721–96), of French ancestry, German birth, and Dutch residence, was a man of broad intellectual interests whom Franklin had apparently met on a visit to the Netherlands in 1766, which led to a correspondence that extended from 1768 to Franklin's death. Dumas, whose long service in behalf of Congress began at this time, enjoyed no formal recognition and was irregularly compensated until October 1785 when provision was finally made for his salary retroactively from April 1775. After Franklin arrived in Paris in December 1776, Dumas was employed in a variety of duties, particularly in the supply and outfitting of American ships in Dutch and French ports. Later he assisted John Adams as translator and secretary and for years functioned virtually as an American chargé d'affaires at The Hague, although he never acquired an official diplomatic title. See Benjamin Franklin, *The Papers of Benjamin Franklin*, ed. Leonard W. Labaree (New Haven: Yale University Press, 1959–), 15:178; *JCC*, 29:835; Jefferson, *Papers* (Boyd), 8:315–16, 340, 12:200–201n; James Madison, *The Papers of James Madison*, ed. William T. Hutchinson and William M. E. Rachal (Chicago: University of Chicago Press, 1962–), 5:136n; Adams, *Diary* (Butterfield), 3:9–10n; and Samuel F. Bemis, *The Diplomacy of the American Revolution* (New York: D. Appleton-Century Co., 1935), p. 126n.

[2] The Dumas extract of this letter preserved in the Algemeen Ryksarchief begins at this point. In that version, the references below to "Mr. Story," "Mr. Alderman Lee, merchant, on Tower Hill, London," and "Messrs. Robert and Cornelius Stevenson" of "St. Eustatia" have also been omitted. The document was copied along with a French translation in a double-column format, which Dumas apparently prepared for the perusal of persons he was to contact in behalf of Congress, deleting those portions of the letter that were not essential to his purpose.

[3] See Committee of Secret Correspondence to Arthur Lee, December 12, 1775.

[4] This postscript does not appear in Sparks' edition of *Franklin's Works* or in the texts that have been printed under both the date December 9 and 19, 1775, in several 19th-century editions of Franklin papers and diplomatic and general historical collections. The letter was apparently first printed in the *Port Folio* 2 (July 31, 1802): 236–37, where it appeared under the caption "Original Letter from Dr. Franklin to Monsieur Dumas."

[5] Dumas' "Mémoire transmis à la Cour de France en conséquences d'Instructions & Créances du Congrès datées du 9–12 Xbr. 1775," can be found immediately following this letter in the collection of his papers at the Algemeen Ryksarchief.

Stephen Hopkins to Nicholas and John Brown

Gentn.[1] Philadelphia Decr. 9. 1775

Your letter concerning the Casting of Cannon I have recd and have made enquiry about Workmen who understand that Business and can hear of but one in this Province who can perform that kind of Work, he an old Countryman and I beleive little to be depended [on.] Him I have treated with but cannot get him to come to New England on any terms, he tells me he knows but of one other man in America who understands Foundery of that kind and that he lives somewhere in Maryland but in what part he dont know so that you can have no dependance on any workmen from this way. The price of heavy Cannon by the information I can get is about Forty pounds this Currency a Ton and whether You can afford to Cast Cannon for 106 2/3 Dollars a Ton or not you who are on the spot can tell much better than I who have as little leisure for Calculations as any body can have. Our Ships of War will be ready for Sailing by the last of next week if we dont wait for Men and one other Necessary article. I am with great regard and Esteem Your assured Friend[2]

Step. Hopkins

RC (RPJCB).

[1] Although Hopkins' salutation indicates that he was addressing more than one person, this letter is clearly a response to Nicholas Brown's letter to the Rhode Island delegates of November 21, 1775. See Clark, *Naval Documents*, 2:1090–92.

[2] Hopkins also wrote a letter this day to Ruth Hopkins, informing her that he and his wife were well, "and have been so ever Since we recovered from Small Pox," and predicting that "the Season of the year is now So far advanced that I think you must not have a great Prospect of Seeing us again before Spring and then I hope Heaven will permit us to Meet Again." MH.

William Livingston to William Alexander

My Lord. Philadel. 9 Dcr 1775

Billy Barnet is appointed Surgeon of the Eastern Battalion according to your Lordships Recommendation.[1] Mr Hatfield is not appointed D Quarter Master, nor like to be. Your Lordship will therefore be pleased to recommend another.[2] I am your Lordship's most humbl Svt

Wil. Livingston

P.S. Your Lordship may direct your Recommendation to me instead of the President, as the appointment of all officers is referrd to a Committee of which I have the Honor to make one.[3] I think Mr Thomas & Mr Dayton are both proper persons,[4] if they would accept, tho' I do not pretend to be a competent Judge.

RC (NHi).

[1] Colonel Alexander had recommended the appointment of William Barnet, Jr., as surgeon of the First New Jersey Regiment in a letter to Hancock of December 3, and Congress made the appointment on December 8. See PCC, item 162, 2:329; *Am. Archives*, 4th ser. 4:164–65; and *JCC*, 3:406, 416.

[2] See Livingston to William Alexander, December 19, 1775.

[3] On December 8 Congress created a standing committee of one delegate from each colony to consider applications for officers' commissions in the Continental Army. *JCC,* 3:416.

[4] Probably Edward Thomas and Elias Dayton. For Alexander's reply to this letter, see *Am. Archives,* 4th ser. 4:246–47, where it is erroneously captioned to the "New Jersey Committee of Safety."

Robert Morris to Unknown

Philadelphia 9th Decr. 1775[1]

Herewith you'l receive some prints by which you'll be much surprized to find the Americans have not only kept the English army pent up in Boston but at the same time have wrested all Canada out of their possession, in short I am unhappy to tell You that as yet nothing is done towards peace & reconciliation but on the contrary every thing breaths Warr & Bloodshed. On this side it seems absolutely necessary to provide for a vigorous defence seeing that every Account we receive from England threatens nothing but destruction. These threats will prove vain whilst the Americans continue united & there is every appearance that the Union will be preserved & grow stronger the longer we are oppress'd. It is but doing bare Justice to assert that nobody wish for Independance on Great Britain; the People all call out for reconciliation on Constitutional Terms, & they do not act against Great Britain untill drove to it by some apparent necessity. From this Cause they attack'd the Ministerial Army at Lexington, defended their Lines at Bankers hill & have kept them there ever since. From Necessity they have taken possession of Canada as it was notorious that the Ministry depended on that Country & its Inhabitants to pierce Us in the Rear, & get Us between two fires, in short it is meer necessity that ever induc'd Us to take up arms, & that now forces Us to depend on them. We love the people of England. We wanted no other Friends, no other Allys, but alas if they cannot be content to Consider Us as Brothers entitled to the same freedom, the same priviledges themselves enjoy, they cannot expect a people descended from their own flesh & blood, long Used to & well acquainted with the blessings of freedom, to sit down tamely & see themselves stripd of all they hold dear. For my part I abhor the Name & Idea of a Rebel, I neither want or wish a Change of King or Constitution, & do not conceive myself to act against either when I join America in defence of Constitutional Liberty. I am now a Member of the Continental Congress & if I have any influence or shoud hereafter gain any it shall be exerted in favour of every measure that has a tendancy to procure Accomodation on terms consistant with our just Claims & if I thought there was any thing ask'd on this side not founded in the Constitution in Reason & Justice I wou'd oppose it. This subject is so Important that it's ever uppermost & you must excuse me for running into it. I will finish with sincerely praying that a Speedy end may be put to the Unhappy Contest.

Tr (PRO: S.P. 94, 200). Enclosed in Josiah Hardy to Lord Weymouth, January 26, 1776, and endorsed: "In Consul Hardy's No. 1." Hardy, British Consul at Cadiz, also enclosed copies of the articles of capitulation relating to Montreal's surrender to General Montgomery.

[1] This Tr bears the heading: "Extract of a Letter from Mr. Robert Morris, Philadelphia dated 9th Decr. 1775."

Naval Committee to Nicholas and John Brown

Gentlemen Philadelphia Decr. 9th. 1775

We have proposed that the small sloop Fly belonging to Clarke and Nightingale is now going immediately to Providence shall return hither again directly and bring as many able seamen as she can carry. If her owners shall agree to this plan to whom we have wrote for this purpose we shall be greatly obliged to you to use your utmost influence for the procuring of such seamen; it being slowly that we raise seamen here has put us upon this project and we hope that the Rhode Island seamen who come to Philadelphia for this purpose will very soon see their own homes again. As this is an essential service to your country, we have no doubt of your engaging Zealously in it. If the small sloop we have mentioned should not be able to bring all the Seamen who are willing to enter into this service, we should be glad that you would procure another vessel that you may think suitable to the purpose to come with the utmost dispatch with such overplus seamen to Philadelphia and a reasonable allowance will be made to her for that service, and she will be permitted if she chooses it to take a load of flour or other provisions back. For this purpose it will be best for her to bring Governor Cooks certificate that such provisions shall be for the use of the inhabitants there or otherwise for the use of the Continental Army. I am in behalf of the Committee for Naval Affairs Your very humble servant Step Hopkins

RC (RPJCB). In a clerical hand, and signed by Hopkins. Addressed: "To Messr. Nicholas & John Brown, Merchants in Providence."

Benjamin Harrison to Wilson Miles Cary

Annapolis, Dec. 10, 1775. "We want at Philadelphia immediately two of your best Pilots;[1] they must be men that can be depended on. . . . I have sent Mr. Middleton in a Boat to Peanhetank, where he is to land and carry this to Col. Lewis who I expect will send it to you in the most secret manner. . . . Immediately on receipt of this look out for two [trusted] men and send them in disguise to Peanhetank where Middleton will wait for them and carry them to the Head of the Bay from whence they may easily get to Philadelphia. If the scheme we have on hand can be executed with secresy I make no doubt but we shall be able at least for the present to rid you of that Nest of Pirates that infest our whole Country. . . .[2] The Pilots . . . shall be rewarded to their Hearts content. Do charge them not to whisper the errand they are going on to any person whatever as I must repeat it again, our whole success depends on secresy. . . . Be so kind as to inform me what force Lord D[unmore] has with him in Ships & Land Forces and where they are stationed."

MS not found; reprinted from extract in *Paul C. Richards Catalog*, no. 11 (April 1964), item 164.

[1] Wilson Miles Cary (1734–1817), wealthy Virginia planter and burgess, was naval officer and receiver for lower James River district, 1760–76, and a member of the Elizabeth City County Committee of Safety, 1775. Fairfax Harrison, *The Virginia Carys, An Essay in Genealogy* (New York: De Vinne Press, 1919), p. 108.

[2] On December 2, in response to an appeal from Northampton County, Va., for protection against Lord Dunmore, Congress had dispatched Harrison to Maryland to work with the delegates of that province in outfitting "two or three armed vessels" to engage enemy ships in Chesapeake Bay. Although Samuel Chase, in conjunction with the ongoing efforts of Congress to acquire a small fleet, had already made preliminary inquiries there into the availability of suitable vessels, news of Dunmore's intensified naval activities underscored the need for a naval force to challenge the Virginia governor. As a result of Harrison's efforts, by early January the Continental sloop *Hornet* and the Continental schooner *Wasp* were ready to join the new American fleet that was preparing to sail from the Delaware with orders to proceed to the Chesapeake and attack Dunmore's naval force. See *JCC*, 3:395, 4:335–36; *Am. Archives*, 4th ser. 3:1669–71; Samuel Chase to John Adams, November 16, 1775; and Naval Committee to William Stone, December ? 1775, and January 10, 1776. For another aspect of Harrison's mission, see also Naval Committee to Samuel Purviance, Jr., January 6, 1776.

Thomas Jefferson to John Page

[December 10? 1775]

De rebus novis, ita est. One of our armed vessels has taken an English storeship coming with all the implements of war (except powder) to Boston. She is worth about £30,000 sterling as General Washington informs us, and the stores are adapted to his wants as perfectly as if he had sent the invoice.[1] They have also taken two small provision vessels from Ireland to Boston; a forty gun ship blew up the other day by accident in the harbor of Boston. Of a certainty the hand of god is upon them. Our last intelligence from Arnold to be relied on is by letter from him: he was then at Point Levy opposite Quebec and had a great number of Cannoes ready to cross the river. The Canadians received him with cordiality and the regular force in Quebec was too inconsiderable to give him any inquietude. A later report makes him in possession of Quebec, but this is not authenticated. Montgomery had proceeded in quest of Carleton and his small fleet of 11. pickeroons then on Lake St. Francis. He had got below him and had batteries so planted as to prevent his passing. It is thought he cannot escape their vigilance. I hope Ld. Chatham may live till the fortune of war puts his son into our hands, and enables us by returning him safe to his father, to pay a debt of gratitude. I wish you would get into Convention and come here. Think of it. Accomplish it. Adieu.

[*P.S.*] The Congress have promoted Brigadier Genl. Montgomery to be a Major General, and on being assured that Arnold is in possession of Quebec it is probable he will be made a Brigadier General, one of those offices being vacant by Montgomery's promotion.[2] This march of Arnold's is equal to Xenophon's retreat. Be so good as to enquire for the box of books you lodged for me at Nelson's and get them to a place of safety. Perhaps some opportunity may offer of sending it to Richmond.

RC (MWA). Jefferson, *Papers* (Boyd), 1:270–71. An extract of this letter was printed in the *Virginia Gazette* (Pinkney), December 23, 1775.

[1] See Washington to John Hancock, November 30, 1775. Washington, *Writings* (Fitzpatrick), 4:132.

[2] Congress promoted Montgomery to the rank of major general on December 9, 1775, and Arnold to that of brigadier general on January 10, 1776. *JCC*, 3:418, 4:47.

Francis Lewis to John Alsop

Dr Sir Phila. 10 Decemr. 1775

I this moment received your favor by the Post and am sorry to find the ordering the Clothg from Albany to Cambridge delayed especialy as it [*will*] at this season of the Year be of no use to the troops in Canada, and those at Cambridge may be in great want of them. Pray do all you can to expedite the forwarding them to Col. Mifflin. The inclosed letter please to forward seal'd. This being Sunday cannot send copy of the Congress's resolve;[1] be assured it is on the Minuts.

I have the money to send you for the Clothing but have not yet an opportunity of sending it.

Congress has resolved to raise four more Battalions in this

Colonie,[2] and purpose sitting all Winter, so hope youl soon be here to relieve your Collegue on duty.

Mr [Philip] Livingston joins me in requesting you would load another Vessell on our Contract with Congress.[3] We shall be [by] next post write you jointly on that head, in the Intrim I am, Sir yr. very Humbl Servt. Frans. Lewis

P.S. Am glad to find our Convention has at last made a House; cannot you get them to fix our pay.[4]

RC (NHi).

[1] That is, Congress' resolve of December 5 stating that since General Schuyler's army probably would be able to obtain clothing at Montreal, all clothing hitherto purchased for this force and sent to Albany should be forwarded instead to Quarter Master General Mifflin for the use of Washington's army outside Boston. *JCC*, 3:407–8.

[2] See *JCC*, 3:418.

[3] See Secret Committee Contract, October 9, 1775.

[4] For attending Congress during 1775, Lewis eventually submitted an account for the following periods of service. "May 7th Sett out for Phila. & returned the 5th August" (89 days @ 32s per diem); "Sepr. 10 Sett out for Phila & returned the 11 October" (32 days @ 32s per diem); and "Novr. 1st arrived at Phila. & return'd to New York 31 Decr." (61 days @ 32s per diem). Francis Lewis account, receipted January 27, 1776, Philip D. Sang deposit, NjR.

Francis Lightfoot Lee to a Friend in London

Decr. 11. 1775

From the little inquiry that has been made concerning your friends Land, upon Susquehanna, in Maryland, It appears to me, that he has a right to that & much more, if he can prove himself the lawfull heir to the person of his Name who died in Maryland. The Gentleman in Maryland is still upon the enquiry, when it is finished you shall know the result.

The Gentleman who brings this will have all our public papers; by which you will see our great success this year, against your infamous ministry. The Associations & Committees of correspondence give us some hopes, that your Hill will soon be graced with their heads. It is my opinion that if the war continues another year, G. Britain & the Colonies are disunited for ever. Our troops now in pay & order'd to be raised amount to 35,000 & will be 8 or 10,000 more in the spring. We have now 10 Ships of war from 10 to 30 Guns in Continental pay, & are determined to exert the whole force of the Continent this winter to fit out as many large Ships as possible against next summer. There are many small Ships belonging to the different Colonies, & private persons to cruise upon the Ministerial transports; and many others getting ready. Ld. Bute will soon make America a great Naval power. The Lee, Capt. Manly, took the other day a store ship called the Nancy, loaded with Musketts, artillery & other stores to a great amount. We thank the Ministry [for] the supply. All Canada is ours.

Yr. ever. Francis Light. Lee

RC (ViHi). A continuation of Lee to a Friend in London, November 29, 1775.

Secret Committee Minutes of Proceedings

C[ommittee] C[hamber] Decr. 11. 1775.

At a meeting of the Com[mittee] of S[ecrecy] present Saml Ward, Francis Lewis, Tho. McKean, Silas Deane & Josiah Bartlett.

A Contract was enterd into between Eseck Hopkins of the Colony of Rhode Island Esqr. & the sd. Committee.[1]

That a voyage be immediately undertaken for the speedy procurg. of thirteen tons good gun powder but if the Gunpowdr. cannot be had as much Saltpetre with a proportion of Sulphur equal to 15 lb to every hundd. weight of Salt petre as will make that quantity of Gunpowder, but if neither gunpowder nor salt petre & sulphur can be had, then as many stand of good Arms as the Cargoe hereinafter mentiond will purchase.

MS (MH).

[1] Esek Hopkins also received an advance of $6,000 on this contract. Secret Committee Account, September 27, 1775–August 26, 1776.

Committee of Secret Correspondence to Arthur Lee

Sir, Philade. Dec. 12, 1775

By this Conveyance we have the Pleasure of transmitting to you sundry printed Papers, that Such of them as you think proper may be immediately published in England.

We have written on the Subject of American Affairs to Monsieur C.G.F. Dumas, who resides at the Hague.[1] We recommend it to you to correspond with him, and to send through his Hands any Letters to us which you cannot send more directly. He will transmit them via St. Eustatia. When you write to him direct your Letter thus, *A Mons. Monsr. C. G. F. Dumas cher Made. le Ve. Loder, à la Hague:* and put it under Cover directed to Mr. A. Stuckey Merchant at Rotterdam.

Mr. Story may be trusted with any Dispatches you think proper to send us. You will be so kind as to aid and advise him.

It would be agreable to Congress to know the Disposition of Foreign Powers towards us, and we hope this Object will engage your Attention. We need not hint that great Circumspection and impenetrable Secrecy are necessary. The Congress rely on your Zeal and Abilities to serve them and will readily compensate you for whatever Trouble and Expence a Compliance with their Desires may occasion. We remit you for the present Two Hundred Pounds Sterling.

Whenever you think the Importance of your Dispatches may require it, we desire you to send an Express-Boat with them from England, for which Service your Agreement with the Owner there shall be fulfilled by us here.

We can now only add that we continue firm in our Resolutions to defend ourselves, notwithstanding the big Threats of the Ministry. We have just taken one of their Ordnance Store Ships, in which are abundance of Carcasses & Bombs intended for burning our Towns.

With great Esteem, we are Sir, Your most obedt humble Servants

B Franklin
John Dickinson } Committee of Correspondence
John Jay

RC (MeHi). Written by Franklin and signed by Franklin, Dickinson, and Jay.

[1] See Benjamin Franklin to Charles William Frederic Dumas, December 9, 1775.

Connecticut Delegates' Memorial to Congress

[December 12? 1775]

The Delegates for the Colony of Connecticut have received the following information which they pray may be inquired into, viz:

That certain persons having formed an Association for the purpose of seizing on, & removing by force of Arms the people settled on the river Susquehannah, under the Government, & protection of sd. Colony of Connecticut, have in pursuance of such designs, raised a Large Sum of Money and with the same employed Agents to inlist Men.[1] That they have also collected, a great Number of Blankets, Shoes, Firelocks, with a quantity of Powder & ball, & other military Stores in this City and conveyed the same to their Agents in this Country who have therewith cloathed, & Armed the Men, they have raised, for sd. hostile purpose. That to induce Men to engage, they have by sd. Agents been promised the plunder of the Inhabitants, they should in this manner seize on & remove, over & above exorbitant Wages given them. That by artful, & wicked Means, the late resolution of Congress,[2] respectg said Inhabitants, which the honorable Presidt. sent forward, for the purpose of preventing hostilities, has been represented as a Forgery, and a Libel propagated, among the people, who were solicited to join in these hostilities, fictitiously signed John Hancock President the purport of which was that This Congress had ordered the removal of sd. Inhabitants.

That the Agents of sd. Association had proceeded to seize on large Quantities of Goods, & Stores, belonging to some of the said Inhabitants of Connecticut & others, which were going up the River Susquehannah, to supply the said Settlers in part, but by much the greater part of sd. Goods, were designed for The Indians of sd. Six Nations at the head of sd. River.

That the detention of sd. Goods, the Total interruption of all Supplies to the Indians, and the hostile preparations making, have given the Indians the most alarming Apprehensions.

That the different parties, engaged in this Hostile invasion, began their March on Monday last, to their place of rendevouz, giving out as they went, that they should be Fifteen Hundred Strong when Collected.

That all passes leading to, & from sd. Settlement are seized on, & guarded by sd. parties.

That the distress'd Settlers have put themselves into the best posture of defence, in their power, having no other alternative, but to Submit to plunder, and ruin, with their Families, or defend them, to the last Extremity. To support the Truth of the above Information, credible persons are ready to be examined, & many Depositions are taken, & ready to be produced.[3]

During this inquiry, which the Delegates desire may be entered upon immediately & pursued untill the whole scheme be detected, and the extensive mischief meditated prevented, They move That some one, or more persons be instantly sent by this Congress, With orders to stop all hostilities above Complained of, To restore to the people, on either side of this unhappy dispute, their property that may be taken from them, To set at Liberty all who may on either side have been made prisoners, to direct that Commerce be open on the Susquehannah with sd. Settlers & Indians, and to give orders that all hostilities between the parties cease, and that every one Continue peaceably to enjoy & occupy those possessions he was in possession & improvement of, before the late disturbances between them.

MS (DNA: PCC, item 69). In the hand of Silas Deane. Endorsed by Charles Thomson: "Affidavits respecting the disputes between the people of Pensylv & Conecticut. Dec. 12, 1775."

[1] A list of subscribers is printed in the *Susquehannah Co. Papers*, 6:366.

[2] See the resolve of November 4, 1775. *JCC*, 3:321.

[3] The despositions submitted by the Connecticut delegates are in PCC, item 69, fols. 31–44. Several of these are printed in the *Susquehannah Co. Papers*, 6:400–401, 404–11; and *Am. Archives*, 4th ser. 3:1965–68.

Benjamin Franklin to Gabriel Antonio de Bourbon

Illustrious Prince Philadelphia Decr. 12. 1775

I have just received through the Hands of the Ambassador of Spain, the much esteemed present your most Serene Highness hath so Kindly sent me, of your excellent Version of Sallust.[1]

I am extreamly sensible of the honor done me, and beg you would accept my thankful acknowledgements. I wish I could send hence any American Literary Production worthy of your perusal, but as yet the Muses have scarcely visited these remote Regions. Perhaps however the Proceedings of our American Congress, just published, may be a subject of some Curiosity at your Court. I therefore take the Liberty of sending your Highness a Copy, with some other Papers which contain Accounts of the successes wherewith Providence has lately favoured us. Therein your wise Politicians may contemplate the first efforts of a rising State, which seems likely soon to act a part of some Importance on the stage of human affairs, and furnish materials for a future Salust. I am very old and can scarce hope to see the event of this great Contest: but looking forward I think I see a powerful Dominion growing, up here, whose interest it will be to form a close and firm alliance with Spain (their Territories bordering) and who being united, will be able, not only to preserve their own people in peace, but to repel the Force of all the other powers in Europe. It seems therefore prudent on both sides to cultivate a good understanding, that may hereafter be so useful to both; towards which a fair Foundation is already laid in our minds by the well founded popular Opinion entertained here of Spanish Integrity and Honour. I hope my presumption in hinting this will be pardoned. If in any thing on this side the Globe I can render either service or pleasure to your Royal Highness, your commands will make me happy. With the utmost esteem & veneration I have the Honour to be Your Serene Highness's most obedient and most humble Servant

Bn. Franklin

FC (DLC). Addressed: "To His most Serene Highness Dn Gabriel of Bourbon." Endorsed: "On receiving his Version of Sallust."

[1] Gabriel Antonio, Infante of Spain, had sent Franklin a copy of the Spanish edition of Sallust that he had translated in 1772. C. Sallustius Crispus, *La conjuración de Catilina y la guerra de Jugurta* (Madrid: J. Ibarra, 1772).

Joseph Hewes to Emperor Mosely

Sir Philadelphia 12th Decemr 1775

Mr. Smith has wrote me he has given you Orders to take in Wine at Spain and then proceed to Saltitudas for a load of Salt.[1] I fear this will not do as you run a great risk of being seized by English men of War among the Salt Islands. I cannot think the profits on the Wine will be equal to the risk, I would rather you should take a Load of Salt and instead of Wine get as much Powder and good Muskets as possible and proceed directly home. Endeavour to make the land to the Northward of Cape Hatteras, get a pilot of, and if any Kings Ship or Cutter should be at Occacock you must land your Powder & Muskets on the Banks and get them sent up to Edenton by small Craft, or you may probably be able to get the Brigg in at New Inlet between Hatteras & Roanoke Inlet. If so you may also send the salt up in small Craft advising Mr Smith of your Arival by a boat sent on purpose, or if you cannot do this, nor get into Ocacock for Kings Cutters I would have you proceed directly for this place. There is not one Kings Vessel in this River nor has there been one for some time past nor any expected 'till April or May next, if then, and you have nothing to fear from the Custom House officers; they dare not look out. If you can get any kind of freight for this place take it, if you cannot get Powder and Muskets you may take Wine and proceed to St. Eustatia or any Dutch or Foreign Port and endeavour to sell the Wine and buy Powder & Muskets. This you may do either with a Load of Salt or without, if you go without Salt reserve as much money as will purchase a Load but be very carefull not to go to any place to purchase Salt where you will be likely to fall in with any of the kings Ships, if you do not return directly from Spain to Carolina you must be very carefull to write to Mr. Backie to get proper Insurance. Be particular in informing him where you intend to go that he may make Insurance Accordingly. I think this will be the Safest Port on the Continent to come too. After you Arive in Spain write by every opportunity you can possibly get to my Brother Josiah Hewes of this City Merchant, inform him of every step you intend to take, advise with Messrs. Duff & Welch on all these Matters and do the best you can for our Interest. If the Brigg can be sold for a good price let her go, if not do the best you can; if you take in both Salt & Wine and cannot do better, that is cannot get into Carolina with Safety, I think you may get in here without much risque, pray dont fail to write by every opportunity. Powder, Salt Petre, Muskets, good Cannon say nine & Six Pounders I believe will Answer if well bought. At any rate Powder & Muskets cannot fail. I am Sir Your very hum Servt

Joseph Hewes

RC (MdBJ-G).

[1] Emperor Mosely was captain of the brig *Joseph*, a vessel owned by Hewes. Clark, *Naval Documents*, 2:396.

Francis Lightfoot Lee to Landon Carter

My dear Colonel, Philadelphia Decr. 12th 1775

Before you receive this, Mr. Colston will have given you all the news of this place when he left it, since which one of our little men of war, called the Lee, capt. Manly, has taken a Store ship, loaded with 2000 stand of arms, a great deal of artillery, 30 tons of shot, a quantity of shells & shott for the bombs & Cannon; and a very great quantity of all kinds of Artillery stores, to the amount of 20,000 £ Str., as tis tho't. We make no doubt but Quebec & Carleton with his powder are in our possession by this time. If we are supply'd with powder from that or any other quarter this winter we shall certainly make Boston too hot for Howe, as the Ministry has kindly supplied us plentifully with Artillery. These successes to the Northward, and the former reputation of Virga. make the present proceedings with you appear in a very odd light. The real friends of liberty are under great concern, & your delegates are mortified with the sneers & reflections of the lukewarm but that is trifling to the uneasiness we suffer, from the apprehension of the consequences that may follow from Ld. Dunmore's being allow'd to get to such a head.[1]

It does not appear to me that Woodford's force is sufficient to effect any thing decisive. In my opinion, our safety depends upon an immediate, & effectual stop being put to that infernal Demon, & his tory associates at Norfolk. The Congress are giving the greatest attention to a Navy, & I hope we shall have ships enough by the spring to oblige the Ministerial fleet to consult their safety by keeping close together, & of course will not be able to do us much injury. I am surprised at not receiving Letters from my friends in Richmond by the Constl. post. The Postmaster assures me there is a post established from Fredericksburg to Portroyal, Hobb's Hole, & Urbanna; And the County Comtees were to direct where the offices shou'd be kept. I wish it was inquired into & the obstruction mentioned; that they may be removed, if in the Postmaster's power. I hope the County chose a Comtee to your liking, & that every thing is quiet. Is it not necessary that the Convention shoud establish some kind of Government as Ld. D. by his proclamation has utterly demolished the whole civil Government. I believe the Congress will adjourn before Christmas, but whether long enough to allow me to see Virga. is uncertain. In the mean time my best wishes attend my friends in Richmond. I am Dear Col. yr. afft. hble Sevt. Francis Lightfoot Lee

RC (ViHi).

[1] For Congress' response to the threat to Virginia posed by Dunmore's operations, see *JCC*, 3:403–4; and Francis Lightfoot Lee to Robert W. Carter, December 2, 1775, note 1.

Samuel Ward to Henry Ward

Dear Bror. Philadelphia 12th Decr. 1775

I am obliged to You for the many very important Hints in your last and hope You will never omit your Sentiments upon every interesting Occasion. The Contest between the two Countries involves a Question of no less magnitude than the Happiness or Misery of Millions & when We extend our Views to future Ages We may say Millions of Millions. Our Views therefore ought to be extensive, our Plans great & our Exertions adequate to the immense Object before Us and such I doubt not will be the Conduct of Congress.

Our Accts. have been presented. There were several large Articles in them which had never been before Us in any Accts. already liquidated. The Comee. of Claims desired the Direction of Congress upon these, Who allowed the Expenses of moving the Stock and the Amount of the Cannon but as the Riflemen & other Soldiers raised in the middle & southern Colonies found their own Arms and were allowed no Bounty The Congress would not pay those two Charges. We hope however when the Difficulty of raising men without a Bounty is better understood and the Accts. from the other Colonies are also before us to obtain a Reversion of this Opinion. Upon a Consultation We all thought best to defer any further Examination of the Accts. until the general Assembly is acquainted with this Resolve & all the N[ew] E[nglan]d Accts. can come under Examination together. We shall move for a Grant to the Colony for a Sum about adequate to the Ball[anc]e as it now stands and as the new Money ordered is now printing We hope to get it for the Comee. in a Week or ten Days.

When you have read the enclosed, seal and deliver it. An objection was made in the Comee. of Secresy that as Mr. Hopkins was going to Sea the Continent would not be safe with his Security. Justice to the Continent, the honor of the Colony & my own Character require me to ask their Obligation and as I had no Motive in this Matter but a Desire of serving them I doubt but they will readily give it. You will take it & deposit it in your office until my Return or a safe Conveyance here presents.

Mr. Nicho. Brown mentions 800 Boxes spermaceti Candles which he would send upon Permission for Powder.[1] If they could do in any foreign Port of Europe & he would export them on Acct. of the united Colonies upon the same Com[missio]ns allowed Clarke & Nightingale & the same Freight that we give others I could serve him & wish to know as soon as possible for our Contracts for Powders are near compleated & People are every Day offering to take up the Remainder & I keep it open on Purpose to serve the Com[pan]y & accommodate that Part of the Country with Arms & Ammunition.[2] We should want a great Part of this Cargoe in good small Arms. I would write to the Comp[an]y but cannot get time being obliged this Moment to attend upon a Comee. I am Dear Bror. Yours most affectionately Sam Ward

P.S. Wish if the proposal be agreable they would write me very particularly their whole Plan or send some proper Person to adjust the whole with the Comee.

My most respectful Regards to the Govr. & all our Friends.

The Congress besides one Battalion in Georgia, two in So. Carolina, two in North, two in the Jersey's & one in Pennsylvania has ordered four more Battalions in Pennsylvania & one in the lower Counties that you see we setting ourselves about the great War in earnest.

RC (RHi).

[1] See Ward to Henry Ward, December 3, 1775, note 1.

[2] The Secret Committee granted contracts for the procurement of gunpowder and other supplies to John Brown on December 26, 1775, and to John and Nicholas Brown on February 6, 1776. See Secret Committee Minutes of Proceedings, December 26, 1775, February 6, 1776; Secret Committee Account, September 27, 1775–August 26, 1776; and Clark, *Naval Documents*, 3:1153–54.

John Jay to Alexander McDougall

Dear Sir Philad. 13 Decr. 1775

Your Letter of the 8th Inst. is now before me. Did you know how much Satisfaction a Line from you gives me, you would not think of apologizing for the frequency of your Letters. I am much obliged to you for your Hints respecting the Command of a certain Post. They are useful and will determine my Conduct, tho some folks here may not coincide with me in opinion. I must confess that I think the Station might be better filled, and wished it consisted with the Interest of the Province to take you from the Convention &c but as I am sure such a Measure would be highly impolitic and imprudent, it must be declined.

I am very glad to hear that the Convention begins to think of us, and am in daily Expectation of hearing from them on the Subject. I wish they would lessen the number of Delegates—it would diminish the Expence, without injuring the Interest of the Colony. As I cant confer with you on this Subject, the Matter must be entirely submitted to your Discretion. It is too delicate to trust to the uncertain Fate of a Letter.

Pray does the Convention mean to take up the New England Expedition? I really think they should thank Connecticut for the Aid they afforded West Chester—and complain loudly of the late improper

Incursion. The Honor of the Colony is at Stake. The Convention is now the only Guardian of it.

Adieu. I am with great Sincerity your Friend John Jay

[*P.S.*] You forgot your Accounts!

RC (NHi).

Naval Committee to Dudley Saltonstall

Sir, Philadelphia Decr. 13. 1775

We perceive by your Letter that you have agreed to accept of the command of the ship Alfred as Captain—and that you wish to know the terms on Which you may engage seamen. For that purpose We herewith send you the Articles to be signed by the seamen, together with the Wages and other Advantages to be allowed them. As we expect these ships to sail in ten days at least, we wish you to make the utmost dispatch you can hither and leave proper persons to bring along as many seamen as can be had Within the time above mentioned. You receive this by express which will intimate to you the dispatch We wish to make in this business. By order of the Committee I am Your humble servant

Silas Deane Chairman of sd Com[mitte]e

N.B. The Wages of seamen is encreased from 50/ to three pounds Pensylvania Currency per month.

RC (MH). Written in a clerical hand and signed by Silas Deane.
[1] See *JCC*, 3:392–93.

Richard Smith's Diary

[December 13, 1775]

Wednesday 13. I was at Congress. The Delegates of Maryland & Georgia all absent. A Report from a Comee. was agreed to for equipping Thirteen Ships of War in several Colonies of 32 Guns 28 and 24 Guns each & the Expence of each at an Average estimated at 66,666 2/3 Dollars. There is a secret Comee. whereof Govr. Ward is Chairman and Thos. McKean Clerk. Mr. Willing resigned his Seat in it & Rob. Morris was chosen in his Room by Ballot. Debates upon the Question Whether to make an Adjornment a few Days hence for some Time and to appoint a Comee. of One out of each Colony to superintend the Treasury and do the Business left unfinished. Agreed to appoint such a Committee if an Adjornt. shall take Place & a Comee. was now nominated to prepare the Business of the other Comee. Debates whether a Comee. of One out of each Colony shall be appointed to take Care of Naval Affairs in the Nature of a Board of Admiralty postponed. Col. Lee moved to raise the Wages of able Seamen in the Armament now fittng out, from 50/ Penna. Cury. which had been before fixed by Congress, to £3 per month and this was carried by Vote. Ablebodied Landmen remained as before at 50/per month. The Order for this day was to consider of giving Gen Washington Directions to storm Boston but various other Matters intervening it was put off till Tomorrow. McKean informed the Congress that many Persons in Pennsa., Maryland and Jersey sell Tea and drink Tea upon a Report that Congress has granted Leave so to do & he doubted Whether the Committees had Power to restrain them. A Day was fixed for considering the Matter. (In April 1776 the Congress gave Leave to sell & use what Tea was in the Country, forbidding any further Importation of it.)[1] Mr Crane went Home, Livingston and myself remain, Kinsey & De Hart have lately resigned.[2]

MS (DLC).

[1] See *JCC*, 4:277–78.

[2] See John DeHart to the New Jersey Assembly, November 13, 1775.

Samuel Ward to Nathaniel Shaw, Jr.

Sir Philadelphia 13th Decr. 1775

I was astonished to find by a Letter from Mr. Mumford that You was shipping live Cattle on Acct. of the united Colonies. There is an express Resolve of Congress that no horned Cattle, Sheep, Hogs, or Poultry should be exported and it must be owing to the great Haste in which your Permit was made out that it was not expressly inserted. You was informed however of the Purport of it by Mr. Deane as he recollects & I think by me. You will therefore if the Vessels have not sailed instantly stop the Exportation of any live Stock mentioned above. The Necessity of the strictest Compliance with every Resolve of Congress you are well sensible of; I doubt not therefore your immediate Compliance as you value the Interest of your Country.[1] I am Sir Your most hbe Servt. Sam Ward

P.S. Be good enough to send me by next Post a Copy of the Permit.

RC (CtNlHi). Addressed: "On the Service of the united Colonies. To Mr. Nathaniel Shaw Jr., Mercht., New London."

[1] Shaw, who had been granted a contract to obtain gunpowder by the Secret Committee on November 8, ignored this warning from Ward, who undoubtedly issued it in his capacity as chairman of the committee, and continued to export

livestock to the foreign West Indies, where he dispatched his ships to procure the gunpowder called for by his contract. See Secret Committee Minutes of Proceedings, November 8, 1775; Clark, *Naval Documents*, 3:679, 817–18, 1111–12, 1197; and *Collections of the Connecticut Historical Society* 23 (1930): 13–15.

John Alsop to Roger Sherman

Sir New York 14th Decem. 1775

The brigt. Polly, Capt. Wm. Thompson, is loaded with a Cargoe of wheat by order of the Congress. She is cleared out for Lisbon and attempted to Sail the day before yesterday, but Capt. Vandepot Stopped her, and Told the master, That his orders from Adm. Graves was not to allow any vessell to pass him but such as were Cleared for Great Brittain, Ireland or the British West Indies, Therefore I thought best to direct him Through the sound. Now shou'd he stop at your, or any adjacent port, you'll please to direct him with the necessary assistance or advice That he may have a safe conduct; and That you'll please to Tra[n]smit such directions with speed to the Committee of New London, That she may not be detained for want of this advice.

My brother Richd Alsop writes that he has prepared a Cargoe of horses in consequence of the advice that I gave, That the Congress permitted horses to be exported, but he writes that you said that resolve was under Some restriction, which I dont recollect, but as you are later from Congress Than I am, shall be Thankfull, if you'll let my brother at Middletown know the circumstance by this post, for his Vessell & horses are waiting for an answer.[1] With Esteem I am Sr Yr Very hble Servt. John Alsop

RC (PHi). Addressed: "On the service of the united Colonies. Roger Sherman Esqr. In his absence, the Chairman of the Committee, New Haven."

[1] On November 1 Congress had decided to exempt the export of horses to the foreign West Indies from the nonexportation agreement. See *JCC*, 3:315; and Samuel Adams to James Warren, November 4, 1775.

Secret Committee Minutes of Proceedings

Philadelphia Com[mittee] Ch[amber] Decr. 14. 1775

At a meeting of the C[ommittee] of Secrecy present Saml. Ward, Benjn. Franklin, Silas Deane, Josiah Bartlett, Frans. Lewis. A Contract was enterd into between Willing Morris & Co. of the City of Philadelphia Merchts. & the sd Com[mitte]e of Secrecy.[1]

That the sd Thos. Willing, Robert Morris & Thos. Morris shall & will, with the utmost speed, & secrecy, send a ship or vessel to some port of Europe & there purchase at the cheapest rate that they can, a quantity of Duck or Sail Cloth to the value of three thousand pounds sterg. or failing to obtain so much value in that article, they are to procure as much thereof as they can & invest the remaining Sum in any of the following Articles—Gunpowder, Saltpetre, vitry, Ticklinburgs, gunlocks, soldiers muskets, or coals fit for Smith's use. As by sd. Contract &c Reg[ister] fol. 26.[2]

MS (MH).

[1] This contract was apparently made in response to the resolve of Congress of December 13 instructing the Secret Committee to procure canvas and powder for the vessels being fitted for naval duty. *JCC*, 3:426.

[2] A footnote keyed to this concluding sentence reads: "They recd. the same day 14000 dol[lar]s on Acct."

Richard Smith's Diary

Thursday 14 Decr. [1775]

Agreed to read the Minutes for the first Half Hour every Morning & also the preceeding Day's Transactions, accordingly the Journal was begun from the 5th. of Septr. last being the Time of Meeting after the last Adjornmt. Ordered that the Votes be sent to the Press as fast as they are revised. Several Matters were marked to be omitted as improper for Public Inspection. Much of the Day was spent upon an Answer to that Part of Gen. Washns. Letters requesting Directions what to do with the Ships & Cargoes lately taken by our armed Vessels which was at length referred after learned Debates & Authorities from Vattel &c.[1] Much Altercation Whether a former Resolution of Congress had passed agt. confiscating the Ships taken in Carrying Military Stores or Goods to Boston, the Colonies on Vote were equally divided upon it, however it was agreed that the Cargoes should be forfeited & that such Matters ought to be tryed in the Admiralty Court and by the Course of the Law of Nations not of the Municipal Law. The President (Hancock) applied to the Congress to release Lieut. Hay taken in Canada & now in Philada. he offering his Parole of Honor to go Home to Scotland, resign his Commission and never serve against America. Lynch, Lee & others for it who were opposed by Nelson and several more, the Question passed in the Affirmative. The Journal of the Indian Treaty lately held by our Commissioners at Pittsburg lies before Congress & is not yet examined. A member from each Colony (Crane for New Jersey, tho now absent) chosen by Ballot to procure or cause to be built and fitted out the 13 Ships of War yesterday ordered. Gadsden moved that the Congress should purchase a handsome Time Piece & set it up in the Assembly Room in the State House where we meet, as a Present for the Use of the Room. Wilson and Willing desired the Motion might be dropt as the Assembly expected no Consideration & it was withdrawn. Duane presented a Petition from Peter Berton of New York praying Compensation for a Vessel taken by the Men of War, it was referred by Ballot to Lynch, E. Rutledge & myself.[2]

MS (DLC).

[1] Congress was at this time considering Washington's letter to Hancock of December 4, 1775. See PCC, item 152, 1:305–12; Washington, *Writings* (Fitzpatrick), 4:141–45; and *JCC*, 3:428.

[2] On December 23 Congress approved a report from this committee calling for the rejection of Berton's petition. *JCC*, 3:454.

Samuel Ward to Henry Ward

Dear Bror. Philadelphia 14th Decr. 1775

I have the Pleasure to acquaint you that upon considering our Instruction for a Navy the Congress has agreed to build thirteen Ships of War. A Comee is to be this Day appointed with full Power to carry the Resolve into Execution. Powder & Duck are ordered to be imported; all other Articles it is supposed may be got in the Colonies; two of these Vessels are to be built in our Colony, 1 in New Hampshire &c; the particulars I would not have mentioned; the Ships are to be built with all possible Dispatch.

We have a Grant from Congress of 120000 Dollars in Advance on our Accts. The Gentn. are determined to wait for the Money, the Printing is begun and I have been to the Treasurers who have engaged to get it signed as soon as possible.

Mr. John Brown arrived last Evening very well. I expect that the Matter mentioned in my last to you about his Bror. Letter can be easily finished now; I am shall see him upon the Occasion in a few Minutes.

The Congress continues to be extrem[ely] hurried yet but I hope to get a [mo]ments Leisure at Christmas. I most heartily congratulate You upon the taking the Transports, & other very good News. I have given the principal Part of your Letter to the Printer; you'll see it in Bradfords Paper.[1] Mr. Adams & several were so highly pleased that they urged me to publish it.

I wrote some time since that I was greatly alarmed about our Army. My Apprehensions are not quieted yet the parsimonious Policy & the Pride of some prevent a Bounty & without it We shall not get Men; We take the Matter again up this Day. May Heaven direct our Councils. Present my most respectful Compliments to the Govr. & all Who deserve & to whom they will [be] acceptable.

The fitting out our small Fleet goes on well. I wrote some time since [. . .] what Wages & Bounty our Col[ony has] given through the two last Wars; do be particular & let Me have it by next Post. I am Your very affece. Brother Sam Ward

P.S. Since writing this I have found some good Paper that you will not be troubled with such vile Stuff again.

Never read my letters to any body till you have gone over them & seen what may be public.

RC (RHi).

[1] See Ward, *Correspondence* (Knollenberg), pp. 141–42.

Silas Deane to Elizabeth Deane

Philadelphia Decr. 15th. 1775

I wrote you one Line yesterday, per Capt Phelps, since which I am fully Convinced this Congress will adjourn before Christmass if nothing New offers.

Naval preparations are Now entering upon with Spirit, and Yesterday the Congress chose a Standing Committee to superintend this department, of which I had the honor to be Unanimously chosen one.[1] This will detain Me here sometime after the 1st of January, indeed I apprehend that the Congress will leave a Number to put into Execution the resolves of the Congress, together with the Naval Committee, as the adjournment will probably be over to the 1st of March. I do not expect to return sooner unless it may be to engage Workmen on the Business, part of which, I shall agree to have carried on in the Colony.

I hear from Connecticut that I am in Irons, & that Your Journey with Mr. Webb was to see me, and as I shall not return with Col. Dyer, & Cyder being plenty, I expect to hear soon, of my being hanged, Drawn, & quartered. I wrote to Governor Trumbull a Lettr. on the Conduct of the Assembly which he will be obliged to read before them when they meet, and I think, some People will look small, in the issue.[2] If the Assembly sit this Winter I shall endeavor to be at home at the Time at all adventures, to demand a hearing before them, how I have discharged the Trust reposed in Me and shall bring with me Vouchers for my Conduct, from the Gentlemen of the Congress. My Enemies designs have been, by superceeding me in my absence, tacitly to Censure Me, & leave by implication a Stigma on my Character, which they know a public hearing must not only clear up, but Tumble them into the Pitt they have (like Moles as they are) been digging for Me. They cloak themselves under Sanction, and Authority of Assembly, and have no Idea of my asking for a public hearing, which as they have not censured Me directly, They imagine I shall not think of, but I can fairly do it, by desiring to give an Acct. of my performance of the Duty reposed in Me, and Justice can never refuse Me.

Col. Dyer joined Me in the Letter, but he somehow grows every Day, more peevish, & is at Times absolutely intolerable, I know the Cause, & You can guess at it. Governor Ward has in a formal Manner, laid Seige to Mrs. House, & I am apt to think the Fortress will surrender, on the first serious Summons. Poor Mrs. Christ. Marshall died this Morning suddenly which has greatly distress'd that freindly Circle of Brothers, and Sisters. You remember, She was D. Mumfords Master's Wife.

I look out, most impatiently, for Your Brother Dudley.[3] His Shipp is a fine one of Thirty odd Gunns & is nearly ready.

The behavior of Our Soldiers, has made Me Sick, but little better could be expected from Men, trained up with Notions of their right of saying how, & when, & under whom they will serve & who have, for certain dirty political purposes, been tampered with by their Officers, among whom, no less than a General has been busy.[4]

I sent you the Silk, Cost four Dollars, the Whole by Capt. E. Phelps whom I sent express to Rhode Island, and ordered him to send you the Silk by the Post from N. Haven. I shall write Brother Bar[naba]s by this Opportunity, You will shew such parts of this Lettr. to such persons as you may judge fitt to be Seen, & to See. My Complts. to Neighboring Freinds, Love to the Family & Connections, I am affectionately Your's S. Deane

RC (CtHi).

[1] See *JCC*, 3:428.

[2] See Connecticut Delegates to Jonathan Trumbull, Sr., December 5, 1775.

[3] See Naval Committee to Dudley Saltonstall, December 13, 1775.

[4] On December 1 a number of Connecticut enlisted men whose terms were about to expire attempted to leave camp at Cambridge before new recruits had arrived to replace them. General Washington, in a letter of December 4 that was read in Congress on the 13th, described their conduct as "scandalous" and expressed fears that a similar "defection" would occur when the enlistment periods of other provincial troops expired. See Washington, *Writings* (Fitzpatrick), 4:141–45; and *JCC*, 3:425.

Richard Smith's Diary

Friday Decr. 15. [1775]

Part of the Journal read and sundry Paragraphs as usual ordered to be omitted in Publication. Controversy Whether a particular Part shall be published, the Colonies were equally divided & the Part is to remain unpublished. Motion by Wilson that all Officers below a Major in the Continental Troops now raising in Pennsa. shall be appointed by the several Committees of Correspondence & Observation was at length rejected & the Mode of Appointment there & in the Lower Counties settled. A Letter & several Papers from some Indians on the Susquehannah, one of them named Jacob Johnson a Preacher, were read and the Indian Messengers ordered to be taken Care of at the Continental Expence.[1] Robert Morris moved that a Comee. be nominated to consider of Ways & Means to bring in Gold & Silver & keep it in the Country, it is reported that Half Joes have already risen to £3–2–6, it was debated & postponed till Tomorrow.[2] Col. Lee moved that George Mead & Co. of Philada. may export from that City to Virginia 6000 Bushels of Salt & carry abroad Produce to the Amount from thence, opposed by Jay, Lewis & others & supported by Nelson, Wyth, Rob. Morris &c. It passed in the Affirmative 7 Colonies to 4. Comee. on Public Accots. reported a Number of Accounts which were allowed & ordered to be paid. (The mode of Payment is the President signs an Order to the joint Treasurers Hillegas & Clymer & then they pay the Money.) Several other Motions & Matters, for these Memoirs only contain what I could readily recollect.

MS (DLC).

[1] There is no mention of this matter in the journals.

[2] Congress apparently did not appoint such a committee but may have instead referred the matter to the committee appointed "to consider what articles are necessary for the army." In any event, on December 23 the latter committee submitted a report to which was appended a recommendation to export produce to the value of $160,000 "to proper Ports in Europe and the West Indies and there disposed of for Gold and Silver to be imported into the Continental Treasury as soon as may be." According to Secretary Thomson's endorsement on the report, however, action on this recommendation was postponed, and it is not clear from the journals that any other action was taken on Morris' motion. See *JCC*, 3:453–54, 467; PCC, item 21, 1:1–3; and Smith's Diary, December 23, 30, 1775.

Eliphalet Dyer to Joseph Trumbull

Sr Philadelphia Decembr. 16th 1775

I receivd your favor of the 8th Instant & one about 2 or 3 weeks since which should have Answerd but was uncertain to send it either to Lebanon or Cambridge. I receivd one or two since from the Govr. & one from your brother. They mentioned Nothing about you whether dead or alive, att home or Abroad. I fear you give your self too much Uneasiness on the hints I gave you some time agoe.[1] I soon found they made no lasting Impression here & were but Transient & gone. My Inducement in giving you some pains on the Subject was rather to put you on your guard as knowing every one has some Watchfull Enemys. Some of the Congress throw out once in a while As tho the Army might be Supplyd at a much less expence & with equally good provisions. They say now the rations Cost the Continent at least a shilling or 14d per diem law[ful]1 & they have heard persons say in Philadelphia they would undertake for 7d or 8d per diem. Indeed one Wharton has undertaken to Supply a Battalion lately raised here for 7d or 8d this Currency per diem with the same rations found in the Army. Perhaps you may make a bargain to advantage. I dare say there will be bidders of this kind which by & by may give Uneasiness. Indeed they want to engross every thing if possible at this place & are Constantly Intriguing with one or another of the Delegates for places, Pensions, Employments, Contracts, &c. Indeed I think we have been Cooped up in this prison of a City long enough. Poor Connecticutt Troops have lost (here) all their fame & all their glory.[2] You will Scarce hear any thing but execrations against them. The Congress astonished & Confounded at their want of every thing laudable, or Impossible they could leave the lines at this Critical moment, and Hazzard their Country & all for Whims for Trifles but however we have excused them as far as possible, but especially the Colony as the Congress had till lately made no application to the Colony for Troops. If they had, the Colony would have seen they were had there by the day, either New or Old, but they would obstinately scorn to apply to Governt. for Troops but would Vainly pursue their own Method. They were told 2 months agoe they would fail in every other Method but by applying to the Colony for such a Number of Troops and the Colony would see they had them tho I know we have had a set of Uneasy fellows in the Army who would spread disaffection wherever they went. I hope my Thomas will behave well & that the ill Treatment he recievd will be no disadvantage too him on the whole; tho for my own part I could allways have wished him not to have gone into the Army at all ⟨*as*⟩ [his?] little Interest will be ruind by it, but however if he behaves well am Content as the Cause is so just, the Contest so glorious. I depend on your & your Friends kind disposition towards him with all friendly advice & assistance. He wants use & acquaintance with or in good Company. His fault has been too much the other way. But guard him against the Vices which attend all. I hope soon to leave this place. I am really tired. I am [*so*] Home sick, that whither I was dismissed out of good will or Envy I rejoice. My respects to Coll Mifflin, Genlls &c &c as occasion and am Sincerely yours Elipht Dyer

[*P.S.*] Post waiting; cannot revise; therefore you must take my letter as it comes. Mr Deen presents his Compliments. He is Very busy, one of the Navy Comtee.

RC (CtHi).

[1] Dyer had previously warned Trumbull to take care to keep complete records of his transactions and expenses as commissary general. Dyer to Joseph Trumbull, September 25, 1775.

[2] See Silas Deane to Elizabeth Deane, December 15, 1775, note 4.

Richard Smith's Diary

Saturday 16 Decr. [1775]

The Journal read & divers Passages marked for omission in Publication. On one Passage there was a vote whether to be printed or not, & the Colonies were equally divided. A Letter read from Gen. Washington advising of some Captures made by our Vessels & that he had released the President of the Island of St. Johns & others who had been taken.[1] A Comee. of 3 prepared a Speech to be delivered by the President to Capt. White Eyes a Chief of the Delaware Indians said to reside on the Muskingham, who was then introduced into the Congress accompanied by One of his Councellors and an Interpreter. The Chief was dressed in a good Suit of Blue Cloth with a Laced Hat & his Counsellor was wrapt in a Blanket, Capt. White Eyes shook all the Members heartily by the Hand, beginning with the President & used the same Ceremony at his Departure, he stayed about an Hour, Our President delivered the Speech & the Chief answered by his Interpreter that he was well pleased to hear such a good Speech and meet his Brethren in the Grand Council Fire, that he would faithfully report to his Friends the kind Disposition of the Congress & proposed to stay in Town all Winter. He wanted a Clergyman, Schoolmaster & Blacksmith established among his People and said they inclined to embrace Christianity & a more civilized Way of Life. A Copy of the Congress's Speech was given to Him when he withdrew, his Councellor said Nothing. A Motion to keep the Officers and Soldiers all together who were taken at St. Johns, took up several Hours & was lost 5 Colonies to 5. A Motion was carried by a bare Majority to permit the Officers to go where they will within the former Orders of Congress till further Order. An Indian introduced Himself by the small Door into the House in the Midst of Debate, he was heard, he wanted Money & was promised a Supply. Several Reports from Committees were made, particularly one relative to Capt. Motts Petition. Jefferson moved that no new Motions shall be offered after 12 oCloc without special Permission till the Order of the Day is satisfyed, which was agreed to. The Comee. appointed to fit out the 13 Ships were impowered to draw on the Treasury for 500,000 Dollars. Sundry other Things transacted in such a Hurry & Want of Order that I find it impossible to remember them.

MS (DLC).

[1] Washington's letter to Hancock of December 7 is in PCC, item 152, 1:329–32; and Washington, *Writings* (Fitzpatrick), 4:152.

George Read to Gertrude Read

My dear Gitty. Phila. 17th Dec. 1775

I have yours of the 14th which I was waiting with impatience for, as I began to suspect that Tatlow might have laid up his Boats; as soon as this shall happen you must make use of the Post for conveyance of your Letters. I find that the News of raising a Battalion in our government has spread amongst you, by the persons you mention intending to apply for Offices. Perhaps when they come to know that their Service will not be confined to the Government, but may be ordered to the most distant parts of the Continent and that as soon as they are raised it may repress the Ardor of some of them.

We have had no certain Accounts from any part of Canada since the Capitulation of Montreal; therefore what you see in the Papers is not to be relied on. The Candles to wit a box of 8's will be put aboard this Evening I expect; there are no 6's ready. I shall not send down my linnen least I shou'd be disappointed in the return of them. I doubt you will not see me in the beginning of the Hollidays. An Adjournmt. of Congress is much talked of and wished for by some but really there is so much that must be done before A seperation that I cannot give you a hint of the time. I was yesterday[1] put upon a committee that is to meet every Evening at 6 o'Clock, which may be obliged to sit regularly for 10 days to come, and as I am considered a great absentee heretofore I must attend constantly for a while. I send you the small [. . .] with 3 old shirts that want mending—some old [. . .] need not be returned as also my uniform Coat [. . .] Jaminey Read tells me Mr. Gardner expected [. . .] other box of Sixes on board. Send the Trunk [. . .] again that in case I shou'd not have an [. . .] of sending my large trunk by the stage. Your friends are all well. My love to our little ones and believe me yours most affectionately. Geo. Read

[*P.S.*] There is a Letter for Parson Thompson in the Trunk with one for George & 2 Evening Posts.

RC (DeHi). William T. Read, *Life and Correspondence of George Read, A Signer of the Declaration of Independence . . .* (Philadelphia: J.B. Lippincott & Co., 1870), p. 117. RC damaged; missing words supplied from Tr.

[1] Read had been named to the committee "for carrying into execution the resolutions of Congress, for fitting out armed vessels." Although this committee was appointed on December 14, it is possible that Read did not become a member of it until the 16th, since in the manuscript journal Secretary Thomson initially wrote

Thomas McKean's name in the list of members and then substituted Read's in its stead. See *JCC*, 3:428; and PCC, item 1, 1:290.

Richard Smith's Diary

Monday Decr. 18 [1775]

The Minutes read & sundry Portions of them marked for Non Publication as usual. An Order passed to allow Capt. Mott who takes Care of the Prisoners at Lancaster £30 more for his Expences. Major Preston allowed to go to Lancaster for 10 Days. Comee. of Lancaster impowered to take the Parole of the Officers who are prisoners there. Chief Part of the Day spent on the Dispute between Pennsa. & Connecticut, various Resolutions were penned by the Delegates of each Colony but the matter was at last postponed.[1] The Chief Point was Whether Pennsylvania shall have the Jurisdiction over the disputed Territory, She agreeing & her Delegates to pledge themselves for it, that private Property shall not be affected. They declared explicitly that they would not abide by the Determination of Congress unless this was conceded.

An Express arrived from Montreal with Letters from Gen. Montgomery, Col. Arnold & others.[2] Eleven Vessels are taken near Montreal by our people who have also seized Brig. Prescot who had caused all the Powder to be thrown overboard, but the Ships contain plenty of Provision. Ethan Allen is sent to England in Irons. Col. James Livingston is about to raise a Regiment of Canadians in our pay for One Year. Arnold is near Quebec but has not Men enough to surround it & his Powder so damaged, that he has only 5 Rounds apiece. Montgomerys Soldiers very disobedient & many of them come Home without Leave. Frauds discovered in some of his Officers. Gen. Washn. in great Want of Powder & most of the Connectt. Troops have left his Army. Accounts of a Skirmish in Virginia and great Preparations in England for an Invasion of Us in the Spring. We sat from 10 oCloc till the Dusk of the Evening.

MS (DLC).

[1] See Connecticut Delegates' Memorial to Congress, December 12? 1775.

[2] According to the journals, this day Congress received "letters from General Schuyler, dated 19, 20, 24 November and 8 December with sundry enclosed papers." *JCC*, 3:436. However, no Schuyler letters of November 19 and 24 have been found, and that of November 20 is endorsed as having been read in Congress on November 30. See PCC, item 153, 1:320–23, 358–61; and *Am. Archives*, 4th ser. 3:1617, 4:219–20. Therefore it may well be that the December 8 letter was the only Schuyler letter that reached Congress this day, and that the other letters mentioned in the journals were actually those from General Montgomery to Schuyler of November 19 and 24, and from Colonel Arnold to Montgomery of November 20, 1775. See PCC, item 161, 1:435–37, 445–47, item 162, 1:36–39; and *Am. Archives*, 4th ser. 3:1682–83, 1694–97.

Thomas Cushing to Robert Treat Paine

Dear Sir Philadelphia Decr 19 1775

I am glad to hear you are Well. I perceive by your Letter to Mr Hancock you are in doubt whether to return to Philadelphia or proceed directly home from Albany, for your Government. I would Inform you that the General Court have Continued our Delegation untill the 31 of Jany next & as affairs are Circumstanced I suppose they will still prolong it.[1] Your presence here is needed especially as you can well Inform us as to the state of our affairs in Canada & Mr John Adams is gone home, the circumstances of his family requiring it. There has been no opportunity to convey your Trunk into our Province as yet, as the waggon by which it was designed to go never went. Hope shall have the pleasure of seeing you soon, in the mean time remain with respect yr Friend & humbl Servt. Thomas Cushing

[*P.S.*] Mr Hancock Send his Compliments.

RC (MHi).

[1] The November 10 resolve of the Massachusetts General Court extending the commissions of the delegates was read in Congress on December 4, and is printed in *JCC*, 3:405.

John Jay to Robert R. Livingston, Jr.

Dear Robert Philad. 19 [December] 1775

How it came to pass I know not, but so the fact is, that neither of your Letters to me came to Hand till the Day before Yesterday, when they were delivered to the President by Gen. Schuylers last Express.

Mr. Duane just now accidentally told me that your Brother was about to leave this Town, and I am now retired to the Lobby, in a Hurry to say a line or two to you.

I confess I was a little hurt at not being favored with a Line from you, especially as your writing to others convinced me that it was in your Power. The Matter is now explained I have only to regret the accident by which the Letter was detained.

I most sincerely console with you on the Loss of your good father & my good friend. The many Instances of Friendship & Attention recd. from him & the family will always command my Gratitude & interest me in every Thing that concerns them.

Something hangs about Harry[1] that I dont understand & probably never shall unless you & I should hereafter confer upon the Subject. On hearing of his being in town I took Ph. Livingston with [*me*] & went to his Lodgings to pay him a Visit Intending unless pre-engaged to take him home to dine with me. I asked him whether he dined out that Day—he told me he should dine with Mr Duane &c at Smiths—on which I replied that I would do myself the Pleasure of dining with him, which I accordingly did. From that Day to this I have not seen his face except in the Street or at some Gentlemans House.

I am not without my suspicions relative to his Behaveour which you will easily guess & which shall induce him to explain to you. Lest this Letter should miss him I must conclude—tho I have much to say. Adieu my dear Robt. I am your afft Friend John Jay

RC (N).

[1] Henry Beekman Livingston (1750–1831), Livingston's younger brother and a captain in the Fourth New York Infantry Regiment, had brought the news of the surrender of Montreal to Philadelphia, in gratitude for which service Congress had resolved on December 12 to provide him with a special sword and the promise of a promotion in rank. *JCC*, 3:424–25; Richard Smith's Diary, December 20; and F. B. Heitman, *Historical Register of the Officers of the Continental Army . . .* (Washington, D. C., 1892), p. 267.

Robert R. Livingston, Jr., to Robert Treat Paine and John Langdon

Clare Mount Decr 19 1775

My abrupt departure from Albany (for which the unhappy occasion will appologize) having deprived me of the pleasure of seeing you or settling such matters as were then undetermined I take the liberty to enclose my account. I have omitted all those articles which tho' not at present necessary may possibly hereafter be of [use] & some other triffles which I have forgot to note & do not know the amount of. The ballance I have in hand & would remit it to you had I safe conveyance. I shall pay it to the order of the congress.

I was much disapointed at not having the pleasure of seeing you on your return as I thought it determined that my house was to have made one of your stages. And I was the more solicitous about it as I fear it will be long before I shall join you at Philadelphia since the sudden death of my father, & the settlement of his affairs will necessarily engage much of my time.[1]

If it would not obtrude too much on the hours which you have devoted to more important purposes I could wish to hear from you when any thing worth communicating turns up as in my present situation I am quite out of the sphere of news or politicks.

Present my comps. to your worthy colleagues, to Mr. Linch & Rutledge, & believe me to be with esteem Your Most Obt &c.

FC (NHi).

[1] Livingston had written on December 17 to his brother, Henry Beekman Livingston, to announce the death of their father. NHi.

William Livingston to William Alexander

My Lord Philadelphia 19 Decr 1775

I inclose you Dr Barnet's Commission as Surgeon of the first Jersey Battalion. The Pay is 25 dollars per month, & I am satisfied the Congress mean to allow for the Chest of Medicines, but I intend to reduce it to a certainty as soon as there is an opening to croud in such a Subject. Mr. Halsted is unanimously voted Quarter Master of your Battalion by the Committee for receiving the Recommendations to officers, & reportd this day, but he must first be confirmed by Congress, which I will push as soon as possible, & then transmit you his Commission.[1]

I cannot imagin the Congress woud give any Directions respecting the Arms you mention, tho' I really believe coud they be got without much Disturbance, it wou'd be convinced as by that Assembly from the Principle of Necessity, & last night I took the opinion of the above Committee, who were unanimous in that Sentiment.[2] But I wou'd not chuse to be mentiond in the Case, nor to have it done under colour of that Committee, unless you shou'd be complain'd of to Congress for the Trespass, & then as far as this Letter woud be your Protection, I give you free Liberty to make use of it for that purpose. I am My Lord your most humble Sert Wil. Livingston

RC (NHi).

[1] Colonel Alexander had recommended the appointment of Matthias Halsted as quartermaster of the First New Jersey Regiment in a letter to Livingston of December 12, and Congress confirmed this choice on December 21. *JCC*, 3:442; and *Am. Archives*, 4th ser. 4:246–47, where the recipient of Livingston's letter is incorrectly identified as the "New Jersey Committee of Safety."

[2] A reference to Colonel Alexander's efforts to obtain arms from the New York Provincial Congress for the troops under his command in that province. See John Hancock to the New York Provincial Congress, November 27, 1775; and *Am. Archives*, 4th ser. 4:173, 387, 391.

Secret Committee Minutes of Proceedings

Philadelpha. C[ommittee] C[hamber] Decr. 19. 1775

At a meeting of the Com. of Secrecy, Present Saml. Ward, Thos. McKean, Josiah Bartlet, Phil. Livingston & Frans. Lewis.

A Contract was enterd into between Ths. York of the City of Philadelphia Mercht. & the sd. Committee. That the sd. C[ommittee] shall advance & pay to the sd. Ths. Yorke the sum of 5350 d[o]ll[ar]s Contl. Money, to be by him laid out in flour & other produce, of these Colonies (hornd cattle, sheep, hogs & poultry excepted) & shippd on board the brig Kitty, Robert French Master, for Cape Nicola Mole, on account & risque & for the benefit of the sd. U[nited] C[olonies] And the nett proceeds thereof laid out in good gun powder or if gunpowder is not to be had, in Saltpetre & a proportion of 15 lb. of Sulp[hur] to every hundred pounds of Salt petre, or in good Soldiers musketts, with double bridled locks (if such are to be had) with bayonets, or in russia or raven's duck.

MS (MH).

Richard Smith's Diary

Tuesday Decr. 19. [1775]

The Votes read & one part only marked not to be made Public. Agreed to request the Comee. of Safety of Pennsa. to lend some Powder & Stands of Arms to the Ships of War now in this Port & almost ready to sail, on an Engagement to use all Endeavors to return them by the 1st of February next.[1] Agreed to use the like Endeavors to return by that Time the Powder heretofore borrowed of New York. A Letter from Gen Washn. read, the Cruizers there (Massachusetts) have taken Two More of the Enemys Ships.[2] Debates upon that Part of the Generals Letters requesting Directions how to dispose of the Captures. A report from a Comee. read on that Head, an Amendment proposed by M[r]. Wyth implying full Leave for any Person to seize all Ships of G Britain wherever found, was lost on a Vote 5 Colonies agt. 4 & 2 divided. Other Resolves were agreed to after Opposition, importing that all Vessels with their Cargoes including all Men of War, found any way assisting the Enemy shall be liable to confiscation. Some Powder just arrived here & at Dartmouth in N England.

MS (DLC).

[1] This request was delivered the following day by Stephen Hopkins, chairman of the Naval Committee. For the response of the Pennsylvania Committee of Safety to this and other requests from the Naval Committee, see *Am. Archives*, 4th ser. 4:502–7, 510.

[2] Washington's letter to Hancock of December 11 is in PCC, item 152, 1:335–38; and Washington, *Writings* (Fitzpatrick), 4:156–58.

James Duane to Robert R. Livingston, Jr.

Philad 20t Decemr 1775

Believe me, my dear Sir, it is with unaffected Sympathy that I condole with you on the sudden Death of your most worthy Father. I know the Tenderness of your disposition, and the full Extent of your

Loss. To dwell upon this painful Subject will administer Consolation to neither of Us. Let us however fortify ourselves against immedeiate Grief by contemplating his Virtues and by a firm assurance that rescued from the Vexations and Calamities of a Jarring world he is translated to the Manshions of eternal Rest and Happiness. This is the sure Reward of a Life directed by a Reverence for the Supreme Being, by a Love of Justice, by Patriotism, and Philanthropy: Qualities for which our amiable Friend was conspicuous! Let us follow his fair Example, and adorn our minds with the same Graces, and after a few more Struggles with the Follies, the Misfortunes and the Sorrows of this transient Scene, we shall meet again never to be disturbed or seperated.

Accept my Thanks for your obliging favour from Albany. Your Brother had already communicated Genl. Montgomerie's Successes which will raise his military Character to an exalted Degree of Eminence.[1] I hope tho' I have had little of Capt. Livingston's Company, owing to Constant Attendance on the Congress, yet I have contributed to his spending the time agreeably here by introducing and mentioning him to my Friends. The Gentlemen you particularize in the Close of your Letter were all pleased with that mark of your Regard and Attention, and I am confident they hold you in high Estimation.

Nothing worthy of particular animadv. has passed in Congress since your departure. The Virginians are distressed by Lord Dumore at the head of a few despicable white people and Slaves. They cry aloud for the Aid of Congress. Nothing less than Six battalions are talked of; nay reported by a Committee, for their Defence! Four Battalions are ordered to be raised in Pensylv., One in the lower Counties. New York I suppose will not be forgotten. In short it is probable that by the spring there will be exclusive of our Province a Southern Army of 16 Battalions besides minute men and militia.

I think I may venture to guess that we shall have a Recess about Christmas. I long for it impatiently and hope soon afterwards to pay you a Visit.

Present my Affectionate Regard to both Mrs. Livingston and Mrs. Montgomerie and the young Ladies; and believe that I am with the highest Regard Dear Sir, Your most Affectionate & most Obed huml servant

Jas. Duane

RC (NHpR: Livingston-Redmond Collection deposit).

[1] See John Jay to Robert R. Livingston, Jr., December 19, 1775, note.

John Jay to Lewis Morris

Dear Colonel Philadelphia 20 Decr. 1775

Nothing worth communicating to you having occurred I have hitherto declined troubling you with a Letter. In order to convince you however that I wish our Correspondence may be punctual & frequent I enclose you a Letter which was designed to have gone by Capt. Shea but he was unluckily on his Journey before the Letter was sent to his House.

A Report is now circulating that some Men of War are at the Capes. This occasions Speculation. Coll. Harrison is returned.[1] He has fitted out two Vessels of some force, one a remarkable good Bermudian. There is no Doubt of there being useful. We have recd. a Letter from Gen. Washingston confirming the Acct. of Manley's having taken two more Prizes with Cargoes of Porter, Cheese, Rum &c.

The Virginians with the Assistance of their Neighbours have made it convenient for Lord Dunmore to retire to his Fleet. Norfolk is again in their Possession. This News is just come to town, and I suppose it to be true. Be so kind as to present my Compts. to all your good Family. I am dear Coll. Your Friend & hble Servt

John Jay

RC (NjP).

[1] See Benjamin Harrison to Wilson Miles Cary, December 10, 1775.

Richard Smith's Diary

Wednesday Decr. 20. [1775]

The Votes read & no Passage erased. David Beveridge allowed to send out Produce for Arms & Ammunition. Capt. Henry Livingston here, the Congress has ordered a handsome Sword to be made & presented to Him as the Messenger, some Weeks ago, of the Surrender of Montreal. Some Money allowed to the Rev. Mr. Spencer & the Rev. Mr. MacWhorter who are going at the Request of Congress, among the regulators of North Carolina. Col. Harrison moved something relative to a Vessel or Two of War ordered heretofore to be fitted out at & for Virginia & a Comee. was appointed. Lord Dunmore is driven to his Ships by the Virginians. Gen. Wash's Letters proceeded upon & Answers agreed to. Debate Whether Butter shall be Continued to his Army and carried in the Affirmative. Motion by Jay to allow it to the rest of the Troops, denied or shuttled off. Application from 2 Inhabitants of Nantucket for Leave to import there various Articles of Goods was thrown out, they are allowed Firing and Provisions. Much Time spent on the Wyoming Dispute. Two resolutions were on the Table, one drawn by the Delegates of Pennsyla. and the other by Connecticut, the former gave Pennsylvania the temporary Jurisdiction & the latter left each Party to exercise Jurisn. on their respective Possessions. The Vote passed in Favor of the Connect[icut] resolve 6 Colonies to 4 & Mr. Livingston & myself declined voting for our Colony. The Delegates of Pennsa. were very angry & discontented with this Determination of Congress.

MS (DLC).

Josiah Bartlett to the New Hampshire Committee of Safety

Gentm Philadelphia December 21 1775

The Congress having Determined to Build at Continental Expence a number of Ships of war in the united Colonies to be ready for Sea if possible by the last of March next; Have agreed that one of the enclosed Dimentions, to Carry 32 guns, be Built in our Colony.[1]

It is proposed that one or 2 persons well Skilled in Ship building, of approved Integrity, be forthwith appointed to provide the materials, Employ workmen, oversee the Business, to keep Exact & Regular accounts of the whole, to Draw on the Marine Committe of Congress for money to Cary on the Business, and to be accountable to said Committe; for all which they will be handsomely Rewarded.

As the Ship Building business is out of my sphere I am unwilling to nominate the Said overseers. I am therefore Directed by Said Committe to Desire you immediately to Consider of proper overseers, also of a proper place for Building said vessel, both for safety & convenience of Materials & workmen. She will be about 700 tons; an Exact Draught will be sent forward in a few Days. In the mean time it will be necessary for the overseers to Buy up without loss of time Every necessary for Building & fitting out [said] Ship and what Cant be had in our Colony must [be] notified to The Marine Committee at Philadelphia [so] they may provide it. The Marine Comtt. [consists?] of one Delegate from Each Colony.

[. . .] You will take Care to name Such Suitable persons [so that] our ship may be as well Built, as Soon & as cheap [as] any of the colonies and that as soon as the [drau]ght of the ship Shall arrive they may be ready [. . .] on the Business immediately.

Four vessels are purchased by the Congress and are now ready for Sea. One Carries 20 guns, the others less. The Ships that are to be Built are 5 of 32 guns, 5 of 28 Do., 3 of 24 Do., one to be Built New H., 2 Massachusetts, 2 Rhode Island, one Conecticut, two New York, four Pensylvania, one Maryland. I hope you have Recd mine enclosing the vote of Congress Concerning our Civil government tho I [have] Recd no account of it. In my last I informed you that the Congress had voted our Colony forty thousand Dollars in part of our Demand till [the] account Can be Setled. The money is yet not ready to be Sent.

I am Gentm your friend and Humble Servt Josiah Bartlett

P.S. I have sent a printed Copy of the Journals of last session of Congress.

FC (NhD). Endorsed by Bartlett: "This was Wrote to [*be*] sent to the Comtte before Mr. Langdons arrival from Tyconderoga. On his return before Sending off the letter at his request I appointed him to build the Ship and he returned home for that purpose." From Bartlett's endorsement and from the appearance of a large "X" across the face of the document, it seems that this letter was not sent.

[1] Congress approved the construction of these ships on December 13, and the following day Bartlett was appointed a member of the committee "for fitting out armed vessels." *JCC*, 3:425–28.

John Dickinson's Notes for a Speech in Congress

[December 21–22? 1775][1]

Questionable shape. Roman sentence in best Times. Themistocles & Aristides. Sextus, Pompey & Menas. Philip 2d & Lewis 14th. Eternal Rules of Justice & Equity. Thucidides, Every Thing just that was useful, every thing honorable that was Profitable.

Liberty & Life may be obtain'd at too dear a Price.

Doubts even if *certain* the Liberty of America depended on the Act, but Event *uncertain*.

May dislodge them to take Post somewhere else. The Destruction of many of our Friends, Women & Children *certain*. Garrison will seize safest Places.[2]

⟨*Question does not properly belong to Us. It is a Point of Generalship. Their authority sufficient.*⟩ 365 Miles distant. In the Room. Nineveh. Injure our Reputation in America. Fatal Consequences. People confined there by our Order (see p. 51.) ⟨*We should leave the Point as it is. Determines Nothing.*⟩ Jehovah. Girah.

The Liberty of America depends not on such a Massacre. Instance of Henry 4th at Siege of Paris. Providence favors Humanity. When We overlook his Laws, The Conclusion not equal to our Expectations. Observe his Laws—& trust to his Goodness. "The skilfulness of the Pilot avails but little, if the Gale of Divine Favor, which governs human Affairs with eternal Providence, does not help to bring our Actions to their desired Port." Davila.[3] War dreadful enough in itself.

Let Us not adopt every horrid Expedient pursuing Advantage. Let us not stain our Counsels with the Blood of our Friends.

Instances of Severity are dishonorable tho advantageous. Cromwells Massacre at Tredah [*Drogheda*]. Lewis 14th burning the Palatinate. Yet against Enemies. Their Misery afterwards. If Convenience & Advantage justify actions, these were justified. Shall We proclaim this to be our Creed to the World.

We may destroy the Town & people & next Day hear of proposals of Accommodation. Let us delay issuing the direful Mandate awhile.

MS (PHi). In the hand of John Dickinson. These notes are strikingly cryptic and are strewn with abbreviations which have been expanded without brackets in this text.

[1] This document is apparently John Dickinson's notes for a speech delivered during the debates of December 21–22, 1775, on the question whether Congress should authorize an attack on Boston even if the assault should result in the city's destruction. The debate was the last in a series stimulated by the report of the Committee of Conference that met with Washington at Cambridge on October 18–24, which led Congress to pass resolutions on a wide range of topics between November 1 and December 2. In the course of those proceedings, however, Congress had deferred action on "that part of the report . . . respecting Boston," and when the subject was resumed on December 12 the delegates were again unable to reach agreement. The matter was postponed to the following day, but it was not until December 21–22 that Congress finally concluded debate over an attack on Boston. Although these notes could have been made for use in an earlier debate, it seems likely that they were intended for either December 21 or 22 when the issue was about to be brought to an affirmative resolution. For further information on the subject, see Committee of Conference Minutes of Proceedings, October 23-24, 1775; and *JCC*, 3:425, 442, 444.

[2] The following paragraph is circled in the MS, suggesting that Dickinson omitted this portion when he spoke. The passages lined out seem to have been marked for deletion even before the entire paragraph was circled.

[3] This quotation, which Dickinson marked for insertion at this point, appears on the verso of the MS.

Richard Smith's Diary

Thursday Decr. 21 [1775]

The Journal read & several Parts to be omitted as usual. Mr. Rogers took his Seat as a Delegate for Maryland, Mr. John Penn from N Carolina had been here some Time.

McKean made report from the Comee. on Gen. Schuylers Letters, it was partly considered & some Articles agreed to. By Ballot Dr. Holmes was chosen Surgeon & Mr. Halstead Quarter Master to the two Battalions (Ld Stirlings & Maxwells) just raised in N Jersey. The Congress resolved itself into a Grand Comee., Govr. Ward in the Chair, to consider Whether to order the General to storm or bombard Boston in Answer to part of his Dispatches, it was made a Question

Whether the Continent should indemnify the Losers. The Gen. says he can, if it is a hard Winter, destroy the Fleet & Army there & at any Rate he can bombard & ruin the Town when he pleases. The Chairman desired Leave to sit again. Leave for M. de Rigouville a Canadian Gentn. one of the Kings Legislative Council there, but now Prisoner at Trenton to come to Town to confess Himself to the Priest. James Livingston Esqr. Colonel & the other Officers of the new Canadian Regiment ordered to be Commissioned. The grateful Acknowledgments of the Congress ordered to Montgomery, Arnold & Easton. A N York Battalion which had returned Home & quitted their Officers ordered to be filled up. Wilson offered a Resolve importing that no more Connecticut People should settle at Wyoming till the Title of the Lands was adjudged, an Amendt. offered that no Pennsylvanians should settle there was voted out & the further Considn. of Wilsons resolve was adjorned.

MS (DLC).

Henry Wisner to Benjamin Towne

Mr. Towne[1] Philadelphia, December 21, 1775.

Having for many months been sensibly affected with the great disadvantage the colonies labour under for want of ammunition, I thought it my duty to apply myself to the attainment of those necessary arts of making SALTPETRE and GUNPOWDER; and having far exceeded my expectations in both manufactures, I think myself still farther obliged to communicate the so much needed knowledge to my country at large. My first trial was on Saltpetre, two pounds of which my son has extracted from about six bushels of stable dirt, perfectly fit for making Gunpowder. This was done by the method of Doctor *Young* and Mr. *Rubsaman,* lately published by the former, for which, and many other useful informations, I take this opportunity to return those gentlemen my publick thanks.[2]

I have lately erected a Powder-Mill in the south end of *Ulster* County, in the colony of *New-York,* at which I have made as good powder as I ever have seen, and will bear the inspection of good judges, in the following manner:

GUNPOWDER is composed of nothing more than the four plain simple articles, Saltpetre, Brimstone, Charcoal, and Water. The three first of which are to be made as fine as possible, so as to be sifted through a gauze sieve, or fine bolt, as fine as for common flour. But it being difficult to make the Saltpetre all fine, those parts that will not be easily got through the sieve, must be dissolved in soft warm water, then let the Sulphur, Saltpetre, and Charcoal, be each separately weighed. Take of the Saltpetre an hundred weight, of the Sulphur fifteen pounds, and Charcoal eighteen pounds, and in that proportion for any greater or smaller quantity. This being done, mix them all well together in some large vessel, such as a potash or any other kettle, and when well mixed, moisten the whole with the aforesaid nitrous water till it is as moist as dough for making bread. Then put an equal quantity in each mortar, and pound it well for at least twenty hours; and if the mill runs slowly, let it run twenty-four hours; and as the paste, by pounding, will naturally grow dry, it must be kept moist by putting in a little of said water, and when pounded sufficiently take it out of the mortar, and put it in some tub or any other proper vessel. As to the graining, it must be done in the following manner, viz. have a box made about five feet square, the sides eighteen inches deep, the bottom tight, and top entirely open; fix across the box two rods or laths near the middle, about four inches below the top, and about ten inches apart, then have six sieves made of wooden splits in the same manner as a wheat riddle, but much finer, the coarsest should be about as fine as a cockle sieve, or a little finer, and so each sieve to increase in fineness till the last is as fine as possible. I believe it were best to make the two coarsest of wire; then take about a quart of the paste, put it into the coarsest sieve, set the sieves on the two rods that are fixed across the box, then work the sieve with a circular motion, which will press the paste thro' the sieve in large and unshapely grains, and when a considerable quantity is passed through, then sift it over again in the next coarsest sieve, and so till the grains are fine enough. The last sieve must be so fine that whatever passes through it will be too fine for Powder, and is to be worked over the next batch. As the paste will naturally roll together in large round balls, when worked in the sieve, a board must be made near as large in circumference as a common pewter plate, and about one inch thick, on the center, declining to the edge, of some hard wood turned in a lathe, and made as smooth as possible. This board must be put into the sieve among the paste, which breaks the lumps in pieces, and forces the paste through the sieve.

When the powder is well grained in the manner directed, it must be rolled in a barrel, the inside of which is to be made as smooth as conveniently may be, with as small a door cut in one side capable of being shut tight, and the barrel to be fixed so as to be turned by the shaft of the mill. Put in a few pounds at a time, and let it be rolled as above, which will make the Powder smooth; then sift it in the finest sieve, till the fine parts that work off in the barrel pass through the sieve, which is to be returned again into the mortars. The Powder must be put in flat trays or dishes, and set by to dry either in a small room kept warm with a large stove, or, if the weather be dry, in the shining of the sun.

I therefore most heartily recommend to the good people of this Continent to enter into these necessary businesses with spirit, being well assured that a greater quantity may, with ease, be made than will be needed for our consumption, even admitting the times to be worse than the threats of the *British* administration would lead us to expect.

Any person inclining to build a powder mill will be shewn a plan, with directions for the constructions of all its parts and utensils, by applying to their very humble servant,[3] Henry Wisner

MS not found; reprinted from the *Pennsylvania Evening Post,* December 21, 1775.

[1] Benjamin Towne (d. 1793), printer of the *Pennsylvania Evening Post,* was noteworthy for the mutability of his political allegiances in the revolutionary era, supporting the American patriot cause until the British occupied Philadelphia, adopting a loyalist position during the British occupation, and returning to the American side after the British evacuated the city. *DAB.*

[2] Thomas Young had published an essay on the manufacture of saltpetre in the December 7, 1775, issue of the *Pennsylvania Evening Post* and had arranged for Towne to print in the December 5 issue some notes on the production of nitre which he had "received from Mr. Jacob Rubsamen, a gentlemen of very liberal education, observation, and experience, some years since from Hesse in Germany." *Pennsylvania Evening Post,* December 5, 7, 1775.

[3] Samuel Adams sent a copy of Wisner's plan of a powder mill with a short covering letter to Paul Revere. Samuel Adams to Paul Revere, December 23, 177[5], MHi; letter damaged but printed in Elbridge H. Goss, *The Life of Colonel Paul Revere,* 2 vols. (Boston: Joseph G. Cupples, 1891), 2:405.

Samuel Adams to John Adams

My dear Sir Philade Decr. 22 1775

My Concern for your Welfare inducd me carefully to watch the Weather till I conjectured you had got to the End of your Journey, and I have the Pleasure of believing it has been more agreable than one might have expected at this Season. I hope you found Mrs Adams and Family in a confirmd State of Health. I will not envy you, but I earnestly wish to enjoy, at least for a few Weeks, domestick Retirement and Happiness. I dare not however, urge an Adjournment of the Congress. It would indeed be beneficial to the Members & the publick on many Considerations, but our Affairs are now at so critical a Conjuncture that a Seperation might be dangerous.

Since you left us, our Colony has sometimes been divided, on Questions that appeard to me to be important. Mr C[ushing] has no doubt a Right to speak his opinion whenever he can form one; and you must agree with him, that it was highly reasonable, the Consideration of such Letters as you have often heard read, which had been assignd for the Day, should, merely for the Sake of order, have the Preference to so trifling Business as the raising an American Navy. I know it give you great Pleasure to be informd that the Congress have orderd the Building of thirteen Ships of War viz five of 32 Guns, five of 28 and three of 24.[1] I own I wishd for double or treble the Number, but I am taught the Rule of Prudence, to let the fruit hang till it is ripe, otherwise those Fermentations and morbid Acrimonies might be producd in the political, which the like Error is said to produce in the natural Body. Our Colony is to build two of these Ships. We may want Duck. I have been told that this Article is manufacturd in the Counties of Hampshire & Berkshire. You may think this worth your Enquiry.

Our Fleet, which has been preparing here will be ready to put to Sea in two or three days, and it is left to the Board of Admiralty to order its Destination. May Heaven succeed the Undertaking. Hopkins is appointed Commander in Chiefe. I dare promise that he will on all occasions distinguish his Bravery, as he always has, and do honor to the American Flag.

General Schuyler is at Albany. By a Letter from him of the 14th Instt.[2] we are informd that there had been a Meeting of Indians in that place, who deliverd to him a Speech, "in which they related the Substance of a Conference Coll Johnson had with them the last Summer, concluding with that at Montreal, where he deliverd to each of the Canadian Tribes a War belt and the Hatchet which they accepted; after which they were invited to feast on a Bostonian and drink his Blood, an ox being roasted for the purpose and a pipe of Wine given to drink. The War Song was also sung. One of the Chiefs of the Six Nations who attended that Conference, accepted of a very large black War belt with an Hatchet depicturd on it, but would neither eat nor drink nor sing the War Song. This famous Belt they have deliverd up, and there is now full Proof that the ministerial Servants have attempted to engage the Indians against us." This is copied from the Generals Letter.

You will know what I mean when I mention to you the Report of the *Committee of Conference*. This has been considerd and determind agreable to your Mind & mine. Mr H[ancock] agreed with me in opinion, and I think, in expressing his Sentiments he honord himself. I dare not be more explicit on this Subject. It is sufficient that *you* understand me.

I have more to say to you but for Want of Leisure I must postpone it to another opportunity. Inclosd you have a Number of Letters which came to my hand directed to you. Had you been here I should possibly have had the Benefit of perusing them. I suffer in many Respects by your Absense.

Pray present my due Regards to all Friends—particularly Coll Warren, and tell him I will write to him soon. Your affectionate Friend

RC (MHi). In Adams' hand, though not signed.

[1] Congress had resolved to build these 13 ships on December 13, four days after John had departed from Philadelphia on his return trip home. *JCC,* 3:425–26. Construction of the ships was allocated to various colonies, and in keeping with her shipbuilding capabilities Pennsylvania was authorized to build four of them. Although only fragmentary information is available on the manner in which Congress managed the preparation of the vessels in Philadelphia, a document in the hand of Robert Morris throws considerable light on the duties and responsibilities of the various officials working under the superintendency of the Naval Committee. According to Morris, the Naval Committee employed "Four Commissioners to Superintend & direct the whole business," who in turn directed a committee of accounts, two procurement committees, a treasurer "to pay the orders of the Commissioners," and "a Superintendant & Clerk to each Ship Yard, to keep an exact Account of the time [of] all persons . . . employed in this Service." This memorandum, bearing the heading "For the Frigates building in Philadelphia the following Boards &c are employed," is printed in Clark, *Naval Documents,* 3:561–62.

[2] Schuyler's letter was read in Congress this day. See *JCC,* 3:443; PCC, item 153, 1:362; and *Am. Archives,* 4th ser. 4:260–61.

John Hancock to George Washington

Sir, Philada. Decr. 22d. 1775.

Your letters of the 30th of November and of the 4th, 7th, & 11 of December being duly received were laid before Congress. To prevent the ill consequences, that might ensue from the backwardness of the men in the present service to reinlist, the Congress, as I informed you in my last, have written to the governors of Connecticut & Rhode Island, the council of Massachusetts Bay and the president of the convention of New Hampshire; In consequence of which letters they have strong hopes & confidence, that measures will be taken to compleat your army. As to the article of butter, the Congress desirous to obviate whatever may have a "tendency to give the soldiery room for complaint" have instructed me to inform you, that the same may be continued, until further order.

The Congress receive, with great satisfaction, your congratulations on the success of Capt Manly. By the enclosed resolves you will perceive their determination on the captures already made, as well as those which may be made hereafter.[1] It is expected the several colonies will erect courts of admiralty, and that the judges in those courts will regulate their decisions by the law of nations, except where it is relaxed by the enclosed resolutions.

I am further directed to inform you, that the Congress approve your taking such of the articles found on board the Concord, as are necessary for the army. The necessity of the case will, they apprehend, justify the measure, even though the vessel, upon trial, should, contrary to their expectation, be acquitted.[2]

I am Authorized to inform you that it is the pleasure of Congress that Mr. Mifflin the Quarter Master General hold the Rank of Colonell in the Army of the United Colonies, and that you Establish his Rank accordingly.

I must Beg leave to Refer you to the Inclos'd Resolutions of Congress for your future proceedings, which I am Directed to Transmitt you. You will Notice the last Resolution Relative to an Attack upon Boston, this pass'd after a most serious Debate in a Committee of the whole house, and the Execution Referr'd to you, and may God Crown your Attempt with Success. I most heartily wish it, tho' individually I may be the greatest sufferer.[3]

I have paid Mr. Fessenden the Express in full for his three Journies as Express to Philadelphia, Deducting only Sixty Dollars, which he Says, you order'd him, that there will be no pay due to him for Services perform'd heretofore, only for his Expences now from this place to you. If this Adjustment be not Right, please to inform me.

I have the Honour to be with sincere sentiments of Esteem, Sir Your most obedt huml sevt. John Hancock Presidt

[*P.S.*] Fessenden being indispos'd, I have Sent a special Express, as Congress were Anxious their Resolves should Reach you as quick as possible.

RC (DLC).

[1] Hancock sent Washington congressional resolves of November 25 and December 20 on the disposition of prize cases. *JCC*, 3:371–75, 439.

[2] These first three paragraphs are in the hand of Charles Thomson; the remainder of the letter was written by Hancock.

[3] For Congress' resolve of December 22 concerning an attack on Boston, see *JCC*, 3:444–45. See also Committee of Conference Minutes of Proceedings, October 24; Thomas Lynch to Washington, November 13, note 3; and John Dickinson's Notes for a Speech in Congress, December 21–22? 1775.

John Jay to Alexander McDougall

Dear Sir Philadelphia 22d Decr. 1775

Few Things have for some time past given me more Pleasure than the address with which you managed the Govrs. Letter on the Subject of Lord Norths Motion. It occasions however both Surprize and Concern that the *Sin of Fear* (as Lewis Morris calls it) should operate so powerfully on some of your Patriots, as it seems to do.[1]

The Provision for the Delegates I imagined Would be similar to that of Connecticut. However as the Convention has thought proper to move on other Principles, I am determined that pecuniary Considerations shall never induce me to quit the Field so long as my constituents will keep me whole. The allowance they have agreed upon will, if I retrench a little, about do that.

It must be obvious that keeping much Company, is necessary to obtain a personal Influence with the members, and that the Colony is interested in their Delegates possessing such Influence. Should we ever converse upon this Subject I will mention some important Instances of its Use.

I am glad you think of reducing our Number. Five is certainly sufficient—3 of them to be a Quorum.[2]

Your Conduct relative to Sear's Expedition so far as it respects Connecticut is certainly proper—but I suspect this will be the first Instance of censuring the Followers without reprehending the Leaders. It is time that your Government should acquire a firmer Tone.

Tomorrow I shall go to Elizabeth Town for a Week—and shall devote the first Leizure Hour I have to telling you twenty things about which want of time compels me now to be silent.

Mr. Duane complains to me that you have taken no notice of a Letter he wrote you some time ago. He says it was friendly & expected you would treat it as such. It respected some Observations made on your Detention from the Army, & his Remarks on that Subject: which were just.

Coll. Morris was very useful at the Indian Treaty & had he not, by being accidentally at Pittsburgh, given the Congress an opportunity of supplying Dr. Franklins absence, by appointing him Com[missione]r pro Tempore, there is Reason to believe our affairs in that Quarter might have suffered.

As to Arms. I think you should take Care how you strip yourselves to cover your Neighbours Nakedness—neighbours too who have no Reason to expect. It is Time that you should look to your own Necessities. New York never stood better with Congress than now. Your Alacrity in raising & arming your Troops last Summer &c. is compared with the Tediousness & slow moving of others.

Some Powder has arrived here, but the Fleet will consume it. More has arrived to the Eastward & the Camp will take that. For the future remember that Charity should begin at Home. God bless you. Yours &c.

John Jay

[*P.S.*] The Congress I am persuaded will not make the Loan you ask.[3]

RC (NHi).

[1] On December 4 Governor Tryon had published a letter to the inhabitants of New York, asking them to express "in a constitutional manner" their sense of the February 20, 1775, parliamentary resolution on conciliation. In response, the New York Provincial Congress, after much debate and amendment, approved a series of resolves on December 14, declaring among other things "that nothing of a salutary nature can be expected from a separate declaration of the sense of this Colony on

the Resolution of the House of Commons of the 20th February last." *Am. Archives,* 4th ser. 4:173–74, 394–95, 406–13; and *JCC,* 2:61–63.

[2] See New York Delegates to the New York Provincial Congress, October 16, 1775, note.

[3] The New York Provincial Congress had asked the New York delegates, in a letter of December 9, to procure a loan of £45,000 from Congress, but on December 23 Congress turned down this request, as Jay predicted. *JCC,* 3:452; and *Am. Archives,* 4th ser. 4:397.

William Livingston to William Maxwell?

Dr Sir Philadelphia 22 Dec. 1775

In Answer to yours of the 18 Instant (since which I have sent the Commissions by Mr Spencer) It can't be expected the Congress will advance the Sum you[1] mention, under the notion of deducting it out of the Men's wages, because the men may die or desert before it is due. The Blankets the men are to find themselves, & if they cannot purchase them I think the Committee should do it. However if Mr. Lowrie who is appointed Commissary was to state to the Congress the Situation of the Battalions, & what articles they are in want of & apply for an advance of Cash, I doubt not he would be attended to. I suppose the same with respect to the Committee, tho' the Commissary must be presumed to be best acquainted with the matter.

I am greatly surprized the Assembly did not on Mr Kinsey's & Mr De Hart's Resignation supply their Places by the Appointment of two other Delegates. 'Tis true they have given the Right of Representation to either of their Members. This is proper enough because it may unfortunately happen that only one might be able to attend. But surely it wou'd not be proper that only one should attend. Admitting then that two attend, who does not see that they may frequently happen to differ in opinion, & then no vote can be given. If to prevent that Inconvenience, all three attend, I leave it to any man to judge of the runinous Consequences to a Man's family to give such constant & perpetual Attendance. I can assure you that nothing but my Devotion to the Public, has kept [*me*] here this long, whereas if we consisted of five as before, we could always have three at the Congress & take turns to see our families, & if only three attended the Expence would be the same. I scorn to quit my Colours thro' Impatience or Discouragement, but I think it reasonable that the Burden should be divided. I do not mean to blame Friend Crane for his last homeward-bound Voyage, because he fairly offered it to me as being my Turn; but as I knew that his Affairs from his Representation, suffered more by his Absence than mine did by my continuing abroad, I consented.

I shall have no objection to giving Dr Harris my Interest for Surgeon in a future Battalion, if he can give me any proof of his skill in

Surgery, either by the Cures he has performed, or the Testimonials of Practitioners of Reputation, because I have been told that he knows but very little about it. I am Sir your most humble Servt

Will Livingston

P.S. I inclose you Dr. Holme's Commission.

RC (PHi).

[1] Presumably Col. William Maxwell, commander of the Second New Jersey Infantry Regiment, a deduction based on the following considerations. About December 14, 1775, Maxwell had written a letter to Congress requesting the appointment of a surgeon for his regiment, to which Congress responded on December 21 by appointing Dr. James Holmes, who is mentioned by Livingston in the postscript of this letter. In addition, the "Mr. Spencer" referred to by Livingston in the opening sentence was probably Elihu Spencer, pastor of the Presbyterian Church in Trenton, who was apparently returning home from Philadelphia, preparatory to departing for North Carolina on a mission for Congress, and bearing with him commissions for Maxwell whose regiment was stationed in Trenton at this time. See *JCC*, 3:335, 442; and *Am. Archives*, 4th ser. 4:295–96. See also North Carolina Delegates to Elihu Spencer, December 8, 1775, note 2.

Secret Committee Minutes of Proceedings

Phild. Com[mittee] Ch[amber] Decr. 22d. 1775

At a meetg. of the Com. of Secrecy Present Saml. Ward, Benjn. Franklin, Silas Deane, Josiah Bartlett, & Thos. McKean. A Contract was enterd into between Blair McClenachan of the City of Philada Merchant & the said Committee that the sum of 4550 dollars be advanced by the sd. Com[mitte]e of Secry. to the sd. Blair Mcclenighan [McClenachan] to be by him laid out in flour & other produce of these Colonies & shippd on board the brigantine John commanded by Chs. Forrest for the port of Nantes, on account & risque & for the benefit of the sd. U[nited] C[olonies] & the nett proceeds thereof laid out in the purchase of 500 stand of good Arms, & as much good gunpowder as the sd. nett proceeds will purchase—or if the gunpowder cannot be had, in saltpetre with a proportion 15 lb of sulphur to every hundred weight of Saltpetre.

MS (MH).

Richard Smith's Diary

Friday Decr. 22. [1775]

The Journal read & some Passages marked. Letters from Lord Stirling & others read, my Lord gives an Account of the Situation & Condition of the 2 Battalions in Jersey & complains of the Increase of Toryism.[1]

The House again in Grand Comee. on the Boston Affair & after much canvassing & sundry Propositions offered, the Vote passed for directing Gen. Washn. to destroy the Army & Navy at Boston in any Way He & a Council of War shall think best, even if the Town must be burnt, 7 Colonies to 2, one not fully represented & our Colony divided, Wm. Livingston being agt. the Resolution & myself for it. Mr. Hancock spoke heartily for this Measure.

Esek Hopkins Esqr. of Rhode Island (the same that commanded their Forces in Quality of Brig. General) appointed Commander in Chief of the American Fleet, he is to sail with the Ships of War now fitting out in the Port of Philadelphia and his Pay was voted to be 125 Dollars per Month 6 Colonies to 4, the latter thought the Pay too high. The Captains, Lieuts. & Warrant Officers as appointed by our Comee. for Naval Affairs were ordered to be Commissioned, the Question was put Whether any Allowance shall be made to the Admiral for Table Expences & negatived by a large Majority. Mr. Hopkins had very generously offered to serve without any Pay. Col. Lee & others gave Him a high Character. A Comee. chosen to confer with the Indians now at the State House. Gen Schuylers Letters finished. Col Harrison the Delegate's Expences ordered to be paid for going lately to Maryland to promote the Equipment of some Frigates there. Motion by Gadsden to publish that Part of Gen Schuylers Letters where the Indians say that Guy Johnson invited them to take up the Hatchet against the Colonists & that he roasted an Ox and gave them a Pipe of Wine asking them to feast on the Flesh & Blood of a New England Man—was deferred.[2] Part of Conollys Letters was ordered to put in the News Papers.

MS (DLC).

[1] See *JCC*, 3:443. Alexander's letter has not been found.

[2] On December 23 Congress ordered the publication of a paragraph of Schuyler's letter to Hancock of December 14 reporting Guy Johnson's efforts to stir up the Iroquois against the Americans. *JCC*, 3:456; and *Am. Archives*, 4th ser., 4:260–61.

John Hancock to the Massachusetts Assembly

Gentlemen Congress Chamber 23d Decr. 1775

I have now only time to inform you that in consequence of your Accounts being laid before Congress, they ordered the Money out of the new Emission which will be ready in three days when it shall be forwarded to you in the cheapest and most expeditious manner.[1]

I have the Honor to be with Esteem, Gentlemen Your most obedient Servant John Hancock

Tr (M-Ar).

[1] See Hancock to the Massachusetts Assembly, December 2, 1775, note 2.

John Jay to Sarah Jay

My dear Wife Philad. 23 Decr. 1775

I have now the Pleasure of informing you that the New York Convention has at Length made some Provision for their Delegates vizt. 4 Dollars per Day for their Attendance on the last, and this Congress, so that I shall not be so great a Sufferer as I once apprehended. The Allowance indeed does by no means equal the Loss I have sustained by the appointment, but the Convention I suppose consider the Honor as an Equivalent for the Residue.

The Congress this Day refused to give me Leave of absence for next Week. There are but five New York Delegates here, Coll. Morris & Mr Lewis being absent, so that should either of us leave the town, the Province would be unrepresented.[1] We expect however soon to adjourn, and your Papa[2] has engaged Mr. Hooper to accompany him to Elizabeth town, where I hope we shall soon be all very happy. My Horses were new shod, Wheels greased, Cloaths put up and every thing ready to set off early in the Morning, when on going to Congress this Morning all my pleasing Expectations of seeing you on Christmas Day were disappointed. Dont you pity me my Dear Sally? It is however some Consolation that should the Congress not adjourn in less than ten Days, I am determined to stay with you till —— and depend upon it nothing but actual Imprisonment will be able to keep me from you.

At present I find the objections of the Congress so reasonable, that I am sure you would blame me, were [*I*] to attempt leaving them without Permission. I must endeavour to resign my self to my fate, and am sure you have too much good Sence and too much Regard for —— to permit the Disappointment to occasion unavailing anxiety. Tomorrow or on Tuesday next the Congress will I believe determine the Time of Adjournmt. so that it is probable I shall have the Happiness of wishing you a happy New Year.

Adieu my beloved. I am most sincerely Your afft. John Jay

P.S. I have recd. a Letter from Rye of an old Date. They were as well as usual. I dined with your Papa toDay. He was very well. Once more let me intreat you to be chearful & keep up your Spirits. I know by my own Feelings that these kind of Disappointmts. are disagreable but when I reflect how much more happy we are than thousands of our Fellow Mortals my Uneasiness is lost in Gratitude.

RC (N).

[1] Until December 21 New York required the presence of five delegates to represent the colony in Congress. See New York Delegates to the New York Provincial Congress, October 16, 1775, note.

[2] William Livingston.

John Jay to Alexander McDougall

Dear Sir Ph. 23 Decr 1775

Since writing my last to You, I find the Congress will not adjourn even for the Holydays. They have not indeed so *determined* but that seems to be the opinion of the majority of the members.

Where does Mr. Alsop stay. Should any thing happen to one of us the Colony would be unrepresented. For my Part I wish some of the absent Gent. would return, we but just make a Quorum. Did not this Circumstance forbid my leaving the Congress I would pay you a short Visit during the Session of the Convention. What has become of Queens & Richmond. Rival Governments or Governors are Solecisms in Politics.

It appears to me prudent that you should begin to impose light Taxes rather with a View to *Precedent* than Profit—suppose salt Petre, wool or Yarn should be recd. in Paymt. I think such a measure would tend to encourage manufactures. They are essential to the Support of the Poor, and care should be taken to increase materials for them. The People of this Place are amazingly attentive to this Object. It keeps People easy & Quiet—by being employed they gain Bread and when our Fellow Mortals are busy & well fed, they forget to complain. I hope your Convention will leave a Com[mitte]e of Safety. Adieu Yours most sincerely John Jay

RC (NHi).

Caesar Rodney to Thomas Rodney

Sir, Phila. Dec. the 23rd. 1775.

I have enclosed you with this the Resolution of Congress for raising a regt. in the lower counties upon the continental establishment.[1] You have also on the same paper the Resolution relative to New Jersey & Penn. setting forth the terms our Regt. being to be raised on the same. You will be pleased to make known the enclosed Resolution to your Brethren of the Commee. of Safety as soon after it shall come to hand as may be convenient for you. I should have wrote to you by Billy or by the post at farthest, had I not been in daily expectation of

John Langdon

your arrival in town, but as the weather is now set in to be very cold, I hardly expect to see you here before I set out for Kent which (if nothing more than I now expect prevents) will be on Sunday-week, The day before New-Years day. The weather is like to continue so cold that I shall travel slow & therefore do not expect to be at Dover before Tuesday or Wednesday following. I sent by Betts Veshell a small box of fine cut Tobacco which I recollect not to have mentioned in my letter & have since put on board of Palmer sewed up in a Bag, one gallon of garden pease & beg you will have these things taken care of. I did not Know whether we were in want of the last article or not but sent them down for fear we should, as has frequently been the case. The intelligence of our having got possession of Quebec, it seems is not true. Lord Stirling who sent us the Express is too credulous. Since then, we have letters both from Arnold & from Montgomery. Arnold says he is before Quebec & Montgom[er]y marched the 25th of Nov. to his assistance, so that I do not doubt we shall have a good account of that place in a little time. I am glad to hear that Betsey is like to get well & desire to be remembered to her & to all the rest of my friends.

I am yours &c. Cesar Rodney

Tr (DLC).

[1] On December 9 Congress had authorized the raising of one battalion in the lower counties. *JCC*, 3:418.

Richard Smith's Diary

Saturday Decr. 23. [1775]

The Journal read & some Parts marked not to be printed. Letter from Ld. Stirling praying to be furnished with Powder & Six Field Pieces to defend some vessels that have taken Shelter on the Coasts of Bergen & Essex, he has seized some Tories.[1] Langdon reported the Proceedgs of Himself & his Two Colleagues who have been sent by Congress to Ticonderoga, which were read & referred.[2] Their Expences reported by the Comee. of Claims and Payment ordered. This Comee. reported other Accounts which were allowed. Dyer read an Act of the Connect[icut] Legislature just passed, forbidding more Settlers to go on the Wyoming Lands on certain Conditions till further Order of that Assembly, Jay moved that it be recommended to Connect[icut] to extend the Time till further Order of this Congress, his Motion was carried 4 Colonies to 3 & the rest either divided or absent. The Delegates of Connecticut wanted to set aside this Vote because it was not carried by a Majority of the Colonies present, sed non allocavit. Duane gave in a Sett of Resolves for Sinking the last 3

Millions of Dollars, similar to those on the former 3 Millions & to be sunk in the same Years. They were all agreed to except the Time of Sinking which required further consideration.[3] Debate Whether to admit Capt. John the Tuscarora Chief and his Companions into Congress terminated in requiring the Comee. to provide them with Food and Raiment for their Return Home. Col. Lee & Cushing had Leave of Absence. Motion by Gadsden to publish the Part of Gen Schuylers Letters mentioned in Yesterdays Notes, was carried in the Affirmative. Jefferson from the Comee. brought in a List of Business before Us. The Comee. on Capt. Peter Bertons Petition reported that the Prayer of it ought not to be allowed & the Report was confirmed. The Prayer from New York for a large Loan of Continental Bills, disapproved of. The Delegates of Pennsa. ordered to inquire what Progress is made in Exchanging Continental Bills for Gold and Silver. A Proposition or Report from a Comee. to send abroad a great Quantity of Produce to be returned in hard Money. A Comee. reported the Draught of an Answer to Gen Montgomerys Letters, advising a General Convention to be summoned in Canada & Delegates to be sent to our Congress &c. Some Suppose we ought to keep up at least 3000 Troops in that Province. Adjorned till Tuesday, Monday being Christmas.

MS (DLC).

[1] See Colonel Alexander's letter to Hancock of December 19 in PCC, item 162, 2:356–57; and *Am. Archives*, 4:354–55.

[2] For the text of Langdon's report, see *JCC*, 3:446–52.

[3] On the final resolution of this issue, providing for the sinking of the bills between 1783 and 1786, see *JCC*, 3:457–59; and Smith's Diary, December 26, 1775.

Samuel Ward to Deborah Ward

My dearest Child Phila. 24th Decr. 1775

Next to the Pleasure of seeing you is that of receiving your Letters; continue therefore to write by every Opportunity. I dare say you want me at home but I believe I am doing you as well as my Country more Service here than I could there. In vain would Heaven smile upon the Labours of a Parent & crown the Year with Plenty if a Tyrant & his Harpies could take it away from him, in vain would paternal affection wish to afford Protection & Support to his dear offspring when a lawless Banditti of armed men could rob them of that Parent & offer every Kind of Injury to his helpless offspring. Now my dearest is the Time to repel this lawless Invasion, Heaven calls us all to the arduous Task. Though of the softer Sex I know you have a generous Mind, endeavour to inspire all your Acquaintance with the Love of Liberty and a fixed Resolution never to part with it but with their last Breath.

You are kind in making the best Apology you can for your little Brothers, but they have behaved ill. I have been from home near four months & have had only one Letter from Ray, charge them all to write immediately. I wish Betsy could write. Cant She be learnt this Winter, a Letter from her would give me much Pleasure. I hope she behaves well. I wish the News of Arnolds taking of Quebec which your Uncle wrote You was true but unhappily one quarter of his Men returned to Cambridge; the rest suffered terribly by fatigue and famine, their Arms & Powder were so damaged & exhausted & the Number of effective men so small 550 only that they were obliged to retire from the City & send to Genl. Montgomery for a Reinforcement. He is gone himself with all his Forces that I hope we shall soon have it. In the mean Time prepare your Mind to part with dear Bror. Heaven only knows where or how he is, if he behaved well he is safe either in Canada or the Mansions of eternal Bliss & I cant doubt it. Arnold's March is considered here as the greatest Action done this War. Some say it equals Xenophons Retreat from Persia, others that nothing greater has been done since the Days of Alexander.

I had a Letter from your Uncle Ward last Post, General Washingtons Difficulties I hope will be removed. If I can get Time to buy some handkers. I will & Pins also. The Poem you desired Polly to write for [me] will send by first Opportunity. Mrs. Li[. . .] Acct. cannot be setled until my Return; pay her twenty Dollars if She wants them.

The Papers inclosed to your Sisters will give you all the News save that Esek Hopkins is made Commander in chief[1]

RC (RHi).

[1] Except for some marginalia pertaining to his personal clothing, remainder of MS missing.

Josiah Bartlett to Mary Bartlett

Philadelphia Decembr 25th 1775
10 of the Clock in the Evening

My Dear

I this moment Receivd yours of the 7th Instant and with pleasure hear you & the family are well. But am Sorry to inform you that I Cannot return to you at present. So much Business lays before the Congress; I fear it wont rise for Some time. When it Does rise, one Delegate from Each Colony must tarry to transact the Publick Business in the recess, So that I think I Shall not be able to return till towards Spring.[1]

Capt Langdon is returned here from Ticonderoga, and I Expect he will return to Pourtsmouth in a few Days and George will return with him. I will Endeavor to Send by him the things you mention in your letter and by George Shall write you more fully.

I am Extremely Sorry for the Disappointment we both have in my not returning So Soon as I Expected & gave you reason to Expect, But I hope all will turn out for the best. Who Knows but that if I had Set out [*in*] this very Severe weather it might have been the means of my Death and So hinder my being Ever able to See you; in Short I Desingn to make my Self as Easy as possible and hope you will Do the Same and make your life as Comfortable as you Can.

I intend to Send you Some mony by George and hope you will lay it out for what you want. I am in good health but very tender, by being Confined here for above 3 months with but little Exercise. This Day being Christmas the Congress Did not Set, So I had an oppertunity to ride about 6 or 7 miles out of town in a Sley, but yesterday and the Day before we had a Severe Cold Storm of Snow which is now about Six inches Deep. Desire Capt Calef to look me out a good faithful Steady hand & hire him for me for 9 months or a year to assist in my farming Business. I am Determined to return as Soon as I Can with propriety. Give my Kind regards to Capt Calef, Col Grely, Leut Pearson and all friends. I remain yours &c Josiah Bartlett

[*P.S.*] I had rather Capt Calef Should give Something Extraordinary than not have a good hand. Ebenr. Hills has the Small pox by innoculation pretty favorable as his Doctr tells me. J B

RC (NhHi).

[1] For the "instructions for the Committee who are to sit during the recess of Congress," adopted on December 15, see *JCC,* 3:430–31.

Samuel Adams to James Warren

My dear Sir Philada. Decr 26 1775

I have receivd your obliging Letter of the 5th Instant by Fessenden, for which I am very thankful to you.[1] The present form of our Government, you tell me, is not considerd as permanent.[2] This affords the strongest Motive to improve the Advantages of it, while it continues. May not Laws be made and Regulations establishd, under this Government, the salutary Effects of which the People shall be so convincd of from their own Experience, as never hereafter to suffer them to be repeald or alterd. But what other Change is expected? Certainly the People do not already hanker after the Onions and the Garlick! They cannot have so soon forgot the Tyranny of their late Governors, who, being dependent upon, and the mere Creatures of a

Minister of State, and subservient to his Instructions or Inclinations, have *forbid* them to make such Laws as would have been beneficial to them or to repeal those that were not. But, I find *every where* some Men, who are affraid of a free Government, lest it should be perverted and made use of as a Cloke for Licentiousness. The Fear of the Peoples abusing their Liberty is made an Argument against their having the Enjoyment of it; as if any thing were so much to be dreaded by Mankind as Slavery. But the Bearer Mr Bromfield, of whose Departure I was not apprisd till a few Minutes past, is waiting. I can therefore say no more at present, but that I am your affectionate Friend[3]
S A

RC (MHi).

[1] James Warren to Samuel Adams, December 5, 1775, Samuel Adams Papers, NN.

[2] The political controversy surrounding the quest for a new constitution in Massachusetts is discussed in Stephen E. Patterson, *Political Parties in Revolutionary Massachusetts* (Madison: University of Wisconsin Press, 1973), pp. 153–247.

[3] For the continuation of this letter, see Samuel Adams to Warren, December 27, 1775.

Eliphalet Dyer to Joseph Trumbull

Sr Philadelphia Decembr 26th 1775

I wrote to you a few days agoe by express to Cambridge which trust you have receivd.[1] I have now only to hint to you what I think I have once before with respect to some further Allowance being made you for your very great services as Commissary Genll.[2] It is thot by your particular friends here that it would be best for you to make a state of your services & what goes thro your hands, the very great Occasional expences &c, in a manner you think best lay before the General & obtain if readily to be had His recommendation to this Congress for some further Allowance or at least his opinion on the Subject. A small Commission I should think best; its coming before Congress in that way believe would not fail of Success, but if it Cannot be done by the way of the General I will Indeavor to get some friend to Introduce the Affair before Congress at some proper time tho how long I shall tarry at this place is very Uncertain As it seems we must wait the Conveniency of the Gentn. (Appointed in our stead) to come, & not when it would be most Convenient for us to return, but fear they will keep us here the most part of the Winter. In your Next you will let me hear how the forming the New Army goes on, what officers of ours are like to tarry, whether my son has joined the Army & his Situation &c. I find Coll Reed has determined not to return to the Army therefore his office of Secrectary will be Vacant. If you preferr that, all things Considered to a Commisy Genll, it is probable to me you might have it. I mentioned it to Coll Reed but he says he knows of no Gentn but your self who could Supply the Army as you have done, and who could fill your place of Commisy Genll. tho doubts not but you would be very agreable to the Genll as his Secrety. but loosing you as Commissy, the loss could not be made up or your place Supplied. I believe you need not be concernd as to the few hints I gave you of some remarks on your Conduct, it makes no Impression, tis Vanished & gone. My respect & regards to whom proper And Am Sincerely Yours Elipht Dyer

RC (CtHi).
[1] See Dyer to Joseph Trumbull, December 16, 1775.
[2] See also Dyer to Joseph Trumbull, January 1 and 15, 1776.

John Hancock to Gunning Bedford

Sir Congress Chamber 26th Decr. 1775

I this morning laid before Congress the severall Muster Rolls you deliver'd me; and Took the Sense of Congress respecting the propriety of your Mustering the Two Battalions of Continental Troops in New Jersey, and have it in Charge to Direct that you as soon as may be Muster the said Troops, and make a Return to Congress.[1]

I am Sir Your most Obedt. Servt. John Hancock Presidt.

RC (PHC). Addressed: "Gunning Bedford D[eputy] Mus[te]r Mas[ter] Gen[era]l."
[1] See *JCC*, 3:457.

Secret Committee Minutes of Proceedings

Philada. C[ommittee] C[hamber] Decr. 26th. 1775

At a meeting of the Com[mitte]e of Secrecy, Pres[en]t Samuel Ward, Benjn. Franklin, Josiah Bartlett, Robert Morris & Thos. McKean.

A Contract was enterd into between John Brown of Providence, Rhode Isld. & the sd. Committee[1]—That a voyage or voyages shall be undertaken for the speedy procuring thirty six tons of good Gunpowder (or if Gunpowder is not to be had) then as much Saltpetre with a proportion of 15 lb of Sulphur to every hundred pounds of Saltpetre as will be sufficient to make that quantity of gun powder, one thousand stand of good Arms, one thousand double bridled gunlocks, twenty tons of lead & one thousand bolts of Russia Duck. If the Arms are not to be had, their value to be laid out in good gunpowder or Saltpetre & sulphur. If neither are to be had, then in Ticklinburgs,

Osnabrigs or Vitrys. Or in case these are not to be had the nett proceeds to be returnd in gold or silver.

At a meeting of the C[ommittee] of S[ecrecy] Present Saml. Ward, B. Franklin, Josiah Bartlett, Robt. Morris & Thos. McKean. A Contract was enterd into between Thos. Green of Providence Rhode Isld. & sd. Commee.

That a voyage or voyages shall be forthwith undertaken, for the speedy procuring of fifty tons of G[un] Powder, five hundred stand of good arms, one thousand good double bridled Gunlocks, twenty tons of Lead, & five hundred bolts of good russia duck, or if those Articles are not to be had, then as much salt petre with a proportion of 15 lb Sulp[hu]r to every hundred pds. Saltpetre, as will be sufficient to make 15 tons good gunpowdr. & the remainder in Ticklinburgs, osnabrigs & Vitrys. If those articles are not to be had the nett proceeds of the Cargo to be shippd shall be returnd in gold & silver.[2]

At a meeting of the Com[mitte]e of Secy. Present Saml. Ward, B. Franklin, Josiah Bartlett, Robt. Morris & Thos McKean. A contract was enterd into between Bayard & Jackson & Co. of the City of Philada. Merchts. & the sd. Committee. That the sd Committee shall advance to the said Bayard & Jackson the sum of 15000 dollars Cont. Mony. to be laid out by them in flour & other produce of these Colonies & shippd on board the Snow Dickenson, ——— Master, for the port of Nantes on account & risque & for the benefit of the sd. U[nited] C[olonies] & these to be disposd of to the best advantage & the nett proceeds laid out in the purchase of 15 tons good gunpowder, or if G[un] P[owder] not to be had as much Saltpetre, with a proportion of 15 lb Sulp[hu]r to every 100 lb Saltpetre as will be sufficient to make that quantity of good G[un] P[owder], 1500 stand arms, 1000 Bolts Russia Duck, & as much more of those Articles as the nett proceeds of the sd. Cargoe will purchase. If any of the sd. Articles cannot be had as aforesaid, the money directed to be laid out in that Article, shall be laid out in good Ticklinburgs, osnabrigs or Vitrys, or otherwise the returns to be made in gold & silver.

MS (MH).

[1] This contract is printed in Clark, *Naval Documents,* 3:879–80.

[2] For the money advanced to John Brown and to Thomas Green, see Secret Committee Account, September 27, 1775–August 26, 1776.

Richard Smith's Diary

Tuesday 26 Decr. [1775]

Votes of Saturday read & Letters from Gen. Washington, from Dr.

John Morgan, from some New England men at Guadaloupe & other Letters.[1] Duanes Propositions for sinking the last 3 Millions of Dollars were gone thro, the Vote was taken Whether that Money shall be sunk in the Years 1779, 1780, 1781 & 1782 as the first 3 Millions, or in the Years 1783, 1784, 1785 & 1786 and carried for the latter. R. Morris informs that Treasurer Clymer says there is about £6000 in Gold & Silver now in the Treasury, Jay moved that it may be immediately sent off to Gen Schuyler which was agreed to. Report from a Comee. recommending inter alia that all Persons who refuse the Continental Bills shall be declared Enemies to their Country was postponed. A Day fixed to consider Whether on the 1st of March next to open the Exportation Trade.[2] Instructions to Lieut. Col. Irwin brought in by Jefferson & passed. This officer is to go from hence to Virginia immedy. with what Companies are ready. Report made from a Comee. recomg. that no more Paper Money may be made by Congress but that the Money wanted for the future may be borrowed and the Treasurers give Notes bearing Interest for 100 Dollars and upwards &c referred till Tomorrow.[3] Jay moved that the several Commees. of Inspection in each Colony should transmit to the Congress Accounts of what Produce has been & shall be exported, with the Returns of Arms and Ammunition and the Prices & Values & to this there was no Objection. An Order took place that all Soldiers in our Service may get their Letters franked & send them free from Postage.[4] Ld. Stirlings Letters were referred to William Livingston, Jay & S. Adams, several other Reports, Motions & Matters acted upon.

MS (DLC).

[1] This day Congress received letters from Washington to Hancock of December 14 and 16. See PCC, item 152, 1:339–42, 347; Washington, *Writings* (Fitzpatrick), 4:162–63; and *Am. Archives*, 4th ser. 4:291. For letters from Jonathan Trumbull, Sr., to Hancock of December 20 and from John Morgan to Washington of December 12, see PCC, item 66, 1:45–49, item 152, 1:343–46; and *Am. Archives*, 4th ser. 4:263, 365. The letter from the "New England men" has not been found, but for its provenance see *JCC*, 3:457.

[2] See Smith's Diary, December 29, 1775.

[3] There is no mention of this report in the journals.

[4] Congress did not pass a formal resolution to this effect until January 9, 1776. *JCC*, 4:43.

Samuel Adams to James Warren

Decr 27th. [1775]

Mr Bromfield who went in a Stage-Coach, set off yesterday before I could close my Letter. I shall therefore forward it by the Post or any other Conveyance that may next offer.

Your last Letter informed me, that "the late Conduct of the ——[1] had weakned that Confidence and Reverence necessary to give a well disposd Government its full operation and Effects." I am sorry for it; and presume it is not to be imputed to a Fault in the Institution of that Order, but a Mistake in the Persons of whom it is composd. All men are fond of Power. It is difficult for us to be prevaild upon to believe, that we possess more than belongs to us. Even publick Bodies of Men legally constituted, are too prone to covet more Power than the Publick has judgd it safe to entrust them with. It is happy when their Power is not only subject to Controul while it is exercisd, but frequently reverts into the hands of the People, from whom it is derivd, and to whom Men in Power ought forever to be accountable. That venerable Assembly the Senate of Areopagus in Athens, whose Proceedings were so eminently upright and impartial, that, we are told, even "foreign States, when any Controversy happend among them would voluntarily submit to their Decisions." "Not only their Determinations might be called in Question and, if Need was, retracted by an Assembly of the People, but themselves too, if they exceeded the Bounds of Moderation, were lyable to account for it." At present, our Council as well as our House of Representatives are annually elective. Thus far they are accountable to the People, as they are lyable, for Misbehavior, to be discarded. But this is not a sufficient Security to the People, unless they are themselves *virtuous*. If we wish for "another Change," should it not be a Change of *Manners?* If the Youth are carefully educated—If the Principles of Morality are strongly inculcated on the Minds of the People—the End and Design of Government clearly understood, and the Love of our Country the ruling Passion, uncorrupted Men will be chosen for the Representatives of the People. These will elect Men of distinguishd Worth to sit at the Council Board, and in time we may hope, that, in the Purity of their Manners, the Wisdom of their Councils and the Justice of their Determinations, our Senate may equal that of Athens, which was said to be, "the most sacred and venerable Assembly in all Greece." I confess I have a strong Desire, that our Colony should excell in Wisdom and Virtue. If this proceeds from Pride, is it not a lawful Pride? I am willing that the same Spirit of Emulation may pervade every one of the confederated Colonies. But I am called off, and must conclude with again assuring you that I am, with the most friendly Regards to Mrs Warren, very affectionately Yours S A

[*P.S.*] Pray write to me often.

RC (MHi). A continuation of Adams to Warren, December 26, 1775.

[1] Probably the Massachusetts Council, which was locked in a battle with the House of Representatives over the power of appointment of state officers. See John Adams to James Otis, November 23, 1775; Samuel Adams to James Otis, November

23, 1775; and Massachusetts Delegates to the Massachusetts Council, November 24 and 29, 1775. Warren's "last Letter" was that of December 5, 1775. Samuel Adams Papers, NN.

Silas Deane to Elizabeth Deane

My Dear Philadelphia Decr. 27th. 1775

I received a Lettr. dated the 19th from one Simeon Deane who is troubled with the Rheumatism, or Gout, at the bottom of which are these Words, "Mrs. Deane says she would write You but not having recd. any Lettrs. lately, She thinks proper to wait." As I can hardly Credit the Story, must leave it with you to inquire into the Truth of it. I have indeed been favored with Two Letters from You since You left Us, & have returned Five in paymt. Mr. Sherman is returned but brings No News from Our assembly. Our Term is up, Saturday Next, but I shall hardly set out for home untill sometime the Middle of January if so soon, as Our Fleet is got stopp'd by the Ice. Your Brother Dudley came here last Saturday & lodges with Me for the present, when he will be able to sail depends on the weather.[1] I wrote you per Capt Phelps & sent the Silk but have no Answer as yet. I had no Time to write by Mr Adams or should have sent one Line. My Complimts. to all Freinds & Love to Jesse & Family. I am my Dear Your's Affectionately Silas Deane

RC (CtHi).

[1] Dudley Saltonstall had recently been appointed captain of the *Alfred,* flagship of the Continental fleet. *JCC,* 3:443.

Benjamin Franklin to Philip Mazzei

Dear Sir, Philada. Dec. 27. 1775[1]

It was with great Pleasure I learnt from Mr Jefferson, that you were settled in America,[2] and from the Letter you favour'd me with, that you like the Country, and have reason to expect Success in your laudable and meritorious Endeavours to introduce new Products. I heartily wish you all the Success you can desire, in that, and in every other Undertaking that may conduce to your comfortable Establishment in your present Situation.

I know not how it has happened that you did not receive an Answer to your Letter from the Secretaries of our Society. I suppose they must have written, & that it has miscarried. If you have not yet sent the Books which the Academy of Turin have done us the Honour to present us with, we must, I fear, wait for more quiet Times before we can have the Pleasure of receiving them, the Communication being now very difficult.

I can hardly suspect Mr Walpole of the Practise against you which you mention,[3] especially as he was then expecting to have Lands of his own in America, wherein the Productions you were about to introduce must have been beneficial. I rather suspect a Person whom you may remember was frequently with him, I mean Martinelli. I rejoice that you escap'd the Snares that were laid for you, and I think all America is oblig'd to the Great Duke [*of Tuscany*] for his Benevolence towards it, in the Protection he afforded you, and his Encouragement of your Undertaking.

We have experienc'd here that Silk may be produc'd to great Advantage. While in London I had some Trunks full sent me from hence three Years Successively, and it sold by Auction for about 19/6 the small Pound, which was not much below the Silk from Italy.

The Congress have not yet extended their Views much towards foreign Powers, and particularly not to those of Italy, who are so distant. They are nevertheless oblig'd by your kind Offers of your Service, which perhaps in a Year or two more may become very useful to them.[4] I am myself much pleas'd that you have sent a Translation of our Declaration to the Grand Duke; because having a high Esteem for the Character of that Prince, and of the whole Imperial Family, from the Accounts given me of them by my friend Dr Ingenhauss and yourself, I should be happy to find that we stood well in the Opinion of that Court.

Mr Fromond of Milan, with whom I had the Pleasure of being acquainted in London, spoke to me of a Plant much used in Italy, and which he thought would be useful to us in America. He promis'd at my Request to send me some of the Seeds, which he has accordingly done. I have unfortunately forgotten the Uses, and know nothing of the Culture. In both those Particulars I must beg Information and Advice from you. It is called *Ravizzone*. I send Specimens of the Seed inclosed.

I received from the same M. Fromond Four Copies of a Translation of some of my Pieces into the fine Language of your Country. I beg your Accpetance of one of them, and of my best Wishes for your Health & Prosperity. With great Esteem & Regard, I have the Honour to be, Dear Sir, Your most obedient and most humble Servant

B Franklin

RC (NhD).

[1] Albert H. Smyth, who reprinted this letter from the *Port Folio,* 4th ser. 4 (July 1817): 94–95, assigned the document an "uncertain" 1776 date on the basis of a reference in the fifth paragraph to "our Declaration of Independence" which had been sent to the Grand Duke of Tuscany. However, the words "of Independence" do not appear in Franklin's letter, although they were inserted in the text printed

by the editor of the *Port Folio,* who also assigned it the date December 3, 1775. Edmund C. Burnett, who took his text from Smyth, printed an extract from the letter under the date [August ? 1776], which he too assigned on the basis of the presumed reference to the Declaration of Independence. See Franklin, *Writings* (Smyth), 6:455–56; and Burnett, *Letters,* 2:65. Mazzei himself published the letter in his *Memoirs* under the proper date and without the two intruded words, but this version is marred by some significant omissions. Philip Mazzei, *Memoirs of the Life and Peregrinations of the Florentine, Philip Mazzei, 1730–1816* (New York: Columbia University Press, 1942), pp. 218–19.

[2] Philip Mazzei (1730–1816), a native of Tuscany, had migrated to Virginia in 1773 after a residence of many years in England as a wine importer, where in 1767 he had met Franklin while attempting to purchase some Franklin stoves, beginning a friendship nurtured by their mutual interest in the propagation of European plants in America. *DAB.*

[3] A reference to a scheme to import textiles from China, which Mazzei explained in his *Memoirs,* p. 219n.

[4] Mazzei never succeeded in interesting Congress in the offer of his services abroad, but in 1779 he embarked on a mission to Europe on behalf of Virginia and subsequently represented the state there for several years, during which time he became embroiled in a dispute with Franklin over the right of individual states to seek foreign loans. See Philip Mazzei, *Philip Mazzei, Virginia's Agent in Europe,* ed. Howard R. Marraro (New York: New York Public Library, 1935); Richard C. Garlick, *Philip Mazzei, Friend of Jefferson: His Life and Letters* (Baltimore: Johns Hopkins Press, 1933), pp. 51–96; and his extensive correspondence with Jefferson in Jefferson, *Papers* (Boyd), especially vols. 2–9.

Richard Smith's Diary

Wednesday 27 Decr. [1775]

A Motion was made to allow an Importation of Salt into Virginia, an Amendt. offered that the Allowance should be general, this Amendt. was strongly opposed by Lynch & others & large Argumts. upon it, the further Considn. deferred till Friday.[1] Report from a Comee. that 6 Battalions are necessary to be raised for the Continental Service in Virginia (their Convention request 8 Battalions). It was largely controverted Whether they shall recieve the Pay of 6 Dollars and Two Thirds allowed to the Troops in N. England, the Two Carolina's & Georgia, or the reformed Pay of 5 Dollars per month allowed to the Forces raised in N York, N Jersey, Pennsa. & the Lower Counties & at length the Determination was postponed by the Interposition of New Jersey according to our Rule that any One Colony may put off the Vote till another Day.[2] Lieut. Hay allowed to negociate a Bill of Exchange to pay his Expences home to Scotland. Complaints of the bad Behavior of Some of the Captive Officers & Capt. Motts Affidavit ordered to be taken thereon. An Allowance made of £3 per man for Capt. Motts Guard on their Return Home to Connectt. This Day, it is said, the King's Post finally stopt & the Postmasters shut up the Office.

MS (DLC).

[1] On December 29 Congress extended to Virginia, Maryland, and North Carolina the privilege of importing salt. *JCC*, 3:464–65.

[2] Congress decided on December 28 that the six Virginia battalions should be paid at the same rate as the Continental troops under Washington's command, unless the Virginia Convention could "raise them on better terms." *JCC*, 3:463; and Smith's Diary, December 28, 1775.

Samuel Ward to Catharine Greene

My dearest Child Phila. 27th Decr. 1775

It is long since I had the Pleasure of receiving a Line from You but I am thankfull to find by your Sisters Letters that you are growing well again, the various Events which We call Pain, Sickness, Trouble & Distress I often think are some of the many Instances of divine Goodness. May Heaven sanctify every thing of this as well as of the more (to human weakness) desirable Kind to my dearest Daughter & long continue her a Blessing to all her Connections.

Let your Aunt Greene know that little Ray is vastly well after the small Pox & exceeding happy: nothing but excessive fatigue & hurry prevents my writing to her. I design it soon. Give my most affectionate Regards to your Uncle & Aunt, to your Uncle Hubbart, & to all your Family. Mr. Greene I heard from at Norwalk in Connecticut; he was like to purchase a load of Wheat very easily. I should have been glad of a Letter from him & wish he had come to Philada. if his affairs would have permitted it. I wrote you sometime since that I was one of a Comee for purchasing Powder &c and that I thought I could serve them in imploying their Vessels &c but never recd. any Answer from you; Mr. Mumford mentioned it to Me to Day. I offered him six thousand Dollars for the Com[pan]y if he would engage they should undertake a Voyage but he was afraid your Vessels were froze in: I fear it will be too late or I would advise one of them to come here.

Every Intelligence confirms the Acct. which I wrote you sometime since that our Enemies would make the greatest possible Efforts in the Spring. We ought to spend the whole Winter in disciplining our People, providing Arms & Ammunition &c and if any thing further is necessary for the Defence of Greenwich I would by all Means advise to have it done as soon as the Weather will admit.

The Virginians have at length defeated Lord Dunmore. They killed two Captains, one of them of the Grenadiers; they killed 52 of that Company & wounded the remaining 10 & have taken them Prisoners, & have taken some others & drove him on board his Ships.

Our Enemies in Boston are vastly distressd. They had not ten days ago above six Weeks Provisions of all Kinds, and no Wood hardly, the Price was £5 Stirg. per Cord. The Soldiery are much intimidated & ready if opportunity presented to desert. The destestable Wretches pulled down the Pews in the old South & turned it into a riding school. I saw a Master of a Vessel who came out of Boston 3rd inst. I have great Hopes Heaven will deliver them into our Hands soon. The Monsters inoculated some People & sent them out of Town & they have since broke out with the small Pox. This is as infamous as[1]

RC (RHi).
[1] Remainder of MS missing.

Samuel Ward to Henry Ward

Dear Bror. Philadelpa. 27th Decr. 1775

A Letter from you tho' ever so short is always agreable. I never allow myself to find Fault with the Ways of Heaven or I should say that Asthma of yours was cruel to take up so much of your Time when your Country & your Friends want every Moment of it.

The Barbarities of a Wallace[1] or any other Savage do not much surprize Me. When I first entered this Contest with Great Britain I extended my Views through the various Scenes which my Judgment or Imagination (say which you please) pointed out to Me, I saw clearly that the last Act of this cruel Tragedy would close in Fields of Blood, I have traced the Progress of the unnatural War through burning Towns, Devastation of the Country & every subsequent Evil, I have realized with Regard to myself the Bullet, the Bayonet & the Halter and compared with the immense Object I have in View they are all less than nothing. No man living perhaps is more fond of his Children [than] I am & I am not so old as to be tired of Life and yet as far as I can now judge the tenderest Connections and the most important private Concerns are very minute objects. "Heaven save my Country" I was going to say is my first, my last and almost my only Prayer.

I have several Times mentioned to you the Anxiety I felt on Acct. of the newmodelling the Army, that cruel Jealousy which the southern Colonies have of the northern has occasioned all this mischief. The Army must be wholly continental, all colonial Distinctions must be at an End, the Troops must be taught to look up not to their several Colonies but to the Continent. For that Purpose the Congress must appoint all officers. Again the British Soldiers have but 6d a Day & shall We give ours 1/. Ours shall have no Bounty & shall find themselves Arms and so far has this stupid Policy been pursued that instead of 20000 Men in the Massachusetts We have not half the Number & in Canada instead of 5000 Men We have not 1500 besides Canadians. In this Province a Battalion was ordered to be raised two Months ago at 5 Dollars a Month; 150 of the best of those enlisted have deserted & they are not full yet and still there is an Idea of raising Men upon the same Terms. I have wrote fully to General Greene & proposed to him that the Generals should recommend at least by private Letters to their Friends the offering a Bounty to the Men, finding them their Arms & recommending to the Colonies the filling up their Troops; this would soon fill up our Army.[2] I mention these things to You that you may use your Influence to prevent the fatal Mischiefs which will atend our being found unprepared in the Spring & may give Me your best Advice upon the Subject. I do not in the least despair for I firmly believe that the Cause We are engaged in is the Cause of God & human Nature & that in Mercy to Mankind Heaven will prosper it.

If the Comee. for building those Vessels in our Colony had been appointed by Congress I should have taken Care to have had you appointed one of the Comee. but as a Comee. of Congress is appointed to carry into Execution the Resolve for building the Fleet it is out of my Power. Mr. Hopkins being on the naval Comee. before is one. I have mentioned it to him or rather I believe read him part of your Letter; through hurry I have forgot to mention it to him again.

I saw on Christmas Day a Master of Vessel belonging to this City who was in Boston Six Weeks & came out 3rd or 5th inst. He says the Acct. which We had of the old Souths being turned into a riding School is true. He saw the Horses exercised in it, the Carp[enter]s he says would not pull down the Pews &c and the officers with their Men did it. He says that all Sorts of Provisions were so scarce that they had not above seven Weeks Provisions including all Sorts. General Washingtons Letters of 16th inst. agree very nearly with this Acct. This Capt. adds that the Soldiery were much intimidated many of them disposed to desert. He mentioned a Conversation which he overheard, "Some of them said if there was another Action & they could get off under the Smoke they would take the fresh Beef Side of the Question." He thinks the Place is easily taken. Genl. Washingtons Letters ascertain the fact that the People who were turned out of Boston were first inoculated & have since broke out with the small Pox, is their a Crime but what these monsters are capable of. Proper Measures are taken to prevent its spreading. Genl. Greene writes me the 10th inst. that our Troops enlist very slowly. He had not received my Letters mentioned above; I wish they may have a good Effect. As the Continent has taken Whipple into their Service I wish the Colony would build such an one as we had the War before last, or a larger one. The Time which we have to prepare in against the Spring is very short; not a Moment is to be lost; besides the general Defence every possible Measure ought to be taken for the Defence of the Colony. I doubt not but you will direct your whole Attention to his important Juncture. Remember Me to all Friends. I am most affectionately yours

Sam Ward

[*P.S.*] Lord Dunmore you will see by the Papers has been defeated & obliged to fly on board his Ships; six Battalions will be raised in that Colony soon & I hope we shall arm all Parts of the Continent soon.

RC (RHi).

[1] See Ward to Henry Ward, October 15, 1775, note.

[2] Ward's letters to Nathanael Greene have not been found, but for further indications of their tenor see Greene's letters to Ward of December 31 in Ward, *Correspondence* (Knollenberg), pp. 152–57.

John Hancock to George Clymer and Michael Hillegas

Congress Chamber, December 28, 1775. Requests Continental Treasurers Clymer and Hillegas to pay the Pennsylvania Committee of Safety $8,000 "for the use of the Battalion of Continental Troops in this city."[1]

MS not found; abstracted from *Am. Archives*, 4th ser. 4:504–5.

[1] See *JCC*, 3:463.

Thomas Lynch to Thomas Lynch, Jr.

Dear Tom Decr. 28 [1775]

I wrote you a long Letter lately by a Vessel bound to Georgia and another to Mr. Neyle,[1] since which the River has been frozen so as to prevent any Vessells getting out. I have sat down to repeat a part of my Letter on the Subject of Salt Petre. A Gentleman here makes from 3 to 4 1/2 l[bs.] every day from less than 2 bushells of earth taken from the Surface, under any old Building. It seems, from his Experiments, that Stables or Cellars are too full of Marine Salts, and that pure Earth, loamy or Clayey which is placed so as to receive the Air, is most useful for this work, as he makes ten times as much as any body who tries the other materials.

He fills his two Kegs with Earth every Morning and pours on soft warm Water, filling it up till the water Stands an Inch above the Earth, letting it remain 2 hours, then draw it off like lees of Ashes (returning the foul). The clear is directly put into a Common Brass Kettle and hung over the Kitchen Fire to boil, the Keggs of Earth again filled with Water, which is to be drawn off and boiled as before. When 2/3 is boiled away, both Boiling are poured on a Bit of wood ashes placed on some straw in order to filter and clarify; when drawn out clear it is to be boiled again till it is so thick as when dropped on the blade of a Knife it will stick when the Knife stands edgeways; tis then to be taken off immediately and poured into another Keg with a Cock 2 Inches from the bottom, where the Sea Salt and any other impurity Settles to the bottom and the Liquor containing the Salt Petre is to be poured of[f] thro' the Cock into dishes & plates to Christallize and set into the coolest plates. This must be done before the Liquor is cold, as the Salt Petre shoots as soon as 'tis cold. Colo. Horrys, Danl Hor[r]ys at Wambaw, our old Place at Santee are exactly of the same soil & under their Piazzas, Negro Houses, & Barns thousands may be got. It is needless to say how material it is to be had among ourselves.

The Bond sent by Mr. Brewton is said to have been paid to the Person to whom it was first given, so there can be no expectation from it.

We have no material News, but daily expect some of most important Nature.

Cold horrid Weather and a most dismal Christmas. We are all well and desire our love to you all.

Your most affectionate Father Tho Lynch

RC (PHi).

[1] Neither of these letters has been found.

Richard Smith's Diary

[December 28, 1775]

Thursday 28.[1] The Journals read & one Passage ordered for Omission. Report of Accounts from the Comee. of Claims allowed. One of them was for maintaining some Prisoners in Goal, Harrison moved to enlarge them. Vote Whether the Virginian 6 Battalions shall have 37/6 or 50/ per month our Curr[enc]y was carried for the latter if their Convention cannot raise Men cheaper, 3 Colonies only in the Negative, then a Motion was made by the Virginians that the 6 Battals. shall be altered to 8. Sed non Allocatur. There was a considerable Controversy on the main Question Whether the 6 Batts. shall be raised, it was carried in the Affirmative. Then a Motion was made by Wilson supported by McKean, Wm. Livingston & others that the Middle Colony Troops shall have the same Pay, after some Time spent therein it was postponed. Some Talk about dispatching Bulls Regiment to Virginia. Montgomery some Weeks ago was created a Major General.[2] 8000 Dollars advanced to the Comee. of Safety of Penna. towards Payment of Bulls Battalion. £5 advanced to the Indians for travelling Charges. A Comee. of 5 ballotted for to consider the present State of N York. A Report brought in on the Petition of Capts. Coffin and Paddock of Nantucket.[3]

MS (DLC).

[1] Robert Treat Paine returned to Philadelphia this date, his diary entry reading: "Very cold, rode to Philada. 7 1/2 m. & went to Mrs. Yards. Went to Congress." MHi.

[2] Congress had made this promotion December 9. *JCC*, 3:418.

[3] Capts. Sylvanus Coffin and Seth Paddock had submitted to Congress on December 23 a petition concerning the exportation of fuel and provisions to Nantucket. The nature of the report by the committee appointed to consider this petition is unknown, but the petition itself was rejected by Congress on January 2, 1776. *JCC*, 3:445, 463; 4:17.

John Rogers to Robert Alexander

Sir, Phila. 29th Decr. 1775.

The inclosed Resolutions passed in Congress today.[1] As the first of them relates particularly to Maryland, I have taken the earliest opportunity of inclosing them to you, that they may be the sooner transmitted to the Convention or Council of Safety. I have long expected the pleasure of seeing you in Philadelphia, but I presume you have been unavoidably detained. Many of the Congress are much dissatisfied that the province of Maryland has been so long without Representation.[2]

I am Yr Obedt. servt. J Rogers

[*P.S.*] No particular news.

RC (MdAA).

[1] See *JCC*, 3:464–65.

[2] Maryland had been unrepresented in Congress for some time. When Rogers took his seat on December 21 he was the sole Marylander in attendance, since Paca had apparently left several days previously, and four of her other delegates—Chase, Johnson, Stone, and Tilghman—had returned to Annapolis to attend the Maryland Provincial Convention which convened on December 7. Rogers, along with Alexander, had been named by the convention on December 9 to replace John Hall and Robert Goldsborough, who had signified their inability to attend Congress, but as Maryland required the presence of three delegates to constitute a quorum, she continued to remain unrepresented for several weeks. Alexander subsequently took his seat January 3, 1776. See Richard Smith's Diary, December 13 and 21, 1775, and January 3, 1776; and *Am. Archives*, 4th ser. 4:712.

Maintaining representation in Congress had been a long-standing matter of concern, particularly since several colonies required the presence of three to five delegates to act in their behalf. See, for example, the resolutions of Congress of November 16 requiring notification of absent delegates "that the Congress expect their immediate attendance," and that in the future delegates were to obtain permission to absent themselves. *JCC*, 3:357. For other aspects of this issue, see

New York Delegates to the New York Provincial Congress, October 16; Francis Lewis to John Alsop, November 19; and John Jay to Sarah Jay, December 23, 1775; and *JCC*, 3:396–97. In response to the inconveniences resulting from their inability to maintain a legal representation in Congress, nine states voted during the ensuing months to reduce their requirements for a quorum. Thus by late 1776 only four states still specified more than a single delegate to cast their state's vote in Congress; and as New York and Virginia reduced their requirement from five to three and from four to three respectively, only Pennsylvania (four delegates) and nearby Maryland (three delegates), with easy access to the seat of Congress, appear to have believed they could continue to ignore such difficulties. See *JCC*, 4:14, 57, 122, 305, 354, 377, 5:712, 6:1000.

Richard Smith's Diary

Friday 29 Decr. [1775]

Journal read & one or Two passages ordered to be omitted in Publication. A Petitn. from Simeon Sellick committed to myself, Col. Floyd & Francis Lightfoot Lee Esqr.[1] The House went into Grand Committee, Gov. Ward in the Chair, when it was agreed after much Debate to allow Virginia, Maryland and North Carolina to import as much Salt as their several Conventions or Committees of Safety think necessary from any foreign Country, & to export Produce therefor. Debates upon opening our Ports to foreign Countries after the 1st of March next, within the Terms of our Association, adjorned. A Recommendation to the several Assemblies & Conventions to encorage the Manufacture of Salt, was offered by Dr. Franklin, agreed to & ordered to be published. R. Morris informed that a person offers to establish Salt Works on the Jersey Coast if the Congress will lend him £200. Mr. Morris & Lynch were desired to inquire more particularly into it. McKean gave Information that a Quantity of Arms, Ammunition & Cannon is buryed near Sir John Johnsons House with his Privity & that some Scotch and other Tories are there enlisted by the Enemy, a Comee. of 3 was appointed to examine the Two Men who brought the report to McKean & to ascertain the Fact as far as they can. Leave granted for a Lieut. a Prisoner, to come to Philada. for 2 Weeks. Andrew Allen presented a Petition from a Number of the Inhabitants of Northampton & other back Parts of Pennsylvania intimating that they will not obey the Recommendations of Congress in the Wyoming Affair, this Petition gave much Offence and was ordered to lie on the Table.[2] An Application from the Virginia Convention praying Means may be used for the Release of 3 Gentlemen, one of them a Delegate in that Convention named Robinson, lately seized by Lord Dunmore, left for Consideration. (The brave Capt. Manly retook & released these Gentn. on their Voyage to Gen. Howe at Boston.)[3]

MS (DLC).

[1] On this point, see *JCC*, 3:463, 467, 4:13; and Smith's Diary, December 30, 1775.

[2] Burnett suggested that this might have been the "Memorial of the Subscribers . . . of the Counties of Northumberland and Northampton," originally presented to the Pennsylvania Assembly on October 25, 1775, but this conjecture seems unlikely since the "Recommendations of Congress" referred to here by Smith were probably those of November 4, 1775. See Burnett, *Letters*, 1:290n6; *Pa. Archives*, 1st ser. 4:669–76; *JCC*, 3:321; and *Susquehannah Co. Papers*, 6:425.

[3] On December 17 Captain John Manley (commander of the schooner *Lee* in Washington's navy) captured the sloop *Betsey*—bearing William Robinson, a member of the Virginia Convention from Princess Anne County, and several other prisoners taken by Lord Dunmore—while it was on its way to Boston with supplies for the British cavalry. William Bell Clark, *George Washington's Navy* (Baton Rouge: Louisiana State University Press, 1960), pp. 21, 94–95, 231.

Virginia Delegate to Unknown

[December 29, 1775][1]

Poor Allen, with his party, who were taken at Montreal, is certainly sent to Great Britain in irons, by general Prescot, who was the commanding officer at that fortress; and shall this injury go unpunished? No, I think I can venture to say that the congress will order Prescot into irons,[2] to remain in them until we have favourable accounts of our colonel and his men. Montgomery, hearing of the treatment of our people, refused to see general Prescot when he was taken, which was shewing a soldier-like spirit.

Howe is carrying on the war at Boston in a manner that would disgrace savages. The very great scarcity of provisions in the town has obliged him to turn several of the inhabitants out, and, to his eternal shame be it spoken, he had them inoculated for the small pox, a short time before they were to come out, in hopes of spreading it among our troops. Is not this as bad as poisoning waters? But notwithstanding this vile scheme, by the vigilance of our people the disorder has been prevented from spreading.

The congress yesterday voted six battallions for the defence of Virginia.

MS not found; reprinted from the *Virginia Gazette* (Pinkney), January 10, 1776. Printed under the heading: "*Extract of a letter from a gentleman of the continental congress to a respectable gentleman in this city.*"

[1] For the date of this letter, see the concluding paragraph below. Congress authorized the raising of six battalions in Virginia on December 28. *JCC*, 3:463.

[2] On January 2, 1776, Congress ordered that Prescott be taken into custody and "safely and securely kept until the further orders of this Congress." *JCC*, 4:16.

Benjamin Harrison to Robert Carter Nicholas

Dr Sir Phida. Decr. 30th. 1775.

I Recd. your Favor[1] by Express inclosing Bills of Exchg. for five hundred Pounds Sterg. which we have agreed to divid amongst us that are left after Deducting the amount of the Paper &c. sent by Capt Innis, and what you have now order'd, and £17.5.0 this Cury. advanced to Singleton. The poor Fellow lost his Horse which made this necessary. We shall also pay fifty Pounds Virga Currency for Mr Jefferson and take up his order on you to Willing & Morris; the Bills are Sold at seventy two and a half per Cent. The Express was Ready to set off yesterday but geting a Letter from the Gen. Inclosing a Number of intercepted Letters from L. Dunmore and both the Carolinas we thought it better to detain him a Day that we might send to the Com[mitte]e of Safety Extracts of such as were interesting, which we have done and refer you to them for a Sight of them.[2] I had a private Letter from Camp by which I think it is certain that Robinson, Mathews and Deane were taken in the Vessel. We have no News from Canada but expect an Express every Day with the good Tidings of our being in possession of Quebec. I am Dr Sir Your affet Servt

Benj Harrison

P.S. We have agreed for 25 Ream of Paper to be Deliver'd in 16 Days which shall be immediately sent to you. The other ten will not be ready in some time longer. We think it best to send what we can get soon that you may not shut up shop.[3]

RC (PHC).

[1] See Robert Carter Nicholas to the Virginia delegates in Congress, December 12, 1775. Jefferson, *Papers* (Boyd), 1:271. See also his letters of November 10 and 25, 1775, ibid., pp. 254–56, 266–68. Nicholas (1728–80), prominent Williamsburg lawyer and member of the House of Burgesses, was the treasurer of Virginia. *DAB*.

[2] See Richard Smith's Diary, this date.

[3] See also Harrison's letters to Nicholas of January 17 and February 13, 1776.

Richard Smith's Diary

Saturday 30 Decr. [1775]

A Letter from Gen. Washn. with a packet of Letters just taken by Capt. Manley in a Vessel sent with Provisions from Lord Dunmore to Gen Howe (the same Vessel mentioned in the last page) these Letters were from Ld. Dunmore, one Mulcaster, said to be the Kings Natural Brother, Hon. John Stuart & many more Persons in the Southern Colonies.[1] One Col. Kirkland of S. Carolina was taken in this Vessel. The Letters took up most of the Day in the Perusal, the S

Cara. Delegates pressed strongly to have the Originals delivered to them & the Virginia Delegates & the Congress to keep attested Copies, but it was opposed & the Letters referred to a Comee. There was no Objection to those Delegates taking attested Copies. Gen. Washn. has sent to Gen. Howe a spirited Letter informing Him that whatever Severities are inflicted on Col. Allen shall be retaliated on Brig. Gen. Prescot & the like as to other prisoners, a Copy of the Letter was read in Congress.[2] Another letter was recd. from Washn. recom[mendin]g 2 French Gentn. who offered to supply this Continent with Powder & these Gentn. being in Town our Secret Comee. were desired to treat with them.[3] Leave given to Major Preston to go for 2 Weeks to Amboy, after much Opposition. A Guard of 5 men ordered immediately to convoy the hard Money to Gen. Schuyler & to take with them the Men who informed agt. Sir John Johnson. 40 Dollars allowed for their Expences. A Comee. directed to give proper orders to Gen Schuyler on this occasion.[4] Myself from the Comee. made Report on Capt. Simeon Sellecks Petition. He commands a small Privateer in Connectt. & lately took at Turtle Bay in the Sound, Kings Stores to the Amot. of £1500 lawful Money of Connectt. We allowed Him £100 like Money as a Reward for his Expences, Trouble and Risque, he gave up his Prize for the Continental Use. Debates Whether to stop Lieut. Moncrief who some Months ago had Leave to go to England & is now about going. He was at length allowed to go.

MS (DLC).

[1] Washington's letter to Hancock of December 18 is in PCC, item 152, 1:351–58; and Washington, *Writings* (Fitzpatrick), 4:172–74. The letters intercepted by Capt. John Manley, most of them originating from St. Augustine, West Florida, and Norfolk, Va., and enclosed in the above Washington to Hancock letter, are in *Am. Archives,* 4th ser. 4:316–52.

[2] See Washington's letter to Sir William Howe of December 18 in PCC, item 152, 1:360–64; and Washington, *Writings* (Fitzpatrick), 4:170–71.

[3] Washington's letter to Hancock of December 14, commending to Congress' attention Pierre Penet and Emmanuel de Pliarne, merchants from Nantes, is in Washington, *Writings* (Fitzpatrick), 4:162–63. By February 8, 1776, to judge from their letter of that date to Nicholas Brown, Penet and Pliarne had obtained a contract from the Secret Committee, presumably for supplying America with gunpowder and possibly other supplies from France. Clark, *Naval Documents,* 3:563, 722, 1176–77. See also Nicholas Cooke to John Hancock, December 18, 1775, PCC, item 64, fols. 356–59; and *Am. Archives,* 4th ser. 4:310.

[4] See *JCC,* 3:466–67.

Samuel Ward to Henry Ward

Dear Bror. Philadela. 31st Decr. 1775

You Favor of 19th I could not acknowledge by the Return of the Post.

I think with You that our Declaration of Retaliation was very proper but that we may go further & believe We shall. Genl. Washington has sent a very spirited Message to Genl. Howe relative to Colo. Allen taken at Montreal; as I recollect his Words are "Whatever may be his Treatment, whatever his Fate, such exactly shall be that of Brigadier General Preston whom We now have in our Power."[1]

The Virginians have at length done bravely. They have defeated Lord Dunmore, killed & taken 62 Grenadiers, their Capn. one of them, and several other privates & forced him to fly on board his Ships. The Congress has taken proper measures for the Defence of the Colony which will soon be carried into Execution.

I am clear with you that our Salvation depends upon effectually supporting the Dignity, Importance & decisive Authority of Congress. How far increasing their Number would answer that Salutary Purpose I have not time to consider at present, our Number is now sixty five, seldom fifty are present, often less than forty. May not the additional Number you propose support by their Influence in their several Colonies the Autho[rit]y of Congress more effectually in Person upon the Spot than when abroad by Letters, surely they may as Difficulties & Disorders arise apply proper Remedies and crush those things perhaps in embrio which in time would become very troublesome and dangerous.

The Plan of Union I agree ought to be setled this Winter but the Terms you propose I dont like. You say Representation ought to be as equal as possible. Agreed, but what is to be represented—not the Individuals of a particular Community but several States, Colonies or Bodies corporate. All Writers agree that a Nation is to be considered as one Person, one moral accountable Person having a Will of its own &c. Your Proposition allows to the larger Colonies several Wills & to the smaller not one, that is not one entire or compleat Will, & thereby makes the smaller wholly dependent on the larger; but You say Justice requires that the larger Colonies having a great number of Inhabitants & a greater Share of Property should have a proportionably greater Share of Representation. Let us see how the Doctrine will apply to individuals. One Man hath a numerous Family & is possessed of a large Estate, another has only a small Family & a little Estate. Is not the Life, the Family, Liberty & Property of the poor man being his all of as much Importance to and as dear to him as the larger all of the rich Man. Most clearly they are, surely then he may be equally intrusted with the Care of that all, and Justice cannot require that he should be deprived of any Part of the Means of self Preservation that they may be transfered to another and yet if you allow to one of them a single Voice, to the other two or three Voices, You certainly (selfish as people in general are) deprive one of the Means of Self Preservation or defence and put him wholly in the Power of the other. Do not the numerous Family & Fortune of the one give him sufficient Weight & Influence, surely they do, he can have no Right to more, the Laws have therefore wisely given to the Man of a fixed moderate Estate an equal Voice with him who is worth a hundred Times as much. Again Towns & Counties are of different Dimensions, contain different Numbers of Inhabitants & various Degrees of Wealth & yet you allow them nearly an equal Degree of Representation. I observed this to the Virginians & asked why they would risque the Introduction of a System of Equality in the States of America which they found impracticable even in a single Colony. Besides the present Sentiments, Prejudices and Jealousies would make it very unsafe. The N. E. Colonies are happily united. Others see it and knowing them to be brave and enterprizing are very jealous especially of the two larger Colonies and it is the Policy of some as far [*as*] the Dread of British Tyranny will admit to lessen the Influence of those Colonies, hence whole Weeks which ought to have been spent in pushing a War vigorously have been employed in ascertaining the Object and Extent of the War, hence the newmodelling the Army the Source of all its Dangers & Difficulties. If the N. E. Colonies had been applied to for their respective Quotas of Men, had appointed their Officers & been permitted to have given a Bounty as usual We might have had a fine Army long since. The ostensible Reasons for the contrary Conduct are Oeconomy & continental Views but the real one is this unhappy & ill grounded Jealousy. Again the Colonies of Pennsylvania N. York, Maryland & N. Carolina would acquire much Weight by the new Mode of Representation and besides the Jerseys, the Lower Counties & Georgia, Rhode Island & New Hampshire would proportionably loose. Can it be for the Interest of America to reduce the Power of those who have risqued all in her Cause & augment that of others who have not & never can or will proportionably serve her. It is impossible; if what I have now said is not satisfactory I will make another Attempt.

Mr. Hewes was surprized at the Hint I gave him but very politely thanked me for it and determined to be upon his Guard for the future.

The Army I wish may be formed soon, but the draughting of Men is vastly disagreable to Me; it distresses Families greatly, & the Men must be paid so that nothing will be saved. On the other hand I cant bear that Quota should be wanting; I had much rather have given a Bounty than be perplex'd in this Manner. I hope the Assembly may be directed to such Measures as may promote the true Interest Honor & Happiness of the Colo[n]y.

The French Gentn. arrived on Friday Evening;[2] Congress has referred them to the Secret Comee. We had a Conference with them last Evening; this Afternoon they paid Mr. Dean & me a Visit and were going to wait on the other Members.

I am grieved for the poor People of Newport; when will there be an End of their Misfortunes. I wish they would nobly resolve to quit it unless it can be fortifyed. I am told Genl Lee was coming up with such a View.

We have very interesting Intelligence in a Number of intercepted Letters from the southward, some Acct. of which I may perhaps be at Liberty to communicate in my next.

I will send you the Pamphlets you write for when I have Opportunity. At present every thing is shut up, our Fleet is just ready to sail but cannot stir without warmer Weather opens the River. My best Regards to all Friends. I am Your very affece Brother

Sam Ward

RC (RHi).

[1] Although Ward wrote "Preston," the reference should have been to Gen. Richard Prescott, whom Congress ordered into close confinement on January 2, 1776. Washington's letter to Howe of December 18, in which he tied Prescott's fate to Allen's treatment, is in Washington, *Writings* (Fitzpatrick), 4:170–71. Since Congress this day also took action on a request from Maj. Charles Preston for leave to visit a relative, Ward's slip is easily understood. See *JCC*, 3:466.

[2] Penet and Pliarne.

Committee of Secret Correspondence to Bonvouloir

[December ? 1775][1]

M. de B . . .[2] is requested by the Secret Committee to consider and reply to the following propositions. It is understood that they are not binding and wholly between private parties.

To wit:

1. Can he inform us what the disposition of the Court of France is toward the colonies of North America, whether it is favorable, and in what way we can be reliably assured of this?

2. Can we obtain two able engineers who are trustworthy and well-recommended, and what steps must we take to obtain them?

3. Can we have directly from France arms and other military supplies, in exchange for the products of our country, and be allowed free entrance and exit to French ports?

M. de B . . . may rest assured that if by means of his efforts we are favorably heard, we shall repose in him all the confidence that one can give a man of distinction whose goodwill toward us has not yet received a sure token of our gratitude.

MS not found; translated and reprinted from Henri Doniol, *Histoire de la participation de la France à l'éstablissment des États-Unis d'Amérique*, 5 vols. (Paris: Imprimerie Nationale, 1886–92), 1:268.

[1] This letter was probably written just before Bonvouloir's letter to comte de Guines of December 28th in which it was enclosed.

[2] Julien Achard de Bonvouloir (1749–83), French secret agent dispatched to America from London in September 1775 by the French ambassador to England, Comte de Guines, had met covertly in Philadelphia with members of the Committee of Secret Correspondence and in his report to Guines of December 28, 1775, had incorporated his translation of this letter from the committee. For Bonvouloir's letter to Guines, see Doniol, 1:287–92, an English translation of which is available in Clark, *Naval Documents,* 3:279–85. Although the French government had taken pains to ensure that Bonvouloir should appear in Philadelphia as a private traveler and that his contacts with Congress should involve no official commitments, the American delegates were undoubtedly aware that high level officials had participated in the planning of his mission. For information on steps previously taken by the committee to determine what support Congress might obtain in foreign capitals, see Benjamin Franklin to C.W.F. Dumas, December 9, and the committee's letter to Arthur Lee, December 12, 1775.

Naval Committee to William Stone

Sir, Philadelphia [December ? 1775][1]

You being Commander of the Sloop Hornet in the service of the United Colonies, are instructed as soon as the said Sloop shall be armed and manned, to proceed down the Bay of Chesapeak so far as to be certain of not being interrupted by the ice, and choose some safe and convenient Station for annoying the Enemy in every way you can. You are also to order the Schooner Wasp to follow or accompany you, and to keep with you in the service. You are to hold yourself in continual readiness to join the Fleet of the United Colonies soon to sail for Chesapeak Bay. And as soon as you shall have joined them, you are to follow such directions and instructions as you may receive from the Commander in chief of the said Fleet.

FC (RHi). In the hand of Richard Henry Lee.

[1] Concern over Lord Dunmore's depredations in the Chesapeake led Congress to dispatch Benjamin Harrison to Baltimore early in December to assist in preparing ships there for a surprise attack on Dunmore's forces. See Benjamin Harrison to Wilson Miles Cary, December 10, 1775. To judge from responses to letters which do not survive, Richard Henry Lee was simultaneously stimulating Virginians to more vigorous naval activity and coordinating preparations involving ships at Philadelphia, the *Hornet* and *Wasp* at Baltimore, and Virginians on the lower Chesapeake who were to provide pilots and marines for the vessels preparing at both Philadelphia and Baltimore. See John Page to Richard Henry Lee, December 9; and Thomas Ludwell Lee to Richard Henry Lee, December 9 and 23, 1775, in Clark, *Naval Documents,* 3:25–27, 219.

This letter to Captain Stone was undoubtedly written in the context of these preparations, and since Lee left Philadelphia on December 23, he almost certainly drafted it before his departure. Although the letter is printed in *Naval Documents,* 3:640, and assigned the approximate date January 5, 1776, on the assumption that this copy was transmitted to Capt. Esek Hopkins, it seems more likely that Lee actually gave his draft to fellow committee member Stephen Hopkins, and that it now reposes in the Hopkins Papers, RHi, because it was in the possession of Stephen rather than Esek Hopkins. In this connection, see Naval Committee to the Virginia Convention, December ? 1775, which Lee drafted on the verso of this document. Although Lee must have drafted both letters before he left Philadelphia, they may not have been copied and sent until some time after his departure. This surmise seems particularly to apply to the letter to the Virginia Convention, in which Lee left a blank, apparently in the expectation that it would be filled in later, and in which passages referring to vessels ordered to the Chesapeake are cast in the past tense, suggesting that the letter was to be sent when the fleet was ready to sail and the orders for its commander were ready. As such orders were not finally prepared until January 5, 1776, it is possible that despite Lee's expectation that the fleet would be able to sail before the end of December, both Stone's orders and the letter to Virginia were not actually sent until January 5. See Naval Committee to Esek Hopkins, January 5, 1776. See also Naval Committee to William Stone, January 10, 1776.

Naval Committee to the Virginia Convention

Gentlemen Philadelphia [December ? 1775][1]

The Congress attentive to the safety and security of every part of the united Colonies, and observing the peculiar distresses that the Colony of Virginia is liable to from a Marine enemy, have with all possible expedition fitted out a small fleet of Armed Vessels, which they have ordered in the first place to the Bay of Chesapeak, if the winds and weather permit, there to seize and destroy as many of the Enemies ships and Vessels as they can. As the best information of the Enemies strength and situation is of the utmost importance to the execution of this service, the Naval Committee request of you Gentlemen to station at Cape Henry a Person of unquestioned honor, understanding, and secrecy, for the purpose of boarding the Fleet when it appears off the Capes of Virginia, and furnish the Commander in Chief with the most accurate information of the then Strength and situation of Lord Dunmores fleet and Land forces. This Fleet will consist of Two Ships, two Brigantines, and one Sloop, with perhaps some smaller Vessel or Vessels. And for still greater certainty, as soon as the Fleet comes within proper distance and until they pass Cape Henry the largest Ship will carry at her Mizen Peak a Jack with the Union flag, and striped red and white in the field. The Person upon the Cape on his part is to fire a Musket, and hoist a white Flag on the most conspicious part of the Cape. A Boat will then be sent on shore to get the intelligence. It is judged of the utmost consequence to the Success of this enterprise that you contrive to place 200 expert Rifle Men on such part of the Shore as that they may be taken on board the fleet before they come in sight of the Enemy, and of this, the Gentleman first at Cape Henry must be able to inform the Commander.

You will discern Gentlemen that the greatest dispatch will be necessary as the Fleet will sail from this Port in .[2]

In contriving the Rifle Men as before mentioned, your judgment will point out the propriety of doing it in such a manner as not to awaken the apprehensions of the Enemy, the success of the Stroke being more sure as it may be most sudden and unexpected.

FC (RHi). In the hand of Richard Henry Lee, and drafted on the verso of Naval Committee to William Stone, December ? 1775.

[1] For an explanation of the circumstances that led to the drafting of this letter, see Naval Committee to William Stone, December ? 1775.

[2] MS blank.

INDEX

In this index descriptive subentries are arranged chronologically and in ascending order of the initial page reference. They may be preceded, however, by the subentry "identified" and by document subentries arranged alphabetically—diary entries, letters, notes, resolutions, and speeches. An ornament (☆) separates the subentry "identified" and document subentries from descriptive subentries. Inclusive page references are supplied for descriptive subentries; for a document, only the page on which it begins is given. Eighteenth-century printed works are indexed both by author and by short title. Other printed works are indexed when they have been cited to document a substantive point discussed in the notes, but not when cited merely as the location of a document mentioned. Delegates who attended Congress during the period covered by this volume appear in **boldface type.**

Advisory Committee

Library of Congress American Revolution Bicentennial Program

John R. Alden
James B. Duke Professor of History Emeritus, Duke University

Julian P. Boyd
Editor of The Papers of Thomas Jefferson, *Princeton University*

Lyman H. Butterfield
Editor in Chief Emeritus of The Adams Papers, *Massachusetts Historical Society*

Jack P. Greene
Professor of History, The Johns Hopkins University

Merrill Jensen
Vilas Research Professor of History, University of Wisconsin

Cecelia M. Kenyon
Charles N. Clark Professor of Government, Smith College

Aubrey C. Land
Research Professor of History, University of Georgia

Edmund S. Morgan
Sterling Professor of History, Yale University

Richard B. Morris
Gouverneur Morris Professor of History Emeritus, Columbia University

George C. Rogers, Jr.
Yates Snowden Professor of American History, University of South Carolina

Note: When the project to publish these congressional documents was initiated, Whitfield J. Bell, Jr., Librarian of the American Philosophical Society, and Adrienne Koch, Professor of American Intellectual History at the University of Maryland, were members of the advisory committee. Professor Koch died in 1971 and Mr. Bell resigned in 1973.

☆ U. S. GOVERNMENT PRINTING OFFICE : 1978 O - 267-213